Dictionary of Literary Biography

151 *British Prose Writers of the Early Seventeenth Century,* edited by Clayton D. Lein (1995)

152 *American Novelists Since World War II, Fourth Series,* edited by James R. Giles and Wanda H. Giles (1995)

153 *Late-Victorian and Edwardian British Novelists, First Series,* edited by George M. Johnson (1995)

154 *The British Literary Book Trade, 1700–1820,* edited by James K. Bracken and Joel Silver (1995)

155 *Twentieth-Century British Literary Biographers,* edited by Steven Serafin (1995)

156 *British Short-Fiction Writers, 1880–1914: The Romantic Tradition,* edited by William F. Naufftus (1995)

157 *Twentieth-Century Caribbean and Black African Writers, Third Series,* edited by Bernth Lindfors and Reinhard Sander (1995)

158 *British Reform Writers, 1789–1832,* edited by Gary Kelly and Edd Applegate (1995)

159 *British Short-Fiction Writers, 1800–1880,* edited by John R. Greenfield (1996)

160 *British Children's Writers, 1914–1960,* edited by Donald R. Hettinga and Gary D. Schmidt (1996)

161 *British Children's Writers Since 1960, First Series,* edited by Caroline Hunt (1996)

162 *British Short-Fiction Writers, 1915–1945,* edited by John H. Rogers (1996)

163 *British Children's Writers, 1800–1880,* edited by Meena Khorana (1996)

164 *German Baroque Writers, 1580–1660,* edited by James Hardin (1996)

165 *American Poets Since World War II, Fourth Series,* edited by Joseph Conte (1996)

166 *British Travel Writers, 1837–1875,* edited by Barbara Brothers and Julia Gergits (1996)

167 *Sixteenth-Century British Nondramatic Writers, Third Series,* edited by David A. Richardson (1996)

168 *German Baroque Writers, 1661–1730,* edited by James Hardin (1996)

169 *American Poets Since World War II, Fifth Series,* edited by Joseph Conte (1996)

170 *The British Literary Book Trade, 1475–1700,* edited by James K. Bracken and Joel Silver (1996)

171 *Twentieth-Century American Sportswriters,* edited by Richard Orodenker (1996)

172 *Sixteenth-Century British Nondramatic Writers, Fourth Series,* edited by David A. Richardson (1996)

173 *American Novelists Since World War II, Fifth Series,* edited by James R. Giles and Wanda H. Giles (1996)

174 *British Travel Writers, 1876–1909,* edited by Barbara Brothers and Julia Gergits (1997)

175 *Native American Writers of the United States,* edited by Kenneth M. Roemer (1997)

176 *Ancient Greek Authors,* edited by Ward W. Briggs (1997)

177 *Italian Novelists Since World War II, 1945–1965,* edited by Augustus Pallotta (1997)

178 *British Fantasy and Science-Fiction Writers Before World War I,* edited by Darren Harris-Fain (1997)

179 *German Writers of the Renaissance and Reformation, 1280–1580,* edited by James Hardin and Max Reinhart (1997)

180 *Japanese Fiction Writers, 1868–1945,* edited by Van C. Gessel (1997)

181 *South Slavic Writers Since World War II,* edited by Vasa D. Mihailovich (1997)

182 *Japanese Fiction Writers Since World War II,* edited by Van C. Gessel (1997)

183 *American Travel Writers, 1776–1864,* edited by James J. Schramer and Donald Ross (1997)

184 *Nineteenth-Century British Book-Collectors and Bibliographers,* edited by William Baker and Kenneth Womack (1997)

185 *American Literary Journalists, 1945–1995, First Series,* edited by Arthur J. Kaul (1998)

186 *Nineteenth-Century American Western Writers,* edited by Robert L. Gale (1998)

187 *American Book Collectors and Bibliographers, Second Series,* edited by Joseph Rosenblum (1998)

188 *American Book and Magazine Illustrators to 1920,* edited by Steven E. Smith, Catherine A. Hastedt, and Donald H. Dyal (1998)

189 *American Travel Writers, 1850–1915,* edited by Donald Ross and James J. Schramer (1998)

190 *British Reform Writers, 1832–1914,* edited by Gary Kelly and Edd Applegate (1998)

191 *British Novelists Between the Wars,* edited by George M. Johnson (1998)

192 *French Dramatists, 1789–1914,* edited by Barbara T. Cooper (1998)

193 *American Poets Since World War II, Sixth Series,* edited by Joseph Conte (1998)

194 *British Novelists Since 1960, Second Series,* edited by Merritt Moseley (1998)

195 *British Travel Writers, 1910–1939,* edited by Barbara Brothers and Julia Gergits (1998)

196 *Italian Novelists Since World War II, 1965–1995,* edited by Augustus Pallotta (1999)

197 *Late-Victorian and Edwardian British Novelists, Second Series,* edited by George M. Johnson (1999)

198 *Russian Literature in the Age of Pushkin and Gogol: Prose,* edited by Christine A. Rydel (1999)

199 *Victorian Women Poets,* edited by William B. Thesing (1999)

200 *American Women Prose Writers to 1820,* edited by Carla J. Mulford, with Angela Vietto and Amy E. Winans (1999)

201 *Twentieth-Century British Book Collectors and Bibliographers,* edited by William Baker and Kenneth Womack (1999)

202 *Nineteenth-Century American Fiction Writers,* edited by Kent P. Ljungquist (1999)

203 *Medieval Japanese Writers,* edited by Steven D. Carter (1999)

204 *British Travel Writers, 1940–1997,* edited by Barbara Brothers and Julia M. Gergits (1999)

205 *Russian Literature in the Age of Pushkin and Gogol: Poetry and Drama,* edited by Christine A. Rydel (1999)

206 *Twentieth-Century American Western Writers, First Series,* edited by Richard H. Cracroft (1999)

207 *British Novelists Since 1960, Third Series,* edited by Merritt Moseley (1999)

208 *Literature of the French and Occitan Middle Ages: Eleventh to Fifteenth Centuries,* edited by Deborah Sinnreich-Levi and Ian S. Laurie (1999)

209 *Chicano Writers, Third Series,* edited by Francisco A. Lomelí and Carl R. Shirley (1999)

210 *Ernest Hemingway: A Documentary Volume,* edited by Robert W. Trogdon (1999)

211 *Ancient Roman Writers,* edited by Ward W. Briggs (1999)

212 *Twentieth-Century American Western Writers, Second Series,* edited by Richard H. Cracroft (1999)

213 *Pre-Nineteenth-Century British Book Collectors and Bibliographers,* edited by William Baker and Kenneth Womack (1999)

214 *Twentieth-Century Danish Writers,* edited by Marianne Stecher-Hansen (1999)

215 *Twentieth-Century Eastern European Writers, First Series,* edited by Steven Serafin (1999)

216 *British Poets of the Great War: Brooke, Rosenberg, Thomas. A Documentary Volume,* edited by Patrick Quinn (2000)

217 *Nineteenth-Century French Poets,* edited by Robert Beum (2000)

218 *American Short-Story Writers Since World War II, Second Series,* edited by Patrick Meanor and Gwen Crane (2000)

219 *F. Scott Fitzgerald's* The Great Gatsby: *A Documentary Volume,* edited by Matthew J. Bruccoli (2000)

220 *Twentieth-Century Eastern European Writers, Second Series,* edited by Steven Serafin (2000)

221 *American Women Prose Writers, 1870–1920,* edited by Sharon M. Harris, with the assistance of Heidi L. M. Jacobs and Jennifer Putzi (2000)

222 *H. L. Mencken: A Documentary Volume,* edited by Richard J. Schrader (2000)

223 *The American Renaissance in New England, Second Series,* edited by Wesley T. Mott (2000)

224 *Walt Whitman: A Documentary Volume,* edited by Joel Myerson (2000)

225 *South African Writers,* edited by Paul A. Scanlon (2000)

226 *American Hard-Boiled Crime Writers,* edited by George Parker Anderson and Julie B. Anderson (2000)

227 *American Novelists Since World War II, Sixth Series,* edited by James R. Giles and Wanda H. Giles (2000)

228 *Twentieth-Century American Dramatists, Second Series,* edited by Christopher J. Wheatley (2000)

229 *Thomas Wolfe: A Documentary Volume,* edited by Ted Mitchell (2001)

230 *Australian Literature, 1788–1914,* edited by Selina Samuels (2001)

Dictionary of Literary Biography Documentary Series

Dictionary of Literary Biography Yearbooks

1980 edited by Karen L. Rood, Jean W. Ross, and Richard Ziegfeld (1981)

1981 edited by Karen L. Rood, Jean W. Ross, and Richard Ziegfeld (1982)

1982 edited by Richard Ziegfeld; associate editors: Jean W. Ross and Lynne C. Zeigler (1983)

1983 edited by Mary Bruccoli and Jean W. Ross; associate editor Richard Ziegfeld (1984)

1984 edited by Jean W. Ross (1985)

1985 edited by Jean W. Ross (1986)

1986 edited by J. M. Brook (1987)

1987 edited by J. M. Brook (1988)

1988 edited by J. M. Brook (1989)

1989 edited by J. M. Brook (1990)

1990 edited by James W. Hipp (1991)

1991 edited by James W. Hipp (1992)

1992 edited by James W. Hipp (1993)

1993 edited by James W. Hipp, contributing editor George Garrett (1994)

1994 edited by James W. Hipp, contributing editor George Garrett (1995)

1995 edited by James W. Hipp, contributing editor George Garrett (1996)

1996 edited by Samuel W. Bruce and L. Kay Webster, contributing editor George Garrett (1997)

1997 edited by Matthew J. Bruccoli and George Garrett, with the assistance of L. Kay Webster (1998)

1998 edited by Matthew J. Bruccoli, contributing editor George Garrett, with the assistance of D. W. Thomas (1999)

1999 edited by Matthew J. Bruccoli, contributing editor George Garrett, with the assistance of D. W. Thomas (2000)

2000 edited by Matthew J. Bruccoli, contributing editor George Garrett, with the assistance of George Parker Anderson (2001)

2001 edited by Matthew J. Bruccoli, contributing editor George Garrett, with the assistance of George Parker Anderson (2002)

Concise Series

Concise Dictionary of American Literary Biography, 7 volumes (1988–1999): *The New Consciousness, 1941–1968; Colonization to the American Renaissance, 1640–1865; Realism, Naturalism, and Local Color, 1865–1917; The Twenties, 1917–1929; The Age of Maturity, 1929–1941; Broadening Views, 1968–1988; Supplement: Modern Writers, 1900–1998.*

Concise Dictionary of British Literary Biography, 8 volumes (1991–1992): *Writers of the Middle Ages and Renaissance Before 1660; Writers of the Restoration and Eighteenth Century, 1660–1789; Writers of the Romantic Period, 1789–1832; Victorian Writers, 1832–1890; Late-Victorian and Edwardian Writers, 1890–1914; Modern Writers, 1914–1945; Writers After World War II, 1945–1960; Contemporary Writers, 1960 to Present.*

Concise Dictionary of World Literary Biography, 10 volumes projected (1999–): *Ancient Greek and Roman Writers; German Writers; African, Caribbean, and Latin American Writers; South Slavic and Eastern European Writers.*

Dictionary of Literary Biography® • Volume Two Hundred Seventy-Six

British Mystery and Thriller Writers Since 1960

Dictionary of Literary Biography® • Volume Two Hundred Seventy-Six

British Mystery and Thriller Writers Since 1960

Edited by
Gina Macdonald
Nicholls State University

A Bruccoli Clark Layman Book

GALE®

Detroit • New York • San Diego • San Francisco • Cleveland • New Haven, Conn. • Waterville, Maine • London • Munich

Dictionary of Literary Biography
Volume 276: British Mystery and Thriller Writers
Since 1960
Gina Macdonald

Advisory Board
John Baker
William Cagle
Patrick O'Connor
George Garrett
Trudier Harris
Alvin Kernan
Kenny J. Williams

Editorial Directors
Matthew J. Bruccoli and Richard Layman

© 2003 by Gale. Gale is an imprint of
The Gale Group, Inc., a division of
Thomson Learning, Inc.

Gale and Design™ and Thomson Learning™
are trademarks used herein under license.

For more information, contact
The Gale Group, Inc.
27500 Drake Rd.
Farmington Hills, MI 48331-3535
Or you can visit our Internet site at
http://www.gale.com

LIBRARY OF CONGRESS CATALOGING-IN-PUBLICATION DATA

British mystery and thriller writers since 1960 / edited by Gina Macdonald.
    p. cm. — (Dictionary of literary biography ; v. 276)
"A Bruccoli Clark Layman book."
Includes bibliographical references and index.
     ISBN 0-7876-6020-5
     1. Detective and mystery stories, English—Bio-bibliography—
  Dictionaries. 2. English fiction—20th century—Bio-bibliography—
  Dictionaries. 3. Novelists, English—20th century—Biography—
  Dictionaries. 4. Detective and mystery stories, English—Dictionaries.
  5. Suspense fiction—Bio-bibliography—Dictionaries. 6. English fiction—
  20th century—Dictionaries. 7. Suspense fiction—Dictionaries.
     I. Macdonald, Gina. II. Series.

PR888.D4B69 2003
823'.0872090914—dc21   2003002268

Printed in the United States of America
10 9 8 7 6 5 4 3 2 1

To Andrew

Contents

Plan of the Series

The advisory board, the editors, and the publisher of the *Dictionary of Literary Biography* are joined in endorsing Mark Twain's declaration. The literature of a nation provides an inexhaustible resource of permanent worth. Our purpose is to make literature and its creators better understood and more accessible to students and the reading public, while satisfying the needs of teachers and researchers.

To meet these requirements, *literary biography* has been construed in terms of the author's achievement. The most important thing about a writer is his writing. Accordingly, the entries in *DLB* are career biographies, tracing the development of the author's canon and the evolution of his reputation.

The purpose of *DLB* is not only to provide reliable information in a usable format but also to place the figures in the larger perspective of literary history and to offer appraisals of their accomplishments by qualified scholars.

The publication plan for *DLB* resulted from two years of preparation. The project was proposed to Bruccoli Clark by Frederick G. Ruffner, president of the Gale Research Company, in November 1975. After specimen entries were prepared and typeset, an advisory board was formed to refine the entry format and develop the series rationale. In meetings held during 1976, the publisher, series editors, and advisory board approved the scheme for a comprehensive biographical dictionary of persons who contributed to literature. Editorial work on the first volume began in January 1977, and it was published in 1978. In order to make *DLB* more than a dictionary and to compile volumes that individually have claim to status as literary history, it was decided to organize volumes by topic, period, or

genre. Each of these freestanding volumes provides a biographical-bibliographical guide and overview for a particular area of literature. We are convinced that this organization—as opposed to a single alphabet method—constitutes a valuable innovation in the presentation of reference material. The volume plan necessarily requires many decisions for the placement and treatment of authors. Certain figures will be included in separate volumes, but with different entries emphasizing the aspect of his career appropriate to each volume. Ernest Hemingway, for example, is represented in *American Writers in Paris, 1920–1939* by an entry focusing on his expatriate apprenticeship; he is also in *American Novelists, 1910–1945* with an entry surveying his entire career, as well as in *American Short-Story Writers, 1910–1945, Second Series* with an entry concentrating on his short fiction. Each volume includes a cumulative index of the subject authors and articles.

Since 1981 the series has been further augmented by the *DLB Yearbooks,* which update published entries, add new entries to keep the *DLB* current with contemporary activity, and provide articles on literary history. There have also been nineteen *DLB Documentary Series* volumes, which provide illustrations, facsimiles, and biographical and critical source materials for figures, works, or groups judged to have particular interest for students. In 1999 the *Documentary Series* was incorporated into the *DLB* volume numbering system beginning with *DLB 210: Ernest Hemingway.*

We define literature as the *intellectual commerce of a nation:* not merely as belles lettres but as that ample and complex process by which ideas are generated, shaped, and transmitted. *DLB* entries are not limited to "creative writers" but extend to other figures who in their time and in their way influenced the mind of a people. Thus the series encompasses historians, journalists, publishers, book collectors, and screenwriters. By this means readers of *DLB* may be aided to perceive literature not as cult scripture in the keeping of intellectual high priests but firmly positioned at the center of a nation's life.

DLB includes the major writers appropriate to each volume and those standing in the ranks behind them. Scholarly and critical counsel has been sought in deciding which minor figures to include and how full their entries should be. Wherever possible, useful references are made to figures who do not warrant separate entries.

Each *DLB* volume has an expert volume editor responsible for planning the volume, selecting the figures for inclusion, and assigning the entries. Volume editors are also responsible for preparing, where appropriate, appendices surveying the major periodicals and literary and intellectual movements for their volumes, as well as lists of further readings. Work on the series as a whole is coordinated at the Bruccoli Clark Layman editorial center in Columbia, South Carolina, where the editorial staff is responsible for accuracy and utility of the published volumes.

One feature that distinguishes *DLB* is the illustration policy–its concern with the iconography of literature. Just as an author is influenced by his surroundings, so is the reader's understanding of the author enhanced by a knowledge of his environment. Therefore *DLB* volumes include not only drawings, paintings, and photographs of authors, often depicting them at various stages in their careers, but also illustrations of their families and places where they lived. Title pages are regularly reproduced in facsimile along with dust jackets for modern authors. The dust jackets are a special feature of *DLB* because they often document better than anything else the way in which an author's work was perceived in its own time. Specimens of the writers' manuscripts and letters are included when feasible.

Samuel Johnson rightly decreed that "The chief glory of every people arises from its authors." The purpose of the *Dictionary of Literary Biography* is to compile literary history in the surest way available to us–by accurate and comprehensive treatment of the lives and work of those who contributed to it.

The *DLB* Advisory Board

Introduction

The period from 1960 to the present spans much of the modern history of the mystery genre and, along with it, many of the political and social changes from the classical detective story, the World War II spy story, and the Cold War thriller to postmodern detective and spy adventures and the politics of terrorism and confrontation of the twenty-first century. The genteel detective of the Golden Age has been replaced by detectives of more-ordinary origins, and the criminal acts are far more heinous. Serial killers are more plentiful, and, as in James Hadley Chase's *No Orchids for Miss Blandish* (1939), sometimes the criminal, not the policeman, is in the limelight. Politics and sociology come into play, as in Raymond Postgate's *Verdict of Twelve* (1940), with its stress on the controlling power of social forces, in which Postgate reveals how each juror's verdict is determined by religious fanaticism, class prejudice, and the dynamics of the jury-room discussion rather than by questions of truth and justice. In spy fiction, as seemingly immutable and permanent political alliances have changed, so has the "enemy" and so have the methods by which that enemy is spied upon and interacted with. Thus, writers such as Alistair MacLean bring to life the conflicts of World War II and the Cold War. In turn, writers such as Gavin Black look back to Japanese encroachments in the Pacific and the Chinese threat to Southeast Asia in the 1950s and 1960s, and writers such as Lionel Davidson deal with the Cold War conflict with the Soviets, in contrast to more recent writers, for example, John le Carré and Adam Hall, who depict a new age of spying and terrorism. Hall experiments with point of view, capturing his warrior hero's psychological preparation for an assault on villains and his moment-by-moment process of analyzing incoming data, evaluating options, and then acting with swift and deadly force. Historian Anthony Price finds in the past the roots of modern confrontations and old hatreds played out in new ways: his argument is that only the methods change, but not the nature of man.

As British society has changed, the cozy village mystery has given way to darker visions of the English small town. Douglas Clark's small-town police investigators doggedly expose hidden relationships among English villagers to get at the heart of the seething passions and hatreds that lead to poisonings. Heron Carvic has his eccentric elderly sleuth, Miss Seeton, encounter vicious gangs and a degree of violence and mayhem impossible in an Agatha Christie tale, while Ruth Rendell, in turn, paints dark images of small-town eccentricity, viciousness, backbiting, hatred, and deceit. Her psychological studies of the criminal mind have more in common with Graham Greene's *Brighton Rock* (1938) than any Miss Marple story. Marion Babson looks at the dangers to innocents and captures the loneliness and alienation of young children, while at the same time making animals, cats in particular, integral to the detection process. (The British love of their pets is carried to new extremes by this expatriate American turned English.) Jonathan Gash's roguish Lovejoy, in a tradition going back to Robert Greene's coney-catching tales, finds con games at work among the most genteel members of village society, including clergymen, and Gash's more-recent team of urban detectives (a doctor and a male prostitute) takes a hard look at the vicious, nasty side of big-city life. Robert Barnard's tales of small-town life are satiric, witty, and scathing, while P. D. James expands the concept of village to include odd modern communities such as the employees of a nuclear plant set on a headland, the isolated religious community of a training school for priests, and a nursing college. Michael Innes likewise captures the academic communities, whether established institutions founded in the Middle Ages or modern redbrick universities.

Even the classic theater mystery is transformed in the hands of Simon Brett into a satiric study of the infighting, jealousies, and nastiness of small-town theater and big-time television drama. Like Brett, Lionel Black examines the changing mores wrought by the sexual revolution of the 1960s and 1970s and makes his heroine, Kate Theobald, daring, feisty, and more sexually available than heroines of the preceding generation. Black contrasts pairs of detectives, whether professional or amateur, and balances qualities to suggest the limits of any one individual and the powerful potential of combinations of thinkers with doers, upper class with working class, and male with female, for example. The comforting English village image has inevitably yielded to harsh modern realities, with the urban criminals preying on the countryside and the countryside producing its own set of nasty types.

The historical mystery has come into its own in this period. Ellis Peters, for example, takes readers back to the Middle Ages and into the life of Father Cadfael, who must deal with a stifling hierarchy, disillusioned soldiers returning from the Holy Land, corruption in the Church, conflicts between the landed gentry and the peasants, a clash of cultures in the tensions between Wales and England, and a society on the edge of chaos. While bringing to life a period and a way of life fewer and fewer readers have learned about in school, Peters also finds in the past the roots of modern conflicts and concerns. In like manner Anne Perry and Robert Barnard bring to life the Victorian age, its hypocrisies and class divisions, its proprieties and improprieties. Perry, in particular, uses the historical mystery novel as a means to explore the foundations of the feminist movement and the injustices perpetrated upon women by a system that denied them education, professional training, or even private lives and private choices. Barnard sets *To Die Like a Gentleman* (1993) in Victorian England and imitates the letter and diary forms popular in works of that period to lend narrative authenticity to his tale of murder. Barnard has also written in a new historical vein, one that takes significant figures from the past, such as Jane Austen, and turns them into investigators. In Barnard's case, the detective is Wolfgang Amadeus Mozart at various stages of his musical career, for example, at age seventy-three, resuscitated as piano tutor to young Princess Victoria in 1830 in *Too Many Notes, Mr. Mozart* (1995).

Scholar Kathleen Klein's *Diversity and Detective Fiction* (1999) provides further insights into the patterns of change at work in the genre, as gender, race, and culture play more and more significant roles. The essays in her collection focus on the ethnic detective, the gay detective, identity politics, feminism, sexism, and the concept of the Other. Her contributors name nearly thirty different general ethnic groups represented by modern fictional detectives, not including the many subdivisions. While most of these detectives are American rather than British, they encapsulate a trend that began first with British writers abroad and only later spread to American writers. British writers abroad, inspired by contact with other cultures and other ways of viewing the world and politics and justice, introduced readers to murder and justice as they had never envisioned it. Although not a mystery writer, James Clavell is typical of this pattern of explaining to Westerners an Eastern worldview, as he does in such novels as *Tai-Pan* (1966) and *Shogun* (1975).

British mystery writers, some of whom had done military service in the Far East or had lived with military families in ports such as Hong Kong, led the way with ethnic mysteries. Gavin Black, for example, makes his Scottish hero, Paul Harris, a former prisoner of war in the infamous Japanese prison camp Changi, now turned Malaysian citizen and businessman with strong ties to the Malaysian community and a strong interest in protecting his adopted land from the encroachments of both Japanese investments and Chinese military invasions. The interest of such stories comes not simply from the exotic locales but from the insights into perspectives, values, and ways of life quite different from those in the West. James Melville's Japanese detective series likewise takes readers into the mind-set of the Japanese, as his Superintendent Otani struggles to understand crimes involving inscrutable Westerners. Such cultural-crossroads stories have become a modern means of educating readers to the other people with whom Westerners must deal in a shrinking modern world and yet whose manners, systems, customs, and world vision are alien to them.

Barnard's *Death of an Old Goat* (1974) captures the disjunction in values, speech, and ways of life between an English university professor teaching abroad and the inhabitants of a distant outpost in the Australian Outback. His *Death in a Cold Climate* (1980), set on the opposite of the globe, captures the alienation travelers feel in a foreign environment (and not simply from different ideas about what is edible), the effects of climate (in this case, long winters) on human psychology, and the problems created by different linguistic patterns. Patricia Moyes dramatizes the breakdowns of communication and the resentments that result in encounters between blacks and whites, particularly in the Caribbean, as in *To Kill a Coconut* (1977), *Angel Death* (1980), and *Black Girl, White Girl* (1989). In *Kolymsky Heights* (1994) Davidson has a Canadian Eskimo hero sent to infiltrate a secret Soviet scientific base in Siberia only to discover that Russian preconceptions of white superiority outweigh British preconceptions about Asian-Aleut influence, while *The Rose of Tibet* (1962) carries readers to India, Sikkim, and Tibet. James McClure uses his Afrikaner and Zulu detective team to explore the injustices and outrages of apartheid in South Africa, and so brings to life the humanity of the Zulu Mickey Zondi and the oppressive conditions under which he and his people suffered; McClure's novels are credited with having helped end apartheid. Like McClure, Brian Cleeve uses the crime novel to explore the abuses and injustices of apartheid, revealed through the fears of light-skinned "coloreds" who pass for white, only to be trapped by their pasts. The British mystery writers' concern with world values and cross-cultural encounters opened the door to American interest in ethnic diversity in mysteries.

Gender issues are an inevitable part of a modern redefining of values and character. Some writers from this period are in the James Bond school, with Chase, for example, in *Twelve Chinks and a Woman* (1940), exploiting the racist, misogynist, and sexually perverse potential of the hard-boiled school. Moyes's *Murder à la Mode* (1963) offers the first of many gay characters in her Henry Tibbett series, a dress designer who is a positive character and out of keeping with gender stereotypes. Lionel Black captures the inevitable marital squabbles that result from women having their own significant careers and an independence impossible in earlier generations. Reginald Hill uses a trio—Superintendent Dalziel; his youthful subordinate, Detective Pascoe; and Pascoe's girlfriend and then wife, Ellie—to dramatize changing attitudes. Ellie is a university-trained child of the 1960s with a negative view of the police, a feminist view of gender relationships, and the commitment of a political activist. She regards Dalziel as sexist and reactionary, and, with the two of them at loggerheads, Pascoe must mediate, explaining the virtues of Ellie's perspective to Dalziel and the virtues of Dalziel's perspective to Ellie, a balancing act and a tension that is a driving force in Hill's series. Perry captures the struggles of competent, headstrong nineteenth-century women to prove their worth in the male workplace, while Cleeve's Regency works show decent women (much like the modern African women of his spy stories) caught up in a criminal underworld: tossed by fate, bound by social manacles, oppressed by brutal males, but finding purpose and strength to overcome victimization. Thus, Perry and Cleeve take a stand on modern gender issues under the guise of historical portraits.

James, in turn, shows modern women performing effectively as lawyers, nurses, scientists, heads of institutions, and even police inspectors. In her Jemima Shore mysteries, Antonia Fraser develops a new kind of woman detective, an independent, cultivated, liberated, and liberal celebrity whose career as a successful television commentator makes her nosiness and curiosity virtues. Like Brett's male detective, Charles Paris, Shore is a happy hedonist, but she takes her reporting seriously, producing documentaries on gender topics such as the mistreatment of women in the Trade Union movement, the legal impediments placed on Asian women, Sri Lankan child brides, and the Russian influence on Afghani social attitudes toward birth control.

The authors in this volume provide compelling reading because of what they tell us about the ways in which our world, our values, and our vision of ourselves and others have changed over the last half of the twentieth century. The detective and thriller genre has been revitalized by an infusion of new perspectives and experiments with new ways of telling stories of basic human interest, of murder and mayhem, loyalties and betrayals, private and national secrets.

–*Gina Macdonald*

Acknowledgments

This book was produced by Bruccoli Clark Layman, Inc. Charles Brower was the in-house editor.

Production manager is Philip B. Dematteis.

Administrative support was provided by Ann M. Cheschi and Carol A. Cheschi.

Accountant is Ann-Marie Holland.

Copyediting supervisor is Sally R. Evans. The copyediting staff includes Phyllis A. Avant, Caryl Brown, Melissa D. Hinton, Philip I. Jones, Rebecca Mayo, Nancy E. Smith, and Elizabeth Jo Ann Sumner.

Editorial associates are Amelia B. Lacey, Michael S. Martin, Catherine M. Polit, and William Mathes Straney.

In-house prevetting is by Nicole A. La Rocque.

Permissions editor and database manager is Amber L. Coker.

Layout and graphics supervisor is Janet E. Hill. The graphics staff includes Zoe R. Cook and Sydney E. Hammock.

Office manager is Kathy Lawler Merlette.

Photography supervisor is Paul Talbot. Photography editor is Scott Nemzek.

Digital photographic copy work was performed by Joseph M. Bruccoli .

Systems manager is Donald Kevin Starling.

Typesetting supervisor is Kathleen M. Flanagan. The typesetting staff includes Patricia Marie Flanagan, Mark J. McEwan, and Pamela D. Norton. Freelance typesetters are Wanda Adams and Rebecca Mayo.

Walter W. Ross did library research. He was assisted by Jo Cottingham and the following other librarians at the Thomas Cooper Library of the University of South Carolina: circulation department head Tucker Taylor; reference department head Virginia W. Weathers; reference department staff Brette Barron, Marilee Birchfield, Paul Cammarata, Gary Geer, Michael Macan, Tom Marcil, Rose Marshall, and Sharon Verba; interlibrary loan department head John Brunswick; and interlibrary loan staff Robert Arndt, Hayden Battle, Alex Byrne, Bill Fetty, Marna Hostetler, and Nelson Rivera.

Dictionary of Literary Biography® • Volume Two Hundred Seventy-Six

British Mystery and Thriller Writers Since 1960

Dictionary of Literary Biography

Marian Babson

(15 December 1929 –)

Mary Jean DeMarr
Indiana State University

and

Gina Macdonald
Nicholls State University

BOOKS: *Cover-Up Story* (London: Collins, 1971; New York: St. Martin's Press, 1988);

Murder on Show (London: Collins, 1972); republished as *Murder at the Cat Show* (New York: St. Martin's Press, 1989);

Pretty Lady (London: Collins, 1973; New York: Walker, 1990);

The Stalking Lamb (London: Collins, 1974; New York: Bantam, 1990);

Unfair Exchange (London: Collins, 1974; New York: Walker, 1986);

Murder Sails at Midnight (London: Collins, 1975; New York: Bantam, 1989);

There Must Be Some Mistake (London: Collins, 1975; New York: St. Martin's Press, 1987);

Untimely Guest (London: Collins, 1976; New York: St. Martin's Press, 1987);

The Lord Mayor of Death (London: Collins, 1977; New York: Walker, 1979);

Murder, Murder, Little Star (London: Collins, 1977; New York: Walker, 1980);

Tightrope for Three (London: Collins, 1978; New York: Walker, 1989);

So Soon Done For (London: Collins, 1979; New York: Walker, 1988);

The Twelve Deaths of Christmas (London: Collins, 1979; New York: Walker, 1980);

Dangerous to Know (London: Collins, 1980; New York: Walker, 1981);

Marian Babson (photograph by Jeremy Hoare; from the dust jacket for the U.S. edition of Break a Leg, Darlings, *1997)*

Queue Here for Murder (London: Collins, 1980); republished as *Line Up for Murder* (New York: Walker, 1981);

Bejewelled Death (London: Collins, 1981; New York: Walker, 1982);

Death Warmed Up (London: Collins, 1982; New York: Walker, 1982);

Death beside the Seaside (London: Collins, 1982); republished as *Death beside the Sea* (New York: Walker, 1983);

A Fool for Murder (London: Collins, 1983; New York: Walker, 1984);

The Cruise of a Deathtime (London: Collins, 1983; New York: Walker, 1984);

A Trail of Ashes (London: Collins, 1984; New York: Walker, 1985); republished as *Whiskers and Smoke* (New York: St. Martin's Press, 1997);

Death Swap (London: Collins, 1984; New York: Walker, 1985); republished as *Paws for Alarm* (New York: St. Martin's Press, 1996);

Death in Fashion (London: Collins, 1985; New York: Walker, 1986);

Weekend for Murder (London: Collins, 1985); republished as *Murder on a Mystery Tour* (New York: Walker, 1987);

Reel Murder (London: Collins, 1986; New York: St. Martin's Press, 1986);

Fatal Fortune (London: Collins, 1987; New York: St. Martin's Press, 1991);

Guilty Party (London: Collins, 1988; New York: St. Martin's Press, 1991);

Encore Murder (London: Collins, 1989; New York: St. Martin's Press, 1990);

Tourists Are for Trapping (New York: St. Martin's Press, 1989);

In the Teeth of Adversity (New York: St. Martin's Press, 1990);

Past Regret (London: Collins, 1990; New York: St. Martin's Press, 1992);

Shadows in Their Blood (London: HarperCollins, 1991; New York: St. Martin's Press, 1993);

Nine Lives to Murder (London: HarperCollins, 1992; New York: St. Martin's Press, 1994);

Even Yuppies Die (London: HarperCollins, 1993; New York: St. Martin's Press, 1996);

The Diamond Cat (London: HarperCollins, 1994; New York: St. Martin's Press, 1995);

Break a Leg, Darlings (London: HarperCollins, 1995; New York: St. Martin's Press, 1997);

Miss Petunia's Last Case (London: HarperCollins, 1996); republished as *Canapés for the Kitties* (New York: St. Martin's Press, 1997);

The Multiple Cat (London: HarperCollins, 1999); republished as *The Company of Cats* (New York: St. Martin's Press, 1999);

A Tealeaf in the Mouse (London: Constable, 2000); republished as *To Catch a Cat* (New York: St. Martin's Press, 2000);

Deadly Deceit (London: Constable, 2001); republished as *The Cat Next Door* (New York: St. Martin's Press, 2002);

Not Quite a Geisha (London: Constable, 2003).

Marian Babson's contributions to the field of mystery and detective fiction lie in both her ten-year service as secretary of the Crime Writers Association from 1976 to 1986 and her steady output of mystery novels, better than a novel per year. The latter have found a wide readership on both sides of the Atlantic, even though reviewers have paid scant attention to her works. At her best, Babson brings to her fiction a keen observer's eye, a fluid, witty style, and an amusement at human foibles, as she explores with wry humor both the American scene of her origins and the British scene of her adoption. Her novels do not adhere to any particular formula: Babson has written in both classical mystery and suspense forms and has created two series with unusual detectives (a publicist who discovers a love for cats and criminal investigation, and two aging actresses who team up as amateur investigators). She has experimented with a variety of storytelling strategies, manipulating point of view and structure and contriving inventive plot scenarios. "I don't think writers ought to be too predictable," she says, and in her novels she strives for surprise. Her works are frequently skillfully crafted and absorbing, with unpredictable backgrounds, characters, and plots. Sometimes her plots include a series of letters, or her characters write out the plots of their mystery stories as they are engaged in Babson's, or the point of view is that of a cat with feline obsessions, or the plot hurtles back and forth between criminal, detective, and victim as the action moves toward sudden death.

Little biographical information is available about Babson, who has preferred to remain mysterious, but readers can intuit a great deal about her interests, experience, and taste from her works. Although born in Salem, Massachusetts, on 15 December 1929, Babson has chosen to make England her home. She moved to London in 1960 and has lived and worked there ever since, with only occasional forays to the United States, for example, when she returned to manage the campaign headquarters of a Boston politician seeking office. Only after living there for decades, however, did she develop the confidence to set some of her novels in England. Even after an adulthood among the English, however, Babson still does not always get the details and facts correct enough for their satisfaction. Yet, she clearly feels comfortable with British reserve, respect for privacy, acceptance and even approval of eccentricity, and love of animals.

Though her résumé is not a matter of record, Babson has worked at a variety of occupations and made use of those experiences in her crime fiction. For instance, she has worked as a temporary secretary for employers in a wide assortment of fields, including a solicitor, a popular singer, and a psychiatrist. Her experiences led to her first detective-series hero, Douglas Perkins, being a publicist, whose occupation brings him into contact with varied people and activities: a "troupe" of American "hillbilly" musicians in *Cover-Up Story* (1971); cat owners, breeders, and fanciers at a cat show in *Murder on Show* (1972), republished as *Murder at the Cat Show* (1989); and tour guides, travel agents, and others connected with tourism in *Tourists Are for Trapping* (1989). Perkins becomes a cat lover after his experiences at the cat show, and cat fanciers become a featured characteristic of Babson's novels thereafter. Her first comic mysteries featuring Perkins served as a form of apprenticeship as Babson learned her trade.

Babson's breadth of occupational experience, coupled with her knowledge of both the United States and England, has enabled her to bring a variety of scene and milieu, crime and means of criminal detection to her crime fiction. She has been particularly skilled at presenting the naive and innocent entangled in violence, as her third novel, *Pretty Lady* (1973), demonstrates. It movingly depicts a retarded man, entranced by a woman he innocently thinks of as a "pretty lady." The young heroine in *The Stalking Lamb* (1974) is much like a Mignon Eberhart heroine–a youth in alien territory terrifyingly at the center of criminal activity. *Unfair Exchange* (1974) features a recurring Babson personality, a selfishly demanding elderly woman who lies, deceives, and reconstructs reality to suit her own self-image. The crime therein is a kidnapping, while in *There Must Be Some Mistake* (1975) it is embezzlement and the question of a missing husband. *Untimely Guest* (1976) follows a pattern unusual for Babson, a psychological study of the passions and character traits that lead to violence, wherein an elderly woman who treats her daughter as a slave, rudely drives away her friends, and insistently demands tea, falls down the stairs to her death (perhaps pushed).

Murder, Murder, Little Star (1977) takes a satiric look at the world of moviemaking. It features a particularly acerbic portrait of an obnoxious, unnaturally knowing, frightened, bratty child star named "Twinkle," and the retinue of hangers-on and parasites who profit from her successful movies. The success of the novel depends on a sympathetic protagonist, Dame Cecile Savoy, a pleasant middle-aged widow who becomes, as she puts it, "a chaperone and sort of secre-

Dust jacket for the U.S. edition of Babson's 1977 novel in which an Irish terrorist uses his five-year-old niece as a decoy in an assassination plot (Richland County Public Library)

tary" to Twinkle. Babson later used Dame Cecile in the Trixie and Evangeline series.

The Lord Mayor of Death (1977) seems to come straight from London headlines with its depiction of an attempted Irish terrorist act. In Babson's suspenseful story the act is the blowing up of the lord mayor of London and those around him. Babson captures the fanaticism of the terrorist by using the circumstance of a missing child to expert effect. Five-year-old Kitty disappears on the day of the Lord Mayor's Show, a time of parading and festivity particularly directed toward children. Her mother, Maureen O'Fahey, an unmarried Irish resident in London, distrusts the English police and yet must depend on them to find her child. Unknown to Maureen, her brother Mike, an Irish Republican Army activist, has taken Kitty with him to use as a decoy so that he can approach the lord mayor without arousing suspicion. The bomb is in Kitty's lunch box, and her uncle intends to make her an innocent sacrifice to his political goals. The narrative shifts skillfully among the points of view of the participants:

Kitty, her mother, her Uncle Mike, the lord mayor, several police officers, and other characters involved in the mad rush toward a potential catastrophe—all well characterized, their motivations clearly captured. *The Lord Mayor of Death* combines swift-moving, tightly plotted action with evocative scenes, depth of characterization, and even humor. It demonstrates Babson's ability to credibly depict children and create adult interest in them.

Like *The Lord Mayor of Death, The Twelve Deaths of Christmas* (1979) experiments with structure and shifting points of view. It follows a tradition of Christmas crime stories going back to Charles Dickens. The setting is a London rooming house in which one of the lodgers is a serial killer. The opening chapter is the first-person narrative of a clearly mad person who impulsively kills a solicitor who has the temerity to suggest that the narrator needs more than legal help. Babson's experience in a solicitor's office comes into play here. In a pattern quickly established, the murderer uses a weapon conveniently at hand, in this first instance an inkstand. Chapters narrated by this unidentified killer recur regularly, each introduced by an epigraph from the carol "The Twelve Days of Christmas" and indicating the temporal movement of the plot toward its climax on Christmas Day. Other chapters are narrated in the third person, some describing the activities of lodgers in the rooming house and offering clues that point toward a variety of possible suspects. A set of chapters center on the two police officers who investigate the murders. Lines from a variety of Christmas songs appropriate to the action introduce a majority of chapters. Only one of the lodgers, Iris Loring, is clearly free of suspicion since the killer unambiguously refers to her. An appealing young artist, Iris becomes the focus of the killer's growing paranoia, compulsive hatred of others, and obsessive dread of the coming Christmas celebrations. Suspense tightens toward the end as her vulnerability becomes particularly clear. Babson cleverly and consistently characterizes the killer through such devices as headaches accompanying violent episodes and subtle allusions to the character's awareness of the potential for ordinary objects to become lethal weapons (a spray can of artificial snow, paraffin-soaked rags, and finally, the carving knife for the festive Christmas turkey). Tautly plotted, with the identity of the insane person skillfully hinted at and yet concealed, *The Twelve Deaths of Christmas* is an absorbing suspense novel.

So Soon Done For (1979) and *Queue Here for Murder* (1980; published in the United States as *Line Up for Murder,* 1981), published a year apart, demonstrate Babson's ability to handle quite different tones. Both examine London streets and how thoroughly the populations of London neighborhoods have changed over time. Babson has walked streets and lived in neighborhoods like those she describes and has been troubled by the social conflicts and changes she dramatizes. The first novel seriously and realistically examines the problem of homelessness and strikingly captures class tensions as urban squatters take over a temporarily vacant house in a fairly well-to-do London neighborhood, and local residents can do nothing legal because the owners are on the road and unavailable. In contrast, the second effectively draws comic characters and comic situations as an odd, highly incompatible assortment of bargain hunters line up overnight in order to be first at the Bonnard's department store New Year's sale. Herein Babson has the sweet, middle-aged Dorothy Witson, who has joined the queue seeking her own bargains, provide a counterpoint of past and present through her firsthand document of the new London. In *Twentieth Century Crime and Mystery Writers,* Babson confirms her pleasure in alternating "straight suspense" with "crime-with-comedy," a combination she employs more and more over time.

Dangerous to Know (1980) is what Beatrice Christiana Birchak calls a "back-of-the-press" novel, with a newspaperman narrator who works the dreary graveyard shift. Throughout her career Babson has been particularly interested in entertainment personalities, such as the resort nightclub singer depicted in *Death beside the Seaside* (1982; published in the United States as *Death beside the Sea,* 1983), the shipboard entertainment director and entertainers in *The Cruise of a Deathtime* (1983), and the "mystery tour" actors who stage a crime at an English country inn in *Weekend for Murder* (1985; published in the United States as *Murder on a Mystery Tour,* 1987). *The Cruise of a Deathtime,* an Agatha Christie–style maritime mystery with Africa the shipboard destination, is memorable for its bizarre murders (five movie viewers "skewered" through their chair backs).

In a pair of interconnected novels published in 1984, two families swap their homes in New England and England for a summer. For readers interested in Babson's experience as an American expatriate turned English, this pair of novels provides interesting observations on the two cultures. In *A Trail of Ashes* an English family visits the United States, and in *Death Swap,* which turns on mistaken identity, an American family visits England. Babson uses the two novels to effectively contrast the countries and to delineate typical attributes of American and British characters; the inclusion of correspondence between the wife and mother of one family to her counterpart in the other family reporting the respective tragedies in personal terms offers interesting possibilities as well. Each novel begins with the arrival of a family in the host country, followed by details of adjustments to the new culture and new complications. Babson tries to connect the novels through thematic ties, for example, English formality versus American informality (as the American family attempts to break through what they see as the standoffishness of the English), well-behaved English children versus their rowdy American counterparts, and even a genteel English cat versus a wide-ranging, randy Maine coon. Each family unwittingly becomes involved in a crime, and hints dropped by letter in one novel relate to events in the other. The solution to the mystery confronted by the American family explains the sudden death of the husband of the Englishwoman, the traumatic event responsible for her agreement to the swap of houses that forms the basis for the pair of novels. Thus, *Death Swap* solves a crime crucial to motivating the protagonist's actions in *A Trail of Ashes,* though in *A Trail of Ashes* this event is not presented as a mystery. The mystery into which the Englishwoman stumbles is not connected to the house swap but is integral to the contrast between countries. The conception of these novels is ingenious, but Babson struggles to set up intriguing parallels. The contrast between the behavior of American and British children seems particularly heartfelt. *A Trail of Ashes* and *Death Swap* were republished as *Whiskers and Smoke* (1997) and *Paws for Alarm* (1996), respectively, and their paperback editions featured charming cats on the front covers, though cats have nothing really to do with the stories.

Weekend for Murder employs a traditional British mystery pattern exploited by writers such as Christie, Ngaio Marsh, and Margery Allingham: the device of an actual murder occurring while a "murder game" or make-believe crime is taking place, so that at first the real murder seems part of the game. The story is set in an English manor turned hotel near Salisbury. The hotel hosts are trying to save the family home. Following another British mystery pattern, *Fatal Fortune* (1987) takes advantage of the dovetailed European train-and-ferry network that permits a passenger who boards a Luxembourg train in the early evening to connect in Ostende with a 2 A.M. ferry to Dover, as the heroine Hope Bradstone flees continental villains with her non-English-speaking nephew.

Reel Murder (1986), the first novel in Babson's second series, features actresses Trixie Dolan and Evangeline Sinclair, amateur detectives who repeatedly find themselves on hand when crime occurs. In *Reel Murder* Babson returns to the subject of movie stardom explored in *Murder, Murder, Little Star.* In both novels American stars differing greatly in age visit London for professional reasons. In *Reel Murder* two mature stars visit London for a "retrospective season" of the career of the older of the two. Evangeline, now in her eighties, plays the "grande dame" with gusto and has had a career that stretches from ingenue roles in silents to

Dust jacket for the U.S. edition of Babson's 1979 novel, in which a mad killer perpetrates a series of Yule-themed murders (Richland County Public Library)

recent grotesques in horror movies. Her unwilling but good-natured companion and the narrator of the novel is sixty-eight-year-old Trixie, who began her movie career as a dancer. A third elderly woman, also a former actress, Juanita Morez, has mysteriously gone into hiding–the victim of a botched face-lift–but plays a significant role as a supposed victim. Comic figures include Trixie's fortyish unmarried daughter, who hovers over her mother much to her irritation and dismay, and Gwenda, a drama student whose speech impediment (*r*s turned to *w*s, so she is "wowwied" about "Twixie") overcompensates for the Welsh accent she tries to hide. Two comic scenes turn on Trixie's dancing skills and physical endurance. In an impromptu dance lesson to Gwenda with photographers present, she unintentionally upstages Evangeline, the intended honoree of the occasion, much to the anger of the great star. Later, discovering an acquaintance busking (playing his clarinet in the London Tube for money), she impulsively dances to his music, high-kicks the hat off an impertinent tourist, and quickly gathers up the coins

*Dust jacket for the U.S. edition of Babson's 1984 novel, the first
of two crime novels involving a British family that trades
houses with an American family for a summer
(Richland County Public Library)*

thrown to them before a staid policeman approaches. Trixie is repeatedly caught between her desire not to embarrass her conventional daughter; her attempts to placate the demanding Evangeline, with whom she has had a long, troubled relationship; and her own free-spirited interests in the London scene and her new friends there. The novel effectively and sensitively contrasts the worlds of young, aspiring English actors and of former stars whose careers are ending or have ended.

Encore Murder (1989) and *Shadows in Their Blood* (1991) develop Trixie and Evangeline further. In the former, they rent a penthouse suite in a dilapidated warehouse and eavesdrop on peculiar and somewhat threatening tenants. In the latter, they are in Whitby, the setting for the English sections of Bram Stoker's *Dracula* (1897), shooting a new movie about vampires. While Babson does not contribute anything new to the literary interpretations of vampirism, she does use both vampire lore and, especially, the Whitby scene in ways integral to plot and character. This amusing novel effectively evokes the old city of Whitby—its ruined abbey, the old church with

its cemetery and the steep steps leading up to it from the town below, and the tourist shops and winding streets of the town. Babson captures the picturesque features of this English city and skillfully uses the chill weather and cold wind from the sea as backdrops. In *Break a Leg, Darlings* (1995) Trixie and Evangeline search for a new play to star in; their strategy, to scour the pub theaters and venues of the London fringe for just the right author, attracts the attention of a murderous stalker. Babson's love of the theater and her own theatergoing make details of place and scene convincing: she describes places she has been and areas of London she knows well.

As a cat lover, with beloved pets of her own, Babson draws on her personal knowledge of cats and cat lore. Like other modern writers who have made cats central to their stories (including Lilian Jackson Braun, Rita Mae Brown, Lydia Adamson, Garrison Allen, Paul Engleman, and Shirley Rousseau Murphy), Babson regularly features one or more cats, not simply as background but as central to plot and solution. *Nine Lives to Murder* (1992), an offbeat theater mystery, and *The Diamond Cat* (1994) include cat characters crucial to the plots and used in unusual, inventive ways. *Nine Lives to Murder* hinges on a somewhat pompous actor's accidental exchange of bodies with a resident feline rodent controller in a theater. This far-fetched device is handled with wit and even some pathos. Both Winstanley Fortescue, the actor, and Montmorency D. Mousa, also known as Monty, retain their own consciousnesses even while physical urges and memories of the bodies they temporarily inhabit are also present, and the strange personality splitting that results is handled, as several reviewers commented, with wit and cleverness. Fortescue, who narrates the novel, becomes a feline detective as he tries to protect his gravely ill human body, now inhabited by a cat's comparatively primitive awareness, to which he hopes somehow to return. His abilities to enter places where no human detective could and his insignificance, so different from the importance he was accustomed to assuming, helps him unravel the mystery, partly with the aid of the backstage crew and other cats. Babson draws on her knowledge of both theater and felines in this comic romp.

The Diamond Cat, on the other hand, centers around an ailurophile, Bettina, and its cat characters are seen only from the outside, with no anthropomorphizing. When a terrible storm blows out all electricity and kills a homing pigeon with smuggled diamonds concealed in the small tube it carries, Bettina, who is caring for four cats while their owners are away on a bank-holiday weekend, becomes entangled in a murder mystery. She discovers the dead pigeon and its freight, and one of the cats inadvertently swallows a diamond. As the weekend proceeds, she stores the pigeon in the freezer; watches for signs the cat will eliminate the diamond; copes with her obnoxious mother; observes strange figures exploring her neighborhood and asking odd questions; and attempts to determine why the pigeon was carrying the diamonds. Babson's characterizations of dictatorial mothers, long-suffering daughters, and antic cats are amusing and also suggestive of insights gleaned from personal experience. Bettina's mother is a recurring Babson type of elderly woman—insufferable, demanding, selfish, and never pleased. Babson viciously satirizes this repellent, dictatorial woman and then kills her off with a heart attack. Bettina, a particularly likable, resourceful young woman, deserves the happier life her mother's death frees her to enjoy with the police inspector she has just met.

Miss Petunia's Last Case (1996; published in the United States as *Canapés for the Kitties,* 1997), is one of Babson's most delightful novels. Her creation of funny, oddly touching personalities and relationships adds a distinctive element to her mysteries, and the three sisters (and village snoops) of *Miss Petunia's Last Case*—Petunia, Lily, and Marigold Pettifogg—are among her most comic figures. Mystery writer Lorinda Lucas has decided to kill off the trio, her most popular fictive creations, but runs into opposition from local fans. The novel juxtaposes a picturesque English village of fiction with Lucas's own village, Brimful Coffers, and the aristocrats of her invention with the informal writers' colony she is a part of. Babson's satiric portrait of a sharp-tongued reviewer who alienates everyone in the colony proves to be a red herring. Chapter 20, typical of the tongue-in-cheek wit that dominates this work, is Babson/Lucas's parody of mysteries such as those by Catherine Aird or Michael Innes, set among Britain's peers of the realm, with death by poison, moat, guillotine, and iron maiden ignored by the "Nob Squad." The cats Had-I and But-Known (as in the "Had I but Known" school of mystery detection, which embraces coincidence) prove integral to the action of the story (actually participating in the detection) as Babson purposefully blurs the line between art and reality.

The Multiple Cat (1999) is another rambling cat mystery, a classic tale of murder with a thin story line, scheming relatives, and a bumbling amateur detective, Annabel Hinchby-Smythe, who pretends to be an interior decorator in order to gather gossip for a scandal sheet. The murder of a reclusive millionaire results in Sally, a precocious stray cat, being heir to a fortune, a fact that provides amusing possibilities as relatives scram-

ble to prove their deep affection for felines. The cat proves more personable than the humans, however, and the idea of it meowing messages on the phone is hard to take, even for cat lovers. Babson's heroines sound arch, but for all her years in England, Babson is simply not in touch with British sensibilities and lacks a sense of regionalism, so that a novel like this one, though set in England, is not recognizably English at all.

Children in Babson's novels are often emotionally needy, neglected, and/or abused, and as a consequence they are shrill, unpredictable, and vulnerable. Eleven-year-old Robin in *A Tealeaf in the Mouse* (2000) is typical. The novel features a despairing youth, a new gang recruit grimly determined to prove his mettle by stealing a prized cat, only to find himself interrupting a murder. The sentimentality about cats expressed throughout Babson's canon, but particularly in her later works, reflects her personal obsession with her own beloved animals and her amusement at their antics. Her anthropomorphizing of cats in her detective stories is a by-product of her personal delight in her own pets, a fact she comments on on-line in "Keep on Purring" in *Mystery Readers Journal* (Winter 1990).

Unlike those authors who rely primarily on series detectives or who stick to a tested formula, Marian Babson offers a new experience with each novel. Her novels are often unpredictable in approach, in plotting, in characterization, and in quality. At their worst, their characters are one-dimensional; their plots strain credulity and verge on the mystical and the ridiculous. At their best, they are carefully crafted and skillfully handled. At times satiric, at times hilarious comedy, at times most serious or absolutely absurd, these novels are as varied as their number. They can be relied on for some wickedly nasty character sketches, some good-humored satire and punning, some slapstick, some interesting cat lore, some unexpected plot complications, and even more unexpected (and often gruesome) means of death.

References:

Mary Jean DeMarr, "Advent of Mystery: Pre-Christmas Rituals and Customs in Novels by Marian Babson, Carol Anne O'Marie, and Isabelle Holland," *Clues: A Journal of Detection,* 14 (Spring/Summer 1993): 49–67;

DeMarr, "Marian Babson: American/English Mystery Novelist," *Clues: A Journal of Detection,* 10 (Spring/Summer 1989): 63–74.

Robert Barnard

(23 November 1936 –)

J. Randolph Cox
St. Olaf College

BOOKS: *Imagery and Theme in the Novels of Dickens* (Bergen, Norway: Universitets Forlag, 1971; New York: Humanities Press, 1974);

Death of an Old Goat (London: Collins, 1974; New York: Walker, 1977);

A Little Local Murder (London: Collins, 1976; New York: Scribners, 1983);

Death on the High C's (London: Collins, 1977; New York: Walker, 1978);

Blood Brotherhood (London: Collins, 1977; New York: Walker, 1978);

Unruly Son (London: Collins, 1978); republished as *Death of a Mystery Writer* (New York: Scribners, 1979);

Posthumous Papers (London: Collins, 1979); republished as *Death of a Literary Widow* (New York: Scribners, 1980);

A Talent to Deceive: An Appreciation of Agatha Christie (London: Collins, 1980; New York: Dodd, Mead, 1980; revised edition, New York: Mysterious Press, 1987);

Death in a Cold Climate (London: Collins, 1980; New York: Scribners, 1981);

Mother's Boys (London: Collins, 1981); republished as *Death of a Perfect Mother* (New York: Scribners, 1981);

Sheer Torture (London: Collins, 1981); republished as *Death by Sheer Torture* (New York: Scribners, 1982);

Death and the Princess (London: Collins, 1982; New York: Scribners, 1982);

The Missing Brontë: A Perry Trethowan Novel (London: Collins, 1983); republished as *The Case of the Missing Brontë* (New York: Scribners, 1983);

Little Victims (London: Collins, 1983); republished as *School for Murder* (New York: Scribners, 1984);

Corpse in a Gilded Cage (London: Collins, 1984; New York: Scribners, 1984);

A Short History of English Literature (Oxford & New York: Blackwell, 1984);

Robert Barnard (photograph by Noelle Barnard)

Out of the Blackout (London: Collins, 1985; New York: Scribners, 1985);

Disposal of the Living (London: Collins, 1985); republished as *Fête Fatale* (New York: Scribners, 1985);

Political Suicide (London: Collins, 1986; New York: Scribners, 1986);

Bodies: A Perry Trethowan Novel (London: Collins, 1986); republished as *Bodies* (New York: Scribners, 1986);

Death in Purple Prose: A Perry Trethowan Novel (London: Collins, 1987); republished as *The Cherry Blossom Corpse* (New York: Scribners, 1987);

The Skeleton in the Grass (London: Collins, 1987; New York: Scribners, 1988);

At Death's Door (London: Collins, 1988; New York: Scribners, 1988);

Death and the Chaste Apprentice (London: Collins, 1989; New York: Scribners, 1989);

Death of a Salesperson (London: Collins, 1989); republished as *Death of a Salesperson, and Other Untimely Exits* (New York: Scribners, 1989);

A City of Strangers (London: Bantam, 1990; New York: Scribners, 1990);

A Scandal in Belgravia (London: Bantam, 1991; New York: Scribners, 1991);

A Fatal Attachment (London: Bantam, 1992; New York: Scribners, 1992);

A Hovering of Vultures (London: Bantam, 1993; New York: Scribners, 1993);

To Die Like a Gentleman, as Bernard Bastable (London: Macmillan, 1993; New York: St. Martin's Press, 1993);

The Masters of the House (London: HarperCollins, 1994; New York: Scribners, 1994);

Dead, Mr. Mozart, as Bastable (London: Little, Brown, 1995; New York: St. Martin's Press, 1995);

The Bad Samaritan (London: HarperCollins, 1995; New York: Scribners, 1995);

Too Many Notes, Mr. Mozart, as Bastable (London: Little, Brown, 1995; New York: Carroll & Graf, 1996);

The Habit of Widowhood and Other Murderous Proclivities (London: HarperCollins, 1996); republished as *The Habit of Widowhood* (New York: Scribners, 1996);

No Place of Safety (London: HarperCollins, 1997; New York: Scribner, 1998);

The Corpse at the Haworth Tandoori (London: HarperCollins, 1998; New York: Scribner, 1998);

A Mansion and Its Murder, as Bastable (New York: Carroll & Graf, 1998);

Touched by the Dead (London: HarperCollins, 1999); republished as *A Murder in Mayfair* (New York: Scribner, 2000);

Emily Brontë (London: British Library, 2000; New York: Oxford University Press, 2000);

Unholy Dying (London: HarperCollins, 2000; New York: Scribner, 2001);

The Bones in the Attic (London: HarperCollins, 2001; New York: Scribner, 2002);

The Mistress of Alderley (London: Allison & Busby, 2002; New York: Scribner, 2003).

OTHER: "The English Detective Story," in *Whodunit? A Guide to Crime, Suspense, and Spy Fiction,* edited by H. R. F. Keating (London: Windward, 1982;

New York: Van Nostrand Reinhold, 1982), pp. 30–36;

"Growing Up to Crime," in *Colloquium on Crime: Eleven Renowned Mystery Writers Discuss Their Work,* edited by Robin W. Winks (New York: Scribners, 1986), pp. 7–22;

"I Could Have Died Laughing," in *How to Write and Sell Mystery Fiction,* edited by Sylvia K. Burack (New York: Writer, 1990), pp. 13–19;

"Keep Taking the Tabloids," in *2nd Culprit: An Annual of Crime Stories,* edited by Liza Cody and Michael Z. Lewin (London: Chatto & Windus, 1993), pp. 275–282; (New York: St. Martin's Press, 1994), pp. 281–288;

"Boxing Unclever," in *A Classic Christmas Crime,* edited by Tim Heald (London: Pavilion, 1995), pp. 166–175; (New York: Berkley Prime Crime, 1998), pp. 190–200;

"Sense and Sensuality," in *Crime Through Time II,* edited by Miriam Grace Monfredo and Sharan Newman (New York: Berkley Prime Crime, 1998), pp. 180–189;

"Nothing to Lose," in *Malice Domestic 9,* edited, with an introduction, by Joan Hess (New York: Avon Twilight, 2000), pp. 22–23;

"The Lost Boy," in *Criminal Records,* edited by Otto Penzler (London: Orion, 2000), pp. 1–26.

SELECTED PERIODICAL PUBLICATIONS–
UNCOLLECTED: "The Choral Symphony: *Our Mutual Friend,*" *Review of English Literature,* 2 (July 1961): 89–99;

"Murder, Cranford Style," *Books and Bookmen,* 15 (June 1970): 30–32;

"Imagery and Theme in *Great Expectations,*" *Dickens Studies Annual,* edited by Robert B. Partlow, 1 (1970): 238–251;

"The Imagery of *Little Dorrit,*" *English Studies,* 52 (December 1971): 520–532;

"Anne Brontë: The Unknown Sister," *Edda: Nordisk Tidsskrift for Litteraturforskning,* 78 (1978): 33–38;

"What the Whispering Glades Whispered: Dennis Barlow's Quest in *The Loved One,*" *English Studies,* 60 (April 1979): 176–182;

"Agatha Christie," *London Magazine,* new series 19 (October 1979): 36–54;

"A Talent to Disturb: An Appreciation of Ruth Rendell," *Armchair Detective,* 16 (Spring 1983): 146–152;

"The Case of the Two Moving Fingers: Have American Editors Butchered Christie?" by Barnard and Louise Barnard, *Armchair Detective,* 18 (Summer 1985): 306–308;

"The Slightly Mad, Mad World of Christianna Brand: What Secret Ingredient Makes Her Novels So Scrumptious?" *Armchair Detective,* 19 (1986): 238–243;

"A Good Deed," *Ellery Queen's Mystery Magazine,* 92 (August 1988): 114–122;

"The Neapolitan Knight," *Armchair Detective,* 22 (1989): 266–270;

"The Face of Violence," *Ellery Queen's Mystery Magazine,* 93 (February 1989): 32–37;

"Not Much of a Life," *Ellery Queen's Mystery Magazine,* 93 (March 1989): 54–60;

"Divine Anger," *Ellery Queen's Mystery Magazine,* 94 (July 1989): 22–30;

"A Good Turn," *Ellery Queen's Mystery Magazine,* 94 (December 1989): 50–56;

"The Nick of Time," *Ellery Queen's Mystery Magazine,* 95 (January 1990): 28–33;

"An Exceptional Night," *Ellery Queen's Mystery Magazine,* 95 (March 1990): 112–120;

"The Man in Her Life," *Ellery Queen's Mystery Magazine,* 99 (February 1992): 58–63;

"A Sure-Fire Speculation," *Ellery Queen's Mystery Magazine,* 99 (June 1992): 103–109;

"Ordinary People: Sheila Radley's Novels," *Armchair Detective,* 25 (Winter 1992): 14–19;

"A Hotel in Bucharest," *Ellery Queen's Mystery Magazine,* 100 (Mid December 1992): 124–138;

"A Statesman's Touch," *Ellery Queen's Mystery Magazine,* 101 (March 1993): 23–31;

"The Eye of the Beholder," *Ellery Queen's Mystery Magazine,* 104 (October 1994): 148–157;

"The Slave Trade," *Ellery Queen's Mystery Magazine,* 105 (April 1995): 121–128;

"Good Time Had by All," *Ellery Queen's Mystery Magazine,* 109 (March 1997): 112–123;

"The Tosca Dagger," *Ellery Queen's Mystery Magazine,* 111 (March 1998): 133–141;

"An Evening with Fred and Rosemary," *Ellery Queen's Mystery Magazine,* 111 (May 1998): 83–91;

"Coming to an End," *Ellery Queen's Mystery Magazine,* 115 (February 2000): 70–83;

"A Slow Way to Di," *Ellery Queen's Mystery Magazine,* 115 (March 2000): 69–75;

"Old Dog, New Tricks," *Ellery Queen's Mystery Magazine,* 117 (March 2001): 82–90;

"A Confusion of Detectives," *Ellery Queen's Mystery Magazine,* 118 (July 2001): 123–129;

"The Path to the Shroud," *Ellery Queen's Mystery Magazine,* 119 (April 2002): 24–31;

"Going Through a Phase," *Ellery Queen's Mystery Magazine,* 119 (May 2002): 111–121;

"Dognapped," *Ellery Queen's Mystery Magazine,* 119 (June 2002): 86–97;

"Checking Out," *Ellery Queen's Mystery Magazine,* 120 (November 2002): 15–21.

Literary critic, academic scholar, and mystery writer, Robert Barnard has achieved the difficult balance between the seriousness the mystery deserves and the bizarre or eccentric characterizations necessary to comment on human frailty in more than ironic terms in a consistently satisfying manner. Working within the varied patterns offered by the classic tradition, he has made the truly comic detective work in contemporary terms, creating a Dickensian social satire founded on the peculiarities and abominable behavior of characters that nonetheless remain recognizable modern personalities and types. Barnard has been called a more sophisticated Agatha Christie; yet, unlike Christie's work, his novels are driven by characterization and satire rather than plot and, consequently, prove satisfying even when the detection itself is weak.

Robert Barnard was born on 23 November 1936 in Burnham-on-Crouch, Essex, England, the son of Leslie and Vera (Nethercoat) Barnard. Barnard was brought up in Brightlingsea, near Colchester, where he attended the Colchester Grammar School. His father, under the name Peter Burnham, wrote women's romance stories for the weekly magazines, turning out what his son has referred to as "very sub-Barbara Cartland" stories. Having a writer as a father might not have given young Barnard the idea of earning a living as a writer, but it might have been responsible for his first effort, a story he wrote as a boy that was published in a children's annual in the late 1940s. Barnard did well in exams and received an Exhibition to Balliol College, Oxford, where he initially read history but soon changed to English. He received his B.A. with honors (a second) in 1959. He worked for a year in the bookshop of the Fabian Society in London, then at a technical college (College of Further Education) in Accrington. During his five years in Australia as a lecturer in English at the University of New England, New South Wales, between 1961 and 1966 he met his wife (Mary Louise Tabor, a librarian) and acquired some of the material and inspiration for his first detective novel. They were married 7 February 1963. During this period he had an opportunity to teach off-campus in adult education, an experience he thoroughly enjoyed. He read deeply in the Victorian period, specializing in Charles Dickens, the Brontës, and Elizabeth Cleghorn Gaskell, and entered the world of publication with articles and reviews for academic journals. In 1968 he tried his hand at a comic novel about a fearsome woman politician, with Margaret Thatcher, then shadow minister of education, in mind, and although it was never finished, the publisher to whom he sent his first effort at a crime novel encouraged him to send another manuscript. His first publication to presage his career as a crime novelist was "Murder, Cranford Style" (*Books and Bookmen,* June 1970), in which he called the classic detective story a mirror of prewar middle-class habits and thought. As a student of the Victorian novel, he recognized as anachronistic even in the 1920s both Christie's portrait of village life and P. G. Wodehouse's literary world.

His first mystery, *Death of an Old Goat* (1974), set in Drummondale University in the outback of Australia, reflects Barnard's own experiences and wry observations while at the University of New England—particularly regarding the snobbish responses of visiting British scholars to a world at odds with their vision of themselves and the conflicted responses of the Australian academics, reverent of the "Oxbridge" ideal but contemptuous of individual representatives as irrelevant to the real world. He says that his central character is a portrait of himself and his reactions to Australia during his first months in the country but notes that his personal reactions changed considerably under the influence of sun and alcohol. In the novel, Professor Belville-Smith, who had bored generations of students with his lectures in England, tours Australia, where he bores new listeners with virtually the same recycled material he has delivered for the past fifty years, such rubbish that even when he mixes up his notes few notice the discrepancies. Of him, Barnard's narrator comments, "The modern world was something he had not seen and didn't want to see," and adds, "he had a vague idea that, if he didn't take any notice of it, it might pass away before very long and his own world come back." The murder of Professor Belville-Smith comes as a kind of grim comic relief to all except the bumbling and bumptious Police Inspector Royle, who has never had to try to solve a real crime before but whose approach to crime is somewhat self-serving, for example, excusing the peccadilloes of important locals in exchange for sex with their wives. Here, as in subsequent novels, Barnard effectively and convincingly portrays the grotesques in life, figures of Dickensian proportions and hilarious satire whose targets are apparent even to those without benefit of a university education. In fact, Barnard has frequently noted the influence of Dickens on his canon, asserting that he is "always pinching things from him" (*Dickens Contemporary Authors,* 1987). Barnard introduces his characters in satirical vignettes in the first chapters, a format he never allows to appear forced or unnatural but one which he varies somewhat in his late novels because of their more serious content.

Although it has been said that he left Australia in reaction to the insufferable heat of the Australian sum-

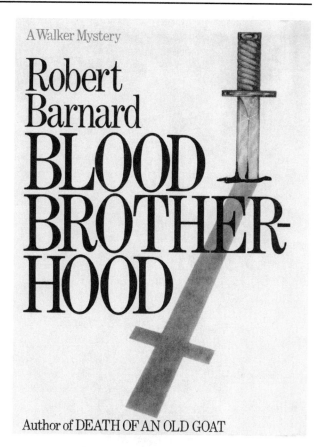

Dust jacket for the U.S. edition of Barnard's 1977 novel, set inside a cloistered religious community (Richland County Public Library)

mer and the boorishness of acquaintances, colleagues, and students, in fact, he claims that he would have enjoyed staying there longer if not for his wife's wish to live in Europe. Consequently, the Barnards moved north to Norway, where he lectured and studied for his Ph.D. at the University of Bergen. His dissertation was titled *Imagery and Theme in the Novels of Dickens,* and he received his doctoral degree in 1971. An analysis of Dickens's *Little Dorrit* (1855–1857) in *English Studies* that same year discusses the weakness of Dickens's plot as irrelevant, a minor drawback since "all else in the book coheres." This observation is telling because it could just as easily be applied to Barnard's own works, where plot takes second place to character and theme.

Upon graduating, Barnard accepted a position as senior lecturer in English at the University of Bergen and held that position until 1976, when he left Bergen for a position as professor of English at the University of Tromsø in Tromsø, Norway. This university, located three degrees north of the Arctic Circle, is the northernmost university in the world. Having begun his professional academic career in Australia, he was now at almost the opposite end of the globe. In contrast

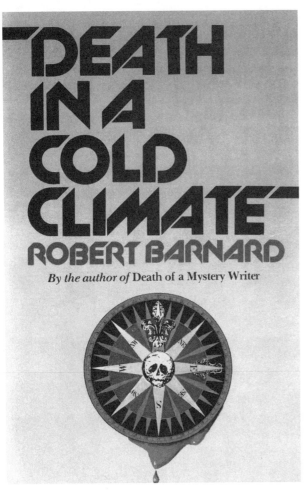

*Dust jacket for the U.S. edition of the 1980 mystery novel
Barnard set in Tromsø, Norway, where he taught as
a professor of English in the 1970s (Richland
County Public Library)*

to Australia, which Barnard took some time to adjust to, he immediately fell in love with Norway. He describes Norway as an ideal place to live, extolling its physical beauties and calling it "the most peaceful and most welcoming" place on Earth.

The year he left Bergen for Tromsø, Barnard published *A Little Local Murder* (1976), set in a closed society, the English village of Twyching. The town is about to gain some publicity by participating in a radio documentary that will be exported to its sister city in Wisconsin, but the plans of Radio Broadwich to place Twyching on the map bring out the worst in its citizens and heighten their individual pretentiousness, affording Barnard an opportunity to display his talent for caricature. The murder does not even take place until some sixty pages into the novel, in part because the satiric characterization is more important to Barnard than the plot. Even in this early period, the victims do not always deserve their fates, but Barnard seldom leaves any doubt which char-

acter has been singled out for the distinction. In *Death on the High C's* (1977), the flamboyant opera singer Gaylene Ffrench is not only the most odious character, a prima donna who goes out of her way to antagonize others, but the murder scene is carefully contrived to make her demise inevitable: scantily clad and perspiring, she touches an electrified doorknob while standing on a metal doormat. The police officers in this story are slow to reach conclusions readers are likely to come to much sooner. The characters herein are flashier and less down-to-earth than in Barnard's previous two novels, but they fit the world of show business he depicts, with the geographically closed society replaced by one of a specific profession. Even the chapter titles referring to opera and music are appropriate to the milieu, with, for example, the chapter in which the murder takes place called "La Commedia E Finita."

The closed society in *Blood Brotherhood* (1977) is even more restricted, the religious community of St. Botolph's, to which each of the main characters makes a pilgrimage. The humor is not as broad as in *Death on the High C's,* but the characterizations are more deeply etched. While Barnard admitted in a 1984 interview in *Armchair Detective* that he is not particularly religious, that irreligiosity has not prevented him from noting those elements that distinguish religious people or from employing religious phrases and symbols with telling significance. Even the title of the novel gains significance when Brother Dominic is found dead in his own gore, a visiting bishop nearby, his hands covered in the blood of a lamb. Barnard takes advantage of his Norwegian experience to introduce into the community of St. Botolph's two Norwegian women, one of whom speaks the correct, but lifeless, English of the typical nonnative speaker.

Having published four detective novels with traditional genre settings (academic, bucolic, theatrical, and religious communities), Barnard makes the detective genre itself the object of his biting satire in *Unruly Son* (1978), published in the United States as *Death of a Mystery Writer* (1979). The chapter titles utilize literary allusions peculiar to detective literature, including "The Unpleasantness at the Prince Albert," "Strong Poison," and "Death Comes as the End," in the tradition of Christie and Dorothy L. Sayers. The murder victim, best-selling thriller writer Oliver Fairleigh, is portrayed in the grand manner, as a poseur who dictates his books to a distracted secretary. Fairleigh dies on his sixty-fifth birthday while sampling a special liqueur in his own library. Few mourn his passing, not even his fellow detective writers, who respond as tactfully as possible. Ironically, the inspector summoned to the case has a voice with a Welsh lilt, much like that of Fairleigh's own detective character, Powys. The book abounds in such parallels between Fairleigh's fiction and Barnard's own, ones a less skillful writer might overplay. Although Barnard has suggested otherwise, the name Oliver Fairleigh echoes that of another fictional detective-story writer, Christie's Mrs. Ariadne Oliver, and there may be some unconscious inspiration at work here.

Barnard satirizes the literary production of critical editions and apparatus connected with the works of prominent literary figures in *Posthumous Papers* (1979), published in the United States as *Death of a Literary Widow* (1980). A researcher who wishes to write a study of a recently rediscovered and newly fashionable writer, Walter Machin, and to interview the great man's widow and his former wife discovers that exhuming the past can be deadly. The two ladies, each of whom claims to be the widow Machin, have little love for each other, and the murder of Hilda Machin, the first Mrs. Machin, can be quite plausibly laid at the door of the survivor, Viola. A published writer and academic, Barnard knows the frailties and abominable behavior of people in the literary world from the inside and possesses a sound sense of how to use literary allusion to powerful effect, without leaving the reader overwhelmed, intimidated, or bored.

As a scholar and theoretician in the detective genre, Barnard published his most extended piece of criticism in 1980, a critical study titled *A Talent to Deceive: An Appreciation of Agatha Christie*. Unlike many other books about Christie, *A Talent to Deceive* is not a compendium of trivia but a solid, readable assessment of what Christie set out to do, how well she succeeded, and what makes her books so popular. Albert A. Bell Jr., in the Salem Press *Critical Survey of Mystery and Detective Fiction* (1988), notes that he is not alone in considering this work "the finest critical study extant" on Christie.

Barnard's next novel, *Death in a Cold Climate* (1980), his first since *Death of an Old Goat* not to be set in England, is also his first written in a fairly serious vein. Set in Tromsø, it conveys the alienation one feels at being in a foreign country and exposed to a foreign culture, a feeling essential to the plot. The murder victim is not initially described as intimately as those in his earlier works, partly because the police must first learn who the man was and where he came from before they can understand why he was buried in the snows of North Norway. Symbolically, the story begins in the darkest time of year, when the sun never appears over the horizon, and concludes in the bright sunlight of spring. The season of resurrection has returned to Norway (an event perhaps only a Norwegian can appreciate fully) and with it, the denouement. *Death in a Cold Climate* offers humorous comments on Norwegian cuisine and depicts the Korvold family with a rare combination of humor and pathos.

In *Mother's Boys* (1981), published in the United States as *Death of a Perfect Mother,* Barnard returns to his special brand of comic realism, in this case, what Peter S. Prescott called in *Newsweek* "a comedy of working-class manners" (19 October 1981). The humor is consistent; the characters are recognizable grotesques; and the death of the murder victim, the odious Lil Hodsden, comes as a relief to all.

Probably no detective in fiction has had as bizarre an introduction to his readers as Peregrine (Perry) Trethowan of the CID in *Sheer Torture* (1981), published in the United States as *Death by Sheer Torture* (1982). Trethowan is Barnard's first recurring detective figure (he follows in three works in succession). Fourteen years after he has been happily disowned by his eccentric aristocratic family, Police Inspector Trethowan reads a newspaper account of his own father's spectacular death on a torture machine. His response is, "That's just how one of my family would die and just how one of my family would murder. . . . I'll be the laughing-stock of the CID the rest of my life." Embarrassed by his family (which includes at least one Nazi sympathizer and one poet) and happily married to a woman working on a degree in Arabic, Trethowan investigates his father's death only when ordered to do so by his superior officer. The bizarre family has long been a traditional ingredient in the detective story, but it has rarely been the detective's own family. Having Trethowan narrate the story gives Barnard a chance to experiment with the first-person point of view, and the fact that traditionally the narrator of the hard-boiled detective story is the detective himself (like Raymond Chandler's Philip Marlowe) may be responsible for Trethowan's tough tone, a tone not previously present in Barnard's books. In its lampoon of British gentlemanly eccentrics, the novel seems like a cross between the works of Roald Dahl and those of Ngaio Marsh, and *Kirkus Reviews* calls it "an oddly Dickensian modern mystery" (15 January 1982).

In *Death and the Princess* (1982), Trethowan, now a superintendent in the CID, is a trifle disappointed to be asked to serve as a bodyguard. The individual in question is the Princess Helena, a diminutive and minor royal person whose specialty is delivering speeches (written for her) about the plight of the elderly. She admits to Trethowan that she has "dreadful difficulty" with the speeches they give her and in fact feels "awfully stupid." Yet, she attracts a circle of men (not all of them admirers), several of whom are found dead under unusual circumstances. The novel is convincingly linked to the previous one by references to the death of Trethowan's father, enough of a cause célèbre for many people to be familiar

Dust jacket for the U.S. edition of Barnard's 1981 novel Sheer Torture, *which introduces his series character Inspector Peregrine Trethowan (Richland County Public Library)*

with it; thus, their comments arise naturally enough in the dialogue. Trethowan needs his wife's help to catch the murderer but then lacks the evidence to keep him. "I had totally misjudged," he says to the readers in unexpected direct address.

Trethowan's third case, *The Missing Brontë* (1983), slightly retitled *The Case of the Missing Brontë* in the United States, is a variant on another traditional genre motif, the search for a missing literary manuscript. While having their car repaired in a Yorkshire village (they are on vacation), Trethowan and his wife relax in a pub, where they meet Edith Wing, a retired schoolteacher who claims to own a previously unknown manuscript by Emily Brontë. Trethowan suggests she take it to the nearest university for verification. Soon afterward he is called back to the village from London when Wing is beaten nearly to death in her home and the manuscript stolen. The background of English literature in this novel is not mere window dressing, with coyly dropped quotations in which the characters try to top each other with their expertise in an ongoing game of intellectual trivial pursuit. Instead, it

serves as an underlying current that arises naturally from the plot and reinforces and substantiates character and action, in part because of Barnard's own thorough knowledge of the field (including a published essay on Anne Brontë) and in part to his instinct for knowing how much detail is enough. The amount of professional lore in a Barnard novel always suggests that he knows the subject thoroughly (the opera, monastic life, or the routes through the stately homes) and holds back much more than he reveals. In reality, it is the result of sound research and the selective use of what he has learned. The university in *The Missing Brontë* is another Barnard institution that strikes a responsive chord for its accurate depiction of familiar types, in this case second-rate intellectuals trying to survive in a society that has not kept pace with the times. Trethowan describes them as "snivelling," "self-important," and "windy and whiney," demanding "special privileges" while doing nothing to deserve them.

For years Barnard maintained a dual existence as professor of English and contributor to academic journals and as a crime novelist. He enjoyed teaching literature at the university level but says that he found crime writing even more stimulating and pleasurable. Finally, in 1983, he made a difficult career decision and requested a leave of absence from the University of Tromsø, during which time he decided to terminate his position as professor of English to devote himself to full-time writing. He had been away from England for so many years that he felt out of touch with the everyday details of life necessary to keep his comic realism from becoming comic fantasy. Even though he left Norway reluctantly, the lure of full-time writing brought him to Leeds, and the same year *Little Victims* was published (published in the United States in 1984 as *School for Murder*). The growing interest in his books in the United States was one reason Barnard felt free to relinquish his dual role as educator and writer. Having an American publisher as well as a British brought him financial freedom to travel occasionally to the United States, to take holidays to the Mediterranean, and to begin a new career writing short fiction as well as novels. He says he plans to continue visiting the United States whenever possible because the enthusiasm of his fans there provides him an ego boost.

Before making the break with his academic career, he arranged to publish *A Short History of English Literature* (1984), intended primarily for use by students in foreign universities, with whom he was thoroughly familiar. The result of seventeen years of lectures to his own students in Australia and Norway, the book is a lively and sound introduction to the field.

Barnard has said he has purposefully avoided repeating himself too often. Villages, the opera, stately homes, and academe have all served as backdrops to the dramas of his devising. Having used a series character in three novels, he dispensed with Trethowan for the next one but kept him in reserve for later stories. The reader coming directly to *Little Victims* after reading the Trethowan books would be surprised at the shift in style and approach. The setting in *Little Victims* is a private day school named Burleigh, where schoolboy pranks become increasingly deadly (such as razor blades in a face towel) and lead to the inevitable murder (critics have noted parallels with Dickens's *Nicholas Nickleby*, 1838–1839). Burleigh is a dying institution in more ways than one and is inhabited by such imaginatively named characters as Headmaster Crumwallis, Onyx Muggeridge, and Hilary Frome. Barnard has always followed Dickens in choosing appropriate names for his characters, ones that guide the reader's attitude toward them while often adding to the humor. The name Sir Oliver Fairleigh in *Unruly Son* should suggest the tradition of "fair play" in distributing clues that provide readers ample opportunity to solve the mystery. The assured, self-centered opera singer Gaylene Ffrench (in *Death on the High C's*) clearly enjoys

calling attention to herself. Even the name of his detective, Peregrine Trethowan, significantly suggests a creature of prey, a falcon. Naming a boys' school—a male bastion—Burleigh (with an aristocratic spelling) suggests further satiric authorial comment. The plot in *Little Victims* is complex, growing out of a fully realized subculture defined by the staff meeting called to find a qualified matron, the penetrating vignettes of the members, and the glimpses into the classroom. At least one reviewer placed the novel in the same category as books that examine the trials of adolescence such as William Golding's *Lord of the Flies* (1954) and J. D. Salinger's *The Catcher in the Rye* (1951).

In his next crime novel, *Corpse in a Gilded Cage* (1984), the satiric target is the landed gentry. When a distant relative of the owner of a stately home inherits the estate and the earldom, it comes as a surprise to his family that he finds the inheritance a burden and decides to unload it. Matters are complicated by the possibility that one of his family would like to succeed him and may be too impatient to wait for his natural demise.

Barnard's works echo his genre predecessors, both in honest tribute and affectionate jest, and his interviews and critical essays on other writers often suggest the direction his next novel will take. For example, when in 1983 he published his appreciation of the work of Ruth Rendell in *Armchair Detective,* he was plotting a psychological novel in the manner of Rendell's insightful works. Barnard described her mind as "unusually attuned to the odd, the menacing, the abnormal," and so is his own mind in *Out of the Blackout* (1985). Like Rendell's works, this novel is serious in tone, lacking the clever chapter titles of past works. The novel takes place over three different periods in time. In 1941 the true identity of five-year-old Simon Thorn, found at the Yeasdon railway station, lies at the heart of the mystery. No amount of questioning will elicit much information from the child. In 1956 the boy, now known as Simon Cutheridge after the family who took him in and raised him, begins to have a clearer image of his past when he recognizes the house where he used to live and wonders if an overdeveloped capacity for guilt might be a clue to his complete story. In 1964 he is confronted with the startling truth. *Out of the Blackout* is as complex as any of Barnard's novels and is wholly compelling, its characterizations and observations of human nature rich and deep, its shifting point of view challenging. The characters in the novel are not the Dickensian grotesques of the early comic novels but the darker side of Dickens, the grim reality of *Hard Times* (1854).

If *Out of the Blackout* was a tribute to Rendell, *Disposal of the Living* (1985; published in the United States as *Fête Fatale*) suggests Jane Austen or Barbara Pym. Barnard returns to the comic novel—his own particular

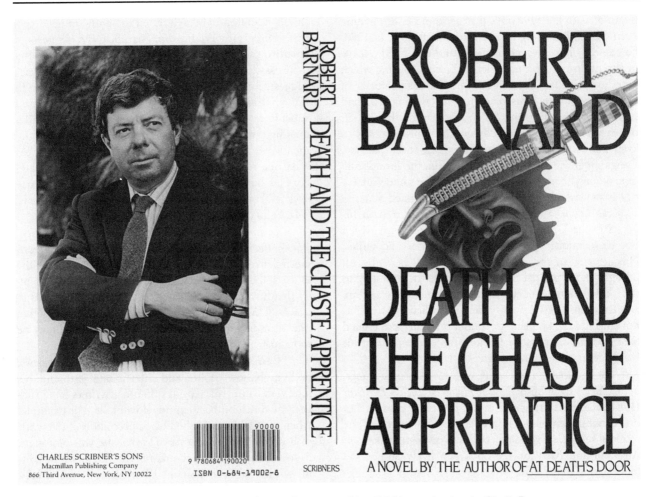

Dust jacket for the U.S. edition of Barnard's 1989 novel in which his recurring detective Charlie Peace
investigates murder at a theater festival (Richland County Public Library)

territory—but the first-person point of view is that of a woman whose husband, the town veterinarian, is the murder victim. The Yorkshire English village setting, Hexton-on-Weir, is unlike any Barnard has used previously, though his humorous characterization of the townspeople is familiar. Barnard does not play totally fair with the reader, for the solution hinges on a knowledge of Scandinavian and obscure British law. The celibate vicar's relationship with the dominant feminine population affords Barnard wide satiric scope. So too does the closely knit profession of politicians in *Political Suicide* (1986). Reviewers have likened Barnard's description of the election campaign to one in Dickens's *The Pickwick Papers* (1836–1837). Once again, the murder has occurred before the opening chapter. Jim Partridge is undeniably dead, though Superintendent Sutcliffe, on the brink of retirement, wonders if the death really was the suicide it appears to be. He is hampered in his investigations to some degree by the fact that no one seems to care how Partridge died, only that he did so.

In an essay for Robin W. Winks's *Colloquium on Crime* (1986), Barnard admits he finds critical praise of his deep knowledge of those areas of life that form the background to his world of crime a source of both amusement and satisfaction. He claims no greater expertise in the backstage world of opera or of life in a stately home than research and reading can provide. Instead, he believes it is the way in which he employs his facts that provides verisimilitude. Thus, when he chose the trade in human flesh (soft-core pornography, child pornography, and bodybuilding) as the background for the aptly titled *Bodies* (1986), he did not need to know more about the subject than his potential readers. Imagination is what counts, he argues, although he says he did seek out the seamier parts of the London underworld, which, he found, were not what they used to be. The grittier style of *Bodies* accompanies the return of detective hero Perry Trethowan. Trethowan's wife is present, but the dottier members of his family have been shelved. There is much to revel in here, but there are also some disappointments. For once the blend of humor and pathos, the balance between the seriousness of the crime of murder and the comic possibilities of the characters, tilts toward the tragic when readers least expect or desire it. On the positive side, Barnard presents the sordid without discomfort or exploitation. He tastefully approaches the possibilities for double entendres and burlesque buffoonery that the underworld of pornography suggests without going over the edge. People behave abominably but are not the grotesques who usually inhabit Barnard's world.

As Trethowan accompanies his sister, Cristobel, a newly published writer, to the convention of the World Association of Romantic Novelists (WARN) near Bergen, Norway, in *Death in Purple Prose* (1987; published in the United States as *The Cherry Blossom Corpse*), Barnard lightheartedly draws on his childhood memories of his father's profession and of his time in Norway to satirize both the romance-novel industry and some areas of Norwegian society. The murder of a famous writer of romance novels exposes the secrets of many other characters. One romance writer asserts, "We're all trash vendors." Barnard's characters are a compelling mixture of stereotype and humanized figure, with, for example, Mary Sweeney's drab, "sensible" attire and "indeterminate" features hiding the "sharp hard glint in the eye" that reveals a piercing intellect. By contrast, the coy and "overly made" romance maven Amanda Fairchild's sugary expressions and romantic prose barely disguise her personal denigration of the male sex.

In a more serious mood, reminiscent of *Out of the Blackout, The Skeleton in the Grass* (1987), set in 1936, contrasts the serenity of a traditional, civilized, and idealized Britain with the destruction of order in the years leading to World War II. *At Death's Door* (1988), another literary mystery, reintroduces Chief Inspector Meridith, the Welsh policeman who works on the Fairleigh case in *Unruly Son*. When Myra Mason, the actress mistress of novelist Benedict Cotterel, is murdered, suspicion falls on their illegitimate daughter, Cordelia, who has arrived at the stately home to write a book about her father. There is no secret that Myra had not been the best of mothers to Cordelia, and the mother-daughter conflict dominates.

Death and the Chaste Apprentice (1989) explores the world of the stage, with the Ketterick Arts Festival performance of a justly forgotten Elizabethan drama, *The Chaste Apprentice of Bowe,* serving as the focus and the motive for the murder. Detective Charlie Peace (who briefly appeared in *Bodies* and whose name also belongs to a notorious nineteenth-century criminal) is a black policeman with the Metropolitan CID who just happens to be in the audience when Des Capper is murdered during the performance. The dialogue is spry and witty, the pages peppered with references to plays

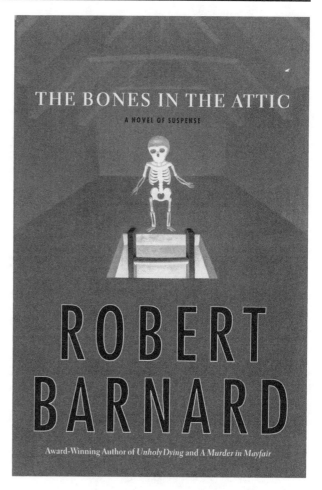

Dust jacket for the U.S. edition of Barnard's 2001 novel, in which the discovery of a child's skeleton leads a soccer star to investigate a mystery from his childhood (Richland County Public Library)

and actors drawn from the rich heritage of English drama. The actor characters behave as readers would expect actors to behave: emoting when they speak and larger than life. Barnard's chapter titles suggest traditional setting designations and stage directions from a script: "The Manager's Office," "People Talking," "The Corridors."

Throughout his writing career, Barnard has produced mysteries on a smaller canvas—short stories, primarily for *Ellery Queen's Mystery Magazine,* that demand a tighter focus and vignettes and characters that do not fit the larger novel format. The short story provides him a forum for ideas and material too good to discard: truly nasty children, dotty aristocrats, and ingenious murderers who use their reading to advantage or who trip themselves up by their own cleverness. The first sixteen of these stories were collected in *Death of a Salesperson* (1989; published in the United States as *Death of a Salesperson, and Other Untimely Exits*). Since the publication of

CHAPTER ONE

When Caroline came in from the garden she was pleased to find that Mrs Hogbin had gone upstairs to do the bathrooms. She had had cleaning ladies whom she'd regarded as friends, whom she'd been more pleased to sit down with over a cup of tea than a letter than those whom she called friends. Mrs Hogbin wasn't one of those. [many of her own generation]

She poked her head round the door of what had once been a bedroom.

"Tea, Alexander? Coffee, milk, coke?"

"No thanks, Mum," he so said, hardly looking up from the screen that mesmerised him. "Mum: I need a whole lot of new software."

"Then you're going to have to wait for quite a while."

"Oh Mum! I've got to have it. I bet Maurice buys all the latest stuff for Guy."

"Guy is really twenty, like Maurice's son, and he's about to start a computer degree course at the City University."

"So what? He's been computer mad for years. You have to start young to really be on top of them. I bet if I asked —"

"Don't even think of asking Maurice. My God — doesn't he do enough for us all?"

She shut the door on his already-opening mouth. At least he'd looked up from that bloody screen. Unfortunately, before she could get to the sitting room she was caught by Mrs. Hogbin descending the stairs with a bucket.

"I'll be finished in half an hour, Mrs. Cawley. If I could have your company, just to the bus-stop —"

"Of course Thora. You never used to be so nervous, though —"

"It's all these paedophiles. It doesn't feel like nobody's safe — their kids any longer."

As she proceeded through it to the kitchen it occurred to Caroline that she not only didn't know how to pronounce paedophile, she had no idea what they were. It had become a synonym for what [——], — Caroline's childhood, used to be called a "sex maniac."

Manuscript draft and typewritten revised draft for the first pages of Barnard's 2002 novel,
The Mistress of Alderley *(Collection of Robert Barnard)*

3134 Words.

CHAPTER ONE

Rural Idyll

When Caroline came in from the garden, she was pleased to find that

Mrs Hogbin had gone upstairs to do the bathrooms. ~~She~~ *Caroline* had had

cleaning ladies in the past whom she'd regarded as friends, whom

she'd been more pleased to sit down with over a cup of tea and a

scone than any of the theatrical people she loosely called her friends.

Mrs Hogbin wasn't one of them.

        She came through to the spacious hallway and poked her head round

the door of what had once been a box-room.

        "Tea, Alex? Coffee, coke, milk?"

        "No thanks, ~~Mum~~." her son said, hardly looking up from the screen

that mesmerised him. "Mum: I need a whole lot of new software."

        "Then you're going to have to need for quite a while."

        "Oh Mum! I've got to have it! I bet ~~Maurice~~ *Marius* buys all the latest

stuff for Guy."

        That was a line Caroline always felt she had to nip in the bud. *

Made, I maybe wh. Anyway "Guy is nearly twenty, he's ~~Maurice~~ *Marius*'s son, and he's about to start

a computer degree course at ~~the City~~ *St. Andrews* University."

        "So what? He's been computer mad for years. *as hos stuff I cald only drawn about* You have to start

young to be really on top of them. I bet if I asked -- "

        "Don't even <u>think</u> of asking ~~Maurice~~ *Marius*. Just think of all the calls

he has on his money. My God -- doesn't he do enough for us all?"

        She shut the door on his already-opening mouth. At least he'd

looked up from that bloody screen. Unfortunately before she could

get to the sitting room she was caught by Mrs Hogbin, descending the

stairs with a bucket.

* *Guy was not the spoilt child of a rich man: he was not given lavish pocket-money, or bought everything his young mind could covet.*

- 2 -

"I'll be finished in half an hour, Mrs ~~Hartley~~ Fawley. If I could have your company, just to the bus stop. -- "

"Of course, Thora. You never used to be so nervous, though -- "

"It's all those feedopiles. It doesn't feel like nobody's safe in their beds any longer."

As she waddled through to the kitchen it occurred to Caroline that ~~she~~ Thora (did) not only not know how to pronounce paedophile, she had no idea what they were. So much for the educational mission of the popular press. The word had become for the tabloids a synonym for what in Caroline's childhood used to be called a "sex maniac."

Luckily when the half hour was up and Mrs Hogbin was pulling on her wholly unnecessary coat Alexander said he needed to go down to the village shop for his chocolate supply. In fact he was going for cigarettes, but so far he had successfully kept this habit from his mother, and even from his sister Stella. He was a naturally secretive boy, who collected > collated information occasionally, but never willingly drawn ~~from whom all information had to be srewed~~.

Caroline went into the sitting room, then crossed to the large window that looked out on to the garden. The roses at the far end were looking ~~much~~ light better ~~after the autumn pruning she had just given~~ in their second flowering than they had = their first ~~them~~. There had been an interesting ~~variety~~ blend in the two big rosebeds when ~~the Falcos~~ Thora she > Caroline had taken ~~took~~ the house over, but she had introduced one or two more unusual types that had enhanced the effect. People commented, and inspected the new varieties closely, and that pleased Caroline.

The lawn had been splendid all ~~summer~~ year, but that had not been due to her. The mowing had mostly been done by Alexander, and Mr Wilks from the village had come to spray the lawn feed and keep down the moss and dandelions. The whole garden had looked a picture ~~all summer~~, and when she ~~was~~ had been asked, in an emergency, if the village fête could be switched to Alderley she had quite happily agreed. Everyone was

that book Barnard has produced enough stories to fill at least two more collections.

In 1990 Barnard returned to the theme of the bizarre family in *A City of Strangers*. The Phelans (suggestive of "felon") are equally known for their dreadful behavior (including petty theft and prostitution) and their squalid living conditions. Then, when Jack Phelan wins the pools and plans to buy an imposing Victorian house in an area above their accustomed station in life, the normally law-abiding, respectable residents plot to stop this encroachment on their tranquillity.

In *A Scandal in Belgravia* (1991) the writer-narrator, Peter Proctor, is not a creator of either belles lettres or popular potboilers but a retired cabinet minister writing his memoirs. Despite his attempts to focus on events in his own life, he is hindered in his labors by his distracting memories of the bludgeoning murder of Timothy Wycliffe, a young aristocrat and colleague in the Foreign Office. Obsessed with these memories, he seeks the truth behind the thirty-year-old murder. The death was originally blamed on one of Wycliffe's boyfriends and consequently was hushed up, but Proctor comes to doubt the official report. Again, Barnard effectively researches a profession to produce a convincing portrait of British society during the 1950s and the people who then walked the corridors of government power.

A Fatal Attachment (1992) provides a glimpse into another kind of writer's life: that of the professional biographer. Lydia Perceval writes popular biographies of George Gordon, Lord Byron and Lord Horatio Nelson that are as elegantly turned out as her name suggests they should be. At work on her latest biography, she struggles to reproduce the inner thoughts of her royal subject. Divorced, with no children of her own, Lydia tends to take over the lives of other people's children and edge out their real parents. This pattern of dominating attachment began with her own nephews but spread to the Bellingham brothers. Despite satiric touches, this novel is another psychological study in the Rendell mode. Detective Peace, newly transferred to the West Yorkshire Police (near Leeds, Barnard's own town), is the investigating officer when Lydia is murdered. He is joined in this endeavor by Superintendent Mike Oddie from *A City of Strangers*.

Detective Constable Peace is on hand as well in the delightfully titled *A Hovering of Vultures* (1993), a reference to the coterie of literary enthusiasts eager to study and exploit the work and personae of Susannah and Joshua Sneddon. These latter-day Brontës did not write great literature, but what career they had was cut short by a murder-suicide. The theme places this novel in the same group as Barnard's other literary society murder stories, especially *The Missing Brontë* and *Death in Purple Prose*.

Given his early academic work in Victorian literature, it was perhaps inevitable that Barnard would write an historical mystery. *To Die Like a Gentleman* (1993), published under the transparent pseudonym of Bernard Bastable, is set in Victorian England and told principally through letters and diary entries that expertly emulate the style of the period. This structure enables Barnard to tell his story from multiple viewpoints and to pay tribute to a predecessor in the genre, Wilkie Collins, whose classics *The Woman in White* (1860) and *The Moonstone* (1868) are narrated through diaries and letters. The next year Barnard published under his own name *The Masters of the House*–a novel imitative of a structure dear to fellow British mystery writer Peter Dickinson, utilizing two time periods with a child or children from one period reexamining the past with adult knowledge. In this case the dates are 1979 and the 1990s. The death in childbirth of his wife shocks Dermot Heenan into retreating from reality. In the aftermath his two older children, thirteen-year-old Matthew and his sister Anne, take over caring for their father as well as for their two younger siblings. Alternating the events of 1979 with glimpses of 1993, when the children, now grown, reconsider this period in their lives, heightens interest and suspense and relieves the extreme tension created by the modern segment of the story. The children, now masters of the house, dare not let anyone learn what has happened to their father for fear of interference with their precarious new lifestyle. When the interference does come in the person of Carmen O'Keefe, she is murdered by person or persons unknown. Matthew and Anne must dispose of the body, an action that accelerates their swift movement toward adulthood. Help comes from a totally unexpected source. This serious novel in the vein of *Out of the Blackout* has little leavening of humor.

Barnard returned to the historical mystery in 1995, again as Bastable, a name he has used for all of his historical fiction, even his short stories. Beginning with the fictional premise that Wolfgang Amadeus Mozart did not die in 1791 but lived into his sixties in England, Barnard sets mysteries for him to solve. In *Dead, Mr. Mozart,* the title of which derives from a conversational exchange about the condition of King George III ("Worse, Mr. Gibbs?" "Dead, Mr. Mozart."), the coronation of a new king occasions a new Mozart opera, a comic opera as befits the mood of the nation. It is also the occasion for a murder–a servant girl found dead in the theater dressing room. The first-person account provides Barnard an opportunity for his satirical comments on English society past and present, and his knowledge of music and the period comes through without being forced.

Barnard's next novel, *The Bad Samaritan* (1995), features a religious community as setting and Detective Constable Peace and Superintendent Oddie as investigators. Barnard divides the book into three parts, assigning a different viewpoint to each part. Barnard explores the relationships between individuals in the parish, primarily as individuals respond to the knowledge that Rosemary, the wife of the vicar, has literally lost her faith and feels a great weight lifted from her. As a consequence she goes to the seaside to rethink her situation and meets a young Bosnian, who has left his wife and child in the war zone. When he follows Rosemary home and a friend of hers who recognizes him dies suddenly, Rosemary's world becomes even more topsy-turvy, and the community responds with various degrees of deliciously un-Christian behavior toward her.

Too Many Notes, Mr. Mozart (1995), published under the pseudonym Bastable, takes the reader a decade forward in the fictional life of the composer, to 1830, with Mozart now seventy-three years old and the piano tutor to young Princess Victoria. The title comes from the suggestion made by Emperor Joseph II in 1782 at the premiere of Mozart's *Abduction from the Seraglio* and dramatized by Peter Shaffer's play *Amadeus* (1980), as well as the 1984 motion picture, that Mozart's compositions suffered from too many notes and would benefit by the removal of some of them. In the novel Victoria requests easy pieces to learn, ones without too many notes. Narrating from his vantage point as her teacher, Mozart observes characters at court, real and imagined, and is plausibly present at a murder as well.

The author remains fond of both his alter ego, Bastable, and Mr. Mozart, but neither has really gained enduring popularity. While there has been a further novel by Bastable, it is unlikely there will be more. Barnard is the first to admit that some of his books are not as good as others, that some were hurried to their completion and that others just do not work out the way he thought they would. Such is the case with *No Place of Safety* (1997), in which Peace's search for two missing teenagers leads to an unofficial refuge for the homeless run by someone with a particular relationship to the young people. Like many of Barnard's later novels, the tone is more serious than satiric.

Originally published in *Ellery Queen's Mystery Magazine,* the seventeen short stories brought together in *The Habit of Widowhood and Other Murderous Proclivities* (1996) are compact dramas, often with only two characters, whose misunderstandings drive the plots. Well-crafted plans still go wrong, and the narrator may be the one planning the crime. There is a revelation of character told in an economy of words, and the conclu-

sions are not obvious to even the most astute reader who plays the game to figure out the solution. Barnard gives new meaning to the term "marriage of convenience" ("The Habit of Widowhood"); his plots twist on demonic jokes ("The Stuff of Nightmares"); and the final sentence can upset the most confident of protagonists and change the tone of the story ("My Son, My Son"). His best short fiction lingers in the mind long after either book or magazine has been set down.

A Mansion and Its Murder (1998), the last work to date Barnard has written as Bastable, concerns the fate of the mansion as much as that of any individual. When a banker's daughter in late-nineteenth-century England enters into a marriage of convenience with a landowner, the result is a murder, but the identity of the victim is unclear. The thread throughout is the relationship of the characters to each other and the revelation of their true natures. The solution to the mystery is suggested through clues in the dialogue. Peace and Oddie return in *The Corpse at the Haworth Tandoori* (1998) to solve a mystery set in Haworth, the community in Northern England where the Brontës once lived. The body of a strangled young man is dumped in an old car outside an Indian restaurant. The main suspect is a wandering Irish minstrel, Declan O'Hearn, a character Barnard makes highly likable and well rounded. The novel also includes an artists' colony and the tense undercurrents among people leading warped lives. *Touched by the Dead* (1999), published in the United States as *A Murder in Mayfair* (2000), is a companion volume to both *A Scandal in Belgravia* (with its parallel political theme) and *Out of the Blackout* (with one character's search for his past). When Colin Pinnock becomes a junior cabinet minister, he finds along with the usual congratulatory messages a poison-pen postcard, which leads him in search of origins he thought he already knew.

Barnard has always maintained his earlier interest in nineteenth-century English literature and has been active in the Brontë Society, serving as chairman in the 1990s. This activity resulted in a slim, well-illustrated volume, *Emily Brontë* (2000), before he returned to crime fiction and the modern moral questions of *Unholy Dying* (2000). Father Christopher Pardoe, a good priest who cares for his parishioners, is suspected of being all too human and having an affair with a young woman he is counseling. The murder of muckraking sex-and-crime journalist Cosmo Horrocks means there is no dearth of suspects (family, colleagues, and other victims), and Peace must discover who bashed in Horrocks's head and why.

The Bones in the Attic (2001) is set in Leeds and is clearly based on Barnard's home territory. Matt, a soccer star turned television and radio personality, is remodeling his newly purchased home when he and his contractor discover the skeleton of a toddler in his attic. Detective Sergeant Peace works alongside Matt, who receives an anonymous letter suggesting that he perhaps knows more about the case subconsciously than he recalls. As a youth Matt spent the same summer in which the child died in the neighborhood. Old playmates help him piece together fragmented memories to narrow the circle of suspects. Again the influence of Dickinson, particularly his novels *The Last House Party* (1982) and *Hindsight* (1983), is clearly at work.

In 2003 he received the Crime Writers Association Diamond Dagger Award for lifetime achievement in crime writing. Nominated eight times for the Edgar Award and winner of the Anthony, Agatha, and Macavity Awards, Robert Barnard provides more than crossword puzzles in narrative form. He consciously builds on long-standing literary traditions, particularly satiric traditions, and draws on the genre patterns of his predecessors to create works that are recognizably his own. Barnard's characters, once met, are worthy of the renewed acquaintance, and his style can be savored from novel to novel. There is more than surface hilarity to his comic realism. Despite critics' frequent use of the term *grotesque* to describe his characters, Barnard argues that his characters are not really life-like because "People can be so much nastier, can act so much meaner than they are usually allowed to do in a book." In a lit-erary tradition going back to the Renaissance, Barnard employs the detective genre to hold up the mirror of fiction in which readers can see reflected their own abominations of behavior much more clearly than they otherwise could.

Interviews:

Rosemary Herbert, "Robert Barnard: An Interview with a Man Called Bob," *Armchair Detective,* 17 (Summer 1984): 290–294; enlarged in Herbert's *The Fatal Art of Entertainment: Interviews with Mystery Writers* (New York: G. K. Hall, 1994), pp. 251–275;

Martin Edwards, "A Very English Writer," *Million: The Magazine about Popular Fiction,* 8 (March–April 1992): 38–40;

Adrian Muller, "The Mystery Scene Interview: Robert Barnard," *Mystery Scene,* 51 (January–February 1996): 32, 39, 42–44.

Bibliography:

William White, "Robert Barnard: A First Bibliography and a Note," *Armchair Detective,* 17 (Summer 1984): 295–297.

Reference:

Herbert, "The Cozy Side of Murder," *Publishers Weekly,* 228 (25 October 1985): 20–32.

Gavin Black
(Oswald Morris Wynd)
(4 July 1913 – 21 July 1998)

Gina Macdonald
Nicholls State University

BOOKS: *Black Fountains,* as Oswald Morris Wynd (Garden City, N.Y.: Doubleday, 1947; London: Home & Van Thal, 1948);

Red Sun South (Garden City, N.Y.: Doubleday, 1948);

When Ape Is King, as Wynd (London: Home & Van Thal, 1949);

The Stubborn Flower, as Wynd (London: Joseph, 1949); republished as *Friend of the Family* (Garden City, N.Y.: Doubleday, 1949);

The Gentle Pirate, as Wynd (Garden City, N.Y.: Doubleday, 1951);

Stars in the Heather, as Wynd (Edinburgh: Blackwood, 1956);

Moon of the Tiger, as Wynd (London: Cassell, 1958; Garden City, N.Y.: Doubleday, 1958);

Summer Can't Last, as Wynd (London: Cassell, 1960);

Suddenly at Singapore (London: Collins, 1961);

The Devil Came on Sunday, as Wynd (London: Cassell, 1961; Garden City, N.Y.: Doubleday, 1961);

A Wall in the Long Dark Night, as Wynd (London: Cassell, 1962);

Dead Man Calling (London: Collins, 1962; New York: Random House, 1962);

A Dragon for Christmas (London: Collins, 1963; New York: Harper & Row, 1963);

The Eyes Around Me (London: Collins, 1964; New York: Harper & Row, 1964);

Death the Red Flower, as Wynd (London: Collins, 1965; New York: Harcourt, Brace & World, 1965);

You Want to Die, Johnny? (London: Collins, 1966; New York: Harper & Row, 1966);

Walk Softly, Men Praying, as Wynd (London: Cassell, 1967; New York: Harcourt, Brace & World, 1967);

A Wind of Death (London: Collins, 1967; New York: Harper & Row, 1967);

Sumatra Seven Zero, as Wynd (London: Cassell, 1968; New York: Harcourt, Brace & World, 1968);

The Cold Jungle (London: Collins, 1969; New York: Harper & Row, 1969);

The Hawser Pirates, as Wynd (London: Cassell, 1970; New York: Harcourt Brace Jovanovich, 1970);

A Time for Pirates (London: Collins, 1971; New York: Harper & Row, 1971);

The Forty Days, as Wynd (London: Collins, 1972; New York: Harcourt Brace Jovanovich, 1973);

The Bitter Tea (New York: Harper & Row, 1972; London: Collins, 1973);

The Golden Cockatrice (London: Collins, 1974; New York: Harper & Row, 1975);

A Big Wind for Summer (London: Collins, 1975; New York: Harper & Row, 1975); republished as *Gale Force* (London: Fontana, 1978);

A Moon for Killers (London: Collins, 1976); republished as *Killer Moon* (London: Fontana, 1977);

The Ginger Tree, as Wynd (London: Collins, 1977; New York: Harper & Row, 1977);

Night Run from Java (London: Collins, 1979);

The Blazing Air, as Wynd (New Haven: Ticknor & Fields, 1981);

The Fatal Shadow (London: Collins, 1983; Bath: Chivers / South Yarmouth, N.H.: Curley, 1991);

A Path for Serpents (London: HarperCollins, 1991).

PRODUCED SCRIPTS: *Tomorrow All My Hopes,* radio, 1951;

Satan and a House in the Country, radio, 1951;

Anna from the Jungle, radio, 1952;

A Medal for the Poachers, radio, 1954;

Killer Lie Waiting, television, 1963.

Dorothy B. Hughes, in *Twentieth-Century Crime and Mystery Writers* (1980), aptly describes Gavin Black, the pseudonym for Oswald Morris Wynd, as "a Scotsman who knows and writes of the Far East quite as if he were a native of Malaysia" and who brings charm, wit, and "irresistible social commentary" to the genre. Like

James Clavell, author of *Shogun* (1975), a stint in the Far East during his wartime service and in a Japanese prison camp gave Black insightful vision with respect to Asia. Unlike Mark Derby, whose thrillers set in Malaysia pit lone westerners against villainous Asians, Black clearly loves Malaysia and appreciates its rural life and its hardworking mix of nationalities. His mystery novels reflect his interests and his special knowledge: they are lessons in geography, history, maritime practices, Asian law, Japanese business practices, Chinese families, Maoist fervor, the Malaysian royal family, cultural distinctions, and much more. His villains come in all types, European and even British, as well as Asian, and he creates sympathy or at least understanding for Tamil laborer, Sikh devotee, Sampan prostitute, and Malaysian playboy alike. His novels realistically assess the interplay of regional politics, inescapable poverty, racial and ethnic hatreds, and competing religions and philosophies common to Malaysia and to Southeast Asia. His stories have quirky twists and turns that hinge on an understanding of locale, custom, the conventional facades behind which Asians and Eurasians hide, and the historical and familial prejudices that drive them. His insights into differences in cultural values and ways of life could have been considered politically incorrect in the 1980s and 1990s, but they could be interpreted as perceptive cultural anthropology in the twenty-first century. Mystery writer Edmund Crispin has praised Black's toughness and his accurate, insightful Eastern backgrounds, while another British mystery writer known for his bent for the historical interplay of past and present, Anthony Price, finds Black's local color "convincing," his action "fast and furious," and his novels "reliable" good reads. Black himself said that readers either like him or they do not but that, unlike some of the best-sellers, he creates "characters who at least vaguely resemble human beings." Significantly, his mysteries are popular in Panang and Kuala Lampur as well as in England and the United States. They are not just slight tales of visitors abroad; instead, like the works of James Melville, H. R. F. Keating, and James McClure, they immerse readers in a foreign milieu, presented from a new perspective.

The son of Scottish missionaries William Oswald and Anna (Morris) Wynd, Gavin Black was born Oswald Morris Wynd in Tokyo, Japan on 4 July 1913. Black spent his first eighteen years in Japan, was totally immersed in the culture, and had dual citizenship in Japan and Scotland. He was educated at the American School in Tokyo, but when his parents left he went with them, attending Atlantic City High School in New Jersey and finally Edinburgh University, Scotland, where he studied for four years. In 1939 he joined the Scots Guard. His service in the British army during World

Dust jacket for the U.S. edition of Gavin Black's 1966 novel, in which adventurer Paul Harris protects an old friend's teenage daughter during an attempted Chinese takeover of the island of Bintan (Richland County Public Library)

War II consisted of six years in the Intelligence Corps, where his knowledge of Japan and his fluent Japanese were put to good use. He achieved the rank of lieutenant, was important enough to be mentioned in dispatches, and eventually was captured by Japanese soldiers. He spent three grueling years as a prisoner of war, first in the Japanese prisoner-of-war (POW) camp at Changi, Malaysia, where 140,000 out of 150,000 inmates died, and then, because of his knowledge of Japanese language and culture and his Japanese citizenship, in the POW camp in Hokkaido, Japan. During this period of imprisonment and torture he kept himself sane by serious writing. Occasional references in his novels to the nightmares of imprisonment, abuse, and dehumanization are drawn from firsthand experience. So too are his complex psychological studies of characters struggling with multiple loyalties and with love of a culture and aversion for its excesses. His writings repeatedly note the things of value in Japanese culture—the art, the subtlety, the sense of community—and yet the potential for extreme cruelty and the insidious, amoral business practices of a people smug in their sense of racial superiority. Upon release from captivity at the end of the war, he spent time in the United States writing and publishing before returning to Scotland.

A freelance writer since 1946, he made a lifetime career of interpreting the East for the West. Black's descriptions of Malaysia, as, for example, in *You Want to Die, Johnny?* (1966), convey his enthusiasm for a country where he could well have died:

> What a country. There is no season of drought, no withering green leaf fighting the old green, hot, but always with relief coming in one of the sudden Sumatras which rattle the shutters, toss the huge hardwoods, batter with rain for twenty minutes, and then let the sun in again. The sun offers eternal largesse, powerful, hard sometimes, but never truly cruel, and the rivers always run full. In the jungle, with the leeches and the mosquitoes, there is fast tumbling water. All around the peninsula is the sea which holds sharks and a gleaming depth of brightness surfaced over in jade and lapis lazuli. There are twenty-mile beaches of gold sand backed by palms and casuarinas without the blot of a single colored hotel umbrella.

In *The Cold Jungle* (1969), when asked what Malaysia is like by a Scots youth who has just saved him from a deadly ambush, Black's hero, Paul Harris, replies, "Gunmen, and death in the dark, and burning villages"; yet, time and again he returns to this chosen home, where he, like Black, will be forever the outsider—one with insights into character, culture, and place but impotent to change the nature of Asia. Throughout his canon Black draws poignant vignettes of Asian life: a tableaux in *A Dragon for Christmas* (1963) describes a river craft with "padded women cooking on deck in the hard winter sunshine," one small boy "urinating into the water," "farther up, a woman . . . washing rice in the flow," and "a vibration of voices, dogs barking, and somewhere a People's Democracy loudspeaker ranting out one of those marching tunes which these days are bullying us even as far south as Singapore."

As a journalist, Black traveled widely in the Far East, the Middle East, Europe, and the United States. His metaphors sum up his attitudes toward the countries he visited. In *A Time for Pirates* (1971), for example, as he waits for an attack, Harris thinks he is caught in a *kabuki* drama just before the enraged samurai character enters, sword drawn; in *The Golden Cockatrice* (1974) Black calls China "the spider's parlor" and one of his fictional characters the fly she seeks to entangle and consume. Black also has Harris praise the rich tonal variations of Chinese that make it a wonderful lan-

guage for quarreling but denigrates the Maoist euphemisms for purges and punishments, such as "Ten Thousand Flowers Unfolding" for a vicious period of "constructive criticism" and human butchery.

Black's short stories have appeared in *The Saturday Evening Post, Woman's Day,* the *Toronto Star,* and other American, Canadian, English, and European periodicals. His first novel, *Black Fountains* (1947), won a $20,000 prize from Doubleday. With the success of his early novels Black became a member of the Society of Authors (Scotland), the Crime Writers Association, and PEN. His novels have been translated into seven languages and sold worldwide.

Black married Janet Muir sometime in the early 1950s, and they settled at St. Adrian's, Crail, in Fife, Scotland, a seventeenth-century National Trust, and lived there for the rest of their lives. Black wrote radio plays between 1951 and 1954. From 1956 to 1957 he served as a Crail town councillor. There he and his family took pleasure in the beautiful vistas and the creatures native to the area. Their garden was an official fulmar nesting site, and a variety of other seabirds also visited, as well as an aged seal that fished under their windows. Black was an avid gardener, and the beauty of nature and landscapes, such as the soothing qualities of an unimpeded view of mountain and valley, is an integral part of his stories.

Black wrote himself into his novels through his hero Harris, who is first introduced in *Suddenly at Singapore* (1961) and then *Dead Man Calling* (1962) and is featured in fifteen of Black's novels. Through Harris, Black provides a running commentary on nature and what man does to it: the spoiled jungles, polluted waters, and stripped hills. A hairy car chase on an island in revolution includes a reference to an aroused cobra by the roadside and the screech of monkeys in the trees, while an escape from Red China aboard a Japanese vessel provides an excuse to eulogize the remote and beautiful islands at the southern tip of Korea—flat and pinnacled, with colored rock and miniature pine trees. In Harris's Scottish adventures Black's writing is similar to Hammond Innes's or Samuel Llewellyn's in its evocation of the pleasures of boats and the sea and in the descriptions of tides and channels, winds and seamanship.

Another of Black's avocational interests that carried over into his fiction was an enthusiasm for ceramics and Japanese color prints. Thus, in *Suddenly at Singapore,* Harris takes care in selecting a well-crafted Chinese vase to give to a Central Intelligence Agency operative who, in the guise of a bored and lonely teacher traveling abroad, has saved his life. In *The Eyes Around Me* (1964) he discusses Chinese silk scroll painters throughout the centuries stubbornly thumbing their noses at reality by putting stylized human figures walking down jadestone paths from red lacquered hermitages amid tumbled rock, pinnacled mountains, and scrub growth on flamboyant islands where no food grows. Later he takes on Zen art—"the carefully placed tree, the slightly phony ocean, and what looked like totally unusable bats"—as a "withdrawal from the facts of life." In *The Bitter Tea* (1972) Harris comments on the poor taste of the rich Chinese villain, who equates quality with price, and on the sterility of Marxist chinoiserie; he also compares a particularly attractive woman to a "piece of Sung porcelain with that extra special glaze on it." Readers thus find out about the interests, values, and taste of Black through statements he attributes to Harris.

Throughout Harris's adventures, and in many of his other books as well, Black comments on such topics as food, architectural styles, manners, genetic features, heritages, and music. In *A Dragon for Christmas,* for example, Harris asks, "Where else but on a Japanese ship could one hope to sit down to a meal of chilling rice, sour pickles, and horse-radish fermented into decay in a sauce which looked like sawdust diluted with liquid garden fertilizer?" and later in the book has him recall some Chinese cuisine: "one surprise heart of lettuce salad which, when you unravelled it with chopsticks, revealed a minute little white mouse which had been stewed in a sugar syrup," ninety-year-old sulfuric eggs, and "glass bowls full of moving locusts," meant to be nabbed and popped into a hot sauce and then one's mouth. He also provides intriguing tidbits of historical fact in *A Dragon for Christmas,* for example, detailing the invention of the ricksha by an Englishman in Yokohama seeking a more economical local means of travel than a horse, or contrasting the fast pace of hard-driven contemporary business executives and the leisurely patterns of nineteenth-century and early-twentieth-century colonial business leaders. He has Harris recognize the smell of Azerbaijani cigarettes, the dated slang of a Russian operative trained in a top KGB language school, the characteristic physique of a South China coolie, and the distinctive facial features of a Manchu aristocrat. Also, he regularly provides readers brief discourses on local politics, for instance in *The Bitter Tea,* in which Lee Kuan Yew's vision of Singapore is described as "something rather like the old Doges' Venice," a city-state serving as a market center for Southeast Asia by avoiding political entanglements with either China or the West and by aiming at a kind of socialism that uses capitalists when needed. Black, thereby, enables readers to see Asia as he does, its charm and fascination, its cultural diversity, and its dangers.

Black's military service and his freelance journalism after the war made Malaysia as familiar to him as

Dust jacket for the U.S. edition of Black's 1969 novel, in which Harris returns to his homeland, Scotland, after an old acquaintance is murdered (Richland County Public Library)

the land of his birth. He expresses this understanding of Malaysia through Harris. Harris is a competent, principled man, who has committed himself to Malaysia with all the complications such a commitment involves and who valiantly battles those outsiders who would take an aggressive colonialist stance toward exploiting the country's people, land, and resources. Raised by a Chinese amah, his proxy mother, he speaks Cantonese, Malaysian, and enough Japanese to translate nursery rhymes. Like Black, Harris was a wartime prisoner of the Japanese, at Changi, with memories of having been "driven by the hunger of a wild dog," as he puts it in *A Dragon for Christmas;* his father died in a Singapore internment camp, and he has not quite forgiven the Japanese for the anguish they inflicted throughout Asia during World War II. Yet, twice his life has been saved by Japanese, and his approach to such nationalistic conflict is pragmatic. He deals with Japanese effectively and courteously when necessity compels. Harris's politics echo Black's in his shift in attitudes from World War II concerns to Cold War concerns, particularly his chilling depictions of Chinese meddling in Southeast Asia and the uneasy Soviet-Chinese relationship.

Black makes Harris neither a spy nor a saboteur. He is a businessman with business values, and yet in Asia business and politics are inseparable. Consequently, in the first novel in the series, *Suddenly at Singapore,* he is already caught up in conspiracies, threatened and injured, and forced to seek remedies outside the law and diplomacy. A magnet for trouble, he is reputedly responsible for the death of a General Sorumbai in Sumatra (as is related in *Dead Man Calling*) because he supported the freedom fighters in that country, and for dozens of other villains in a variety of nationalistic and political causes. Always with Harris, nothing is what it seems: in *The Golden Cockatrice* his partner in Hok Lin Shipping turns out to be a Maoist spy, and other associates betray him for politics, money, or spite. Though skilled in Malaysia boxing techniques (particularly a snake-like kick) and clever at avoiding confrontation, throughout the series he is repeatedly beaten and knocked out, nearly blown up, shot, or drowned, and yet somehow he survives to fight again. Self-described as a retired gunrunner, Harris tells readers that he has picked up a few tricks for traveling quietly through sodden jungle (tricks Black learned while spying in Malaysia), but he is defeated by the new safety locks on cars that make a quick theft difficult. In *Suddenly at Singapore* he loses three boats to Indonesia but gets all three crews home safely and now produces armor-plated junks to even the odds. His personal contacts suggest both the variety of cultural patterns and the inhumanity that results from overpopulation, poverty, and hunger. His personal experiences confirm the vulnerability of individuals in community-centered societies. As Harris notes in *The Bitter Tea,* five millennia before Jean-Paul Sartre the Chinese rejected "the importance of a man as a separate entity within the mass" and opted instead for survival of race over individual. As a westerner, Black values individualism, but as a man born and raised in Asia, he understands the heritage of overpopulation and crowding that drives community-centered cultures, where survival of the group is paramount to survival of the individual.

Suddenly at Singapore establishes Harris as "responsible," an adjective that drives his action throughout the series as he blames himself for the plights of others and feels obliged to help in some way. Occasionally, those for whom he feels personal responsibility prove undeserving of his sacrifices or even dangerous to him, but in many cases they prove a loyal and often unexpected friend. Black's mystery-story pattern is to depict this Scotsman abroad (or other pragmatic yet responsible characters like him) in situations requiring a combination of circumspection, intuition, expertise, esoteric and often exotic knowledge, and aggressive action. Often the hero has traveled somewhere on business and found himself caught up in covert Chinese-Russian competition. Only more travel can lead him to understand the subtle action that swirls around him.

Having taken up Malaysian citizenship and developed a prosperous maritime engine business there, Harris (like his creator, Black) sees the world with the dual vision that Edward W. Said ascribes to exiles. This vision includes a commitment to the values of a Western-style democracy, a nostalgia about Scotland and things Scottish, but also an appreciation of the subtlety and caution of Asian business practices and diplomacy and a real-world understanding of the threat of Red Chinese Communism in Southeast Asia. In several stories he forms alliances with Japanese businessmen in order to undercut their goals and make sure that Malaysia benefits instead. Yet, he cannot help but appreciate Chinese realism, as he admits in *The Eyes Around Me,* "which goes back through four thousand years of adult experience, a cool assessment of living that includes large areas of our prehistory." Through Harris, Black captures the psychology of colonialists who see their world fading, of women coming to terms with grief and readjusting their memories of the dead to fit their needs, of Chinese women trained in submissive patterns but driven to excel in a competitive modern market. His other positive characters share this dual vision of peoples and cultures.

In *A Dragon for Christmas* Harris goes to Red China to negotiate a sale of riverboat engines and to discover what happened to his vanished partner but finds himself caught up in the one-upmanship of Cold War competition and betrayed by an attractive doctor, Florence Yin, to whom he has strong emotional ties dating to their childhood in China. The novel marks Black's coming to terms with the nightmare of Changi, for herein he creates a likable Japanese character, a marked change from the negative or carefully neutral portraits of the past. Harris's closest ally is a Japanese businessman and spy, with whom he shares a drink and straight talk sitting on the bathroom tub with Chinese martial music reverberating to keep their conversation secret from the hidden microphones in their rooms. A Scotsman taken captive in Korea and forced to renounce his citizenship reminds Harris of how easily one can lose one's identity and hope imprisoned under totalitarian conditions. The descriptions here reflect Black's own experiences as a prisoner of war. Black also understands the importance of personal pride for survival in an inhumane system, so he has Harris sympathize with his cold, hungry Red Chinese translator, a former opera star now in disgrace, and assert that it is "hideous to see a human being reduced to a frightened shell of obedi-

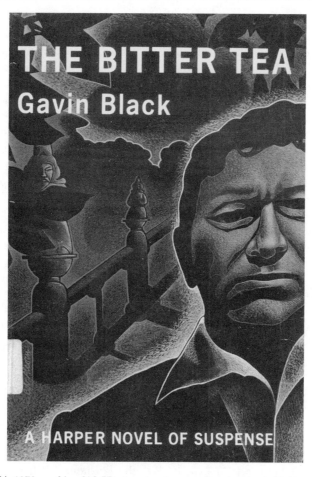

Dust jacket for Black's 1972 novel in which Harris roots out a smuggling operation inside his own shipping company
(Richland County Public Library)

ence." Harris finds ways not only to force the fearful woman, as part of her duties, to share his food and the warmth of his heater but also to escape to the West. Harris is put off by the puritanism of modern Singapore and so punctuates his first-person narrative with succinct predictions, for example, that "boredom" is what will ultimately defeat Communism or that Chinese villages will remain pretty much as they are, with dogs and pigs and children, long after the Maoist regime falls. With tongue in cheek, he calls William L. Shirer's *The Rise and Fall of the Third Reich* (1960) "light reading" for travel in China. As an Asian expert, Black had begun to make the psychological shift in understanding from viewing Japan as the wartime enemy to seeing China as the Cold War threat, and he records this personal shift in attitude through his series hero.

In 1963 Black wrote his first and only television play, *Killer Lie Waiting.* He did not, however, find the television medium as congenial to his goals as a social commentator and cultural investigator as radio had been.

A visit to Hong Kong led to *The Eyes Around Me,* which pays tribute to that capitalistic bridge between East and West, with wonderful descriptions of the city and its people, the Hong Kong Club with its Victorian furnishings and colonial sensibilities, and the Chinatown section of the city amid the glass and steel of modern financial establishments. An old friend of Harris, a rich Scottish heiress with a penchant for secret lovers, is found murdered in her lavish Hong Kong mansion, and houseguest Harris, as both the man on the scene and the major beneficiary under her will (a matter of a quarter of a million pounds), is the obvious suspect.

A melancholy inspector, another Scotsman, does not really believe Harris when he reports that the money is entrusted to his care for a single purpose, as an endowment with which to found an orphanage for Chinese children in Singapore. Through her Chinese secretary, Harris learns how deeply troubled his friend was before her death and what vast sums she had been investing in a project encouraged by her wastrel brother. The brother claims philanthropic motives, but Harris intuits personal investment. Also, his friend has provided so well for her former husband that the consequences are highly troubling. Events turn so nasty that Harris has occasion to note the value of a knife "for that moment when metal touches skin," and the wielder can use "the second of your adversary's paralyzing terror, in the dark," to good advantage.

In *You Want to Die, Johnny?*, an old friend, the British resident of Bintan, needs help with a worrisome teenage daughter who has run off once with a famous rock star and who threatens to do so again despite her angry father. When Harris takes the contrary young lady home to Bintan, he finds himself in the midst of an attempted coup. Their plane is shot down, and they are chased by Chinese with Czechoslovakian rifles. Ultimately, Harris must take refuge with a tantalizing woman, a member of the Malaysian royal family. As a Malaysian he must juggle political options to thwart the Red Chinese takeover of Bintan but also to keep the British from having an excuse to set up troops in the region. At the same time, he must help a teenager come to terms with the loss of her father, disillusionment in love, and the need for adult reactions to dangerous and unfamiliar situations. In response to Harris's responsible actions, one British officer describes him as "a public servant who can't be bought, bribed or cajoled."

The Cold Jungle is set in familiar territory for Black—Scotland and the Scottish coast. An old acquaintance begs Harris for a shipbuilding contract to save a dying family shipbuilding business, but competitive bidders have hidden political agendas that lead to violence, murder, and a frightening chase down a mountainside. Here Harris is at his most sentimental, as he (like Black) longs for a foothold in the country of his ancestry, is pleased at having his genetics recognized and his identification with Scotland confirmed, and feels a personal obligation to a friend in trouble. Ultimately, Harris buys into the Scots shipbuilding company out of nostalgia for the homeland of his imagination and a desire to thwart those who killed his friend because of his dealings with Harris. He is, as a British agent points out, "of the West" despite his immersion in Eastern cultures, and "still a man with some motivations that aren't just money." He prefers known problems to the hidden agendas of other bidders for his investment funds; he comforts a widow and protects her from greedy relatives bent on manipulating and exploiting her. Furthermore, he buys a boat (the *Tanjong Pudu*) for the sheer pleasure of its hardy craftsmanship and even takes it on a test trip to feel the way she handles in rough weather and strong tides (the lyrical passages reflect Black's deep-seated love for the sea and sailing vessels). In contrast to his respect for the daring, attractive women in earlier books, here Harris has difficulty respecting the self-imposed invalidism of his friend's widow and wishes she would try harder on her own instead of leaving her obligations to others to fill. He realizes that there is no way he can tell her that her husband has been murdered and that her brother was involved. Instead, he simply takes care of the situation himself. Thus, he goes to Europe to rescue a kidnap victim he does not like, and he engages a cousin, Jeremy, in his business affairs out of family feeling.

A Time for Pirates opens with armed street conflict between Chinese and Malaysians in Kuala Lumpur—the Chinese are throwing pork at Moslem Malays, and the Malays are running amok with bamboo staves. As Malaysian rioters rampage through a Chinese section of town, Harris endangers his own life to rescue a young woman who is caught up in the riot. Behind the scenes, Chinese, Japanese, and Malaysians (pushed by Harris) race to claim oil fields discovered by prewar Japanese. Caught in the middle and playing one group against the other, Harris strives to do what is best for his adopted country without injuring a part of the country he finds so peaceful and beautiful that he had hoped to retire there. A Sikh employee proves his mettle and his trustworthiness during these threatening times, and a wastrel Malay prince meets Harris's challenge to do what is best for his country after a reminder that his older brother at age nineteen had been decapitated by the Japanese, his head displayed on a bamboo pole. Harris does what must be done but is not totally content with some of the results. When an associate burns down the storage shed of a remote rubber plantation and the harvest for the year as well, he buys the owner out with an extremely generous sum, yet the damage has been done. The story ends on an ambiguous note with a crowing cock and Harris's memory of the prince's fighting cocks, fitted with steel spurs and trained to kill. The novel reflects Black's understanding that change does not come easily and that centuries-old cultural patterns are hard to break.

In *The Bitter Tea* Harris gets caught outside his hotel just when armed soldiers are pursuing the would-be assassin of a visiting Chinese dignitary. His attempt to reenter the hotel after a stint in the jungle raises the suspicions of the authorities and puts him on the outs with his longtime friend, Kuala Lumpur police inspector Superintendent Kang, a recurring character in the series. Harris has recognized the shooter as the beloved granddaughter of another friend and tries to protect him by directly confronting the young woman. Thus, he learns firsthand of the hatreds that drive her and the extremes to which she is willing to go to foment trouble. In the meantime, someone, clearly an insider in his business, is using his shipping line to smuggle goods and weapons. He is kidnapped and drugged, only to be rescued by a disappointed Kang, who had hoped to find a more important kidnap victim instead. The bitter tea of the title is a reference to poison served with tea, betrayal in the guise of friendship and hospitality. It reflects the way Kang views Harris's failure to be forthright about his knowledge and observations, and the way Harris views the young girl's betrayal of him and of a loving grandfather on whom the weight of authority will fall. Everyone suspects Harris's new assistant of treachery and terrorism because of his lack of family connections (his entire family was wiped out in a Shanghai purge), but Harris stands by him, and the true villain turns out to be someone much closer to home.

The exciting fight scenes in *The Bitter Tea* are typical of Harris's physical confrontations in all of Black's mystery stories:

> They weren't faces, just heads masked by nylon stockings. . . . one . . . had got across the ditch and was waiting for me. I turned back towards the other man still in the road. . . . I went straight for him . . . jack-knifed my body down, putting my head in his stomach. The man's breath exploded, . . . a snake's head with nylon sucked into the hole of a mouth. It wasn't a contest between two. A kick in the groin reminded me of that. I balled up from the agony. A second kick got me in the chest, just below my head. And then I saw a hand with a cosh in it.

Harris is neither superhero nor superman. He has effective fighting skills, but he is no martial-arts hero who can take on a dozen attackers with ease.

The Golden Cockatrice gets its name from "a fabulous monster produced from a cocks egg, hatched by a serpent" and thought to possess deadly powers, poisoning all living things by touch or look. In the book a shipping scheme on the gambling island of Macao, a neutral territory where belligerents can battle, spawns a potentially deadly and monstrous scheme for using Chinese slave labor. A Japanese shipping tycoon who has undercut Harris's business with a price war has been softening him up for a takeover that seemingly will give Japanese shipping power a cover for doing business throughout Southeast Asia and the China Sea. Harris, who is kidnapped and fed a series of lies, is vulnerable because of his stolen passport and his distance from official friends on whom he can normally rely for assistance. With time he realizes that he is caught between a Red Chinese plot to secretly develop its maritime power and a Russian effort to undermine it.

Furthermore, on a personal level he is caught up in disturbing and dangerous relationships. The wife of a longtime acquaintance comes to him for marital advice,

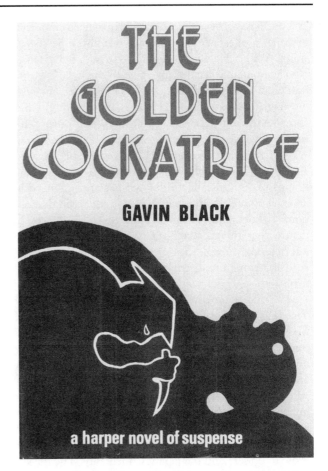

Dust jacket for the U.S. edition of Black's 1974 novel, in which Harris uncovers a Red Chinese plot to use slave labor on the island of Macao (Richland County Public Library)

and he offers her practical Asian wisdom instead of Western romantic illusion; her husband repays Harris's efforts at reconciling them by setting him up to be burned to death in his bed. When Harris realizes that his so-called friend is involved in even greater villainy, he says, "Like a fool I had taken friendship at face value, and there must have been many times when he laughed at me because of this. I was being softened up now, for what I could only guess." Even Superintendent Kang warns that his behavior warrants deportation and will not be tolerated, especially after his escapades in *The Bitter Tea*.

Harris is attracted to strong women, but often their devotion to a cause or their ruthlessness places him at odds with them, or their financial practicality coupled with their concept of sex as simply a physical exercise or a manipulatory strategy disturbs the romantic in him. In *The Golden Cockatrice* he admits that he has "never shown any skill at all in the art of arranging a satisfactory private life." Ranya Nivalahannanda, the owner of a Bangkok restaurant whom he had encountered in earlier Malaysian novels and whom he takes on as a business associate at a time when he needs financial backing, proves a resourceful ally but also a persistent suitor. With what Black identifies as Asian practicality, Nivalahannanda decides marriage to one's boss is the best of all possible worlds: love and money intertwined. Through several novels Harris is dependent on her competence but flees her prying eyes and purposeful sexual advances.

A Big Wind for Summer (1975; republished as *Gale Force,* 1978) returns Harris to Scotland. He travels to the islands of the Outer Hebrides and becomes engaged in an exciting sea adventure with chases and vivid descriptions of tides and storms and the herculean forces of nature that thwart man's petty schemes. Here again international conspiracies and personal betrayals are all part of a game that begins as business competition and turns into something far more destructive.

Critics have attributed the success of *The Ginger Tree* (1977), written under Black's real name, Oswald Morris Wynd, to its author's ability to knowledgeably bridge several worlds and to convincingly capture divergent points of view. The first is that of an innocent and protected twenty-year-old Scots girl who travels with her chaperon in 1903 to meet her fiancé (a British military attaché) in Peking; the other is that of Count Kentaro Kurihama, the Japanese soldier with whom she has an affair and through whom she and the reader grow to understand the Japanese mentality. The epistolary style brings to life the viewpoint of this turn-of-the-century young woman, her reactions to China and the Chinese and then Japan and the Japanese. The book was described in *The Japan Times* in 1977 as "honest," "sensitively written," "beautifully understated," and "one of the few contemporary novels to show Japan as it was and is." Although Black somewhat (perhaps with

tongue in cheek) denigrated his mysteries as bread-and-butter hackwork meant to subsidize his more ambitious work, all of his novels provide intriguing, realistic images of and perspectives on an Asia to which many westerners are blind.

Black's production of novels was greatly reduced to three books in the 1980s and 1990s. His last two novels were published eight years apart: *The Fatal Shadow* in 1983 and *A Path for Serpents* in 1991. Gavin Black died on 21 July 1998 at age eighty-five.

A Gavin Black mystery guarantees a cross-cultural mix of businessmen and spies, a clash of ideologies and values, unexpected and deadly action set amid exotic Asian settings. The hero relies on a combination of intuition, competence, pragmatic experience, and plain good luck to see him through the dangers hiding behind illusions.

Black's dramatization of the ways in which culture shapes perceptions, values, and attitudes and of the driving economic and political forces that separate nations and individuals continues to resonate with current day readers who discover in his works insights into modern geopolitics. As one who was himself divided in loyalty between the nation of his birth and the nation of his ancestral heritage, Black speaks through a uniquely divided self, a perspective and a voice that is possibly more comprehensible in post modernist times than in his own. As long as his novels remain in print, he will continue to stimulate and engage readers with his insightful depiction of multicultural encounters.

Papers:
A collection of Gavin Black's papers is in the Manuscript Collection of the Mugar Memorial Library, Boston University.

Lionel Black
(Dudley Barker)
(25 March 1910 – 1980)

Daryl Y. Holmes
Nicholls State University

BOOKS: *Laughter in Court,* as Dudley Barker (London: Methuen, 1935);

Palmer, The Rugley Poisoner, as Barker (London: Duckworth, 1935);

Lord Darling's Famous Cases, as Barker (London: Hutchinson, 1936);

Coastal Command at War, by Black (as Barker), Gordon Campbell, and Tom Guthrie (as Tom Dudley-Gordon) (Cairo: Schindler, 1943; London: Jarrolds, 1943); republished as *I Seek My Prey in the Waters: The Coastal Command at War* (Garden City, N.Y.: Doubleday, Doran, 1943);

A Few of the People, as Barker (London: Jarrolds, 1946);

Harvest Home: The Official Story of the Great Floods of 1947, and Their Sequel, as Barker (London: His Majesty's Stationery Office, 1947);

People for the Commonwealth: The Case for Mass Migration, as Barker (London: Laurie, 1948);

Berlin Air Lift: An Account of the British Contribution, as Barker (London: His Majesty's Stationery Office, 1949);

Grandfather's House, as Barker (London: Heinemann, 1951);

The Voice, as Barker (London: Heinemann, 1953);

Green and Pleasant Land, as Barker (London: Heinemann, 1955); republished as *This Green and Pleasant Land* (New York: Holt, 1956);

Toby Pinn, as Barker (London: Heinemann, 1956);

Private Company, as Barker (London: Longmans, 1959);

The Commonwealth We Live In, as Barker (London: Her Majesty's Stationery Office, 1960);

Grivas: Portrait of a Terrorist, as Barker (London: Cresset, 1959; New York: Harcourt, Brace, 1960);

A Provincial Crime (London: Cassell, 1960);

The Man of Principle: A View of John Galsworthy, as Barker (London: Heinemann, 1963); republished as *The Man of Principle: A Biography of John Galsworthy* (New York: Stein & Day, 1969);

The Young Man's Guide to Journalism, as Barker (London: Hamilton, 1963);

British Aid to Developing Nations, as Barker (London: Her Majesty's Stationery Office, 1964);

Chance to Die (London: Cassell, 1965);

Swaziland, as Barker (London: Her Majesty's Stationery Office, 1965);

Writer by Trade: A View of Arnold Bennett (London: Allen & Unwin, 1966); republished as *Writer by Trade: A Portrait of Arnold Bennett* (New York: Atheneum, 1966);

The Bait (London: Cassell, 1966; New York: Paperback Library, 1968);

Two Ladies in Verona (London: Cassell, 1967); republished as *The Lady Is a Spy* (New York: Paperback Library, 1968);

Outbreak, as Barker (London: Cassell, 1968; New York: Stein & Day, 1968);

The Ladder, as Barker (London: Cassell, 1968);

Prominent Edwardians (London: Allen & Unwin, 1969; New York: Atheneum, 1969);

Swinging Murder (London: Cassell, 1969); republished, as Anthony Matthews (New York: Walker, 1969);

A Pillar of Rest, as Barker (London: Cassell, 1970);

Breakaway (London: Collins, 1970); republished as *Flood* (New York: Stein & Day, 1971);

Death Has Green Fingers (London: Collins, 1971); republished, as Matthews (New York: Walker, 1971);

Ransom for a Nude (London: Collins, 1972; New York: Stein & Day, 1972);

G. K. Chesterton: A Biography, as Barker (London: Constable, 1973; New York: Stein & Day, 1973);

The Life and Death of Peter Wade, as Barker (London: Collins, 1973; New York: Stein & Day, 1974);

Death by Hoax (London: Collins, 1974; New York: Avon, 1974);

Arafat Is Next! (New York: Stein & Day, 1975);

A Healthy Way to Die (London: Collins, 1976; New York: Avon, 1979);

Paperback cover for the U.S. edition of Lionel Black's 1966 novel, the first of two thrillers featuring spy Emma Greaves (Bruccoli Clark Layman Archives)

The Foursome (London: Collins, 1978);

The Penny Murders (London: Collins, 1979; New York: Avon, 1980);

The Eve of the Wedding (London: Collins, 1980; New York: Avon, 1981);

The Rumanian Circle (London: Collins, 1981).

PRODUCED SCRIPT: *Visiting Airmen,* radio, 1960; *Obedience Test,* radio, 1961.

Called "a leading crime writer" of his day by mystery critic Donald C. Ireland, Lionel Black is a versatile mystery writer, uneven at times but nevertheless representative of his period with its revolution in gender relationships. Black strives for authenticity of time and place, provides thoroughly English settings and situations, and enjoys the give and take of pairs of con-

trary characters or characters with different backgrounds and perspectives. It is his detective teams that stand out in his works as distinctive and memorable.

Lionel Black was born Dudley Raymond Barker in London on 25 March 1910. His parents were Theodore Edwin and Katie Bradgate Barker. Educated at Bournemouth School from 1920 to 1929, he obtained his bachelor's degree from Oriel College, Oxford, in 1933, graduating with honors. Black began his career in journalism in 1933, working for the *Evening Standard* (London), serving as reporter and news editor during his seven years with that paper. He married Muriel Irene Griffiths in 1935, and the couple had two children, Raymond and Jane. In 1940 he started working for the *Daily Herald* (London) but shortly thereafter joined the war effort, serving in the Royal Air Force from 1941 to 1945 and becoming a wing commander who was mentioned in dispatches. Barker returned to the *Daily Herald* in 1945 and remained with that newspaper until 1954, first as a reporter and later as a features editor. His next career move was to associate editor for *John Bull* (London) from 1954 to 1959, and from there he became a staff member of the literary agency Curtis Brown Ltd. from 1960 to 1965. Even before turning full-time to freelance writing and broadcasting in 1965, Barker was a prolific writer, producing seven novels, a mystery, a biography of John Galsworthy, and eleven other works ranging from pieces on courts and criminals to studies of Britain as a commonwealth and as a participant in World War II. "Lucid," "shrewd," and "sensible" are terms frequently applied to his nonfiction. His detective stories draw heavily on his long career as a journalist. During his lifetime he was a member of the Crime Writers Association, the National Union of Journalists, the Savage Club, and the Whitefriars Club. Barker died in London in 1980 at age seventy, and his last works were published posthumously.

The suspense novels Barker wrote under the pseudonym Lionel Black fall into four main categories based on the presence or absence of a recurring protagonist or set of protagonists and on the occupations of those protagonists. The earliest novels are espionage thrillers revolving around the character Emma Greaves, a British spy, and her coworker, Nick Wiffen. The second series features Kate and Henry Theobold, a reporter and her barrister husband. Where Greaves's adventures are international in scope and involve foreign politics, terrorists, and threats to world peace, Kate and Henry's rarely extends beyond the borders of England and seldom beyond London. Their search for criminals takes them into an individual family, a private company, or at most, a small community, and the motives of their criminals—"sex, greed, or secrets," as the Theobolds put it—are personal. Though not as unhindered in movement and independent in thought as Emma, Kate is a fine sleuth in her own right. Her instincts and theories take her deeper and quicker to the heart of a story than do the careful, sometimes plodding procedures of the police or the logical thinking of her husband, Henry. Furthermore, she and Henry are as frequently tied up or knocked out by criminals they are pursuing as Greaves, but their world is the safer one associated with what are conventionally called "cosy" British mysteries, a world of jobs that keep them close to home amid a comfortable network of friends and associates, yet with policemen only a step behind them.

The third series, not always recognized as such, features Francis Foy, chief detective-superintendent from Scotland Yard, and Detective Sergeant Ronald Madge. The reason Foy and Madge do not stand out as obviously as Emma Greaves and Kate Theobold is the keenness with which Black portrays the essence of police work—quiet and largely behind the scenes. While Foy's brilliant intellect, keen instincts, insight into human character, and experience lead him quickly to the criminals he seeks, he and Madge are inevitably upstaged by riveting settings, dramatic interactions among criminals, and sudden heroic acts of otherwise ordinary people. The remaining nonseries mysteries share in common with all three series the emphasis on the individual willing to place his or her life on the line for the greater good.

As a whole, all of Black's mysteries affirm the basic goodness and generosity of the majority of human beings while exploring the social and sexual revolutions of the 1960s and 1970s. Pairs, whether policemen, spouses, spies, or doctors, more often than not have one formally educated person and one person who has risen to the top through hard work and experience, with the scales tipped slightly in favor of the latter. The woman is usually rescued by the man, but the husband sometimes finds his wife more successful in her career than he in his. Women as well as men have casual sex; husbands sometimes wish their wives were as "progressive" in the bedroom as they are in their child-rearing practices; and homosexuality is treated as simply another choice of relationship.

The Bait (1966) involves Emma Greaves in both espionage and the apprehension of a serial rapist. Emma's assignment from her boss, Colonel Chase, who reports directly to, and only to, the prime minister, is to move into the apartment of a former female agent, Violet Bridgewater, suspected of having been killed because she got too close to learning the identity of the spy who has infiltrated England's defense departments. Emma is used to lure the spy, who will know that she too is an agent and who will want to know whether she

knows as much as Violet did. In considering the assignment, she reveals some of the less glamorous aspects of espionage: "For three months, ever since she arrived from South Africa, she had sat idly in that crumby hotel, waiting to be given the next job. They congratulated her on the job she did in South Africa and then seemed to forget all about her." Besides the seemingly interminable waiting and the less than congenial accommodations, espionage is by its nature lonely and dangerous: "She was excited all right, but frightened too. It sounded so lonely. There would be people watching, of course. . . . But once it started, she wouldn't always be able to get in touch with them. She'd be on her own. And defenceless." Such points might be so taken for granted by someone with greater experience as a spy that they would not bear mention. Emma is new to the game, however: she has only worked on two assignments before, both in South Africa, where she was born and where her family has lived for two hundred years, and during the second of the assignments her cover was blown, so she had to leave the country.

Little more information is given about Emma's character. In the scene leading up to her going to bed with Nick, she briefly summarizes her history. The only child of a wealthy family in the Cape district whose father was a lawyer and then a judge, she is well educated and decidedly liberal. "Mother died young. . . . He gave me everything I wanted, including the freedom to think what I wanted. That costs a lot of money in South Africa these days."

In the next work of the series, *Two Ladies in Verona* (1967; published in the United States as *The Lady Is a Spy,* 1968), Emma is called upon to do some spying as part of her vacationing in Verona. This time the trouble involves a man who has escaped from Russia and a Chinese plot to start a Vietnam-type war elsewhere to get American forces out of China and to exhaust Britain. She uses the same phony last name, Glanville, that she did in *The Bait;* has a casual sexual encounter with a man she barely knows, similar to her one-nighter with Nick Wiffen in *The Bait;* once again comes close to being raped; and blows her cover so that she can no longer work in Italy. A little more is revealed about Greaves in this work, however: she is inept in setting up electronic listening devices but quite good at the quick thinking and maneuvering necessary to escape from the wine cellar where she is left bound and to dodge enemy agents chasing her through the streets of Verona.

Of Black's novels that do not form a part of any series (although both *Outbreak* [1968] and *The Foursome* [1978] have in common a character introduced in the Theobold series, Bill Comfort), *Outbreak* is the only one that develops plot and characters in any depth. A modern English version of the 1950 American movie *Panic*

*Dust jacket for Black's 1969 novel, which introduces
married detectives Kate and Henry Theobold
(Bruccoli Clark Layman Archives)*

in the Streets, *Outbreak* probes the minds and spirits of a pair of medical officers faced with the task of containing a smallpox epidemic before it overwhelms London. Reviewing the work for the *Library Journal* (1 July 1968), Anne Kincaid summarizes the appeal of the novel: "Excitement all the way, with the plus of a detailed description of the doctor's role in public health." Dr. Henry Laverack, within three months of retirement after a disappointing twenty-three-year career as a routine town-hall employee rather than the great surgeon he once showed promise of being, is a cynic who views human nature as contemptible in general. For him, containing the smallpox outbreak set off by a smuggler is his last chance to distinguish his otherwise unremarkable career. David Gregson, whose marriage is rocky because his wife, a research scientist, has little but contempt for his career as a practitioner, is further faced with the consequences his pursuit of the original smallpox carrier's contacts may have for his family.

A. J. Hubin in the *New York Times Book Review* (19 May 1968) aptly suggests that "The framework of the epidemic disease is a standard item of mainstream fiction; it is not so often used in mysteries, and seldom as successfully as in *Outbreak*, a fast-moving thriller. . . . Dr. David Gregson's effort to halt the epidemic, and a nice predicament involving both him and his wife are skillfully woven into a fine storyline." Marital squabbles amid a medical nightmare humanize what could otherwise be relentlessly grim.

Beginning with *Swinging Murder* (1969), the Kate and Henry Theobold series follows in the tradition of many charming husband-wife detective teams. Art Bourgeau in *The Mystery Lover's Companion* (1986) describes Black's stories of Kate and Henry as "nice English updates of Elizabeth Daly"–creator of the detectives Henry and Clara Gamadge–with the mysteries "light," "well-drawn," and "written with a touch of humor and warmth." Other such couples include Richard and Frances Lockridge's Mr. and Mrs. North, Dashiell Hammett's Nick and Nora Charles, and Ngaio Marsh's Roderick and Troy Alleyn. The introductory page to the Avon paperback edition of *Death by Hoax* (1974) calls the Theobolds "today's answer to Lord Peter and Harriet Vane." Kate is the inquisitive, intuitive, and insightful half of the pair, whose job as a reporter gives her a large network of resources on which to draw. Henry is the solid, grounded barrister who provides the logical thinking, the head for figures, and the additional resources of college friends, legal colleagues, and membership in a men's club. Henry's work as a barrister rarely occupies him, so he is almost always available to help Kate pursue whatever her current line of inquiry might be. He works conservatively, within the establishment; she works on the fringes of the law, toys with danger, and often needs rescuing. As a result of these differences in strategy, however, they cover twice the ground Kate could cover alone, and the time saved allows them ample opportunity to drink scotch or gin and compare notes. Further, their going off in separate directions allows Black to build suspense, ending a chapter with Kate at a climactic point and turning attention to Henry in the next chapter.

In *Swinging Murder* Henry and Kate are invited to a costume party at the home of an eccentric earl, Godfrey Marston, Lord Wilmington, who attended Oxford with Henry in the days before Marston became an earl. The wild party is, however, brought to a halt when a dead body is found beneath a bush in the back of the house. Lord Wilmington believes the police think he is the prime suspect and asks Kate and Henry to assist him in clearing his name. Their search for the truth leads the Theobolds from London to Glasgow and involves another man's claim to the title of eleventh earl of Wilmington and a venture into the violent world of gambling and thugs.

In this first novel of the series Kate is not yet a crack reporter. In fact, toward the opening of the novel she tells Henry that because of an office battle in which her editor "got the chop," she has been reduced to recipe writing in the cooking column of the magazine section. What is established, however, is that Henry's practice is rather slow, giving him a great deal of free time. Their mutual lack of financial success is the cause of their having only a "small, top-floor, walk-up flat" in Chelsea, though the narrator notes that "of course, it had to be Chelsea." Moreover, Henry is portrayed as a moderately "modern" husband, nurturing Kate when she is shaken up, bringing her her favorite nightcap (hot milk with shaved chocolate in it), even cooking pork chops when she is tired. He is also a moderately "modern" barrister, swigging ale straight from the bottle at times and able to enter into the party spirit of "the 11th Earl and all his queer friends" by donning a velvet smoking jacket and a plum cravat for the occasion. Kate is established as having an active imagination, not only in the nosing out of a story that will take her out of the cooking column and back into the heart of news reporting but also in its susceptibility to the nuances of a setting. She is enchanted to realize she is viewing the "gloaming" during her first evening in Scotland, and she readily imagines vengeful ghosts on the site where a body is being exhumed. Black also briefly hints at Kate's tendency to put on weight around the hips, a tendency that will be referred to in several novels. Further, the pattern for their solving of the mystery is established—Kate pursuing leads through her job as a reporter and Henry pursuing them through colleagues, friends, and his knowledge of law, with chapters alternating between them, and their getting back together to analyze the information they have gathered. Finally, the novel introduces Ronnie James, Kate's former boyfriend whose marriage proposal she turned down and who remains on such good terms with Henry that he helps Henry in his investigation. Other regulars include Bob Ritchie, a fellow reporter who appears again in *Death Has Green Fingers* (1971), and Sergeant Chin and Inspector "Bill" Comfort, a pair of detectives who appear in several works both in the series and outside of it. Each time Black introduces Comfort in a story, he tells readers that Comfort looks like Charles Dickens's Mr. Pickwick.

Breakaway (1970; published in the United States as *Flood,* 1971) introduces Detective Inspector Foy and Detective Sergeant Madge. Madge, who respects Foy, describes him as a methodical man who came up through the ranks (unlike Madge, who is university educated) and who appears to be plodding but in fact

possesses a "restless, questioning intellect darting about behind the stolid façade—far keener than that of superior policemen who had come in through universities."

Here, as in the Theobold series, Black pairs education and "nose," with the scales once again tipped slightly in favor of "nose." Not a major issue in his works because his pairs form good working teams, one supplying the other's deficiencies, this tension remains an undercurrent that feeds the dynamic relationships between members of these teams. Given less emphasis but mentioned briefly in the course of Foy's search for bank robbers in the flooding fens is the tension between local constables and Scotland Yard detectives. As earlier noted, however, the workings of the detective take a backseat to the excitement created by the descriptions of the fens and of the local inhabitants' attempts to stay the encroaching water. Ireland, in *Twentieth Century Crime and Mystery Writers* (1980), clearly articulates Black's greatest achievement in the book: "the action was set in the Fens and the reader was left with a deep impression of Eastern England in all its moods."

The next Theobald novel, *Death Has Green Fingers,* begins, like *Swinging Murder,* with an invitation, this time with one of Henry's old college friends inviting the couple for a visit. Jonathan Sims needs some legal advice and hopes Henry and Kate will oblige if they come to his house for the weekend. Kate, who has not been impressed with the college friends of Henry's she has met so far, finding them "either dull or dissolute—most of them both," is pleasantly surprised to find Sims attractive. Jonathan and his wife, Stella, are among the people invited for drinks at Nick Bell's house the afternoon of the Theobolds' arrival, so Kate and Henry are there on the scene when Nick is discovered dead in his greenhouse, stabbed in the throat with a pruning knife. Nick's activities in the past and his two current foci, cultivating roses and seducing women, provide sufficient reasons for the entire population of the village of Ashworth to be suspects, and Kate and Henry are soon investigating, though not with the approval of the police. Two of the policemen who become involved in the case appear in the next work of the series as well: Detective Chief Superintendent Roger Wake and Detective Inspector Sam Kippis. Kate describes the former as "County force, of course; not the Yard," a temperate nonsmoker whose cases "had been little classics of steady, patient routine police method, applied by a keen, deductive intelligence. 'Never takes a short cut,' one of the *Post'*s crime men had once told her, 'and never misses a hint.'" Since Wake does not like the press, he is not overly fond of Kate, but he recognizes that she has a good mind and good instincts. They do not converse so much as gather information from each other, Wake usually ending the session with a warning

Dust jacket for Black's 1970 novel, the first to feature his
recurring characters Inspector Foy and Sergeant Madge
(Bruccoli Clark Layman Archives)

lishes only on Sunday, a day the *Daily Post* does not. Theirs is a pleasant working relationship, each helping the other get information for their stories.

Ransom for a Nude (1972), another nonseries novel, involves the theft of a painting to be auctioned by Sir David Bullen, an eccentric baronet whose experiences in World War II have caused him to devote his life and energies to philanthropy. Bullen becomes personally involved in Scotland Yard's efforts to recover the painting, and his boyish excitement during the first attempt to retrieve the painting, along with the somewhat technologically outdated policeman whispering instructions from the trunk of the car, gives the entire episode a comical feel. The interactions among the criminals are convincingly portrayed, however, and Bullen's effort to regain the painting at the end of the novel is serious and touching enough to make him the most charming and likable of all of Black's heroes.

In *The Life and Death of Peter Wade* (1973), a novel Barker published under his real name, former reporter Johnny Trott gets an assignment from his literary agent, who happens to be his former wife as well, to write the biography of a remarkably undistinguished actor, Peter Wade. For the somewhat down-and-out writer, this assignment proves to be perhaps the greatest test of his reportorial skills and his sense of responsibility.

The setting for the next Theobald novel, *Death by Hoax,* is Loxham Bay in August, a "grotty little seaside town on the South coast" during "the silly season." Kate's assignment is to help Geoff Hayward, a young stringer who does not know how to write a good story, cover a series of hoaxes. On her first visit to an electronics store, the target of two hoaxes (including a bomb threat that day), Kate is just in time to hear a real bomb explode and to witness its effects on its intended victim, the owner of the store. The question for Kate, Geoff, Henry, and the police is what connection, if any, exists between the hoaxes and the active bomb. Ronnie James again helps Henry investigate as he did in *Swinging Murder,* and Black reintroduces Kate's struggle to maintain her weight. When she mentions to Henry that she is gaining weight in the hips, his almost comforting response is that she is "comfortable in bed . . . but perhaps a little too much when you're dressed."

Kate's struggle with her weight problem is the springboard for the next Theobald novel, *A Healthy Way to Die* (1976). Butch also notices Kate's weight gain, so when he receives an invitation from the exclusive fat farm, Gorsedene, to send a reporter out for a week free of charge, he calls Kate and tells her that "he couldn't think of anyone more suitable to send" than she. On a diet of a grapefruit a day and all the boiled water she can drink, one-hundred-and-forty-two-pound Kate still manages, in spite of mental and physical lethargy, to get

to Kate to steer clear because the situation is far more dangerous than she realizes. Kippis is Wake's good-natured companion, a detective inspector with a "jolly face," a "very beery nose," and a "rotund smile."

Although a variety of Kate's coworkers are mentioned in this novel, the two of note because they appear in later works as well are Kate's editor, Butch, and the obnoxious photographer Horace. Good-natured and strongly supportive of Kate, Butch's behavior is at times male chauvinistic. Pleased with one of Kate's stories, he pats her bottom "approvingly." Horace, whatever his other failings might be, is a fine photographer and especially good at getting sneak shots. In *Death Has Green Fingers* he also proves invaluable for his professional connections. The picture he helps Kate find not only assists her in solving the case but also highlights Kate's qualities of intuitiveness and insight, qualities that make her such a good reporter. Also worthy of mention is Dereck Andrews, an old friend of Kate's who writes for the *Recorder,* which pub-

kidnapped and rescued, solve the murder of financier Philip Antrobus, and lose nine pounds, six ounces, in six days. The novel concludes with a nice salute to Kate's private moral and ethical standards—and perhaps a nod to Sherlock Holmes—when Kate chooses to report to her editor that Antrobus's death was a suicide and to write a sensational piece instead on her dramatic weight loss.

The Penny Murders (1979) begins with the exposure of a new aspect of Henry's character, his interest in rare coins. Henry's father, Luke Theobold, a well-known leading criminal-defense lawyer with a fine coin collection, is mentioned for the first time. A barrister unable to afford more than a modest coin collection, Henry appears to be a bit overshadowed by his father. The sense that modern men do not quite live up to the stature or standards of their fathers is further suggested when Kate goes out to meet Henry for their weekly lunch at his club, in "the ladies annexe of course, through a side entrance. But after all, Henry pointed out, they did allow women in the dining-room. Several older members had resigned when that decision was reached by the committee." After seeing Kate undertake dangerous assignments before, Henry's sudden declaration in this novel that being intrepid does not suit her is peculiar, suggesting, perhaps, an unusual amount of discomfort at the moment with Kate's typical behavior as a reporter. Interestingly too, The Penny Murders is the only novel of the series in which Henry is kidnapped and has to rely on a woman to call the police to rescue him.

For all that, Kate and Henry's world is more traditional than otherwise. They have their cozy little walk-up apartment in Chelsea, which Kate especially loves in the winter for its warmth, and Kate will always need Henry's logical mind and ability to balance a budget: "My dear man," Kate says at one point, "I can scarcely add up the household accounts. Ask Henry." The main plot of the story concerns discovering who killed rival coin collectors Miles Cabral and Cornelius Ball. Except for Butch, none of the other characters readers have met before are present, except the pair of detectives from Scotland Yard, Detective Chief Inspector Bill Comfort, whose Christian name is revealed to be Aloysius, and Detective-Sergeant Chin.

James Girdin, in The St. James Guide to Crime and Mystery Writers (1996), draws attention to one of Black's particular strengths in this and the two previous novels: Black's interest in the way things work and the appeal given to the novels as a result of his research and skill in presenting journalism:

The reader is given extensive information on breeding roses (Death Has Green Fingers), dismantling explosive

Dust jacket for the U.S. edition of Black's 1972 novel, in which an eccentric aristocrat becomes involved in police efforts to apprehend a gang of art thieves (Richland County Public Library)

devices and booby traps (Death by Hoax), both arcane numismatic lore and the process of counterfeiting coins (The Penny Murders), and the legal system in all of the novels. Often beginning with a conventionally impossible problem like breeding a blue rose or finding a 1933 or 1954 penny (years in which none was minted, although dies were cast), the author supplies extensive and fascinating information on the subject. . . .

This attention to detail and purveying of esoteric knowledge is a feature of the best fiction from this period.

In The Eve of the Wedding (1980) Comfort and Chin along with Kate and Henry investigate the murder of Gregory Letheridge in the family mansion, TongKing House, on the night of a Polterabend party (during which dishes and crockery are smashed) to celebrate the wedding of his younger brother. Here Black is particularly good at capturing the various effects of indulging or overindulging in alcohol—from Kate's romantic thoughts about Henry, her happy wonderment that they have been married ten years, and her desire to be a "soft-boiled" newspaperwoman for the evening to the assault on a young woman who is too inebriated to resist. Here Black also creates two of his most memorable eccentric characters, an elderly brother and sister. Rupert Letheridge spends his time making pictures out of seashells. Sybil "dresses like something out of *Great Expectations*" and spends hours alone in her room playing her grand piano. When they dance together at the party, however, their antiquated attire, grace, and elegance reveal a charm and decorum that attracts the attention of everyone at the party and creates a memorable scene.

Black also picks up a thread he earlier worked into *The Penny Murders,* identifying some distinctions between British and American customs. In the earlier work, American Cornelius Ball complains to Kate that the only trouble with England is that it does not make its drinks as strong as they are in the States. Ball also observes that the American "happy hour" begins at 5:30, whereas the British do not begin theirs until 6:00. In *The Eve of the Wedding,* Kate explains to a visiting American the British use of the drawing room: "After the meal the ladies retire to the withdrawing room, and the gentlemen sit around the dining room table discussing the port wine and telling dirty stories. Nobody does it any more except old-fashioned gentlemen like my husband. He insists on it, in his quaint way." Immediately following, and in contrast to Kate's mod-

ern ideas of custom, is Henry's explanation that his port was a gift from his father who, presumably according to custom for those who could afford it, "put down a pipe [around 600 bottles] of port against my twenty-first birthday."

Black was clearly showing his age in two of the stand-alone novels published in the last decade of his life, and they lack the quirky interest of his early work. The plot of *Arafat Is Next!* (1975), in which two brothers from England set out to assassinate Yasser Arafat because their other brother was killed by a terrorist bomb in England, is so thin and the characters so one-dimensional that the book fails to create any of the intended suspense. *The Foursome,* a mystery novel concerning a man who moves his mistress and eventually her seventeen-year-old son into his and his wife's home, is heavy on sex and callousness, heavy-handed in plot, short on believable characters, and devoid of any suspense or shock value. The only saving graces are new information concerning the home of Comfort and his wife, Grace, and the introduction of their friends Vivian Duke, a social worker, and his schoolteacher wife, Mary.

Nonetheless, despite an erratic quality to these late efforts, Lionel Black offers readers insights into the changing morality of the 1960s and 1970s, some interesting details of time and place, and some highly readable mysteries notable for their balanced detective teams and good-natured and forgiving view of human foibles. Readers can laugh with Black at human pretensions.

Christianna Brand

(17 December 1907 – 11 March 1988)

Nancy Ellen Talburt
University of Arkansas

and

Juana R. Young
University of Arkansas

BOOKS: *Death in High Heels* (London: John Lane, 1941; New York: Scribners, 1954);

Heads You Lose (London: John Lane, 1941; New York: Dodd, Mead, 1942);

Green for Danger (New York: Dodd, Mead, 1944; London: John Lane, 1945);

The Single Pilgrim, as Mary Roland (London: Sampson Low, Marston, 1946; New York: Crowell, 1946);

The Crooked Wreath (New York: Dodd, Mead, 1946); republished as *Suddenly at His Residence* (London: John Lane, 1947);

Danger Unlimited (New York: Dodd, Mead, 1948); republished as *Welcome to Danger* (London: Foley House, 1949);

Death of Jezebel (New York: Dodd, Mead, 1948; London: John Lane, 1949);

Cat and Mouse (London: Joseph, 1950; New York: Knopf, 1950);

London Particular (London: Joseph, 1952); republished as *Fog of Doubt* (New York: Scribners, 1952);

Tour de Force (London: Joseph, 1955; New York: Scribners, 1955);

The Three-Cornered Halo (London: Joseph, 1957; New York: Scribners, 1957);

Starrbelow, as China Thompson (London: Hutchinson, 1958; New York: Scribners, 1958);

Heaven Knows Who (London: Joseph, 1960; New York: Scribners, 1960);

Nurse Matilda (Leicester: Brockhampton, 1964; New York: Dutton, 1964);

Nurse Matilda Goes to Town (Leicester: Brockhampton, 1967; New York: Dutton, 1968);

What Dread Hand: A Collection of Short Stories (London: Joseph, 1968);

Court of Foxes (London: Joseph, 1969; Los Angeles: Brooke House, 1969);

Brand X (London: Joseph, 1974);

The Radiant Dove, as Annabel Jones (London: Joseph, 1974; New York: St. Martin's Press, 1974);

Nurse Matilda Goes to Hospital (Leicester: Brockhampton, 1974);

Alas, for Her That Met Me! as Mary Ann Ashe (London: Star Books, 1976);

A Ring of Roses, as Ashe (London: Star Books, 1977);

The Honey Harlot (London: W. H. Allen, 1978);

The Rose in Darkness (London: Joseph, 1979);

The Brides of Aberdar (London: Joseph, 1982; New York: St. Martin's Press, 1982);

Buffet for Unwelcome Guests: The Best Short Mysteries of Christianna Brand, edited by Francis M. Nevins Jr. and Martin H. Greenberg, introduction by Robert Briney (Carbondale: Southern Illinois University Press, 1983);

No Flowers by Request, by Brand, Dorothy L. Sayers, E. C. R. Lorac, Gladys Mitchell, and Anthony Gilbert, published with *Crime on the Coast,* by John Dickson Carr and others (London: Gollancz, 1984; New York: Berkley, 1987).

Editions: *Green for Danger,* introduction by Otto Penzler, includes "The Author Comments" by Brand (Del Mar: University of California Extension Press, 1978);

Fog of Doubt, introduction by Brand (New York: Carroll & Graf, 1984);

London Particular, introduction by P. D. James (London: Pandora, 1988);

Green for Danger, preface by H. R. F. Keating (New York: Carroll & Graf, 1989).

PRODUCED SCRIPTS: *Death in High Heels,* motion picture, Hammer-Marylebone, 1947;

Christianna Brand (from The Armchair Detective, *Summer 1988)*

The Mark of Cain, motion picture, by Brand and Francis Crowdy, based on the novel *Airing in a Closed Carriage* by Joseph Shearing, Rank Organization and Two Cities Films, 1947;

The Secret People, motion picture, screenplay by Thorold Dickinson, Joyce Cary, and Wolfgang Wilhelm, additional dialogue by Brand, Ealing Studios, 1952.

OTHER: *Naughty Children,* compiled and edited by Brand (London: Gollancz, 1962; New York: Dutton, 1963);

"Miss Marple: A Portrait," in *Agatha Christie: First Lady of Crime,* edited by H. R. F. Keating (London: Weidenfeld & Nicolson, 1977; New York: Holt, Rinehart & Winston, 1977), pp. 193–204;

"Inspector Cockrill," in *The Great Detectives,* edited by Otto Penzler (Boston: Little, Brown, 1978; Harmondsworth, U.K. & New York: Penguin, 1979), pp. 59–66;

Certain Members of the Detection Club, *The Floating Admiral,* introduction by Brand (Boston: Gregg Press, 1979).

SELECTED PERIODICAL PUBLICATIONS– UNCOLLECTED: "Upon Reflection," *Ellery Queen's Mystery Magazine,* 70 (August 1977): 136–141;

"Over My Dead Body," *Ellery Queen's Mystery Magazine,* 74 (August 1979): 34–40;

"My Small Personal Tribute to the Late, Alas, Ned Guymon," *Clues: A Journal of Detection,* 6 (Spring–Summer 1985): 133–135.

Christianna Brand was a meticulous and street-smart writer whose plots and surprises rival those of the best of Golden Age mystery novels, while her characters, with their verve, sparkling talk, and matter-of-fact morals, extend the boundaries of such fiction. Underscoring Brand's achievement is the enduring acclaim for her best-known work, *Green for Danger* (1944), which is included in *Crime and Mystery: The 100 Best Books* by H. R. F. Keating (1987). In addition, her *Cat and Mouse* (1950) was included by Julian Symons in "Crime: The Hundred Best Stories" in 1959 in *The Sunday Times* (London), and her second novel, *Heads You Lose* (1941), was a "$1,000 Red Badge Prize Mystery" in the United States in 1942. She received additional achievements and recognition, including awards for short stories, throughout her career. Brand published a dozen crime and mystery novels, twice that many crime stories, and one nonfiction crime work. In addition to her crime works, she wrote half a dozen other novels, four works for young readers, and short pieces including sketches and horror and ghost stories. She also edited an anthology of works for children.

Born in Malaya on 17 December 1907 to Alexander Brand Milne, a rubber planter, and Nancy (née Irving) Milne, Mary Christianna Milne lived in India in early childhood and was sent to live in Ipswich with the family of her cousin, Edward Ardizzone, following the death of her mother in 1911. Educated at a Franciscan convent in Taunton, Somerset, she was left to support herself at age seventeen as a result of family financial reverses. Of this period in her life she reported being often poor, cold, and hungry. Among other occupations, she worked as a nursery governess, interior decorator, gadget demonstrator, organizer of a girls' club, nightclub hostess, dancer, model, and (least successfully) secretary. While employed to sell Aga cookers, she began to write. "The Rose," Mary Brand's first published work, appeared in *The Tattler* (London) in 1939 (reprinted in *What Dread Hand: A Collection of Short Stories,* 1968). This brief story introduces key features of her work, such as the surprise ending and equal duplicity in relationships between the sexes. Also in 1939, Mary Brand married Roland Swaine Lewis, a surgeon. Her first novel, *Death in High Heels,* was published in 1941 under the name of Christianna Brand, and she is said to have written it out of frustration over unhappy experiences with a bossy woman supervisor. The novel was rejected by fifteen publishers before being accepted, without revision, by publisher John Lane. Brand points out in "The Author Comments" in the 1978 Mystery Library edition of *Green for Danger* that she was "the complete amateur," having "never had a day's 'education' in writing, never been a journalist, never had any family literary experience to draw upon and had no handhold whatsoever in the publishing world."

Death in High Heels introduces Inspector Charlesworth of Scotland Yard and is full of informal but informative chat among the employees at Christophe et Cie, a fashion house where an employee is murdered. Brand creates a set of characters with convincing behavior and aspirations. One is a divorced parent and another is a sometime prostitute. Victoria David, a salesperson happily married to a painter, is central to the action and is the inspiration for yet another of Charlesworth's many romantic passions. Her good sense and warm relations with the rest of the employees, along with her natural curiosity, allow her to assist in the investigation and draw conclusions. The crime springs from the employer's casual liaisons and attempted seductions involving most of his attractive young employees, and one woman takes violent exception to another taking her place in his affections.

Inspector "Cockie" Cockrill, chief constable of the Kent County police, makes his first appearance in *Heads You Lose.* Brand's essay in *The Great Detectives* (1978) points out Cockrill's acute powers of observation, understanding of human nature, integrity, and commitment—and perhaps overlong experience of the criminal world. Despite empathy for many of the crimi-

nals whose crimes he uncovers, his strict ideas of justice never soften. Cockrill tests hypotheses while observing suspects and searching for confirmation. As a result he is often on the wrong track until the eleventh hour before another murder. As with Sir Arthur Conan Doyle's model for Sherlock Holmes, the original for Cockrill was a doctor. Brand says Cockrill is the "dead spittin' image" of her father-in-law, William James Lewis, who was for more than fifty years a medical practitioner in a Welsh mining town. Cockrill is identified by his white hair, small stature, nicotine-stained fingers, and ill-fitting hats.

In *Heads You Lose,* Cockie, like the guests at the country house, is a longtime friend of the owner of the manor, Stephen Pendock. He investigates by taking up residence in the manor house and spending most of his time in the midst of the suspects, even conferring with them regarding key events as the investigation moves toward resolution. Both murder victims are outsiders with a history of interconnections with the inhabitants of and guests in the manor. Passion erupts into violence when it is thwarted and carries the murderer over the line into madness. The revelation of the murderer is painful for the house-party members and nearly fatal for one. As in her first novel, Brand here utilizes her talent for presenting young, lighthearted women and their talk, fondness for fun, and easy acceptance of different lifestyles.

When Lewis entered military service in the early 1940s, he was first posted to a hospital in Kent. Mary Lewis was able to join him by taking lodgings in the nearby village, and she spent nights in the underground air-raid shelters with the nursing staff, experiences reflected in *Green for Danger.* Published in 1944, the novel has enjoyed continuing recognition and popularity and was brought to the screen in 1946 with Alastair Sim as Inspector Cockrill. Brand's knowledge of wartime Britain is tellingly represented in this novel of human challenges and frustrations and brilliantly staged murder. One of Brand's strengths is the ability to create characters who fill up the cast of needed suspects and also display a wide range of human behavior, including foolishness and culpability. As in most of the Brand novels, relationships afford as much frustration as satisfaction, a point emphasized in the last chapter, an epilogue. Excellent red herrings, one of the great murder devices of the genre, and the shocking identity and chilling motive of the culprit are also reasons for the reputation the novel possesses. Cockrill gambles to unmask the killer and nearly pays with the life of a third person. The suspects conspire to prevent his taking the killer alive, and he mistakenly spills the antidote to the drug the killer has taken. Brand's ability to surprise with revelations throughout the unfolding of a

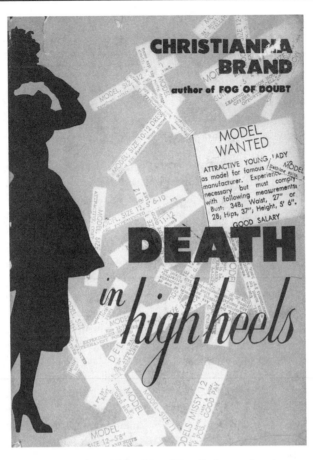

*Dust jacket for the U.S. edition of Brand's first novel, set in
a fashion house where an employee is murdered
(Bruccoli Clark Layman Archives)*

work is one of her memorably satisfying qualities. In this novel is the added drama that wartime and the Blitz provide to the characters' lives, heightening both danger and excitement. In his essay identifying the novel as one of the hundred best crime and mystery books, Keating calls it "perhaps the last golden crown of the Golden Age detective story" and describes it as a "splendidly worked-out detection puzzle, as good as any in the field," with "substantial characters in acknowledgment of the gradual move in detective fiction away from mere mechanical figures and toward characters who evince the darknesses of real life."

The third Cockrill novel, *The Crooked Wreath* (1946; published in England as *Suddenly at His Residence,* 1947), has a country-house setting and a typical closed circle of suspects, all of whom belong to one family. Within these confines there is conflict, passion, and intrigue, including a second murder, the incarceration of a family member later found innocent, blackmail, a dying message, and family concern about whether the fits of young Edward Treviss, a fifteen-year-old grandson, are genuine. Edward's own torment in this regard

is well evoked, and the murderer callously fans the flame of doubt. Brand offers an interesting change on the use of footprints to limit and misdirect suspicion. The death of the wealthy patriarch results directly from his cruelty to a family member, and that cruelty is apparent in his treatment of most of his family, particularly his second wife and former mistress. Similarly, the gardener's greed and attempted blackmail lead to his demise. As in many classic mysteries, a will and the financial need of the would-be inheritors play a central role in *The Crooked Wreath,* but, surprisingly, the murderer's need is not primarily for money. Cockie deliberately accuses an innocent person but fails to provoke a confession from the killer. A bomb brings justice and levels the country house, freeing the widow from living in what amounts to a mausoleum. Plot defines this novel, of which the noted crime writer Edward Hoch writes, in a foreword to the 1997 Linford edition, that Brand has produced in the novel not one but two impossible crimes.

Brand worked in the war effort as a tea girl in a munitions factory before earning a job in the Emergency Bed Service (intended to get patients into the nearest hospital in the shortest time) through the intervention of the minister of health, whom she knew. In 1946 Brand's first nonmystery novel was written at the request of the minister. *The Single Pilgrim,* published under the pen name of Mary Roland, depicts the experiences of a woman infected with syphilis. The book is a frank and outspoken work that emphasizes the dangers of the disease when left untreated.

By the late 1940s Brand was reunited with her husband, who was home from service abroad, and they adopted a daughter, Victoria (Tora), a name and nickname shared with the main character in Brand's first novel. The family moved to a Regency house in Maida Vale with a mulberry tree in the garden, and, though the days of cold and hunger were behind, Brand continued to write and in 1947 became a member of the Detection Club.

Brand expanded the dimensions of her crime writing in 1947, when she turned *Death in High Heels* into a screenplay and collaborated on another screenplay, *The Mark of Cain.* She published her first piece of juvenile fiction, *Danger Unlimited,* in 1948. A sheltered squire's son, Bill Reddenen, is abandoned on Dartmoor by a villainous chauffeur and befriended by the astonishingly able Patch and his sister. Patch saves Bill and himself time after time, including escapes from a knife, poison, and grenades, as the two follow the sinister and violent thieves of the Red Star of Devon, a jewel stolen from Bill's mother. All the while Bill is incidentally tutored in Welsh. Pulling off a particularly effective surprise at the end, Brand reveals the clever and tough Patch to be a girl.

By the fourth novel in the Cockrill series, *Death of Jezebel* (1948), Brand appears to have exhausted the obvious possibilities of her special formula. The plot intricacies of this novel do not work well, and the lead characters are down-at-heels and sordid. The fencing between Cockie and Inspector Charlesworth continues, although they eventually form an alliance. After three beers each, they decide that reenactment of the crime is a contrivance of fiction, and after six they decide to have the crime that baffles them reenacted. The conclusion seems highly improbable; yet, Brand's gift for surprise is evident. Once again, the murderer is a more engaging character than the victims.

In *Cat and Mouse* Brand turns to a different kind of mystery. The impetus for the plot is a series of intriguing letters written to an advice columnist for the magazine *Girls Together* in London. Katinka Jones, who writes under the name "Miss Friendly-Wise," embarks upon investigative journalism leading to a small town in her native Wales. The result is a contemporary Gothic mystery of suspense and adventure recalling Charlotte

Brontë's *Jane Eyre* (1847), with a secluded house, domestic mysteries, a tragic past, and violent deaths at the conclusion. The attractive and masterful villain's machinations are the result of greed rather than personal tragedy or madness. The story is focused on the naive but spirited journalist, whose wrongheaded attraction to the villain nearly makes her an additional victim. The Welsh detective on the case, the handsome Inspector Chucky, saves her life and provides the love interest her life in London had been lacking. The couple reappears, happy and with children, in one of the last Brand crime novels, *A Ring of Roses,* published in 1977 under the pseudonym Mary Ann Ashe.

Many of Brand's works, such as *Danger Unlimited* and *Cat and Mouse,* reflect her interest in Wales and its language. Short glossaries inform the reader of key words and usage, and characters' names include epithets to indicate the occupation of the person ("Evans the milk," "Dai trouble") in a region where many surnames are shared.

In 1951 Brand was employed to write new dialogue for the lead character, Maria (played by Valentina Cortese), in the movie *The Secret People* (1952). An account of the making of this thriller refers to Brand being employed to improve the dialogue and working sometimes at home and sometimes at the Ealing studio, where *The Secret People* was produced.

Brand's own Maida Vale house is copied as a setting for the Cockrill novel *London Particular* (1952; published in the United States as *Fog of Doubt*), in which Brand returns to top form. An introduction by P. D. James to a 1988 edition of the novel cites it as Brand's favorite and identifies the "expected Christianna Brand virtues: a zest and liveliness which are typical of the writer herself and characters who are observed with an affectionate but unsentimental eye." The method of the murder—which shatters one of many "firm" alibis—is revealed only in the last line of the novel, and Brand creates one of her most sympathetic murderers in this account of domestic relationships and an indulged and wayward young girl. Among the many ways in which Brand moves outside more standard practice in the classic detective novel is the use of casual slang associated with everyday activity. Rosie, unwed but unashamedly pregnant, spends most of the morning in the "huh-ha" (toilet) while her sister-in-law slavishly follows a regimen of child care that involves "potting the baby" (toilet training) at specific hours regardless of dinner guests left downstairs to their own devices. The household Siamese cat, Annaran, is named after a popular movie of the day, *Anna and the King of Siam* (1947), starring Rex Harrison. The grandmother continues a long tradition of dotty dowager figures but more than holds her own with fantasies of seduction and life in the

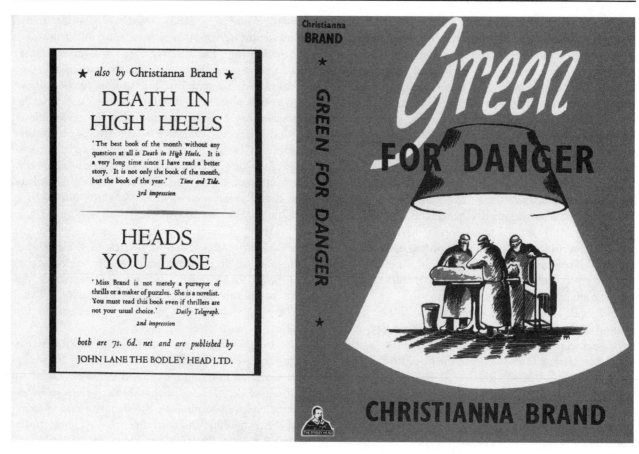

Dust jacket for British edition of Brand's best-known novel, in which her series character, Inspector Cockrill,
tracks a murderer during the London Blitz (Bruccoli Clark Layman Archives)

desert and a habit of tossing her wig and the contents of her bedroom out into the garden during moments of aberration or inattention on the part of the family.

In 1953 Brand contributed to a round-robin novella by some members of the Detection Club, *No Flowers by Request,* which was serialized in *The Daily Sketch* (London). It was eventually published in book form in 1984 along with another collaborative novel, *Crime on the Coast.* It fell to Brand to write the concluding three chapters of the novella, following sections written by Dorothy L. Sayers, E. C. R. Lorac, Gladys Mitchell, and Anthony Gilbert. In Brand's contribution, Mrs. Merton, the housekeeper, solves the abundant crimes and penetrates the intrigues in the novella; she is one of Brand's most interesting (and mature) female characters, a resourceful widow who has chosen to take up housekeeping rather than be unpaid labor in her daughter's home. As with younger characters in other works, her pluck, intelligence, and energy have their reward in the form of the love and hand of her employer, an offer she at first declines on the grounds of his having taken to drink.

The last of Brand's Cockrill novels is *Tour de Force* (1955). For reasons soon regretted, Inspector Cockrill has yielded to the temptation to take a holiday tour and signed on with a group headed for Mediterranean destinations, including the fictional island of San Juan el Pirata. Planning to catch up on his reading of detective fiction, he is immediately befriended by a fellow passenger, Louli, who engages his affection and attention, as do many other attractive young women in the novels. Fellow tourists are suspects when a reclusive tour participant is viciously stabbed to death. The exotic setting on an independent, feudal island creates a situation in which the solution to the crime must be found despite the absence of moral impetus by the political system and the ineffectiveness of official crime fighters. As it turns out, the lack of law and morality on an island on which the chief livelihood is smuggling and pirated goods makes possible a doubly surprising conclusion. The mood of comic opera and farce on the island yields to darker truths that require Brand's most elaborate concluding description of who did it and how. Mr. Cecil from *Death in High Heels* reappears, ostensibly on holiday to gain inspiration for new fashion designs, and Brand's recurring motifs of true love and passionate jealousy spur characters to drastic measures.

Tour de Force is not only the last novel to feature Inspector Cockrill, but it is also the last detective novel published by Brand for twenty years. During this period in her life she continued to publish but was, for personal reasons, either unable to write or unable to publish detective novels of her characteristic kind. As she was quoted in *Contemporary Authors* (1979), "for many years, for personal family reasons, I was able to write hardly at all so that there has been a long gap in my work. It was a bitter sacrifice. . . ." Possibly Brand's ability and time free to develop highly structured and focused mystery plots came to be undercut by domestic and family responsibilities.

With *The Three-Cornered Halo* in 1957, Brand tried a new format. Returning to the fantasy island of San Juan el Pirata for setting and making the grand duke of the island a main character, she wrote a satirical and farcical crime caper novel centered upon a faction determined to capture a sainthood for the most venerated figure in island history, Juanita "the Pearl of San Juan," who lived on a table. The tourist heroine, who foils a murder plot in the cathedral and figures out the grand duke's elaborate counterplot, is Henrietta Cockrill, Inspector Cockrill's equally talented sister. In another departure from novels of crime and detection, Brand's historical mystery *Starrbelow* (1958), written as China Thompson, recounts the battle of Sophie Devign (nicknamed Sapphire) against scandal and intrigue to recover her name and her lover without revealing a friend's secret.

Heaven Knows Who (1960) is Brand's first nonfiction publication. It is a retelling of the story of Jessie McLachlan, a Glasgow woman convicted of murder in 1862. Brand comes up with some conclusions of her own through personal research and analysis, and the events leading to murder in the mean streets of Glasgow are presented with Dickensian detail. This work was nominated for a Mystery Writers of America (MWA) Edgar Award.

In 1962 Brand compiled and edited an anthology of excerpts and stories, *Naughty Children,* including a short story of her own introducing the character Nurse Matilda, and in 1964 she wrote the first of three books about Nurse Matilda and the magical transformation of the terribly naughty and innumerable Brown children. Nurse Matilda will remind some readers of Mary Poppins in her child-minding success and the magic with which it is accomplished. Two others followed in 1967 and 1974. These books, illustrated by Brand's cousin, the noted children's illustrator Edward Ardizzone, have drawn an appreciative audience for many years and

were based on their family storytelling tradition dating back to a great-grandfather.

During the years in which she did not publish detective novels, Brand turned with an equally deft hand to the creation of outstanding short stories, and in 1966 her story "Twist for Twist" (collected in *What Dread Hand* as "The Hornets' Nest") won a competition for members of the Crime Writers' Association (CWA) sponsored by *Ellery Queen's Mystery Magazine*. Brand was a member of the MWA and earned Edgar nominations for best short story in 1967 and 1969. She published the first of three collections of short fiction in 1968 as *What Dread Hand*. This volume collects her first published mystery story, "The Rose," three Inspector Cockrill stories ("The Hornets' Nest," "Blood Brothers," and "After the Event"), and other crime, ghost, and horror stories, most of which had been published between 1957 and 1968. In her short stories Brand utilizes a greater variety of plot structures than in her novels, including use of an inverted structure in which the reader knows the criminal's identity. Her short fictions and serializations were published in such periodicals as *Ellery Queen's Mystery Magazine, The Saturday Evening Post,* the *Chicago Tribune, Good Housekeeping, Australian Women's Weekly,* and *Woman's Journal* (U.K.). Her crime stories were also regularly collected in volumes of the year's best and in collections by *Ellery Queen's Mystery Magazine,* the CWA, and the MWA.

Concluding a decade of varied works is *Court of Foxes* (1969), an historical romance and adventure set in the time of George III. The toast of London society, Marchesa Marigelda, also totes a silver pistol in her belt and heads a band of outlaws as Gilda the Vixen. Another historical romance, *The Radiant Dove* (1974), published by Brand as Annabel Jones, centers on the dilemmas of the governess as a well-born working woman. Also published in 1974, *Brand X* collects crime, mystery, and horror stories along with several sketches or essays, including a wartime journal memoir and appreciations of life in Wales not previously published. Among the stories most characteristic of Brand's crime works are "The Niece from Scotland," "Madame Thinks Quick," and "The Scapegoat," all of which include seemingly unbreakable alibis and surprise conclusions. "The Kite" and "Pigeon Pie" reveal Brand's talent for domestic horror. "The Scapegoat," first published in *Ellery Queen's Mystery Magazine* in 1970, was the winner of a special CWA award.

Almost twenty years after her last classic detective novel, Brand published a new one, *Alas, for Her That Met Me!* (1976) under the name of Mary Ann Ashe. It is set in Glasgow in the mid nineteenth century and recalls the well-known Madeleine Smith murder case of 1857. There is a murder and a trial, and a

HEAVEN
KNOWS
WHO

*A fascinating, scrupulously
accurate recreation of a
famous Scottish murder case
a century ago.*

CHRISTIANNA BRAND

*Dust jacket for the U.S. edition of Brand's 1960 nonfiction account
of nineteenth-century Glasgow murderer Jessie McLachlan
(Richland County Public Library)*

surprising reversal is exposed at the conclusion of the novel. Sibling rivalry in love precipitates the action and illustrates adolescent psychology with chilling accuracy. In much of Brand's fiction, the depth of love is tested by significant challenges. In this novel the challenge is a murder trial of the beloved, Adelina, in which the verdict is "not proven" and the victim is believed to have been her lover. Adelina owes a considerable debt to Emma Woodhouse, the title character of Jane Austen's *Emma* (1816).

In *A Ring of Roses* the action originates in the United States and includes a credulous English journalist, some creaky American gangsters, and a popular but fragile actress. This melodrama takes the reader into the entertainment industry and sensational journalism, where old and new crimes threaten the central characters and lead to murder. Despite Brand's typical inventiveness of plot and capable handling of character, the effect is of strain and exaggeration and not a little unpleasantness.

The Honey Harlot (1978) is another foray into historical mystery. This novel is a fictional re-creation of the voyage of the *Marie Celeste,* a sailing ship found adrift in the Atlantic Ocean in 1872 with no evidence of the fates of her passengers and crew. Brand's imaginative account of the history of the ship focuses on another of her passionate and obsessed characters, in this case the captain, who is a religious zealot. Told from the perspective of the sole survivor, the mystery is explained by means of the fatal attractions and shrewd manipulations of a female stowaway, the Honey Harlot.

Brand returns to a more typical mystery form in *The Rose in Darkness* (1979). A memorable plot device is the meeting of two identical new-model cars facing one another but separated on a road made impassable by a tree felled in a storm. The drivers, in order to continue their vital journeys, swap cars, turn them around, and continue on their way. When a body is found in one next morning, the hunt is on, with Charlesworth, now a superintendent, investigating and the ruling family of San Juan el Pirata (from *Tour de Force* and *The Three-Cornered Halo*) involved on behalf of the heir apparent. Similar to the central figure of the actress in *A Ring of Roses,* an actress in this novel follows a descending spiral of failure and drugs along with her set of Eight Best Friends. The novel reflects Brand's talent for plot and surprise, but the characters, while interesting and well drawn, elicit less sympathy than those of early Brand mysteries.

Brand wrote several ghost stories, and her last work was a Gothic novel, *The Brides of Aberdar* (1982), about a haunted family and the bitter sacrifices required to end the spell. The first collection of Brand short mysteries to be published in the United States, *Buffet for Unwelcome Guests: The Best Short Mysteries of Christianna Brand* (1983), includes stories from both previous collections and uncollected works, as well as an excellent introduction and bibliography.

During the late 1970s and early 1980s, Brand enjoyed spending time in the United States and participating in special events such as those sponsored by the University of California at San Diego in the company of such friends and acquaintances as Keating, John Ball, and Otto Penzler. She was even made an honorary sheriff. The dedication of *A Ring of Roses* is to Ball, and the dedication of *The Rose in Darkness* is "To all my friends in America, so loving and generous and ever kind; and so much loved in return." Robert Briney's introduction to *Buffet for Unwelcome Guests* pays personal tribute to Brand's ability to enthrall an audience in person as well as through her fiction, citing appearances from 1976 to 1981 for the Mystery Library, at Bouchercon meetings in Culver City, California, and New York, and at the Third International Congress of

Crime Writers in 1981 in Stockholm, Sweden, where Brand was named a grand master. She died on 11 March 1988 at the age of eighty.

As a body of work, Brand's novels and stories are well written, tightly plotted, and peopled with developed and convincing characters. Humor, clues, and spirited dialogue add further value. Robert Barnard's praise in *The Armchair Detective* (Summer 1986) identifies the spirit of her eight detective novels as "Christiannity" (or "Brand X"). He sees it as a collection of qualities—gaiety, gallantry, insouciance, effrontery, and wit— and finds the qualities in both her characters and her treatment of them. As he puts it, "Their most characteristic activity is cocking a snook, and they do it with style." Brand's views of her own work can be found in occasional essays and comments reported from interviews. In *Contemporary Authors* she says that her aim is to write good, readable (and sellable) entertainment books and, above all, to write them well. Colleagues recall her personal attractiveness and the vivacity and the skill she displayed in directing events during her presidency of the CWA in 1972–1973. In a 25 August 2001 unpublished interview, a fellow writer in the CWA, Jean McConnell, pointed out Brand's talent for drawing and her use of hand-drawn and colored caricatures on specially printed postal cards with which to communicate with friends.

Christianna Brand achieved significant recognition despite her best-known character. Inspector Cockrill fails to achieve the highest rank among the great detectives, perhaps because of his unimpressive appearance, his lack of off-duty life or pastimes, and his failure to establish a patterned approach to the solution of crimes. Despite Cockrill's human but less than heroic stature and Brand's relatively small output of detective novels, she received awards and tributes from her peers throughout her life for her accomplished and readable fiction and left a body of work still deserving of the attention of discerning readers.

References:

Babener, "Christianna Brand's 'Cockie' Cockrill," in *Cops and Constables: American and British Fictional Policemen,* edited by Earl Bargainnier (Bowling Green, Ohio: Bowling Green University Popular Press, 1986), pp. 125–142;

Robert Barnard, "The Slightly Mad, Mad World of Christianna Brand," *Armchair Detective,* 19 (Summer 1986): 238–243;

Otto Penzler, "Christianna Brand: In Memoriam 1907–1988," *Armchair Detective,* 21 (Summer 1988): 228–230;

Julian Symons, "Crime: The Hundred Best Stories," *Sunday Times* (London), 1959.

Simon Brett

(28 October 1945 –   )

T. R. Steiner
University of California at Santa Barbara

BOOKS: *Cast, in Order of Disappearance* (London: Gollancz, 1975; New York: Scribners, 1976);

So Much Blood (London: Gollancz, 1976; New York: Scribners, 1977);

Star Trap (London: Gollancz, 1977; New York: Scribners, 1978);

An Amateur Corpse (London: Gollancz, 1978; New York: Scribners, 1978);

Frank Muir Goes Into–, by Brett and Frank Muir (London: Robson, 1978);

A Comedian Dies (London: Gollancz, 1979; New York: Scribners, 1979);

The Second Frank Muir Goes Into–, by Brett and Muir (London: Robson, 1979);

The Dead Side of the Mike (London: Gollancz, 1980; New York: Scribners, 1980);

The Third Frank Muir Goes Into–, by Brett and Muir (London: Robson, 1980);

Situation Tragedy (London: Gollancz, 1981; New York: Scribners, 1981);

The Fourth Frank Muir Goes Into–, by Brett and Muir (London: Robson, 1981);

Murder Unprompted (London: Gollancz, 1982; New York: Scribners, 1982);

Murder in the Title (London: Gollancz, 1983; New York: Scribners, 1983);

Molesworth Rites Again (London: Hutchinson, 1983);

The Child Owner's Handbook (London: Unwin, 1983);

Bad Form; or, How Not to Get Invited Back (London: Elm Tree, 1984);

Not Dead, Only Resting (London: Gollancz, 1984; New York: Scribners, 1984);

A Shock to the System (London: Macmillan, 1984; New York: Scribners, 1985);

A Box of Tricks: Short Stories (London: Gollancz, 1985); republished as *Tickled to Death, and Other Stories of Crime and Suspense* (New York: Scribners, 1985);

Dead Giveaway (London: Gollancz, 1985; New York: Scribners, 1986);

Dead Romantic (London: Macmillan, 1985; New York: Scribners, 1986);

People-Spotting: The Human Species Laid Bare (London: Elm Tree, 1985);

The Wastepaper Basket Archive (London: Sidgwick & Jackson, 1986);

The Three Detectives and the Missing Superstar (London: Scholastic, 1986; New York: Scribners, 1986);

A Nice Class of Corpse (London: Macmillan, 1986; New York: Scribners, 1987);

The Three Detectives and the Knight in Armor (London: Macmillan, 1987; New York: Scribners, 1987);

What Bloody Man Is That? (London: Gollancz, 1987; New York: Scribners, 1987);

After Henry (London: Viking, 1987);

Mrs. Presumed Dead (London: Macmillan, 1988; New York: Scribners, 1989);

A Series of Murders (London: Gollancz, 1989; New York: Scribners, 1989);

The Booker Book (London: Sidgwick & Jackson, 1989);

How to Be a Little Sod (London: Gollancz, 1989);

Mrs. Pargeter's Package (London: Macmillan, 1990; New York: Scribners, 1991);

The Christmas Crimes at Puzzel Manor (London: Hodder & Stoughton, 1991; New York: Delacorte, 1992);

Corporate Bodies (London: Gollancz, 1991; New York: Scribners, 1992);

Mrs. Pargeter's Pound of Flesh (London: Macmillan, 1992; New York: Scribners, 1993);

A Reconstructed Corpse (London: Gollancz, 1993; New York: Scribners, 1994);

Look Who's Walking: Further Diaries of a Little Sod (London: Gollancz, 1994);

Murder in Play (London & New York: S. French, 1994);

Hypochondriac's Dictionary of Ill Health, by Brett and Sarah Brewer (London: Headline, 1994);

Mr. Quigley's Revenge (London & New York: S. French, 1995);

Sicken and So Die (London: Gollancz, 1995; New York: Scribners, 1995);

Singled Out (London: Macmillan, 1995; New York: Scribners, 1995);

Simon Brett (photograph by Christian Doyle; from the dust jacket for the U.S. edition of The Body on the Beach, *2000)*

Mrs. Pargeter's Plot (London: Macmillan, 1996; New York: Scribners, 1998);

Not Another Little Sod (London: Gollancz, 1997);

Dead Room Farce (London: Gollancz, 1997; New York: St. Martin's Press, 1998);

Crime Writers and Other Animals (London: Gollancz, 1998);

Silhouette (London & New York: S. French, 1998);

Mrs. Pargeter's Point of Honour (London: Macmillan, 1998; New York: Scribner, 1999);

The Body on the Beach (London: Macmillan, 2000; New York: Berkley, 2000);

Death on the Downs (London: Macmillan, 2001; New York: Berkley, 2001).

PLAY PRODUCTIONS: *Mrs. Gladys Moxon,* London, Soho Theatre, 19 May 1970;

Did You Sleep Well? and *A Good Day at the Office,* first produced together, London, 1971;

Third Person, London, 1972;

Drake's Dream, script by Brett, music and lyrics by Lynne Riley and Richard Riley, Worthing, 1977; London, 1977;

Silhouette, National Tour, 1997.

PRODUCED SCRIPTS: *Semi-Circles,* radio, 1982;

Gothic Romances, radio, 1982;

A Matter of Life and Death, radio, 1982;

Cast, in Order of Disappearance, radio, 1983;

The Crime of the Dancing Duchess, television, 1983;

A Promising Death, television, 1983;

So Much Blood, radio, 1985;

After Henry, radio, 1985;

Molesworth, radio, 1987;

After Henry, television, 1988–1990.

RECORDINGS: *Situation Tragedy,* read by Brett, Boston, G. K. Hall Audio SSO 12, 1981;

Cast in Order of Disappearance, read by Brett, Bath, Chivers Audio Books CAT 4007, 1986; Boston, G. K. Hall Audio, 1986;

A Comedian Dies, read by Brett, Boston, G. K. Hall Audio CAT 4014, 1987;

A Nice Class of Corpse, read by Brett, Oxford, Isis Audio Books IAB 87122, 1987;

Mrs. Presumed Dead, read by Brett, Oxford, Isis Audio Books IAB 89042, 1989;

A Series of Murders, read by Brett, Bath, Chivers Audio Books CAB 427, 1989; Boston, G. K. Hall Audio, 1989;

Mrs. Pargeter's Package, read by Brett, Oxford, Isis Audio Books IAB 91061, 1991;

What Bloody Man Is That? read by Brett, Bath, Chivers Audio Books CAB 632, 1991; Boston, G. K. Hall Audio, 1991;

Murder Unprompted, read by Brett, Bath, Chivers Audio Books CAB 686, 1992; Boston, G. K. Hall Audio, 1992;

Murder in the Title, read by Brett, Bath, Chivers Audio Books CAB 769, 1992;

Corporate Bodies, read by Brett, Bath & Hampton, N.H., Chivers Audio Books CAB 814, 1993;

Dead Giveaway, read by Brett, Bath & Hampton, N.H., Chivers Audio Books CAB 893, 1993;

Mrs. Pargeter's Pound of Flesh, read by Brett, Oxford, Isis Audio Books IAB 93051, 1993;

A Reconstructed Corpse, read by Brett, Bath, Chivers Audio Books CAB 1040, 1994;

So Much Blood, read by Brett, Bath & Hampton, N.H., Chivers Audio Books CAB 934, 1994;

Star Trap, read by Brett, Bath, Chivers Audio Books CAB 1097, 1995; Ashland, Ore., Blackstone Audiobooks 2554, 2000;

An Amateur Corpse, read by Brett, Bath & Hampton, N.H., Chivers Audio Books CAB 1233, 1996;

Sicken and So Die, read by Brett, Bath & Hampton, N.H., Chivers Audio Books CAB 1314, 1996;

Singled Out, read by Brett, Oxford, Isis Audio Books IAB 960207, 1996; Wrentham, Mass., Dual Dolphin, 1996;

Mrs. Pargeter's Plot, read by Brett, Oxford, Isis Audio Books IAB 961001, 1996;

The Dead Side of the Mike, read by Brett, Bath & Hampton, N.H., Chivers Audio Books CAB 1354, 1997;

Dead Room Farce, read by Brett, Bath & Hampton, N.H., Chivers Audio Books CAB 1573, 1998;

Mrs. Pargeter's Point of Honour, read by Brett, Oxford & Winter Springs, Fla., Isis Audio Books IAB 981201, 1998;

Dead Romantic, read by Brett, Bath & Hampton, N.H., Chivers Audio Books CAB 1943, 2000;

The Body on the Beach, read by Brett, Oxford & Winter Springs, Fla., Isis Audio Books IAB 000607, 2000;

Death on the Downs, read by Brett, Oxford & Winter Springs, Fla., Isis Audio Books IAB 010601, 2001.

OTHER: *Frank Muir on Children,* compiled by Brett and Frank Muir (London: Heinemann, 1980);

The Faber Book of Useful Verse, edited by Brett and Muir, with an introduction by Brett (London: Faber & Faber, 1981);

Frank Muir Presents the Book of Comedy Sketches, edited by Brett and Muir (London: Elm Tree/Hamilton, 1982); revised as *The Penguin Book of Comedy Sketches* (London: Penguin, 1992);

Take a Spare Truss: Tips for Nineteenth-Century Travellers, compiled by Brett (London: Elm Tree, 1983);

The Faber Book of Parodies, edited by Brett (London: Faber & Faber, 1984);

The Faber Book of Diaries, edited by Brett (London: Faber & Faber, 1987).

Simon Brett's multifarious and intense mystery productivity includes psychological suspense and an innovative female sleuth, but the invention of the middle-aged actor-sleuth Charles Paris and his London theater milieu remains his signature creation. Such writers as Edmund Crispin, Ngaio Marsh, and Anne Morice had popularized the theater mystery as a combination of crime fiction and the comedy of manners. Brett's titles alluding to the stage—including *Cast, in Order of Disappearance* (1975), *Star Trap* (1977), *A Comedian Dies* (1979), *Situation Tragedy* (1981), and *Murder Unprompted* (1982)—indeed place him in that tradition, as do his stage-oriented settings, with one-man shows, Shakespearean parallels, and farces both onstage and off. Brett expanded the potential of the theater mystery to incorporate satire and social critique, however. Despite his avowed goal to entertain, he clearly strives for more. As E. D. Huntley observes in the *Critical Survey of Mystery and Detective Fiction* (1988), Brett's "intimate knowledge of backstage society and activity" enabled him to paint "devastatingly accurate scenes of competition and deceit, ambition and lust in provincial theatrical venues and West End houses alike" and thereby to capture through wit, caricature, burlesque, and farce a critical image of humans at their worst. Brett turns a critical eye on modern society and through witty characterizations deflates human pretensions, probes motives, exposes vices, and satirizes one and all.

Simon Anthony Lee Brett was born at Worcester Park, Surrey, on 28 October 1945, the son of Alan John and Margaret Agnes Brett. Educated at Dulwich College from 1956 to 1964, Brett won a major scholarship in history to Wadham College, Oxford. He graduated in 1967 with First Class Honours in English. While there, Brett was president of the University Dramatic Society and in 1967 director of the Oxford Late-Night Revue on the Fringe at the Edinburgh Festival. In 1968 he joined the BBC for a ten-year career as producer with BBC Radio Light Entertainment. His first play, *Mrs. Gladys Moxon,* was produced in London in 1970. He married Lucy Victoria McLaren, with whom he had two sons and a daughter, the next year. Two more plays, *Did You Sleep Well?* and *A Good Day at the Office,* were produced together in 1971. *Third Person* was produced in 1972. Brett received the Writers Guild of Great Britain Award for best radio feature script in 1973. Though he continued to write plays, he turned more and more to radio and then television scripts.

Brett published the first in his ongoing Charles Paris mystery series, *Cast, in Order of Disappearance,* in 1975. Paris, called simply Charles throughout the novels, is a fresh, appealing character. A libertine and alcoholic, the middle-aged actor nonetheless proves a good detective and a decent man. Ominously born on Guy Fawkes Day (5 November), he is at the mature but reckless age of forty-seven when the series starts. He is a divorcé, amicably separated for fifteen years from his former spouse, Frances, the attractive headmistress of a girls' school, to whom he occasionally returns. Bored by bourgeois routine, he seeks variety and excitement in acting, amateur detection, and the restless pursuit of shallow sexual encounters of momentary satisfaction (which is why his marriage floundered). On occasion he works part-time as a house painter or a char, accepts a minor role in some rural production, or assists friends and acquaintances.

Critics acclaimed *Cast, in Order of Disappearance* an impressive start to the series, which featured a new volume nearly every year until 1997. Some of its memorable characters, such as the aging comedian Harry Chiltern, appear only in the first novel. Others recur in subsequent novels, such as Charles's incompetent agent, Maurice Skellern; his college friend and "Dr. Watson," the successful solicitor Gerald Venables; Frances Paris; the couple's daughter, Juliet, and her insufferably boring husband, accountant Miles Taylerson; and the Swedish girls living in Charles's building who butcher the English language. In *Cast, in Order of Disappearance* blackmail photos, suburban estates, hired toughs, a corrupt doctor, a convoluted plot, and a powerful man with a shady past echo Raymond Chandler's *Farewell, My Lovely* (1940) and *The Little Sister* (1949).

Jacqui Mitchell, Charles's onetime bed partner, asks him to give Marius Steen, her recent celebrity lover, some "naughty" photographs of her and Steen, blackmail photos Jacqui bought to protect Steen, a sixty-plus, larger-than-life theater impresario who no longer answers her phone calls and who writes that they are through. Steen's office and his son Nigel claim Steen is at his country house, but when the blackmailer is discovered dead, Charles suspects Steen of murder and of having Jacqui harassed. Charles breaks into the country house and finds Steen dead, apparently of natural causes. Charles suspects murder, however, so he investigates, spurred on by Jacqui, pregnant with Steen's child and convinced that Nigel murdered Steen to prevent their marriage. A final will generously providing for the unborn child confirms Jacqui's claim. The mystery is why, given Steen's complicated will, Nigel attempted to control the perceived time of his father's natural death, and why his thugs kidnap Jacqui to abort her baby.

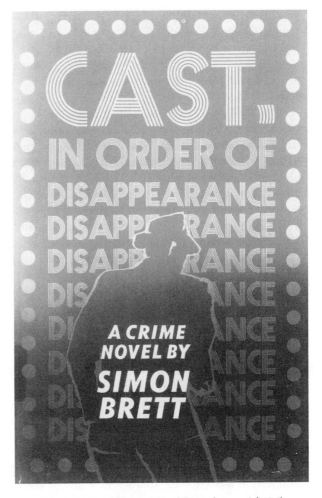

Dust jacket for the U.S. edition of Brett's first novel (1975), which introduces actor and amateur detective Charles Paris (Richland County Public Library)

Such plot complications typify a Charles Paris mystery, and this volume establishes the series pattern: one or more murders, questions of motive, puzzling clues, much misdirection, and much coming and going that guides the amateur detective to a solution others miss. Other genre conventions Brett employs include red herrings, locked-room mysteries, villains perfectly alibied, a village circle of suspects, and murder onstage, to which Brett adds interesting details of place and community, an insider's knowledge of British theater productions and companies (William Shakespeare naturally features importantly), and an intuitive detective. No spiffily dressed, self-confident Sherlock Holmes with logic ever his guide, Charles muddles about indirectly, puzzled by trivial discrepancies or minor incidents but always guided by a deep-seated personal need to discover the truth. An actor himself, he effectively hides his emotions, plays the part occasion demands, and disguises himself creatively, convincingly mimicking rustic or urban accents. Despite his closed circle, his world is far removed from the cozy mystery world of Agatha Christie–it is thoroughly modern and thoroughly nasty, with sexual jealousies; class hatreds; business rivalries; political maneuvering; tough union bosses; lazy, empty television stars; and unscrupulous characters in various fields.

So Much Blood (1976), the only Charles Paris mystery set outside England, describes the Edinburgh Festival of experimental drama (the Fringe), which Brett himself attended in 1967 and where Charles gives a one-man show of Thomas Hood's poetry (which the chapter headings quote). He domiciles with Derby University Dramatic Society (DUDS) members, whose artistic and social life the novel satirizes. Their landlord, James Milne, recently moved into the residence, having sold his other house to Willy Marinello, a former rock musician now acting in a DUDS production. During a rehearsal of *Mary, Queen of Sots,* Martin Warburton, the author of the play who is also playing Lord Darnley, strikes Marinello (playing Mary's secretary, David Riccio) with the stage prop knife, really killing him. Warburton, a talented but emotionally disturbed young playwright, feels wretchedly guilty. Suspecting murder, Charles informally explores Marinello's place in the company and the circumstances of his death, consulting Milne, a willing Dr. Watson. Charles considers Milne's theory that Warburton identifies with the violent Darnley in the history of Mary. A bomb planted in Charles's bag at Holyrood Castle leads police to bomb-making materials connected with Warburton, who, pursued, leaps to his death from the Edinburgh Castle walls; jaded, Charles accepts him as a murderer. He persuades Frances, in Edinburgh for the festival, to take a holiday in the Highlands, where a murderous attack helps him reconfigure the facts: in the house bought from Milne, Marinello discovered evidence of murder and blackmailed Milne, who retaliated by substituting a real knife for the stage prop. Appalled that Milne unforgivingly drove the distraught Warburton to suicide, Charles turns him over to the police. Such intricate plot twists and repeated suspenseful misdirection are signature features of Brett's canon.

The first novels are impressive, but the third is strikingly better in its theatrical material, characterization, and detective narrative. *Star Trap* explores the talent, single-mindedness, and ruthlessness of stars, a subject Brett has personal experience with and elaborates on in several Paris series volumes. Charles plays Old Marlowe in a musical adaptation of Oliver Goldsmith's *She Stoops to Conquer* (1773) titled *Lumpkin!* and starring powerful, enigmatic television star Christopher Milton as Tony. Milton overrides the director and tailors the production to his talents, thereby alienating nearly all the company, including Charles. Yet, his ideas make the production brilliant theater. Uncanny in intuiting what works, he indefatigably orchestrates every element of the production. Venables, a secret member of the show's investment group, recruits Charles to investigate "accidents" affecting *Lumpkin!,* for backers fear sabotage. As the incidents intensify from serious injuries to homicide, Charles theorizes that Milton's "messianic" belief in his total responsibility for the success of the show and a violent nervous breakdown early in his career have made him a paranoid madman bent on eliminating all who cross him. A "star trap" (a trapdoor) operates improperly, nearly killing Charles and exposing the saboteur as "Spike," Gareth Warden, the stage manager. A contemporary of Milton who could not continue his promising acting career after childhood, Warden tries to exact revenge for Milton's psychological destruction of a beloved fellow child actress and for Milton's "evil" by framing him. Warden fails to understand that Milton's life–his obsessive ambition, his schizophrenic lack of real identity, his vicarious living in a "fictional self," and his constant need for mental relief–is his punishment, his ineluctable "star trap."

While writing these early novels, Brett served as the producer of Light Entertainment for London Weekend Television from 1977 to 1979. His 1977 musical *Drake's Dream,* written in collaboration with Lynne and Richard Riley, had a successful run in Worthing, Sussex, and London. His depiction of a pretentious, self-important suburban amateur theater group, the Breckton Backstagers of *An Amateur Corpse* (1978), reflects his personal life and early career experiences. The Backstagers' star, Charlotte Mecken, is the wife of Charles's college friend Hugo Mecken, whose production of Anton Pavlovich Chekhov's *The Seagull* (1897) Charles is to critique. Only the male lead, Geoffrey Winter, is a professional. On the night of the critique, when Charles and Hugo find Charlotte strangled, the police arrest Hugo, who had publicly raged about his wife's infidelity. Hugo's drunkenness, violence, and lack of an alibi negate his innocence. Even his solicitor believes him guilty, but friendship makes Charles investigate. Cryptic entries in Charlotte's diary confirm her affair with "Geoff." Winter readily admits the affair, but his grief suggests lack of motive, and his alibi seems unshakable. Eventually, a vital clue–an unerased phrase ("-ed coal") on a music tape borrowed from Winter–leads practiced Shakespearean Charles to identify "dead coals" as from a speech by Leontes (Winter's next role) in *The Winter's Tale* (1611). Winter is a cool, calculating genius (his name is revealing) who used the tape of himself rehearsing to help establish his alibi. Winter tacitly accepts Charles's analysis but is untouchable until Charles patiently retraces the crime and conclusively proves his theory. The opposition of Winter and Paris resembles that of genius criminal and genius detective in a Golden Age whodunit. In the last scene, Winter "keeps on laughing" as a policeman holds up the fatal evidence.

In *A Comedian Dies* Charles and Frances, briefly reunited, attend a provincial music hall. On the bill are two comedians, Lennie Barber, a nearly forgotten star of the music halls and early television, and rising featured performer Bill Peaky, who is electrocuted by a faulty microphone. Charles suspects murder. He learns that Peaky was an unpleasant chap, universally disliked. Meanwhile, Barber has begun a comeback. With Charles standing in for his former straight man, Pole, they appear on a highly rated television interview program. The milieu of popular comedy gives this novel special force, and each chapter begins with a classic joke alluding to its content. Charles's early deductions all prove wrong, and the least likely suspect turns out to be the actual murderer. A consummate professional comedian and a likable character, Barber, dying of a stroke, reveals that he murdered Peaky because the untalented young man insulted the memory of Barber's idol, his father, an underpaid, underrecognized comic genius of the music halls. Brett presents powerful themes: the superiority of old to new comedy, of music-hall popular art to the mere packaging of television, of the traditional experienced craft to contemporary gadgetry and flash.

At the same time that his novels were coming out regularly, Brett's career in radio and television producing was marked with notable successes. Yet, he turned to full-time writing in 1979 and in the early 1980s moved from London to Burpham, a village on the South Downs, near Arundel, West Sussex, where he and his family have now long resided. His next novel, *The Dead Side of the Mike* (1980), however, continues to reflect his media interests. While Charles finishes a job at BBC Radio, stage manager Andrea Gower, back from an exhausting New York trip, apparently commits suicide. Charles is skeptical, and between other jobs at the BBC he investigates the likeliest suspects: Gower's most recent boyfriend–a philandering producer–and her former husband, Keith Nicholls. When a visiting New York music producer, Daniel Klinger, also dies, an apparent suicide, the unsettling coincidence leads Charles to surmise a connection with Gower and her New York visit. In New York for Frances's mother's funeral, he uncovers a complicated transatlantic music piracy involving Klinger and an unknown English associate, probably his former fellow disc jockey "Mike Fergus," and evidence that Gower knew of the criminal activity. A New York informant reveals that on the air Fergus and Klinger communicated in a code using song

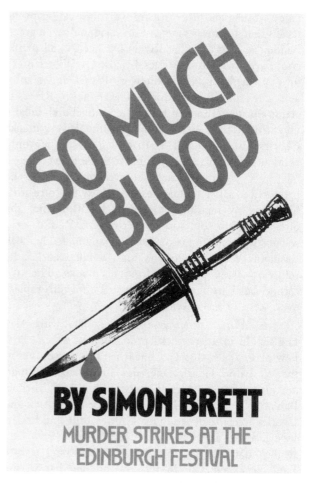

Dust jacket for the U.S. edition of Brett's 1976 novel, in which Charles Paris investigates a murder at the Edinburgh Fringe drama festival (Richland County Public Library)

titles and place references, like the one the popular Dave Sheridan radio show used when Nicholls was producer. Coded directions in a tape-recorded Sheridan broadcast lead to evidence of music piracy and Klinger's murder, and Sheridan is revealed to be the elusive Mike Fergus.

In *Situation Tragedy* the television comedy *The Strutters* is in deep trouble after losing crew members to accidental deaths. The alcoholic Charles plays Reg, a bartender, alongside old acquaintance George Birkitt and the grande dame of British actresses, septuagenarian Aurelia Howarth. Aurelia retains her charm and beauty and travels in a prewar Bentley with her former leading man, husband Barton Rivers, now a dotty eighty-year-old, and her beloved Yorkshire terrier, Cocky. Aurelia's excessive worries about her aging dog make Charles suspect murderous senile dementia until a falling portable light standard kills the stage manager while Aurelia is with Charles. As he desultorily searches for a copy of a 1930s mystery novel that provided Aurelia and her husband with a movie script, he recalls that a witness to one of the incidents saw a green Bentley nearby and that Rivers has been at all of the crime scenes. The mysteries by "B. Q. Wilberforce" turn out to have been written by Rivers and feature analogues for all the murders. The deranged Rivers is acting out the crimes of his mystery-novel arch-villain, von Strutter, with Aurelia protecting him. Rivers attacks Charles, and Aurelia claims that the death of their only child in World War II drove him mad. Aurelia confirms Charles's new theory that she accidentally killed the production assistant and responded to the director's blackmail by sending the unwitting Barton after the director, supposedly von Strutter's agent. With a star's self-absorption, Aurelia repeatedly manipulated her sick husband. When she orders him to kill Charles, he refuses, lacking a pattern from his books. The two escape, but Barton drives the Bentley off a cliff–replaying a scene in a Wilberforce novel.

In *Murder Unprompted* Charles stars with Alex Household in a provincial production of an excellent new play, *The Hooded Owl,* but when the play moves to the West End, Charles and Alex are replaced by marketable television stars: George Birkitt and Michael Banks, a World War II hero and movie great. Alex and Charles accept understudy roles. Alex's girlfriend, Lesley-Jane Decker, the featured ingenue in *The Hooded Owl,* seems infatuated by the genuinely charming Banks. Banks has been away from theater so long that he cannot learn his lines, but Household ingeniously feeds him his lines by earphone, averting disaster and enabling a powerful performance. On opening night, however, as Banks concludes his most powerful speech, he is shot from the wings where Alex stands. Bank's last words were seemingly a plea for mercy. When Alex flees the theater, all conclude that he killed his artistic and sexual supplanter in a jealous rage. With Banks dead and his stand-in decamped, Charles plays the lead. Feeling something does not "ring true" about Alex's guilt, he studies four others with motive and opportunity, but Alex remains the likely suspect. Later, however, Charles plays with his grandsons, who automatically repeat his words, and he surmises that Banks's last words merely repeated what a threatened Alex said into his transmitter. In rural Somerset he finds a frightened Alex, who identifies the murderer as Lesley-Jane's mother. Once a hopeful actress "betrayed" by pregnancy, Valerie Cass shot at her pregnant daughter's "seducer" but killed Banks instead. With Charles as the replacement lead, *The Hooded Owl* opens to West End success, but fate once again turns unkind as Lexington's financial juggling bankrupts the production company: Charles's brief stardom ends when the play closes after three weeks.

In addition to publishing *Murder Unprompted* in 1982 Brett produced three radio scripts: the *Semi-Circles* series, *Gothic Romances,* and *A Matter of Life and Death.* The following year he turned *Cast, in Order of Disappearance* into a radio script of the same title and produced his first two television scripts: *The Crime of the Dancing Duchess* and *A Promising Death.* Thus, Brett's mystery novels grew out of his theater and production experience, and his scriptwriting for radio and television grew out of his experience writing novels.

Provincial Rugland Spa is the location for *Murder in the Title* (1983), one of several novels in which Brett counterpoints Charles's detection with another detective story. In a revival of a second-rate 1950s thriller, *The Message Is Murder,* Charles plays the corpse. Despite some good acting, the play is hopeless, and many foul-ups suggest that the Regent Theater's longtime artistic director, Tony Wensleigh, cannot handle the job. One evening a drunken Charles is nearly stabbed while awaiting his "entrance" as the corpse. Charles, a last-minute replacement, surmises that he substituted for the intended victim, possibly Wensleigh. The theater board opposes the local council's wish to sell the property to the large developer Schlenter Estates. Yet, every bad review or unsavory incident pushes the venerable Regent nearer closing. Managing director Donald Mason wants the theater's books checked for an "inconsistency," but Charles suspects Wensleigh of embezzlement, covered up by the recent "accidents." When Wensleigh dies, apparently a suicide, his widow has Charles investigate. To Charles's surprise, Wensleigh's papers reveal his considerable business acumen, his lack of culpability for the season's bad plays, and sabotage. A web of business mergers and associations leads to the local peer, Regent patron Lord Kitestone. Kitestone, whose conglomerate owns Schlenter Estates, manipulated the board to secretly undermine the Regent, appointing as managing director the Schlenter Estates "winkler" (one who induces unwilling tenants to move from development properties), Mason. Mason's theater credentials were faked, and his assignment was to oust the Regent to clear the town-center site for development. Doing so led to Wensleigh's murder, secretly recorded on a tape recorder that Charles finds. Charles's cynical assessment that nevertheless the Regent will close and Schlenter develop the property is not immediately borne out, but the prospects for the survival of the theater are dubious.

In *Not Dead, Only Resting* (1984), Charles's friends Bartlemas and O'Rourke, London's most prominent first-nighters, take him to dinner at trendy new Tryst, the joint creation of Tristram Gower and his lover, chef Yves Lafeu. The couple have a public spat about Yves's sexual adventuring, and Tristram threatens Yves with a chef's knife. Several days later the out-of-work Charles contracts to paint Tristram and Yves's unoccupied apartment, where painters find the mutilated corpse of Yves. Everyone assumes that the missing Tristram killed Yves in a jealous fit and fled to France, where indeed his car and a shadowy figure resembling Tristram have been sighted. O'Rourke, Tristram's cousin and legal heir, has Charles investigate. Though convinced Tristram murdered Yves, Charles successively "convicts" then exonerates Yves's homophobic sister, Tristram's angry former wife, and an actor with whom Yves may have had a relationship. When Charles learns that Yves was a playful blackmailer, whose victim, the television star Bertram Pride, years ago may have viciously knifed a career rival, he realizes that the "Tristram" who was spotted in France could have been Pride in disguise. Symbolically named, Pride murdered Yves to protect his secret, but gave his crime the trappings of homosexual jealousy. He also murdered Tristram and created red herrings to throw off the police. The setting of the novel is gay London, its "escort services" and expensive gay clubs; as Charles investigates, he suffers the comic discomfiture of being frequently mistaken for an aging queen.

In 1984 Brett wrote his first suspense novel, *A Shock to the System*. Built on detective-fiction conventions, it is his most chilling and perhaps best novel. The novel combines exceptional suspense with keen satire of British business and social life. Graham Marshall, the protagonist, is a "new man," situated between the traditional Britain of class labels and class loyalty and the newer Britain of computers and ruthless business practice. Enabled by family sacrifices to receive a red-brick-university education, Marshall has attained personal and material success. He has played the success game expertly, crafting himself as the loyal assistant to his department head, old-school conservative George Brewer, whom everyone expects Marshall to succeed. The world and the company take new turns, however, and Marshall's tie to George proves a liability: the directors choose the department's computer expert, Robert Benham. Marshall's first "failure" drives him mad. Drunk from a tippling session with Benham, in a "fury" at "forty-one wasted years," he strikes and kills an old beggar. Brett exploits the detective-fiction truism that it is easier to kill a second time, with Marshall initially fearing detection, then feeling liberated and special. Benham may have a flashy car and flashy girlfriend, a perfect vacation cottage, and a sailboat, but Marshall feels superior, for he has killed and continues meticulously to kill everyone in his way: his wife, Benham, and finally Brewer, when Brewer accidentally acquires evidence of Marshall's murder of Benham. Marshall lacks common human affect. Only the games

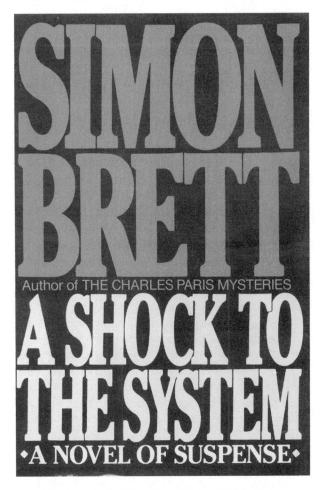

Dust jacket for the U.S. edition of Brett's 1984 novel about a ruthless corporate executive who kills to achieve success (Richland County Public Library)

of corporate life, rage at slights, and the secret joy of murdering move him. Without compunction or retrospect, he shucks off his children, personal associations, and new mistress—his unwitting alibi—and assumes a single life of freedom and material pleasures. His seemingly ineffectual mother-in-law doggedly seeks evidence that he murdered her daughter, but her despairing self-poisoning seems to remove this danger until the false testimony of his vengeful cast-off mistress frames him for a murder he did not commit: "The random gods of chance had changed their allegiance. . . . they had made the false seem real; now, with savage impartiality, they were making the real seem false." This unsettling novel assaults moral and institutional systems, while the void of Marshall's spirit shocks cherished traditional beliefs in love and community. *A Shock to the System* was made into a motion picture, starring Michael Caine as Marshall, in 1990.

The first hundred pages of Brett's second suspense thriller, *Dead Romantic* (1985), are equally chilling.

The brief first part reports a grisly murder at Winter Jasmine Cottage, identifying neither victim nor murderer. The novel then backtracks to detail the circumstances of a romantic triangle involving the English tutor Madeleine Severn, her teenage pupil Paul Grigson, and her colleague Bernard Hopkins. Madeleine is a beautiful, thirty-seven-year-old Oxford graduate stalled in self-adoration, myopic snobbery, and a long-maintained virginity. She teaches English to foreigners at the small provincial Garrettway School of Languages and occasionally prepares a student for university entrance. Paul is a virgin, a troubled adolescent in love with Madeleine. The newly hired Bernard seems burdened by a sick wife. As Madeleine and Bernard move closer to a tryst, Paul develops a murderous hatred of his rival. Madeleine underestimates the danger of Paul's obsessive love and tries to soothe his despair by liberal applications of the Romantic poets and "maternal" understanding, not recognizing that Paul, driven by sexual hysteria, misunderstands and misuses these "mature" perspectives. While Paul stumbles through adolescent sexual misadventures, Madeleine and Bernard share literary chitchat, intimate gourmet suppers, and mounting unconsummated desire. Paul, with a newly purchased knife and wild behavior, seems even more dangerous—possibly the mysterious figure who fails at sex with a Soho prostitute and strangles her. When Bernard arranges a weekend with Madeleine at Winter Jasmine Cottage, infuriating Paul, the three converge toward a fatal rendezvous, but the police detain Paul for erratic driving. Bernard is revealed to be wifeless and virginal, as well as the strangler of five prostitutes, but he convinces himself his romantic passion for Madeleine will enable sexual success. In the surprise ending, only Madeleine, who kills Bernard in self-defense, survives "unchanged," a hollow "dead romantic" in her flirtatious virginity and blind fraudulence.

The lively *Dead Giveaway* (1985) returns to Charles Paris, long unemployed, accepting a marginal acting job on the pilot for a new television game show, *If the Cap Fits*. Charles finds the sexy, hard-boiled, young television molls "daunting," most of all Sydnee Danson, the researcher for the show, who maneuvers contestants and secret guests around the studios to keep them apart. At the climax of the pilot, as the winning contestant spins a wheel for the grand prize, host Barrett Doran, a thoroughly unlikable brute, crashes to the floor, dead from cyanide poisoning. Witnesses and suspects include contestants, celebrity guests, and production staff, whom Doran has insulted and humiliated, as well as the owners of the American version of the series, which Doran had belittled. Amid this gallery of characters, Brett is often at his comic best. A likely suspect is Danson's roommate and former lover, Chippy Postgate, because she recently threatened Doran when he threw her over; besides, she was assistant stage manager on a show demonstrating poisons and had fiddled with his glass. Now, "numb and totally fatalistic," she will not fight the accusation. Danson recruits Charles to prove Chippy innocent. He and Danson, with her fellow researchers assisting, discover various chicaneries (a fixed wheel, sexual assault, and Doran's affair with celebrity guest Bob Garston's wife); the turning point comes when Charles realizes that the drink glasses had been moved and the wrong person murdered. The intended victim was celebrity guest Joanie Bruton, a beloved advice columnist, whose sexual coldness and patronizing of her peccant husband led him to murder. Bruton confesses and commits suicide. Charles's success brings no erotic reward, however, only awareness of himself as alien amid young television girls.

In 1986 Brett significantly departed from the successful Charles Paris series in the first of the Mrs. Pargeter novels, *A Nice Class of Corpse*, in the main an imitation of Agatha Christie's mysteries. Set in a small seaside hotel, the Devereux, with a "nice class" of eccentric, dotty old residents, it is a classic whodunit that weaves the diary of an unidentified criminal with a clever elderly female amateur's systematic detection. Unlike Christie's Jane Marple, however, Melita Pargeter is a financially well-endowed and sexually attractive widow, occasionally assisted by the "business associates" of her mysterious late husband, apparently a hugely successful though eminently respectable master criminal. Mrs. Pargeter and Miss Marple share the intelligence, inquisitiveness, and understanding of human nature that a detective needs, but Pargeter taught his wife intimately about both crime and detection, and when she needs expert information on safe combinations or jewelry reproduction his address book provides the right shady "expert" to call. Her somewhat flashy elegance and questioning of the hidebound procedures and attitudes of the Devereux disturb the starchy proprietress.

Investigating a series of deaths judged "old people's" accidents, Mrs. Pargeter assumes murder, a judgment confirmed for the reader by periodic diary entries revealing criminal intent. Mrs. Pargeter, discovering expert imitations in place of jewels in the hotel safe, catches a hotel employee who secretly converted an aristocratic lady's jewels into needed cash but who also stole from another resident. Later, she smokes out the "diarist," Colonel Wicksteed, who murdered the first old lady to resurrect his blighted finances and a second to silence a witness but who commits suicide rather than kill his best friend, who intends to expose his crimes. Not ready "to spiral down to a genteel death"

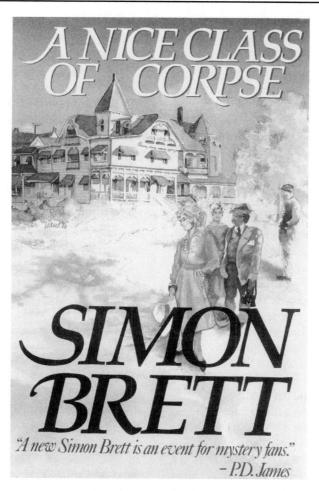

Dust jacket for the 1986 novel in which Brett introduced Mrs. Pargeter, who solves mysteries with the help of associates of her late husband, a master criminal (Richland County Public Library)

like the other hotel residents, Mrs. Pargeter leaves the Devereux.

While writing mysteries, Brett continued his activities in radio, television, and other venues of British entertainment. He turned his radio play *After Henry* into a television series that ran from 1988 to 1990. Since the mid 1980s Brett has alternated his crime publications from Pargeter to Paris to suspense novels. *What Bloody Man Is That?* (1987) returns to the fortunes of Charles Paris. Though its plot is transparent, the book is crammed with Shakespearean text and issues of interpretation and succeeds because of the variety and richness of its theater material: high jinks during rehearsals and performances, a send-up of the pomposity of the Royal Shakespeare Company, and a fascinatingly obnoxious old actor-queen. Charles and his fellow professionals know Shakespeare's plays intimately, extemporize whole passages, and recollect their every appearance in past productions. Charles has several minor roles in a calamitous production of *Macbeth*,

whose director is an old acquaintance, Gavin Scholes. Heading the cast are George Birkitt, now more successful in television than in earlier novels, and his Lady Macbeth, Felicia Chatterton, a brilliant young member of the Royal Shakespeare Company. A source of trouble in the production is boozy homosexual Warnock Belvedere, who plays King Duncan and alienates almost everyone (he propositions every male, including Charles). His principal target is Russ Lavery, an extremely talented newcomer, who idolizes Felicia even though she constantly interrupts rehearsals with questions of interpretation. An impatient, jealous Belvedere, angry at the delays, berates her as a "jumped-up little tart," and she, in turn, threatens "you've got to go."

When Belvedere dies in the theater bar's storeroom, his death is ruled accidental: while stealing liquor, he passed out, and carbon dioxide escaping from a broken pump hose asphyxiated him. Because Charles knows that the police theory is wrong and that he would be their chief suspect, he investigates. Lavery is the most likely suspect (Macbeth to Felicia Chatterton's unknowing Lady Macbeth, he has murdered her enemy), then Scholes, whose shaky theater company Belvedere's disruption endangered, and finally Norman and Sandra Phipps, box-office manager and theater-bar manager. Inspired by a hilarious school production in which the boys underline every bawdy hint of the text, even unintended ones, Charles surmises that Belvedere sexually targeted a young boy with a minor role who left the company suddenly and that the boy's parents revenged their son: "It was like *Macbeth*, the woman urging the man to murder."

Notably less like Christie's novels than the first, the second Pargeter novel, *Mrs. Presumed Dead* (1988), maintains the whodunit form, having five suspects with motives and actions to account for, but also satirizes affluent suburban life. Mrs. Pargeter finds her women neighbors at Smithy's Loam pretentious, materialistic, and indifferent to one another, engaged in affairs or bitter about men or family life. The night before Mrs. Pargeter moved into her new house, the previous owner was strangled and her body hidden in a freezer. No one questions whether she and her husband arrived at their new residence until Pargeter finds the address false. Her husband's former associates learn that Theresa Cotton had joined an ascetic religious sect but never arrived at the retreat and that Rod lost his prestigious, high-paying job six months before and disappeared. When Theresa's body turns up, the missing Rod becomes chief suspect, until a Pargeter associate finds him—a homeless, vagrant alcoholic. Mrs. Pargeter, thinking the murderer a woman from Smithy's Loam, sets a trap and unexpectedly catches a Swedish au pair, who murdered to protect her international drug trafficking and who almost succeeds in making Pargeter another victim.

In the next Paris mystery, *A Series of Murders* (1989), no one grieves when Sippy Stokes, a limited actress improperly cast in a television mystery series, dies accidentally. She starred in an adaptation of W. T. Wintergreen's Golden Age mysteries about the improbably dashing genius detective Stanislas Braid, in which Charles plays a befuddled police sergeant. The elderly author, Winifred Railton (who wrote under the pen name "Wintergreen"), and her sister, Louisa, haunt the set to keep the adaptation of their creation true to its original. *A Series of Murders*, like *Star Trap*, devotes much attention to company dynamics, filming, and the economics and contingencies of a show. Charles suspects Rick Landor, the director and Sippy's lover, of murdering her; then Jimmy Sheet, a pop singer turned actor who also was having an affair with Sippy; next the strange assistant stage manager, Alex Rees; and finally producer Ben Docherty. Charles mistakenly expects a stiletto murder to follow the candlestick murder of Sippy because of parallels between reality and incidents in the Wintergreen novels. Then, Winifred Railton wounds the actor playing Braid, escapes to her London cottage, and calmly confesses to killing to protect the Wintergreen novels as sacred memorials to the sisters' revered late father, the model for Braid. She killed her sister, Louisa, because she could not have survived alone. Charles counters that Louisa was the crazed murderer, protecting the family icons from revision and keeping secret the incestuous relationship between her and their father—a fact Louisa only dimly understood. Winifred's mercy killing protected Louisa from the consequences of her tragic madness. When Winifred dies in custody, only Charles attends her funeral.

Mrs. Pargeter's Package (1990) demonstrates the new freedom the Pargeter series gave Brett in its loving, idyllic portrait of the beautiful island of Corfu, where Mrs. Pargeter and her recently widowed friend, Joyce Dover, vacation. This rich, complex mystery weaves clues from Corfu and England, with Spiro Karaskakis's *taverna*, the Hotel Nausica, and the Mediterranean coast of Agios Nikitas serving as key locations for drama. Shortly after arriving in Corfu, Joyce dies, in what the tourist police say is a suicide. Mrs. Pargeter is unconvinced because of unsettling evidence at the scene, the fact that Joyce had her carry an unidentified package through customs, and the ambiguous relationship of Joyce's shadowy late husband to Corfu. Mrs. Pargeter again calls on her husband's associates for help, starting with Larry Lambeth, a Greek-English crook living in Corfu, already assigned by an English associate to protect Mrs. Pargeter. She suspects that Joyce's late husband was actually Karaskakis's evil twin brother, Christo, supposedly killed thirty years earlier in an explosion set to kill Spiro and give Christo the *taverna*. Meanwhile, the Dovers' daughter, Conchita, is kidnapped in Corfu, and Mrs. Pargeter and Lambeth are captured in a rescue attempt. They learn that Spiro, in reality Christo, is the mastermind. After the true Spiro fled for his life (becoming Chris Dover), Christo usurped his identity and enforced family silence. A sudden change of wind turns the fire Christo sets to kill his prisoners on him, fulfilling his dying father's prophecy that this treacherous firebrand would himself die from fire.

Of the many acting venues into which Brett thrusts Charles Paris, the industrial movie of *Corporate Bodies* (1991) may be the least propitious. Charles portrays a forklift driver at the Delmolene Corporation. During a filming at the Delmolene warehouse, the forklift that Charles switched off causes some pallets to fall, killing an employee, Dayna Richman. Charles, accused of carelessness, has a personal motive to investigate this so-called accident. As Charles becomes better acquainted with the employees and management team at Delmolene, principally Brian Tressider, the managing director, and Ken Colebourne, the marketing director, he learns that Dayna sought career advancement by sleeping with her bosses and videotaping the trysts for blackmail purposes. A Delmolene sales convention confirms that Tressider is sexually impaired and therefore motiveless. Meanwhile, to protect his terminally ill wife from painful revelations of his affair and blackmail, Colebourne leaps to his death from a hotel balcony. Dayna's murderer proves to be Heather Routledge, the warehouse dispatcher, a girlfriend of Tressider in their youth, who did not follow him to his London posting because of her mother's apparent neediness. Still in love with Tressider, she protects both him and the company by impulsively killing Dayna when Dayna reveals her sexual designs on Tressider. In the rather perfunctory conclusion, Charles remains silent about Heather's guilt, deeming her loss of Tressider and her continued domination by her shrewish mother sufficient punishment.

Brett's satiric target in *Mrs. Pargeter's Pound of Flesh* (1992) is the modern craze for health, dieting, and exercise. Mrs. Pargeter takes a friend to Brotherton Hall, a spa managed by Pargeter associate Ankle-Deep Arkwright. Kim Sturrock giddily accepts the stern regimen the spa offers while Mrs. Pargeter, claiming allergies, eats and drinks sumptuously and avoids exercise. One night she sees a young girl's corpse wheeled out of the building, possibly the missing Jenny Hargreaves, a Cambridge undergraduate paid to test a diet program. When physical trainer Lindy Galton also dies, Pargeter uncovers the dark side of the spa and of popular health guru Sue Fisher, whose corporate empire is associated with Brotherton Hall. A growing cast of Pargeter associates helps Mrs. Pargeter investigate the deaths. In the background of events is Julian Embridge, the trusted lieutenant who betrayed Mr. Pargeter and then disappeared. Mrs. Pargeter uncovers misdemeanors and crimes on the part of Arkwright, Fisher, and Dr. Potter, Brotherton Hall's resident physician and health experimenter. After Potter's thugs capture Mrs. Pargeter, the diabolical doctor invents a novel murder weapon, an exercise machine speeded up to overstress her heart. After Mrs. Pargeter's rescue, Dr. Potter proves to be the surgically altered, long-missing Embridge. In bringing Embridge to punishment, Mrs. Pargeter finally gets the pound of flesh he owed her husband.

In *A Reconstructed Corpse* (1993) Charles portrays a missing man who may be dead. After Chloe Earnshaw reports her husband Martin's disappearance, the true-crime television program *Private Enemies* joins the investigation. The program showcases brilliant and beautiful Detective Inspector "Sam" Noakes and hires private detective Ted Faraday, Noakes's former colleague in the

Dust jacket for the 1995 novel in which Charles Paris hunts a murderer among the participants in an avant-garde adaptation of William Shakespeare's Twelfth Night
(Richland County Public Library)

metropolitan police, to compete with her in solving the case. In response to reported sightings of Earnshaw and body parts identified by Chloe, Charles presents a short scene of the victim's supposed activity. An array of police officers, ranging from unrespected Chief Inspector Roscoe to depressed Sergeant Greg Marchmont, provides the program information. Noakes has been the department's sexual bombshell, going through affairs with many policemen, including Faraday. Faraday informs *Public Enemies* that he will take his investigation "under cover." Often at the investigative scenes, though disregarded by both television staff and the police, Charles confirms Marchmont's and perhaps Faraday's involvement in the apparent murder and dismemberment of Martin Earnshaw. Charles suspects collusion to provide suspense between the program and the murderer, an exhibitionist, who controls the flow of clues to *Public Enemies*. Ultimately, however, Earnshaw turns out to be alive. The villain is Inspector Roscoe, near retirement, who contrived the scheme to kill his hated critic on the force, Faraday, and to show up "all those smug young bastards" who belittled him. Roscoe exploits television's exploitation of crime to highlight his own cleverness. In this drama all the players are corrupt: the television audience with its lust for sensationalism and horror; the network producers, who pander to this taste and subvert truth and law to better ratings; and the complicitous police, who chase after publicity and career advancement.

Sicken and So Die (1995) richly satirizes trendy modern reinterpretations of Shakespeare through the Great Wensham Festival production of *Twelfth Night,* in which Charles plays Sir Toby Belch, a dream role for an aging actor. In the company are old acquaintances such as director Gavin Scholes, actor John B. Murgatroyd, and Russ Lavery, a young actor when Charles first worked with him, now a television star, returning to his roots in legitimate theater. Lavery plays the male twin, Sebastian. Another former television star, Sally Luther, plays his sister, Viola. Three weeks before the opening, Scholes suffers serious stomach distress and cannot continue as director. His replacement is Alexandru Radulescu, a young Romanian currently a favorite in British theater circles. *Twelfth Night* is "about sex," he tells the company, every kind of sex, between all the characters, and in particular homosexual sex. Charles and Murgatroyd hold out for real Shakespeare as the others buy into Radulescu's radical reinterpretation, until even Murgatroyd finally goes over. One night at dinner, Murgatroyd is felled by apparent food poisoning, which Charles suspects was meant for him, Radulescu's last opponent. After Sally Luther dies from injected poison during a dress rehearsal, Radulescu enlists Lavery to portray both Sebastian and Viola, and he performs brilliantly. Charles realizes Sally was the intended victim all along and suspects Lavery, whom a witness saw near the scene with a hypodermic syringe. When the unknown murderer poisons Charles—adulterating his beloved Bell's whisky—Charles confronts Lavery, whose secret is heroin addiction and fear for his career, not murder. In a perfunctory ending to a novel with some of Brett's keenest satire, Charles flushes the murderer, a young company member who killed the idol he stalked because she derided his obsessive devotion.

Amid these novels Brett published what challenges *A Shock to the System* as his most substantial work, *Singled Out* (1995), a complex whodunit with graphic sex, turn-of-the-screw suspense, realistic characters, and serious contemporary concerns. Successful Laura Fisher, who as an adolescent was a victim of her father's sexual abuse, decides to have a child by an anonymous partner (apparently a murderer) and to raise her son, Tom, alone while pursuing her career. Twenty years later, a new cycle of violence connected to Laura suggests the work of a serial killer. When a young woman who resembles the young Laura is mur-

dered, Tom's secret father (recently released from prison) is the prime suspect. Shocks and revelations follow with dizzying speed. The killer is Laura's brother, Kent, a policeman, whose thwarted lust for Laura has led him to five murders (he killed their mother and framed Tom's father). Tom is a homosexual, whose "troubles" resulted from masking his sexual orientation and who, out of the closet, normalizes relationships with his mother. The title refers to the single person or single parent as typically an outsider to married society, and to those who are socially ostracized because of sexual difference from the so-called norm, such as Laura's best friend, Rob, a decent, aging homosexual. *Singled Out* demonstrates Brett's maturation as a more realistic and more serious writer than the creator of the delightful and generally lighthearted Charles Paris novels.

From 1995 to 1997 Brett served as chairman of the Society of Authors. During this period he also wrote more Mrs. Pargeter novels. *Mrs. Pargeter's Plot* (1996) is mostly a comic romp. As former Pargeter associate Concrete Jacket builds Mrs. Pargeter's new house, he finds at the construction site the body of a former employee with whom he was on bad terms. Since Jacket's gun killed him, he is arrested and imprisoned. His wife and Mrs. Pargeter, convinced of his innocence, gather Pargeter's associates to investigate. Brett makes the comic turns and misadventures the main interest, with music-hall comedy, movie chases, and even a pet monkey named Erasmus throwing bananas. A tough career criminal, Fossilface O'Donahue, has a spiritual conversion and offers "restitooshun" to mates he disappointed or betrayed. His restitutions cause the recipient unexpected trouble (when he delivers burgling tools to an incarcerated master burglar, for example). Especially funny is the niche magazine for career criminals, *Inside Out,* which records prison news and offers advice on the "coming out" party and "Amateur Dramatics for a Captive Audience." Using inside and outside sources, Mrs. Pargeter and cronies target a confidence game to sell to dozens of buyers—all aging criminals wanting a retirement residence—a single Brazilian villa that Jacket built. Car and tractor chases and threats of bodily harm to a captured Mrs. Pargeter lead to a finale in which the criminals are grievously discomfited when a gift from Fossilface, a barn full of neatly stacked tires, falls on their Jaguar. Erasmus steals their keys and enables Mrs. Pargeter's rescue.

In *Dead Room Farce* (1997) Charles acts in *Not on Your Wife*, a bedroom farce touring the provinces, its first stop Bath. Charles has both a voice-recording job in Bath and a liaison with a company actress, Cookie Stone. The co-owner of the recording studio is fifty-year-old Mark Lear, a longtime BBC acquaintance of Charles, an alcoholic and philanderer whose wife left him. His new partner in business and life is Lisa Wilson, a younger woman, Mark's opposite in activity level and personal style. She does most of the studio's work while Mark broods over his life and sinks deeper into drink. In a drunken stupor Mark may have locked himself in a soundproof studio–the "dead room"–and suffocated, but the studio door being locked from the outside tells Charles that he was murdered, and personal affinities with the victim compel him to investigate. Charles is strongly attracted to Lisa, with whom he continues the recording jobs. They have sex, and Lisa challenges him to stop drinking. He does not know how to break it off with Cookie, a needy woman often disappointed in love, but the affair with Lisa fails too, for Lisa wants merely good sex, not a future companion. Charles focuses on four men whom Mark had known in the BBC days, one of whom feared the exposure of pornographic videotapes on which they had collaborated years before. The solution of the crime depends on the fact that the tapes were of homosexual activity and that actors often change their names: the killer made the tapes while he still bore his birth name. Of greater interest in *Dead Room Farce* are long, funny passages from the play, the theme of aging, Charles's relationship with women, and the women themselves. Lear's life and doom heighten Charles's questioning of his own life. The mechanical round of liaisons in the onstage farce parallels his multiple unsatisfactory affairs: Cookie, Lisa, an old sex partner who dies, and his former wife, Frances. Alone at the end, Charles feels like "an emotional cactus, someone whom no woman could approach without getting hurt."

The high-spirited comic novel *Mrs. Pargeter's Point of Honour* (1998) reverses a typical criminal caper, for the crooks return great paintings to the galleries from which they were stolen. Bennie Mason, one of Mr. Pargeter's associates, stole the pictures to decorate his manorial home, but his widow, the aristocratic Veronica Chastaigne, wants Mrs. Pargeter and associates to return the paintings to prevent her greedy son from selling them. Brett invents two outrageously comic characters: the dismal, ineffective police detective Inspector Craig "Craggy" Wilkinson and the pathetic art forger Reg Winthrop, or "VVO"–"Vincent Vin Ordinaire"–to friends. Wilkinson, an absurdly incompetent bumbler, speaks with an air of experienced professionalism and browbeats his intelligent sergeant. While Winthrop readily paints brilliant forgeries in every style, his original paintings, of which he is inordinately proud, are irredeemable kitsch, featuring "winsome" scotties in "natty little tartan" coats and "fluffy" white pussycats. Although failure dogs both men, Wilkinson once almost caught the "criminal mastermind" Mr. Pargeter; with Pargeter dead, Wilkinson's

last chance for redemption is to recover the stolen masterpieces. Meanwhile, crooks learn that the paintings are to be moved and steal nearly all of them. While interrogating Mrs. Pargeter, Wilkinson falls in love with her. As in any classic comedy, everything goes wrong for the fools and villains and succeeds for the good guys. To recover the stolen paintings from boss Rod D'Acosta and his thugs, Mrs. Pargeter's crew stages a complex automobile dance of timing and misdirection in which Inspector Wilkinson loses both the paintings and then Mrs. Pargeter. Surprising turns of plot reveal the hidden plotters, Toby Chastaigne and Palings Price (a former Pargeter associate gone bad), and their excessive punishments. Because Price had been for years the hidden betrayer of Mr. Pargeter and later his widow, Mrs. Pargeter satisfies an outstanding point of honor while Mrs. Chastaigne revenges herself on her bad son.

In *The Body on the Beach* (2000), the first of a series of mysteries set in the seaside village of Fethering, Brett weaves into his complicated detection plot a story of growing friendship between two ill-matched women: Carole Seddon, retired from the Home Office to Fethering to lead a quiet, well-ordered private life, and her next-door neighbor Jude, a flamboyant, fifty-year-old flower child, her last name and private history secret. The starched Seddon distances herself from the warm, open Jude, until, on a beach walk near the Fethering Yacht Club, Seddon discovers a body, its throat oddly slashed. When the body disappears and the police dismiss her as a middle-aged hysteric, Jude believes her. A day later the corpse of a drowned teenager, Aaron Spedding, washes up, and his mother demands silence. Jude suggests they investigate.

Opposites, Jude and Seddon make an odd couple, and Jude's company and example change her companion. As they question village residents, they uncover potentially lethal tensions in the regulars at the local pub, the Crown and Anchor. Neighbors Bill Chilcott and club vice commodore Denis Woodville feud. Dentist Rory Turnbull's pretentious wife, Barbara, and her even more pretentious mother belittle his midlife crisis and hatred of dentistry. Nick Kent, a local working-class youth, reveals that he and two friends broke into the yacht club, found a body in a boat, and, high on marijuana and beer, performed a voodoo throat-slashing rite before throwing the body over the seawall. When the tide returned the body, the impressionable Spedding, terrified of black magic, jumped to his death in the river. The villain turns out to be Turnbull, who embez-zled money from the Yacht Club and falsified £10,000 of dental insurance claims in a plot to free himself from his family and to amass wealth for a new life. He planned for the body on the beach to stand in for himself in a staged suicide to hide his tracks. Seddon rescues Jude from Turnbull's clutches just as he starts to send his BMW off the seawall. Seddon has unalterably entered a world of friendship, variety, and action.

A prolific writer, repeatedly characterized as witty, urbane, satiric, acidic, and always engaging and cultured, Simon Brett writes detective and suspense novels that reflect his good humor, theater training, and empathy with those humiliated or emotionally damaged. *Booklist* reviewer Peter Robertson aptly praises Brett for avoiding the "treacly simpering" of British cozy mysteries and for instead keeping readers entertained by his "steady stream of dryly noted cultural tidbits." Brett sometimes writes at a level below his best. Yet, his Charles Paris series and his suspense novels are distinguished contributions to contemporary mystery fiction, bringing a modern sensibility to traditional patterns.

References:

Martha Alderson, "Death at the Stage Door: Anne Morice's Theresa Chrichton and Simon Brett's Charles Paris," *Clues: A Journal of Detection,* 4 (Fall/Winter 1983): 21–29;

Earl F. Bargainnier, "Simon Brett," in *Twelve Englishmen of Mystery,* edited by Bargainnier (Bowling Green, Ohio: Bowling Green University Popular Press, 1984), pp. 302–325;

Rosemary Herbert, "The Cosy Side of Murder," *Publishers Weekly,* 228 (25 October 1985): 20–32.

W. J. Burley

(1 August 1914 –   )

Margaret Kinsman
South Bank University

BOOKS: *A Taste of Power* (London: Gollancz, 1966);

Three Toed Pussy (London: Gollancz, 1968); republished as *Wycliffe and the Three-Toed Pussy* (London: Corgi, 1995);

Death in Willow Pattern (London: Gollancz, 1969; New York: Walker, 1970);

To Kill a Cat (London: Gollancz, 1970; New York: Walker, 1970); republished as *Wycliffe and How to Kill a Cat* (London: Corgi, 1993);

Guilt Edged (London: Gollancz, 1971; New York: Walker, 1972);

Death in a Salubrious Place (London: Gollancz, 1973; New York: Walker, 1973); republished as *Wycliffe and Death in a Salubrious Place* (London: Corgi, 1995);

Death in Stanley Street (London: Gollancz, 1974; New York: Walker, 1974); republished as *Wycliffe and Death in Stanley Street* (London: Corgi, 1990);

Wycliffe and the Pea-Green Boat (London: Gollancz, 1975; New York: Walker, 1975);

Wycliffe and the Schoolgirls (London: Gollancz, 1976; New York: Walker, 1976);

Centenary History of the City of Truro (Truro, U.K.: Blackford, 1977);

The Schoolmaster (London: Gollancz, 1977; New York: Walker, 1977);

The Sixth Day (London: Gollancz, 1978);

Wycliffe and the Scapegoat (London: Gollancz, 1978; Garden City, N.Y.: Doubleday, 1979);

Charles and Elizabeth (London: Gollancz, 1979; New York: Walker, 1981);

Wycliffe in Paul's Court (London: Gollancz, 1980; Garden City, N.Y.: Doubleday, 1980);

The House of Care (London: Gollancz, 1981; New York: Walker, 1982);

Wycliffe's Wild Goose Chase (London: Gollancz, 1982; Garden City, N.Y.: Doubleday, 1982);

Wycliffe and the Beales (London: Gollancz, 1983; Garden City, N.Y.: Doubleday, 1984);

Wycliffe and the Four Jacks (London: Gollancz, 1985; Garden City, N.Y.: Doubleday, 1986);

W. J. Burley (photograph from the dust jacket for the United States edition of Wycliffe and the Dunes Mystery, *1994)*

Wycliffe and the Quiet Virgin (London: Gollancz, 1986; Garden City, N.Y.: Doubleday, 1986);

Wycliffe and the Winsor Blue (London: Gollancz, 1987; Garden City, N.Y.: Doubleday, 1987);

Wycliffe and the Tangled Web (London: Gollancz, 1988; Garden City, N.Y.: Doubleday, 1989);

Wycliffe and the Cycle of Death (London: Gollancz, 1990; New York: Doubleday, 1990);

Wycliffe and the Dead Flautist (London: Gollancz, 1991; New York: St. Martin's Press, 1992);

Wycliffe and the Last Rites (London: Gollancz, 1992; New York: St. Martin's Press, 1993);

Wycliffe and the Dunes Mystery (London: Gollancz, 1993; New York: St. Martin's Press, 1994);

Wycliffe and the House of Fear (London: Gollancz, 1995; New York: St. Martin's Press, 1995);

Wycliffe and the Redhead (London: Gollancz, 1997; New York: St. Martin's Press, 1998);

Wycliffe and the Guild of Nine (London: Gollancz, 2000).

Editions: *The Wycliffe Omnibus* (London: Gollancz, 1996)–comprises *Wycliffe and the Winsor Blue, Wycliffe and the Four Jacks,* and *Wycliffe and the Quiet Virgin;*

The Second Wycliffe Omnibus (London: Gollancz, 1997)– comprises *Wycliffe and the Last Rites, Wycliffe and the Dead Flautist,* and *Wycliffe and the Schoolgirls.*

W. J. Burley published his first mystery novel, *A Taste of Power,* in 1966 at the age of fifty-one. With two professional careers already behind him, by 1974 Burley had become a full-time writer. Although he has experimented with various types of mystery novel, Burley is best known for the long-running police series featuring Detective Chief Superintendent Charles Wycliffe of the Criminal Investigation Department in the West Country of England. After two early novels featuring the amateur investigator Henry Pym, and some non-series psychological mystery stories, from 1980 Burley concentrated on the successful Wycliffe series. He has since produced a Wycliffe novel nearly annually, making a total of twenty-two to date, with plans for more. "I will keep going as long as my health holds out," he told Geoff Tibballs, author of *The Wycliffe File: The Story of the ITV Detective Series,* in 1995. While Burley's Cornish detective series is located within the mainstream British police procedural tradition, the novels also carry hallmarks of the classic British cozy mystery and the whodunit traditions of the 1920s and 1930s. Burley writes cozy dramas in a scenic setting, with the machinery of an official murder inquiry working quietly away in the background, novels that appeal to fans of the classic English mystery.

William John Burley was born in Falmouth, Cornwall, England, on 1 August 1914, on the eve of World War I. His parents, William John (a builder) and Annie (Curnow) Burley, were both descended from long lines of Cornish people. Burley was raised and educated in Cornwall. From 1933 to 1949 he made his living as an engineer, assistant manager, and then manager in the gas industry in Southwest England. In 1938 he married Muriel Wolsey, a school secretary. They have two children, Alan John (born in 1940) and Nigel Philip (born in 1943), and three grandchildren. Upon leaving the gas industry, Burley returned to full-time education as a mature student at Balliol College. He read zoology and obtained his degree from Oxford University in 1953. On leaving Oxford, Burley went into teaching, taking up an appointment in the biology department at Rich-

mond Grammar School in Surrey. Shortly afterward, Burley took up a similar appointment at the Newquay School in Cornwall, where he remained as head of the biology department and sixth-form tutor until his retirement in 1974. He and his wife have lived continuously in Cornwall since 1953.

Burley began his writing career with the series character of an amateur detective, Dr. Henry Pym, a science teacher at the Huntley-May Grammar School. His choice of detective enabled him to draw on his personal experiences as a grammar-school science teacher and to project his attitudes and concerns onto his central figure. Burley briefly explained his start as a writer in *Contemporary Authors* (1984): "my intention was to try to write interesting detective fiction which did not exploit extreme forms of violence or sex and was relatively free of 'four-letter' words. In doing this I thought I might help fill a gap that was left in the market by the gradual disappearance of the traditional whodunit." In *A Taste of Power* and *Death in Willow Pattern* (1969) Pym investigates similar outbreaks of anonymous poison-pen messages and letters at his coeducational secondary school. Burley's use of an autobiographical setting and profession gives the short series a true-to-life atmosphere. He successfully utilizes the device of the poison-pen letter, demonstrating its effects on the recipient (loss of peace of mind) and giving his protagonist ample opportunity to speculate on the individual mind and complex motivation behind the letters. Burley told Tibballs that his first fictional detective "was a bit like Lord Peter Wimsey." He realized that Pym probably had limited potential and so set about creating a new central character.

Between the two Pym books, Burley introduced the thoughtful police inspector Charles Wycliffe in *Three Toed Pussy* (1968; republished as *Wycliffe and the Three-Toed Pussy,* 1995). Wycliffe is a taciturn and kindly middle-aged policeman in the Cornwall region who has risen in the police hierarchy in spite of his reputation as someone who does not take well to discipline and who often becomes too emotionally involved in his cases. The inspector has a good record in catching villains and so has been promoted. In spite of his rank and profession, Wycliffe is an intuitive rather than a procedural investigator. He involves himself in cases that interest him, like the great amateur sleuths of the genre, and he still does much of his own legwork, inviting comparisons to Georges Simenon's police detective, Maigret. Like Maigret, Wycliffe solves his cases through a combination of gifted intuition and a methodical immersion in the ambience of the crime. Wycliffe's name, and some of his characteristics, were inspired by the fourteenth-century theologian John Wycliffe, a master of Balliol College, who was instrumental in translating the Bible into English and also famous for challenging the spiritual authority of the Church. The detective Wycliffe is developed through his idiosyncratic, even unorthodox, interpretation and execution of his job as superintendent, then chief inspector, and, finally, detective chief superintendent. This first novel in the series establishes a formula used in many of the subsequent Wycliffe novels: atmospheric descriptions of the author's native Cornwall; the violent death of a sexually attractive and available young woman living in a quiet community; Wycliffe's understated and intuitive approach to the investigation of the crime; and a recurring cast of police characters attached to the procedural side of the investigation.

In *Three Toed Pussy* and throughout the series Burley individualizes his main character by making Wycliffe a transplanted Cornishman enamored of the beauty of his adopted territory. Doing so allows Burley to describe details of the region familiar to him and beloved from childhood. Born and reared in the Midlands, Wycliffe loves his adopted West Country and displays a keen historical appreciation of the local area and a neverending enchantment with the landscape of sea and sky. Readers come to know his wife, Helen, their two children, and eventually some grandchildren over the course of the series. Their peaceable domestic life on the Tamar Estuary in Cornwall becomes part of the backdrop to the novels. Wycliffe's team of police officers are also developed as series characters, including the cynical Chief Inspector James Gill, the more compassionate Detective Inspector Kersey, the jocular pathologist Dr. Franks, Detective Constable Potter, and Detective Sergeant Dixon.

Throughout the series Wycliffe specializes in investigating old-style domestic homicide with a powerful personal element. Usually his cases bring him up against an extended and multigenerational family group, apparently functioning on the surface but seething underneath with historical grievances and memories of misdeeds. When the long-suppressed feelings and tensions between family members come to the surface, murder results. This is the sort of case Wycliffe engages with best. He talks to witnesses, strolls around the town, gets to "know" the victims, and elicits family history from the closed group of suspects. He prefers on the whole to leave the formal investigation procedures to his able police team. His favorite methodology is to gather a myriad of impressions, memories, and fragments of information and then to let these form patterns in his mind until one pattern emerges and makes sense to him. Burley's character, like Burley himself, has a fondness for puzzles, expressed in frequent textual references to crosswords, Scrabble, and other word games, and literary quotation and allusion.

The second Wycliffe novel, *To Kill a Cat* (1970; republished as *Wycliffe and How to Kill a Cat*, 1993), repeats the motif of the young woman victim and fur-

Dust jacket for the U.S. edition of Burley's 1974 novel, in which his recurring character, Cornish police inspector Charles Wycliffe, investigates the murder of a prostitute (Richland County Public Library)

ther establishes the idiosyncratic Inspector Wycliffe. The fact that he is on a walking holiday in Cornwall with his wife again provides Burley opportunities to comment on the natural beauty and way of life of his region. Wycliffe becomes involved in the local investigation of the death of a beautiful prostitute and striptease artist found strangled and mutilated in a sleazy seaside hotel. Wycliffe mildly antagonizes the local police force with his casual holiday clothes and his cerebral references to, for example, William of Occam's axiom that the simplest possible explanation is probably the right one. His habits of taking walks, ruminating, and talking to witnesses in preference to the more mundane demands of police paperwork are tolerated, although somewhat mystifying to some of his colleagues. Wycliffe's rank (he is now chief superintendent of the Area CID in South Devon) places him at the center, coordinating all aspects of the investigation, but his execution of official duties departs from the norm.

Wycliffe observes people closely and tries to develop a feeling for the texture of another life. He enjoys his encounters with people as the reward, and not the penalty, of his work, though he frequently comes perilously close to emotional identification with the suspects he is trying to wear down.

The next three novels repeat the pattern of young women meeting violent deaths. In *Guilt Edged* (1971) Wycliffe investigates the death of the wife of a prominent businessman, in a case full of family quarrels over company policy, money, and sex. *Death in a Salubrious Place* (1973; republished as *Wycliffe and Death in a Salubrious Place,* 1995) concerns the murder of a young woman and the local community's suspicions of a young pop singer, an outsider in their midst. In *Death in Stanley Street* (1974; republished as *Wycliffe and Death in Stanley Street,* 1990) Wycliffe again finds himself investigating the murder of a prostitute who also runs a local real-estate business. Although there are similarities in Burley's choice of murder victims, these early novels also show his interests in moving the plot along through lively dialogue and by including plenty of action within the tight time frame of the first intensive days of an official murder investigation. The novels further establish and develop the police team behind Wycliffe. Somewhat prudish in speech and attitude, Wycliffe's "austere, almost puritanical approach" contrasts with the "earthy realism" of Kersey. Both are tolerant men, with a firm but compassionate approach to policing, and together they make a good team. As the series develops, both the main character and the regional setting of Southwest England become more fully realized and are the features that make the series distinctive. Burley knows the West Country well and uses it to vary the more usual setting of the police procedural in the mean city streets of the urban milieu. Thus, the Cornwall settings for the Wycliffe series serve to locate the novels in the English classic tradition of the Agatha Christie village mystery, as well as in the police procedural convention.

In the next five Wycliffe novels, Burley begins to vary his formula in order to explore the violent consequences that arise from long-repressed emotions and intergenerational feuds in introverted village life. Burley effectively portrays the time bomb of festering family quarrels and betrayals and the inevitability of violence. In *Wycliffe and the Pea-Green Boat* (1975) sexual jealousy and material greed link two cousins, twenty years apart, who may both be murderers. Part 1 of the novel evokes the rural England of Coronation Year, 1953, when Cornwall is still full of working fishing villages. Twenty years later Wycliffe's investigation of the murder of one cousin's father gives Burley the opportunity to chronicle a changing way of life. The Cornish village has become a commercial racket, dependent on tourism and pleasure boating, full of day-trippers and holiday rentals in place of the dying fishing industry. In addition, Burley experiments with the traditional resolution to a police investigation; Wycliffe, who is not officially on duty on this case, finds the truth and, rather than following the police routine of arrest and prosecution, lets natural justice prevail.

In these novels Burley effectively exploits the claustrophobic aspects of family life in the small towns and villages of the West Country, which he chronicles vividly in terms of landscape, village life and its gossip, and the dying industries of Cornwall (fishing, tin, and copper). He varies the settings of Wycliffe's cases, putting him into recognizable Cornish towns and villages and using schools, a small hotel, local family businesses, and the decaying homes of members of the British upper and middle classes fallen on hard times. The village settings and self-contained world of the family allow Burley to bring together a closed group of people with a broad range of emotions and fears and to explore time-honored motives of greed, envy, sexual jealousy, repression, and lust. Against the small family unit and village, Burley sets the long distances involved when police traverse Cornwall, the annual holiday and summer influxes of tourists, and the Cornish folklore tradition, using all of these features to heighten suspense and danger. Burley also effectively exploits holiday settings and seasons (May Day, Christmas, school and summer holidays) by contrasting seasonal expectations with the scandal, corruption, and murder taking place behind the scenes.

In *Wycliffe and the Schoolgirls* (1976) Burley returns to a school setting, which he portrays realistically. Here Wycliffe investigates the murders of two women whose only apparent connection is their shared schoolgirl past. The next year Burley wrote *The Schoolmaster*, a departure from the Wycliffe series. It is a chilling study of the effect of a profound sense of guilt in a rigid secondary-school history teacher who goes to pieces psychologically after his wife leaves him. Burley explores the theme of self-denial and the thesis that unleashed sexual urges have the potential to manifest themselves in unscrupulous and uncontrolled behavior. *The Sixth Day* (1978) and other stand-alone novels that followed over the next few years, all psychological mysteries, explore lust and repression in romantic Cornwall settings. Along with exhibiting "a skill in developing atmosphere and suspense," as Susan Oleksiw characterizes them, these works also show the deepening psychological focus that Burley takes further in the Wycliffe series.

Wycliffe and the Scapegoat (1978) shows Burley going further afield for plot. Cornwall is again the backdrop, and an old Cornish ritual involving a human effigy provides the ingenious murder method. The male murder victim in this novel is the local undertaker and business tycoon who, estranged from his family and his community, disappears just before Halloween. *Wycliffe in Paul's Court* (1980) again uses a young woman as the murder victim and explores the tensions between the teenage victim, her attractive mother, and the neighbors who disapprove of the mother's nude sunbathing. Before the case is resolved, another murder takes place, and Wycliffe has to work out how the two are connected.

In two nonseries novels, *Charles and Elizabeth* (1979) and *The House of Care* (1981), Burley experiments with the use of supernatural elements to heighten suspense. In *The House of Care* a troubled daughter dabbles in the occult, and her susceptibility to a staged "manifestation" has tragic consequences. *Wycliffe's Wild Goose Chase* (1982) returns to the series, with Wycliffe's discovery of a stolen gun leading to the investigation of a murder, an earlier suicide, and the story that links them.

During the period in which he wrote these novels, Burley developed his skills in the portrayal (both victims and suspects) of sad, lonely middle-aged men, full of self-denial and aspirations to be better or different than they are. Though they long for stability, comfort, and distinction, they are often stuck with reproduction furniture, disintegrating family relationships, and unfulfilling work. The Wycliffe series also begins to include a running commentary, most often expressed through the ruminations of the main character, on the state of England during the last three decades of the twentieth century. Though minor in relation to plot, this concern with the state of England expresses aspects of Wycliffe's character that show him as rather old-fashioned, prone to the occasional sweeping judgment, and struggling to adjust to changes in society and behavior of which he does not wholeheartedly approve. Wycliffe often casts himself in the mythical mode of figures such as Canute, Quixote, and Sisyphus, all of whom were condemned to fruitless attempts to halt the tide. Readers might well conclude that Burley has made Wycliffe an extension of his personal voice and political concerns.

Through the next two decades Burley produced some of his more psychologically complex and skillfully realized novels. In *Wycliffe and the Beales* (1983) he constructs a tight plot, including a series of convincing red herrings, around the repressed hatreds and jealousies within the wealthy Beale household and their connection to poor cottager Bunny Newcombe, who dies in suspicious circumstances after making inquiries about his parentage. The novel makes effective use of traditional crime-fiction plot devices: the anonymous letter to the police; the innocent family member who lies; the skeleton-laden well-to-do local family; the recently

Dust jacket for the U.S. edition of Burley's 1977 novel, in which a history teacher suffers a psychological breakdown after his wife leaves him (Richland County Public Library)

released prisoner returning to the community. The family secrets of hidden homosexuality, obsessive gambling, and illegitimate pregnancy are effectively counterpointed to the psychological disintegration of Newcombe, a decent community member traumatized after his mother's death.

Wycliffe and the Four Jacks (1985) finds Wycliffe again on holiday in a beautiful corner of Cornwall and drawn into the investigation of the murder of a best-selling novelist, David Cleeve. The case comes to involve another murder, arson, and a series of crimes that stretches back over many years. Again, use of the anonymous-message device effectively creates suspense and fear. The young and ambitious Detective Inspector Lucy Lane joins Wycliffe's team in this novel, reflecting the increasing presence of women police officers in the United Kingdom during the 1980s. Lane continues thereafter as a series character, and Wycliffe's initial suspicions of her lessen as she makes the most of her initiative and capabilities.

Wycliffe and the Quiet Virgin (1986) exploits a Christmas setting, with the festive seasonal rituals masking an edgy and preoccupied atmosphere in the Bishop household, where Wycliffe is spending the holiday as a guest. For Wycliffe, the holiday is over when a local woman is found shot dead on Christmas morning, and her husband meets the same fate later the same day. In this novel Burley contrasts new scene-of-crime forensic police procedures with Wycliffe's depressed awareness that he is increasingly out of step with the direction his profession is taking. The novel accurately reflects the ascendence of criminology, which, like other social studies in the early 1980s, is struggling to qualify as a science. Wycliffe finds the changes make him feel old, like having to wear reading glasses. He is also trying to give up his pipe, which contributes to his feeling out of sorts. The villain of the novel, the local member of Parliament, gives a talk on the need to maintain high standards of integrity and independence in the face of the growing domination of professions by central and local government, again showing Burley's interest in charting the state of contemporary England. Burley depicts the coma-like atmosphere of a 1980s Christmas as a metaphor for England: with no trains, buses, newspapers, or mail delivery, families are marooned for several days in front of soporific television programs. In the course of this novel Wycliffe reveals a horror of social and economic disorder: "the prospect of anarchy appalls me and I suppose I'm helping to stave it off."

In *Wycliffe and the Winsor Blue* (1987) Wycliffe is again on a holiday, in Falmouth, a once-important commercial port that now largely caters to nautical amateurs who enjoy boats. Wycliffe, still preoccupied by his advancing years, worries about what he will do in retirement without a hobby but is soon caught up in a murder investigation. The case involves sudden death among a coterie of Falmouth artists, whose feuds and fame (or lack of) are the source of murderous acts and witty, enigmatic jokes in a will. More murders are committed before the killer, the young wife of the deceased artist, is uncovered, and before Wycliffe understands the purpose of the Winsor blue pigment signaled in the title. Burley effectively counterpoints the orderly routine of a holiday Sunday in Falmouth—a leisurely hotel breakfast, church bells, a stroll around the harbor, morning church services, evensong—with the grim business of a murder investigation. Detective Inspector Lane becomes more of a presence in Wycliffe's area squad, and another officer uses a computer. Wycliffe, not entirely at ease with these modern developments, admits that he is unaccustomed to working closely with

women and clearly is still more interested in human nature than in forensic clues and computers.

Wycliffe and the Tangled Web (1988) has Wycliffe investigating the disappearance and possible murder of a schoolgirl. Burley returns to familiar territory in his portrayal of a complex web of family relationships and rivalries centered on the girl. Under the surface of an apparently normal community in a small Cornish village, Wycliffe finds bubbling hatreds and resentments as well as the surprise discovery of the body of an elderly woman in a freezer. Burley again depicts the landscape of Cornwall and the claustrophobic atmosphere of small-town family feuding to suspenseful effect, along with some macabre extras.

Wycliffe and the Cycle of Death (1990) is set in Penzance, and in the character of Matthew Glynn, bookseller and district councillor, Burley demonstrates increasing skill at portraying disappointed and failed middle-aged men and at keeping the reader guessing until the final pages. Glynn is found strangled, and then one of his two estranged brothers is found dead of strychnine poisoning. The motives for the murders have lain dormant for thirty years in another family story of festering hatred and sexual jealousies. In spite of the ever-modernizing police force, which is "becoming as adept at verbal evasion as politicians, far outstripping bishops and trade union leaders," Wycliffe sticks to his favored methods of interviewing witnesses in their own surroundings and cogitating on the pattern of the case during long walks on the Cornish coast. Increasingly cynical about the influence of the judicial system on police procedure and always more interested in motive and psychology than forensic detail, Wycliffe reluctantly agrees that his team needs to establish which bottle the strychnine came from: "The courts like to know these things; it creates a comfortable illusion of precision and that's what justice is about." Matthew Coady in his 5 July 1990 crime review column in the *Guardian* (London) describes the novel as a "smooth combination of police procedure and Wycliffian instinct . . . a rewarding read." In the early 1990s some of the Wycliffe novels and additional original stories based on the characters were serialized on British network television, with Jack Shepherd starring in the title role.

Wycliffe and the Dead Flautist (1991), seventeenth in the Wycliffe series, centers on a distinguished Catholic Cornwall family with secrets, the apparent suicide of their estate manager, a character with a sinister interest in Victorian pornography, illicit romantic liaisons, and a particularly chilling ending that relies on the convention that the landed gentry are a law unto themselves. The next two novels, *Wycliffe and the Last Rites* (1992) and *Wycliffe and the Dunes Mystery* (1993), both use the familiar device of the anonymous letter, exploring how

Jack Shepherd as Charles Wycliffe and Helen Masters as Lucy Lane in one of several adaptations of Burley's fiction for British television (photograph by Mike Alsford © HTV)

the writers of such messages are able to work their cruelty at a distance. In the earlier novel a series of unsigned letters, framed around four biblical quotations, heralds a woman's death. In the next novel a series of anonymous communications threatens the stability of six well-established community members who, as teenagers, had been linked to the unresolved disappearance of the son of the local member of Parliament. The discovery of a body in the sand dunes brings Wycliffe to the scene and, inevitably, to a reconsideration of events fifteen years earlier.

These novels continue to develop characteristics and qualities of Wycliffe's personal life. In *Wycliffe and the Dunes Mystery* Wycliffe and Helen disagree over their daughter Ruth's professional and personal relationship with a man who Wycliffe describes as one of "that faceless breed of currency manipulators." As this novel opens, Wycliffe, bored and lacking a case to focus on, broods on his successful ascendency up the career lad-

der. Mystified at the strange twists of fate that have brought him to the rank of detective chief superintendent and an air-conditioned, double-glazed, and sound-proofed office, Wycliffe suffers a sudden lack of self-confidence. Such misgivings are quickly pushed aside as the investigation takes over, however. The police team and up-to-date forensic procedures continue to play a more prominent part in the investigations, though Wycliffe and his intuitive approach still dominate the proceedings. Lane, who represents one of the modernizing faces of the police profession and has by this point been a member of Wycliffe's team for six years, is someone Wycliffe has come to rely on for "her no-nonsense logic which nicely opposed his own tendency to woolliness and Kersey's inclination to flog dead horses."

In the subsequent Wycliffe novels Burley continues to explore the themes of how the past intrudes on the present, and the power of greed. A once-prosperous

Dust jacket for the U.S. edition of Burley's 1994 novel,
in which poison-pen letters lead Inspector Wycliffe
to investigate a fifteen-year-old disappearance
(Richland County Public Library)

Catholic family, the Kemps, has fallen on hard times in *Wycliffe and the House of Fear* (1995); the survival of the ancestral home, Kellycoryk, now depends on its potential as an upmarket leisure complex and hotel. Family feeling is divided and runs high. The disappearance of Roger Kemp's wife, Bridget, leads Wycliffe and his team to investigate the murder of his first wife five years earlier. Wycliffe and the local general practitioner debate the subjects of crime, criminology, the role of individual responsibility, and heredity versus environment in the makeup of criminals. This case takes place against a background of national and international news, overheard periodically by Wycliffe on the radio, of the "usual mix of terrorism, famine, street crime and political chicanery spiced with sex and scandals." In *Wycliffe and the Redhead* (1997) Wycliffe is involved in "the most disturbing case of his career" when he investigates the disappearance of a young woman assistant from a Falmouth antiquarian bookstore that Wycliffe himself patronizes. On

familiar ground with the bookstore setting and the character of the odd, reclusive bookseller Simon Meagor, who is suspected of having done away with his young employee, Burley weaves a tight plot around the missing girl. As usual, menacing elements from the past, including an unwanted pregnancy, an illegitimate and crippled child given up for adoption, and a long-lost sibling, all play a part in the case. Burley sets *Wycliffe and the Guild of Nine* (2000) in an artists' colony near St. Ives, using the location as effectively as ever and returning to some of the characters who first appeared in *Wycliffe and the Quiet Virgin*. The newest member of the artists' group, Francine (the "quiet virgin" ten years later), is found dead of carbon monoxide poisoning. The murderer is a classic Burley portrayal of psychological complexity: someone who feels disproportionately threatened, is tortured by a blend of hatred and fear, and who kills with a detachment that is, as Wycliffe says to Lane, "the essence of wickedness." In the most recent book, *Wycliffe and the Guild of Nine*, Wycliffe, by now detective chief superintendent and still the cerebral and introspective investigator, uses a mobile phone and mulls over possible retirement.

To date, Burley is still writing the Wycliffe series, and the next title, "Wycliffe's Last Lap," is due out in 2003. This fact makes the Wycliffe novels one of the longer-running British crime series still in publication. Moreover, Burley's Wycliffe novels have been published in the United Kingdom, the United States, and, in translation, in Germany, Switzerland, Denmark, Sweden, France, Holland, Spain, and Italy.

Critical comment has drawn attention to both strengths and weaknesses of the Wycliffe series. Martin Edwards praises Burley's long series for having consistently and powerfully conveyed "the atmosphere of the author's native Cornwall." Julian Symons, writing in his regular crime-fiction column in the 11 February 1989 edition of *The Independent* (London), also finds that "the local colour is well done." Burley uses a range of small Cornish villages to exploit the small-town atmosphere in several ways. First, it links him to the tradition of Agatha Christie, whose cozy village settings conceal complex social mores and disturbing human motives. In addition, the small-town setting limits the number of suspects, as did the country-house setting, and gives the novels a personal flavor. Beyond that, the series as a whole chronicles the tensions and difficulties faced by small, closed rural communities no longer able to make a living from the traditional occupations of fishing and mining. Forced to turn to tourism and leisure activities for income, old fishing and mining villages have to adjust to the influx of day-trippers and holiday visitors with expectations and ways of their own. The result is a simmering atmosphere just underneath the surface which Burley uses effectively.

According to Oleksiw, however, the Wycliffe novels are limited because "the repeated use of a young woman as the murder victim gives a sameness to his mystery novels which cannot be alleviated by varying the range of suspects." Bruce F. Murphy concurs, noticing the proliferation of women victims and the predilection for cases involving sex and commenting that the "narrowness of subject matter leads to some repetition and also a suspicion that shock value has been used as a crutch." In addition, his work is not altogether free of stereotyped character references, such as "virgin" spinsters and "pouf" homosexuals. Burley's unvarying formula has, paradoxically, ensured his reliability and predictability for those readers who return to him and limited his appeal for others who look for more variety and development in their mystery reading. The series character is one of the most consistent conventions of crime and mystery writing. Burley's protagonist, Wycliffe, is taken up again and again, by both author and reader, in comfortable and familiar expectation of a novel in which the policeman is still the hero and the supporting characters are convincing in their ordinariness and devotion to routine, small-town life.

The Wycliffe oeuvre of twenty-two novels sits comfortably within mainstream British crime writing of the last twenty years, one recurrent feature of which is a renewed concentration on the charismatic individual detective character. W. J. Burley has, along with other contemporary writers such as P. D. James, Ruth Rendell, Colin Dexter, Reginald Hill, Ian Rankin, Peter Lovesey, and John Harvey, created a widely recognized individual personality in the figure of Wycliffe. The modern British police procedural is moving in the direction of the novel of character and personality with greater psychological and ethical complexities. In the Wycliffe series the police are an honest and industrious group of individuals, who implement policies, rules, and procedures handed down to them. Their job requires efficiency, care, courage, and fortitude. *Financial Times* crime-fiction reviewer William Weaver aptly wrote on 18 March 1989 that Burley "inevitably guarantees a good story, straightforward prose, convincing characters, and . . . appealing landscape and seascape." Through the Wycliffe series Burley offers readers a sympathetic and unorthodox police detective, some good puzzles and studies in obsessional hatred and frustration, an informative account of a country police force in changing times, and a successful rendition of Cornwall as a setting.

Reference:

Geoff Tibballs, *The Wycliffe File: The Story of the ITV Detective Series* (London: Boxtree, 1995).

Heron Carvic
(1917? – February 1980)

Ellen Kocher Plaisance
Dillard University

and

Gina Macdonald
Nicholls State University

BOOKS: *Picture Miss Seeton* (London: Bles, 1968; New York: Harper & Row, 1968);

Miss Seeton Draws the Line (London: Bles, 1969; New York: Harper & Row, 1970);

Miss Seeton Bewitched (London: Bles, 1971); republished as *Witch Miss Seeton* (New York: Harper & Row, 1971);

Miss Seeton Sings (New York: Harper & Row, 1973; London: Davies, 1974);

Odds on Miss Seeton (New York: Harper & Row, 1975; London: Davies, 1976).

PLAY PRODUCTIONS: *The Widow of Forty,* London, 1944;

Beggars' Union, London, 1947.

OTHER: "Little Old Ladies," in *Murder Ink: The Mystery Reader's Companion,* edited by Dilys Winn (New York: Workman, 1977).

Heron Carvic's fame as a mystery writer rests on his Miss Seeton series, which features a dotty little old lady who lives in the small English village of Plummergen. Miss Seeton is a familiar enough type, reminiscent of a beloved former schoolteacher or a kindly elderly friend or relative. This unlikely heroine becomes involved in a surprising amount of criminal activity and tangled predicaments and manages through unexpected methods to escape horrifying situations and aid in catching the criminal or criminals. Readers are entertained by the humorous twists to the mysteries and their hilarious parodies of scenes and types popularized in Golden Age mysteries such as those featuring Agatha Christie's Miss Marple or Patricia Wentworth's Maud Silver, both septuagenarian sleuths with noses for trouble and fingers on the pulse of a village or community.

Elderly, fragile, and endangered, Miss Seeton faces a modern world of chaos and street gangs, drugs and thuggery. Where her amateur-detective counterparts are unquestionably aware of events and personalities, she is blithely unaware. She is a nondetective, an amateur sleuth who has clairvoyant artistic visions but no conception of the identity of a detective and no impulse to investigate. Nefarious events happening around her are transformed by her, without her understanding or acknowledgment. Carvic thus plays against mystery conventions.

Little has been written about Heron Carvic's life or writing. He was born in London, England, but was closemouthed about when, though it was probably some time during World War I. He attended Eton College and then accepted employment in a variety of positions, many of them connected to the stage and to television. At one time he produced and marketed vegetables. At various other points in his lifetime he was a dancer, an actor, and a stage and set designer. He worked in the theater and as a radio actor from 1937 to 1944, performing in stage productions of Mary Roberts Rinehart and Avery Hopwood's *The Bat* (1920), Walter Reynolds's *Young England* (1930), and William Shakespeare's *The Taming of the Shrew* (1594) and *Twelfth Night* (1601?), all in London theaters. He was Latimer Lord in a 1944 radio production of Emery Bonett's *One Fine Day* and wrote an episode of *Meet Dr. Morelle,* a *Monday Night at Eight* BBC radio series featuring an eminent criminologist. He directed and produced his own plays, *The Widow of Forty* (1944) and *Beggars' Union* (1947), playing the part of John Blister in the former. In the postwar years he wrote for television and played occasional television roles on series such as *Doctor Who, The Avengers, Police Surgeon,* and *Dick Barton, Special Agent.* He married actress Phyllis Neilson-Terry in 1958.

At the prompting of his wife, Carvic recalled in "Little Old Ladies," an essay for *Murder Ink: The Mystery Reader's Companion* (1977), he started writing short stories. The first–based on a true incident, about an actual artist whose failed attempt to paint a mother and son became personally significant when the sulky son murdered his mom–provided the seed for an idea that grew to full flower in the Miss Seeton novels. Although that story was never published, it led to two others that were the first portraits of Miss Seeton, and the original concept reappeared in *Miss Seeton Draws the Line* (1969), when Miss Seeton finds that each time she attempts to draw a child she unconsciously sketches him as a corpse. Yet, because of his involvement in his television career, Carvic did not return to the character until he wrote the first Miss Seeton novel, *Picture Miss Seeton* (1968), some fifteen years after her conception. He received an Edgar Award from Mystery Writers of America the next year for *Picture Miss Seeton,* and he joined the Writers Guild of Great Britain and Crime Writers Association.

Carvic's theater background is apparent in his vivid characterization, his visual conception of action, and his sense of parody and satire. The action in each book moves rapidly and is as clearly visualized as that in a movie (or a light-hearted theatrical production), with slapstick, drama, and the irony of highly professional police detectives depending on the erratic and symbolic drawings of an accident-prone old lady who at times seems to be approaching senility. Having lived in London most of his life, Carvic took advantage of his move to Kent, the garden region of England, as a setting for his mysteries. It is so closely located to London that urban crime easily spills over, and yet the region itself is rural and in some spots seemingly untouched by the passage of recent years. Carvic's wife died in 1977, and Carvic himself died three years later. Yet, the Miss Seeton novels were so popular that after his death, in February 1980, several other authors, at the urging of the publishers, have continued the series.

As Pearl G. Aldrich comments in her piece on Carvic in *Twentieth Century Crime and Mystery Writers,* Carvic's enduring contribution to the genre is a character: "an unlikely combination of the quintessential Victorian lady who is also fey," the latter a characteristic she strives to repress. *Picture Miss Seeton* paints a portrait of the heroine of Carvic's five books: a slim, elderly art teacher near retirement. She wears plain clothes and a hat that is constantly being squashed by events. Always prepared for the weather, she keeps an umbrella at her side. She has thin, wispy hair, drinks weak tea, and worries about saying the exact truth, an obsession with precision that makes her speech halting and disjointed. She certainly seems conventional enough, making other characters feel they clearly understand exactly who and what she is. She breaks type in many unexpected ways, however; she performs yoga, for example, and as a result is surprisingly supple and spry for her age. She uses her trusty umbrella as a most dangerous weapon–at various times a rapier, a fencing sword, or a club–and it becomes a savior in many situations. Miss Seeton firmly confronts both police questioning and criminals with the strength of a conservative English grandmother who knows what is proper behavior, no matter how unusual the situation. She is clairvoyant, and once made a lot of money stepping in for a gypsy fortuneteller, though her sense of morality and decorum did not let her keep the money. Part of the pleasure of her character is her absolute predictability amid unpredictable chaos. She is completely incapable of acknowledging her "gift" of artistic and prophetic vision and character insight, but, fortunately, those around her see her capabilities clearly on their own. Her surreal, modernistic drawings that fluster her, as her hand and eye take on a volition of their own, involve her in many situations she would never personally deem proper.

The contrast between Christie's Miss Marple and Carvic's Miss Seeton is significant and purposeful. Both elderly spinster ladies live in an English village, but the similarities intentionally stop there. Where reason, logic, and close observation normally characterize the investigator and result in solutions to criminal puzzles and reasonable answers to questions of who did what and why, Carvic's amateur does not even turn to intuition as the traditional standby explanation of nonrational crime-solving strategies. Instead, his detective is no detective at all, just a doddery, aging artist, her head in the clouds, her eye on decorum, her manner Victorian. Miss Seeton's pictures take on symbolic meaning in the hands of detectives who know the players and the details of the crime and, having experienced her clairvoyance in the past, intuit meaning from seeming scribbles. She is completely unobservant, except when drawing with her artist's eye. She is more of a "catalyst" of events than a detective on the prowl. Put her into any situation, and violence and chaos will ensue, while she remains disconcertingly blind to the criminal and to the gossip, jealousy, and unwholesome or unforgiving thoughts of her village neighbors. She breezes through her daily life unaware of the danger she is in, seeing only a series of disjointed, unconnected, unfortunate events. She has the eccentricity or idiosyncrasy of the generic senior-citizen detective, but is, at the same time, a radical departure from tradition, attracting trouble and newspaper headlines wherever she goes. Aldrich complains of the farcical nature of the Miss Seeton plots, the lessened credibility, the "pompous" irony; yet, these are the inevitable and

Dust jacket for Heron Carvic's 1973 novel, in which an amateur detective, the eccentric psychic-artist Miss Seeton, encounters an international gang of counterfeiters (Richland County Public Library)

intentional results of Carvic's satiric method. If the plots were credible and serious and the irony missing, there would be no Miss Seeton.

As with all the characters in this series, Miss Seeton is not developed nor complicated over time. Instead, she has a fixed and basic persona from the beginning of the series. In *Picture Miss Seeton* she is contentedly walking to the bus stop after having seen a production of Georges Bizet's *Carmen* (1875), an opera featuring what she thinks of as some rather badly behaved foreigners, when she inadvertently witnesses a murder by stabbing. She does not recognize the crime as a crime, but instead sees an impolite young man rudely pushing a young woman. Naturally, she pokes him in the back with her umbrella and ends up on the ground with the assailant. Later, at police headquarters, her recounting of events becomes confused with the events in *Carmen,* but the quick sketch she produces when asked to draw the man who stabbed the young woman captures his essence and provides an impression

of a prison association that enables Superintendent Delphick of Scotland Yard to name the suspect immediately. Thus, from the beginning Miss Seeton's reputation as a reliable, though unusual, sketch artist is assured at Scotland Yard. The newspapers make much of her use of her umbrella and call her "Battling Brolly," a moniker that defines her public image throughout the series.

Delphick, a recurring series character, attributes her firmness and successes to her strict following of manners and to the fact that she has no understanding at all of the severity of the situations in which she becomes embroiled. She is secure in her worldview of people as good but imperfect. As Delphick explains in *Picture Miss Seeton,* the only distress or upset Miss Seeton experiences is shock at bad manners, though in *Odds on Miss Seeton* (1975) he adds that for her this term encompasses her distaste for injustice and unkindness. Although she has no grasp of the danger she is in, luckily for her the situations resolve themselves with Miss Seeton still well in mind and body. While Delphick (known as "the Oracle" to colleagues, as he sees all) and many other characters in the novels (such as Detective Sergeant Bob Ranger) give Miss Seeton their seal of approval, some villagers consider her an unrepentant troublemaker, bringing waves of evil from the big city. Criminals, in turn, are convinced that she is a cool, unflinching detective (she sees right through them) and try at every opportunity to outwit and eliminate her–without success. No matter how she is viewed, Miss Seeton's appearance deceives all, including Miss Seeton herself. These various views of Miss Seeton are established in Carvic's first novel and set the pattern for the rest of the series. Each novel includes the same Scotland Yard officials and the same villagers; only the criminal changes, though his or her defeat is inevitable and results from a similar set of comic incidents.

In *Picture Miss Seeton* Battling Brolly leaves London for the village of Plummergen, Kent, where she has inherited a cottage, Sweetbriars, from her godmother. Plummergen becomes her home and in a sense acts as an important character in the series in its own right. Her arrival is greeted with curiosity since her reputation has preceded her. Several of the villagers become Miss Seeton's allies: Reverend Arthur Treeves and his sister, Miss Treeves; Lord and Lady Colveden and their seventeen-year-old son, Nigel; and Martha Bloomer and her husband, Stan, who prepare Miss Seeton's cottage and welcome her. Other recurring series characters consider Miss Seeton a negative element, particularly the "Two Nuts" of the village, Miss Nuttel and Miss Blaine, spinsters who live together downtown and see evil everywhere. The pair is Carvic's satiric take on the small-mindedness of some English villagers.

Interestingly, however, the Two Nuts are not entirely incorrect about problems in Plummergen: drugs have infiltrated their town. A local woman and her daughter are involved in a drug ring that brings death and mayhem to town. Miss Seeton is in the middle of events since the solicitor involved in her inheritance of the cottage is a drug dealer, who makes Sweetbriars his own. Moreover, he tries to make off with her inheritance and drives out anyone connected with the police. Likewise, a London murderer wants the only witness to his crime eliminated. Attacked on every side, Miss Seeton thwarts repeated plans to dispose of her, escaping from a panel truck, for instance, and surviving by landing in a pond, held up by her open umbrella, or causing a criminal to shoot himself in the foot, until she eventually, indirectly, leads the police to solve the crime. Superintendent Delphick, looking over her shoulder as she absentmindedly draws in charcoal, notes the brooding sky, the dangerous cliff, and the girl, lying half in the water, a bottle smashed at her side. Underneath this drawing lies a quick pen sketch, "a portly, pompous figure . . . delivering a speech while holding up a phial in his right hand: a wicked likeness to Mr. Trefold Morton in the role of a huckster selling quack medicines." The image of a con man and the odd coincidence of a bottle or phial in both drawings send the police investigating in the right direction. Although Miss Seeton believes she had nothing to do with the recent unfortunate events, police and readers know that she lies at the heart of darkness, a guardian against it. This pattern repeats itself throughout the series, so that the value of these books lies not in their plots but in the nature of their main character and her interaction with her village and her world.

In the second novel in the series, *Miss Seeton Draws The Line,* the ambitious newspaper reporter Amelita Forby of the *Daily Negative* befriends Miss Seeton and protects her secrets but has learned that all the trouble stirred up around the heroine makes for good copy. Criminal elements run rampant in Plummergen, with a gang perpetrating a set of burglaries, a strangler killing six children, and a bank clerk disappearing with a lot of money. In each case Miss Seeton brings the villains to justice. After her umbrella slaps into the windshield of the burglars' car, sending it off the road into the canal, she jumps into the water and seizes the loot. She unnerves the embezzler/murderer when she accurately draws his portrait, and he chooses suicide over exposure and imprisonment. Her umbrella trips the strangler and sets lawn equipment loose, crushing the strangler's leg, and thus Miss Seeton unwittingly saves her own life and closes the case for Scotland Yard. Those villagers who love her gallantly defend her;

while the Nuts, per usual, point out that she is just another outsider involved in crime.

In *Miss Seeton Bewitched* (1971; published in the United States as *Witch Miss Seeton*) Sergeant Ranger of Scotland Yard worries protectively about "MissEss" (a clerical error that caught on), even calling her "Aunt Em" when he plays interference for her and stands by his newly adopted relative. Several cults have infiltrated Plummergen, ritualistically slain a cow, and then begun to mesmerize the villagers out of their money. Carvic's heroine gets to the bottom of the corrupt cults by literally falling into the underground cave where their money is stashed. She manages to lead a group of Satan worshipers to safety, but the church goes up in flames. Miss Seeton ends up crouched on the roof, like a gargoyle ready to take flight, convincing Miss Nuttel and Miss Blaine of her supernatural powers.

In *Miss Seeton Sings* (1973), the heroine takes her form of mayhem to an international level. Her reputation earns her a trip to Switzerland to look into missing money and counterfeiting for a bank, but her poor French gets her into trouble, especially since she has somehow ended up unawares in Italy. When she finally makes it to Switzerland, she knows nothing about banking, but she spots several missing masterpieces hidden behind new works. When she hums the criminal ring's secret song, a forger is unnerved and decides she has the evil eye. In Paris she unwittingly makes her stage debut and steals the show. Eventually, she returns to England, where customs agents find a human arm in the wedding gift she has brought for Sergeant Ranger. When the murderer tries to give her a bomb in a package, she kindly places the bomb in his car (unbeknownst to him), since good manners do not allow a lady to receive a gift from a stranger.

Miss Deirdre Kenharding in *Odds on Miss Seeton* finds moral guidance when Miss Seeton tells her, "it's simply a question of whether you believe in law and order or you don't." During the course of that novel, the police ask Miss Seeton to look into racketeering and blackmail involving a casino and a member of Parliament. She knocks a thug down the Gold Fish Casino steps with a swing of her little black bag and frightens her would-be kidnapper when she speaks out—ghostlike—from behind the curtain of her darkened bedroom. When the case spills over into Plummergen again, the Nuts petition for Miss Seeton's expulsion from the village. Lord Colveden, as magistrate, denies their appeal, however, leaving Miss Seeton free to wreak havoc in Plummergen.

Accident and dumb luck are the two main qualities that have made the innocent and kindly Miss Seeton the greatest force against evil in modern times, according to various authorities in Carvic's series.

Likewise, Carvic makes it clear that criminals detest Miss Seeton. It is, after all, embarrassing to be thwarted by a gray-haired old lady with good manners. Yet, neither racketeers nor bandits on motorbikes can stand against her.

Ultimately, the Miss Seeton series is a study in human nature, a comic view of how gossip can affect the public image of a person and of how wide the dichotomy is between outward labels and an individual's self-understanding. Carvic explains Miss Seeton's denial of her abilities, her exciting life, and the evil around her in *Odds on Miss Seeton:* "Many people tend to forget or to translate experiences in their lives which do not fit with their own conception of themselves and Miss Seeton was a past mistress of this art." The series sets truth against reputation, public against private, and, in the tradition of the British stage, appearance against reality. Miss Seeton is exactly what she seems to be, an eccentric and fuzzy-minded old lady, but she is also exactly what she does not seem to be: an active force for good in an evil world. The pleasure of these books, then, comes from the sharp dichotomy between village and urban crime, between the appearance of rural virtues and the reality of modern obsessions, between the true dottiness of those who jealously guard their insider status and the eccentricities born of a unique world vision. Carvic takes on the Golden Age detective tradition, retaining its essential elements and at the same time turning them on their heads. His is a world turned upside down, first by criminals who threaten decent folk, and then by his heroine, whose unexpected and unpredictable behavior questions proprieties while advocating and defending them and both destroys and restores order. Furthermore, his books are quintessentially English, turning ordinary features of suburban and rural life topsy-turvy. It is no accident that in a female revue dress rehearsal, Miss Seeton takes center stage as "Miss England."

Critics from *Harpers* and *The New York Times Book Review* to *Best Seller,* the *Christian Science Monitor,* and *Critic* have praised Carvic's novels, frequently in terms of antitheses: classical but not so classical, procedural but in unprocedural ways. After Carvic died, Harpers commissioned two other authors to continue the Seeton tradition, with the request that they use pen names whose initials matched those of Heron Carvic. Thus, writer James Melville (Roy Peter Martin) wrote three Miss Seeton novels under the pseudonym Hampton Charles in 1990, and Sarah J. Mason wrote fourteen more under the name Hamilton Crane between 1991 and 1999. The large number of Seeton novels produced after Carvic's death is testimony to the popularity of the series. As implausible as they seem, Miss Seeton's adventures somehow touch and amuse readers. Indeed, Miss Seeton, a sweet, elderly innocent, always does what is right and always wins in the end—with a lot of luck and plenty of comic relief to make up for the rampant criminality that encompasses her world. Thus, the works that Carvic wrote for fun have come to represent his good humor, his tongue-in-cheek sensibility, and his optimism.

James Hadley Chase
(René Raymond)
(24 December 1906 – 6 February 1985)

Charles L. P. Silet
Iowa State University

BOOKS: *No Orchids for Miss Blandish* (London: Jarrolds, 1939; New York: Howell, Soskin, 1942); republished as *The Villain and the Virgin* (New York: Avon, 1948); revised as *No Orchids for Miss Blandish* (London: Panther, 1961; New York: Avon, 1961);

The Dead Stay Dumb (London: Jarrolds, 1939; New York: Pocket Books, 1973); republished as *Kiss My Fist!* (New York: Eton, 1952);

He Won't Need It Now, as James L. Docherty (London: Rich & Cowan, 1939); as Chase (St. Albans, U.K.: Panther, 1975);

Lady–Here's Your Wreath, as Raymond Marshall (London: Jarrolds, 1940); as Chase (London: Hamilton, 1961);

Twelve Chinks and a Woman (London: Jarrolds, 1940; New York: Howell, Soskin, 1941); revised as *Twelve Chinamen and a Woman* (New York: Diversey, 1948; London: Novel Library, 1950); republished as *The Doll's Bad News* (London: Panther, 1970);

Miss Callaghan Comes to Grief (London: Jarrolds, 1941);

Just the Way It Is, as Marshall (London: Jarrolds, 1944);

Miss Shumway Waves a Wand (London: Jarrolds, 1944);

Blondes' Requiem, as Marshall (London: Jarrolds, 1945; New York: Crown, 1946);

Eve (London: Jarrolds, 1945);

Make the Corpse Walk, as Marshall (London: Jarrolds, 1946); as Chase (London: Hamilton, 1964);

More Deadly Than the Male, as Ambrose Grant (London: Eyre & Spottiswoode, 1946); as Chase (London: Hamilton, 1960);

I'll Get You for This (London: Jarrolds, 1946; New York: Avon, 1951);

No Business of Mine, as Marshall (London: Jarrolds, 1947);

Last Page (London: S. French, 1947);

The Flesh of the Orchid (London: Jarrolds, 1948; New York: Pocket Books, 1972);

James Hadley Chase (from W. J. West, The Quest for Graham Greene, *1998)*

Trusted Like the Fox, as Marshall (London: Jarrolds, 1948); as Chase (London: Hamilton, 1964);

The Paw in the Bottle, as Marshall (London: Jarrolds, 1949); as Chase (London: Hamilton, 1961);

You Never Know with Women (London: Jarrolds, 1949; New York: Pocket Books, 1972);

You're Lonely When You're Dead (London: Hale, 1949; New York: Duell, Sloan & Pearce, 1950);

Figure It Out for Yourself (London: Hale, 1950; New York: Duell, Sloan & Pearce, 1951); republished as *The Marijuana Mob* (New York: Eton, 1952);

Lay Her Among the Lilies (London: Hale, 1950); republished as *Too Dangerous to Be Free* (New York: Duell, Sloan & Pearce, 1951);

Mallory, as Marshall (London: Jarrolds, 1950); as Chase (London: Hamilton, 1964);

But a Short Time to Live, as Marshall (London: Jarrolds, 1951); as Chase (London: Hamilton, 1960);

In a Vain Shadow, as Marshall (London: Jarrolds, 1951); as Chase (London: Hale, 1977);

Strictly for Cash (London: Hale, 1951; New York: Pocket Books, 1973);

Why Pick on Me? as Marshall (London: Jarrolds, 1951); as Chase (London: Hamilton, 1961);

The Fast Buck (London: Hale, 1952);

The Double Shuffle (London: Hale, 1952; New York: Dutton, 1953);

The Wary Transgressor, as Marshall (London: Jarrolds, 1952); as Chase (London: Hamilton, 1963);

The Soft Touch (Toronto: Harlequin, 1953);

The Things Men Do, as Marshall (London: Jarrolds, 1953); as Chase (London: Hamilton, 1962);

This Way for a Shroud (London: Hale, 1953);

I'll Bury My Dead (London: Hale, 1953; New York: Dutton, 1954);

Mission to Venice, as Marshall (London: Hale, 1954); as Chase (St. Albans, U.K.: Panther, 1973);

Tiger by the Tail (London: Hale, 1954);

Safer Dead (London: Hale, 1954); republished as *Dead Ringer* (New York: Ace, 1955);

The Sucker Punch, as Marshall (London: Jarrolds, 1954); as Chase (London: Hamilton, 1963);

Mission to Siena, as Marshall (London: Hale, 1955); as Chase (London: Panther, 1966);

You've Got It Coming (London: Hale, 1955; New York: Pocket Books, 1973; revised edition, London: Hale, 1975);

There's Always a Price Tag (London: Hale, 1956; New York: Pocket Books, 1973);

You Find Him—I'll Fix Him, as Marshall (London: Jarrolds, 1956); as Chase (London: Panther, 1966);

The Guilty Are Afraid (London: Hale, 1957; New York: New American Library, 1959);

Hit and Run, as Marshall (London: Hale, 1958); as Chase (London: Hale, 1977);

Not Safe to Be Free (London: Hale, 1958); republished as *The Case of the Strangled Starlet* (New York: New American Library, 1958);

Shock Treatment (London: Hale, 1959; New York: New American Library, 1959);

The World in My Pocket (London: Hale, 1959; New York: Popular Library, 1962);

What's Better Than Money? (London: Hale, 1960; New York: Pocket Books, 1972);

Come Easy—Go Easy (London: Hale, 1960; New York: Pocket Books, 1974);

A Lotus for Miss Quon (London: Hale, 1961);

Just Another Sucker (London: Hale, 1961; New York: Pocket Books, 1974);

I Would Rather Stay Poor (London: Hale, 1962; New York: Pocket Books, 1974);

A Coffin from Hong Kong (London: Hale, 1962);

Tell It to the Birds (London: Hale, 1963; New York: Pocket Books, 1974);

One Bright Summer Morning (London: Hale, 1963; New York: Pocket Books, 1974);

The Soft Centre (London: Hale, 1964);

This Is for Real (London: Hale, 1965; New York: Walker, 1967);

The Way the Cookie Crumbles (London: Hale, 1965; New York: Pocket Books, 1974);

Cade (London: Hale, 1966);

You Have Yourself a Deal (London: Hale, 1966; New York: Walker, 1968);

Well Now, My Pretty— (London: Hale, 1967; New York: Pocket Books, 1972);

Have This One on Me (London: Hale, 1967);

An Ear to the Ground (London: Hale, 1968);

Believed Violent (London: Hale, 1968);

The Vulture Is a Patient Bird (London: Hale, 1969);

The Whiff of Money (London: Hale, 1969);

There's a Hippie on the Highway (London: Hale, 1970);

Like a Hole in the Head (London: Hale, 1970);

Want to Stay Alive? (London: Hale, 1971);

An Ace Up My Sleeve (London: Hale, 1971);

Just a Matter of Time (London: Hale, 1972);

You're Dead without Money (London: Hale, 1972);

Knock, Knock! Who's There? (London: Hale, 1973);

Have a Change of Scene (London: Hale, 1973);

Three of Spades (London: Hale, 1974);

Goldfish Have No Hiding Place (London: Hale, 1974);

So What Happens to Me? (London: Hale, 1974);

Believe This, You'll Believe Anything (London: Hale, 1975);

The Joker in the Deck (London: Hale, 1975);

Do Me a Favor, Drop Dead (London: Hale, 1976);

I Hold the Four Aces (London: Hale, 1977);

My Laugh Comes Last (London: Hale, 1977);

Consider Yourself Dead (London: Hale, 1978);

You Must Be Kidding (London: Hale, 1979);

Can of Worms (London: Hale, 1979);

Try This One for Size (London: Hale, 1980);

You Can Say That Again (London: Hale, 1980);

Hand Me a Fig-Leaf (London: Hale, 1981);

Have a Nice Night (London: Hale, 1982);

We'll Share a Double Funeral (London: Hale, 1982);

Not My Thing (London: Hale, 1983);

Hit Them Where It Hurts (London: Hale, 1984);

Get a Load of This (London: Hale, 1988).

NO ORCHIDS
FOR
MISS BLANDISH

by
JAMES HADLEY CHASE

579th Thousand

JARROLDS *Publishers* (LONDON) LTD

FOUNDED IN 1770

LONDON   NEW YORK   MELBOURNE   SYDNEY   CAPE TOWN

*Title page for the first edition (1939) and paperback cover for the 1951 edition of Chase's first novel, which George
Orwell likened to "a header into the cesspool" (left: Frank Melville Jr. Memorial Library, State University of
New York at Stony Brook; right: from Richard A. Lupoff,* The Great American Paperback, *2001)*

PLAY PRODUCTIONS: *Get a Load of This,* by Chase
and Arthur Macrea, music and lyrics by Manning
Sherwin and Val Guest, London, 1941;
No Orchids for Miss Blandish, by Chase and Robert Nesbit, adapted from the novel by Chase, London,
Prince of Wales Theatre, 1942;
Last Page, London, 1946.

OTHER: *Slipstream: A Royal Air Force Anthology,* edited
by Chase, as René Raymond, and David Langdon (London: Eyre & Spottiswoode, 1946).

George Orwell, in his essay "Raffles and Miss
Blandish," first published in *Horizon* in October 1944,
applied what he described as a "sociological" reading to
E. W. Hornung's "amateur cracksman" stories and to
René Raymond's best-selling novel *No Orchids for Miss
Blandish* (1939), published under his best-known pseudonym, James Hadley Chase. Orwell chose these two

crime writers because they both played "the limelight
on the criminal rather than the policeman," and he was
concerned about the "immense difference in moral
atmosphere between the two books and the change in
the popular attitude that this probably implies."
Although Orwell describes the writing in *No Orchids for
Miss Blandish* as "brilliant . . . with hardly a wasted word
or a jarring note," he did feel that reading it was to take
"a header into the cesspool," an assessment consistent
with his politics, since he saw *No Orchids for Miss Blandish*
as pure fascism and primarily concerned with a will to
power. He calls it a "daydream appropriate to a totalitarian age."

In spite of Orwell's reservations, his essay provides a fairly comprehensive examination of Raymond's writing. For example, Orwell notes that the
language, plot, and moral attitudes in the novel so carefully copied its predecessors in the school of hard-boiled
crime fiction that many in Great Britain thought it a

reprint of an American import. Orwell also pointed out what a departure the novel was from the traditions of English sensational fiction, in which there had always been "a sharp distinction between right and wrong and a general agreement that virtue must triumph in the last chapter." While Orwell deplored the corruption of British sensibilities that the popularity of the novels suggested, he unwittingly uncovered a shift that crime fiction made after World War II, a shift that *No Orchids for Miss Blandish* prefigured. Certainly, the novels of Raymond have a contemporary feel that most other crime fiction written during his most productive period lack. Orwell's insights provide the reasons for retrieving Raymond's fiction from its current neglect.

René Brabazon Raymond was born in London, England, on 24 December 1906. His father, Colonel Francis Raymond, was a veterinary surgeon. Raymond was educated at King's School, Rochester, Kent; Reading Grammar School; and Hastings University School. He left home at age eighteen, apparently because of a quarrel with his father, and in 1924 he became a door-to-door encyclopedia salesman in his hometown of Hastings on the south coast of England. Two years later he moved to London and worked for Simkin and Marshall, a wholesale bookselling firm. During World War II he served in the Royal Air Force, becoming a squadron leader, and he was the editor of the *RAF Journal*. Raymond married Sylvia Ray and had one child, a son.

While working for Simkin and Marshall, Raymond realized that the demand by British readers for the fiction of the American crime writers Dashiell Hammett, Raymond Chandler, and James M. Cain offered him an opportunity for employing his own talents as a writer. According to legend, during six weekends over the summer of 1938 he wrote his first novel, *No Orchids for Miss Blandish,* which was published under the pseudonym of James Hadley Chase by Jarrolds in London in 1939. The novel was immediately successful and was quickly published in the United States, France, Germany, Spain, Norway, Sweden, Denmark, Finland, Canada, Japan, Russia, and South America. A play based on it ran for seven months at the Prince of Wales Theater in London in 1942 and for an additional seven years on tour in the provinces. The novel was first adapted for the screen by the Renown Film Company in 1945. When a revised edition of *No Orchids for Miss Blandish* was issued in 1984, the publishers claimed that it was the most popular work of fiction read by the armed forces during World War II, and they estimated that more than four million copies had been sold worldwide. *No Orchids for Miss Blandish* has remained Raymond's best-known book.

The formula Raymond created when writing his first novel he followed throughout his career. He once described it in four words: "speed, violence, women, America." As he had discovered while employed by Simkin and Marshall, British tastes in crime fiction were changing, and when he began to write fiction himself he adopted the style and content of the American hard-boiled school of mystery fiction. Unlike his fellow British crime writer Peter Cheyney, who also wrote hard-boiled novels featuring an American-style private investigator, Slim Callaghan, as well as the Lemmy Caution series, Raymond set most of his novels in the United States. Although he only visited the country a few times and never actually saw the locations for most of his novels, Raymond managed to capture the atmosphere of the American locale with skill and verisimilitude. Most of his knowledge of his American settings was largely drawn from United States maps, police reports, timetables, and slang dictionaries. Raymond did not always restrict himself to an American setting, however. For example, after a trip to the Far East in 1960, he wrote two novels, *A Lotus for Miss Quon* (1961) and *A Coffin from Hong Kong* (1962), which were praised for their locale. Furthermore, his spy thrillers often take place in Europe.

His plots are fast paced and complex, and his narratives are populated not only by private eyes and former government agents but also by an array of petty crooks, pimps, prostitutes, and gangsters. His stories are often strongly violent and sadistic and include every sort of perversion. It was a formula that worked well, and writing primarily as James Hadley Chase, but also as James L. Docherty, Ambrose Grant, and Raymond Marshall—multiple pseudonyms are characteristic of writers who write and publish several books per year—Raymond produced almost one hundred crime novels, some thirty of which were adapted into motion pictures, especially in Italy and France.

Raymond wrote several series featuring a variety of protagonists. Dave Fenner, a former reporter turned private detective, is featured in his first novel and in a sequel, *Twelve Chinks and a Woman* (1940; revised as *Twelve Chinamen and a Woman,* 1948). Brick-Top Corrigan is an unscrupulous private eye who often fails to solve his clients' cases while still pocketing the fees. Steve Harmas, an insurance investigator who lives in Los Angeles, is aided in his cases by his beautiful wife, Helen. Mark Girland, a former Central Intelligence Agency (CIA) agent, lives in Paris, enjoys the good life, and operates as a freelance operative for his former employers. Don Micklem is a millionaire playboy who is also involved in international intrigue. Frank Terrell is a private investigator who works in Paradise City, Florida, as does Al Barney, a dissolute former skin

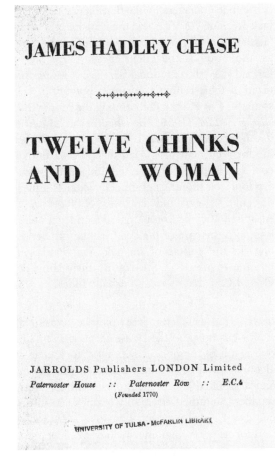

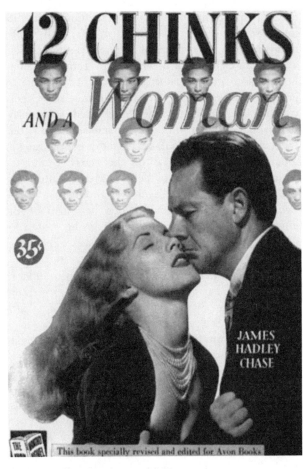

Title page for the first edition (1940) and paperback cover for the 1948 edition of a hard-boiled detective story influenced by Dashiell Hammett's 1930 novel, The Maltese Falcon *(left: McFarlin Library, University of Tulsa; right: from Lupoff,* The Great American Paperback, *2001)*

diver. In addition to these series, Raymond also wrote novels with central characters such as Vic Malloy, Herman Radnitz, Helga Rolfe, and Lu Silk, as well as many one-off thrillers.

Sixty years after its publication it is difficult to gauge the immediate impact of *No Orchids for Miss Blandish*. The book garnered phenomenally good sales both in English and in various translations. The play and movie version helped to extend its popularity. It was still sufficiently well known five years after it had appeared for Orwell to use it as an example of the direction modern crime fiction was taking in 1944. In fact, the novel did indicate some of the directions mystery and detective writing took in the postwar period with such writers as Mickey Spillane, Brett Halliday, and a score of authors of paperback originals working in the late 1940s through the 1950s.

In many ways *No Orchids for Miss Blandish* is a traditional crime story out of the prewar pulp magazines. The action is fast and nonstop, the plot complex and at times a bit outlandish, the characters tough; there are plenty of killings, loose women, hard drinking, and heavy smoking. The story begins with a gang of small-time crooks planning to heist a diamond necklace after the birthday party given for Miss Blandish by her multimillionaire father. The gang decides to kidnap her as well, hoping for a larger share of the Blandish millions, but they in turn are robbed of both the necklace and Miss Blandish by a larger, more vicious mob. The rest of the fiction follows the fate of Miss Blandish as she is kept as a plaything for the psychotic, mother-dominated Slim, who has been compared to Cody Jarrett of the movie *White Heat* (1949), until she is finally rescued through the efforts of the police and Fenner, who is hired independently by Miss Blandish's father. Raymond apparently borrowed the kidnapping plot and the sexually dysfunctional psychotic from William Faulkner's *Sanctuary* (1931).

The pace of the novel is relentless, the language economical, and the violence pervasive. All of the original gang of small-time crooks are killed by the second mob, who are in turn wiped out by the police and Fenner. Perhaps the most daring part of the novel is its ending, however. Once Miss Blandish has been finally removed from the clutches of Slim and is safely tucked away in an eighth-floor hotel room by Fenner awaiting her reunion with her father, she takes her own life by jumping out a window, thereby violating all of those traditional crime-fiction rules Orwell cited in his essay. It leaves the reader with a profound letdown. Moreover, as Orwell points out, the narrative concentrates as much on the criminals as on the detective and the police, shifting the focus of the novel. For example, Fenner is not introduced until midway through the narrative. Orwell is also correct when he mentions the importance of the reward for Fenner in his search for Miss Blandish, although he overemphasizes the detective's greediness.

Fenner's behavior squares solidly with that of other hard-boiled gumshoes of the period, especially Hammett's Sam Spade, the protagonist of *The Maltese Falcon* (1930). Self-protective, independent, and with a flexible moral attitude, the traditional American private investigator had already established a literary type different from the traditions of Sherlock Holmes, the gentleman school of detectives such as Lord Peter Wimsey, and the cozy crime fiction of Hercule Poirot and Miss Marple created by Agatha Christie. Fenner is not a new kind of private eye; it was just unusual for a British writer to employ such a character. Raymond primarily used American-style models for his protagonists throughout his career, whether in his spy novels, private-eye fiction, or his solo thrillers.

Fenner appears again in *Twelve Chinks and a Woman,* in which Raymond's indebtedness to Hammett is even more pronounced. The introduction of the private eye is reminiscent of the opening of *The Maltese Falcon:* a woman arrives at Fenner's office, is shown in by his trusty girl Friday, Paula Dolan—who is not a little in love with her reluctant boss—and asks the detective's help in locating her lost sister, who eventually turns out to be bogus. Once again, the novel is economical, violent, and full of constant action. *Twelve Chinks and a Woman* also exploits the racist, misogynist, and sexually perverse nature of the hard-boiled school—in this case, elements taken to the extreme, in the way Spillane does later in *I, the Jury* (1947). By the early years of the war, in some half a dozen crime novels, Raymond had created the moral atmosphere and had exploited the excesses that characterize much of postwar crime writing. After *No Orchids for Miss Blandish,* Hornung's gentleman burglar, Raffles, and his ilk forever appeared as quaintly anachronistic throwbacks.

Another of Raymond's private eyes is Vic Malloy, who operates out of his agency, International Services, in Orchid City, California, along with his partner-

cum-office-manager, Paula Bensinger, and his legman, Jack Kernan. As Vic says, their business is essentially a "millionaire's service," but then millionaires are almost as numerous as the grains of sands on the beach in Orchid City. International Services is more of an organization than Fenner's one-man operation, and it has something of a reputation among the moneyed. *Lay Her Among the Lilies* (1950; published in the United States as *Too Dangerous to Be Free,* 1951) involves the office working for a client who is dead when Paula finds in Vic's coat a letter that has remained unopened since its delivery fourteen months before. The letter is a plea for the detective's help and encloses $500 as a retainer. Although Vic and company have no legal obligation to look into the case of the dead woman, there is a moral one. In the course of the tale Vic, Paula, and Jack become involved in uncovering the seamy depths of Orchid City that its wealth usually hides.

Raymond hinges the plot on one of his favorite devices: the switched identity ploy he occasionally used, as, for example, in *The Double Shuffle* (1952). The narrative is full of many of Raymond's stock characters: an alcoholic lawyer, a quack healer, a playboy gambler, and a crooked cop or two, plus assorted thugs, family retainers, and the flotsam of working-class stiffs who are employed by the wealthy. The novel is packed with various forms of wrongdoing, including kidnappings, blackmail, murder, embezzlement, fraud, drug addiction, and gambling. Raymond never stinted on the number and kinds of crime he employed in his fiction.

In *Lay Her Among the Lilies* Raymond works variations on the principal characters in his other detective novels. Jack Kernan gets the most salacious dialogue, freeing Vic to be marginally more refined. Paula is more than just a secretary—she loaned Vic the money to start the agency in the first place—and functions as business manager, fact finder, and assistant detective. Investigating the case, they work as an ensemble. As a result Vic is less on his own and relies on help from the other two, and he is even rescued by each of them at various points in the story. Unlike Fenner, Vic is not the lone detective in the mold of Sam Spade, Chandler's Philip Marlowe, and Ross Macdonald's Lew Archer.

In his long writing career Raymond explored other crime-fiction genres besides the conventional hard-boiled private-eye novel. For example, he wrote several works featuring insurance investigator Steve Harmas and his wife, Helen. Although Harmas retains many of the characteristics of Fenner, he is married (which curtails his womanizing, if not his attraction to other women) and is more domestic as a result; relies heavily on his wife's intelligence and especially her intuition in solving his cases; and is somewhat hampered by the restrictions placed on him by his bosses at the San Francisco–based National Fidelity Insurance Company.

In *The Double Shuffle* Harmas is asked to investigate a $100,000 life policy taken out for publicity purposes by a young stripper who does an act with a snake. She also has taken out similar policies from nine other insurance companies. The case demands Harmas and his wife go to Los Angeles and other places in southern California as they sort out multiple murders, the kidnapping of a movie star, and a case of bigamy and fraud involving a pair of identical twins. Steve and his wife, although employed by the insurance industry, operate much in the style of traditional private eyes: he is shot at, knocked out, lied to, and in general bulls his way forward, and she uses her feminine charms to beguile and otherwise manipulate her way through the plot. Although there is plenty of violence and some sex in *The Double Shuffle,* it is far less perverse and has a more conventional ending, where everything is satisfyingly wrapped up, than does *No Orchids for Miss Blandish.*

Writing under the pseudonym of Raymond Marshall, the one he used most often after James Hadley Chase, Raymond published more than a dozen books, several of them featuring Don Micklem, a millionaire playboy who often finds himself engaged in various sorts of international intrigue. Inheritor of £5 million, Micklem has houses in London, Nice, New York, and a modest palazzo in Venice. He also has a long-suffering staff: his secretary, Marian Rigby, and his "man," Cherry, a majordomo, valet, butler, and general factotum of the old school—sort of a combination of P. G. Wodehouse's Jeeves and Dorothy Sayers's Bunter. They keep Micklem's household and business interests running smoothly. With his wealth and his cosmopolitan connections, both social and professional, Micklem is a perfect amateur sleuth who is able to meddle in international affairs without being restricted by official associations.

In *Mission to Venice* (1954) Micklem searches for an old wartime friend who both the American CIA and British secret service think has defected to the Russians. Raymond works in the locale more thoroughly than he do in the novels set in the United States. Rather than a series of street and city names and a generic American landscape, Venice provides a nuanced background against which is set the plot of the novel. Micklem, as do all of Raymond's protagonists, exhibits the characteristics of the competent man of action, but with the added sophistication of a man of wealth and position. Micklem allowed Raymond to extend his repertoire of central figures.

The advent of the Cold War and the success of the early James Bond novels by Ian Fleming stimulated the production of spy fiction during the 1950s and 1960s, and a new kind of espionage hero emerged with

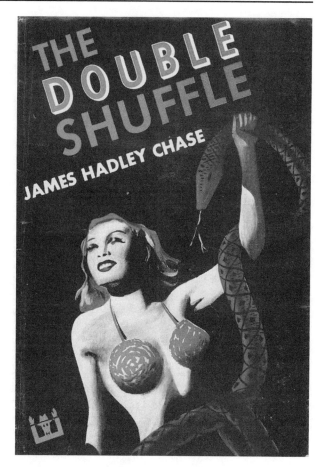

Dust jacket for the first U.S. edition of Chase's 1952 novel, in which detective Steve Harmas and his wife investigate an insurance case involving an exotic dancer and the snake she uses in her act (Bruccoli Clark Layman Archives)

a set of attitudes unlike those of the interwar period in novels by John Buchan, W. Somerset Maugham, and Eric Ambler, whose reluctant spies dominated the genre. Raymond joined the ranks of those who explored this new terrain. Writing his spy thrillers, he also had an opportunity to move his locales outside the United States and break the hard-boiled detective formula he had first adopted.

One of his spy heroes is Mark Girland, who is scraping by working as a street photographer in Paris in *You Have Yourself a Deal* (1966), the second book in the series (the first being *This Is for Real,* 1965). He is drawn back into the world of espionage when his former boss at the CIA employs him as a freelance agent to extract information from a woman suffering from amnesia, who the agency believes knows some vital military secrets. She is also being sought by the Russians and the Chinese for the same reason, and the plot revolves around their attempts to kidnap or kill her while Mark waits for the effects of the amnesia to wear off. Raymond uses multiple parallel stories as the Russians,

Dust jacket for Chase's 1966 novel, in which an alcoholic
crime photographer becomes caught up in the racial
tensions of a small southern town (Bruccoli
Clark Layman Archives)

Raymond could also use different kinds of protagonists, and since they were not in a series, they were also expendable and less subject to the standard characteristics of the detective model. A good example of one of his single books is a late novel in the crime noir genre, *Cade* (1966).

Cade is the story of a former ace photographer for the *New York Sun,* now an out-of-work alcoholic, who is sent on a last-minute assignment to get some pictures of the racial tensions in a small southern town. Val Cade immediately arouses the suspicions of the local police department, who are wary of strangers who might reveal the racism and violence toward African Americans rampant in Eastonville. The assignment leads Cade beyond his adventures in the southern town, and he becomes involved in a secondary plot that carries him to Europe and finally to Geneva in pursuit of a mysterious woman. On a mountain in the Swiss Alps an assassin's bullet ends his short and miserable life.

Raymond uses his single novels to explore more topical current events such as racism and perverted small-town justice. He also creates darker characters, who, like Cade, have reached the end of their tether and become enmeshed in hopeless, endgame plots. Unlike the series books, which demand that the central character somehow survive even the most hostile environment, the noir stories allowed Raymond to vent his more pessimistic, existentialist, darker side, the side of him that had first appeared in *No Orchids for Miss Blandish* and later appealed to Continental moviemakers. This darkness, with its later postwar angst, makes Raymond's fiction so modern and still so accessible.

The critics are divided about the quality of Raymond's fiction. Julian Symons, who thought Raymond's work was at worst shoddy and at best competent but unimaginative, agreed with Orwell that the novels were about the pursuit of power and that such power fantasies were responsible for their popularity. On the Continent, however, Raymond has been compared to Fyodor Dostoevsky and Louis-Ferdinand Céline, although such an evaluation may rest as much with the quality of the motion pictures made from the novels as from the fiction itself. Ernest Mandel, the Marxist critic, found in *No Orchids for Miss Blandish* a social critique of the sick society that was a phenomenon of social decomposition, although Raymond himself denied that his books reflected any such commentary.

Some critics have derided Raymond's fiction for its sexism, racism, amorality, and violence, while others have pointed out that these aspects are merely the conventions of the hard-boiled writers and their stylized fiction that preceded him. As Vicki K. Robinson has remarked, this seemingly callous attitude toward conventional morality simply underscores contemporary,

Chinese, and Americans all continuously stumble over one another in pursuit of the elusive secrets thought to be held by the amnesiac woman. From Paris to the south of France to Hong Kong, in typical spy-novel fashion, the plot thickens and twists, finally to end in a futile search for a rare, black pearl that promises to yield millions.

Girland is the usual surly, independent, wise-cracking, insubordinate loner reminiscent of Raymond's detectives, but he is also resourceful, tough, and wily: the perfect man for the job. He is only slightly reminiscent of James Bond, however. Girland likes his booze and cigarettes throughout, but he lives in a seedy flat in Paris, is in desperate need of money (the only reason he takes the job), and dresses down most of the time. There are none of the sophisticated affectations to his character that so defined Bond.

Raymond's series books are perhaps better known because of their recurring characters than his single novels, of which he wrote more. In these solo books he works in a variety of crime genres, including thriller and noir. Since he was not restricted by a series, he had greater flexibility in developing his plots and could explore themes and locations not tied to the American hard-boiled tradition or to the spy novel.

post-Darwinian life, in which raw survival is more effective than idealism. Raymond's use of the American idiom generally has been praised; nevertheless, he does at times lapse into Briticisms, using "torch" for flashlight, referring to "trunk" roads and bank managers, and occasionally retaining British spellings such as "tyres" for tires.

For all of the controversy his fiction stirred up during his lifetime, the large number of books he wrote, and the successful movie adaptations of them, Raymond is among the least read and least appreciated of postwar British crime writers. Popular fiction always reflects the deeper concerns of the times in which it was written. The fact that his novels were popular should alert critics that there is more to them than a casual reading would suggest and that he was providing his reading public with something more than power fantasies.

René Raymond was a retiring man and little is really known about his personal life. He was once described by a reporter for *The Times* (London) as "a typical quiet Englishman." Raymond did not like to talk about his work or waste time giving interviews, writing introductions to his novels, or reading what the critics said about his writing. In a rare interview he once confessed that, "An introduction to my work would certainly not be of use to my general readers. They could care less." All they wanted from him, he remarked, was a "good read." His philosophy of writing was simple: "My job is to write a book for a wide variety of readers. I do this job conscientiously." He died on 6 February 1985 in Corseaux-sur-Vevey, Switzerland.

References:

Theodore P. Dukeshire, "The Caper Novels of James Hadley Chase," *Armchair Detective,* 10 (April 1977): 128–129;

Dukeshire, "James Hadley Chase," *Armchair Detective,* 10 (April 1977): 128–129;

George Orwell, "Raffles and Miss Blandish," in his *The Decline of English Murder and Other Essays* (Harmondsworth, U.K.: Penguin, 1988), pp. 63–79;

Jacques Robichon, "Un Virtuose de sadisme: James Hadley Chase," *Nouvelles-Litteraires,* 11 March 1965, pp. 1, 11;

Susan Harris Smith, "No Orchids for George Orwell," *Armchair Detective,* 9 (February 1976): 114–115.

Douglas Clark

(1 December 1919 – 22 February 1993)

B. J. Rahn
Hunter College, City University of New York

BOOKS: *Suez Touchdown: A Soldier's Tale,* as D. M. J. Clark (London: Davies, 1964);

Nobody's Perfect (London: Cassell, 1969; New York: Stein & Day, 1969);

Death after Evensong (London: Cassell, 1969; New York: Stein & Day, 1970);

Deadly Pattern (London: Cassell, 1970; New York: Stein & Day, 1970);

Sweet Poison (London: Cassell, 1970);

The Miracle Makers, as Peter Hosier (London: Cassell, 1971);

Sick to Death (London: Cassell, 1971; New York: Stein & Day, 1971);

You're Fairly Welcome, as James Ditton (London: Hale, 1973);

The Bigger They Are, as Ditton (London: Hale, 1973);

Escapemanship, as Ditton (London: Hale, 1975);

Premedicated Murder (London: Gollancz, 1975; New York: Scribners, 1976);

Dread and Water (London: Gollancz, 1976; New York: Harper & Row, 1984);

Table d'Hote (London: Gollancz, 1977; New York: Perennial Library, 1984);

The Gimmel Flask (London: Gollancz, 1977; New York: Dell, 1982);

The Libertines (London: Gollancz, 1978);

Heberden's Seat (London: Gollancz, 1979; New York: Perennial Library, 1984);

Poacher's Bag (London: Gollancz, 1980; New York: Harper & Row, 1983);

Golden Rain (London: Gollancz, 1980; New York: Dell, 1982);

Copley's Hunch, as Ditton (London: Gollancz, 1980);

Roast Eggs (London: Gollancz, 1981; New York: Dodd, Mead, 1981);

The Longest Pleasure (London: Gollancz, 1981; New York: Morrow, 1981);

Shelf Life (London: Gollancz, 1982; New York: Harper & Row, 1983);

Doone Walk (London: Gollancz, 1982);

Douglas Clark (photograph by Andy Williams; from the dust jacket for the U.S. edition of Premedicated Murder, *1975)*

Vicious Circle (London: Gollancz, 1983; New York: Perennial Library, 1985);

The Monday Theory (London: Gollancz, 1983; New York: Perennial Library, 1985);

Bouquet Garni (London: Gollancz, 1984);

Dead Letter (London: Gollancz, 1984; New York: Perennial Library, 1985);

Jewelled Eye (London: Gollancz, 1985; New York: Perennial Library, 1988);

Performance (London: Gollancz, 1985; New York: Perennial Library, 1986);

Storm Centre (London: Gollancz, 1986); republished as *Storm Center* (New York: Perennial Library, 1988);

The Big Grouse (London: Gollancz, 1986; New York: Perennial Library, 1988);

Plain Sailing (London: Gollancz, 1987; New York: Perennial Library, 1988).

PRODUCED SCRIPTS: "The Appointed House," radio, *Saturday Night Theatre,* BBC, 1 July 1972; "Late Night Final," radio, *Afternoon Theatre,* BBC, 24 August 1974.

Douglas Clark's novels make a distinctive contribution to the genre of detective fiction because of his ingenious means and methods of murder. His work draws upon his extensive knowledge of natural bacterial, plant, and mineral poisons; manufactured chemical poisons; and lethal combinations of normally benign substances. Clark's expertise derives from his geological studies at university, his military training, and twenty-plus years of working in the pharmaceutical industry. Of his twenty-six police whodunits, only five include violent deaths by means of gunshots, strangulation, blows from a blunt instrument, a hit-and-run car crash, or electrical shock. Instead, villains commit crimes with botulinum bacteria, arsenical gas released from iron pyrites, sodium aurothiomalate (gold salts), and deuterium oxide (heavy water). The plant poisons employed are derived from castor oil beans, laburnum seeds, croton oil seeds, and lily of the valley leaves. Manufactured chemical poisons include barbiturates, paracetamol, diazepam, promethazine chloride, hexachlorophone, monoamine oxide inhibitors, etorphine, and cyanide. His thorough knowledge of poisons and his imaginative use of them sets Clark apart from most other writers.

As Clark states in *St James Guide to Crime and Mystery Writers* (1996), "The books are for the most part medical mysteries and I try to make their appeal lie in the technical problems they present." The various settings for the crimes include the corporate headquarters of a drug company, a girls' school, a police training college, a concert hall, and a mountainside in the great outdoors. Although the weapons are esoteric and the settings diverse, except for two political abductions the motives for the crimes are personal and fall into conventional categories such as sexual desire or jealousy, misguided love, greed, ambition, and revenge.

The other noteworthy aspect of Clark's writing is his dynamic Scotland Yard team. At first glance these whodunits might appear to be police procedurals, but close scrutiny reveals that George Masters evinces many of the traits of the Great Detective in the tradition of Edgar Allan Poe's C. Auguste Dupin and Sir Arthur Conan Doyle's Sherlock Holmes. Masters relies on his intuition and keen powers of analysis to form a hypothesis that will lead to a solution of the crime. The team follows routine, and evidence is gathered according to police regulations, but just as Dupin and Holmes are not candid with their associates until the confrontation with the villain is imminent, so Masters often does not share his ideas with his colleagues until they are about to make an arrest. Thus, the solution to the puzzle does not emerge only from employing police methods but usually results from Masters's brilliant insight. Because the Yard team is brought in from outside, Masters often leaves the local officers to make the arrest, which deprives the reader of the traditional confrontation between detective and villain. Although there is no dramatic climax, Masters's explanation to his colleagues provides the denouement. Clark retains the Holmes/Watson partnership between Masters and his second in command, William (Bill) P. Green, but modifies it in the early books by giving the two characters personalities that grate against each other. The subordinate officers do the legwork, perform useful tasks such as fingerprinting and photography, and act as the reader's surrogate in asking questions that elicit needed information and propel the narrative, all the while manifesting admiration for their chief.

The personal lives of the team members develop concurrently with their professional lives and play a greater role in the stories after Masters and Wanda Mace become engaged in *Table d'Hote* (1977). Their cozy domesticity provides a counterpoint to the grim duties of police work. After Green's wife, Doris, is introduced, the Greens play a larger part in George and Wanda's social life, especially following the birth of Masters's son, Michael William. The two couples spend weekends together and even go away on holiday with each other. These informal get-togethers provide Clark with an opportunity to discuss social questions of all kinds from table manners to changing sexual mores and also provide positive models of behavior. The cases supply a framework for discussing ideas on relations between the police and the public, capital punishment, individual accountability, and other aspects of the social contract.

Born on 1 December 1919 to Walter Clark, a regular soldier, and Sarah Annie Fenwick, at Cleethorpes, Humberside, Douglas Malcolm Jackson Clark had three successful careers. He spent his youth in Cleethorpes and received his early schooling at the Humberstone Foundation school, where he qualified for a Higher

*Dust jacket for the U.S. edition of Clark's first novel (1969),
which introduces his series characters, Scotland Yard
inspectors George Masters and William Green
(Bruccoli Clark Layman Archives)*

School Certificate and won several school prizes. He
was studying geology at University College, Nottingham University, in 1939 when World War II broke out.
He joined the Royal Horse Artillery and served in the
Eighth Army with the Desert Rats in the Middle East,
Italy, France, and Germany during the war, attaining
the rank of captain. He remained in the army as a member of the Ninety-fifth Amphibious Warfare Regiment
from 1945 until 1956.

Clark was placed on the list of Regular Army
Reserve officers at the end of June 1956 and was still in
the process of finding employment and settling his
small family into civilian life when he received orders
on 11 August to report to the Royal Artillery Depot at
Woolwich during mobilization related to the Suez War.
The call-up was particularly unwelcome because he was
reluctant to leave his wife, Patricia (they were married
31 October 1952), who was expecting their second
child and was kept busy looking after their two-year-old

son, Roderick. Unexpectedly, a cease-fire was declared
almost immediately after the initial invasion, so Clark
returned from active duty on 28 December, having
spent only a few weeks in Egypt. He was just in time to
take over care of Roderick when his wife delivered
their second son, Richard, on 30 December.

Clark's first book, *Suez Touchdown: A Soldier's Tale*
(1964), recounts his experience during the Suez crisis
and points the way toward the type of detective novel
he later wrote, in which a group of highly trained, disciplined men work cooperatively to solve a problem
under a senior officer who may have been modeled on
Colonel Peter Norcock of the Royal Marine Commandos. Certainly, Clark's description of Norcock's skills
as a commanding officer are reflected in Masters of
Scotland Yard. Clark also draws upon his military
experience through the character of Masters's colleague
Green, who purportedly served in the Gunners during
World War II.

Clark, as a highly experienced forward-observation
officer—an expert in the direction and control of gunfire
from offshore naval ships against beachhead targets—
landed at Port Said in the first assault wave of the Royal
Marine Commandos. His book describes their assembly and training in Malta, the convoy through the Mediterranean, and their meeting with the American Sixth
Fleet as well as the landing at Port Said on 6 November
and subsequent operations at Suez. Clark's narrative is
a warm and lively account of the men and conditions
involved in a carefully plotted military operation as well
as the maneuvers they executed, rather than a clinical
or pedantic record. It reveals the close camaraderie and
cooperation existing between various military units plus
their interaction—both hostile and humanitarian—with
the Egyptians. After the British withdrawal from Suez,
Clark again spent a brief time as a civilian before
returning to the Royal Artillery and serving in Scotland
until 1962.

During the same year that he finally left the army,
Clark joined Sterling Winthrop, a multinational pharmaceutical firm, and stayed for more than twenty
years, first as a promotional copywriter and later as art-design director. During the 1970s Clark tried his hand
at writing adventure novels under the pseudonyms
James Ditton and Peter Hosier. He also created a series
of crime novels—featuring a police team from Scotland
Yard—that directly relied on his wide knowledge of
drugs and their toxic effects on the human body. So he
pursued his second and third careers simultaneously.
Not only did he write fiction but he also wrote radio
dramas. On 1 July 1972 the British Broadcasting Corporation (BBC) aired "The Appointed House" in the
series *Saturday Night Theatre,* and on 24 August 1974
"Late Night Final" was broadcast as part of the BBC

program *Afternoon Theatre*. Clark retired from his business career in 1984, when he reached the age of sixty-five, and published his final crime novel in 1987. An intensely private person, he joined few, if any, professional organizations or private clubs. During his retirement he spent his time enjoying the quiet pleasures of family life and pursuing his hobbies—reading, doing crossword puzzles, and cooking.

Although possessed of extensive knowledge of esoteric drugs and their effects, Clark preferred to use substances that the average reader would be familiar with, such as the castor beans in *Premedicated Murder* (1975), croton seeds in *The Gimmel Flask* (1977), laburnum seeds in *Golden Rain* (1980), and lily of the valley foliage in *Vicious Circle* (1983). By the same token, Clark did not employ nonexistent substances or ones ordinary readers could not find in the reference section of the local library. When working on *Premedicated Murder* he was scrupulous enough to consult a professional technician to verify details for extracting the toxic poison ricin from castor beans but also careful to omit significant facts so that readers could not use his novel as an instructional manual. Clark did resort to manufactured substances in some works, including *Nobody's Perfect* (1969), *Sweet Poison* (1970), *Poacher's Bag* (1980), *Shelf Life* (1982), and *Plain Sailing* (1987).

For professional reasons Clark read most medical journals and kept extensive files; however, he insisted that except for one instance he did not usually begin a book with a conscious decision to use his clippings. In the case of *Dread and Water* (1976) an article on nystagmus—uncontrolled rapid eye movements—published in the journal *Nature* inspired him. In August 1980 the *British Medical Journal* asserted that Clark's whodunits were "acclaimed as much for their medical knowledge as for their detection," and *Pharmaceutical Journal* has commended Clark's accuracy.

From 1969 to 1987 Clark produced twenty-six detective novels featuring a four-man team from Scotland Yard headed by George Masters, who rises from detective chief inspector to chief superintendent during the two decades of the series. William P. Green begins as a detective inspector and is promoted to detective chief inspector on Masters's recommendation in the ninth book, *The Gimmel Flask*. The detective sergeants Hill and Brant are replaced in the same story; Hill is promoted, and Brant moves to a private security firm because he is to be married to a medical doctor with an important job outside of London. Paul Reed becomes Masters's assistant, and Tom Berger is taken on as Green's second. In the final two novels, when Reed is promoted and simultaneously becomes engaged, he is replaced by a female sergeant, Irene (Tip) Tippen, who works with the team briefly in *Dead Letter* (1984).

Initially, Clark carefully develops a tension-fraught working relationship among members of the team based on differences of social class, politics, age, and personality. The interpersonal dynamic does not remain static but evolves as the books progress. In the first novel the team is on its fifth case, so battle lines have already been drawn. Masters does not want "a passed-over old has-been tied to his tail forever," and Green feels that Masters has become "too big for his boots" because he had caught somebody's eye and had been promoted too soon. He also believes that Masters only has an average flair for detection, whereas Masters thinks that Green's highly retentive memory is his only asset. Socially they are at opposite poles: Masters is a well-mannered, educated, cultured man of taste from an upper-class background; Green's working-class origins include minimal schooling and social refinement along with maximum resentment of those more privileged. Their political views are antithetical as well: Masters is conservative, while Green assertively expresses his socialist views in an offensive manner. Another source of friction is the disparity in their ages with resultant generational differences in attitudes and values. Finally, Masters is tall and well built, with long, slim aristocratic hands, as well as expensively and stylishly dressed. Green is short and stocky with stubby hands and invariably wears an unattractive, wrinkled cheap suit. In his pipe, which he carries upright in his breast pocket next to his immaculate silk handkerchief, Masters smokes Warlock Flake from a brass tin with a distinctive black sphinx on the lid. Green's packet of down-market Kensitas cigarettes, which he smokes incessantly, is always crumpled. At the outset Masters is a bachelor living with his doting mother who collects newspaper cuttings about his successful cases, but Green is married. When attracted to a woman, Masters appreciates her physical beauty but also relates to her character; Green regards women as sexual objects and refers to their physical attributes in extremely vulgar language. Both Masters and Green attempt to break up the team, but their superior officers refuse because they have such a high success rate. Their negative energy produces positive results.

This pattern gradually changes as Green becomes less hostile and much more civilized. The tide turns in *Table d'Hote* (1977), when he considers leaving the team but discovers that no other division will have him. In fact, Hill has been selected in preference to him. When Masters offers Green a chance to stay on with him, Green agrees. In this book Green shows unaccustomed sensitivity and consideration toward his colleagues and others. For example, he offers to deal with an awkward witness to spare Masters; furthermore, with a certain amount of self-serving calculation he abandons his

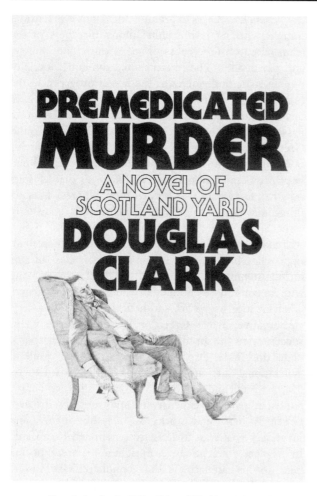

Dust jacket for the U.S. edition of Clark's 1975 novel in which Masters and Green investigate the murder by poisoning of a crippled World War II veteran and civic leader (Bruccoli Clark Layman Archives)

In Green's honor they even choose William as the child's middle name. Green is extremely pleased and makes an inordinate fuss over young Michael William whenever he gets a chance. He and Doris, who are childless, become surrogate grandparents. As time goes by, Green becomes Masters's greatest admirer, bragging that he is "jammy," or lucky. Their working relationship becomes almost symbiotic. After Masters and Green solve the problem in a cryptic dialogue over coffee in *Shelf Life,* they explain to a bewildered constable that this sort of team thinking and understanding only comes with years of working together.

As the old man of the team, in the penultimate novel Green befriends the new female recruit and helps to train her. Following Masters's lead, both Berger and Tip show concern for Green's health in *The Big Grouse* (1986), and Tip tries to "daughter" him. His reformation extends beyond interpersonal relationships to loss of resentment of educated vocabulary and the ability to quote poetry in appropriate circumstances, everything from William Shakespeare to skipping rhymes. He displays heretofore undiscovered reserves of knowledge from homely folklore to science. Although he never loses his intolerance for pomposity and pretentiousness, his working-class taste, and his irreverent, even earthy style of speech, he becomes less "bolshie" and more comfortable with middle-class social life. He displays intense concern for children, and during their final case he is quite sentimental about a stray border collie and gets up early to feed her. This portrait is a far cry from the insensitive, irascible one of the early novels.

Masters also mellows after he marries and becomes a father. His affection for children extends beyond his own son, as seen in his concern for Oliver Holtby in *Doone Walk* (1982). References to his vanity disappear. The final example appears in *Table d'Hote,* when he revels in the attention Wanda attracts as she enters the bar where he meets her: "he knew that together they would catch any eye that still had the power to see and appreciate." He grows more tolerant, and his natural compassion and consideration for others, evident in his concern to alleviate Green's traffic phobia and protect the self-respect of Mrs. Huth in *Nobody's Perfect,* develop further. They surface in his desire to improve the life of the victim's hapless Cinderella daughter in *Death after Evensong* (1969), to spare Sarah Harte the humiliation of arrest in *Premedicated Murder,* to secure a job for Brant so he can marry in *Dread and Water,* and to smooth the entry of young Irene Tippen to the all-male team in *The Big Grouse.*

A locked-room mystery, Clark's first title in the series, *Nobody's Perfect,* is set in a large international pharmaceutical company. Scotland Yard is called in when an admired director of the Barugt Company, Adam Huth,

abrasive manner and treats the chief suspect, Wanda Mace, gently. Masters falls in love with her and proposes marriage, but she does not accept immediately. In the next book, *The Gimmel Flask,* Masters recommends Green for promotion. In an uncomfortable scene Green thanks Masters and offers to buy him a celebratory drink. In this novel Masters and Wanda have become engaged. Green's admiration for Wanda becomes a positive force in changing his attitude toward Masters, whose increased goodwill for Green is expressed in his use of the nickname "Greeny." Their relationship has progressed to the point where Wanda has invited Green and his wife to spend the weekend with her and Masters at her cottage.

From this point on Green and his wife offer a domestic complement to Masters and Wanda. Doris Green and Wanda become good friends, and when the Masters's child is born (in *The Longest Pleasure,* 1981) George and Wanda ask Green to become his godfather.

is found dead at his desk. The divisional surgeon opines that it looks like a case of poisoning from an overdose of barbiturates, but only an empty bottle of nontoxic Nutidal with Huth's prints is found next to the body. The only other physical evidence is a cigar end of an unfamiliar brand in the ashtray, indicating that Huth had a visitor. An interview with the commissionaire convinces Masters that internal security cannot be breached, so he decides that the murder was an inside job and sets the team on tracing the source of the phenobarbitone identified in the autopsy report from internal sources. He also focuses on motive, smoking and brooding rather like Sherlock Holmes with a three-pipe problem: "he sat for two hours considering the people he had met in the last three days and going over carefully in his mind what each one had said, recalling their expressions and their attitudes."

Neither Masters nor Green is presented as an entirely sympathetic character; each has traits that alienate the reader. Although Masters has commendable qualities and few faults, his arrogance is off-putting. "Masters' rating of his own importance when he was on a job was as high as Everest. Failure by others to recognize it usually led to a display of temper." For example, when he is challenged by the commissionaire as he is heading for the VIP elevator upon arriving at the Barugt offices, he says: "I'm a senior police officer. I go where I like, when I like and how I like. Understood?" His vanity is displayed unattractively when en route to the pharmacy department he is conscious that all the typists are watching him closely, and "he felt the egoistic thrill of pleasure that being the centre of attention always gave him." Halfway along the room he stops to use the ashtray of the prettiest secretary and then reflects as he continues on that "he'd made the girl's day by giving her himself to talk about when she got home." Yet, just as he is compassionate regarding Green's phobic traffic fears, Masters is chivalrous with the victim's wife, Mrs. Huth, denying that Huth had a mistress, although he has certain knowledge of it. In addition to bad manners, lack of taste, and general abrasiveness, Green also exhibits meanness of spirit and intense self-promotion. "Green rarely discovered anything of use, but when he did he tried to make the most of it." Furthermore, he frequently jumps to superficial conclusions.

In *Sweet Poison* the villain employs the latest in pharmaceutical technology to commit murder. A young widow, Fay Partridge, and her two poodles die of necrosis of the liver, caused by an unidentified substance. A couple of local doctors, Laurence and Meg Meeth, suggest that Partridge was exposed to a type of poison that acts in two stages: the victim suffers a mild first reaction and recovers for a day or two but then dies after five or six days. Mrs. Partridge had suffered a

severe bilious attack on the previous Friday before her death, so she could have succumbed to second-stage poisoning. Although the solution to the crime is highly technical, Masters and Green solve it principally through interviews. Masters focuses on motive as well as means. Through speaking with Mr. Sprott, one of the guests, who good-heartedly distributes samples of his company's headache medicine, Masters discovers that the product is a time-release paracetamol capsule. Mrs. Partridge's symptoms match those of death from an overdose of paracetamol.

Having identified the means, Masters tries to determine how and when the poison was ingested and focuses on food eaten only by the victim. He realizes that a lethal dose of the particles could be added, without being noticeable, to the icing sugar in the sweets Mrs. Partridge favored. He then sets about discovering where her private supply came from and when she indulged her appetite. In the meanwhile, the team mingles with the guests and staff of the hotel to try to discover motive. The sergeants even don cowboy costumes and dance at a fancy dress party. Suspicion centers at first on the two daughters from Mr. Partridge's first marriage, who will inherit the business. Ultimately, however, Masters traces Sprott's samples to Mr. Compton, the hotel manager, who complained that Mrs. Partridge interfered with his running of the hotel. Compton, an expert sweet maker, confesses missing the friendship of the first Mrs. Partridge and her daughters, who had treated him like one of the family.

In *Deadly Pattern* (1970), set in a small resort community in Lincolnshire in February, the team proceeds from the previous case in *Sweet Poison* without returning to Scotland Yard. The mystery in this book is simple in that the puzzle is finite—locating the common factor in the murders of five women who disappeared within one month and were buried with arms and legs extended in shallow circular graves among the sand dunes near a group of seaside bungalows. The proximity of the graves and position of the bodies suggest some kind of ritual or symbolism. All of the women had broken noses and had died from manual strangulation, but there were none of the usual scratches or bruises on the bodies indicating struggle had taken place and no sign of drugs to render the victims unconscious. The women were all known to each other from school days but were not necessarily good friends as adults. The investigation is based on a series of interviews with the families of the victims, who are requested to make lists of people known by the deceased. These lists are then collated and compared for similarity.

At Masters's request, Green determines the exact sites on a map where the bodies were discovered, which he does by employing artillery surveying techniques learned during his military service. After much consideration Masters realizes that the graves form a perfect cross pointing east–the basic plan of most Christian churches and cathedrals. By following the logic of this design, Masters then determines that the missing body of the fifth woman would be located where the diagonals intersect at the center of the cross, under a bungalow. After the body is recovered, Masters also volunteers to tell the victim's husband: "If I do the bad bits myself, none of my people can call me selfish when I accept the best chair available, or the best bedroom in a pub."

Over drinks the local pathologist reports on the postmortem examination of the latest cadaver, which exhibits the same physical characteristics as the others, and claims the deaths are the work of a madman. Masters borrows the doctor's psychiatry texts to look for behavioral traits discernible in the killer's actions. At the same time, another focus of his investigation is finding an explanation for the broken noses and lack of bruises or lacerations on the victims. Ultimately, he turns up a suspect among the students of a jujitsu instructor, as well as a potential sixth victim from the lists of acquaintances of the murdered women. The woman tells Masters and Green that she alone among a group of teenagers was kind to the suspect when they went to school together. Her remarks support Masters's theory of the culprit's mental state and supply motivation for what is essentially a series of revenge killings. The killer, an architect of cathedrals named Tintern after a well-known English abbey, is an obvious suspect from the beginning of the narrative, which robs the ending of surprise.

Premedicated Murder requires the team to unravel both means and motive for the murder when a man seemingly without an enemy, as in *Nobody's Perfect* and *Sick to Death* (1971), dies in the home of a disagreeable neighbor. The victim is killed with a highly potent poison, ricin, distilled from the residue of castor beans after the oil has been extracted from them. The victim, Roger Harte, was a crippled World War II veteran who made a name for himself devising and creating prosthetic devices for disabled people. Apart from his professional achievements, Harte was a leader who molded opinion in the neighborhood by force of character, never raising his voice. The murder occurred on a Saturday evening in a confined area, a tennis-racquet-shaped close of semidetached houses, while Harte was drinking coffee with his neighbors Milton and Maisie Rencory. From interviewing the neighbors in Lowther Close, Masters and his team learn that Harte was universally beloved and Rencory was universally detested.

Harte and his wife were the only residents in the close who were friendly with the Rencorys.

Green feels at ease with Rencory, whose bad manners and working-class background match his own; moreover, they reminisce about being Gunners during the war. Nevertheless, Green is ready to arrest him when Masters discovers that there are castor beans on the premises of the animal-feed factory that Rencory owns. Rencory seems to have no motive; he admired Harte's courage in dealing with his disability and appreciated his friendship.

Another neighbor of the Hartes gives some of the couple's history: the Hartes were married in 1944 and Sally, an assistant pharmacist during the war, nursed Harte from the time of his initial injuries. Harte was run over by a British tank in August 1944 as he was emerging from a trench in a French farmyard. Based on this information, and after another round of interviews and another search of Harte's house, Masters can confirm his hypothesis and prove means, motive, and opportunity. He reverses the perceived villain/victim relationship between Rencory and Harte. Actually, Harte victimized Rencory through a series of vicious pranks because he realized that Rencory had driven the tank that maimed him for life. Rencory was the intended murder victim; Harte ingested the ricin by accident when using some of Rencory's artificial sweeteners, which Sally Harte had replaced with tablets she had laced with ricin. Masters decides not to leave the arrest of Harte to the local officer because it might impair his relationship with members of the community. When they go to make the arrest in the small hours of the morning, however, Mrs. Harte swallows another ricin tablet and dies. Hill accuses Masters and Green of colluding to allow her plenty of time to do so, and indeed they act with tacit accord that prefigures their future behavior. The team all agree that justice was served in the most merciful manner, but Clark never addresses the immorality of the intended revenge killing.

Green's uncouth manners are revealed throughout the narrative. He sucks his teeth, yawns without covering his mouth, wipes crumbs from his mouth with the back of his hand, and picks a strand of meat from between his front teeth with his fingers. Unjustifiably, he accuses Masters of making facts fit theories while preaching the opposite. Masters is fed up with Green when he objects to working after dinner: "The trouble with Green was that he was always a nuisance, whether for putting obstacles in the way of suggestions, opposing requests, or simply stinking out the inside of the car by sucking cough lozenges." In a confrontation with the local inspector whom Green baits from the outset, Masters is ironically forced to defend Green: "You must forgive Mr. Green. We all have our methods. He has years of success behind him based solely on gaining information from people stung into replying unwisely to his particular brand of abrasiveness."

Masters and Green are introduced to the rivalries and romances at the Pottersby Research Centre, a top-secret government facility, in *Dread and Water*. This time their orders emanate from government offices in Whitehall. They are to investigate whether three nuclear physicists who fell to their deaths while mountain climbing were murdered. All three were experienced mountaineers, who fell in conditions deemed to be well within their competence. Moreover, they were all working within the same unit on the same research problem: how to make small tactical nuclear reactors economically practical. Because the research being done is highly technical and classified, the movements of Masters's team are subject to scrutiny by Chief Security Officer Toinquet, who seems to be unnecessarily officious.

Masters decides to focus on the common factor among the victims, their work in Group 6, while ferreting out personal relationships among the community. There was some dissension among the members of the unit about the best approach to the problem, particularly with respect to the use of deuterium oxide (heavy water). Meanwhile, the sergeants and Green gather information about the organization and practical arrangements of the climbing club plus details of the climbing accidents, which reveals a remarkable number of parallels in the incidents such as drinking from water bottles forty minutes prior to falling. The autopsy reports all include the same types of injuries and same cause of death. The most recent mentions nystagmus from brain damage. Research indicates to Masters that heavy water causes nystagmus and that it probably caused the accidents.

Interviews with remaining members of Group 6 disclose that the group is in disarray from poor management. Those who complained most about the direction of the team's research have been silenced. Masters feels confident he has found ample grounds for motive. A search of the quarters of one of the remaining group members, Dr. Clay, reveals a second water bottle with the numeral 6 on it, which could be substituted at the site for one filled by the climber. Masters explains his case to the director and the head of internal security, Toinquet, and then Green arrests Clay. Green is savage in his treatment of Toinquet and his men throughout the novel, with many rude references to the British pantomime character Widow Twankey. He is also surly and hostile with Masters and his team, but at the end both he and Masters pave the way for Brant to join the security staff at the Centre: Green complains to his

superiors about Toinquet, and Masters recommends Brant in the right quarters.

Table d'Hote occupies a significant place in the series because murder is committed with a benign substance, and because Masters falls in love with the chief suspect and proposes marriage. Once again, Clark applies his extensive knowledge of pharmacology to create an ingenious crime in which a woman taking tranquilizers to combat chronic depression dies of seemingly natural causes in the home of her husband's mistress. When the love triangle is revealed, the local police naturally suspect the victim's hostess of poisoning her, but an autopsy discloses no traces of toxic substances in the body. Because the death seems inexplicable, the dead woman's doctor and the police surgeon refuse to sign a death certificate. In these baffling circumstances Scotland Yard is called in.

The death occurs at Pilgrim's Cottage in a small village called Little Munny on the first night of a visit by Dr. David Bymeres and his wife, Daphne, to her old friend Wanda Mace. From all reports Daphne appeared normal during a small dinner party and ate heartily but excused herself early and went to bed with a headache. Wanda found her dead in a rumpled bed with a pool of vomit congealing by the bedside on Saturday morning.

When Masters and Green interview Wanda, she gives an account of the evening, including the dinner menu. She also admits her intimate relationship with David but claims Daphne knew nothing about it. Not only was their liaison one of convenience, but she and David had been seeing less of each other lately. Both Masters and Green are impressed by her good looks and her manner. Daphne's general practicioner, Dr. Spiller, tells the investigators that she had recently begun taking a form of antidepressant known as monoamine oxide inhibitors (MAOIs). People taking MAOIs must avoid tyramine, an organic compound present in a variety of foods. Every dish on the menu the night of Daphne's death was a tyramine-bearing food.

Having learned the means, the team concludes it unlikely that such a meal was prepared by chance, leaving only Bymeres and Wanda as reasonable suspects. Because Masters is attracted to Wanda, he assigns Green to interview her. Green discovers that the menu duplicated that of a meal Bymeres ordered for lunch on the previous Monday, claiming that the dishes were his favorite foods. Masters himself interrogates Bymeres, who is combative and conceited. He expresses surprise at Daphne's switch to MAOIs, horror at the contents of the menu, and ignorance of Wanda's intention to surprise him with his favorite dishes. Masters remains suspicious of Bymeres, however, because of his attitude of self-satisfaction. Eventually they find the piece of evidence that confirms his plot: a list of proscribed foods

which it was poured onto the victim's food; nor can he find anybody who saw the perpetrator going or coming from the crime scene. So his solution is based on speculation and probability. The means of murder, colorless and tasteless croton oil, was substituted for ordinary salad oil in a double cruet called a gimmel flask. The victim, a middle-aged local councillor and head of an auction house, died after mixing it with vinegar in a tablespoon and sprinkling it on his luncheon salad. The oil is traced to an antique medicine chest of the sort often carried by travelers, which was bought at auction by an elderly collector.

In this novel Green is promoted to detective chief inspector, and Reed joins the team, replacing Hill, while Brant is superseded by Berger. Green is pleased with his new rank and grateful to Masters for recommending him but embarrassed to admit it. The working relationship has changed because they have chosen to remain together, whereas in the past they worked together on sufferance. Green has decided to stay because he found it difficult to find another posting for his final few years, and Masters has agreed to keep Green on the team out of sympathy for his plight. Because they have worked so closely together for so many years, they can almost read each other's minds. Both have striven to cooperate, so the gap between them has narrowed, reflected in the fact that Green now refers to Masters by his first name and Masters calls him "Greeny." Since Masters's engagement to Wanda Mace, they have begun seeing each other socially as well. Green's antisocial behavior does not vanish entirely, but Masters deals with it forthrightly. Instead of ignoring a hostile political jibe from Green, as he might have done in the past, Masters confronts him and Green backs down. Green helps train the new men and supports Masters throughout the investigation. He even acts as peacemaker when the local investigating officer and Masters cross swords, for which Masters thanks him.

In part to smooth relations with the local officers and partly to initiate the new sergeants to the team's methods, Masters focuses a great deal on official police routine. Yet, these methods produce poor results. In the end he posits a theory that is logical but unsupported by evidence. Masters, who is told of a ring of dishonest antique dealers as well as illegal property schemes, then uncovers some records supporting the allegations. Based on a psychological profile of the victim, who cheated his partners and thus provoked his own death, Masters claims that the motives for the murder are revenge and greed. The putative murderer, who supposedly killed his senior partner and framed his junior partner for the crime, never appears as a character and is never confronted. From the reader's viewpoint, Clark

Dust jacket for Clark's 1976 novel, in which Masters and Green hunt for a murderer who uses heavy water to kill scientists at a government research facility (Bruccoli Clark Layman Archives)

for takers of MAOIs, sent by the pharmacist to Daphne but intercepted by Bymeres before she could see it. Bymeres, it is revealed, wanted to get out of his marriage, not because of Wanda but because of another lover, whom he wanted to marry.

After wrapping up the case, when Masters stops at Wanda's cottage to give her the news, he also proposes to her. Wanda replies that her first marriage was a mistake that she does not intend to repeat. In trying to persuade her to marry him, Masters asserts that he has been in exactly the same situation previously, referring to his frustrated pursuit of Joan Parker in *Nobody's Perfect;* however, this time he intends to succeed.

The Gimmel Flask is an unsatisfactory case on several counts, but principally because Masters cannot build a chain of physical evidence to link his primary suspect to the source of the poison or to the flask from

seems more interested in antiques and the antique trade than in constructing a tight puzzle.

In *Poacher's Bag* Masters and Wanda, along with Bill and Doris Green, visit Wanda's mother, Isobel (Bella) Bartholomew, for the weekend. Unbeknownst to them, she has lured them to Winterbourne Cardinal under false pretenses to conduct an informal investigation into the recent death of Haydn Prior, the man she was about to marry, who was shot by a poacher in a nearby wood at 3 A.M. Although the police pathologist attributes the death to a massive heart attack brought on by the panic induced by the gunshot wound, Bella is dissatisfied with the local police inquiry and does not think the poacher should be blamed for her fiancé's death. She raises troubling questions concerning the circumstances of the shooting accident and about the strange erratic behavior of Prior for several days before he died.

In this story Clark returns to a theme familiar from Roger Harte's persecution of Milton Rencory in *Premedicated Murder*. The original goal of the villain in *Poacher's Bag* was not murder, but it ensued accidentally. Bella explains that Prior could not sleep at all for several days before his death and was troubled, even ringing her in the middle of the night complaining of being possessed by the devil. The autopsy reveals the presence of an experimental drug called PCPA (parachloraphenylalanine), which in high doses can cause hallucinations, intermittent blackouts, disorientation, and paranoia. Under its influence, Prior could have startled the poacher into firing at him.

The villain is Harry Gooding, who identifies himself as Prior's natural son and makes claim to Prior's estate. Bella rejects the claim as fraudulent because Haydn told her he had been tested and found infertile during his first marriage. The doctor who performed the tests corroborates this fact, so the team must discover whether Gooding actually believes Prior was his father or whether he is out to defraud the estate. Actually Gooding arranged an elaborate plan to have the PCPA slipped into Prior's food, with the intent of ruining his marriage plans by having him declared non compos mentis so he could claim to be next of kin. Even if Prior had been hospitalized, his rejection of Gooding's claims would have been discounted because of his mental derangement, as long as his infertility was unknown. When arrested, Gooding and Vignal confess in order to avoid a murder charge. Lunn the poacher is released because he cannot be blamed for firing inadvertently, given Prior's erratic behavior.

Nicknamed "The Great Dictator," Wanda's mother is a dominant personality, but she and Green get along well. He is sensitive to her need for discretion about her intended remarriage and sympathizes with her

desire to solve the puzzle of Prior's death. Green blossoms in the comfort of Bella's beautiful home, and Clark indulges his love of cooking as his characters exchange recipes and anecdotes about country life and employ old-fashioned terms unknown to the others. Green reminisces about his mother's cooking, while Bella spoils him by serving his favorite dishes of wood pigeon and jugged hare (provided earlier by the jailed poacher).

In *Golden Rain* Clark uses another familiar poison when Mabel Holland, the headmistress of Bramthorpe, a well-known girls' boarding school, is discovered dead in a pool of vomit among disordered bedclothes by her housekeeper. The pathologist's report establishes the cause of death to be cytisine found in seeds from the laburnum, or golden rain tree. After Masters testifies at an inquest that the death was unlikely to be suicide or an accident, his team investigates the case as a murder. Masters relies principally on police methods rather than intuition to solve the case. Having ascertained that the seeds had to be brought into the premises, he then focuses on opportunity for internal access to the victim's flat from the school and external entry using a key. Masters also attempts to establish motive, although only one person disliked the victim and is candid enough to express hostility—Miss Lickfold, the former deputy headmistress who was gradually relieved of her teaching responsibilities by Miss Holland and moved into the position of bursar.

A search of Holland's kitchen produces evidence of a prank: plaster of paris substituted for corn flour, powdered color paints for paprika and curry powder, and laburnum seeds for peppercorns. Masters infers that Holland dropped the seeds into a food chopper without looking closely while preparing dinner. The prank is eventually traced to some students at the school, but the girls swear they had no laburnum seeds. Ultimately, the culprit is revealed to be Miss Bulmer, a teacher at the school, who found out about the prank and had been looking for an opportunity to poison Miss Holland with the laburnum seeds she had already collected. Masters attributes Bulmer's motive to ambition to become headmistress and bases his arguments on reports of her undermining Lickfold to become deputy headmistress, evidence that she was on the premises, and her strongly hostile attitude toward the police investigation.

The new shared sensitivity between Masters and Green is registered when they interview Miss Lickfold; after she expresses her intense hatred of Miss Holland, they make eye contact and silently get up and leave. Later, attempting to sympathize with the pranksters' parents over their embarrassment and exasperation, Masters announces his own impending parenthood. Green is delighted with the news and rushes to tele-

Dust jacket for the U.S. edition of Clark's 1981 novel, in which a house fire turns out to be part of a man's elaborate scheme to murder his wife and claim her inheritance (Richland County Public Library)

Newly promoted Detective Inspector Hill of the Elmhurst Criminal Investigation Department (CID) conducts the police inquiry and is confident he has an open-and-shut case against James Laurence Connal, husband of the deceased, but things go awry at the trial when Connal makes a good impression on the witness stand and paints a portrait of his wife as a neurotic haunted by guilt and grief over the premature death of their son, whose death has led her to fabricate a charge of his infidelity. The police cannot locate the woman alleged to be his mistress in a poison-pen letter sent to his wife; nor can they find his fingerprints on a supposedly incriminating photograph of a nude woman found by the housekeeper in his jacket pocket. Since she has cut him out of her will and was suing for divorce, he seems to have no material motive to kill her. Moreover, Connal was out of town during the blaze, and no physical evidence can be found proving he set the fire.

Hill's case is dissolving before his eyes, so he consults Masters and Green on an unofficial basis. They deduce that Connal built a fake case of infidelity against himself, expecting to be exonerated in court and simultaneously demonstrating that his wife was unstable and her judgment untrustworthy. He could then contest her will and probably win, thus inheriting the shares in the family business left her by her father, which would have been impossible had their son lived. They also reconstruct the mechanism by which he started the fire using a time switch and demonstrate from the serial-number plate of Connal's typewriter that it could have been used to type the poison-pen letter. When Connal is confronted in court with the typewriter evidence and a model of the apparatus employed to start the fire, he develops hysterical aphasia, the inability to speak, and is taken to hospital. While waiting for a report on Connal's prognosis, the team and the attorneys meet in the judge's chamber for an off-the-record discussion over drinks. Masters, who has been promoted to detective chief superintendent, answers everyone's questions. Be it with military men, police officers, or civilian professionals, this scene, with characters sharing and admiring each other's expertise in an informal atmosphere of camaraderie, is the kind that Clark handles well.

As Clark utilizes his own military experience in *Dead Letter,* Green becomes the main character in an investigation that relies on his technical training as well as his memories of the campaigns in which he fought in World War II. He receives an anonymous letter by a former comrade in arms who is reluctant to identify himself but asks for help because he has witnessed a murder in which a senior policeman has been involved. The team's investigation as to whether the letter is genuine leads Green to his former fellow Gunners, whom he locates through War Office and Retired Army Asso-

phone his wife, having jokingly told Masters that they are both crazy about Wanda and only tolerate him because of her.

Roast Eggs (1981) takes its name from the 1601 essay "Of Wisdom for a Man's Self" by Francis Bacon: "It is the nature of extreme self-lovers, as they will set a house on fire, and it were but to roast their eggs." This statement defines the personality of the murderer, a man of overweening vanity. At first Clark seems to depart from his usual choice of murder weapon because Angela Connal dies in a suspicious fire when her home burns to the ground, but investigation reveals that she had probably been given an antihistamine in warm milk to soothe a sick headache before going to bed for a nap. The fire started while she was in a deep sleep, so she did not awaken. The drug had originally been prescribed for her young son; the victim confided to her lawyer, while consulting him about changing her will and filing for divorce, that she believed her husband had given their son an overdose of the pills, which had caused his death, and that she feared he might kill her.

ciation lists. They must work clandestinely to protect their informant and to avoid alerting the corrupt police officer, if he exists.

As requested by their correspondent, Green inserts a reply in the personal column of *The Daily Telegraph* signed with the name Stinky Miller, Green's gunlayer for a limited time when the battery was in the Mareth Line in Italy. Inquiries disclose that Miller had recently died unexpectedly. After interviewing a succession of fellow veterans, Green is led to the conclusion that the correspondent is Stanley Pearce, a signaler's specialist assistant. When the team goes to the coastal town of Chinemouth to find Pearce, however, they learn that he has also died recently, the victim of a hit-and-run accident. Pearce's sister-in-law, Mary Brunton, confirms that he had been nervous after being out taking photographs at night just prior to Green's receiving the letter and that he anticipated a visit from Green.

The investigation of Miller's and Pearce's suspicious deaths leads the team to uncover drug trafficking and police corruption in Chinemouth, which the two men were killed to hide. Masters and Green even bring their wives in on the covert search for the body at the site described by Pearce in his letter. Masters holds a briefing at his own home and organizes a military-style operation on a strict timetable like those described by Clark in *Suez Touchdown,* including coded radio contact. The team finally closes in on a corrupt detective chief inspector named Shepherd, who kills himself rather than face arrest. In handing out accolades to the team, the assistant commissioner likens Masters and Green to an architect and a mason and asserts that no sound edifice is built without both.

In Clark's last book, *Plain Sailing,* the team returns to the locale featured in *Performance* (1985). Masters and Green are specially requested to investigate by Chief Superintendent Matt Cleveland of the North Eastern Counties Force when his son Jimmy collapses while sailing in a race; cyanide poisoning is diagnosed. Since Masters and Green and their wives are on holiday in the area, they respond quickly when Chief Constable Pedder requests an immediate conference. The sailing club in Cullermouth, which is hosting the weeklong Supranational sailing races, becomes the center of activity. The victim acted as crew on a two-man dinghy whose owner, Harry Martin, was a casual acquaintance. The puzzle to be solved is how the toxic substance was ingested, because the victim neither ate nor drank anything within thirty minutes of setting sail. Cyanide is a fast-acting poison causing death within five minutes, so Jimmy must have taken it at sea. To com-

plicate matters further, there appears to be no motive since Jimmy seems to have no enemies.

Masters and Green do not view the body but go to the crime scene. With so many people moving casually in and around the club, Masters realizes that it will be difficult to identify the villain. He deploys the team, including Doris and Wanda, to mingle and listen to gossip while he learns as much as he can and watches for anomalies. As with other books, Clark furnishes a great deal of background detail about the setting and about sailing. As the team circulates, they learn of professional and personal rivalries among the yachtsmen and their partners. They also discover a great deal of sexual promiscuity and infidelity. Green thinks sexual jealousy is a likely motive, so they investigate Jimmy's relationships with women in the club.

When he discovers that Jimmy was a last-minute replacement for the usual crew member, however, Masters decides that he was killed by mistake and seeks to learn whether the other man has enemies. When they ascertain that he is having an affair with the wife of a yachtsman whose boat is parked next to the one crewed by the victim, they can prove opportunity as well as motive. The retrieval of a rope impregnated with cyanide from Jimmy's boat completes the physical chain of evidence, for Jimmy habitually put the rope in his mouth when lowering sails.

Because this case occurs while the two couples are on holiday, the day-to-day events of the investigation merge with domestic routine and the holiday activities of the sailing club to produce a cheerful atmosphere even though the young son of a close professional colleague has died. In order to resume their vacation as soon as possible, Masters leaves the final arrest to the local police force.

Clark died six years after *Plain Sailing* was published, on 22 February 1993. Because of his concentration on death contrived by a remarkable range of toxic substances, displaying knowledge not only of the agents themselves but also ingenuity in their administration, Douglas Clark occupies a unique position among creators of scientific detectives such as R. Austin Freeman, with his Dr. John Evelyn Thorndyke; Jacques Futrelle, with Professor Augustus S. F. X. Van Dusen; and Arthur B. Reeve, with Dr. Craig Kennedy. Furthermore, Clark molded a Scotland Yard team of compelling personalities who evolve over time in a realistic fashion.

Reference:

"With Crime in Mind: Douglas Clark," *British Medical Journal* (2 August 1980): 378.

Brian Cleeve

(22 November 1921 –   )

Gina Macdonald
Nicholls State University

BOOKS: *The Far Hills* (London: Jarrolds, 1952);

Portrait of My City (London: Jarrolds, 1952);

Birth of a Dark Soul (London: Jarrolds, 1953); republished as *The Night Winds* (Boston: Houghton Mifflin, 1954);

Colonial Policies in Africa (Johannesburg: St. Benedict's House, 1953);

Assignment to Vengeance (London: Hammond, 1961);

Death of a Painted Lady (London: Hammond, 1962; New York: Random House, 1963);

Death of a Wicked Servant (London: Hammond, 1963; New York: Random House, 1964);

Vote X for Treason (London: Collins, 1964; New York: Random House, 1965); republished as *Counterspy* (London: Lancer, 1966);

Dark Blood, Dark Terror (London: Hammond, 1966; New York: Random House, 1966);

The Judas Goat (London: Hammond, 1966); republished as *Vice Isn't Private* (New York: Random House, 1966);

The Horse Thieves of Ballysaggert, and Other Stories (Cork: Mercier, 1966);

Violent Death of a Bitter Englishman (New York: Random House, 1967; London: Corgi, 1969);

Dictionary of Irish Writers, by Cleeve and Anne M. Brady, 3 volumes (Cork: Mercier, 1967–1971); revised as *A Biographical Dictionary of Irish Writers* (Mullingar, U.K.: Lilliput, 1985; New York: St. Martin's Press, 1985);

You Must Never Go Back (New York: Random House, 1968);

Exit from Prague (London: Corgi, 1970); republished as *Escape from Prague* (New York: Pinnacle, 1973);

Cry of Morning (London: Joseph, 1971); republished as *The Triumph of O'Rourke* (Garden City, N.Y.: Doubleday, 1972);

Tread Softly in This Place (London: Cassell, 1972; New York: John Day, 1973);

The Dark Side of the Sun (London: Cassell, 1973);

Brian Cleeve (photograph by Morgan-Wells; from the dust jacket for The Triumph of O'Rourke, *1972)*

A Question of Inheritance (London: Cassell, 1974); republished as *For Love of Crannagh Castle* (New York: Dutton, 1975);

Sara (London: Cassell, 1976; New York: Coward, McCann & Geoghegan, 1976);

Kate (London: Cassell, 1977; New York: Coward, McCann & Geoghegan, 1977);

Judith (London: Cassell, 1978; New York: Coward, McCann & Geoghegan, 1978);

Hester (London: Cassell, 1979; New York: Coward,
    McCann & Geoghegan, 1980);
The House on the Rock (London: Watkins, 1980);
The Seven Mansions (London: Watkins, 1980);
The Fourth Mary (Dublin: Capel, 1982);
1938: A World Vanishing (London: Buchan & Enright,
    1982; New York: State Mutual, 1982);
A View of the Irish (London: Buchan & Enright, 1983;
    Topsfield, Mass.: Salem House, 1985);
A Woman of Fortune (Dingle, U.K.: Brandon, 1993).

OTHER: "Death," *London Mystery Magazine* (September
    1953);
"Vendetta!" *Suspense* (March 1961);
"Angela's Satyr," in *The 8th Annual of the Year's Best Sci-
    ence Fiction,* edited by Judith Merril (New York:
    Simon & Schuster, 1963);
"Foxer," in *Best Detective Stories of the Year,* edited by
    Anthony Boucher (New York: Dutton, 1966);
"The Devil and Jake O'Hara," in *Magazine of Fantasy and
    Science Fiction,* 35, no. 2 (August 1968);
"The Devil Finds Work for Jake O'Hara," *Ellery Queen's
    Mystery Magazine* (December 1969);
W. B. Yeats and the Designing of Ireland's Coinage, edited,
    with an introduction, by Cleeve (Dublin: Dol-
    men, 1972);
"The Devil in Exile," in *Isaac Asimov's Magical Worlds of
    Fantasy 8: Devils,* edited by Asimov, Martin H.
    Greenberg, and Charles G. Waugh (New York:
    New American Library, 1987);
"The Devil and Democracy," in *Great Irish Tales of the
    Unimaginable: Stories of Fantasy and Myth,* edited by
    Peter Haining (London: Souvenir, 1994);
"Mr. Murphy and the Angel," in *Great Irish Tales of Hor-
    ror: A Treasury of Fear,* edited by Haining (London:
    Souvenir, 1995).

Brian Cleeve is one of the best-known modern
Irish writers, having achieved international attention
for his analyses of national and international conflicts
that grow out of personal ambitions, animosities, and
quirks. He draws on his personal experience and
knowledge of South Africa, Ireland, and England to
define and expose in a brutal, straightforward manner
the conflicts, passions, and injustices he sees inherent in
these cultures. Prior to 1980 most of his books were
light entertainment, relying on the conventions of spy,
murder, and Gothic romance novels. His hard-boiled
crime novels, which critics described as frightening and
provocative tales of horror and sadism, combine the
spy, mystery, and adventure genres. As he related in
Twentieth-Century Crime and Mystery Writers (1980), Cleeve
finds crime thrillers appealing because, like fairy tales
and myths, they directly confront the battle of good

and evil and "touch the most fundamental levels of
human experience." Since 1980, to deal with serious
questions in a new, more effective way, Cleeve has
turned to a format he calls "mystical" or "metaphysi-
cal," because it delves into the heart of philosophical
questions about human purpose, the function of evil
and suffering, the possibility of discovering God, and
what he calls the inexplicable cruelty of traditional religion to women.

Born in Thorpe Bay, Essex, on 22 November
1921, the son of a businessman, Charles Edward
Cleeve, and his wife, Josephine née Talbot, Brian Talbot Cleeve attended Selwyn House in Broadstairs,
Kent, from 1930 to 1935 and St. Edward's School,
Oxford, from 1935 to 1938, before joining the war
effort by entering the British merchant navy. He began
writing novels for personal amusement while on watch.
After demobilization in 1945 he married Veronica
McAdie, a business director, on 24 September 1945,
and they had two daughters, Berenice and Tanga. In
1948 he began working as a freelance journalist in
Africa and continued to do so to pay his way through
school. He began classes at the University of South
Africa in Pretoria in 1951.

While working on his degree he published his
first short story, "Death," in *London Mystery Magazine* in
1953 and three novels, each about South Africa: *The Far
Hills* (1952), *Portrait of My City* (1952), and *Birth of a Dark
Soul* (1953; published in the United States as *The Night
Winds,* 1954). His first efforts are somewhat traditional
tales of rape, murder, and robbery, involving a "murder time clock" or a detailing of motives, but they fore-
shadow his later themes in their exposure of man's dark
soul—the hypocrisies, promiscuities, foibles, and sadism
that lead respected citizens to let the innocent suffer to
hide personal acts and motives. *Birth of a Dark Soul* is
ostensibly a crime novel about the scheme of a "colored" criminal gang to rob a wealthy white European
during a large party given at his home; it is really about
the abuses and injustices of apartheid, however,
revealed through the fears of light-skinned "coloreds"
who pass for white, only to be trapped by their past. A
young girl becomes the mistress of a white employer in
hopes of escape, but, when her brother and friends
break into his safe, her experiences with police brutality
make her realize that breaking the color barrier is
another illusion. Yet, the book ends hopefully as the
most violent and murderous of the burglary gang
rejects his past of thieving, killing, and "dog-eat-dog
preying on his own kind" that apartheid encourages
and sets out "on the night wind" to find hope in his
rural roots: "For a timeless moment he felt Africa in his
soul, felt his kinship with the land and its thousand
sleeping nations. But they would wake, and he would

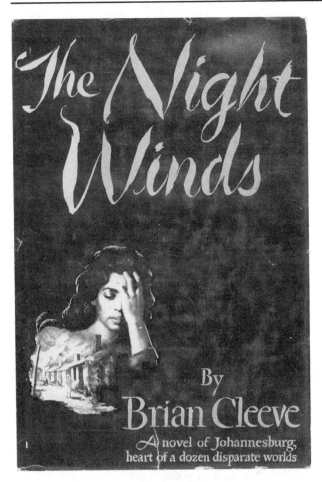

*Dust jacket for the retitled U.S. edition of Cleeve's 1953
novel,* Birth of a Dark Soul, *in which a light-skinned
African woman is caught between her European lover
and the criminal gang that wants to rob him
(Bruccoli Clark Layman Archives)*

be with them in their wakening, and his love flowed out
to them across the sleeping land."

Cleeve completed his B.A. in 1953 and then
worked for one more year as a journalist in South
Africa, finishing up *Colonial Policies in Africa* (1953) before
moving on to Ireland early in 1955. Continuing his
education, he received his Ph.D. from the National University of Ireland, Dublin, in 1956 and did freelance
work as a journalist. In the 1960s he published short
stories and articles and continued to write novels such
as *Assignment to Vengeance* (1961), *Death of a Painted Lady*
(1962), and *Death of a Wicked Servant* (1963). These novels are set in Ireland, with Irish themes and social criticism bound up in crime plots. In *Death of a Painted Lady,*
for example, the rape and murder of an artist's model
leads to the conviction of an innocent man and a bitter
exposé of the Dublin art world, a world of promiscuity,
drunkenness, and sadism, in which everyone, from
tramp to art critic, is hypocritical and warped.

Between 1963 and 1972 Cleeve was a broadcaster
for Radio Telefís Éireann in Dublin. During this time he
continued to write short stories (some of which are collected in *The Horse Thieves of Ballysaggert, and Other Stories,*
1966). He also turned to a new genre, the spy story, and
produced a series of novels following the violent and varied career of Sean Ryan, a paroled Irish terrorist, a self-
styled revolutionary—explosive, embittered, and hardened
into cynical survivor by his years in prison. Ryan
begins his career in *Vote X for Treason* (1964). Rescued
from prison by one of the better representatives of an
elite British intelligence organization anxious to exploit
his special skills, Ryan renews within himself the moral
values that led him to fight for the Irish cause, values
that his new superiors find disturbing because they lead
him on private vendettas sometimes at odds with his
assignments. The nature of his recruitment, his past life,
and his cultural heritage keep Ryan an outsider, a loner
whose successes win approval but never true acceptance.
In *Vote X for Treason* he spies on a new "anti-fascist," right-
wing party that threatens Irish and English security.
Pursuit of these plausible, menacing fascists traps Ryan
in a crossfire between conflicting British agencies. Intricate, unexpected turns of plot, a tragic sensibility, and
what *The New York Times Book Review* critic Anthony
Boucher, in his 20 November 1966 review, called "heroism and death cheapened into the base coinage of politics," lend this novel force.

As the series progresses Ryan experiences guilt
for past wrongs and betrayals, self-doubt about his identity and his work, and Sisyphean despair at battling
forces he can never fully overcome. Nonetheless, he
endures, personally opposing large-scale operations that
threaten British security; infiltrating the opposition;
exacting and savoring pitiless revenge for personal and
state wrongs; protecting weak, dependent, victimized
females from rape, torture, and death; and countering
the enemies' use of hallucinogens, electroshock, castra-
tion, and even crucifixion with ingenious uses of the
readily available—such as boiling coffee, gasoline, a
plank, or a nail—or his own skills at physical combat.
Ryan may be a tortured soul, fearful of personal injury,
but his natural instincts transform him into an avenging
angel who routs diabolical schemers. These villains
include the repressive, power-hungry lords and members of Parliament of *Vote X for Treason,* who direct the
hatreds of Iraqi militants and English teddy boys to produce violence, chaos, and the overthrow of the liberal
government. Likewise, in *Dark Blood, Dark Terror* (1966)
Ryan undermines an Afrikaner lieutenant and his special-
branch task force, who plan to assassinate the South
African prime minister and to blame the British for
their deed. They terrorize a Jewish liberal fund-raiser
and his African mistress, who are privy to their plan.

Dark Blood, Dark Terror moves from London slums to a Swiss insane asylum, but at its heart is South Africa and Ryan's struggle between forbidden love for a mixed-race mistress and his duty to British intelligence. Assigned by a South African agency to track liberation movement fund-raisers, Ryan uncovers plots and counter-plots involving black African racists, South African white supremacists, and multiracial communists vying for power.

Throughout the Ryan series Cleeve's villains are bigots, chauvinists, and hypocrites, obsessed with power, acting out age-old prejudices in the name of enlightenment and progress, and indifferent to the plights of others. Sadists who delight in torture and in inflicting pain, they abuse the weak, the helpless, and the disenfranchised. The moody, indestructible Ryan returns injury for injury as a spontaneous natural reaction to bullies. When reason proves futile, he beats sense into recalcitrant opponents. He may question the justice of the system for which he works, but he has no doubts about the villainy he fights. In *The Judas Goat* (1966), a study of horror and sadism, Ryan battles the British Mafia and killers from his own side as he first arranges the prison escape of a convicted murderer with explosive knowledge of the home secretary's perverted sexual vices and then leads a wild chase to Belgium and home again in pursuit of villainy amid his superiors. Thus, the home secretary's secret propensities lead to public murder and mayhem.

In *Violent Death of a Bitter Englishman* (1967) power politics force Ryan's trusted superior into early retirement, but, suspecting foul play, he unofficially assigns Ryan to discover whether the death of Olaf Redwin was suicide or murder—an assignment that uncovers violence, betrayal, and treachery. Ryan battles fascistic "superpatriots" plotting to enact their own "Kristallnacht" to expel or kill English "coloreds"—a catch-all term including Asians, Indians, and mixed-race Africans. Cleeve's suspense and spy thrillers communicate a vivid sense of time and place and a perceptive understanding of diverse characters. Although often relegated to the "slug-and-slay" school of espionage because of their violent action, like the spy stories of Len Deighton they are subtle and reflect a complex moral view. Without exception their underlying messages are more significant than is typical in this genre. They demonstrate the crippling force of taboos and social stratification based on race, religion, and class; they suggest the primitive heritage behind modern civilization; and despite their portrayal of destruction and despair, they find hope in people's common humanity and in the fact of survival that leaves open opportunities for reconstruction.

At this stage of his career Cleeve began work on a three-volume reference encyclopedia, *Dictionary of Irish Writers* (1967–1971), which he co-authored with Anne M. Brady. The work is an exemplary set of scholarly books covering 1,500 years of Irish literature and 1,800 authors writing in English, Irish, and Latin, from St. Patrick to the present. It includes interesting lore and objective evaluations and faces Irish questions directly and uncompromisingly. While working on this project Cleeve continued to produce exciting thrillers in which racism and class conflicts are bitter spurs to violence and treason.

In *You Must Never Go Back* (1968), as in the works that proceeded it, Cleeve's view of human nature is cynical and resigned. In the novel a young man returns fifteen years later to the scene of his parents' unsolved murders and becomes tangled in a web of Italian intrigue, vengeance, and murder that spans generations. Reliving the childhood terror of a peaceful camping trip that turned into a massacre and his desperate flight through dark mountain forests, his dying mother's cries still ringing in his ears, he tracks his parents' murderers. Youthful dreams of easy revenge prove false, however, and reality complex. Those he pursues were his father's confederates in a scheme to steal booty from Benito Mussolini, and their motive for past murder leads to present pursuit. In *Exit from Prague* (1970; published in the United States as *Escape from Prague*, 1973) a television reporter is caught up in Orwellian nightmares: a repressive society that tortures Jews, that plots with black South Africans to replace one tyranny with another, and that aims to destroy individuality and the human will to resist.

Work on *Dictionary of Irish Writers* led Cleeve to turn to Ireland as a source for further stories. His Irish novels dramatize the varied contradictions and self-destructive extremes he sees in the Irish character, contradictions that make men fear plots everywhere, that encourage frustrated teenagers to play commando and impoverished gentry to destroy their heritage. Cleeve captures the ironies of Irish life—Irish Republican Army sympathizers playing into the hands of the non-Irish capitalist developers they oppose, as in *Cry of Morning* (1971; published in the United States as *The Triumph of O'Rourke*, 1972) and *A Question of Inheritance* (1974; published in the United States as *For Love of Crannagh Castle*, 1975); xenophobes playing pranks that their neighbors interpret as symptoms of international communism, as in *Tread Softly in This Place* (1972); rigid Catholics inciting drunkenness, lechery, violence, and hatred. Cleeve portrays Irishmen, united in distrust of outsiders but also torn by distrust of each other and engaging in meaningless acts born of outrage. He has a good ear for Irish dialogue, and his plots are ingeniously manipu-

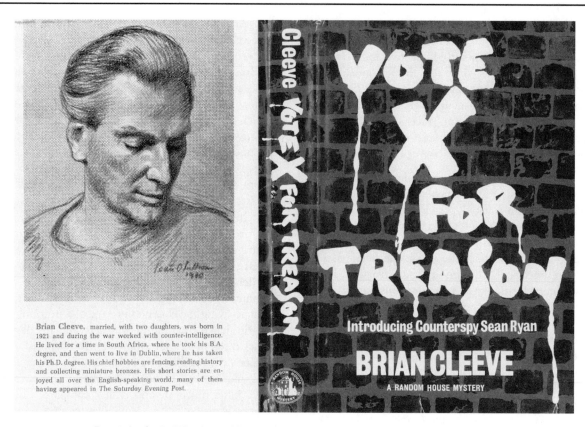

*Dust jacket for the U.S. edition of Cleeve's 1964 novel, the first to feature Sean Ryan, a reformed
terrorist turned British intelligence agent (Bruccoli Clark Layman Archives)*

lated. At their best his Irish works are novels of manners. As such, they capture shifting Irish scenes, interweaving themes and subplots interspersed with social commentary and drawing a variety of vivid character portraits from fanatical communist and radical priest to itinerant tinker, posing artist, real estate tycoon, television commentator, or even small-town girl made good. *Cry of Morning*, in particular, was called–by R. J. Thompson in *Best Sellers* (15 April 1972)–"one of the best recent novels in modern Ireland," partly because it renders the metamorphosis of the country from a nineteenth-century holdover to a modern, economically important nation and partly because it questions the values that place country above citizens. Cleeve also edited the scholarly study *W. B. Yeats and the Designing of Ireland's Coinage* (1972).

The *Dark Side of the Sun* (1973) brings together Cleeve's Irish and African interests. An Irish speculator invests goodwill and know-how in an African state only to discover he is playing with human lives. After barely surviving his time in Africa, his only possessions a plastic bucket holding his manuscript and a cheap nylon suit (compliments of the embassy), he finds that he has also been toying with his black African daughter's life and must give her the freedom she has never had. His

story is told through the diary the man keeps while in prison, his letters to and from old friends, and his reminiscences as he surveys his life and ancestral heritage to determine, after so thorough a failure and decline, whether his life is worth continuing. When the Irishman's sister rejects his impassioned plea to help him escape the tortures of imprisonment in Africa and to care for his helpless daughter, her excuses for evading her moral and sororal obligations are that he must be exaggerating and that it would be too embarrassing to have to deal with his mixed-blood daughter socially. Later she and her stingy husband refuse to honor a small bequest of property made by her father to a faithful employee, a bequest that means security for the man's old age and little loss to them. Such depictions of moral blindness are central to Cleeve's canon.

From 1976 to 1979 Cleeve wrote four novels–*Sara* (1976), *Kate* (1977), *Judith* (1978), and *Hester* (1979)–for Regency, a publisher of romance novels. In keeping with the conventions of the genre he focused on female characters instead of male and thus added a new twist to his previous concerns: women as victims of fate, bound by social conventions and oppressed by brutal males but finding purpose and strength to overcome victimization. Like Cleeve's mysteries, these novels link poverty to crime and power to abuse, so the criminal underworld is a significant feature. They are Dickensian in their exposure of nineteenth-century abuses and the snares and seductions of London of the time. They provide vivid images of initially defenseless young people trapped economically, psychologically, and physically—locked away in private homes, in prisons, and in insane asylums. They explore the evil that Cleeve finds inherent in class differences, as powerful, ruthless villains take advantage of the poverty, naïveté, and vulnerability of Cleeve's heroines.

The women's battle is to liberate themselves and those who depend on them from the strictures of a hypocritical society and to overcome cruelty, prejudice, and greed. As with Cleeve's spy and mystery heroes, these women must learn to trust instinct, to reassess old values, and to seize their own destiny. In *Sara* the titular heroine's parents are slaughtered by Napoleon Bonaparte's soldiers, and she slaves in a disreputable gambling house. In *Kate* the female protagonist is the sole survivor of a political massacre who helps London "Upright Men" promote smuggling. Judith, in the novel of the same name, is pressured by an ill father and financial necessity to consort with smugglers and chooses the terrors of poverty and the infamous Bedlam asylum over a loveless marriage to a rich pervert, while the heroine of *Hester,* stunned by the injustices of the French Revolution, chooses principle over necessity, takes to the road, and learns to face discomfort and possible death with strength. At the end of *Sara* the heroine, an orphan herself, takes in other orphans, an act some reject as mad, but she argues, "When you see a child cold and hungry and naked and afraid, it is quite a natural thing to wish to take care of it." Her humane act is at odds with the deeds of most Cleeve characters, who kill, maim, and persecute without remorse. Cleeve values passion, pride, resourcefulness, and daring, regardless of sex, for he believes such qualities help human beings rise above chains of gender, race, and economics and find personal meaning, purpose, and strength. Cleeve equates the abuse of women with the same limited and twisted mentality at work in his vivid portraits of South African racism.

By his account, in 1977 Cleeve underwent a series of strange psychic and spiritual experiences that led him to rejoin the Catholic Church after a twenty-three-year absence and to write biblical stories that he attributes to divine inspiration. Cleeve's controversial religious studies, best-sellers in Ireland, tell the stories of people who lived in Jerusalem at the time of Jesus' Crucifixion: "to convey a particular spiritual view and description of this world and the next that is clearly linked to Catholic doctrine, even if the presentation is unorthodox, and even if some of the details may seem

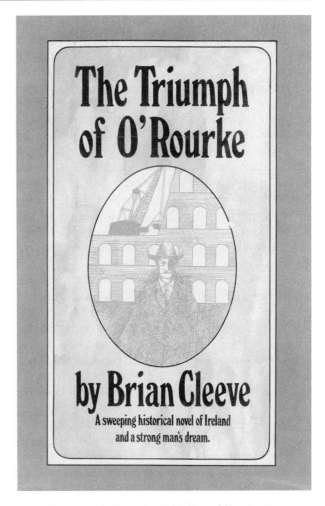

Dust jacket for the retitled U.S. edition of Cleeve's 1971 novel, Cry of Morning, *about Irish Republican Army sympathizers (Richland County Public Library)*

at first reading to be in conflict with details of Church teaching," as he put it in the introduction to *The Fourth Mary* (1982). *The House on the Rock* (1980) and *The Seven Mansions* (1980) provide the historical background preparatory to the Crucifixion. *The Fourth Mary* has a striking point of view. It tells of the Crucifixion as a murder story seen through the eyes of Jesus' enemies, particularly a servant girl who is attached to the high priestess of a sadomasochistic cult. She is Judas's lover and considers the Crucifixion a triumph for her sect. Despite their religious focus, the books in this series graphically portray the criminal mind at work plotting the malicious destruction of good, as well as the hatred, sadism, and sexuality of characters caught up in events of historical moment.

1938: A World Vanishing (1982) examines modern historical events in a personalized way, just as *A View of the Irish* (1983) provides Cleeve's personal views as an Anglo-Irish Catholic convert, as a Dubliner with strong emotional ties, but also as an outsider. Its examination of Irish history, literature, society, and politics is tart and witty, laced with jokes, anecdotes, and tongue-in-cheek analyses. Cleeve attacks Irish alcoholism, "visual" illiteracy, self-advertising, and unfair treatment of women but sees himself as sharing in the faults and charms of the paradoxical land of his heritage. *A Woman of Fortune* (1993), a feminist-style novel about Margaret Gurney, a Dublin shopkeeper, provides a vivid image of Dublin life from the 1920s to the 1950s, with a focus on the strong Irish puritanical streak; it is a close psychological study of a woman obsessed with making money to provide a security society denies her. Cleeve has continued to explore Irish themes in stories such as "Mr. Murphy and the Angel," published in *Great Irish Tales of Horror: A Treasury of Fear* (1995).

Throughout his canon Cleeve captures the nuances of street slang and dialect, includes highly sensory, detailed descriptions of place, and enters the minds of minorities to give readers convincing images of their doubts and fears, shame and animosity and to make their choices understandable. His main characters are alienated from each other and from their world, absurdist figures who are out of place and out of step in a sinister universe. They puzzle over what certainties are left in a world gone mad and feel guilty about mistakes that cannot be paid for. At times they seem carried helplessly, blindly forward, sometimes toward disaster, sometimes toward unlooked-for success. They question the nature of honor and require a human touchstone to maintain their sense of perspective. They sometimes feel that nothing matters, but a sense of responsibility for the weak, the injured, and the vulnerable compels them to action. Cleeve's historical works are accurate and credible; his modern ones vividly reflect an interplay of culture and values. Cleeve opposes philosophies and values to expose the reality behind the masks and takes a moral stance against political and social oppression and inhumanity in its varied forms. His images of human cruelties, whether in czarist or Marxist Russia, colonial Africa, Nazi Germany, a divided Ireland, or nineteenth-century France and England, are indelibly graphic and realistic. He demonstrates how the best of motives can produce the worst of effects and contemplates the thin curtain between civ-

ilized man and darkness: "the Ice Age . . . waiting . . . behind the mask," as he puts it in *The Dark Side of the Sun*. He faces pain and human misery directly and makes vivid the shivers of a malaria attack and the pangs of chronic dysentery. What Cleeve portrays most conclusively is that political ideologies change, but any system that violates the dignity and the freedom of the individual returns to the animal savagery of the not-too-distant origins of the human species and must be fought for humanity and civilization to endure.

Cleeve's omniscient narrative voice, employed throughout his works, heightens the sense of a complex clash of philosophies, for the narrator enters the minds of key characters and records their perceptions, values, and motivations. His narratives include exchanged letters, reminiscences of bygone times, and synopses of attitudes and worldviews. Such multiple perspectives make it difficult for readers to judge characters or acts in clear-cut moral terms and instead impose moral shades of gray requiring care and understanding and imparting a sense of shared human weakness but also shared responsibility. There are no comic-book heroes and villains, only vulnerable human beings whose motivations are mixed and whose results sometimes differ greatly from motive and wish. Cleeve's imagery reflects such attitudes: images of helplessness, blindness, human degradation, night, chaos, and bestial powers. Oppression transforms the human to the less than human.

Brian Cleeve brings a social conscience to genres traditionally concerned with intrigue, detection, adventure, and romance. His goal is to shock readers into rethinking issues vital to their future but seemingly outside their daily lives: questions of social justice, national character, and personal responsibility. He is especially powerful at presenting the excuses that ordinary men and women invent to avoid involvement and to deny the realities of the suffering and the oppressed. His religious books reverse his early pattern, bringing the conventions of detective fiction—its violence, betrayals, guilt, and murder—to an historical, religious topic.

Papers:
A collection of Brian Cleeve's manuscripts is at the Mugar Memorial Library, Boston University.

Liza Cody

(11 April 1944 –   )

Anna Wilson
Birmingham University

BOOKS: *Dupe* (London: Collins, 1980; New York: Scribners, 1981);

Bad Company (London: Collins, 1982; New York: Scribners, 1982);

Stalker (London: Collins, 1984; New York: Scribners, 1984);

Head Case (London: Collins, 1985; New York: Scribners, 1986);

Under Contract (London: Collins, 1986; New York: Scribners, 1987);

Rift (London: Collins, 1988; New York: Scribners, 1988);

Backhand (London: Chatto & Windus, 1991; New York: Doubleday, 1992);

Bucket Nut (London: Chatto & Windus, 1992; New York: Doubleday, 1993);

Monkey Wrench (London: Chatto & Windus, 1994; New York: Mysterious Press, 1994);

Musclebound (London: Bloomsbury, 1997; New York: Mysterious Press, 1997);

Gimme More (London: Bloomsbury, 2000).

OTHER: *1st Culprit: An Annual of Crime Stories,* edited by Cody and Michael Z. Lewin (London: Chatto & Windus, 1992); republished as *1st Culprit: A Crime Writers' Association Annual* (New York: St. Martin's Press, 1993)–includes Cody's "In Those Days";

2nd Culprit: An Annual of Crime Stories, edited by Cody and Lewin (London: Chatto & Windus, 1993); republished as *2nd Culprit: A Crime Writers' Association Annual* (New York: St. Martin's Press, 1994)–includes Cody's "Where's Stacey?";

3rd Culprit: An Annual of Crime Stories, edited by Cody, Lewin, and Peter Lovesey (London: Chatto & Windus, 1994); republished as *2nd Culprit: A Crime Writers' Association Annual* (New York: St. Martin's Press, 1995).

Liza Cody is an innovative producer of feminist detective fiction and novels of suspense. While the majority of feminist revisions of the hard-boiled genre

Liza Cody (photograph © 1988 by Kate Butler; from the 1993 U.S. edition of Bucket Nut, *1992)*

locate their private investigators on American mean streets and endow their wisecracking women with guns and violent tendencies, Cody's British serial detective moves more tentatively through the murk of London. Like her American contemporaries, however, Cody uses the detective genre to question and destabilize gender boundaries; her feminist approach to problems of knowledge and authority threaten the institutional and intellectual certainties that crime fiction could once be counted on to reproduce. Cody's detective mysteries are notable for their refusal to provide the reader with neat solutions and closures: investigation may lead to understanding, but it rarely leads to the administration of justice or punishment. A second series of novels, beginning with *Bucket Nut* (1992), marks a further development in Cody's work away from either detective or feminist convention. Featuring an unreliable narrator who has the physical prowess and determination, but none of the mental agility or social skills, of the feminist private eye, these suspense stories focus on a view from below, animating the consciousness of a representative of a marginal underclass.

Cody was born Liza Nassim on 11 April 1944 and grew up in London, where she studied painting and graphic art at the City and Guilds of London Art School and at the Royal Academy School of Art. She worked as a painter and in related fields, including photography, graphic design, and as a studio technician at Madame Tussaud's wax museum before publishing her first novel, *Dupe* (1980), which won the British Crime Writers' Association John Creasey Memorial Award for best first crime novel in 1980. Cody's work has met with continued critical and popular acclaim. *Bucket Nut* won the Crime Writers' Association Silver Dagger Award in 1992, and in 1993 London Weekend Television produced *Anna Lee,* a series of dramas based on Cody's detective.

Although Anna Lee, the detective introduced in *Dupe*, is a private investigator, she is not a lone operator in the heroic mold cast for Philip Marlowe by Raymond Chandler but rather the most junior employee of a small firm. She remains in this position, prey to her employer's patriarchal condescension and her colleagues' routine sexism, through subsequent additions to the series until in *Backhand* (1991), the last of the Lee novels, she finally achieves an office of her own. This small rise in status and material success, signaled, with Cody's typical attention to tellingly precise detail, by the gradual improvement in the cars she drives from rusted heap to faintly sporty subcompact, leads neither to greater freedom nor greater happiness. Where in *Dupe* Lee chafes under her assignment to the most unchallenging cases of "missing minors," *Backhand* finds her as deeply buried in routine, feeling herself to have become only an effective saleswoman for security devices. This sense of entrapment, both personal and institutional, defines Cody's take on the feminist detective. Rather than fulfilling a fantasy of female empowerment, Lee's agency is consistently limited by events beyond her control; despite her commitment to a philosophy of "self-determination," she is more often defeated by events than their triumphant manipulator. *Bad Company* (1982) makes this predicament literal: Lee is kidnapped by mistake early in the text and spends the bulk of the novel locked in a dank basement, unable to free herself or her fellow victim and awaiting rescue at the hands of her male colleagues. In a striking departure from feminist convention, Cody gives her heroine

both professional skills and feminist practice—the ability to pick locks and talk back—but neither prove effective against brute male strength.

In *Stalker* (1984) the challenge to the detective's competence comes from her having to follow leads on a missing person to bleak moorland country, where horse-handling skills would be more useful than her urban street smarts. In this novel the involvement of the police in protecting informers, as well as the power of drug cartels, prevent Lee from putting the information she acquires to use in pursuing criminals. Knowledge is not power; in fact, knowledge and successful investigation lead only to a more acute sense of powerlessness and futility. Cody shows the individual, however resourceful, as having little autonomy or influence.

Head Case (1985) is the most tightly plotted of the Lee mysteries, offering some of the elements of the more traditional detective story: Lee's search for a missing teenager leads her to the mystery of an unidentified corpse in a hotel room; when the teenager becomes a suspect in the murder, Lee must protect her by unraveling a complex mesh of false identities, lying witnesses, and overlapping deceits. Key feminist concerns emerge in the treatment of the missing girl, who has been sexually exploited by her tutor and possibly by her father (an element made explicit and focal in the less-than-faithful television adaptation of this novel), as well as in Lee's own awareness of and vulnerability to male predation. While Cody abundantly portrays the systemic victimization of women in this story and other novels, she also frequently examines women's capacity for villainy. In *Head Case* a suburban adulteress will go to any lengths to keep up appearances, while in *Under Contract* (1986) the lesbian lover of the woman whom Lee is paid to protect turns out to be the instrument of her father's violent extortion.

Under Contract revisits and enlarges upon the themes of constraint and lack of agency laid down in earlier novels in the series. Lee's embattled status as the lone female investigator in a male world is exacerbated by her temporary transfer as a bodyguard to a much larger, still more male-dominated, firm, where her competence is constantly questioned. Unable to persuade her new employers to take her fears seriously, she cannot prevent her charge from being attacked and disfigured, nor can she pursue further the various betrayals and duplicities that she uncovers.

Lee inhabits the hard-boiled detective's corrupt world in which, classically, no one but oneself is to be trusted. True to this tradition, her clients are often not who they appear to be, those in both *Stalker* and *Backhand* using Lee in hopes of murdering the missing person she is set to find. Like other feminist detectives, however, Lee forges alliances and relationships that provide a fragile community and comfort. Estranged from her family of origin (in several novels, a letter from her respectable, bourgeois sister remains unopened), Lee finds alternatives in her neighbors, who provide protection and solace in return for her manly competence in mechanical matters.

As *Backhand* opens, Lee seems as constrained as ever by her circumstances but also in danger of losing this community because the house in which she and her neighbors live has been sold. As the narrative develops, Lee escapes on assignment to the United States, which briefly seems to offer both new personal and narrative opportunities: in the denouement of the novel Lee confronts her devious client, an act of aggression apparently enabled by the shift of the action to Florida, where the private investigators wear guns and mob hits are an everyday fear. Yet, the results of such self-assertion are equivocal: if Lee and the reader acquire knowledge, it is at a price—the cost of the client's disabling stroke, probably brought on by the stress of Lee's interrogation, while no justice or restitution results. In the fulfillment of an anxiety that has haunted every earlier case, Lee loses her job as well as her home at the end of the novel, providing an open and uneasy finale to the last case in the series. Cody consistently refuses the neatness that the detective fiction formula used to require, producing endings that leave not resolution but rather what Glenwood Irons and Joan Worthing Roberts identify in *Backhand* as a "Cody trademark," "preferring to leave Anna with a sense of emptiness at the desperate future faced by her clients and even by herself."

The revision of both generic and gender boundaries in feminist detective fiction focuses attention on the detective's own sexuality, as well as on the behaviors she observes in others. Lee, although described by Irons and Roberts as an updated version of Agatha Christie's spinster detective Miss Marple, differs from this precursor in being active in pursuit of sexual amusement. Following a male model of sexual desire, Lee's only difficulty comes from her need to avoid emotional intimacy and commitment; like hard-boiled heroes before her, she leaves partners with relief and without regret.

Lee's sexual autonomy is one aspect of her character that lines her up closely with detectives created by contemporary American authors. Cody also endows Lee with the hard-boiled investigator's wit and verbal power, but, lacking the lone operator's sense of himself as a knightly avenger, she routinely silences herself in contests with employers and colleagues. Lee's capacity for absorbing violent assault without ill effects, as well as for retaliating in kind, is also well below the generic norm; although she can defend herself against minor assaults, she never wins a fight against serious opposi-

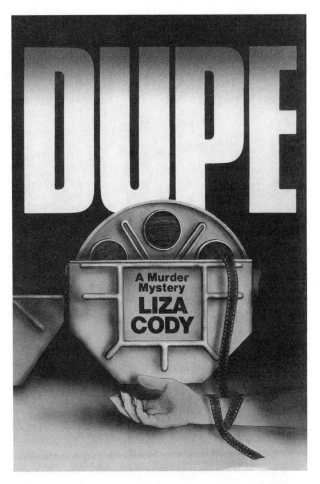

Dust jacket for the 1981 U.S. edition of Cody's first novel (1980), which introduces her series character, private detective Anna Lee (Richland County Public Library)

tion. In general, Cody's detective operates in a world much closer to realism and further from fantasy than other hard-boiled characters, and despite her allegiance to a code of self-reliance, her observations of that world have an edge of fatalism in the face of immovable circumstance. While Sally Munt's *Murder by the Book? Feminism and the Crime Novel* (1994) describes this atmosphere of constraint and the focus on "mundane problems" as "indefinably British," Kathleen Gregory Klein argues in *The Woman Detective: Gender and Genre* (1988) that by writing a character who is "one of a long line of women detectives who have been portrayed as less able or less complete than their male counterparts, Cody . . . undercuts her own efforts to revise the genre."

Rift, published in 1988 at a time of hiatus in the Lee series, represents Cody's first departure into suspense fiction. Set in the 1970s, the novel chronicles a young woman's geographical and psychological journey of discovery on a trip through Ethiopia. Although the narrative provides the pleasures of a thriller, as the naive heroine negotiates the dangers of a strange coun-

*Dust jacket for the 1993 U.S. edition of Cody's 1992 novel, the
first to feature security guard, part-time wrestler, and petty
criminal Eva Wylie (Richland County Public Library)*

try in the midst of a civil war, Cody's primary concern
is with the narrator's interior struggle. To survive, she
must learn not only whom to trust but also, in encounters with the insuperable otherness of lives constructed
by different circumstances and experiences, how to
develop and protect her own independent identity.

The series of three novels beginning with *Bucket
Nut* develops Cody's interest in class, female identity,
and the individual's battle against social constraints,
from a different angle. The hero and narrator, Eva
Wylie, struggles to subsist at the edges of the criminal
underclass of London. Huge, irascible, and slow, psychologically scarred by a neglectful mother and a series
of grim foster-care and remand homes, Wylie leads a
precarious existence as a security guard and minder for
various more-or-less dubious employers. She plans to
escape from penury by wrestling her way to fame in
the ring as the London Lassassin, but she is trapped
both by rigid class hierarchies and by her own limita-

tions. Wylie's muscles and insults are blunt though
sometimes effective weapons in her war against the
world. Cody's use of an unreliable narrator who is a
source of humor, but who is incapable of sharing the
reader's enlightenment as the suspense plot unfolds,
provides the novel with an additional originality
beyond that lent by Cody's careful and plausible rendering of a subculture in which moonlight flits are the
norm and honesty is defined as leaving the car you
steal in a place where it is likely to be easily found. Lee,
now a partner in her own security firm, reappears in
Bucket Nut and its sequels, but seen through Wylie's
eyes she is transformed into "the Enemy," a member
of the despised "boss class" and a representative of the
forces of social control, a shift that reinforces Cody's
play with point of view.

In *Monkey Wrench* (1994) Cody uses Wylie's limited, distorted perspective in service of further exploration of women's experience. The daughter of a woman
who worked intermittently as a prostitute, Wylie is hostile and vituperative to the group of hookers who ask
her to teach them self-defense after several of them are
brutally attacked. The dangers and hardship of their
lives—and their resourcefulness in resisting degradation—thus emerge between the lines, a counternarrative
to Wylie's contemptuous slurs on their character and
physical capacities. In a dark world strewn with people
damaged by deprivation and neglect, Wylie's's angry
outbursts are both survival mechanism and symptom.
The novel ends with her and the prostitute group plotting murderous revenge in response to violence they
have suffered, but since they have identified the wrong
perpetrator, even these primitive attempts at restitution
cannot be seen as either justifiable or effective.

Wylie's marginality is reflected not only in her
propensity toward violence but also her vulnerability to
it; having barely escaped being murdered by more-
powerful villains in both *Bucket Nut* and *Monkey Wrench,*
she is both target and perpetrator in *Musclebound* (1997).
In this last and bleakest novel of the series, Wylie, alcoholic and barred from wrestling, teeters on the edge of
dissolution. Cody's subversion of sentimental visions of
family, a constant but low-key presence in the Lee
series, takes a much sharper form in her Wylie novels.
This preoccupation reaches a climax in *Musclebound,* in
which Eva's blind and misplaced loyalty to her long-lost
sister finally leads her into accidental murder, and the
novel ends with her betrayed by the idol of the family
she worships. The reader, if not the protagonist, is compelled to recognize that relationships outside the family,
however provisional, may offer some hope of solace in
a hostile world.

Gimme More (2000)—while linked to earlier works
by the appearance of a character reminiscent of Lee,

again as a secondary character to be hoodwinked by the narrator–signals a further extension of Cody's innovative use of the suspense form. Praised by H. R. F. Keating in a May 2000 review on the Tangled Web U.K. website as "a giant step forward" in Cody's development as a writer for its revelatory depiction of the music industry and its advocacy of "values of the spirit" over "material acquisitions," the novel again draws the reader effortlessly into an act of imaginative identification with a marginal, unorthodox character. The protagonist of *Gimme More,* Birdie, a superannuated "rock chick," is another woman forced to survive on her wits and a freewheeling interpretation of property laws. The object of suspicion and manipulation by greedy, resentful members of the rock scene, Birdie must scheme and cheat to keep her independence and her secrets.

Liza Cody's creation of a British version of a popular contemporary form, hard-boiled feminist detective fiction, has brought her success and recognition, but the lasting appeal of the Lee series may lie in Cody's departures from generic convention toward a more nuanced, less phantasmic account of the possibilities of female self-determination. Cody's woman on the streets of London provides more than local color, giving the reader a route to exploring both the outer trappings and the inner workings of a new version of womanhood. As Cody's work moves further from the traditional detective format, it becomes clearer that her most original contribution to the field lies in the compellingly realized depiction of subcultures, on the one hand, and on the other in her focus on presenting versions of reality from different standpoints. Increas-ingly, a Cody novel immerses the reader in an alien consciousness, requiring that they identify across chasms of cultural difference and recognize the relativity of truths and viewpoints.

Interviews:

Charles L. P. Silet, "Murder in Motion: An Interview with Liza Cody, Michael Z. Lewin, and Peter Lovesey," *Armchair Detective,* 28 (Spring 1995): 188–195;

Charles L. P. Silet, "Eva Wylie, Anna Lee, and the Contemporary Crime Novel: An Interview with Liza Cody," *Mystery Scene,* 49 (September–October 1995): 20, 59, 65–68.

References:

Glenwood Irons and Joan Worthing Roberts, "From Spinster to Hipster: The 'Suitability' of Miss Marple and Anna Lee," in *Feminism in Women's Detective Fiction,* edited by Irons (Toronto: University of Toronto Press, 1995), pp. 64–73;

Kathleen Gregory Klein, *The Woman Detective: Gender and Genre* (Urbana: University of Illinois Press, 1988);

Sally Munt, *Murder by the Book? Feminism and the Crime Novel* (London & New York: Routledge, 1994), pp. 50–55;

Priscilla L. Walton and Manina Jones, "'She's Watching the Detectives': The Woman PI in Film and Television," in their *Detective Agency: Women Rewriting the Hard-Boiled Tradition* (Berkeley: University of California Press, 1999), pp. 220–272.

Desmond Cory
(Shaun Lloyd McCarthy)
(16 February 1928 –   )

Marcia J. Songer
East Tennessee State University

BOOKS: *Secret Ministry* (London: Muller, 1951); republished as *The Nazi Assassins* (New York: Award, 1970);

Begin, Murderer! A Detective Novel (London: Muller, 1951);

This Traitor, Death (London: Muller, 1952); republished as *The Gestapo File* (New York: Award, 1971);

This Is Jezebel (London: Muller, 1952);

Dead Man Falling (London: Muller, 1953); republished as *The Hitler Diamonds* (New York: Award, 1979);

Lady Lost (London: Muller, 1953);

Intrigue (London: Muller, 1954); republished as *Trieste* (New York: Award, 1968);

The Shaken Leaf (London: Muller, 1955);

The Phoenix Sings (London: Muller, 1955);

The Height of Day (London: Muller, 1955); republished as *Dead Men Alive* (New York: Award, 1969);

The City of Kites, as Theo Callas (London: Muller, 1955; New York: Walker, 1964);

High Requiem (London: Muller, 1956; New York: Award, 1969);

Johnny Goes North (London: Muller, 1956); republished as *The Swastika Hunt* (New York: Award, 1969);

Pilgrim at the Gate (London: Muller, 1957; New York: Washburn, 1958);

Johnny Goes East (London: Muller, 1958); republished as *Mountainhead* (London: New English Library, 1966; New York: Award, 1968);

Johnny Goes West (London: Muller, 1958; New York: Walker, 1967);

Johnny Goes South (London: Muller, 1959; New York: Walker, 1964); republished as *Overload* (London: New English Library, 1964; New York: New American Library, 1966);

Pilgrim on the Island (London: Muller, 1959; New York: Walker, 1961);

Ann and Peter in Southern Spain, as Theo Callas, Kennedys Abroad (London: Muller, 1959);

The Head (London: Muller, 1960);

Desmond Cory (photograph by The Western Mail; from the dust jacket for the U.S. edition of The Circe Complex, *1975)*

Jones on the Belgrade Express (London: Muller, 1960);

Stranglehold (London: Muller, 1961);

Undertow (London: Muller, 1962; New York: Walker, 1963);

Hammerhead (London: Muller, 1963); republished as *Shockwave* (New York: Walker, 1964; London: New English Library, 1966);

The Name of the Game (London: Muller, 1964);

Deadfall (London: Muller, 1965; New York: Walker, 1965);

114

Feramontov (London: Muller, 1966; New York: Walker, 1966);

Timelock (London: Muller, 1967; New York: Walker, 1967);

The Night Hawk (London: Hodder & Stoughton, 1969; New York: Walker, 1969);

Sunburst (London: Hodder & Stoughton, 1971; New York: Walker, 1971);

Take My Drum to England (London: Hodder & Stoughton, 1971); republished as *Even If You Run* (Garden City, N.Y.: Doubleday, 1972);

A Bit of a Shunt up the River (Garden City, N.Y.: Doubleday, 1974);

The Circe Complex (London: Macmillan, 1975; Garden City, N.Y.: Doubleday, 1975);

Bennett (London: Macmillan, 1977; Garden City, N.Y.: Doubleday, 1977);

Lucky Ham, as Shaun McCarthy (London: Macmillan, 1977);

The Modes of Comedy, as McCarthy (Hythe, U.K.: Volturna, 1980);

Strange Attractor (London: Macmillan, 1991); republished as *The Catalyst* (New York: St. Martin's Press, 1991);

The Mask of Zeus (London: Macmillan, 1992; New York: St. Martin's Press, 1993);

The Dobie Paradox (London: Macmillan, 1993; New York: St. Martin's Press, 1994).

PRODUCED SCRIPTS: *Orbit One,* as Shaun McCarthy, BBC, 1961;

England Made Me, motion picture, by Cory, as McCarthy, and Peter Duffell, Atlantic Productions, Centralni Filmski Studio, and Two World Film, 1973.

OTHER: "Switchblade," in *Midwinter Mysteries 2,* edited by Hilary Hale (London: Little, Brown, 1992).

Desmond Cory is a pseudonym of suspense-fiction writer Shaun McCarthy, who also wrote two books under the name of Theo Callas and used his birth name for several works. Much of Cory's work can be divided into groups according to the protagonist. The most prominent protagonist is Johnny Fedora. The Fedora series consists of sixteen novels written during a period of twenty years. Cory also has written four novels with Lindy Gray as the protagonist, two with Mr. Pilgrim, two with Mr. Dee, and three with John Dobie. In addition, Cory has written seven self-contained novels and one children's book.

Cory was born Shaun Lloyd McCarthy on 16 February 1928 in Lancing, Sussex, England, the son of William Henry Lloyd and Iris Mary (née Chatfield) McCarthy. From 1945 to 1948 Shaun McCarthy

served as a commando in the Royal Marines, then began his higher education. In 1951 he earned a B.A. from St. Peter's College, Oxford, taking honors in English. While at Oxford, McCarthy edited a university review called *Viewpoint.*

The publication of McCarthy's first two novels, *Begin, Murderer!* and *Secret Ministry,* coincided with his 1951 graduation from Oxford. The novels, both written under the pseudonym Desmond Cory, introduce two different series protagonists. Lindy Gray of *Begin, Murderer!* is an urbane man-about-town who solves murders that baffle the Oxford police. Self-described as "a one-time private detective of one-time private means," Lindy is not ashamed of living a dissolute life. *Lady Lost* (1953), the third novel to feature him, opens with a scene that succinctly exemplifies Lindy's character. He is groping for something to help his hangover, while his fiancée, Richarda Baddeley, grouses from her bed. He says of her, "Her virtue as a fiancée is that she hasn't got any." Chapter headings in *Lady Lost* are the titles of jazz songs, including "Lady, Be Good," "I Can't Get Started," and "Mood Indigo." The books use a first-person narration with attempts at sophisticated humor.

By contrast, *Secret Ministry,* the other 1951 novel, introduces Johnny Fedora, a secret agent whose forte is the ability to outshoot, outwit, and outmaneuver his Cold War opponents. Although he is often teamed with Sebastian Trout, who is attached to the Foreign Office, Johnny's connection with British intelligence is unofficial, and he is hired only for specific assignments. Unlike Trout, Johnny lacks a solid education. In *Intrigue* (1954) he does not recognize lines from Lewis Carroll's *Alice's Adventures in Wonderland* (1865) or William Shakespeare's *Julius Caesar* (1599), and when Trout mentions that someone is descended from the Medici, Johnny asks what a Medici is. He relies on native cunning rather than acquired knowledge to outsmart his opponents. His one cultural distinction is his love of music. Thanks to a benefactor, Johnny received piano lessons, and he developed into a pianist who is equally proficient playing classical music, jazz, or boogie-woogie. He is protective of his hands, as a delicate touch is needed on the ivories as well as on the trigger.

Immediately after completing his baccalaureate, Cory began work in Europe as a freelance writer and translator. By 1953 he was living in Cordoba, Spain, where he served as a technical translator for an electrical-engineering company and began teaching at Academia Britanica, a language school. Cory produced both a Lindy Gray book and a Johnny Fedora book every year from 1951 through 1954. Thereafter, he dropped Lindy Gray and for awhile concentrated on Fedora and self-contained novels. The first two self-contained works appeared in 1955, although only one was written under

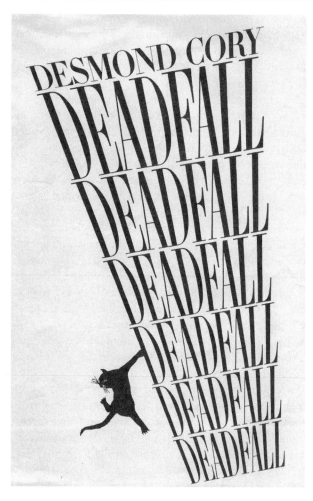

*Dust jacket for the U.S. edition of Cory's 1965 novel,
about a jewel thief and his homosexual accomplice
(Richland County Public Library)*

the Desmond Cory pseudonym. On 16 February 1956 Cory, still living in Spain, married Blanca Rosa Poyatos. The couple eventually had four sons—John Francis, Alexander Justin Lloyd, Richard Charles, and Dewi Anthony.

The Fedora books all take place in exotic locales, but starting in 1956 Cory used specific directions in several titles, sending Johnny north, east, west, and south. In *Johnny Goes West* (1958), the setting is Venezuela. Jimmy Emerald, Sebastian Trout, and Fedora, "three outstanding wartime operatives of Western Europe," have established Emerald Investigation and Exploration Co. Ltd. (E.I.E.), a company offering to "do practically anything, from inaugurating a rebellion in Mexico City to babysitting for a millionaire's infant." Both Emerald and Trout have left government service, and Emerald runs the company while Trout and Fedora work in the field. In this case, the field is the jungle far from Caracas. Trout and Fedora must put up

with heat and mosquitoes as well as a sadistic robber baron as they attempt to discover what happened to Robert West, who died soon after reporting a new source of carnotite, a uranium ore.

In many ways Cory makes Johnny the prototype of a hard-boiled hero. He refers to one of Trout's former girlfriends as "that little blonde piece." He indulges in alcohol, cigarettes, and women with no physical or emotional aftereffects, and despite beatings, he wins at cards and gunplay. Some aspects of the Fedora books are not typical, however. Cory's facility for language is apparent not only in his idiomatic use of Spanish but also in his apt inclusion of French, German, and Latin. In addition, Cory unexpectedly uses humor in both action and description. In *Johnny Goes West* a mining engineer hired by E.I.E. wears a black suit to impress the locals. He succeeds in impressing them: everyone thinks he is a hit man. He belatedly discovers he is in a part of the country where only professional killers wear black. Later, Cory refers to him as "Hendricks, the ex-professional gunman." In another example of unexpected humor, Trout, remembering his exclusive public-school education, realizes that "of late, he had found himself mixing more and more frequently with companions whom he would have been decidedly reluctant to present on a formal occasion to 'the Reverend the Provost.'"

In 1957 Cory chose a different approach to Cold War high jinks. In *Pilgrim at the Gate* (1957) members of a West Berlin travel agency called Pilgrim Tours arrange trips for their special clientele. Hoffmann, a former Nazi who has changed his name to Pilgrim, transports other former Nazis to South America, where the climate is better for their health than that of postwar Germany. The business is thriving, successfully providing "tours" for those from East Germany and Poland, when the real Mr. Pilgrim enters the office. The two men had met before, when Hoffmann was in charge of disciplining those subjected to Nazi experiments. Pilgrim eliminates Hoffman and takes over the business, sending the onetime Nazis where their former activities will be appropriately dealt with and concentrating instead on providing egress from behind the Iron Curtain. James Sandoe of the *New York Herald Tribune* (23 March 1958) said of the book, "Mr. Cory's manner is lightly wry with a quizzically furrowed brow and space for ethical speculation as to the implications of all of this lethal hanky-panky." Cory wrote only one more Pilgrim book, *Pilgrim on the Island* (1959).

Cory worked for the Academia Britanica until 1960, when he was awarded an M.A. from Oxford. Cory moved that year to the University of Wales at Cardiff. He was a lecturer in modern English literature there in the Institute of Science and Technology from

1960 to 1977. In 1976 he earned his Ph.D. from the University of Wales.

While teaching, Cory continued to write, including the last of the Johnny Fedora books, sometimes called the Feramontov Quintet. They share a common antagonist, Feramontov, a Soviet secret operative. The quintet begins with *Undertow* (1962) and includes *Hammerhead* (1963), *Feramontov* (1966), *Timelock* (1967), and *Sunburst* (1971), all set in Spain. Fedora and Feramontov are archenemies, meeting in increasingly unreal situations. In *Hammerhead,* Johnny takes a leave of absence from E.I.E. to investigate a sudden death. He does so as a favor even though he does not care much for murder investigations. They lack "the familiar tingle of expectancy, the illogical but unmistakable promise of violent action, of danger, of the risk of death." The investigation, however, quickly escalates into that kind of dangerous, violent adventure, as Fedora must foil a plot to drop an atomic bomb on Madrid.

Some reviewers compared the Fedora books with Ian Fleming's James Bond series. When *Hammerhead* was republished in the United States as *Shockwave* in 1964, the book jacket carried a quote from Anthony Boucher of *The New York Times* saying that Johnny Fedora "more than deserves to take over James Bond's avid audience." Reviews of *Feramontov* and Ian Fleming's *Octopussy* (1966) appeared side by side in *The New York Times Book Review* (10 July 1966). Of *Feramontov* the reviewer said, "As one has come to expect from Cory, colorful action, copious carnage, elaborate intrigue, frequent surprises." *Octopussy,* however, was dismissed as "a thin and even emaciated volume." In reviewing *Timelock* in *The New York Times Book Review* (6 August 1967) Boucher commented, "I must say once more that I find Cory's Johnny Fedora a much more persuasive, violent, sexy and lucky agent than James Bond." Boucher also considered Johnny's love interest "a more provocative girl than Bond ever met." All did not agree, however. *Sunburst,* the last novel in the quintet, elicited this comment from Newgate Callendar, also writing for *The New York Times Book Review* (16 May 1971): "If Cory can rid himself of his Ian Fleming syndrome, he can develop into quite a good writer." *Sunburst* was the last Fedora novel.

During the years when Cory was developing the Feramontov Quintet, he also wrote the two Mr. Dee novels and several self-contained works, one of which, *Deadfall* (1965), set the tone for several novels to come. The first of several psychological novels, *Deadfall* examines the life of the solitary jewel thief, his vulnerability, and his sensitivity. It also probes the role of the homosexual in the criminal world. *Deadfall,* like the Feramontov Quintet, is set in Spain, with some forays into North Africa. The book met with conflicting reviews.

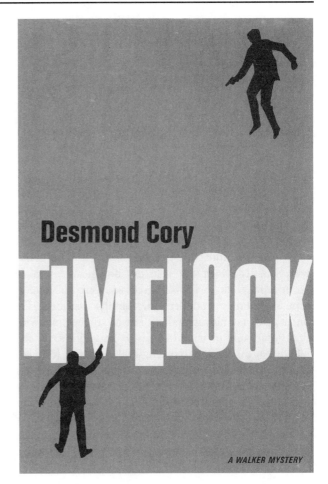

Dust jacket for the U.S. edition of Cory's 1967 novel, which features his Cold War secret agent Johnny Fedora (Richland County Public Library)

M. K. Grant, writing for the *Library Journal* (1 September 1965), called it "a serious psychological study of crime, and of the criminal mind, its motivations, and its aspirations, combined with all the tension, fast action, and suspense expected from one of Mr. Cory's adventures." R. Z. Sheppard dismissed it in *Book Week* (10 October 1965) as "unconvincing" and "pseudo-psychology." *Deadfall* was made into a movie by the 20th Century-Fox Film Corporation in 1968.

Deadfall was followed by two other psychological novels with Spanish settings. *The Night Hawk* (1969) concentrates on family relationships, while *Take My Drum to England* (1971) features Henry, a disaffected young Englishman with a genius for explosives. Cory convincingly examines the causes of Henry's impotence and his lack of sociability, but he is less convincing in elaborating the causes of Henry's political allegiance. While terrorist companions maintain Communist leanings as their part in the fight against Spanish Fascism, Henry seems to participate as an attempt to do something well, to erase the anonymity of his life.

While writing the psychological novels, Cory was living in Penarth, Glamorgan, Wales, as well as in Torreblanca, Spain, but he did not use Wales as a setting until 1974. That year he published *A Bit of a Shunt up the River* and the following year *The Circe Complex. A Bit of a Shunt up the River* is a thriller with a suspenseful car chase and investigates the relationship that develops between the pursuer and the pursued. *The Circe Complex,* as its name implies, centers on the effect a woman has on several men who are hunting stolen jewels. In addition, it scrutinizes concepts of honesty, since three of the men are "honest," while one is a former convict. *The Circe Complex* was presented as a four-part drama by Thames Television, London, in 1980.

The last book benefiting from Cory's familiarity with Spain is *Bennett* (1977). Its psychological bent takes an unusual twist. A British detective named Hunter is sent to Spain to find Bennett, a murder suspect. He finds a journal indicating that there are two people with that name, one of whom seems to be taking over the identity of the other. According to the journal, to try to find the imposter, Bennett starts carrying a book he has written, titled *Bennett.* As Hunter reads the journal, he thinks it "full of endless figures, circling round, circling." The plot becomes so convoluted that Callendar thought it a bore. He did admit in his review for *The New York Times Book Review* (1 January 1978), however, that "the writing is urbane."

Cory used his real name when he published *Lucky Ham* (1977). Set in fictional Mauxldever College, the novel is a satirical look at Oxford featuring allusions to Shakespeare's *Hamlet* (circa 1600–1601)–the characters Hamilton and Ophelia, a scene with a grave digger, and parodies of Hamlet's soliloquy and other well-known lines, and sophisticated wordplay.

In the late 1970s Cory began a series of associate professorships of English in Arabic-speaking countries: at the University of Qatar from 1977 to 1980, at the University of Sanaa from 1978 to 1985, and at the University of Bahrain from 1985 to 1987. In 1987 he began a three-year position as an adviser to the Ministry of Education in the Sultanate of Oman. Cory did not write any fiction during the thirteen years he lived in and around the Arabian Gulf, although he did write a work of serious criticism, *The Modes of Comedy* (1980), under his own name.

He left the Arabian Gulf in 1990 to take a position as associate professor of English at Eastern Mediterranean University in Famagusta, Cyprus. Within the next few years he published three books with a new protagonist, a Welsh math professor who relies on intellect and logic to solve his mysteries. The first John Dobie novel, *Strange Attractor* (1991), was enthusiastically received. The reviewer for *Publishers Weekly* (17 May 1991) called it a "near perfect puzzler, written with intelligence and laced with wit." Although in *The Mask of Zeus* (1992) Dobie leaves Wales for a visiting professorship in Cyprus, he returns in *The Dobie Paradox* (1993).

John Dobie appeared forty years after Johnny Fedora. Fedora is a young man's creation; Dobie is the product of a wiser, more experienced writer who prizes finesse above speed and brawn. The contrast between the two represents the evolution of Desmond Cory. Cory's concern for style is a notable characteristic of the post-Fedora books. Although Cory includes witty sentences and clever allusions in the Lindy Gray books, such stylistic plums are scarce in the spy novels. By limiting Johnny's education, Cory limited himself in writing about him. Once he quit writing about Fedora, those strictures were lifted, and the mature Cory is confined only by the sophistication of the new characters he creates.

Lionel Davidson

(31 March 1922 –   )

Michael J. Tolley
University of Adelaide

See also the Davidson entry in *DLB 14: British Novelists Since 1960.*

BOOKS: *The Night of Wenceslas* (London: Gollancz, 1960; New York: Harper, 1961);

The Rose of Tibet (London: Gollancz, 1962; New York: Harper & Row, 1962);

Soldier and Me, as David Line (New York: Harper & Row, 1965); republished as *Run for Your Life* (London: Cape, 1966);

A Long Way to Shiloh (London: Gollancz, 1966); republished as *The Menorah Men* (New York: Harper & Row, 1966);

Making Good Again (London: Cape, 1968; New York: Harper & Row, 1968);

Smith's Gazelle (London: Cape, 1971; New York: Knopf, 1971);

Mike and Me, as Line (London: Cape, 1974);

The Sun Chemist (London: Cape, 1976; New York: Knopf, 1976);

The Chelsea Murders (London: Cape, 1978); republished as *Murder Games* (New York: Coward, McCann & Geoghegan, 1978);

Under Plum Lake (London: Cape, 1980; New York: Knopf, 1980);

Screaming High, as Line (London: Cape, 1985; Boston: Little, Brown, 1985);

Kolymsky Heights (London: Heinemann, 1994; New York: St. Martin's Press, 1994).

Lionel Davidson (photograph © Jerry Bauer; from the dust jacket for the U.S. edition of Kolymsky Heights, *1994)*

Lionel Davidson has won three Crime Writers' Association Golden Dagger Awards, one for his first novel, *The Night of Wenceslas* (1960), which also won an Authors' Club Award for best first novel of its year. His other award-winning novels are *A Long Way to Shiloh* (1966; published in the United States as *The Menorah Men*) and *The Chelsea Murders* (1978), the latter a Book Society choice in Britain and a Book-of-the-Month Club choice in the United States, where it was published as *Murder Games.* Perhaps none of these novels is his best, however, which may be *The Rose of Tibet* (1962), *Making*

Good Again (1968), *Smith's Gazelle* (1971), or *Kolymsky Heights* (1994). Although his output has been relatively small, Davidson's consistently high quality ranks him among the best thriller writers, and in the 1960s, critics often compared his writing to that of Graham Greene or Kingsley Amis. He is distinctive in his versatility and in the range and diversity of his canon. As H. R. F. Keating notes, Davidson moves from one subgenre to another instead of sticking to a successful formula. The result is that each book offers surprises for readers.

Born in Hull, Yorkshire, on 31 March 1922, Lionel Davidson was one of nine children of a Polish father and a Russian mother. When he was two years old, his father died, and four years later his mother moved the family to London. Necessity compelled Davidson to leave school at the age of fourteen and work as an office boy. His first job was in a shipping firm, and then he worked at *The Spectator*. At age fifteen he submitted to the journal a story of his own, which was accepted. The story led to a job with a Fleet Street agency. When war came he joined the Royal Navy and served in the Submarine Service from 1941 to 1946. Before his success as a novelist, Davidson worked as a freelance magazine journalist and editor from 1946 to 1959. He married Fay Jacobs in 1949 and has two sons. In 1971 he and his family moved to Israel, a nation that Davidson characterizes without undue reverence (he is no less impartial toward the neighboring countries). They lived there ten years before moving to north London. After the death of Davidson's first wife in 1988 he remarried, to Frances Ullman, in 1989.

Davidson's novels are characterized by good humor, ingenuity, and scholarship. The hero is usually rather self-centered and egocentric, unaccustomed to the type of life in which he finds himself plunged. He drinks, womanizes, and makes witty observations. There is some form of genre parody, perhaps a touch of satire, and an exciting and fast-paced final chase. The writing also includes some linguistic play and imitation of accents. Davidson incorporates metaphors and similes appropriate to characters and environments; where people come from is always important.

The Night of Wenceslas, an enjoyable comedy thriller, is remarkable for its vivid evocation of Prague, a city that the author had never visited. His hero, narrator Nicolas Whistler, is initially in the mode of P. G. Wodehouse's Bertie Wooster, envisaging himself as "the young master" and showing a kind of timidity unbecoming a young man of twenty-four with the equivalent of a student's income. He hopes to receive a financial legacy from a distant, asthmatic uncle who cans fruit in Canada. Meanwhile, he serves as dogs-body to Karel Nimek, who has taken over the Whistler family business of glass importing (originally from Czechoslovakia) and is unfondly labeled "the Little Swine" by Nicolas's steady girlfriend, Maura. Young Whistler's greatest love is not Maura but an MG sports car, the expense of which makes him easy prey for spies, such as Stephen Cunliffe, who wish him to transmit messages to Prague (they convince him he is procuring a secret formula for unbreakable glass). Whistler's mother was once the toast of Prague, so Nicolas speaks Czech, though he has not been back to the country since the age of six. Prague brings out unlikely qualities of toughness, improvisation, and even lust in "hende Nicolas," though he proves to be an ungrateful lover, having hardly left Vlasta Simenova, his driver to the glass factories, before he is proposing

to Maura, in the false euphoria of a safe, successful return to London.

After Nicolas is sent back into Czechoslovakia, on the frail pretext that the glass formula was defective, his serious adventures begin, and he experiences his "night of Wenceslas" when on the run from the SNB (the State Security Police) in an enclosed group of streets near the Wenceslas statue. He uses hilarious disguises and escapes to Vlasta's home for an energetic night with her, marred only by the discovery that she works for the SNB. The dawn arrival of a milkman gives him an idea for entering the heavily guarded British Embassy; by the time of his eventual escape he has learned, "If experience taught anything, it was not to think too much, but to sharpen up the responses."

The Rose of Tibet deliberately follows the adventure-story tradition of H. Rider Haggard, particularly his *Ayesha: The Return of She* (1905). In *Ayesha* the narrator, Holly, returns from Tibet with an arm mauled and broken by an attack from a beast; in Davidson's novel, the hero, Charles Houston, returns from Tibet with an arm so badly savaged by a bear that it has to be amputated. Houston's encounter with the bear is a vivid episode. Although both Haggard and Davidson profess their stories to be true, Haggard almost ignores the problem of credibility, while Davidson (placing himself as narrator in a frame story) instead offers the reader almost obsessively detailed marks of authenticity, among them an outdated map, with references, giving the point of Houston's entry into Tibet. When Hugh Whittington, a member of a movie crew, is reported missing and then dead near Mount Everest, his half brother, Charles, sets out to find him and ends up in the forbidden monastery of Yamdring, with a reincarnated eighteenth-century she-devil as abbess. Having fallen into a trap, his cover compromised, he is isolated and scared but, despite his wish to escape, is overcome by family loyalty and curiosity.

The Rose of Tibet, an unusual romance in which many strange events occur, satisfies the reader's sense of wonder, yet never offends credulity and continually defers to the skeptic. Davidson seems to be able to get the reader to believe a great deal by not asking for too much belief. He uses his method so confidently that he can mock the means by which his witch heroine foists superstition on the gullible populace (her "miraculous" movement between an island temple and a mainland monastery is effected by a secret passage, the key to which is the salient feature of a phallic statue of a monkey). The realism is underpinned by reliance at several points on Heinrich Harrer's *Sieben Jahre in Tibet* (1952; translated as *Seven Years in Tibet*, 1953), among other sources. Both Daphne du Maurier and Graham Greene

Dust jacket for the 1961 U.S. edition of Davidson's first novel (1960), in which a feckless young
man travels to Prague as an unwitting pawn of British intelligence agents
(Richland County Public Library)

were impressed by Davidson's re-creation of Tibet and its exotic ways.

Much of the action in the novel is graphically brutal; one of the episodes presents a revolting account of murder, piled on top of a chilling rape and torture scene. Davidson exposes with remarkable force a paradox that the hard stuff of romance is the passage of the human body through almost unbearable anguish. Ideas about life and death are exchanged between the characters, and the Westerners are baffled by the Tibetan reliance on "superstition" and rigmarole, while the Chinese invaders are given merely temporal excuses for their brutal behavior, despite the fact that the heroine, the Abbess Mei-Hua, is part Chinese (and many of the Tibetans welcome the change in rule and even the enforcement of reign by pregnancy).

Davidson next produced *A Long Way to Shiloh,* set mainly in Israel in the 1960s. As Keating points out, the setting is not merely an "exotic or unusual back-

ground," though it is that; instead, Israel becomes "a major character in its own right" and the book a political "hymn to hopefulness." This novel is more assured in manner than *The Night of Wenceslas,* as is partly reflected by the more aggressive and consciously libidinous hero, Caspar Laing, who is a young appointee to a chair in Semitics at the University of Beds (horrid puns are the bedrock humor of the book). Laing tells his own story—a quest narrative. At one level it is a search for hidden treasure (the ancient, true Menorah, made of gold, supposedly concealed before the destruction of the Temple at Jerusalem); at another level, it is a search for love (with Lieutenant Shoshana Almogi, who desires to bring herself as a virgin to her betrothed, a giant Moroccan called Shimshon or Samson); more broadly it is a search for light in darkness, for peace (*shiloh*) in a life of sojourning. Two sets of scrolls, each describing the transport of a mysterious treasure to a secret place, are discovered simulta-

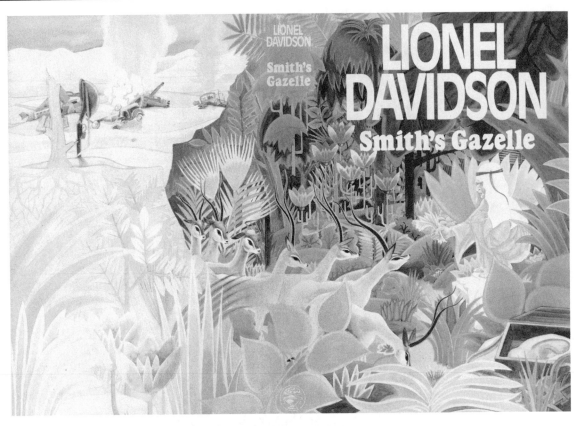

Dust jacket for Davidson's 1971 novel, in which an Arab man protects nearly extinct gazelles in a ravine on the border between Israel and Syria around the time of the 1967 Six-Day War (Special Collections, Thomas Cooper Library, University of South Carolina)

neously, one with the Israelis, one with the Arabs. The text from the scrolls is presented as a prologue to the book. Professor Agrot of the Jerusalem University calls on Caspar for help. One practical problem is the excavation of a tel on the shores of the Dead Sea, which must be completed before a builder, Teitleman (one of the villains of the novel), drives a water pipe under it for a big resort project. A tel, a place of excavation (from an Old Testament word meaning a heap), presents layer upon layer of history.

What is of timeless value for all people is set against the ephemeral demands of a wealthy philistine. Once Caspar gets the scroll photographed, his helper is killed, and he is abducted, hit severely on the head, and driven toward the border. Caspar's equally violent escape is effectively rendered. In an unreliable narrative, he and his friends enjoy a drunken celebration in Tel Aviv, during which Caspar discovers a new reading of the scroll. He needs yet a third set of scrolls from a place across the border of Israel in Jordan. There he becomes trapped in a cave but escapes across the Dead Sea, only to find that the menorah he seeks is already partly buried by Teitleman's building.

Davidson ends philosophically, or perhaps cynically, suggesting that personal survival matters more than the *shiloh* of faith.

Making Good Again, despite elements of mystery and suspense and some humorous passages, is a serious novel that addresses questions about the Nazi regime and the postwar continuation of Nazism. While, in other novels, Davidson pokes fun at Zionists, his obvious target here is the phenomenon of Nazism, the specter of which still haunts Germany thirty years after World War II. As the title implies, Davidson is less concerned with past evil than with the problems of healing and of maintaining sanity and faith in the wake of evil actions.

Three lawyers come together in Munich to consider new evidence in a reparations case concerning the distribution of funds from the estate of a Jewish banker, Helmut Wolfgang Bamberger, who remained in Prague after the war began and who disappeared when the Germans overran Europe. One lawyer, an eminently reasonable Englishman appropriately called Raison, represents the interests of the principal heir, Bamberger's daughter. Raison's wife, Hilda, is being treated

for insanity, and, sexually frustrated, he is strongly susceptible to women though determined to remain a faithful husband. A second lawyer, Dr. Grunwald, an
elderly Jew who survived Dachau and who represents
an Israeli agency, is aggressively Orthodox and burdened by physical infirmity. He often appears mad to
others and is claiming the money for himself in order to
build a home for the mentally ill in Israel. The third
lawyer is Heinz Haffner, a German who hides a deep
sense of collective guilt under a cover of irascible righ-
teousness; his patient wife suffers from the strains of
this hypocrisy. He deplores the "swinishness" of other
Germans, notably that of his daughter, Elke, who is
having an affair with a deformed Hungarian Jewish
poet, Tibor, and that of his promiscuous sister, Magda.

Raison is drawn ineluctably into infidelity with
Elke, a betrayal that goads Haffner almost to committing suicide, because of his previously high belief in the
Englishman's integrity. One of the rules of the novel,
propounded by Grunwald, is that "Every action we
take brings into a major context some minor context."
He and Raison survey the crematorium at Dachau in a
rather somber section of the novel. Grunwald is almost
killed in a Bavarian forest, where he is set upon by
some German students. A quest for Bamberger himself,
who is thought to have returned to Germany to operate
a numbered account in Zurich, also occupies part of the
action. The complex layers of understanding expressed
in *Making Good Again* are only gradually revealed.

A lyrical and allegorical book for young readers,
Smith's Gazelle received the President's Prize for Literature in Israel. Davidson offers an alternative explanation for the Six-Day War than that found in the history
books: it was a survival plot to keep a near-extinct
gazelle alive in a ravine between Israel and Syria.
According to Hamud, a deformed Arab, God's real
purpose (spoiled by the typical unfaithfulness of the
Children of Israel) was to establish not the Jews but a
herd of Smith's gazelles in the Promised Land. Hamud
shepherds the herd, providing for them during years in
which their number grows from one pregnant female
to six hundred gazelles. Hamud, as resourceful with
sparse materials and as isolated as Robinson Crusoe
on his island, fled to the ravine after murdering his
unfaithful wife's brother and father, after they had
murdered her and her lover. He believes the place is
haunted by djinns and souls, and the sight of such an
uncanny creature as the gazelle tells him that he is
entering a period of trial; caring for her and her prog-
eny becomes his mission.

Hamud is encouraged in his belief by a young
boy, known to him only as "the messenger," a redheaded Jewish runaway, Jonathan, who descends into
the ravine with a Bedouin boy, Musallem. Musallem,

who lives on the Syrian side of the ravine, is torn
between the two worlds of tent and settlement; he
never learns that Hamud once killed his father when he
followed a sheep into the ravine, but curiosity about
that occurrence brings him there at the same time as
Jonathan. Musallem is a nicer boy than Jonathan:
Jonathan is a notorious liar whose behavior becomes
almost sociopathic when he learns that his mother is
pregnant. Other important characters are Motke Bar-
tov, who first sights the gazelle, and his commander,
Major General Naftali Mor, who photographs it. It falls
to Motke to play Joshua to the gazelle herd and lead
them into the Promised Land, and to the general to
explain to Jonathan that the Six-Day War was caused
not by the gazelle situation but by the need to protect a
kibbutz's beetroot field from Syrian shelling. Jonathan's
inventive father, Amos, and his patient teacher, Esther,
represent in different ways the scientific worldview. A
rich ironic humor pervades the novel, rendering even
the horrendous war farcical.

The Sun Chemist (1976), a clever espionage story,
supposes that the Zionist leader and first president of
Israel, Chaim Weizmann, successfully discovered how
to extract cheap energy from sweet potatoes by a process that, Davidson assures readers, actually works. In
the context of an oil crisis, such a discovery constitutes
an industrial secret and involves the scientists concerned in danger and intrigue. The first-person narrator
hero, historian Igor Druyanov, who is editing Weizmann's correspondence, is the son of a well-known
Russian dissident. He has a somewhat chaotic bachelor
lifestyle and a passive personality. When his research
assistant is mugged in an attempt to steal some of the
Weizmann papers, Igor becomes involved in intrigue
surrounding Weizmann's discovery. Davidson's settings vary between the United Kingdom and Israel and
include Weizmann's home at Rehovot, now a museum,
as well as the ruins of Caesarea by moonlight. The use
of real figures in the narrative is elaborate, and the
book becomes a kind of philosophical survey of history,
as Igor finds that his attempt to recover the particular
variety of potato in combination with a particular kind
of bacteria seems doomed to failure by the system of
scientific research. Sexual complications confuse his
quest, and he seems unable to keep secrets from his colleagues and lovers. There is a mixture of ironies and
humor in the work alongside tragic happenings.

The Chelsea Murders, set in the fashionably bohe-
mian art district in London, is a highly elaborate murder mystery. The police—led by Ted Warton,
described as looking like a warthog—and a freelance
journalist, Mary Mooney, are on the trail of "the
Chelsea maniac," a serial murderer whose methods are
both gruesome and bizarre. The victims all have the

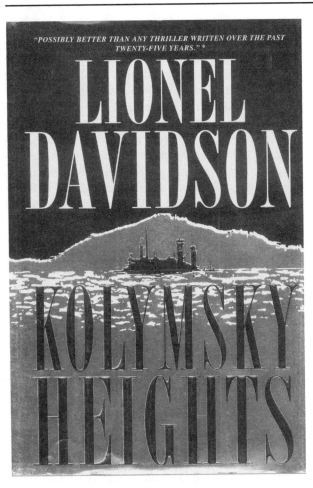

"POSSIBLY BETTER THAN ANY THRILLER WRITTEN OVER THE PAST TWENTY-FIVE YEARS." *

LIONEL DAVIDSON

KOLYMSKY HEIGHTS

Dust jacket for the U.S. edition of Davidson's last novel, in which a Canadian Eskimo infiltrates a Siberian research facility that experiments with creating intelligent apes (Richland County Public Library)

former medical station in Siberia has become a research station at which biological experiments to create intelligent apes are performed. Near Kolymsky, an ancient, pregnant woman preserved in the ice has been discovered. A former student of Lazenby's, a Canadian Eskimo named Jean-Baptiste Porteur (also known as Johnny Porter), is recruited to reach the laboratory from the outside and to return with secret information.

Porter is good at languages and codes, physically courageous, and also detests spies and people in uniforms. He plans to enter the research station disguised as a reindeer-hunting Eskimo, but he must first endure a complicated and dangerous process, including joining the crew of a trading ship and surviving a rare fever, to enter Siberia. Most of the book pits Porter against formidable opponents, who themselves use advanced detection techniques, which he must anticipate and avoid. The climax is a hair-raising pursuit as the Russian defense general, though competent and intelligent, thinks in terms of classic military maneuvers while Porter does not. Davidson's novel is in the tradition of those of Martin Cruz Smith and Stuart Kaminsky, whose stories of crimes inside Russia capture the alien perspectives and lifestyles there (although all these authors show that the basic conflicts in human values remain). Porter, in effect, tries to carry a new light to the world outside, contradicting his mother's prediction that he would bring universal darkness and tears.

Davidson also wrote three thrillers under the pseudonym David Line, each about friendships between a "normal" boy, the narrator, and a social misfit. These friendships suggest comparisons with those of Jonathan, Musallem, and Hamud in *Smith's Gazelle*. In *Soldier and Me* (1965; published in the United States as *Run for Your Life*, 1966), the narrator is Jim Woolcott, a schoolboy who befriends a smaller, immigrant boy, Istvan Szolda, whom Jim calls Soldier. Soldier overhears a conversation in Hungarian between men plotting to murder a cripple. He persuades Jim to help him save the man's life, but the police show no interest, and before long Jim and Soldier find themselves on the run after witnessing the shooting of the cripple. They take a train, on a snowy Christmas Eve, to King's Lynn, where Jim would have been holidaying with his friend Nixon, if Nixon had not been jealous of Soldier. One of the Hungarians follows them onto the train, but the boys jump off in the middle of a snowy field. They hide, are captured, and suffer pain, hunger, and exposure. In *Soldier and Me*, as in all three narratives, the strength of the characterization is evident, even in the peripheral characters.

In *Mike and Me* (1974), the outsider who Jim befriends is a tall, thin cousin, Mike Mitchell, who limps and is a year behind in his classes because of an

initials of poets who have resided in the district, and messages to the police in the form of quotations from these poets are left at the crime scenes. The victims are also linked to three amateur moviemakers, Artie, Frank, and Steve, at least one of whom must be the killer. Mooney puts the evidence together in such a way that she almost becomes the final victim. The mystery is intriguing, the characters interesting, the action rapid and lively, and the misdirection clever, with amusing false trails and a parody of genre conventions. Dramatized for television by Jonathan Hales as part of the *Armchair Detective* series, the story succeeds in its ironic references to other detective stories.

In *Kolymsky Heights* Davidson parodies the spy-fiction conventions popularized by Greene, John Buchan, and Eric Ambler. A coded message does not reach the hero directly but is received almost accidentally by an Oxford academic, Lazenby, who is also employed by the Central Intelligence Agency. British and American spies collate material to show that a

accident. The setting is a vague urban place, a north Midlands woollen town with a well-known grammar school. An art teacher, A. S. Morgan (called Moggy), becomes central to this story as the target of violent property developers who wish to destroy evidence he has found, in the form of an old title deed, that will ruin their scheme to destroy old almshouses. The dynamics of school friendships, as well as of staff-student relationships, are explored through the medium of an elaborate, well-plotted story. Soldier appears again, but this time his Jewishness and trustworthiness are stressed more than his foreignness and pluck. There are again exciting chases, and the denouement relies, as it does in *Soldier and Me,* on Nixon's father, a doctor, though in *Mike and Me* it also involves nail-biting dependence on the egotistical, unreliable Nixon. In both narratives the boys dare not hide in their own homes; Jim has to protect his mother and has no father to turn to for help.

Both of these novels show how befriending a difficult, apparently overly dependent boy may be rewarding for both partners. Soldier becomes a hero, and Mike's intuitive artistic gifts are recognized. The third novel Davidson published under the David Line pseudonym, *Screaming High* (1985), develops this idea further. Ratbag, whose real name is Paul Mountjoy, is black, poor, undependable, and somewhat fey but also a closet prodigy as a trumpet player. Ratbag joins the school orchestra, and because the music teacher has ambitions, the orchestra wins a national championship and travels to Amsterdam for a European competition. Ratbag will not go anywhere without his friend Nick,

and the two of them have an adventure, stumbling upon the headquarters of drug racketeers. The police are told but decide not to intervene until Nick and Rat can lead them back to the house in Amsterdam. Such an opportunity arises when Rat auditions for a music scholarship; the boys are captured by the gang, and Nick proves his usefulness in their escape, especially after Ratbag hurts himself as they fall into a canal. In this story the thriller element takes second place to the personal story of friendship and musical success.

Lionel Davidson's fiction encompasses the idea of hope with longing for *shiloh,* a desire for love and friendship, and an attitude of ineffable irreverence toward the encumbering realities of life. In recent years he has become popular in Italy and, most especially, in Germany. Davidson is never politically correct or simplistic. He toys with his readers' prejudices and their expectations, turns the conventions of whatever genre he employs on its head, and therefore is always intellectually challenging and highly amusing. As a descriptive writer he is particularly good at presenting clearly what is seen through impoverished vision in the stories, whether through ignorance, illogic, intoxication, darkness, or the inebriation of romantic love. He perhaps seems obsessively interested in technical or political matters at times, but the thriller elements are by no means as obfuscated as they are in James Buchan's *Heart's Journey in Winter* (1995), for example, or Tom Clancy's *Red Rabbit* (2002). The crispness of Davidson's fiction is always welcome, whether on first or subsequent readings.

Peter Dickinson

(16 December 1927 –   )

Daryl Y. Holmes

and

Gina Macdonald
Nicholls State University

See also the Dickinson entries in *DLB 87: British Mystery and Thriller Writers Since 1940, First Series* and *DLB 161: British Children's Writers Since 1960, First Series.*

BOOKS: *Skin Deep* (London: Hodder & Stoughton, 1968); republished as *The Glass-Sided Ants' Nest* (New York: Harper & Row, 1968; Harmondsworth, U.K.: Penguin, 1981);

The Weathermonger (London: Gollancz, 1968; Boston: Little, Brown, 1969);

A Pride of Heroes (London: Hodder & Stoughton, 1969); republished as *The Old English Peep Show* (New York: Harper & Row, 1969);

Heartsease (London: Gollancz, 1969; Boston: Little, Brown, 1969);

The Seals (London: Hodder & Stoughton, 1970); republished as *The Sinful Stones* (New York: Harper & Row, 1970);

The Devil's Children (London: Gollancz, 1970; Boston: Little, Brown, 1970);

Sleep and His Brother (London: Hodder & Stoughton, 1971; New York: Harper & Row, 1971);

Emma Tupper's Diary (London: Gollancz, 1971; Boston: Little, Brown, 1971);

The Lizard in the Cup (London: Hodder & Stoughton, 1972; New York: Harper & Row, 1972);

The Dancing Bear (London: Gollancz, 1972; Boston: Little, Brown, 1973);

The Iron Lion (Boston: Little, Brown, 1972; London: Allen & Unwin, 1973);

The Green Gene (London: Hodder & Stoughton, 1973; New York: Pantheon, 1973);

The Gift (London: Gollancz, 1973; Boston: Little, Brown, 1974);

The Poison Oracle (London: Hodder & Stoughton, 1974; New York: Pantheon, 1974);

Peter Dickinson (photograph by Jerry Bauer; from the dust jacket for the U.S. edition of Death of a Unicorn, *1984)*

The Lively Dead (London: Hodder & Stoughton, 1975; New York: Pantheon, 1975);

Chance, Luck, and Destiny (London: Gollancz, 1975; Boston: Little, Brown, 1976);

King and Joker (London: Hodder & Stoughton, 1976; New York: Pantheon, 1976);

The Blue Hawk (London: Gollancz, 1976; Boston: Little, Brown, 1976);

Walking Dead (London: Hodder & Stoughton, 1977; New York: Pantheon, 1977);

Annerton Pit (London: Gollancz, 1977; Boston: Little, Brown, 1977);

Hepzibah (Twickenham: Eel Pie, 1978; Lincoln, Mass.: Godine, 1980);

One Foot in the Grave (London: Hodder & Stoughton, 1979; New York: Pantheon, 1979);

Tulku (London: Gollancz, 1979; New York: Dutton, 1979);

The Flight of Dragons (London: Pierrot, 1979; New York: Harper & Row, 1979);

City of Gold and Other Stories from the Old Testament (London: Gollancz, 1980; New York: Pantheon, 1980);

A Summer in the Twenties (London: Hodder & Stoughton, 1981; New York: Pantheon, 1981);

The Seventh Raven (London: Gollancz, 1981; New York: Dutton, 1981);

The Last House-Party (London: Bodley Head, 1982; New York: Pantheon, 1982);

Hindsight (London: Bodley Head, 1983; New York: Pantheon, 1983);

Healer (London: Gollancz, 1983; New York: Delacorte, 1983);

Death of a Unicorn (London: Bodley Head, 1984; New York: Pantheon, 1984);

Giant Cold (London: Gollancz, 1984; New York: Dutton, 1984);

A Box of Nothing (London: Gollancz, 1985; New York: Delacorte, 1987);

Tefuga: A Novel of Suspense (London: Bodley Head, 1986; New York: Pantheon, 1986);

Mole Hole (London: Blackie, 1987; New York: Bedrick, 1987);

Perfect Gallows: A Novel of Suspense (London: Bodley Head, 1988; New York: Pantheon, 1988);

Eva (London: Gollancz, 1988; New York: Delacorte, 1989);

Merlin Dreams (London: Gollancz, 1988; New York: Delacorte, 1988);

Skeleton-in-Waiting (London: Bodley Head, 1989; New York: Pantheon, 1989);

AK (London: Gollancz, 1990; New York: Delacorte, 1992);

Play Dead (London: Bodley Head, 1991; New York: Mysterious Press, 1992);

A Bone from a Dry Sea (London: Gollancz, 1992; New York: Delacorte, 1993);

Time and the Clockmice, etcetera (London: Doubleday, 1993; New York: Delacorte, 1994);

The Yellow Room Conspiracy (London: Little, Brown, 1994; New York: Mysterious Press, 1994);

Shadow of a Hero (London: Gollancz, 1994; New York: Delacorte, 1994);

Chuck and Danielle (London: Gollancz, 1994; New York: Doubleday, 1996);

The Lion Tamer's Daughter and Other Stories (New York: Delacorte, 1997; London: Macmillan Children's, 1999)–comprises *The Lion Tamer's Daughter, Touch and Go, Spring,* and *Checkers;*

Suth's Story (New York: Grosset & Dunlap, 1998);

Noli's Story (New York: Grosset & Dunlap, 1998);

Po's Story (New York: Grosset & Dunlap, 1998; London: Macmillan Children's, 1999);

Mana's Story (London: Macmillan Children's, 1999; New York: Grosset & Dunlap, 1999);

Some Deaths before Dying (New York: Mysterious Press, 1999; Sutton, U.K.: Severn, 2001);

The Ropemaker (London: Macmillan Children's, 2001; New York: Delacorte, 2001);

Water: Tales of Elemental Spirits, by Dickinson and Robin McKinley (New York: Putnam, 2002); republished as *Elementals: Water* (London: Random House, 2002).

Editions: *The Changes: A Trilogy* (London: Gollancz, 1975)–comprises *The Weathermonger, Heartsease,* and *The Devil's Children;*

The Kin (London: Macmillan Children's, 1998)–comprises *Suth's Story, Noli's Story, Po's Story,* and *Mana's Story.*

PRODUCED SCRIPT: *Mandog,* television, BBC, 1972.

OTHER: *Presto! Humorous Bits and Pieces,* collected by Dickinson (London: Hutchinson, 1975);

"Who Killed the Cat?" in *Verdict of Thirteen,* edited by Julian Symons (London: Faber & Faber, 1978; New York: Harper & Row, 1978), pp. 203–220;

Hundreds and Hundreds, edited by Dickinson (London: Penguin, 1984);

"Flight," in *Imaginary Lands,* edited by Robin McKinley (New York: Greenwillow, 1985), pp. 63–96;

"Barker," in *Guardian Angels,* edited by Stephanie Nettell (London: Viking, 1987), pp. 105–117;

"The Spring," in *Beware! Beware!: Chilling Tales,* compiled by Jean Richardson (London: Hamilton, 1987), pp. 1–12.

SELECTED PERIODICAL PUBLICATIONS–
UNCOLLECTED: "Fantasy: The Need for Realism," *Children's Literature in Education,* 17 (Spring 1986): 39–51;

"Murder in the Manor," *Armchair Detective* (Spring 1991).

Dust jacket for Dickinson's first mystery novel (1968), the first of five that feature Inspector James Pibble (from John Cooper and B. A. Pike, Detective Fiction: The Collector's Guide, *1988)*

Peter Dickinson categorizes his special brand of mystery as science fiction with far more fiction than science. When he imagines the closed world of a classic detective story, he tries to invent it as if it were an alien planet. The result is a tendency toward the grotesque in characterization, what he calls "a twist" that sets his fictive creations "apart from the outside world." At times this sense of the grotesque carries over into setting and crime, such as a corpse pickled in a solution of vodka and brandy or an antler prong used as a murder weapon, thrust through the eye. Although Dickinson's early works feature more science-oriented, original, and bizarre plot elements, his later works continue to explore otherworldliness in everyday people and situations. Dickinson approaches mystery writing in a manner that parallels both William Wordsworth's and Samuel Taylor Coleridge's roles in *Lyrical Ballads* (1798) by showing the extraordinary within the ordinary and making the extraordinary seem commonplace through attention to realistic detail. Dickinson creates multifac-

eted male characters and is especially skillful at sensitive and accurate depiction of female characters. His women are competitive, clever, and highly competent; his men, as he himself says in *Twentieth Century Crime and Mystery Writers* (1980), are "weedy." He intensely illuminates both individual characters as well as the complex weave of human relationships. Dickinson is also a children's author, creating credible adolescent characters and writing fantastic plots.

Peter Dickinson was born on 16 December 1927 in Livingston, Northern Rhodesia, now Zambia, the son of a colonial civil servant, the Honorable Richard Sebastian Willoughby Dickinson, and May Southey (Lovemore) Dickinson, the daughter of a South African farmer. The Dickinsons belonged to the upper bourgeoisie, or squirearchy, mainly lawyers and high-ranking military officers. Peter Dickinson's father was assistant chief secretary of the Rhodesian colonial government, and his grandfather was a noted barrister, member of Parliament, and one of the originators of the League of Nations, who in 1930 was created first Baron Dickinson (hence the courtesy title of "Honorable" carried by his father, and in time by Dickinson and his two younger brothers, his elder brother inheriting the barony on their grandfather's death).

Dickinson's father died in 1935, shortly after the family returned to England when Dickinson was seven years old. Dickinson attended St. Ronan's, an English preparatory school, from 1936 to 1941, and his experience with the regimen and regulations of educational institutions, the interactions between boys and masters, and the effects of wartime relocation to rural areas to protect youngsters from urban bombing raids was later used in *Hindsight* (1983). Dickinson attended Eton College during the war years from 1941 to 1946 as a King's Scholar. He served as a signals officer in the British army from 1946 to 1948 and then attended King's College, the University of Cambridge, as an exhibitor in classics, and he completed his B.A. in 1951. His broad reading in the classics and his erudition are exemplified in many of his works, from references in *A Pride of Heroes* (1969, also published as *The Old English Peep Show*) to one set of characters as "heroes from the age of Sophocles who had survived with endearing absurdity into the age of Menander" to the distinction he makes in *The Last House-Party* (1982) between "the rounded, sardonic, mature and genuinely heroic Byron of *Don Juan* and the Greek liberation" and "the young, glum, intense *poseur* presented in *Childe Harold.*"

Dickinson began his seventeen-year career as assistant editor of and reviewer for *Punch* in 1952. On 20 April 1953 he married artist Mary Rose Barnard, the daughter of Vice Admiral Sir Geoffrey Barnard. The couple settled in London and had four children: Philipa Lucy Anne, born in 1955; Dorothy Louise, born in 1956; John Geoffrey Hyett, born in 1962; and James Christopher Meade, born in 1963. Dickinson's work for *Punch* included several years reviewing crime novels, a natural lead-in to trying mystery writing himself. He began his writing career shortly before leaving the staff of *Punch,* publishing his first two books, *Skin Deep,* a crime novel, and *The Weathermonger,* a children's adventure story, almost simultaneously in 1968. For the next thirty-plus years, writing both adult and children's works, Dickinson used several name combinations for his writing, including Peter Malcolm de Brissac Dickinson, Peter Malcolm Dickinson, and Malcolm de Brissac.

The first of Peter Dickinson's mysteries, *Skin Deep* (1968), published in the United States as *The Glass-Sided Ants' Nest* (1968), introduces Inspector James Willoughby Pibble, a character who appears in five subsequent works. Pibble is well into his career and given small, odd cases to investigate. In the first in this series, the case involves the death of New Guinea tribal leader Aaron Ku, whose tribe (every member of which is called Ku) is housed in the middle of London and cared for by anthropologist Eve Mackenzie, who for cultural reasons has been accepted into the tribe as a man. Mackenzie is the daughter of a former missionary to the tribe. When the missionary and the majority of the tribe were wiped out by Japanese soldiers, Aaron Ku decided to leave New Guinea and make a fresh start in a Christian country. The alien landscape and way of life, however, cause many of the tribe to want to return to their native land, and some revert to their pre-Christian practices. Because of the discord in the community, Pibble initially believes that the murderer is a tribesperson, but the guardians to the men's and women's quarters, themselves proven innocent, are sure that no one left his or her room at all on the night the murder was committed. The tribe is equally sure that no outsider committed the murder because the outsider's scent would have alerted Aaron to his presence.

The classic locked-door mystery proves especially challenging for Pibble. He must strive to understand the Kus' beliefs, traditions, reasoning, history, art, and methods of communication. Moreover, he must question whether his own cultural perspective prevents him from seeing what would be obvious to a member of the Ku culture. An example of the difficulty he faces is Eve's relationship with Paul, a member of the tribe. From Pibble's initial perspective, theirs is a heterosexual relationship; to the Kus, aware of her status in the tribe, the relationship is homosexual–irregular, but neither criminal nor taboo. Pibble realizes the danger of becoming so hypnotized by the idea of otherness that recognition of basic human motivation is lost.

Within this closed community, Dickinson, through Pibble, questions the nature of identity, knowledge, communication, love, and loyalty. Dickinson closely examines the small, tightly woven subcommunity, an approach he takes in most of his later works. Pibble's nature is also established here in his self-questioning, self-doubt, and awareness of both his fallibility and the negative manner in which his investigations into the peculiar are perceived by his colleagues and superiors at Scotland Yard. An ordinary, humble, reasonably intelligent man with a gift for investigating the peculiar, Pibble is an Everyman, flawed and questioning where his loyalties should lie. This novel received the 1968 British Crime Writers Association Gold Dagger Award for best mystery of the year.

Dickinson was also working at this time on a fantasy trilogy for children set in an England at some undefined period in the future, when the English have actively and forcefully rejected technology, returned to a pastoral way of life, and rediscovered the magic of the past, a new Merlin and a new Camelot. In *The Weathermonger* a brother and sister seek the cause of these mysterious changes, while *Heartsease* (1969) reveals a darker side to the changes–xenophobia and fear of witchcraft–and *The Devil's Children* (1970) follows the problems of a community of Sikhs living in Britain, the sole remaining advocates of technology and its advantages. The Sikhs settle in a remote region and trade goods with the more primitive British. Dickinson takes great pleasure throughout his works in reversing expectations and poking gentle fun at the British sense of superiority, satirically undercutting prejudices and preconceptions.

Shortly after the publication of his first two books, Dickinson took over his in-laws' large country home, driving down weekends and spending school holidays gardening and repairing the house. The second book in the Pibble series is *A Pride of Heroes*. It is set in "Herryngs," an eighteenth-century, revitalized grand home noted for its lion pit. There is also a zoo on the grounds, and the inhabitants wear period costumes to meet tourist expectations of "Old England" in a Disneyland fashion. The pride of the title refers in part to the estate's pride of lions and in part to the pride of its eccentric, aristocratic owners, the Claverings, Sir Richard and Sir Ralph–twin brothers and World War II military heroes who hid their major failures well. The brothers' pride results in their being eaten by their lions. There seem to be plenty of red herrings to distract Pibble from his investigation of the supposed suicide (really a murder) of the family mechanic. These red herrings include one Clavering twin pretending to be both brothers, a machine for grinding up bones, a particularly fierce man-eating lion, a family tradition of dueling and competitive womanizing, and porno-

*Dust jacket for Dickinson's 1972 novel in which Pibble is called on to help a shady
Greek tycoon (from Cooper and Pike,* Detective Fiction: The
Collector's Guide, *second edition, 1994)*

graphic Hindu-style temple carvings featuring cavorting local historical personalities. The seeming red herrings prove integral to Pibble's placing of blame. As he becomes more deeply immersed in his investigation, his original eulogy to the grand house as a vision of balance and decorum is replaced by a sense of the house reflecting its inhabitants, a superficial semblance of propriety but in truth "monstrous," "an alien mass leaning its elbows on the landscape." Likewise, his original irritation with the pretensions of the family is replaced with horror as he realizes that they truly believe in and live out eighteenth-century aristocratic values and that behind the facade lies a clever madman who carries those values to their ruinous end. This novel received the British Crime Writers Association's Golden Dagger Award for the best mystery of the year. As in the other books in this series, it develops the character and background of Pibble, who contemplates retirement and

repeatedly faces the absurdity of the universe and of his thankless task. He describes himself as "the chosen vulture spiraling down onto a dying line," and later, disgusted by the ease with which the family thinks they can manipulate his case, he warns "the lion would feel the talons of this vulture, blunt, bourgeois talons though they were." Luckily, as the vulture spirals down after a prey still capable of deadly attack, he is joined by others of his kind–in this case other policemen who save Pibble from the same fate the mechanic suffered.

In Dickinson's third novel, *The Seals* (1970), published in the United States as *The Sinful Stones,* Pibble uses some of his vacation time to answer the summons of millionaire Sir Francis Francis, two-time winner of the Nobel Prize and Pibble's father's employer and betrayer. Currently on an island in the Hebrides, the richest and most notable "convert" to a religious sect constructing "the eternal city," the elderly and sickly

Sir Francis, sharp-tongued, spiteful, suspicious, and arrogant, has discovered that portions of his memoirs have been stolen and published. The investigation of the religious sect is secondary to Pibble's interest in gaining knowledge of his father, who died while James was still young. By establishing a quid pro quo arrangement with Sir Francis, Pibble slowly uncovers his brilliant father's history, a process that causes Pibble's own recollections of his father to surface. The recollections twice help Pibble escape from danger. His memory of his father's lesson about the strengths and weaknesses of arches shows him the way to escape from a locked cell, and later, his memory of his father attempting without success to get his homemade kite more than a few feet off the ground helps Pibble to bring down a pursuing helicopter. In spite of his strong sense of his own shortcomings, Pibble proves himself his father's son not only in using practical lessons learned from his father but also in his looking past the shortcomings of other people and seeing them as worthy of risking his life.

While writing adult mysteries, Dickinson was also producing novels for young people in science fiction and other genres. Among them was *Emma Tupper's Diary* (1971), which received the Notable Book Award from the American Library Association the year of its publication.

By the next novel in the Pibble series, *Sleep and His Brother* (1971), Pibble has been sacked after thirty-four years of service. The mystery opens with this announcement, noting that Pibble's self-confidence has been stripped from him. He calls himself a "minor expert in beer and murder and the treatment of ailing lawns." In an attempt to lessen her husband's sense of being at loose ends, Mary Pibble arranges for him to meet the secretary of the McNair Foundation, a charitable institution that has been established to care for children with an illness called "cathypny." Reluctant at first, Pibble finds that he likes the children and is offered two jobs, one by a resident doctor because of Pibble's apparent ability to receive telepathic messages from the children, and the other by the secretary, Posey Dixon-Jones, who believes there is something illegal about a sudden influx of funding and who would like a discreet investigation.

Limited to a collective vocabulary of about three hundred words, more often asleep than awake, and apparently telepathic, the cathypnic children are otherworldly and difficult to communicate with. Marilyn Goddard, the stepdaughter of serial killer Samuel Gorton, is one of the cathypnic children, though different from the others because she has nightmares rather than pleasant dreams. Pibble believes that Gorton, recently released from prison, is planning to sneak into the home and kill Posey and to retrieve Marilyn, whose telepathic powers make her a kind of familiar. Pibble also investigates the two resident doctors, neither of whose work presents clear, unambiguous research or motivations. Reuben Kelly's research into the cause of the children's illness at once helps to prolong the children's lives and tempts him to use the children as guinea pigs to be sacrificed in the pursuit of a Nobel Prize. Ram Silver's research into the afterlife, supported by millionaire Thanassi Thanatos, is by its very abstractness open to fraudulence. So when the house is set on fire, the question becomes whether the children's words have been warnings that confirm Pibble's suspicions about Gorton, or whether the words have been meaningless and the danger was really coming from the doctors.

The difficulty of separating legitimate causes for concern from false alarms is likewise a central theme in *The Lizard in the Cup* (1972), featuring Pibble and Thanatos. Contrary to his name, Thanatos is the embodiment of relished life, and his concern in this work is whether to take seriously the rumor of a pending assassination attempt by the Mafia. Pibble, whose vacation with his wife in Greece is being bankrolled by Thanatos, leaves Mary on Corfu when he is summoned by Thanatos to the island of Hyos. Like the royal court Pibble compares it to, Thanatos's realm is filled with the trappings of wealth and power—food, drink, a host of mechanical conveniences, servants, and toys such as powerboats and dune buggies. Thanatos himself is kingly, with a beautiful, pampered mistress, a network of contacts and spies, his tests of the loyalty of his "courtiers," and the continually swirling galaxy of orbiting satellites—beautiful women and artists—who hope for patronage or a place in court. Among the dangers Pibble assesses are the potential access to Thanatos's stronghold from the cliff-side monastery run by two drunken monks, the discovery of a person wanted by the police, the hints of the island being used for the production of morphine or heroin, the possibility of priceless mosaics being stolen from the monastery, and the sentiments of each of the courtiers, all men who know they owe everything they have to Thanatos. Pibble's discoveries frequently cause him to question to whom he owes loyalty. At times, protecting Thanatos conflicts with his policeman's knowledge of right and wrong; yet, that knowledge in turn reminds him that his own dismissal from Scotland Yard was not right. Also, his strong attraction to Thanatos's mistress, Tony d'Agniello, conflicts with his loyalties to himself, Mary, and Thanatos. Although in the end he does what he considers right, it is not without a painful sense of loss.

This same year Dickinson wrote a screenplay, *Mandog,* which Lois Lamplugh turned into a six-episode

*Dust jacket for the U.S. edition of Dickinson's 1984 novel
in which a woman connects the actions of her twin
sister and mother to the death of her lover
(Richland County Public Library)*

teleplay of the same title produced by the British Broadcasting Corporation (BBC) in 1972. The next year Dickinson's children's novel and science-fiction mystery *The Green Gene* was published. The novel postulates an alternative world in which a rigidly authoritarian England is divided into Celts (green humans) and Saxons (blacks and whites), with separate laws for each, an apartheid situation that provides Dickinson the opportunity for effective satire, as the Saxons oppress and intimidate the Celts. A gentle Indian medical statistician, whose knowledge of English ways is gleaned from popular magazines, disrupts the politics of the day by developing a surprising method of predicting the green mutation. He eventually elucidates a murder and, in self-defense, ends up double-crossing everyone. Dickinson's ability to move outside conventional perspectives and provide an Indian view of English life lends both comedy and realism to his sharp-edged projection.

The Gift (1973), a children's novel, was the basis for a television serial produced by Red Rooster and

broadcast on BBC television in 1990. *The Changes: A Trilogy* (1975), comprising *The Weathermonger, Heartsease,* and *The Devil's Children,* likewise provided the basis for a television serial produced by the BBC in 1975.

In *The Poison Oracle* (1974) psycholinguist Wesley Morris, anxious to study the complex language of the Stone Age marsh people of the Arab kingdom of Q'Kut, has been hired at a huge salary to cater to the wishes of a charming, ruthless, Oxford-educated sheik. Morris introduces into a group of captive chimpanzees an intelligent chimpanzee, Dinah, with whom he communicates through colored blocks of varying shapes. He hopes that the study will go beyond the well-known (and factual) study by behaviorists Ann and David Premack of the learning skills of another chimpanzee, Sarah, as indeed it does. The setting is a modernistic Arab palace in a desert surrounding oil-rich marshlands. The inhabitants of the marsh have ancient treaties of loyalty with the royal line. The sultan is poisoned by his Arab chief adviser, in a manner that ensures that the Sultan's hereditary bodyguard, himself one of the marsh people, will be blamed. His apparent motive is his passion for an Englishwoman; newly installed as the sultan's favorite concubine, she escapes with him into the marshes. To prevent the destruction of the marshes for oil exploitation, which will follow from the breaking of the treaties, Wesley must travel there to bring the runaways out as witnesses, and as a result finds himself undergoing trial by the poison oracle of the marsh people and seeing firsthand the complex but primitive nature of their culture. He confirms the trustworthiness of his witnesses during a convincing demonstration in which Dinah uses her blocks to answer questions about the past and identify the murderer. Ultimately, the novel warns of potential ecological disaster as human tampering disrupts the slow, evolutionary patterns of nature and poisons the world.

The heroine of *The Lively Dead* (1975), Lydia Timms, is an interesting contradiction. She is the daughter of an earl, occasionally invited to hobnob with heads of state and minor government officials, but she is also the tough-minded, hardworking landlady of a run-down, five-story apartment house in Notting Hill. Throughout the novel Timms is engaged energetically in restoring the apartments room by room and board by board, testing for dry rot, replacing damaged wood, hanging wallpaper, and refinishing. Her goal is partly to enhance her own finances but also, in small ways, to help the downtrodden. She is as comfortable with a crowbar, hammer, and nails as she is with entertaining her young son and babysitting a renter's squalling infant. She rents the top floor to the exiled Livonian government, a group of eccentric, elderly gentlemen whose national hero has supposedly recently died in a

Siberian work camp, but who turns up instead in the grave of an elderly renter who passed away suddenly. The body of the renter, in turn, has been buried in the flowerbed, and Timms must face the truth that a conspiracy is afoot among her renters. Timms manages to provide hope for the dead renter's imprisoned daughter, thwart a thug and his cohorts, block a real estate swindle, and prove an intellectual match for a younger, stronger opponent with a political agenda.

Praised for its inventive irreverence and for its delightful heroine, *King and Joker* (1976) provides an alternative universe, one in which the eldest son of Albert Edward, Prince of Wales (King Edward VII from 1901 to 1910), did not die in 1892 and instead produced a modern successor, King Victor II–a frustrated medical doctor with a live-in mistress and a vegetarian son. Buckingham Palace is plagued by pranks, including a frog under a breakfast tray and a plethora of pianos delivered all at once. The Osmonds draw a larger crowd than do the royals, the king seriously considers giving a party for all claimants to be "Rightful Kings of England" (including two blacks and a Chinese), and the princess is getting ready for her O-level school examinations. By moving out of the real world, Dickinson is free to describe royalty in ways that would otherwise be libelous, and the introduction of a murder (the king's double propped up on the throne, dead) simply adds spice to a witty satiric spoof. At one level of seriousness, however, Dickinson's goal is simply to humanize those whose public status demands of them a facade quite at odds with their reality.

In 1977 Dickinson received the Boston Globe-Horn Book Award for Nonfiction, for *Chance, Luck, and Destiny* (1975), and the Guardian Award for Children's Fiction, awarded to *The Blue Hawk* (1976), a children's book that Don D'Ammassa of *Twentieth-Century Science Fiction Writers* says may be "the best single work Dickinson has written." By rescuing a sacred blue hawk, despite taboos against such action, the protagonist, a young trainee for the priesthood, totally disrupts his society, brings about the death of the king, and almost dies himself in the power struggle that he precipitates.

Walking Dead (1977) is set on two Caribbean islands whose people and dictator resemble Haiti's population and Papa Doc Duvalier. The central character, David Foxe, is a mathematician, statistician, and laboratory researcher, testing the effects of a supposed goodness-enhancing drug on rats. In fact, however, the scientific experiments prove to be a cover for a spy and intelligence agency, as Foxe learns to his dismay. The government is battling voodoo out of mixed motives, to bring the population into the twentieth century but also to eliminate the opposition. Yet, ironically, they find

voodoo the only means to fight voodoo effectively. A murdered woman provides the government with an excuse to take Foxe prisoner and intimidate him into applying the test methods and drugs used on rats to particularly recalcitrant prisoners, a religious sect that believes in mystical powers. Foxe, who is in a pit with the prisoners and who has listened to tapes of their prolonged torture, uses a mixture of science and voodoo to carry out an escape plan. After much bloodshed on both sides and a revolution of sorts, Foxe manages to overcome his voodoo nemesis. The title refers to the voodoo concept of zombies, to the effects of totalitarianism on an impoverished and tyrannized populace, and to the hero, whose choice of love and an acceptance of the mystical over experimentation bring him back to the world of the living. Dickinson helps readers enter minds different from their own, yet humanizes his alien islanders through his attention to the details that provide insight into the helplessness and vulnerabilities that have produced their patterns of behavior and belief.

Dickinson served as chairman of the management committee for the Society of Authors from 1978 to 1980. In 1979 *Tulku,* an adventure fantasy for younger readers set in Tibet and influenced by Rudyard Kipling's *Kim* (1901), won the Whitbread Award, the Library Association Carnegie Medal, and, along with *The Flight of Dragons* (1979), was named to the American Library Association's "Best Books for Young Adults 1979" list.

As Patrick Meanor points out in *Critical Survey of Mystery and Detective Fiction* (1988), with each successful novel Pibble is more greatly humanized, his vulnerabilities and limitations exposed. His Victorian sensibilities nurture his sense of personal responsibility and guilt, even for events beyond his control. A good man in a wicked world, he comes more and more to understand the futility of his efforts. The last in the Pibble series, *One Foot in the Grave* (1979), appeared seven years after *The Lizard in the Cup* and returned to the style of the first books in the series. The death of Pibble's wife, Mary, leads to his complete physical and mental breakdown. Committed to an exclusive sanatorium/mental hospital and contemplating suicide, he is at the mercy of nurses and doctors working to cure him of his physical ailments and to awaken him to a sense of reality and self-identity. When he stumbles on a corpse and falls in love with a kindly nurse, his will to live and his desire to solve criminal mysteries are both restored, and, though he drifts in and out of reveries about the past, he reexperiences the thrill of the hunt and the sense of moral principle that drove his earlier investigations.

On 1 January 1982 *The Flight of Dragons* was adapted as an animated television movie by the Ameri-

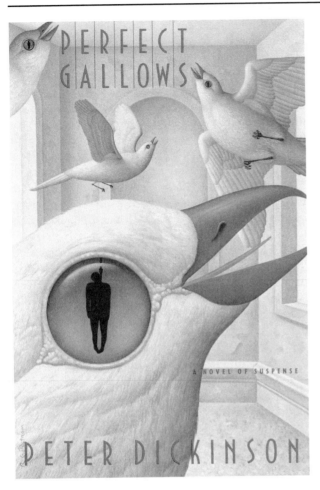

*Dust jacket for the U.S. edition of Dickinson's 1988 novel
about an actor haunted by a murder in his past
(Richland County Public Library)*

can Broadcasting Company. That same year Dickinson received the Library Association Carnegie Medal for his retelling of Old Testament stories in *City of Gold* (1980) and *The Last House-Party,* a reminiscence of prewar country life and an homage to the Golden Age detective story, was published. It is a farewell to the prewar British way of life and to long-cherished traditions, a farewell epitomized in the final action of the book, the selling of the ancient estate by the impoverished British inheritor to a rich Arab potentate and a restructuring of the ancient castle clock tower, burned in 1937, to make the Saracen behead the Christian as the hour turns, rather than the original pattern of Christian beheading Saracen. Allusions to real personalities such as Vita Sackville-West and her estate at Sissinghurst add greater depth and realism to the portrait. This is the only one of Dickinson's adult novels to be written from entirely outside the minds of any of the participants, so that all motives and purposes remain uncertain. The novel bridges two time periods, with an adult seeking explanations of childhood experiences. The story begins

with an introduction to Snailwood through the voice of a tour guide and then turns to 1937 and the lavish weekend parties of the countess of Snailwood, a beauty whose sympathies with the Nazis are hidden by her willingness to bring together significant and conflicting multinational personalities representing the prewar political spectrum, with Jews and Arabs at odds over the British plans for Israel and a Jewish state, with pro-Hitler British fascists and antifascist soldiers and politicians in a countdown to war. Pedantic assertions denigrating Winston Churchill as weak and ineffectual are ironic in context, and speculation about the German willingness to gas civilians suggests how unimaginable the later Nazi atrocities were. Amid the festivities and the confrontations, a seven-year-old child is raped and the castle clock tower set afire. The closed circle of acquaintances brought together under a single roof limits the possible suspects. The fire is blamed on a disgruntled employee whose head is caved in by an anvil used as a weight to drive the clock, while the child accuses the young heir to the estate of the rape, and he flees the scene, sending a message from abroad giving up his inheritance.

The action of the novel alternates between the past and the attempt of the child-victim forty years later to reassess and come to terms with the trauma that still brings her nightmares. Through a quirk of fate she has inherited the house in which she was violated and has consulted a clock maker whom she begins to think may be the missing accused. As she gathers testimony and rethinks events, she realizes that there were a multitude of hidden adult motives affecting responses to the crime and, just as she convinces herself of the identity of the clock repairer with the missing man and of his innocence, his explanation of what could have happened and why matches testimony from another witness, and she is appalled to discover that he is indeed the man who not only raped her but in effect murdered one or possibly two others. Her second loss of innocence parallels the reader's final shocking understanding that the intelligent and seemingly kindly soldier turned clock maker is a pedophile who still has to struggle to control his impulses and may be on the verge of raping another child on the same estate.

Using an experimental form similar to the alternating time pattern of *The Last House-Party, Hindsight* is a detective story exploring questions about creativity and the ties between fiction and fact. The narrator, a mystery writer named Paul Rogers, has been engaged by a dying man to recall childhood memories about a great man of letters, whose biography the dying man is trying to complete. Rogers is trying to work these remembered vignettes into a fictional mystery, but he comes to realize that a true mystery is before him. Rogers recalls his harsh, respected preparatory-school master of Latin—who was at one time the male lover of the great man. Rogers also describes his youthful pleasure in being allowed to attend the weekend parties of an attractive, liberated woman who claimed to have been an intimate friend of his dead father and who, he learns from the biographer, resisted the advances of the great man. He also describes a horrific and bungled drive to cull the growing herd of deer on the school grounds and his discovery of a body while searching for wounded deer. The fact that these three memories stand out from his past makes the adult Rogers explore them more fully in the light of new knowledge. The interest of the book lies in part in the portrait of youth coping with war, physical violence, and puzzling adult behavior. It also lies, however, in the contrast in understanding between Paul Rogers as a youth, enchanted with the rural setting and naively innocent of the sexual repercussions of adult encounters he observed, and Paul Rogers as an adult, who sees his craft as a means to "truth" and, in attempting to recapture incidents and memories from his youth, realizes that a supposed accident was murder. He understands fully who did what, why, and with what consequences. In the end, Dickinson's book supposedly becomes itself the fictional rendering of the cruel truths that Rogers' exploration of facts and hindsight revealed.

Death of a Unicorn (1984) makes use of Dickinson's experiences at *Punch,* most effectively in advice to a younger writer to employ contrasting voices to lend depth and complexity to otherwise lightweight fare, in the sparring between writers, and in the portraits of journalistic types. By tracing the career of a young woman who obtains a writing position, in large part because of her aristocratic social connections, at a *Punch* competitor in 1952, Dickinson suggests biographical parallels. The writing and editorial force is an odd mix of class and political affiliations, with one close colleague revealed years later as a communist plant. The give-and-take of the staff rings true, as does their odd mix of respect for the old families and their desire for shocking gossip and exposés about them. H. R. F. Keating, in his article on Dickinson for *Twentieth Century Crime and Mystery Writers* (1980), criticizes the occasional showiness of Dickinson's vocabulary, but herein words and phrases such as *aposiopesis, haruspication,* and "neither mathematical nor hippophatical my bent" characterize the pretensions of writers for whom snobbery is their meat and potatoes, as well as their sheer pleasure in linguistic dueling.

The story hinges on Cheadle, a grand but financially burdensome country house in the Midlands, to which Lady Margaret Millett (Mabs) is the heir. (His family's less imposing home in Gloucestershire has been an important source for various houses in Dickinson's books both in its layout and for the century-long struggle to keep it financially viable.) Again, Dickinson contrasts two periods. In the events set in 1952–1953 the twenty-year-old Mabs, while participating in the London debutante season, begins her writing career and falls in love with and becomes the mistress of an entrepreneur with tangled financial affairs, until he is mysteriously gunned down in the streets of Rio de Janeiro. Thirty years later she is a writer of romantic novels whose success has enabled her to establish Cheadle as a major tourist attraction, when a chance encounter leads to her gradual discovery that her identical twin sister and her mother set in motion the chain of events that produced her lover's death, in part to bring her back to the family estate and her inherited obligations. The novel captures not only the niceties of the British class system but also the equally complex relationship between natives and plantation owners in a colonial situation (in this case the Barbados). Just as the heroine is a slave to her inheritance, the man of mystery in the story is part black because his grandfather married a beautiful quadroon, and his mother's much-trusted black retainer is also his brother by a slave mistress, and many of his drives and actions spring from that inheritance.

Tefuga (1986) is a mainstream novel with some mystery element. Set in colonial Nigeria, and in the same country after independence, it concerns a television journalist's attempt, with the help of his mother's diary, to make a movie portraying the events leading up to his father's suicide, before he himself was born.

Perfect Gallows: A Novel of Suspense (1988) explores the making of actor Adrian Waring. Alternating between 1944 and 1986, the story of Adrian's obsession with his theatrical talents unfolds. Driven by the knowledge of his own potential greatness and willing to protect his gift at any cost, Andrew Wragge loses his mother in a bombing raid with no more regret than the loss of his birth name when he adopts his stage name. When he travels to relatives and learns that he is likely to inherit money from his ailing uncle, Waring scorns the money, wanting to be able to say he made it to the top of his profession on the basis of his talent alone. He does, however, take the opportunity to act that an aunt offers when she decides to put on a production of William Shakespeare's *The Tempest* (1611). While rehearsing, Adrian deliberately sets out to seduce the girl playing Miranda, just to test his powers of acting. Now in 1986 a famous, successful actor, Waring's current girlfriend probes too deeply into his past, reminding him of the death of Samuel Mkele, his uncle's black butler and a natural actor whose performance of Caliban displayed acting ability equal to Waring's. Publicly deemed a suicide, Mkele's death haunts Adrian because

Dust jacket for Dickinson's 1999 novel in which an elderly, paralyzed widow investigates a mysterious disappearance with the help of her nurse and her daughter (Richland County Public Library)

he knows it was murder and knows why Samuel was killed. Perhaps the most chilling of Dickinson's works, *Perfect Gallows* picks up themes of obsessiveness and loyalty raised in earlier works, particularly *Sleep and His Brother* and *The Lizard in the Cup*. Most frightening is the question with which the reader is left at the end: is Adrian haunted by the murder of a human being, the loss of a great talent, guilt for having never revealed what he knew, or fear that his knowledge of what happened might be discovered and his career ruined? In 1988, the same year that *Perfect Gallows* was published, Dickinson's first wife died.

A sequel to *King and Joker, Skeleton-in-Waiting* (1989) features as its protagonist an adult Princess Louise, with her new baby, Davy, balancing the roles of motherhood, family arbiter and peacekeeper, and one of the representatives of the monarchy at public functions. When Louise's grandmother Princess Marie, mother of the king and last of the Romanovs, dies after falling off a piano while chasing her parrot, her collection of letters becomes a bone of contention among three parties: the

man she named as her literary executor, Louise's aunt Beatrice and the woman Beatrice hired to translate the letters from Russian, and the other members of the royal family, who do not want their secrets or Princess Marie's malicious gossip published. In addition to trying to assure that the letters and their contents remain within the family, Louise is called on to stamp out fires of scandal when her brother's wife has a nervous breakdown, all the while trying to live as normal a life as possible among security guards, multiple diaries scheduling her life, and the ever-present threats of abduction, kidnapping, and bombings. In 1989 as well, Dickinson received a Boston Globe-Horn Book Award for Fiction honorable mention for *Eva* (1988) and in 1990 the Whitbread Award for *AK* (1990). He married writer Robin McKinley on 3 January 1992. He had previously contributed the story "Flight" to her collection *Imaginary Lands* (1985).

Set wholly in contemporary London, *Play Dead* (1991) returns to the form of the orthodox crime novel. Nannies, their charges, and the families they work for form the small community explored. The protagonist is Poppy Tasker, a fifty-year-old divorcée currently baby-sitting her grandson Toby while his mother stays busy with her political campaign to become a Labour Party representative in Parliament. Not ready to resign herself to old age or to identify herself solely as a grandmother or a babysitter, Poppy's membership in what she calls the "Nafia" introduces her not only to the variety of lif-estyle possibilities presented by the different nannies but also to three men who will alter the course of her life: a young pedophile whose murder she helps solve, a Romanian national with whom she shares a love of opera, and Inspector Firth, with whom she shares a "sense of order, structure, the feel for the network of other lives you've got to respect and cherish if you're going to live among them."

The Yellow Room Conspiracy (1994) is a story told in flashback of the events leading up to the fire that destroyed the Vereker family's mansion, Blatchards, along with the evidence that might have explained the death of Gerry Grantworth in the Yellow Room of the mansion that same evening. For the five Vereker sisters and some of the men who loved them, Blatchards was both a force that drew them together and the represen-tation of a way of life on the verge of being lost in the chaos resulting from World War II. Told in chapters alternating between the now elderly Lucy Vereker and her lover, Paul Ackerley, the tale reveals the power of their romantic attachment despite their suspicions about each other as responsible for Grantworth's death and the tangle of marriages, espionage, sexual liaisons, secrets, and shady financial dealings that threatened to break them apart while the war tore apart the world.

The power of love is likewise at the heart of *Some Deaths before Dying* (1999), in which Rachel Matson, a ninety-year-old widow of a World War II veteran, par-alyzed below the neck and in the final stages of her ill-ness, uses her lifework as a photographer, her devoted nurse, and the daughter with whom she is living to solve the mystery of the disappearance of one of a pair of rare pistols she gave her husband when he returned from the war. The investigation is as much a final put-ting of her life in order for Rachel as it is the solution of what turns out to be several mysteries. In the process of examining the record of her life captured in her photo-graphs and tracing the current owners of the gun,

Rachel pieces together the events that led to the dimin-ishment of her married life after Jocelyn came home from the war, to two murders, and to the creation of the Cambi Road Association, which Rachel believed was simply a group of veterans talking out the horrors of their experience on the Cambi Road, where they were prisoners of war, enslaved and abused by their Japanese captors.

In 2001 Dickinson received the Phoenix Award for *The Seventh Raven* (1981). The Phoenix Award is given by the Children's Literature Association to young-adult books of high literary merit that have been neglected or obscured.

Peter Dickinson brings the power of an out-sider's vision and the force of a classical education to his mystery writing. Where others find simplicity, he finds complexity. His characters are restless, at times in the grip of change even against their will. His existen-tial perceptions and sensibilities have led to compari-sons with Samuel Beckett and Albert Camus. Behind socially acceptable facades lie hidden drives, fears, obsessions, guilt, and murderous intent. Yet, his char-acters, faced with the discovery of hidden crimes, often think that the past is the past and the only question is what to do to keep on going. Like the exiles of whom Edward Said speaks, Dickinson sees with a dual vision that enables him to puncture deeply cherished preten-sions and convictions. Thus, he takes on the absurdi-ties of apartheid and of racism in general, debunks Victorian restraints and hypocrisies, and challenges readers' preconceptions. At the same time, he draws readers into the special features of closed worlds and the eccentrics who inhabit them and provides thought-ful and challenging questions of crime, criminality, social obligation, and justice.

Interview:

"Peter Dickinson," *Achuka* (19 February 2003) <www.achuka.co.uk/guests/dickinson/int01.htm>.

References:

Kit Alderice, "Notes from a Crossover Novelist," *Pub-lishers Weekly* (11 May 1992): 29;

Eden Ross Lipson, "Write, Then Research, Then Rewrite," *New York Times Book Review* (20 April 1986): 26.

Joan Fleming

(27 March 1908 – 15 November 1980)

Gina Macdonald
Nicholls State University

BOOKS: *Dick Brownie and the Zagabog: A Collection of Tales* (London: Fairston, 1944);

Mulberry Hall (Bognor Regis, U.K.: Crowther, 1945);

The Riddle in the River (London: Hammond, 1946);

Button Jugs (London: Hammond, 1947);

Two Lovers Too Many (London: Hutchinson, 1949);

The Jackdaw's Nest (London: Hammond, 1949);

A Daisy-Chain for Satan (London: Hutchinson, 1950; Garden City, N.Y.: Doubleday, 1950);

The Gallows in My Garden (London: Hutchinson, 1951);

The Man Who Looked Back (London: Hutchinson, 1951; Garden City, N.Y.: Doubleday, 1952); republished as *A Cup of Cold Poison* (London: Hamilton, 1969);

Polly Put the Kettle On (London: Hutchinson, 1952);

The Good and the Bad (London: Hutchinson, 1953; Garden City, N.Y.: Doubleday, 1953);

He Ought to Be Shot (London: Hutchinson, 1955; Garden City, N.Y.: Doubleday, 1955);

The Deeds of Dr. Deadcert (London: Hutchinson, 1955; New York: Washburn, 1957);

You Can't Believe Your Eyes (London: Collins, 1957; New York: Washburn, 1957);

Maiden's Prayer (London: Collins, 1957; New York: Washburn, 1958);

Malice Matrimonial (London: Collins, 1959; New York: Washburn, 1959);

Miss Bones (London: Collins, 1959; New York: Washburn, 1960);

The Man from Nowhere (London: Collins, 1960; New York: Washburn, 1961);

Shakespeare's Country in Colour (London: Batsford, 1960);

In the Red (London: Collins, 1961; New York: Washburn, 1961);

When I Grow Rich (London: Collins, 1962; New York: Washburn, 1962);

Death of a Sardine (London: Collins, 1963; New York: Washburn, 1964);

The Chill and the Kill (London: Collins, 1964; New York: Washburn, 1964);

Joan Fleming (photograph by Jerry Bauer; from the dust jacket for the U.S. edition of . . . To Make an Underworld, 1976)

Nothing Is the Number When You Die (London: Collins, 1965; New York: Washburn, 1965);

Midnight Hag (London: Collins, 1966; New York: Washburn, 1966);

No Bones about It (London: Collins, 1967; New York: Washburn, 1967);

Kill or Cure (London: Collins, 1968; New York: Washburn, 1968);

Hell's Belle (London: Collins, 1968; New York: Washburn, 1969);

Young Man, I Think You're Dying (London: Collins, 1970; New York: Putnam, 1970);

Screams for a Penny Dreadful (London: Hamilton, 1971);

Grim Death and the Barrow Boys (London: Collins, 1971); republished as *Be a Good Boy* (New York: Putnam, 1971);

Alas Poor Father (London: Collins, 1972; New York: Putnam, 1973);

Dirty Butter for Servants (London: Hamilton, 1972);

You Won't Let Me Finish (London: Collins, 1973); republished as *You Won't Let Me Finnish* (New York: Putnam, 1974);

How to Live Dangerously (London: Collins, 1974; New York: Putnam, 1975);

Too Late! Too Late! The Maiden Cried: A Gothick Novel (London: Hamilton, 1975; New York: Putnam, 1975);

. . . To Make an Underworld (London: Collins, 1976; New York: Putnam, 1976);

Every Inch a Lady: A Murder of the Fifties (London: Collins, 1977; New York: Putnam, 1977);

The Day of the Donkey Derby (London: Collins, 1978; New York: Putnam, 1978).

OTHER: "Cat on the Trail," *Saint* (June 1964);

"Gone Is Gone," in *Tales of Unease,* edited by John Burke (London: Pan, 1966; Garden City, N.Y.: Doubleday, 1969);

"Still Waters," in *Winter's Crimes 1,* edited by George Hardinge (London: Macmillan, 1968);

"The Bore," in *Winter's Crimes 4,* edited by Hardinge (London: Macmillan, 1972).

During her writing career, Joan Fleming wrote some thirty-three mystery novels, some historical, all quite varied in approach, with finely delineated characters, surprising twists of plot, and amusing or compelling eccentricities. Her principle series character, Nuri Bey Iskirlak, a Turkish philosopher, represents part of the growing British interest in ethnicity in the 1960s and 1970s, reflected, for example, in the works of Gavin Black, Arthur Upfield, H. R. F. Keating, and James McClure. In keeping with this interest, she set several of her novels in exotic locales, for example, Paris in *The Good and the Bad* (1953), a Portuguese fishing village in *Death of a Sardine* (1963), and Helsinki in *You Won't Let Me Finish* (1973; published in the United States as *You Won't Let Me Finnish,* 1974). Most of her novels are psychological studies of a community's response to murder rather than reports of investigative methods. Kathleen Klein in *Twentieth Century Crime and Mystery Writers* has compared Fleming to a less complex

Patricia Highsmith in her study of the criminal mind and of the criminality latent in others and in her inclusion of what the *San Francisco Chronicle* called "charming oddities." In this way her works are also somewhat like those of Richard Hull, in their unusual narrative perspectives and deceptive voices, or Ruth Rendell, in their cruelty, viciousness, and criminality at the heart of the English village. Fleming's villagers are not at all kindly but instead are capable of deep-seated malice, unwarranted suspicions, and xenophobia. D. B. Hughes in *Book Week* asserted, "There are not enough superlatives to do justice to the Joan Fleming works."

Born Joan Margaret Gibson in Horwich, Lancashire, England, on 27 March 1908, she was the daughter of David and Sarah Elizabeth (Suttcliffe) Gibson. She attended Brighthelmston School in Southport, Lancashire, before moving on to Grand Belle Vue in Lausanne, Switzerland, and then Lausanne University. Her youthful adventures abroad stirred in her an interest in cultural differences and a desire to travel to distant lands. On returning to England, she worked as the medical secretary of a London doctor from 1928 to 1932, seeing human nature close up—sometimes at its worst. In June 1932 she married Norman Bell Beattie Fleming, an eye doctor. The couple had three daughters and a son—Penelope, Lalage, David, and Rowan Whitfield. Fleming's religious affiliation was Church of England, and she was a self-declared freethinker in politics. She took pleasure in photography, gardening, travel, and her four Yorkshire terriers. Fleming once told *Contemporary Authors* that she got her plot ideas and characters from simply observing people around her, and she does indeed look closely at her characters in her novels. Unmotivated jealousy, selfishness, egotism, narrow-mindedness, dependency, fear of change, suspicion of outsiders, greed, backbiting, a pleasure in bullying, a willingness to reinterpret reality to suit one's prejudices or needs, a tendency to believe the worst about those around one—these are but a few of the characteristics at play in her fictive creations.

Fleming had been writing children's books since *Dick Brownie and the Zagabog* in 1944. She published *Mulberry Hall* in 1945, *The Riddle in the River* in 1946, and *Button Jugs* in 1947. In these books she honed skills that gave her the confidence to attempt writing for adult readers. Consequently, in 1949 she published not only another children's book, *The Jackdaw's Nest,* but also her first adult novel, *Two Lovers Too Many.* She produced a novel a year thereafter until 1978. In *A Daisy-Chain for Satan* (1950) the narrator, Mr. Ravensden, the uncle of Saul Jones, is first stunned by the breathtaking beauty of Saul's wife, Sigtuna, but when her disagreeable father drowns and Sigtuna clearly schemes to force Ravensden's silence, he begins to understand the trouble his nephew is in. The night Sig-

Dust jacket for Fleming's 1949 novel, her first for adult readers (from John Cooper
and B. A. Pike, Detective Fiction: The Collector's Guide, 1988)

tuna dies along the local towpath, Saul goes for a walk alone along that same towpath in a forty-mile-an-hour gale, and it takes all of Ravensden's power to save Saul from the gallows and reunite him with his small son. At the end of the novel, Saul reflects on how wrong he was when he asserted that his wife had not sold her soul to Satan and how "beautiful, neat, clean, and above all timely" her end was.

The Deeds of Dr. Deadcert (1955) concentrates on the psychological and emotional reactions of the victims—both direct and indirect—rather than on the psychology of the criminal mind or on the detective's investigation. The book was turned into the movie *Family Doctor* by 20th Century-Fox Film Corporation in 1958.

The continually ironic and slyly witty *Maiden's Prayer* (1957) features a vulnerable middle-aged spinster, Miss Maiden, who is courted by a charming but scheming Mr. Aladdin. Mr. Aladdin hopes to replenish his finances through whatever inheritance she will bring him through marriage. Mr. Aladdin then plans to rid himself of her by murder, but in this case Miss Maiden and her mother, Mrs. Maiden, prove more for-

midable. The setting is a shabby Georgian house in London. The characters are carefully and plausibly drawn, and the suspense is indeed effective. *Malice Matrimonial* (1959), called wry, sardonic, malicious, intelligent, and amusing by various reviewers, follows the cause-and-effect outcome of an unhappy marriage, while in the grim *Miss Bones* (1959) a skeleton is exhumed from a shop courtyard; a burglar plays detective; and dual identities mislead.

In 1960 Fleming, whose works regularly reflect her practical understanding of William Shakespeare's characters and comments, published a nonfiction book titled *Shakespeare's Country in Colour,* a study of and guide to the Stratford-upon-Avon area. The same year she published *The Man from Nowhere,* a mystery that Klein considers one of Fleming's best works because of the skill with which it probes the psychological effects of crime on a closed community. A quiet stranger, Rockambole, disturbs the rural villagers because of his highly visible birthmark, his silence about his origins and his past, and his lack of concern for what most of the locals worry a great deal about: possessions and monetary success. The villagers see in each of these traits cause for suspicion and distrust, especially when a murder occurs. The fiancée of the cleric finds the stranger attractive and grows to love him, which adds to the villagers' distrust of him. The ending is both ironic and disturbing. Anthony Boucher in *The New York Times Book Review* (1960) called *The Man from Nowhere* "quietly satisfactory," while *Springfield Republican* (1960) praised its "sharp analysis of human nature" and of life in rural England.

In 1962 Fleming's first Nuri Bey Iskirlak novel, *When I Grow Rich* (1962), received the Gold Dagger Award of the Crime Writers' Association of London. The novel is initially set in Istanbul, a locale that is neither Eastern nor Western but has a special exotic flavor of its own, "at times deadly dull and at other times causing such a penetrating wave of emotion that those who feel it never forget it nor do they get quite the same thrill anywhere else." Iskirlak, a contemplative hero, bookish and educated, nonetheless travels frequently across the Bosporus from Europe to Asia and engages with a criminal class quite at odds with his own scholarly and philosophical style and manner. At odds, too, is Iskirlak's perception of Oxford and a Westerner's understanding of that reality. Although he claims to be neither Muslim, Christian, nor Buddhist, but a combination of the best of all three, a British Council friend named Landrake regularly reminds Iskirlak of the limits of his perspective; for example, the impossibility of his questioning whether or not a marriage is a success. In *When I Grow Rich* an English girl becomes dangerously involved in Turkish opium smuggling and, when Iskirlak comes to her aid, his house is burned down and his books destroyed.

When I Grow Rich was followed by *The Chill and the Kill* (1964), an intriguing novel about Rita Side, who receives the power of second sight when inadvertently knocked over by the vicar of Marklane in his old Bentley. Rita suddenly can foretell the future, particularly the possibility of sudden death. Her newly acquired gift wins her much publicity, to the great disruption of her peaceful village. One particular prediction takes place in Marklane itself and is of murder. The details Rita sees in connection with the crime seem to fit the situation of the accused, but, in fact, Fleming takes pleasure in recounting how, seen through the prism of truth, Rita's details could add up to a different situation, with the accused murderer actually the intended victim.

In 1965 Fleming published a second volume in the short series featuring Iskirlak, *Nothing Is the Number When You Die*. The suspicious death of the husband of Iskirlak's long-time friend Tamara Yenish and the fact that her son is missing, possibly because of a father-son involvement in the opium trade, once again takes him to Oxford.

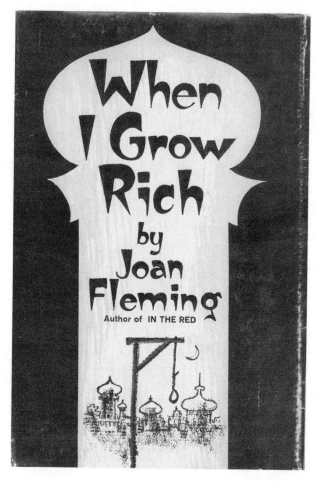

Dust jacket for the U.S. edition of Fleming's 1962 novel, the first to feature Turkish detective Nuri Bey Iskirlak (Richland County Public Library)

There he encounters an eighty-two-year-old English eccentric, Lady Mossop, who, on first meeting, is hauling horse manure by wheelbarrow to fertilize her magnolia tree. Fleming is interested in cross-cultural differences, such as the Turkish desire to appear serious and distant with strangers as opposed to the smiling Lady Mossop. The portraits of Mme. Miasma of Turkey and Lady Mossop demonstrate adaptation to changing circumstances of place and time. The effects of the destruction of Iskirlak's home and library on the young hero are a major psychological interest. Suspense, death, the opium trade, and detection take second place to Fleming's interest in how culture affects perspective, despite a common humanity. Klein finds Tamara's destruction of her dead husband's opium field too easily accomplished, given the potential danger, but the descriptions of Turkish life in the sultan's time are "fascinating."

Midnight Hag (1966) is another study of a malign village that protects and rewards the guilty, who are known and trusted, and turns with malice and spite

*Dust jacket for the U.S. edition of Fleming's 1967 novel, about
an elderly man who discovers the loot from a bank robbery
in his backyard (Richland County Public Library)*

against the innocent, merely because they are outsiders. Despite the third-person narration, the perspective is that of Sister Cramp, a lovely, highly competent nurse, who knows all the secrets of her patients, whom she assists in their homes, and understands the psychology of the townspeople. She nurses old Mr. Crumlock, an inordinately wealthy and mean-spirited man who, surprisingly, leaves his estranged adopted son all his worldly goods. Fleming captures the nurse's attitude toward this patient: "She could not but show a certain interest in the final disposal of this antique and she wondered at the courage of someone who was to die unrepentant, to storm out into whatever lay in store, as pugnacious and aggressive, as selfish and inconsiderate, as opinionated and altogether beastly as he had always been."

In point of fact, his final deathbed wish brings about the destruction of the son, Valentine, he had resented for a lifetime. Crumlock had married a beautiful pregnant girl and then driven her to her death with his cruelty; later he impregnated a sexually loose local girl and forced his despised adopted son to marry her. When she accidentally drowned, he wrote the police, accusing his son of murder. Acquitted, the son had fled to the British Virgin Islands and had become a reclusive, impoverished painter. Stunned at his good fortune in receiving recognition from his putative father, Valentine returns home, to the resentment of locals, who thought they surely would share in the inheritance. With time, he begins to see a "fearful symmetry" in his life. He marries a young woman with whom he quickly becomes bored, and, when she commits suicide, the townspeople assume he has committed murder a second time and turn on him maliciously. Sister Cramp relentlessly seeks and finds the truth, but during the time she is confronting the liars, the town's young people drive Valentine to his death. This novel is vintage Fleming, sharing with Rendell's work a negative image of the English small town, with its seething hatreds and vicious secrets just below the placid surface. Klein believes the ability of love to prosper in a setting where such hatreds and villainy thrive is one of the ironies that makes Fleming's tale most poignant.

No Bones about It (1967) is also Fleming at her best. On the edge of the story and not really introduced until almost two-thirds of the way through the book is a major bank robbery, involving a large amount of money, all in old, unmarked bills. The main perpetrators were caught almost immediately, but the loot is still at large, sought both by the mastermind of the robbery and by the pregnant wife of one of the imprisoned robbers. Fleming's focus, instead, is on a frail grandfather who accidentally discovers two bags of cash in his garden and decides to use the money to help cheer up his dreary family for a while. He finds, however, that the more he gives, the more the family needs—a kiln and other equipment for throwing pots for his daughter, the wherewithal to start a new school to direct for his son-in-law, a London apartment to attract a rich husband for a granddaughter, and so on. Some of the family members accept his lie that he has sold a little property to a company planning a large commercial development, but most believe he has done something criminal. Fleming tells her story through the point of view of each family member and the son of the housekeeper. Midway through the story they all know something unspeakable has happened, and eventually the whole family is accused of criminal indifference: ignoring the fact that the pregnant wife has been locked in the walk-in Victorian safe to suffocate and die as she gives birth. The interaction of the family members, their personal preoccupations and obsessions, their sense of guilt or lack thereof, the blame they are willing to cast on others, and the absence of common sense in the main is of far more interest to Fleming than "whodunit," because basically the whole family to varying degrees is both psychologically culpable but technically innocent. *No Bones about It* is a minor work in her canon, but it is representative of why her works are so often described as wry, odd, and yet charming. Fleming's husband died in 1968.

In 1970 Fleming won her second Gold Dagger Award of the Crime Writers' Association of London, this time for *Young Man, I Think You're Dying* (1970). She captures the adolescent mind, both good and bad, playing off two young men from the same neighborhood, Winston Sledge, a leader, indulged by his parents and self-indulgent as an adult, and Joe Bogey, a follower, a hard worker, devoted to his parents, but anxious to fit in with his peer group. Sledge has learned to get his way by a mixture of cajoling and intimidation, torturing animals, abusing his Indian girlfriend, and choosing from his neighborhood "gang" those who will drive his Jaguar while he commits petty robberies. Bogey, in turn, works in a pizza parlor and dreams of opening his own pizza place, cares for his invalid and dying father, and, behind his facade of teenage surliness, is really tender and reliable. Everything changes when Sledge kills an elderly woman who interrupts his robbery of her home, then kills his girlfriend without provocation, and frames Bogey for the first murder. Bogey's friends and family close ranks to protect him, and a lovely, upper-class runaway proves instrumental in arranging Sledge's comeuppance, a demise anticipated by the local fortune-teller, and hence the title of the novel. Fleming's portrait of the adolescent male mind is wonderfully conceived, as the following description of Bogey confirms:

> He was compelled to put on this parent-hating act, if he did not do so, he could not tolerate living at home, he would have gone off on his own somewhere long ago. So for pride's sake he swore and looked sulky and banged about the place, left his room a great deal more untidy than any pigsty, told them nothing about what he did during the day or night, and behaved most of the time like a dissatisfied lodger.

In *Grim Death and the Barrow Boys* (1971) young Gideon Price, a crippled orphan, decides to make a firm break with Towser, the peddler, con artist, petty thief, fence, and "prestidigitator" who has taught him the trade since Gideon was sixteen years old. Gideon blackmails Towser out of £1,000 and starts a pizza bar in Craigness, a town where he spent a lovely holiday and met a girl whom he has determined to marry. Though Gideon starts off on the right foot by saving a drowning child, he soon faces disappointments. Craigness in winter is not like Craigness in summer, and he finds that the money Towser gave up so easily is mainly newspa-

Dust jacket for the U.S. edition of Fleming's 1976 novel, in which a successful industrialist is wrongly suspected of rape and murder (Richland County Public Library)

per. Gideon ends up working in a geriatric home, helping the vicar with teenage youths prone to crime. Gideon continues to do good, simply because it is in his nature to do so, until a lovely girl the vicar is in love with turns up murdered. Towser, who is in town to bring Gideon back to work for him, finds the body, and Gideon, who had a flirtatious relationship with the deceased, is the main suspect. Fleming captures the gossipy nature of small-town life, the complications of human motivations, and the illogic of loyalty.

In *Alas Poor Father* (1972) Brigadier Basil Patricroft, an expert in Arab affairs newly returned to England and ready to retire, finds himself unknowingly caught in an Irish conspiracy involving an eccentric recluse who was teaching the brigadier's sons to raise racing pigeons. Mrs. Desirée Furnish, a woman the brigadier has found attractive, but not enough so to marry, is shot and killed. Since he is known to have quarreled with her and to have left behind his briefcase, he seems a prime suspect. Fleming has fun with the father's speculating about his sons as possible murderers and the sons' speculating similarly about their father. When one son disappears, however, the brigadier blows up every room in his mansion to find him, setting off the secret cache of illegal ammunition hidden in the basement as well.

In *How to Live Dangerously* (1974) the retired and somewhat stuffy Martin Pendle Hill, once an intelligence officer, has, for thirty-five years, resided in an eleven-room maisonette above the flat of the owner of the building; the elderly Miss Smite. Yet, he only truly gets to know his landlady when he asks permission to take in lodgers to share his large space. She is shocked, but he is determined. He goes against her wishes and the warnings of the colorful and loyal housekeeper to take in one lodger, who brings in a girlfriend as well. Nonetheless, Smite and Pendle Hill gradually become friends, only to have their blooming friendship ended by Smite's murder. Despite his frailty from a mending broken hip, Pendle Hill thrusts himself innocently into an investigation that taxes his strength and determination. He eventually uncovers a conspiracy between his lodgers and a rather well-organized fence with a quality cover as an expert in antiques. Encounters with a dwarf who repairs antiques and with Smite's missing cat, who left in the car with the loot, enable Pendle Hill to recover two of the stolen ceramics, enough to make his final days comfortable, and to point the police toward Smite's killer. The story began with Pendle Hill at loose ends because of the death of his beloved black Labrador retriever and of a close friend, and it ends with his call to obtain another black Lab and thus to get his life back on track.

In *. . . To Make an Underworld* (1976) a highly successful industrialist named Robert, tired of his life and no longer in love with his spouse, retires to a newly renovated seaside cottage in Cornwell, where he hopes to build a new life with his devoted black Lab, having left his wife, son, and name behind. He discovers a young, mentally handicapped waif locked in the bathroom, and, when he finally persuades her to come out the next day, the police discover that she has been raped. Later, when she is found dead, the village readily believes him guilty, simply because he is the mysterious outsider. Thus, he must investigate to save himself, and, in doing so, unexpectedly finds love and a truly new start in life.

Joan Fleming died on 15 November 1980 at age seventy-two, leaving behind a legacy of understated, slightly eccentric, but highly readable tales, notable in the variety of their framework, narrative voices, and approaches. These works are neither flashy nor unusually innovative, but they are reliably interesting with often surprising twists of action and motive. Fleming had the art of making rather boring people into characters worthy of reading and of making the psychological effects of crimes on families and communities more interesting than the crimes themselves. Her stories transform the ordinary into matters of great interest and bring to life the dynamics of English small towns and the contradictions of the adolescent mind. They move credibly across the barriers of gender, class, age, and ethnicity. The police come only rarely into the action but are a knowing force behind the scenes, understanding more than most of the characters in the novels. Readers who take pleasure in the works of Doris Disney Miles, Patricia Flower, Highsmith, and Rendell will find pleasure in Fleming's novels.

Papers:
A collection of Joan Fleming's manuscripts can be found in the Mugar Memorial Library at Brown University, Providence, Rhode Island.

Antonia Fraser

(27 August 1932 –   )

Katherine Staples
Austin Community College

and

Gina Macdonald
Nicholls State University

BOOKS: *King Arthur and the Knights of the Round Table,* as Antonia Pakenham (London: Heirloom Library, 1954; New York: Knopf, 1970);

Robin Hood, as Pakenham (London: Heirloom Library, 1955; New York: Knopf, 1971);

Dolls (London: Weidenfeld & Nicolson, 1963; New York: Putnam, 1963);

A History of Toys (London: Weidenfeld & Nicolson, 1966; New York: Delacorte, 1966);

Mary, Queen of Scots (London: Weidenfeld & Nicolson, 1969; New York: Delacorte, 1969);

Cromwell, Our Chief of Men (London: Weidenfeld & Nicolson, 1973); republished as *Cromwell, the Lord Protector* (New York: Knopf, 1989);

Mary, Queen of Scots, and the Historians (Ilford, Essex: Royal Stuart Society, 1974);

King James VI of Scotland, I of England (London: Weidenfeld & Nicolson, 1974; New York: Knopf, 1975);

Quiet as a Nun (London: Weidenfeld & Nicolson, 1977; New York: Viking, 1977);

The Wild Island (London: Weidenfeld & Nicolson, 1978; New York: Norton, 1978);

King Charles II (London: Weidenfeld & Nicolson, 1979); republished as *Royal Charles: Charles II and the Restoration* (New York: Knopf, 1979); republished as *Charles II* (London: Mandarin, 1990); republished as *Charles II: His Life and Times* (London: Weidenfeld & Nicolson, 1993);

A Splash of Red (London: Weidenfeld & Nicolson, 1981; New York: Norton, 1981);

Cool Repentance (London: Weidenfeld & Nicolson, 1982; New York: Norton, 1982);

The Weaker Vessel–Woman's Lot in Seventeenth Century England (London: Weidenfeld & Nicolson, 1984; New York: Knopf, 1984);

Antonia Fraser (photograph © Sophie Baker; from the dust jacket for the U.S. edition of Political Death, *1996)*

Oxford Blood (London: Weidenfeld & Nicolson, 1985; New York: Norton, 1985);

Jemima Shore's First Case and Other Stories (London: Weidenfeld & Nicolson, 1986; New York: Norton, 1986);

Your Royal Hostage (London: Weidenfeld & Nicolson, 1987; New York: Atheneum, 1988);

Boadicea's Chariot: The Warrior Queens (London: Weidenfeld & Nicolson, 1988); republished as *The Warrior Queens* (New York: Knopf, 1989);

The Cavalier Case (London: Bloomsbury, 1990; New York: Bantam, 1991);

Jemima Shore at the Sunny Grave and Other Stories (London: Bloomsbury, 1991; New York: Bantam, 1993);

The Six Wives of Henry VIII (London: Weidenfeld & Nicolson, 1992); republished as *The Wives of Henry VIII* (New York: Knopf, 1992);

Political Death (London: Heinemann, 1994; New York: Bantam, 1996);

Faith and Treason—The Story of the Gunpowder Plot (London: Weidenfeld & Nicolson, 1996; New York: Doubleday, 1996);

Marie Antoinette: The Journey (London: Weidenfeld & Nicolson, 2001; Garden City, N.Y.: Doubleday, 2001).

PRODUCED SCRIPTS: *On The Battlements,* radio, BBC, 1975;

The Heroine, radio, BBC, 1976;

Penelope, radio, BBC, 1976;

Charades, television, BBC, 1977;

"Quiet as a Nun," television, *Mystery!* 1982;

Jemima Shore Investigates, television, Thames Television, 1983;

"Mister Clay, Mister Clay," television, *Time for Murder,* 1985.

OTHER: Jean Monsterleet, *Martyrs in China,* translated by Fraser as Antonia Pakenham (London: Longmans, Green, 1956);

Christian Dior, *Dior by Dior: The Autobiography of Christian Dior,* translated by Fraser as Pakenham (London: Weidenfeld & Nicolson, 1957);

The Lives of the Kings and Queens of England, edited by Fraser (London: Weidenfeld & Nicolson, 1974; New York: Knopf, 1975);

Scottish Love Poems: A Personal Anthology, compiled by Fraser (Edinburgh: Canongate, 1975; New York: Viking, 1976; enlarged edition, Edinburgh: Canongate, 2002);

Love Letters: An Anthology, compiled by Fraser (London: Weidenfeld & Nicolson, 1976; New York: Knopf, 1977);

"Death of an Old Dog" and "The Case of the Parr Children," in *Winter's Crimes 10,* edited by Hilary Watson (London: Macmillan, 1978);

"The Case of the Parr Children," in *The Fourth Bedside Book of Great Detective Stories,* edited by Herbert Van Thal (London: Barker, 1979);

Heroes and Heroines, edited by Fraser (London: Weidenfeld & Nicolson, 1980; New York: A & W, 1980);

Mary, Queen of Scots: An Anthology of Poetry, compiled by Fraser (London: Eyre Methuen, 1981);

Oxford and Oxfordshire in Verse, edited by Fraser (London: Secker & Warburg, 1982);

"Who Would Kill a Cat?" in *Winter's Crimes 15,* edited by George Hardinge (New York: St. Martin's Press, 1983);

Love Letters: An Illustrated Anthology, edited by Fraser (London: Barrie & Jenkins, 1989; Chicago: Contemporary Books, 1989);

"The Moon Was to Blame," in *Winter's Crimes 21,* edited by Hilary Hale (London: Macmillan, 1989);

"Getting to Know You," in *A Woman's Eye,* edited by Sara Paretsky (New York: Delacorte, 1991);

The Pleasure of Reading, edited by Fraser (London: Bloomsbury, 1991; New York: Knopf, 1992);

"Boots," in *1st Culprit: A Crime Writers' Association Annual* (London: Chatto & Windus, 1992; New York: St. Martin's Press, 1993);

"The Bottle Dungeon," in *Midwinter Mysteries 2,* edited by Hale (London: Little, Brown, 1992);

"A Witch and Her Cats," in *Women on the Case,* edited by Paretsky (London: Virago, 1996; New York: Delacorte, 1996);

Maurice Ashley, *The Stuarts,* edited by Fraser (Berkeley: University of California Press, 2000);

Anthony Cheetham, *The Wars of the Roses,* edited by Fraser (Berkeley: University of California Press, 2000);

John Clarke and Jasper Ridley, *The Houses of Hanover and Saxe-Coburg-Gotha,* edited by Fraser (Berkeley: University of California Press, 2000);

John Gillingham and Peter Earle, *The Middle Ages,* edited by Fraser (Berkeley: University of California Press, 2000);

Andrew Roberts, *The House of Windsor,* edited by Fraser (Berkeley: University of California Press, 2000);

Neville Williams, *The Tudors,* edited by Fraser (Berkeley: University of California Press, 2000).

Although Lady Antonia Fraser is best known as an historian with a strong interest in biography and women's studies, she has also written a series of elaborately plotted mystery novels featuring television commentator Jemima Shore, works reflecting the author's background and scholarly interests. Fraser has said that the mystery writers she most admires are principally women, and her own mysteries are influenced by them: the intricate plots of Dorothy Sayers, the carefully researched backgrounds of Elizabeth Peters, the business insights of Emma Latham, the exposure of village nastiness amid picturesque rural settings of Agatha Christie and Ruth Rendell, the psychological complexities of P. D. James, and the dry, dark humor of Patricia Highsmith. Critics have described Fraser's works as witty, droll, stylish, sophisticated, and literate, and they praise her skill at deftly bringing together history, scholarship, theater, and detection. Fraser aims for straightforward mystery stories against a variety of backgrounds that allow her to explore the possibilities of her amateur sleuth and to emphasize the subtleties of human behavior more than the enactment of bloody deeds.

Antonia Pakenham was born 27 August 1932 into a distinguished socialist family–"the literary Longfords." She was the first of eight children born to University of Oxford–trained Francis Aungier and Elizabeth Harmon Pakenham. Her parents both supported the Labour Party in the 1930s and became Catholics in the 1940s. Both dabbled in politics and social reform and ran for political office (her father successfully; her mother not). Her father, an Oxford historian, became the seventh earl of Longford in 1961 and assumed a seat in the House of Lords (he had previously been a member of the House of Commons); her mother, a relative of the Chamberlains, became Lady Longford. Both parents wrote scholarly books, and Fraser reports not being able to remember a time when her mother was not researching or writing–a pattern she imitated in her own life.

Educated at Dragon School, Oxford, and at Saint Mary's Convent, Ascot (which later inspired *Quiet as a Nun*, 1977), Fraser was attracted to Catholicism by its rituals and converted at age thirteen. She received her B.A. and M.A. in history from Lady Margaret Hall, Oxford, in 1953. She then worked as an editor for Lord Weidenfeld's publishing house, Weidenfeld and Nicolson, for three years, during which time she published her first book, *King Arthur and the Knights of the Round Table* (1954). Her eldest brother, Thomas Pakenham, and two sisters, Rachel and Judith, are also published authors, a fact that Fraser attributes to upbringing and constant intellectual stimulation. Her father wrote the first biography of John F. Kennedy to be published in Great Britain and, according to Alice Painter in *An Encyclopedia of British Women Writers* (1988), was nicknamed "Lord Porn" for his exhaustive official inquiries into pornography.

On 15 September 1956 Antonia married well-to-do Conservative Scots member of Parliament Sir Hugh Charles Patrick Joseph Fraser, a Tory who had formerly served as secretary of state for air, who was fifteen years older than she and whose involvement in Scottish politics later inspired her second mystery, *The Wild Island* (1978). They settled down in a Georgian home with traditional gardens in Kensington. Parents of three sons and three daughters, the Frasers became noted as politically active socialites. Fraser worked as a broadcaster

Dust jacket for Fraser's first novel (1977), which introduces celebrity journalist and amateur sleuth Jemima Shore (from John Cooper and B. A. Pike, Detective Fiction: The Collector's Guide, *second edition, 1994)*

and lecturer, was a panelist on the BBC radio program *My Word!*, and appeared on television talk shows–experiences that later provided inside knowledge of television broadcasting for her Jemima Shore mysteries. In interviews she reported being impressed by the needs of her husband's constituency, but she continued to lead the glamorous life of a celebrity and to be noted for her expensive, fashionable attire. She served as chairwoman of the Prison Committee, a member of the Arts Council, chairperson of the Society of Authors (1974–1975), and a judge for the Booker Prize. The Frasers traveled extensively in the United States, the Far East, Australia, and Ethiopia, locations that later served as settings for the Jemima Shore novels. Her journey through Ethiopia (partly by muleback) was reported in fashion magazines, and a feature article on her in British *Vogue* led to her becoming a contributing editor of that magazine. A privileged aristocrat, wealthy, well known, and sought after, Fraser also enjoyed challenging through her historical writings the establishment positions of university scholars about notable personalities.

In 1975 Fraser fell in love and moved in with a married man, dramatist Harold Pinter. Divorced from their mutual spouses in 1977, Fraser and Pinter were married in a civil ceremony and currently reside in London. The free-spirited Jemima Shore mysteries, with their lively sexuality and their cynicism about establishment figures, are a product of this second marriage. Fraser has said that the series reflects qualities within herself that she could not express through writing histories. These qualities certainly include her love of theater, opera, ballet, and motion pictures as well as her interest in women's issues. Since her marriage to Pinter she has served as vice chairwoman and then chairwoman of the Crime Writers Association, as a fellow of the Royal Society of Literature, and as the English PEN vice president and then president, in which capacity she worked against apartheid. Fraser won the Wolfson History Prize and the Pris Caumont La Force for her seventeenth-century studies and was awarded an honorary doctorate from Hull University in 1986 and from Sussex University in 1990.

Fraser's responsibilities as a parent did not hinder her writing and research as an historian, and, in fact, her children's books on King Arthur and Robin Hood and her books on dolls and toys were written with them in mind; her later mysteries include precocious children such as the ones in "A Witch and Her Cats" (collected in *Women on the Case,* 1996) and *The Cavalier Case* (1990). Encouraged by her mother, the countess of Longford, a noted biographer best known for her study of Queen Victoria and the duke of Wellington, Fraser began her serious writing career with popular histories that captured the romance and intrigue of sixteenth- and seventeenth-century personalities. Mel Gussow, writing in *The New York Times Magazine* (9 September 1984), noted her impressive research and her readability (thanks to a strong sense of narrative) but pointed out that professional historians criticize her "storybook" approach to history. She writes best about subjects to which she feels a personal commitment and about personalities who engage her at a deep-seated emotional level. For example, as a child, she had been fascinated by Queen Mary of Scotland and had even acted out historical events from Mary's life with her brothers and sisters. Later, the St. Mary's Convent nuns encouraged her to write about Mary, and she even had an opportunity to model Mary's wedding dress. Finally, as a convert to Catholicism and disturbed by the traditional Anglican interpretations of Queen Mary as unrelentingly monstrous, Fraser wrote *Mary, Queen of Scots*

(1969) to test and repudiate the apocrypha that had encrusted Mary's story over the years. The result was a warm, sympathetic portrait of a controversial personality, which won the James Tait Black Memorial Prize and which infused history with intuitive, sometimes romantic, insights to make understandable the longing and loneliness that drove Mary Stuart's actions, and the betrayals that produced her bitterness. It was followed by other contrasting biographies also meant to rehabilitate figures repudiated by historians: *Cromwell, Our Chief of Men* (1973), *King James VI of Scotland, I of England* (1974), and *King Charles II* (1979). In general, positive reviewers found Fraser's biographies well written, well-researched, and convincing popular studies, but critics found them overly favorable, superficial, cursory, and sometimes distorted and misleading. Fraser's revisionist attempts to humanize the notorious and to discover extenuating circumstances for their unconventional behavior is in keeping with her approach to detection in the Jemima Shore series.

Fraser's *The Weaker Vessel—Woman's Lot in Seventeenth Century England* (1984) is an exciting and informed study of women from all levels of seventeenth-century English society. It laid the groundwork for the Jemima Shore mystery *The Cavalier Case* and demonstrates Fraser's willingness to question untested assertions about the historical role of women, much as Jemima takes on those in her profession and shakes their preconceptions. *Boadicea's Chariot: The Warrior Queens* (1988) explores the historical depiction of women who were both martial leaders and rulers, beginning with Queen Boadicea and ending with Margaret Thatcher, and their contradictory treatment as both "supernaturally chaste" and "preternaturally lustful." Given such interests, Fraser predictably explores women's issues in her fiction, introducing strong female characters in the Jemima Shore series as well as characters who reverse traditional expectations for their respective sexes. *Faith and Treason—The Story of the Gunpowder Plot* (1996) reads like a detective story as Fraser untangles the complex web of religious and political personalities involved in this early case of terrorism. The issues raised in these books are further examined in Fraser's mystery series, in what Painter calls "an obvious extension" of Fraser's earlier work.

Fraser's mysteries reflect her wide-ranging interests and broad education, and their narrative perspective is in keeping with a heroine who got a first in English at Cambridge. Readers of Fraser's mysteries will find references to William Shakespeare's Coriolanus and Volumnia, Cleopatra, Marie Antoinette, Niccolò Machiavelli, Christopher Marlowe, Lord Byron, Richard Strauss's *Der Rosenkavalier* (1909), Wolfgang Amadeus Mozart's *Don Giovanni* (1787), the Lilliputians

Dust jacket for the U.S. edition of Fraser's 1986 collection of short stories, including mysteries set during
Jemima Shore's teenage years in convent school (Richland County Public Library)

of Jonathan Swift's *Gulliver's Travels* (1726), Percy Bysshe
Shelley at Lerici (where he drowned), William Wordsworth's poem "The World Is Too Much with Us"
(1806), an Annunciation scene by Dante Gabriel Ros-
setti, and paintings by Thomas Gainsborough. In *Political Death* (1994) Jemima finds in a dramatic
performance of Shakespeare's *Twelfth Night* (circa 1601)
and in Viola's unrequited and undeclared passion for
Orsino parallels in the behavior of murder suspects,
and sometimes a well-known quotation will be explored
through a variety of relationships. For example, in *Cool
Repentance* (1982) Jemima's clue to character is a line
about "a virtuous mind" and "Conscience" from John
Milton's *Comus* (1637), while in *Political Death* Byron's
comment that love is "a woman's whole existence" is
tested and found true for some, false for others, but a
dangerous concept for all.

Fraser's metaphors are delightful. A character in
Cool Repentance looks "both greedy and cheerful, like a
gourmet cat who expected to be fed on lobster for the
rest of his life," while another looks "sad and very distinguished, like a French marquise at an eve-of-guillotine
feast." A character in *The Cavalier Case* looks as if she
would play tennis "like a stately galleon in full sail" and

is as imperious as Cleopatra: "so would Cleopatra in
ripe middle age have commanded some slave to a tennis game." Occasional digressions about variations in
manuscripts and incunabula confirm Jemima's good
humor and scholarship.

In Jemima, Fraser develops a new kind of woman
detective, an independent, cultivated celebrity whose
career as a successful television commentator makes her
nosiness and curiosity into virtues. She is in her early
thirties in the first few books but ages into her forties in
later works. Her parents died in a car crash when she
was eighteen, and her only inheritance was her father's
medals and her mother's photograph albums of life as
an army wife in India. Jemima considers herself a no-
nonsense rationalist. She is shrewd, commonsensical,
and adept at cutting deals and making compromises
that ultimately increase her clout in the business world.
She is mobile, maintaining an expensive London flat
but spending much of her time on the road, and she
uses her public notoriety as a television commentator to
good advantage. For British readers her name embodies
the contradictions of her personality–Jemima from the
Hebrew word for "dove," a popular Puritan name associated with virtue–and Shore after Joan Shore, the mis-

tress of King Edward the IV of England. Her bright smile hides a barbed wit and an ambitious cynicism.

Her liberal views frequently clash with those of her conservative employer (and one-time lover), Cy Fredericks, the profit-minded chairman of British Megalith Television. Though she continues to come to Fredericks's aid, she and Cherry Bronson, her former personal assistant at MegaTV, found JS Productions, which packages the long-standing and successful series of social inquiries *Jemima Shore Investigates* and sells it back to MegaTV. Bronson runs JS Productions with great energy while Jemima continues to turn out challenging programs on controversial social topics. Her documentaries link private motives with public acts and expose social abuses, the excesses of the wealthy, the exploitation of the poor, and the indignities of aging. Single and unattached, Jemima values her sexual freedom as much as her personal independence, and even long-standing relationships are interrupted by fleeting affairs and one-night stands (sometimes several in one book). She is a happy hedonist, untouched by guilt about her sexual adventures with cameramen, artists, and lords, married or not. In *Political Death,* for example, the foreign travels of Ned Silver, her mercurial barrister lover, leave her restless and susceptible to the advances of a handsome, popular actor, whose reputation makes him a challenge, while in *The Cavalier Case* she becomes enamored of a seventeenth-century cavalier poet who supposedly haunts a family's stately Elizabethan mansion and enjoys a romp with his descendant, a handsome tennis star and womanizer who has fathered several children in multiple marriages and whose recent cavorting provokes murder. Her major personal loyalty is to her cat, Midnight, who shares his mistress's propensity to roam, her curiosity, and her territoriality.

Jemima never seeks out detective cases: her media fame attracts them, and her own curiosity involves her in their solution. People in trouble or with secrets or seeking revenge have seen her programs and feel as if they know her, so they come to her with their stories and their danger. Sometimes gathering information for her television program places her on the spot to investigate murder, or else her shows provide background information that allows her to connect events the police cannot. Every murder she investigates means physical and emotional risk, and Jemima's investigative style depends as much on sensitivity and intuition as on deduction. She works amicably and quietly with the police, particularly Chief Detective Superintendent John Portsmouth, whom she first met during a television interview in connection with a missing child and whom she teasingly calls "Pompey of the Yard" in reference to the Portsmouth Football Club. Yet, her solutions to public crimes usually remain private: her

detective discoveries provide Jemima introspective self-knowledge rather than sensational newscasts. Her great asset as an interviewer is her ability never to be riled, no matter the provocation, to maintain a cool composure that instead riles others into revelatory outbursts. Anne Wallach, in *The New York Times Book Review* (6 January 1991), calls her "prettier, sexier, and far more in tune with today's London" than Peter Wimsey, Jane Marple, Hercule Poirot, or Sherlock Holmes, though, as in the stories of these genre predecessors, Fraser's villains predictably get their just deserts, and conventional order is preserved.

Despite critical complaints about their predictability and their departure from the genre convention of ratiocinative detection, Fraser's mysteries have all been best-sellers. Furthermore, *Quiet as a Nun* was made into a PBS *Mystery!* presentation, and the Jemima Shore stories were the basis for a series produced by Thames Television, *Jemima Shore Investigates.*

The first Jemima Shore novel, *Quiet as a Nun,* reflects Fraser's Catholic education. Jemima, invited by the mother superior, returns to her old convent school to quietly investigate the suspicious death of a nun (starved to death in a ruined tower), her old schoolmate, an invalid whose inheritance included the convent lands. Jemima's motivation is mixed: she feels loyalty to the nuns, guilt about the schoolmate whom she failed to help years before, curiosity about an involved set of schoolgirl conspiracies, and alarm about a kidnapping and second convent death. She discovers that a crooked land reformer had hoped to use the convent's inheritance for his own self-promoting schemes; the wicked are conveniently eliminated in a car wreck; and the secrets of the convent remain hidden.

The only novel in the series to use first-person narration, *Quiet as a Nun* introduces and develops Jemima as a series character. She speaks of her feelings about the past and the present: her school days, her adulterous affairs, her cultivated pleasure in fine things, and her amusement at gratuitous snobbery and insular zeal. While she is able to accept the nuns as women with purpose, faith, practicality, direction, and real wisdom, her own vocation is far different, and her own life tempers discipline with indulgence. She observes the distraught nuns with calm detachment and looks on gothic extravagance with rational common sense. The gothic setting of *Quiet as a Nun* reflects Fraser's interest in history and social context, an interest that appears throughout the other Jemima Shore novels. In *Quiet as a Nun* the hidden secrets of the convent include a dank, secret passageway to an ancient tower, a crypt full of coffins, and a supposed ghost—the Black Nun. The maze of subplots in the novel and its many minor characters are tied together by Jemima's memories, sensibilities, and experience and unraveled by her discoveries. Daniel Coogan, writing in *America* (8 October 1977), was disappointed in *Quiet as a Nun* as "too slick" and "tidy" and in Jemima as a detective, calling her "unprepossessing" and lacking the "undoubted charm of Lady Antonia," despite their circumstantial similarities, while Susannah Clapp of the *New Statesman* (27 May 1977) longed for "more vigorous action and rather fewer general reflections." Crime novelist P. D. James, writing in *TLS: The Times Literary Supplement* (27 May 1977), was more positive, however, calling the mystery "a judicious mixture of puzzle, excitement, and terror" and praising both its adherence to Gothic horror conventions and Fraser's confident depiction of "an alien and vaguely disquieting world" where her nuns may all look "like black crows" but where their characters are "nicely differentiated."

The *Wild Island* reflects Fraser's interest in Scottish history. Jemima's vacation on a secluded island involves her with murder, an adulterous affair with an attractive laird, a tangled, violent family history, and publicity-mad Scots revolutionaries (who have never forgiven the English for the massacre on Culloden Moor and other such historical "outrages"). The murdered man, her host, is Charles Edward Beauregard, called by locals "His Late Majesty King Charles Edward of Scotland." Jemima discovers that the killer is the laird's crazed wife, who has murdered repeatedly to punish her husband's lovers, to bring the succession to her sons, and to conceal her own crimes. When the laird gallantly dies protecting Jemima, his wife hurls herself from a cliff. Their deaths are recorded as accidents, the revolutionaries are disbanded, and the new heir restores order on the island, marrying an English princess. *The Wild Island* is crowded with subplots, minor characters, local color, and historical allusion and wavers between parody and melodrama, but at times it is disconcertingly serious. Its Highland setting is compelling, if corny, and Fraser indulges satire at the expense of the vanities and pretensions of all the characters—including Jemima.

Reviewer Frederick Guereson of *Best Seller* praised the novel for its interesting mix of history, local folklore, distinctive setting, and a plot dependent on the universal themes of "greed, jealousy, and power," while T. J. Binyon, writing in *TLS* (5 May 1978), was disappointed by Jemima's passivity, her "preferring to reflect on the quality of her Yves St. Laurent beige silk shirt, to wonder whether her long dark green jersey dress from Jean Muir is discreetly sexy enough (it is), or to worry about the effect of Scotch [*sic*] mist on her honey-coloured suede skirt and waistcoat"; he found the novel "pleasant," "amusing," "civilized," and "well-written" but the violence and murder "curiously unreal." Despite the

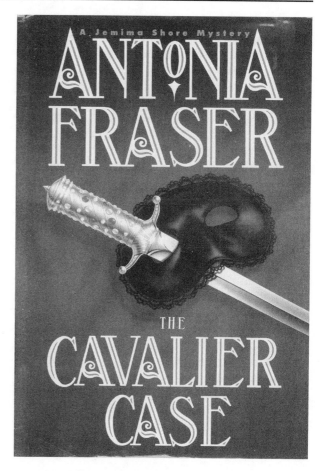

Dust jacket for the U.S. edition of Fraser's 1991 novel, in which Jemima Shore solves a series of murders in a haunted great house (Richland County Public Library)

assertion in the *Virginia Quarterly Review* (Spring 1979) that Jemima is the new Miss Marple, she is not an adventurous, active investigator; instead, as Patricia Craig and Mary Cadogan point out in "A Curious Career for a Woman?" (1981), she is "as startled as anyone when the truth comes out" but is quick to make sense of what had previously seemed puzzling.

In *A Splash of Red* (1981) Jemima becomes involved in the tangled affairs of a Cambridge friend, promiscuous best-selling novelist Chloe Fontaine, whose cat and flat Jemima agrees to watch. When Jemima finds Chloe's mutilated body on the premises, the suspects abound. The police fasten on Chloe's recently discarded lover, an alcoholic painter who is violently jealous of her current lover, a married real-estate magnate, but the new lover's wife, a handsome young stranger, and a fashion editor are suspects as well. Chloe's cat helps Jemima ferret out the real but unlikely killer: the weak, effeminate publisher who was Chloe's confidant and a secret voyeur. When the murderer dies of a heart attack, Jemima allows all of his secrets to die with him. The sexual and social intrigue of *A Splash of Red* forces Jemima to question her own loyalty, motives, and role in the London scene. While she finds herself excited by some of Chloe's behavior, she is also repulsed by its excesses. Jemima must understand and accept Chloe's weaknesses and dishonesty in order to remain honest in accepting some of her own. Alice Painter finds both the victim and the detective projections of Fraser herself and notes particularly Chloe's beauty, which "hid a considerable talent as a novelist," her "series of admirers, lovers, and husbands," and the "odd contrast of her disorderly private life and the careful formality of her work."

In *Cool Repentance* Jemima, covering a rural theater festival, becomes involved in scandal when an aging actress returns to the stage from retirement. The actress, Christabel Cartwright, had engaged in a notorious and humiliating affair, abandoning her family for a youthful rock star, the son of family servants. Although Christabel has returned home, someone in the Cartwright estate hates her and intends to kill her. Jemima soon discovers motives. Julian Cartwright, his two daughters, the servants, the housekeeper, and Christabel's playwright-in-residence (and lover) all feel bitter resentment. A series of theater-related deaths soon follow. Christabel's suicide reveals the killer, Christabel herself, the one person most unable to forgive her faithlessness, her aging body, and her failure both as a woman and as an artist. *Cool Repentance* skillfully throws suspicion on every major character while also developing an accurate psychological portrait of the disintegrating actress. The theme of the novel appears in the alienation of a woman who cannot accept herself or the love of the people around her. Forced into a role of her own creation, Christabel remains completely self-centered, a risk Jemima herself also runs. The story allows Fraser to explore the inducements and stresses that afflict pop performers, playwrights, and television documentary crews, and, more particularly, the behind-the-scenes realities of country theaters. Likewise, a planned performance of Anton Chekhov's *The Seagull* (1896) allows her to draw parallels between her creations and Chekhov's and between her themes and his. Several reviewers praised Fraser's theatrical world as sharply observed and intimate and called the sexual intrigue volatile and carefree but dismissed the psychological explanations as trite. Harriet Waugh, writing in *The Spectator* (26 June 1982), called Jemima "prissy" but Fraser's mystery "jokey, accomplished, and action-packed."

In *The New York Times Book Review* (20 December 1992) critic Beverly Lyon Clark placed *Oxford Blood* (1985) in the tradition of the British "Tea Cake and Country House" mystery, recast as a "Champagne and Maserati" mystery; Margaret Cannon of the *Toronto Globe and Mail* found the upper-class settings through which Jemima moves both fascinating and modern: "There's nothing in the detective code of ethics that says you have to dress badly, get married or pass up an interesting one-night-stand." The story takes Jemima to Oxford (Fraser's childhood home) to cash in on the popularity of the television series based on Evelyn Waugh's *Brideshead Revisited* (1945) by documenting the spoiled and dissolute student aristocrats at the university, foremost among whom is handsome Saffron Ivy. Jemima learns that Saffron is adopted and that someone is trying to kill him, as a series of related deaths soon shows. Many hate Saffron: jealous classmates, moneyless relatives, jilted lovers. When Saffron becomes engaged, his promiscuous fiancée, the daughter of a beautiful classicist, is found dead at the family estate, seemingly of a drug overdose. The murderer is a bumbling and apparently harmless professor who jealously hates Saffron and has discovered the secret of his birth: a liaison between Saffron's aristocrat father and the fiancée's mother–the professor's own lover.

Oxford Blood, with its setting reminiscent of Dorothy L. Sayers's *Gaudy Night* (1935) and its Oedipal web of hidden relationships, develops themes of alliance and identity. By the end of the novel Saffron has discovered his real identity: he wants the stability and values he had previously rejected. After her brief encounter with Saffron, Jemima also seeks stability. When her barrister lover proposes marriage at the end of the novel, she agrees to consider it, even at the cost of compromising her own independence. Through Jemima's documentary Fraser sets the privileged world of the indifferent and self-indulgent English aristocrat against famine abroad and widespread unemployment at home.

Jemima Shore's First Case and Other Stories (1986) consists of short mystery, detective, or supernatural puzzles. Four of the stories in this collection involve Jemima's earliest detective work, at age fifteen in convent school, and the remaining thirteen stories feature ironic or supernatural events, each with what the *Publishers Weekly* reviewer (24 April 1987) calls "a satisfying shock." The same reviewer calls "Have a Nice Death," the story of two women who successfully commit a particularly nasty crime, both "funny" and "hackle-raising." "On the Battlements" is an understated dramatic piece. As an actor and his faithless wife explore the turrets of a Tuscan castle, he recites poignant passages on infidelity and jealousy from Shakespeare's *Othello* (1604); she slips and nearly falls but he saves her, leading her to say with feeling "I'll never slip again."

In *Your Royal Hostage* (1987) Jemima has been deserted by the barrister she refused to marry, fired by Megalith, and hired by Television United States to cover the Anglo-Catholic royal wedding of the spoiled and petulant Princess Amy and the world-weary Prince Ferdinand. The wedding is interrupted by a bizarre and disparate group of animal-rights activists who decide to kidnap the princess to promote their own cause. The case is complicated by dysfunctional families, gender reversal, and Prince Ferdinand's past lover, the sultry animal-rights advocate Mirabella Prey. Jemima plays an active role in forestalling blackmail and rescuing the kidnapped princess. Leaving her studio post at the wedding, she prevents assassination at the church door. *Your Royal Hostage,* with its play on gender roles and mother-daughter relationships, allows Jemima her most actively heroic detective work. She collaborates quietly with the police and uses her knowledge of protocol and people to discreetly save the day. She is also triumphantly restored to Megalith, where Cy has staged a takeover. Although *Library Journal* reviewer Rex Klett finds Jemima "largely incidental to a rather negligible plot," he praises the mystery as "stylishly presented . . . with a dash of satire."

In *The Cavalier Case* lonely Jemima is infatuated by the compelling portrait of Decimus Meredith, Viscount Lackland, a handsome poet who died young and under mysterious circumstances in 1615. Her investigation of famous ghosts in English great houses soon involves her in the tangled personal and financial relationships of the Meredith family and raises questions of English mansions being converted into tennis centers and of such irreplaceable antiquities as furnishings, art, and manuscripts being secretly sold off to pay the bill collectors and replaced by cheap imitations. The current viscount Lackland, a randy, aging tennis star, is surrounded by children from two marriages and by his past and present mistresses. When two murders take place around the ghostly appearance of the poet, Jemima solves the problem: the jealous current wife has killed to protect her own interests in the estate, her marriage, and her husband. In *The Cavalier Case* Jemima must again discover where her loyalties lie. She has brief encounters with Viscount Lackland and with her former lover, finding a happy relationship at last with a television executive untroubled by her independence or his own. Anne Wallach calls attention to the Fraser formula (a country-house setting, a touch of the gothic, and sexual intrigue) and praises the "zest and verve" with which she combines history and detection.

Jemima Shore at the Sunny Grave and Other Stories (1991), a second collection of short stories, includes more of Jemima's adventures abroad—on Bow Island in the Galapagos and on the Greek island of Corfu—and of incidents that changed her view of her work. In "Getting to Know You," for instance, Jemima gains sympathy for rape victims. She interviews many rape

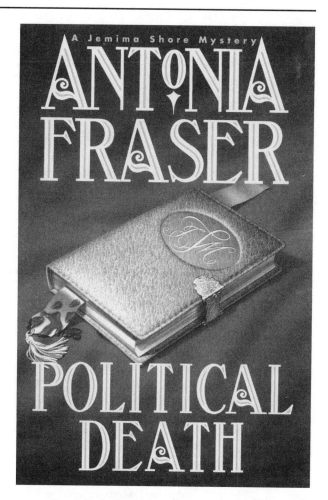

Dust jacket for the U.S. edition of Fraser's 1996 novel, in which Shore's association with an eccentric elderly socialite leads her to investigate a thirty-year-old murder (Richland County Public Library)

victims who, when asked why they did not scream or fight back, talk about being paralyzed with fear or experiencing a sense of helplessness that the self-confident Jemima finds inexplicable. In this story she is nearly raped herself, however, and discovers that her own behavior follows the patterns of other victims, in contradiction to what she assumed she would do. "The Blude-red Wine" follows a pattern Fraser uses repeatedly, drawing parallels between literature—in this case, the seventeenth-century poem *The Ballad of Sir Patrick Spens*—and life, while "Jemima Shore at the Sunny Grave" is a traditional story of would-be heirs killing their benefactor, set on exotic Bow Island. "The Moon Was to Blame" is told from the point of view of a murderer and "Dead Leaves" from the point of view of someone who precipitates murder for personal ends, while "Out for the Countess" involves a revenge murder that seems to backfire but in fact accomplishes its goals.

Political Death begins with a confused and elderly former beauty and socialite, Lady Imogen Swain, talking mysteriously of threats to her life and promising Jemima diaries and letters that expose the sexual escapades of the distinguished Tory foreign secretary Burgo Smyth Oust before elections and that connect him with the disappearance thirty years earlier of a homosexual journalist on trial for selling government secrets. Jemima is hesitant to take the clearly dotty old woman seriously until she suddenly plunges to her death from an upper floor of her crumbling mansion. The murder of a minor actress in a production of *Twelfth Night,* the discovery of the skeleton of the missing journalist, and permission to investigate granted by all members of the Swain family place Jemima in a position to puzzle out psychological responses born of a genetic and cultural heritage and to confirm the old adage "Like mother, like daughter." The *Publishers Weekly* reviewer (5 February 1996) calls *Political Death* an "intelligent tale," "filled with atmosphere" but with characters that seem "a bit remote."

Antonia Fraser's charm for American readers is her wide-ranging intellect revealed by copious allusions and references to matters historical, literary, scholarly, and cinematic, her personal identity as a British celebrity, and her heroine, whose independence and self-assurance are the product of a distinctly British perspective. In Jemima Shore, Fraser develops a central character whose detection is more passive than active; her ingenuity, her knowledge of human nature, and her examination of her own motives, values, and commitments—personal, political, and ethical—help her discover psychological nuances that others miss. Jemima is caught up in complex marital and familial relationships that force her to question and evaluate her own sexual identity and her role as a successful professional who tries to live a full life as a free and single woman. In addition to the elaborate plots, intriguing social contexts, and character studies of the formal detective-novel tradition, Fraser brings to the genre a fantasy heroine who manages to have life her way.

Interviews:

Stephanie De Pue, interview with Fraser, *Newsday Ideas* (20 January 1974): 19;

Rosemary Herbert, "PW Interviews: Lady Antonia Fraser," *Publishers Weekly,* 231 (19 June 1987): 104–105.

References:

Bonnie Angelo, "Not Quite Your Usual Historian," *Time,* 135 (15 January 1990): 66–68;

L. Christopher, "Romantic Spirit of Lady Antonia," *Macleans,* 92 (31 December 1979): 7–8;

Patricia Craig and Mary Cadogan, "A Curious Career for a Woman?" in their *The Lady Investigates: Women Detectives and Spies in Fiction* (New York: St. Martin's Press, 1981), pp. 223–246;

Mel Gussow, "Antonia Fraser: The Lady Is a Writer," *New York Times Magazine* (9 September 1984): 60–61.

Celia Fremlin
(20 June 1914 –   )

L. R. Wright
East Tennessee State University

BOOKS: *The Seven Chars of Chelsea* (London: Methuen, 1940);

The Hours Before Dawn (London: Gollancz, 1958; Philadelphia: Lippincott, 1959);

Uncle Paul (London: Gollancz, 1959; Philadelphia: Lippincott, 1960);

Seven Lean Years (London: Gollancz, 1961); republished as *Wait for the Wedding* (Philadelphia: Lippincott, 1961);

The Trouble-Makers (London: Gollancz, 1963; Philadelphia: Lippincott, 1963);

The Jealous One (London: Gollancz, 1965; Philadelphia: Lippincott, 1965);

Prisoner's Base (London: Gollancz, 1967; Philadelphia: Lippincott, 1967);

Possession (London: Gollancz, 1969; Philadelphia: Lippincott, 1969);

Don't Go to Sleep in the Dark (London: Gollancz, 1970; Philadelphia: Lippincott, 1970; London: Gollancz, 1979);

Appointment with Yesterday (London: Gollancz, 1972; Philadelphia: Lippincott, 1972);

By Horror Haunted (London: Gollancz, 1974);

The Long Shadow: A Novel (London: Gollancz, 1975; Garden City, N.Y.: Doubleday, 1976);

The Spider-Orchid (London: Gollancz, 1977; Garden City, N.Y.: Doubleday, 1978);

With No Crying: A Novel (London: Gollancz, 1980; Garden City, N.Y.: Doubleday, 1981);

The Parasite Person (London: Gollancz, 1982; Garden City, N.Y.: Doubleday, 1982);

A Lovely Day to Die, and Other Stories (London: Gollancz, 1984; Garden City, N.Y.: Doubleday, 1984);

Listening in the Dusk (London: Gollancz, 1990; New York: Doubleday, 1990);

Dangerous Thoughts (London: Gollancz, 1991);

The Echoing Stones (Sutton, U.K.: Severn House, 1993);

King of the World (Sutton, U.K.: Severn House, 1994);

Celia Fremlin (from the dust jacket for the U.S. edition of Possession, *1969)*

Duet in Verse: Some Occasional Poems, by Fremlin and Leslie Minchin (London: Pioneer Arts, 1996).

OTHER: *War Factory: A Report by Mass-Observation,* new preface by Fremlin (London: Cresset Library, 1987).

SELECTED PERIODICAL PUBLICATIONS– UNCOLLECTED: "The Special Gift," *Ellery Queen's Mystery Magazine* (1967);

"From the Locked Room Upstairs," *Ellery Queen's Mystery Magazine* (April 1968);

"Don't Be Frightened," *Ellery Queen's Mystery Magazine* (1970);

"Golden Tuesday," *Ellery Queen's Mystery Magazine* (April 1972);

"The Coldness of a Thousand Suns," *Ellery Queen's Mystery Magazine* (1972);

"Waiting for the Police," *Ellery Queen's Mystery Magazine* (February 1973);

"A Case of Maximum Need," *Ellery Queen's Mystery Magazine* (March 1977);

"Anything May Happen," *Ellery Queen's Mystery Magazine* (July 1981);

"The Summer Holiday," *Ellery Queen's Mystery Magazine* (November 1983);

"The Sensory Deprivation Tank," *Ellery Queen's Mystery Magazine* (March 1986);

"Guilt Feelings," *Ellery Queen's Mystery Magazine* (February 1987);

"Yellow Ken," *Ellery Queen's Mystery Magazine* (January 1991);

"Mother's Clever Idea," *Ellery Queen's Mystery Magazine* (October 1992);

"Accommodation Vacant," *Ellery Queen's Mystery Magazine* (1993);

"The Sound of Silence," *Ellery Queen's Mystery Magazine* (December 1994);

"The Coincidence," *Ellery Queen's Mystery Magazine* (September–October 1998);

"The Do-Gooder," *Ellery Queen's Mystery Magazine* (April 1999);

"Revenge Is Sweet," *Ellery Queen's Mystery Magazine* (August 1999).

Celia Fremlin is one of the most underrated British mystery writers; yet, her stories share striking qualities with works by Patricia Highsmith and Patricia Flower, which provide unusual perspectives and unexpected shifts of perception. Fremlin's works also share Flower's concern with the plight of young women who find themselves caught up in seemingly ordinary situations that prove most unordinary and who find good cause to suspect their nearest and dearest. In her novels Fremlin explores the common experiences of everyday men and women and uses these experiences to create stories filled with wit, terror, and a deep understanding of the complexities of relationships. Fremlin takes the smallest details and turns them into moments of chilling significance. Her plots are sharp, allowing the reader to discover secrets along with the investigator.

Fremlin uses the psychological-thriller genre to create mysteries of domestic horror in decidedly English settings. She has said that publishers and critics usually categorize her works as suspense novels because they often do not involve policemen, detec-

tives, procedures, or even murder, as do traditional crime, police, and detective stories. Instead, her self-proclaimed goal is to create a "mysterious threat hanging over someone and escalating . . . chapter by chapter." Her novels are most effective in presenting tales of terror that lurk beneath the surface of familiar situations. Instead of taking the reader into a dark, menacing environment, Fremlin sets the tale in the supposed safety of the home, with all its common minutia and daily banalities. Her stories create fear from the ordinary events of day-to-day life, placing characters in thrilling and often life-threatening situations. Her forte is not extravagant exhibitions of action-packed drama but a slow luring of the reader, allowing the quiet, increasing uneasiness to build to a climax. The feelings of terror and panic are sometimes more horrific than the acts that precipitate them. Her plots move slowly and deliberately. Usually not until the last chapter of the novel do all of the carefully placed details culminate in a shocking revelation. Most of her novels focus on a female protagonist forced to deal with a newly developed, tension-filled situation. Fremlin's antagonists appear ordinary and harmless but ultimately are not. Fremlin says she intends to create a view of ordinary life from a nonordinary angle.

Fremlin was born in Ryarsh, Kent, on 20 June 1914 to Heaver Stuart, a bacteriologist, and Margaret Addiscott Fremlin. She attended the Berkhamsted School for Girls in Hertfordshire. After graduating from Somerville College, Oxford, with a B.A. in classics and B.Litt. in philosophy in 1937, Fremlin moved to north London, where she spent most of her life. Fremlin held several menial jobs after graduation, including that of a charwoman and a shop assistant. During World War II Fremlin worked as an air-raid warden and an interviewer for Mass-Observation, a social research organization. She published at least one report with them, in a March 1939 issue, on air-raid shelters and precautions.

Fremlin married Elia Sidney Goller, a schoolteacher, on 6 July 1942. They had three children: one son, Nicholas, born 20 January 1943; and two daughters, Geraldine, born 14 March 1947, and Sylvia, born 10 May 1949. After her husband's death, Fremlin lived alone for many years before marrying her second husband, Leslie Minchin, a musician, in 1984.

Fremlin wrote her first novel, *The Hours Before Dawn* (1958), when she was forty-four years old. Her experiences dealing with a baby who cried incessantly throughout the night inspired the work. The novel paints a vivid, bleak picture of characters trapped by their domestic life. Fremlin carefully structures the story, leaving many hints and clues along the way, and, using a touch of humor and a wealth of irony, unravels

*Dust jacket for the U.S. edition of Fremlin's 1958 novel, in which a woman gradually realizes that a female lodger
in her home intends to take her baby away from her (Bruccoli Clark Layman Archives)*

the mystery occurring under the family's roof. Deliberate in pace, the novel may seem slow and out-of-date with current suspense fiction, but the purposefully lingering quality of the story allows the reader to understand the psychological tension and stress that affect all of the characters. Its general themes of familial distress, underlying terror, and psychological confusion are typical of most of Fremlin's succeeding novels.

Louise Henderson, the protagonist, is a wife and the mother of two rambunctious young girls and a newborn baby boy, Michael. For Louise, every single night is the same. At two o'clock, Michael begins to cry and does not stop until the early morning. Louise's hours before dawn are most often spent in the dark, dank scullery, propped up against the mangle, trying to quiet the baby by bouncing him on her knee and hoping desperately that the noise does not wake anyone else in the house. Finally, at sunrise, when Michael drifts off to sleep, Louise sleeps too, usually sitting up in a chair. Soon the household awakens, however, and another

day of gray fog, grinding misery, and fear descends upon her.

The family takes in a lodger, the respectable and well-educated Miss Vera Brandon, in order to make ends meet. Fremlin creates an unassuming antagonist in the character of Miss Brandon, a classics teacher at the local grammar school. Louise slowly becomes convinced that Miss Brandon did not come to be their lodger by coincidence but deliberately sought them out. Louise's suspicions prove correct. Miss Brandon, as Louise reads in her lodger's diary, is convinced that Michael is actually her biological child and that the hospital staff purposefully had switched him with Louise's stillborn son because she was a single mother. In her diary Miss Brandon plots to recover her son and do away with Louise. When that plot goes awry, Louise saves Michael from her burning home, and Miss Brandon dies in the fire. *The Hours Before Dawn* won the Mystery Writers of America Edgar Award for best mystery novel in 1960.

The Long Shadow
Celia Fremlin

A Crime Club Selection

Dust jacket for the U.S. edition of Fremlin's 1975 novel, in which a family is plagued by a series of seemingly supernatural events (Richland County Public Library)

In *The Long Shadow: A Novel* (1975), Fremlin creates a family that is frightened by inexplicable events after the death of their patriarch. The novel explores the theme of a blended family, where stepchildren, former wives, and stepmothers try to live cohesively.

Imogene Barnicott has recently lost her husband, Ivor, in a horrible car accident. She wishes to be left alone, to mourn in private, but Ivor's son, second wife, daughter, and her two children all move into Imogene's house. On top of all the family now living with her, Robin, the son, also invites a university student to board in Imogene's home. In this novel Fremlin introduces the element of supposed supernatural events. Ripe with chaos, several strange things begin to occur around the house. Ivor's daughter's children believe they have seen their grandpa during the night and claim they hear his voice calling to them. Then, Robin's room is mysteriously vandalized behind a locked door. To everyone's horror, Cynthia, the second wife, finds a note in Ivor's drawer, stating simply, "Please Leave My Things Alone." Even Imogene begins to believe she is

sensing Ivor's ghost around her when she finds that a book he started writing years before suddenly has new additions to it.

The novel culminates in an unexpected fashion. Imogene receives a letter in the mail that states, "I've taken my cat back and tomorrow I'll come for my grandsons." Imogene remembers that the cat she has just retrieved from the grandchildren's home is actually Ivor's first wife's cat. In a moment of clarity, Imogene sees the pieces of the puzzle fall into place. As she is looking for her missing grandsons, she meets an old woman on the path also looking for her grandsons. The woman on the path is Ivor's first wife, Lena. Lena has been responsible for all of the tricks from the beginning. She is highly unstable. Fremlin's antagonist has not been any of the characters explored in the novel. Instead, the antagonist is never seen or talked about until the last pages of the novel. The novel concludes quite bleakly. In a moment of psychological turmoil, Lena believes she sees her children, Robin and Dot, in the water and goes after them, drowning.

Fremlin again visits the dynamics of an everyday family existing in fear in *The Spider-Orchid* (1977), this time with a worried father, Adrian, as the protagonist. Adrian's lover of four years, Rita, has decided to leave her husband, Derek, and move in with Adrian. Rita feels threatened by the bond between Adrian and his ten-year-old daughter, Amelia. Rita tries to step in and influence Amelia, much to Adrian's dismay. Desperate to replace Amelia in Adrian's eyes, Rita finds Amelia's diary and uses her crush on her English teacher, Mr. Owen, to try to win back Adrian's favor. Fed up with his lack of attention, Rita makes veiled threats about the secret of Amelia's "homework." When she confronts Adrian with Amelia's diary and reveals the information inside it, he does not believe the attraction between teacher and student is real, tells Rita that she is absurd if she believes it, and eventually breaks off his relationship with her.

The story picks up quickly in the last few pages when Adrian's former wife and Amelia go on vacation in Seaford. Adrian finds out that Derek and Rita are there as well. Adrian becomes suspicious of Rita. Derek had earlier warned him about her mental instability, and Myra Owen and her husband tell Adrian that Rita has been blackmailing them with Amelia's diary. As Adrian becomes painfully aware of the threat to his daughter, he takes off to Seaford. Meanwhile, Rita invites Amelia out for a day trip, and even though she does not want to go, the child accepts. Rita "drops" her belt over the cliff, and Amelia volunteers to get it. Rita uses a stick to jab at Amelia in an attempt to knock her off the cliff. In the ensuing struggle, Rita herself falls over the cliff and dies. Later, the police find in her purse a note written by Rita and addressed to Adrian. The note discusses Amelia's death, and it is clear that the whole afternoon was a setup. The only person who does not seem to know about the scheme is Derek, who will not talk about the events of that day. Though he claims he was not involved in Rita's plan, he tells the police that he was hunting for spider orchids when she fell off the cliff; the only problem is they do not grow in the area he says he was in.

In her novel *Listening in the Dusk* (1990), Fremlin writes about a woman striving to survive after her devastating divorce. Desperate to strike out on her own after her husband leaves her for another woman, Alice Saunders rents an upstairs attic room in a boardinghouse. Over the years, everyone in the house has stored his or her belongings in the attic room. As Alice tries to make the most of her new situation, she decides to arrange the boxes and use them as her furniture. Looking through them one day, she finds what she thinks is a novel about murder and death, then casually lays it aside. The house is filled with a variety of intriguing characters, including Mary, a highly neurotic girl who seems perpetually on edge. Alice finds it odd that such a young, vibrant girl refuses to leave the house and hides in her room most of the time. Mary is clearly terrified of something–or someone. One day Mary tearfully reveals that the novel is really a diary written by her brother, a mass murderer who was convicted years before. In an attempt to keep her brother's twisted ideas private, Mary took the diary, left home, kept her identity a secret, and hid the diary in the neglected attic room.

Alice now understands Mary's unusual behavior. They struggle together to face a life that has, in different ways, robbed them both of time. Mary gets a job at a local store, and Alice continues her tutoring. It seems as if they have both finally broken free of their past. Then, in an instant, both of their lives are thrown into a whirlwind of activity. It is reported on the news that Julian, Mary's brother, has broken out of jail. Mary, desperate to find him before he commits another act of violence, goes after him. Alice, concerned for Mary's safety, tries to find her. A reporter desperate for the story kidnaps Mary and forces her to take him to her brother. Luckily, Alice's young student notices the strange event and creates a diversion, enabling Mary to escape. She immediately heads to the house she and Julian grew up in. There, in a climactic scene, Julian accidently shoots Mary and then shoots himself. In the aftermath, both Mary and Alice must face life alone.

In a genre where action, murder, and detectives culminate in a fast-paced environment, Celia Frem-

Dust jacket for the U.S. edition of Fremlin's 1990 novel, in which a neurotic young woman attempts to keep her brother, a mass murderer and escaped convict, from killing again (Richland County Public Library)

lin's novels seem to be an aberration. Using a deliberately slow pace, Fremlin creates mysteries that expose themselves slowly, gradually opening up to the terror within them. By exploring the setting of the humdrum, everyday home, with a protagonist who is struggling to thrive within the framework of domestic life, Fremlin presents tales of terror that hide beneath a seemingly normal surface. Fremlin herself has stated that the intent of her novels is not to present some graphic murder or crime, but instead to present how the everyday person deals with a mysterious threat or mysterious person hanging over them. Though her pace may seem slow for some, this writing technique allows the tension to build in Fremlin's characters. Fremlin's mysteries are precisely calculated journeys for the reader that always pay off.

Jonathan Gash
(John Grant)
(30 September 1933 –)

Gina Macdonald
Nicholls State University

BOOKS: *The Judas Pair* (London: Collins, 1977; New York: Harper & Row, 1977);

Gold from Gemini (London: Collins, 1978); republished as *Gold by Gemini* (New York: Harper & Row, 1978);

The Grail Tree (London: Collins, 1979; New York: Harper & Row, 1979);

Spend Game (London: Collins, 1980; New Haven, Conn.: Ticknor & Fields, 1981);

The Incomer, as Graham Gaunt (London: Collins, 1981; Garden City, N.Y.: Doubleday, 1982);

The Vatican Rip (London: Collins, 1981; New Haven, Conn.: Ticknor & Fields, 1982);

Firefly Gadroon (London: Collins, 1982; New York: St. Martin's Press, 1984);

The Sleepers of Erin (London: Collins, 1983; New York: Dutton, 1983);

The Gondola Scam (London: Collins, 1984; New York: St. Martin's Press, 1984);

Pearlhanger (London: Collins, 1985; New York: St. Martin's Press, 1985);

The Tartan Ringers (London: Collins, 1986); republished as *The Tartan Sell* (New York: St. Martin's Press, 1986);

Moonspender (London: Collins, 1986; New York: St. Martin's Press, 1987);

Jade Woman (London: Collins, 1988; New York: St. Martin's Press, 1989);

The Very Last Gambado (London: Collins, 1989; New York: St. Martin's Press, 1990);

The Great California Game (London: Century, 1991; New York: St. Martin's Press, 1991);

The Shores of Sealandings, as Jonathan Grant (London: Century, 1991);

The Lies of Fair Ladies (Bristol: Scorpion, 1991; New York: St. Martin's Press, 1992);

Storms at Sealandings, as Grant (London: Century, 1992);

Paid and Loving Eyes (London: Century, 1993; New York: St. Martin's Press, 1993);

Jonathan Gash (photograph © Jerry Bauer; from the dust jacket for the U.S. edition of A Rag, a Bone, and a Hank of Hair, *1999)*

The Sin within Her Smile (London: Century, 1993; New York: Viking, 1994);

Mehala, Lady of Sealandings, as Grant (London: Century, 1993);

The Grace in Older Women (London: Century, 1995; New York: Viking, 1995);

The Possessions of a Lady (London: Century, 1996; New York: Viking, 1996);

Different Women Dancing (London: Macmillan, 1997; New York: Viking, 1997);

The Rich and the Profane (London: Macmillan, 1998; New York: Viking, 1999);

Prey Dancing (London: Macmillan, 1998; New York: Viking, 1998);

A Rag, a Bone, and a Hank of Hair (London: Macmillan, 1999; New York: Viking, 2000);

Die Dancing (London: Macmillan, 2000; New York: Viking, 2001);

Every Last Cent (London: Macmillan, 2001; New York: Viking, 2002).

Collections: *Lovejoy at Large* (London: Arrow, 1991)—comprises *Spend Game, The Vatican Rip,* and *The Tartan Ringers;*

Lovejoy at Large Again (London: Arrow, 1993)—comprises *The Judas Pair, Gold from Gemini,* and *The Grail Tree.*

OTHER: "Eyes for Offa Red," in *Winter's Crimes 11,* edited by George Hardinge (London: Macmillan, 1979; New York: St. Martin's Press, 1979);

"The Hours of Angelus," in *The Year's Best Mystery and Suspense Stories,* edited by Edward D. Hock (New York: Walker, 1982);

"The Julian Mondays," in *Winter's Crimes 18,* edited by Hilary Hale (London: Macmillan, 1986);

"The Contras of Bloomsbury Square," in *Winter's Crimes 21,* edited by Hale (London: Macmillan, 1989);

"The Mood Cuckoo," in *1st Culprit: An Annual of Crime Stories,* edited by Cody Lewin and Michael Z. Lewin (London: Chatto & Windus, 1992); republished as *1st Culprit: A Crime Writers' Association Annual* (New York: St. Martin's Press, 1993).

PLAY PRODUCTION: *Terminus,* Cheshire, England, Chester Festival, November 1978.

PERIODICAL PUBLICATION: "The Trouble with Dialect," *Journal of the Lancashire Dialect Society,* 38 (September 1989): 2–6.

Jonathan Gash (Cockney rhyming slang for "trash" in the sense of "good-for-nothing") is the main pseudonym of John Grant, a distinguished English medical doctor who has turned out more than a mystery a year since he began publishing in 1977. The majority of his humorous and witty fictive creations focus on antique dealer and sometime investigator Lovejoy (his full name is never revealed), an unscrupulous, conniving antihero; a lecherous connoisseur of anything old, rare, beautiful, and valuable; a "divvy" who can mystically separate the genuine from the fake; a master of inspired fakery himself; and a dealer in dreams. He has highly flexible ethics and a cheeky manner as he engages in outrageous scams and counterscams in the name of justice, revenge, and a quick profit. Lovejoy is an idealist corrupted by everyday circumstances: his life is a constant quest for the rare, the exquisite, the irreplaceable; yet, he is always caught up in villainy and murder and easily imagines the worst in everyone. Through him, Gash satirizes the pleasures, pretensions, greed, and self-delusions of the antiques world and its hangers-on, from millionaire collectors to down-and-out barkers. The Lovejoy series follows a basic formula, but there is such a variety of information and experience bound up in it that each book is a new, intriguing experience. Unlike Agatha Christie, whose stories are plot-driven, Gash makes narrative voice his driving force, with Lovejoy's anecdotes about history, antiques, and human behavior, his advice, warnings, diatribes, and antics, taking precedence over story line. In the late 1990s Gash introduced a second series, with an unusual detective team that allowed him to focus on urban England and grim realism and to effectively employ his medical knowledge (the heroine is a doctor).

Jonathan Gash was born John Grant in Bolton, Lancastershire, on 30 September 1933, the son of Peter and Anne (Turner) Watson, both mill workers. He grew up in Bolton as one of a large family of boys. He married Pamela Richard, a nurse, on 19 February 1955, at age twenty-one, and they had three children: Alison May, Jacqueline Clare, and Yvonne. He attended the University of London, where he received his M.B. and B.S. in 1958, and the Royal College of Surgeons and Physicians, where he earned his M.R.C.S. and L.R.C.P. and became a member of the International College of Surgeons.

While a penniless premed and then medical student, Grant held a variety of odd jobs to pay for his education. Once he began working in the Cutler Street Antiques Market in London's East End, however, he had found a lifelong avocation. He carted around antiques and had them appraised by a real-life expert who, as Peter Gambaccini reports, became the model for Lovejoy. Gash's interest in antiques reveals itself particularly in his mysteries, where readers learn an array of information about a variety of unusual collectibles. Even British country lanes reveal "antiques," the legacy of the old Romans versus the heritage of the ancient Britons. Gash finds intriguing the idea that treasures abound everywhere, or, as he has Lovejoy point out in *The Grail Tree* (1979): "Right from our sinister prehistory to the weird present day, mankind's precious works are scattered in the soil, under walls, on beams, in rafters, in chests and sunken galleys, in tombs and tumuli. . . . I've seen an early Chinese black-ink jade cup used for tiddlywinks. And a beautifully preserved genuine 1751 Chelsea dish stuck under a penny plant pot out in a garden." Gash learned enough from this hands-on experience in the trade to be able to make his own forgeries (a practice he continues in order to make sure his descriptive details in his books are accurate). Unlike his characters who sell fakes as the real thing, Gash signs his creations and donates them to charity.

Once his main medical degrees were completed, Grant turned to full-time medical practice, but, while doing so, earned specialized degrees–D.Path., D.Bact., D.H.M., M.D., and D.T.M.H. He was a general practitioner in London from 1958 to 1959, a pathologist in London and Essex from 1958 to 1962, and a clinical pathologist in Hanover and Berlin from 1962 to 1965. A stint in the Medical Corps of the British Army from 1965 to 1968 earned him the rank of major.

In 1968 Grant moved to Hong Kong, where he served as head of the clinical pathology division at Queen Mary Hospital and as lecturer in the faculty of medicine of the University of Hong Kong. There he learned a great deal firsthand about tropical medicine. Grant grew to love the city and to have contempt for authors who researched their books on it from conversations in the Hong Kong Club. Grant learned Cantonese and used it in his professional dealings as physician and pathologist, and, as a result, attained a level of awareness of culture and perspectives most Westerners miss. This distance from his own culture made him quite capable of seeing through English social pretensions and of satirizing British sacred cows. He left Hong Kong in 1971 to become head of the bacteriology unit of the School of Hygiene and Tropical Medicine at the University of London. He also became a member of the Royal Society of Tropical Medicine.

His first work under the pseudonym by which he is best known among readers of the detective-fiction world, *The Judas Pair,* was published in 1977 and was, he says, an attempt to find "light relief" from medical duties. He began the Lovejoy series on a commuter train to London and from then on wrote on his lap while commuting to work and to lunch. He writes in longhand in small letters, changing the color of his ink each time he rewrites, and after four or more drafts finally turns the manuscript over to a typist before continuing revisions (up to as many as thirteen drafts). He has remarked that he finds writing both a pleasure and a game. His escape from urban drudgery was to write about a rural village, and his escape from his own medical persona was to produce a fun-loving, womanizing rogue, Lovejoy of Lovejoy Antiques, an impoverished but resilient and knowledgeable antique dealer with a flair–a nose for antiques and a nose for trouble. Through Lovejoy, Gash builds on the knowledge of antiques developed and refined as he worked his way

through medical school and then developed outside the trade as an aficionado. He also works in a British literary tradition going back to Robert Greene and his tales of coney-catching. Gash, like Greene, makes his rogue lovable, and, because it is Lovejoy's narrative voice addressing readers, Gash can escape into the skin of a witty, lively character, with a short temper, few scruples, and an obsession with antiques first and women second. These consuming interests take precedence in his life to the exclusion of almost everything else.

Newgate Callendar, writing in *The New York Times Book Review* (19 August 1979), called Lovejoy "flawed indeed"–scrambling "for a living" and "turning a dishonest deal or two," his speech "ribald," his manner "offensive"–yet "a genuine hero . . . faithful to himself," seeking the "unattainable . . . backed by a tremendous knowledge and a rapt love for what he is doing." Writing in the same source on 29 April 1984, Callendar captured Lovejoy's essence: "always broke, always hustling, always randy, always seedy and unsavory, always resourceful . . . never an admirable character . . . always ready to forge an antique, to bend the law, to lie outrageously, always managing to justify himself by specious reasoning . . . a male chauvinist . . . [without] one redeeming characteristic," but also "a true artist" and "a visionary who loves beautiful antiques more than life itself and who knows as much about them as Bernard Berenson did about Renaissance art." In fact, Lovejoy's antiheroic nature is the key element in the series. His impromptu, informed lectures on a wide range of curiosities are, of course, another important part of the charm and attraction of the novels. These lectures reveal the author behind the series character–a man fascinated by history, the arts, and human behavior and forgiving of human foibles.

The Judas Pair won the Creasey Award of 1977 for the best first crime novel of the year. Lovejoy's scout, Tinker Dill, brings him a promising customer, a Mr. Field, who employs Lovejoy to track down a legendary pair of dueling pistols, the Judas pair of the title, which may not actually exist but which the would-be buyer claims recently killed his brother. As Lovejoy explains in the opening, "This story's about greed, desire, love and death–in the world of antiques you get the lot." Motivated by the hope of an enormous fee, he follows the trail to Norfolk, where he is caught up in violence. When his latest girlfriend is murdered, he pursues the culprit, spurred on by vengeance and aided by luck, and stirs things up enough to cause another murder, to be attacked with a crossbow, and to find himself entombed in his own burning cottage. He survives, thanks to his own ingenious construction of an air-pumping device, but is left frustrated and distraught: "All life in that moment seemed utterly mad. No won-

Dust jacket for the U.S. edition of Gash's first novel (1977), which introduces the rascally antique dealer Lovejoy (Richland County Public Library)

der people just set out determined to simply get what they could. Who could blame them? The proof was here, in ashes above me. And I, honest, God-fearing Lovejoy, finished up buried underneath the smoking ruins of my own bloody house, cut, filthy, bleeding, weary, and as naked as the day I was born."

Bent on revenge, he confronts the insane murderer in a deadly final duel with ice bullets and weapons as warped as their owner. Lovejoy's ethics, labeled "situational" by Robin W. Winks of the *New Republic* and "stretchable" by Callendar in *The New York Times Book Review,* do indeed bend with the wind. Lovejoy is not above selling a fake to an expert who should know better, but he gives a cautionary tip to the amateur buyer who has no way of determining value for himself. Such, implies Gash, are the shifting ethics of the antique trade, in which gamesmanship and trust are in constant competition. Lovejoy lies without hesitation and grabs what he can while he can—then spends it on feeding birds and assisting the down-and-out. When his latest girlfriend whimpers, "All you think of is antiques," he stands amazed at her self-centeredness and points out to readers that "Women have no sense

of priorities." At the end of *The Judas Pair* the valuable dueling pistols for which he has searched throughout most of the book quietly disappear into his own secret hideaway, as do many other valuable items throughout the novels. Lovejoy waxes eloquent about shady possibilities. He may be seedy and unscrupulous and a perpetual complainer, but he is not a man to be trifled with, for, when cheated, he retaliates in full. When an interrogation subject tells him to "Get stuffed," Lovejoy's forehead turns white hot; he struggles for control, then pushes the man back, knees him in the crotch, and butts his nose with his head: "heaven knows where I learned it. I honestly am a peaceable chap," he tells readers as the other man scrambles away in terror.

This first novel establishes the pattern of the Lovejoy mysteries, a pattern that remains surprisingly similar beneath the surface variations that keep the pace fast, the action exciting, and the details fascinating. The novels are told in the lively, eccentric, first-person narrative voice of Lovejoy, who speaks directly to the reader as a sympathetic confidant. They are each dedicated to an ancient Chinese god such as Wu Ch'ang Kuei, who "brings a fortune in treasure." They begin with Lovejoy's general comments on the importance of antiques and the mysteries of women and his affirmation that he is the only person the reader can trust. Lovejoy then proceeds to a tale centered around some intriguing antiques scam, the larger and the more complex the better. Usually, Lovejoy, short of cash and hungry enough to take on anything (paper-delivery route, day labor on local farms, and so on, much like Grant the impoverished student), accepts a commission related to antiques (finding a particular item, tracking down a dealer, replacing a stolen treasure with a credible forgery) and works hand in hand with a woman (either the person who commissioned the work or an employee of that person). As he halfheartedly pursues his assignment, Lovejoy becomes caught up in some sort of caper involving forgery, burglary, or some outrageous con perpetrated by outsiders rather than the closed circle of his neighboring antiquarians. Often an older bystander who has been close to Lovejoy or whom he considers part of his world is threatened, injured, or killed, and Lovejoy decides on revenge. The police are less than tolerant of his motives and methods, but he uses them and they use him. Consequently, he is always taking justice into his own hands; a friend is murdered and his automatic response is "I was going to kill somebody." One judge begs him to simply point the way and let the police round up the murderers, but Lovejoy feels compelled to handle the dirty work himself. Lovejoy gravitates toward peculiar predicaments and perpetual trouble—with women, with fellow dealers, with wealthy clients, with thieves and forgers and con artists of all sorts. He is a bit of a coward but daring when driven by a lust for antiques or revenge. These unpredictable shifts keep reader interest in the character lively, for Lovejoy is always capable of surprises. Episodic action sends Lovejoy ranging far afield from East Anglia, the center of his trade, to changing locales—from nearby villages to the Isle of Man, Guersey, Jersey, or even foreign lands. Interspersed are intriguing, often scholarly disquisitions on antiques and art.

Throughout this first novel and the series that follows, Lovejoy's detective method is to talk to large numbers of people, observe their behavior, trust his instincts, gather gossip, and watch and wait until clues fall into place, plots are unraveled, and murderers exposed. He trusts neither motive nor alibi, both of which he calls "the falsehoods of murder" in *The Grace in Older Women* (1995). His charm, his wit, his deductive powers, his eye for detail, his doggedness, his cavalier approach to life, and his luck eventually lead to the affair being settled—to Lovejoy's satisfaction if to no one else's. During the course of these events Lovejoy usually juggles several amorous ladies (most-often married), one of whom outrages his sensibilities by

destroying an exquisite antique or by manipulating and controlling his life. At the same time, he exposes the limitations and hypocrisy of upstanding citizens and manages to spread around a lot of IOUs to acquire valuable antiques, create a couple of faked "antiques," feed an assortment of robins, budgerigars, squirrels, kittens, hedgehogs, and the occasional small child, and aid the impoverished (abandoned mothers, out-of-work craftsmen, alcoholics, indentured servants, and aged pensioners). Inevitably, Lovejoy must do something heroic, all the while complaining of his fear and reveling in his cowardice. Again, part of the character's appeal is his exaggerated human frailty combined with sometimes startling romantic gestures.

Starting in *The Judas Pair* and continuing throughout the series, Gash tosses out gems of Lovejoy wisdom: "Information, like statistics, is rubbish," "Ditching a priceless necklace . . . in a temper is still basically an unreasonable act," "Removing people is the ultimate crime," "Embarrassment's my life style," "There's mileage in groveling," "Love creates art; precision makes fakes," "Man doth live on bread alone, if antiques are thrown in as well," "Greater love hath no man than that he gives up his life for his collection," "A woman marries because a man is less trouble than her mother," and "Modern means lunatic." Through Lovejoy, Gash gives vent to that side of him that takes pleasure in turning the world upside down and shocking the stuffy and conventional.

In *Gold from Gemini* (1978), a Crime Club Choice published in the United States as *Gold by Gemini,* a brilliantly forged picture puts Lovejoy in search of a dead artist whose cryptic diaries and Roman coins cause the death of a broken-down dealer. Lovejoy follows the diaries and the Roman clue in search of a treasure trove of early Roman coins. His adversary, "one of those sick cold people who impelled more normal people into lunacy," threatens him and wins over his companion. Lovejoy can understand greed and even murder, but when he learns his pet birds have been killed, gruesome deaths ensue.

Though clearly a genius possessed of all-inclusive knowledge in his profession, a diviner who intuitively and mystically responds physically to genuine antiques, Lovejoy remains perpetually hard-up for funds throughout this book and the others in the series. His water, electricity, and telephone are regularly cut off for nonpayment, and he depends on water from a well in his overgrown garden; his cottage is, says Gash, "grotty with a flagged floor." Yet, possessing genuine antiques so consumes his life that he has no time or money for anything else. He is forced to baby-sit, do farmwork, and even sell stolen handkerchiefs in the rain to survive from day to day; he borrows where he can, owes friendly waitresses the price of an occasional meal, jerry-rigs his ancient car, and in emergencies finds himself caught short without change for a vital telephone call. He squirrels away his treasures in a basement room whose only entrance is a trapdoor hidden beneath a worn rug; adjacent to his cottage is a jumbled workshop where he plies his trade, restoring, reproducing, and downright forging.

Gash's enthusiasm for antiques and for the techniques by which they were originally made and later forged is an essential feature of the series. A reviewer in *Library Journal* (1 December 1977) argued that Gash's novels "could almost be used as . . . primer[s] for the trade in small antiques." Readers learn the ease with which fakes can be created and the distinctions between some fakes and the real goods, in other words, tricks of the trade whose exposure antique dealers probably resent. As he moves in and out of antique shops, shows, and private homes, Lovejoy provides a running monologue of tips about purchases and repairs. He also explains with care and love the skill involved in producing fine craftsmanship. The joy of antiques for both Lovejoy and his creator is the risk of human error and the infusion of human love. The precision of the technical process description is indicative of Gash's expertise in this area: he has tested out the strategies he has Lovejoy describe and advise.

In his third adventure, *The Grail Tree,* another Crime Club Choice, Lovejoy is asked by Reverend Henry Swan to authenticate the Holy Grail. He decides something of value must be at stake when Swan's longboat blows up with the reverend aboard. The killers have not only blown up an old man who believes beautiful objects are sanctified by use, a sentiment Lovejoy shares, but they have also maliciously poured acid over antique medallions—an offense against reason from the point of view of Lovejoy and his associates. Lovejoy deduces who is involved, gathers incriminating evidence, blackmails the criminal conspirators, and ends up in a violent showdown in a castle museum—a Galileo pendulum up against a flintlock amid fireworks. He rips a woman's dress down the back, batters her murderous companions, and roughs up some bully-boys he suspects of vandalism: "I heard one of them move suddenly forward, but he caught his shin on my heel and took a nasty tumble. It was quite accidental. Worse still his hand got trodden on as I stepped to one side." Amid such aggressive activities, he is also engaged in training a new assistant in the mysteries of his trade and avoiding the police who want either a scapegoat or an informant. Antique dealers and aristocrats, here and throughout Gash's novels, are dismissed with disdain. Bearing

Dust jacket for the U.S. edition of the 1979 Lovejoy mystery in which the antique dealer goes on a quest for the Holy Grail (Richland County Public Library)

names such as Alvin Honkworth, they are incapable of distinguishing between "a priceless Sung dynasty imperial jade butterfly and reinforced concrete"; they are duped by sloppy forgers passing off clearly modern scrawl as ancient documents and have no appreciation for the poverty and passion that compelled artisans.

Another Lovejoy gripe that emerges in *The Grail Tree* is his detestation of fresh air and the rigors of outdoor life. He prefers smoky towns and dim antique shops to "lurking around in reeds." When a young lady admires the countryside, Lovejoy dismisses it as "obnoxious," because not "man-made," and eulogizes instead the toil and struggle of the impoverished that produced true beauty. He finds beauty not in "a bit of dirt and a blade of grass" but in "an old viaduct" because "If mankind made it by his own gnarled hands, it has love in every crack. And love's all there is." For Lovejoy, true love is loving craftsmanship, "not a casual glimpse of a posh field or a bored cow."

Lovejoy is also contemptuous of "bratty" young-sters, though his soft heart shows through as he gives them rides on a donkey he inherits by default, shares candy with them, and helps their mothers provide for them, perhaps because they, like Lovejoy, are free spir-its, desperate to escape the restraints of convention and of the adult world. For a similar reason, Lovejoy also feels a camaraderie with wild birds and feeds them expensive tidbits whenever he can. At the close of the novel, trapped by his young female assistant who moves in with him as the price for eventually handing over the prized Grail, Lovejoy notes, "You can't beat a woman for trickery. I don't think they'll ever learn to be honest and fair-minded, like me," just as he has plot-ted to end the affair by secretly arranging for the girl's unsuspecting mother to pay a visit.

These first three books point the direction that the rest of the series takes. In large part they are satiric spoofs on the glittering, greedy, and glitzy world of antiques: the pretensions, the hypocrisy, the cons, and the rip-offs. Lovejoy, who, oddly enough, seems to have joined the priesthood for a short while at some distant point in his life, has authored a little-known but monumental work on antiques, one that betrays secrets he now regrets revealing. In *The Grail Tree* he asserts, "Antiques, women and survival are my only interests. It sounds simple, but you just try putting them in the right order." When it comes to antiques, Lovejoy is willing to sacrifice all else. When someone destroys a genuine article, a white rage takes hold of him and he plots retribution. He even rhapsodizes about valuable furnishings while making violent love or fighting a foe: "Even as Jimmo kicked at me while we tumbled scrap-pily among the furniture I knew it was a memorable piece . . . 1785. Wheezing with the chest pain I got to my knees a second before Jimmo and managed to kick him. There was one almighty crack. For a terrible instant I thought it was the chair, but it was only Jimmo's bone, thank God."

The Incomer (1981), written under the pseudonym of Graham Gaunt, is not part of the Lovejoy series. Instead, it is a mystery in the vein of those of Ruth Ren-dell, a study of the vigilante "justice" of English villag-ers whose prejudices predate Oliver Cromwell; the novel pits "incomers," those not born and bred in the village, against locals over the treatment of Les Taun-ton, a simple man accused of murdering a local girl but freed for lack of evidence. Behind the gossip, the affairs, and the secret spying of neighbor on neighbor lurks a cruel self-righteousness that evokes "the dark days of past ages when folk were half-mad with superstition." The tensions in the novel depend on a love-hate rela-tionship between a self-assured doctor, Clare Salford, and a hesitant priest, Reverend Shaw Watson. Their combined efforts reveal the truth and save a life, while proving that a courageous heart is perhaps more impor-tant than technological expertise. The style and tone of *The Incomer* are more traditional than those of the Love-joy series.

Spend Game (1980), one of Gash's best novels, begins with Lovejoy and a lady friend seeing a car go over an embankment and finding its driver—an old army friend and local antique dealer—dead. Investigat-ing, Lovejoy tries to trace the missing escritoire the friend had purchased the night before and, in the pro-cess, takes up with another lady and finds a message and key in the desk of a deceased doctor. Although a massive black saloon automobile tries to drive him off the road, much to the regret of its driver, Lovejoy's "industrial archaeology" uncovers a solid silver Victo-rian steam engine hidden in an underground tunnel. Nearly entombed permanently by outsiders who had murdered his friend, he finds solace in an effective, vio-lent, and devastating use of the engine as a weapon.

In this novel, and throughout the series, when not obsessed by antiques, Lovejoy is beleaguered by women, the joy and bane of his life. The women who surround him (and they are plentiful) end up mothering him, bringing him food, cuddling him for warmth, try-ing to clean up his cottage against his protests. Nonethe-less, they always fail, for he is incorrigibly set in his ways: "Honestly, I just can't see the point of moving things to a fixed spot for the sake of mere tidiness. Things only wander about again. I find it more sensible just to stay vigilant, simply keep on the lookout for essentials like towels and the odd pan. In fact, I'd say neatness is a time-waster." After spending several hours scrubbing a floor, he sees little accomplished and resolves to leave such obsessive tidying to others; more-over, he bemoans the negative effects of excessive cleaning on antiques, which lose their value from the absence of an aged fingerprint or grime identifiable from a significant locale.

In *The Vatican Rip* (1981), an Italian checks Love-joy out at Seddon's auction rooms (where Lovejoy, angered at the auctioneer's ill treatment of Tinker, pub-licly points out the fakes on sale). The Italian then shad-ows Lovejoy at the Three Cups and threatens his friends in the hope of forcing Lovejoy to go to Italy, learn Italian, and steal from the Vatican a Chippendale table the Italian claims was stolen from his family. The opening lines set the tone: "The trouble with life is, you start off worse and go downhill." In Rome, Lovejoy forms an alliance with a seemingly elderly female con artist, who enlivens the action with a repertoire of dis-guises, tasty tidbits on the Vatican, and an irrepressibly larcenous approach to life. He works part-time in an antique shop while perfecting the plan for the heist and plotting revenge on his employer. When he makes his move, however—a "fiddle switch"—he finds a fake already in place, his employer a cardinal, and himself an intended dupe. The caper is, as Callendar wrote in *The New York Times Book Review* (21 February 1982), "well-planned and executed" and the writing "urgent, realistic, amusing," but the explanations "lame" and the motivations "less believable than in the past." Nevertheless, the shooting of Pope John Paul II the week the novel was published and its detailed description of the Vatican's security system resulted in the initial printing selling out in two days.

Firefly Gadroon (1982) begins with Lovejoy trying to master one of the lost arts of silver craft—the reverse gadroon—and ends with him on his way to jail but with agreements already made to exploit his mastery of that art. In between he is consulted about a firefly cage carved in coal and a carving that holds the secret to a giant slab of chrysoberyl, a metamorphic rock of incredible value. As a result, his friend and teacher (the gadroon master) is killed, and Lovejoy goes after the murderers, a gang of thieves with their stash of portable antiques in an old sea fort. There is an exciting chase sequence that begins in the depths of the fort and leads to the nearby reeds and tidal flats. Lovejoy turns his stolen boat into a fire ship and explodes the ship of those responsible for his friend's death: a blackened, blistered hand reaches from the oily water; one of the villains, his legs blown off, drowns in a foot of seawater. In this novel and throughout the series, Gash captures through Lovejoy the fanaticism of the true fan, the self-destructive commitment to a single goal that can lead to honor and prestige but also to ruinous, almost pathological single-mindedness. Gash suggests that the line between genius and eccentricity is a thin one: one man's drive toward excellence is another's lunatic compulsion. Lovejoy's lifestyle is eccentric, but his instincts for true antiques are unerring. Time and again he sets up a scam or perpetrates a forgery to earn enough to pay expenses while trying to outwit and undo those who have done him or his wrong, but once the funds are in his hands he cannot rest until they are spent on acquiring more antiques: "I felt on top of the world—money in my pocket, antiques nearby and vengeance at hand," he says in *The Firefly Gadroon*. "Of course I should have first [fulfilled my duties]. . . . Instead I finished up an hour later with the stumpwork box . . . the collection of old theatre playbills . . . a carved beechwood chair of the Great Civil War period." He defends such actions as not all self-indulgence since his buying and selling also involves collecting useful gossip, in this case about "thirty-one antiques nicked in the past three months."

As a consequence of his compulsions, his thatched cottage is a rat's nest of disorder and filth—grime and dust and bits and pieces of antiques everywhere, heating nonexistent, and cupboards bare, except perhaps for a forgotten pastry, his main source of nourishment. His divan folds into his only bed. However, despite his perpetual need of funds, he feels superior to snobbish aristocrats who have sold their heritage, replaced valuable antiques with modern reproductions, and lack his good taste, appreciation, skill, and expertise. He is the ultimate snob about true value and takes pleasure in berating the limited visions and pedestrian tastes of aristocrats with no understanding of the deep sacrifices made by impoverished craftsmen to create beauty of form and function. Lovejoy argues that he normally hates "tricks with antiques" and calls such activities "evil" and "sin," but then concludes that the practice is "so common nowadays" and that "antique dealers—and even real people—think it's perfectly proper," so his occasional trickery in a good cause is perfectly acceptable. Lovejoy is capable of justifying anything in the name of expediency or rogue's justice. He constantly points out, "A couple dozen of these forgeries will keep you in idle affluence a year or so—if you're unscrupulous, that is." Even if you end up destitute on the streets, says Lovejoy, "you'll be one of the few owners of . . . Greenwich . . . armour."

In *The Sleepers of Erin* (1983) Lovejoy is framed for stealing church valuables by the real thieves, who cut his artery. After recovering (aided by a sympathetic nurse) and a bit of revenge, he unwittingly precipitates the murder of an Irish antique dealer (the nurse's brother), and then travels to Kilfinney, Ireland, to investigate links between the frame, the murder, and the theft. There, while avoiding "teams of rich, homicidal, fraudulent con merchants," he is caught up in a complicated plot involving a priceless set of silver Irish artifacts, the Derrynaflan Hoard. He takes a hilarious ride through the byways of rural Ireland accompanied by a would-be poet whose lilting ramblings are entertaining and whose skill as an archer proves valuable. During his travels Lovejoy stumbles on a ring fort, a Stone Age house, a lone burial tumulus, and a set of gold Celtic torc "sleepers" that are at the heart of a daring fraud. At the same time, he gets involved in complicated sexual affairs, so much so that a local policeman describes Lovejoy's liaisons with women as crossing "all known marital boundaries." The conclusion of this plot is a triple con with a team within a team to con the conners and with Lovejoy beating the Irish in retaliation for friends trying to defraud friends. The twists and turns of plots and motives make this one of Gash's best creations. When a dealer tries to con him with a fake edition of John Milton's *Paradise Lost* (1667), Lovejoy drives the dealer's own car through the man's storefront window. Later, when two

Dust jacket for the U.S. edition of Gash's 1982 novel, in which Lovejoy exacts violent revenge on a gang of antique thieves who killed his friend (Richland County Public Library)

Everything . . . in sight was man-made. Boats, canals, houses, wharves, bridges, hotels, churches. . . . It gave me a funny feeling, almost as if I'd come safe home. . . . Venice is singing caged birds at canal-side windows . . . exquisite shops and window dressing . . . inverted-funnel chimneys, leaning campaniles, wrought iron at doors and windows, grilles at every fenestration, little flower sellers, droves of children and noisy youths . . . bridges every few yards, narrow alleys where you have to duck to get under the houses which have crammed so close they've merged to make a flat tunnel. Venice is patchy areas of din—from speedboats racing to deposit their owners in cafes to do nothing hour upon hour—and silence. It's uncanny. . . .

For Lovejoy, Venice is a joy because it is all man-made. Nonetheless, he discovers that Venice has a darker side that also means "fright, evil, everything sinister," "perverse secrecy of the most surreptitious and malevolent kind," "secret trials, silent stabbings, spies, clandestine murder, and sudden vanishing without trace," "a slit throat while sleeping, and violent unfathomable assassination," "poison—it took a Venetian priest to murder a communicant by slipping poison into the very Host," "refined treachery and skullduggery," "a reign of hidden terror," and "stark cold cruelty." In the name of art, Lovejoy steals a gondola, breaks into a palazzo, forges a piece of art, saves an injured woman shot in his stead on a reedy island, and outwits a large-scale forgery ring run by killers. A "borrowed" dredger, a funeral barge, and the Venetian police's art squad further his actions. Ultimately, he buries the killers under tons of stone and water.

Pearlhanger (1985) focuses on a scam to pass off a fake bepearled siren as a priceless heirloom. Lovejoy (and obviously his creator as well) appreciates any highly developed skill, whether it is that of a master plowman or of a master painter. A "clamorous sixth sense," "a bell" in his chest, a sudden "bong" warns Lovejoy he is in the presence of a genuine antique, and when that happens all else loses significance. "Tinker really can't see the point in actually loving antiques," Lovejoy says of his assistant, and adds, "I can't see the point in loving anything else." Lovejoy's constant complaint is restoration that removes all traces of "human warmth," of "the precious care" lavished for centuries on a "priceless" piece. As he regales readers with odd bits of knowledge ("Did you know that Confucius was a police inspector . . . And Gandhi . . . a stretcher-bearer . . . Standards are falling"), he waxes eloquent about the power of antiques. Hired by a pushy woman to find her missing husband, Lovejoy follows the man's trail from antique to antique, only to be framed at the end of the trail for a murder he did not commit. The whole chase has been a setup, with crooks using Lovejoy's reputa-

church robbers frame him, he methodically stones them with a homemade slingshot, breaks their arms, and throws them over a bridge, thinking: "Sooner or later somebody has to chuck in the sponge on a vengeance. Otherwise we're all at war for ever and ever, and life's nothing but one long holocaust." After this noble sentiment, however, he queries angrily, "why should that somebody be me?" At the end, he arranges a cave-in that wipes out a full gang of murderers.

The Gondola Scam (1984) strains credulity but is nonetheless exciting and clever. It begins with a mugging and a robbery and moves on to a rich, elderly collector who, fearing Venice will sink into the sea and its treasures with it, resolves to remove every treasure for the sake of posterity and his private collection. He plans to replace the originals with accurate reproductions—with Lovejoy's assistance—and has a forger's factory to do so. The setting provides Lovejoy an opportunity to eulogize the magnificence of Venice, its beauty, its wonders:

tion as a divvy to con buyers, and with cops using Lovejoy's known shadiness to lull criminals. The con games do not bother him as much as buying art for investment—a "villainy" that makes him indignant: he calls those who do so "the worst sort of criminals," for they "steal our antiques, then hold them to ransom." What disturbs Lovejoy even more, however, is the senseless murder of a dotty old woman whose séances he deplored but whose friendship he appreciated. With this motivation, he outwits crooks and cops, gets his revenge, and makes a profit, too. With the police watching his every move, he tries to substitute an obvious fake for a more clever one so the buyer, a powerful and ruthless thug, would wreak vengeance for him. Afterward his comment is predictable: "I was only after justice. Honest truth."

Lovejoy's private life in this book, as in all the others in this series, is always a mess, for he has the sensibility of a tomcat and moves from lover to lover at a heart-stopping pace. "If it weren't for women my life would be tranquility itself," he quips, and warns, "Women get to you. You have to take proper precautions because female means sly." He describes them as "aching to belt you one yet simultaneously wanting to use you in their designs." Several of them, when angered, call him a male chauvinist pig; and he definitely makes a lifestyle out of unashamedly exploiting women's attraction for him and their desire to protect or change him. He continually abuses women, not physically, but psychologically and financially. He takes their money, uses their cars, eats their food, and then makes them stand outside in the mud or rain or harsh sea air while he confers with a "pal" or passes them on to a friend when the relationship begins to bore him. His preference is for married women (particularly ones with brutish, hulking spouses), for they are more of a challenge but less of a threat, more willing to accept his eccentricities, and less shrill.

While working full-time as a practicing physician and turning out mysteries on the side, Gash was approached by the BBC about making a television series starring Ian McShane as Lovejoy. McShane had read the novels, imagined himself in the starring role, and pushed scriptwriter Ian LaFrenais to adapt the books to screen. Gash says he literally signed the contracts for the BBC Lovejoy television series "between ward rounds in a busy London hospital." The producers did not seek his assistance in the production, but they did pay him author's rights for three separate limited-run series. The first series aired in 1986, the second in 1991, and the third in 1992. The series (with more than eighty episodes) was so successful that it sent viewers back to the books and literally made Gash's fame and fortune. The series captured the setting but

sanitized Lovejoy (particularly his randy sexual exploits with a continually changing cast of nubile young and middle-age women). McShane aimed for a slightly disreputable demeanor and chummy confidences (his Lovejoy confesses to shady deals and clever cons, exposes the insider tricks of his trade, and cynically comments on the way of the world) but made the television Lovejoy lovable, fairly faithful, and even honorable. Gash was most disturbed by these changes, because for him the goal of his books was to make readers grudgingly like Lovejoy in spite of his grasping, selfish nature. In an unpublished letter to Gina Macdonald, Gash contrasted the two. Instead of the "scruffy, shop-soiled article with the unruly thatch of hair, who baby-sits for a living between antiques carry-ons" and who is particularly fond of budgerigars, wild birds, and other creatures (he has a cat on occasion and a dog in *Gold from Gemini*), the glamorous television Lovejoy is "hygienically squeaky clean." Unencumbered by babies or pets, he is "dramatically dressed in faultless black Dakkar leather and trendy jeans, drives a Volvo instead of a derelict Austin Ruby, and knowledgeably drinks expensive wines at polo meets in Windsor among the gentry." Only the first series, for which much of the dialogue was taken verbatim from Gash's novels, includes the violence of village life and of Lovejoy. Whereas in *Gold from Gemini* Lovejoy ruthlessly relishes murderous revenge on a devious and grasping female who had contemptuously and maliciously killed his budgerigars, in the television series she "accidentally" falls to her death. Furthermore, the BBC series gives Lady Jane Felsham greater prominence than do the books and discreetly makes her the main love interest.

In *The Tartan Ringers* (1986), published in the United States as *The Tartan Sell,* after a truck driver transporting fake antiques that prove genuine turns up dead, another death follows quickly, and both suspicious bobbies and murderous thugs turn on Lovejoy. The intrepid divvy goes underground, joining a traveling carnival and divining "treasures" for a fee to fund his travels north, where the scam originated. After unwillingly helping carnival toughs roust rivals, Lovejoy leaves his love of the moment and sneaks away to Scotland, where he is educated about historical Scottish shams: "The bagpipe?—the only invention ever to come out of Egypt. . . . The kilt?—invented by Thomas Rowlandson, an English iron-smelter, in 1730." He gets caught up in the troubles of the McGunn clan and helps them save Tachnadray mansion by organizing a complex scam, a "paper job," an auction of household goods swollen and multiplied by offerings that dealers gain an instant provenance for, enhanced by a tricky auctioneer and "steganography" (secret pricing). The auctioneer, Cheviot Yale, embodies the skilled artistry

Ian McShane as the title character in Lovejoy, *the BBC television series based on Gash's antihero that was broadcast between 1986 and 1994 (Everett Collection)*

of the truly great con artist as he sets up elaborate systems of ruses and counterruses to arouse the competitive spirit of bidders, manipulates pacing and presentation, and meets all the legal requirements of authentication while building in subtle disclaimers.

Lovejoy equates love and antiques and argues, "Hatred and evil are their opposite. I'm an antique dealer, in bad with the law, and I should know." Thus, the book incorporates a wealth of details about legal and not-so-legal antique cons but never loses sight of its original double-murder mystery. There is comedy too, often mocking pretensions and pretenses, as in the irreverent comment about the Scotsman who had a stroke "the day after two immigrant Pakistanis registered a Clan MacKhan tartan." The final scenes, an exciting chase sequence and a surreal and deadly parade at the Edinburgh festival, bring all the subplots together in a clever, comic way. Maslow, a policeman who appears in multiple novels in the series and always seems to classify murders as accidents, attacks Lovejoy as "pathetic," haunting "junk shops," and "shagging" his way "through women's handbags," but he is obviously jealous of both Lovejoy's success with women

and his ability to detect crime. Lovejoy despises the police, particularly Inspector Maslow, and concludes, "the law has no sense of what's right."

Moonspender (1986) intertwines several plotlines: Lovejoy is asked to validate the source of rumors about a genuine Roman bronze found locally; coerced into arranging a large wedding for a womanizing friend; manages a failing farm at the bequest of a wealthy lover; is forced to participate in a rigged television quiz show about antiques; helps redecorate a new restaurant and helps its conservative owners deal with the wild tastes of their gay decorators; and is intrigued by high-tech, midnight treasure hunters. Outraged by an irritating television hostess, Lovejoy bursts into inventive name-calling, denounces the fakes, and in general creates chaos and havoc that results in the death of a forger, run down by a bull. There are a barrage of lawsuits and romantic complications as Lovejoy moves from bed to bed and scheme to scheme. Readers learn how to fake a Roman bronze artifact and how to make falsehoods ring true: believe in them at the moment of delivery. All is unraveled at the end. Gash's portrait of Lovejoy's "swishy" associates, Sandy and Mel (and Cyril and Keyveen in later novels), adds tongue-in-cheek humor to the satiric mix, especially their campy come-on to embarrassed village cops and their multicolored Rover with angel wings projecting from the mudguards, orange-striped curtains, and "a dazzling array of painted flowers, stripes, zigzags, and twinning greenery." Despite their heavily exaggerated lifestyle, they are basically benign, in contrast to the vicious, greedy hypocrites preying on the unwary, whom Lovejoy foils.

By 1988 Gash could afford to retire from his daily round of medical duties. He opted to serve as a private consultant, a specialist in infectious diseases. He also spoke in libraries throughout Britain on his personal, intuitive theory about the impulses that motivate and produce creative writing.

He was also free to pursue his interest in dialects. In 1989 he published an article on dialect for the *Journal of the Lancashire Dialect Society* under his real name. For some time he has regularly contributed poems in Lancashire dialect to the *Record,* and in the Lovejoy series he has his protagonist regularly translate arcane terminology, underworld slang, and gypsy terms such as *jinney-mengro, chohawno,* and *moskey.* Moreover, Lovejoy's attitudes and concerns are expressed in colorful slang that suits his casual lifestyle and carefree ways. Lovejoy and his drunken barker, Tinker, converse in dealer's slang about "whifflers" and "vannies," all of which Lovejoy carefully explains. Other examples of such slang are "knocking down" (stopping at the highest bid), "naughty" (deliberately falsified), "cloth job" (raiding a church), "flocking" (gradually releasing antiques and fakes claimed to be from a single source), and "twinning" (the practice of dividing up a piece of antique furniture and using the parts to create two pieces, each half genuine, half false). The novels also include technical terms such as "electrochemical abrasive stripping voltammetry," "depletion gilding," and "Fourier transform interferometry," and antique terms such as "japanned," "thurible," and "arctophiles" (teddy bear collectors). Such a mix of slang and specialized jargon reflects Lovejoy's working-class origins, his knowledge of arcane historical terms, his expertise, his individualism, and his close acquaintance with underworld activities. It also reveals Gash as an amateur linguist with a good ear for dialect and a deep-seated interest in language.

Jade Woman (1988) is a loving tribute to Hong Kong, a city Gash knows intimately from his time there in the 1960s. In this novel Lady Jane, one of Lovejoy's many wealthy liaisons, engages in a carefree destruction of Lovejoy's way of life in order to force him into marriage. She not only has him "evicted, bankrupted, sued and dispossessed," but also pursued by an angry mobster who had depended on a confiscated fake, eight months in the making, to save a tricky financial exchange. When Lovejoy escapes to Hong Kong, he finally meets his match: the city itself, a benchmark of affluence and of poverty, a legendary showplace of capitalistic venture with everyone engaged in nefarious scams. Lovejoy falls asleep at the airport and awakens to find all his possessions gone, including his passport, and he is trapped in a city of far cleverer con artists than he has ever encountered. Where he could eke out a subsistence-level livelihood in England, on the lam in Hong Kong he is reduced to starvation and bondage. Though on the edge of the world of James Clavell's *Noble House* (1981), Lovejoy is trapped in a much lower social level, where the wheeling and dealing is literally cutthroat. His sex appeal proves effective only in work as a gigolo, and only his skills as a divvy save him from a life of prostitution, as he becomes caught up in murder, theft, seduction, and the machinations of a triad "Jade Woman" named Ling-Ling. To the question "Is every moral man up for grabs?" his experience answers, "quite possibly, in Hong Kong." To his attempts to make sense of triad schemes, Ling-Ling rightly responds that Chinese tactics might be "too duplicitous" for his "romantic soul."

In *The Very Last Gambado* (1989), the title of which refers to the last jump in a tumbler's routine, a theft on a gigantic scale is planned with a movie production as cover. Lovejoy, as technical consultant and extra for a caper movie set in the British Museum and involving the theft of priceless art and archaeological objects,

must save Britain's national treasures and himself. Though the plot of the novel is weak, the narration is as lively and informative as ever. The story begins with the death of an eminent local forger and the disappearance of an antique dealer, turns on rumors of a local hoodlum sending full containers of antiques to the United States and on an aged Russian countess with an enticing collection of family heirlooms, and ends with a shoot-out and a roundup of the villains.

The Great California Game (1991), a result of Gash's visit to the United States, is one of the author's weaker efforts, mainly because his treatment of American lingo and social interaction rings false. What works well in a contained environment goes out of control as Lovejoy tackles an international antiques conspiracy. Lovejoy, fleeing Hong Kong, tends bar in a Manhattan eatery, until an opportunity to wait tables at an expensive dinner party gives him a chance to reveal his expertise: recognition of a guest's diamonds as fake and of an abused old table as a valuable antique. The party hosts entangle him in extortion and cons that result in the death of a fellow bartender. Joining forces with a streetwise eight-year-old boy and his down-and-out mother, a prostitute, Lovejoy heads for Malibu in hopes of raising sufficient backing to participate in a grand-scale gambling tournament with monumental stakes. He finds himself disturbed at the idea of antiques treated as commodities, however, and paves the way for a huge explosion that does in the game and its more-sinister players. Though federal agents engaged in a sting operation try to further involve him in exposing other antiques scams, Lovejoy, mother, and child flee to Kansas. Far from the soil that nurtures his personality and the class differences that compel his behavior, even Lovejoy's narration rings hollow in this novel.

The Lies of Fair Ladies (1991) begins with Lovejoy's friend, Prammi Joe, being suspected of stripping a carefully secured mansion of its valuable antiques. When Joe is killed, Lovejoy tracks down the real mastermind behind the heist, an anonymous but sinister broker who is engineering a major swindle that has local dealers feverishly stockpiling antiques in the hope of a quick profit. Lovejoy is aided by a sexy fortune-teller famous for full-body massages and a pet python, and by his prim apprentice, Luna, the mayor's wife. Readers share in Luna's apprenticeship, as Lovejoy instructs her in the fine points of his trade (buying, selling, bidding, faking) and regales her with pearls of philosophic wisdom ("Plastic spoons are the end of civilization").

Under the name Jonathan Grant, Gash produced a trilogy titled *The Mehala of Sealandings,* comprising *The Shores of Sealandings* (1991), *Storms at Sealandings* (1992), and *Mehala, Lady of Sealandings* (1993). With its mythological and ecological concerns, it is a major departure from his mystery stories.

Paid and Loving Eyes (1993), the plot of which critics have labeled "baroque," "cryptic," and "mindboggling," has a confusing array of characters, including a bevy of scheming females sexually conquering and manipulating Lovejoy (his former wife, Cissie, among them). Lovejoy's women come from all classes and backgrounds, but most are high-handed and scheming and even the good-hearted and innocent eventually find Lovejoy incorrigible. About them Lovejoy asserts "women talk in the pluperfect vindictive" and, even with the best of motives, unsettle a man's life. Nevertheless, he believes, "the lusts for antiques and women are one and the same" and "the sin within a woman's smile," to paraphrase the title of another Lovejoy novel, offers him a passion akin to the passion and the sin that antiques embody for him. While moonlighting as the driver of a van engaged for clandestine sexual encounters, Lovejoy ends up judging an illicit contest of antiques, spotting the fake, and thereby unwittingly dooming its forger. Then, compelled by Cissie's faked (or real) death, he becomes enmeshed in a complicated Continental antiques scam involving an underworld ring, a Swiss repository, defrauded insurance companies, and a hunt by the "paid but loving" eyes of SAPAR (Stolen Art and Purloined Antiques Rescue), a group of watchdogs of the antiques trade, out to expose fraud and exploitation. In addition to witty descriptions of France as a "gentle" land of "lies," "cruelty," and "preconceptions," tips on French antiques and on master fakers, and negative portraits of drug abuse, Gash's social conscience shines through, and the book exposes the horrors of debt-bonded indentured servitude in the European antiques trade—the use of young children to duplicate the injurious, bloody eighteenth- and nineteenth-century techniques of polishing and finishing furniture—and of white slavery for similar purposes in Third World countries: "the exploitation of over 3 million child slaves." The pain of children reproducing mahogany furniture in Dickensian workshops leaves him overwhelmed at the craftsmanship but physically ill at the human cost. Thus, Lovejoy blows up an antiques repository and with it a gang of unscrupulous antiquarians whose frauds depend on child labor.

In *The Sin within Her Smile* (1993) Lovejoy is sold as a "slave for a day" at a charity auction, a position villagers assume is a humorous guise for sexual hanky-panky but which proves in addition a serious bondage in which Lovejoy is expected to help divvy Romano-Celtic gold artifacts. The divvying is part of a major scheme to revive ancient Roman gold mines in Wales. Furthermore, Lovejoy is commandeered to assist on a fund-raising mental-health caravan, an

excursion for kleptomaniacs, nudists, murderers, philanderers, senile oldsters, and an infant. Of his situation Lovejoy jokes, "Suddenly it's like I'm watching a kabuki play blindfold with commentary in lost Tasmanian." The wagon loads of "loonies" begin to seem far saner than the greedy "good" citizens who use them and mock them. There are discursive lectures on gold, silver, diamonds, and Wales—its language, customs, history, and antiques. Ultimately, Lovejoy makes sure the murderers get their comeuppance, the indigent along the journey benefit from his expertise and softheartedness, various possessive women are foiled, and a sympathetic American colonel is inspired to cut from the Welsh mountains and transport to the United States a new Stonehenge to teach Americans about Wales.

The Grace in Older Women is a tribute both to lovingly, skillfully faked "antiques" and to the virtues of women who are ugly and aged by conventional standards but whose grace, understanding, and mercy can "sanctify a saint." The story begins with Lovejoy making love with a lady in a forest to get close to her valuable Bilston enamels and ends with him trapped into initiating two aging spinsters (the proprietors of the Lorelei tearooms and of various tourist tours for gullible Americans) in the mysteries of sex. He is later sacrificed to the insatiable appetites of a female pretender to the British throne (by way of Charles Edward Stuart, or "Bonnie Prince Charlie"), who forcibly enlists him to raise funds for her cause, and his mounting of a huge auction of forgeries and fakes (all lovingly described and some perhaps genuine). His able assistant is the highly competent but unattractive mistress of one of Lovejoy's old friends, Tyrer, who is drowned in the local pond and whose mobile "Sex Museum" is torched; the auction is meant to flush out his killer. In the process Lovejoy exposes a mail-order priest and a criminal cop, reveals the source of decay behind the atrophied village of Fenstone, and denounces Bonnie Prince Charlie as a total sham, "Yanks" as litigious and obsessive handshakers, and nature as "lurking." In this novel, as throughout the series, Lovejoy's love of antiques is balanced by his sympathy for birds and beasts, as he nearly faints from the exquisite beauty of a seventeenth-century tortoise-shell fan and then from his recollection of the monstrous cruelties perpetrated on turtles in the process of collecting such shells.

In 1997, with *Different Women Dancing*, Gash launched a new detective series featuring an unusual detective team: Clare Burtonall, a medical practitioner, and Bonn, a streetwise gigolo of growing importance in her life. The duo meet for the first time when they both stop to assist at a fatal road accident. The accident begins to look suspiciously like murder, however, and Clare's husband, an influential property developer, seems somehow involved: the dead man is a business associate, and his battered briefcase is furtively delivered to the Burtonall home. Bonn, who heads his own team of men for the Pleases Escort Agency, draws Clare into unfamiliar territory–the criminal underworld of urban England. Unlike the ribald and jovial village tales involving Lovejoy, these novels share a darkness akin to that of Graham Greene's *Brighton Rock* (1938). They depict a world inhabited by the down-and-out, the dregs of society, and the predators. They are graphic explorations of hard-boiled urban settings and personalities. In *Prey Dancing* (1998), the second novel in the series, Clare, determined to pass on the dying words of an eighteen-year-old drug addict and street person to the man to whom they were addressed, discovers he is an angry, threatening criminal, a weapons man for a gang of murderous thugs with revenge in mind.

Until this new series, Grant had, in the main, avoided medical concerns in his novels, but since he had retired from medicine, he was no longer writing to escape his daily routines and the human problems they involved. Thus, in addition to the introduction of Clare Burtonall, Grant began to introduce some medical concerns into the Lovejoy series, for example, having Lovejoy respond sympathetically in *The Rich and the Profane* (1998) to a paraplegic youngster who paints credible forgeries with a toothbrush clenched between her teeth. Lovejoy provides the youngster lessons in his art. Typical is his advice on putting together an antique hunter's kit, which he concludes with "If technology scares you, forget the little microscope and make do with the tape measure, the colour chart, the hand lens and the torch. They'll save you a fortune, and maybe earn you one." The novel takes Lovejoy to Guernsey, seeking revenge for the supposed death of a companion in crime whom he believes has been tossed into the bottomless, bubbling hot mud of an ancient pool on priory grounds. When Lovejoy pulls together a musical and gambling extravaganza as part of his revenge strategy, he finds how far afield his assumptions have been. In the process he brings wealth and fame to many, but is lucky to barely escape with his life.

In *A Rag, a Bone, and a Hank of Hair* (1999), Lovejoy, as a favor to a friend, breaks his usual patterns and goes to London to check out who is passing off fake gemstones. There he is reminded of why he so despises the city. In this novel, he travels between the antiques markets of Bermondsey, Camden Passage, and Portobello and takes on a dangerous German entrepreneur responsible for the death of a fellow antique dealer and the destitute existence of the friend's wife.

Die Dancing (2000) returns to Gash's new detective team. Clare is newly divorced, Bonn has become

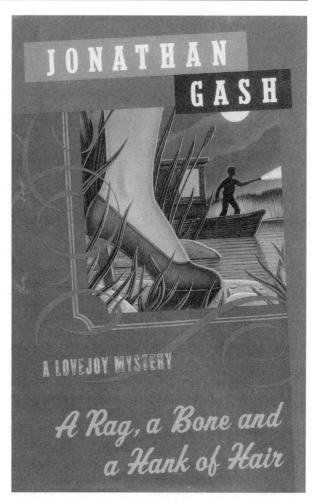

Dust jacket for the U.S. edition of Gash's 1999 novel, in which Lovejoy investigates a murderous fabricator of gemstones (Richland County Public Library)

her lover as well as partner in amateur detection, and, unbeknownst to Clare, the Pleases Escort Agency is the secret sponsor of her own new medical practice. While the pair merrily dance away an evening, a "fixer" for important businessmen is brutally beaten to death. The death has political implications because of the man's ties to a member of Parliament and personal associations for his similar links to Clare's former husband. While the detective inspector on the case follows these leads, Clare and Bonn follow other leads that end in more murder.

Every Last Cent (2001) involves another large-scale antiques scam, in which Lovejoy divines antiques as his alleged son, Mortimer, denounces fakes, and dozens of characters engage in a variety of nefarious doings. The loose-jointed plot spins off in colorful vignettes and informative and entertaining discourses on a variety of historical and artistic topics.

A family man whose personal persona is both witty and gentle, Gash lives with his wife in West Bergholt, Colchester, in Essex and enjoys the company of his three daughters and four grandchildren. As part of his activities in the new millennium, he has been negotiating with the UK Cable company to do a new Lovejoy series, this time with a new cast of actors and with Grant/Gash clearly involved in the production and decision making so that this time around the series will be much closer to the mocking irreverence of his books. At this stage in his life too he has more time for mystery conventions and occasionally makes appearances to speak about his books and characters.

Barbara Bannon of *Publishers Weekly,* in a review of *Spend Game,* called Gash's works "volatile and raffishly comic mysteries" and Lovejoy "a folk hero" with a "rapscallion" nature. Lovejoy in the twenty-first century has not evolved. Instead, he is a stable figure built solidly on English institutions: the small-town eccentric, the lovable rascal, the boyish philanderer, the honest thief with a heart of gold, the righteous avenger, the experienced con artist revealing to a privileged few his stock-in-trade, the magician creating illusions, the realist exposing falsity. He mocks respectable society and yet depends upon it. He is an obsessive person, truly talented in his narrow area, one who does not care about the opinions of others and who lives a notoriously naughty life. He exposes the shams of life, the realities behind illusionary appearances. The Clare Burtonall series has added a complexity and darkness to the Gash canon that takes the investigation of hypocrisy and of human foibles in new directions, with grimmer exposés and sharper contrasts.

In sum, a Jonathan Gash mystery promises convincing English settings, both physical and social, roguish characters, deflation of snobs and proprieties, and authoritative details about the medical world, architecture, the world of antiques, pets, and intriguing tidbits of history. Gash provides processes and lessons that, in the best English tradition, both instruct and delight.

Interview:

Matthew R. Bradley, "The Jonathan Gash Interview," *Mystery Scene,* 44 (1994): 18, 26–30.

References:

Earl F. Bargainnier, "Antiques, with a Vengeance," *Armchair Detective,* 20 (Spring 1987): 127–134;

Peter Gambaccini, "Alias Jonthan Gash," *Diversion* (November 1989);

Michael O'Hear and Richard Ramsey, "The Detective as Teacher: Didacticism in Detective Fiction," *Clues: A Journal of Detection,* 21 (Fall/Winter 2000): 95.

William Haggard
(Richard Clayton)
(11 August 1907 – 27 October 1993)

Anita Tully

and

Marie D. Sheley
Nicholls State University

See also the Haggard entry in *DLB Yearbook: 1993*.

BOOKS: *Slow Burner* (London: Cassell, 1958; Boston: Little, Brown, 1958);

The Telemann Touch (London: Cassell, 1958; Boston: Little, Brown, 1958);

Venetian Blind (London: Cassell, 1959; New York: Washburn, 1959);

Closed Circuit (London: Cassell, 1960; New York: Washburn, 1960);

The Arena (London: Cassell, 1961; New York: Washburn, 1961);

The Unquiet Sleep (London: Cassell, 1962; New York: Washburn, 1962);

The High Wire (London: Cassell, 1963; New York: Washburn, 1963);

The Antagonists (London: Cassell, 1964; New York: Washburn, 1964);

The Powder Barrel (London: Cassell, 1965; New York: Washburn, 1965);

The Hard Sell (London: Cassell, 1965; New York: Washburn, 1966);

The Power House (London: Cassell, 1966; New York: Washburn, 1967);

The Conspirators (London: Cassell, 1967; New York: Walker, 1968);

A Cool Day for Killing (London: Cassell, 1968; New York: Walker, 1968);

The Doubtful Disciple (London: Cassell, 1969);

The Hardliners (London: Cassell, 1970; New York: Walker, 1970);

The Bitter Harvest (London: Cassell, 1971); republished as *Too Many Enemies* (New York: Walker, 1972);

The Little Rug Book (London: Cassell, 1972);

The Protectors (London: Cassell, 1972; New York: Walker, 1972);

William Haggard (photograph by Clayton Evans; from the dust jacket for the U.S. edition of The Antagonists, *1964)*

The Old Masters (London: Cassell, 1973); republished as *The Notch on the Knife* (New York: Walker, 1973);

The Kinsmen (London: Cassell, 1974; New York: Walker, 1974);

The Scorpion's Tail (London: Cassell, 1975; New York: Walker, 1975);

Yesterday's Enemy (London: Cassell, 1976; New York: Walker, 1976);

The Poison People (London: Cassell, 1978; New York: Walker, 1979);

Visa to Limbo (London: Cassell, 1978; New York: Walker, 1979);

The Median Line (London: Cassell, 1979; New York: Walker, 1981);

The Money Men (London: Hodder & Stoughton, 1981; New York: Walker, 1981);

The Mischief Makers (London: Hodder & Stoughton, 1982; New York: Walker, 1982);

The Heirloom (London: Hodder & Stoughton, 1983; Bath: Chivers / South Yarmouth, Mass.: Curley, 1985);

The Need to Know (London: Hodder & Stoughton, 1984; Bath: Chivers / South Yarmouth, Mass.: Curley, 1986);

The Meritocrats (London: Hodder & Stoughton, 1985; Bath: Chivers / South Yarmouth, Mass.: Curley, 1987);

The Martello Tower (London: Hodder & Stoughton, 1986; Bath: Chivers / South Yarmouth, Mass.: Curley, 1987);

The Diplomatist (London: Hodder & Stoughton, 1987; Bath: Chivers / South Yarmouth, Mass.: Curley, 1988);

The Expatriates (London: Hodder & Stoughton, 1989; Bath: Chivers / South Yarmouth, Mass.: Curley, 1990);

The Vendettists (London: Hodder & Stoughton, 1990; New York: Curley, 1992).

OTHER: "Night Train to Milan," in *Best Secret Service Stories 2*, edited by John Welcome (London: Faber & Faber, 1965);

"Why Beckett Died," in *Blood on My Mind: A Collection of New Pieces by Members of the Crime Writers' Association about Real Crimes, Some Notable and Some Obscure*, edited by H. R. F. Keating (London: Macmillan, 1972);

"The Hirelings," in *Winter's Crimes 4*, edited by George Hardinge (London: Macmillan, 1972);

"Timeo Danaos," in *Winter's Crimes 8*, edited by Hilary Watson (London: Macmillan, 1976; New York: St. Martin's Press, 1977);

"The Great Divide," in *The Rigby File*, edited by Tim Heald (London: Hodder & Stoughton, 1989).

In his spy fiction William Haggard created a handful of memorable characters, most especially security expert Colonel Charles Russell, who appears in nearly all of his books. Russell is generally considered his author's representative in political and cultural matters, an assumption that brought Haggard warm endorsements from the conservative press and attacks from a liberal press that interpreted his impatience with incompetence as condemnation of the weak. Haggard's espionage novels are short (rarely two hundred pages in paperback) and briskly paced. Most were reprinted as paperbacks a year or two after hardcover publication. Closer to novella length when compared to John le Carré's lengthy and intricately detailed yarns of fatigue and desperation, Haggard's stories have little room for subplots or complications apart from the main problem, little development of character beyond the changes and growth of a few central characters over the thirty-plus years of the author's work on the series. A change in setting and a new, sharply contrasted set of supporting characters from book to book substitute for more-complex ingredients of psychological analysis or the interplay of themes.

Haggard was born Richard Henry Michael Clayton on 11 August 1907, in Croydon, Surrey, England. His parents were Anglican minister Henry James Clayton and Mabel Sara Haggard Clayton. The young Haggard attended Lancing College and Christ Church, Oxford, graduating with a B.A. degree in 1929. Haggard lived in India from 1931 to 1939, a turbulent period during which Mahatma Mohandas Gandhi pushed reform and independence; Haggard worked in the Indian Civil Service as a magistrate in 1931 and a sessions judge in 1937. In 1939 he married Barbara Myfanwy Sant, and they had two children, Michael Edward and Julia Katharine. From 1939 to 1945 he saw service in the Indian Army, rising to lieutenant colonel. Like George Orwell, Haggard's experiences in India provided him a close-up view of the dirty work of the empire and made him wary of officialdom and private motives and prejudices for public policies. Like Orwell, too, he learned to look with cold, hard eyes at a system Indians had good reason to both loathe and imitate, and at a diverse and divided country with high potential but with competing religions and philosophies and regional rather than national perspectives.

With postwar independence for India, Haggard, like so many British colonialists, sought safer positions elsewhere. After a brief posting in Buenos Aires, Argentina, he joined the British Civil Service Board of Trade in 1947, where he served until 1949. During the early years of his tenure, he worked on and received an M.A. from Oxford in 1949. For the last twelve years of his tenure, until 1969, he served as Controller of the Enemy Property Branch. Haggard's long career as a writer began at age fifty-one with the publication of *Slow Burner* (1958), which he wrote as he commuted by train to and from work. A series of successful spy novels followed at the rate of roughly one per year. Many of these books grew directly out of his work experience, as did *The High Wire,* the runner-up for the Crime Writers' Association's Gold Dagger Award in 1963. In fact, Haggard's avocation became so lucrative and enjoyable that he left government employment in 1969 to become a full-time writer. Haggard wrote until the final years of his life, with *The Vendettists* (1990) being his final novel. He died on 27 October 1993, having written more than thirty novels.

Haggard's admirers praise the consistency and dependable craftsmanship of a majority of these espionage novels. Haggard excels at dramatic plotting, staying close to a formula of explosive action growing out of volatile political circumstances. His experiences abroad lend this fiction the authenticity of the insider's view, and he exploits heavily the characters, historical events, and cultural mores of India, the Middle East, Russia and its satellites, and, somewhat less believably, South Africa. Even more interesting is Haggard's realistic and often contemptuous look at the inner workings of the British government. The balance Haggard strikes between individualism and a measured obedience to authority is a primary source of interest in the development of his central character, Russell. He also sharply differentiates his characters, preferring strong and decisive personalities even in minor characters. In several Haggard novels a character other than Russell takes center stage. In a few Russell is not present at all. Minor characters who rise to leading roles include William Wilberforce Smith, the aristocratic Caribbean operative who becomes a valued staff member, and Major Mortimer, another Russell protégé who evolves into a highly competent investigator. Paul Martiny, another of Haggard's series characters, whose stories mark a significant departure from the themes and characters of the Russell novels, has no connection to the cast of characters in those works.

The precisely worded opinions of Russell about international affairs, proper behavior around the great and mighty, and even proper behavior as a human being are thought provoking and occasionally simply provoking. Some of these opinions are dated—what modern readers might call sexist or racist or even chauvinistic—but Haggard was a product of his times, one for whom pragmatism and objectivity were far more admirable than political correctness. Haggard's early characters speak directly to 1950s contemporaries about events of their time. Yet, many of his assessments of international political trends have proved to be prophetic, as nations and factions have aligned themselves in ways Haggard anticipated. Russell's musings on many subjects is the most engaging fea-

Dust jacket for Haggard's first novel (1958), about a security leak involving British nuclear secrets (Special Collections, Thomas Cooper Library, University of South Carolina)

ture of the series. Through Russell, Haggard brings his readers into a circle of intimates in much the same way as did earlier novelists of manners such as Jane Austen and Dorothy L. Sayers: by using irony and understatement to make readers feel smarter than they might otherwise have reason to feel—as if they alone have caught the point. This illusion of being one of Russell's cognoscenti persists even when Haggard includes details that few readers, even his British contemporaries, could have fully interpreted.

Most often, a Haggard novel sets Russell's wry phrasing and epigrammatic humor amid exotic settings and glimpses behind the throne into the dominions of the most powerful persons on Earth. Haggard's is the highly tuned ear of a professional listener: Russell can detect not only languages, dialects, and registers, but he can also read motive, deception, and deflection in the spaces between words. Mystery critic Robin Winks, in *Detective Fiction: A Collection of Critical Essays* (1988), notes: "What has given Haggard

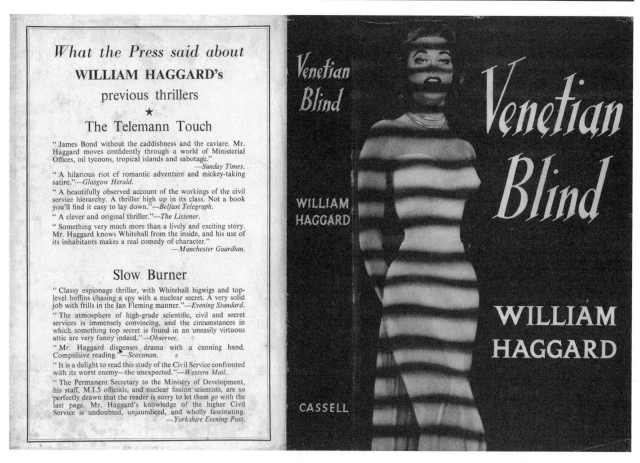

Dust jacket for Haggard's 1959 novel, which features an early example of his strong female characters
(Special Collections, Thomas Cooper Library, University of South Carolina)

his readership is his unwillingness to shed blood unnecessarily, his sympathy and insight into all of his figures, who are seen less in the traditional roles of villain and hero than as actors in a stylish drama in which all are motivated by a reasonable self-interest, and his subtle, ironic, detached voice. His books are not for the impatient." Undeniably respectful of principled authority and willing to employ his own powers of office to extremes of deadly force, Russell never seeks opportunities to exploit his power or his influence. Rather than riding the coattails of Ian Fleming, as some reviewers have suggested, Haggard provides a corrective for many of the comic-book elements in characters such as James Bond, bringing gritty, hard-nosed realism to a genre that could become submerged in male adventure fantasy.

The first of Haggard's books, *Slow Burner,* about a security leak of restricted nuclear information, received strong critical approval and attracted a wide readership. *The Telemann Touch,* considered by many to be one of Haggard's best, followed immediately the same year. It features a sympathetic assassin, one who fails to

arouse automatic condemnation. This reversal of stereotype became a stock technique for Haggard, who throughout his books enjoys jarring expectations and questioning assumptions about "typical" individuals or cultures. Additionally, the title carries forward a Haggard fondness for phrases with multiple applications to plot: the assassin whose touch is deadly to his victims is ironically gifted with a tender touch with people. The plot of *Venetian Blind* (1959) revolves around security leaks of nuclear secrets and includes one of the author's early female characters of startling strength. *Closed Circuit* (1960) is set in South America, where Haggard had a brief posting in 1946.

One of Haggard's better early novels (and one of his personal favorites), *The Arena* (1961), takes the City, the central financial district of London, as its setting and financial predators as its villains. Haggard clearly knows these new emperors of international finance well from his work administrating millions of pounds in money and valuables connected with the Enemy Property Office. In this book, new money tied to Naples, Brussels, and Paris corrupts members of

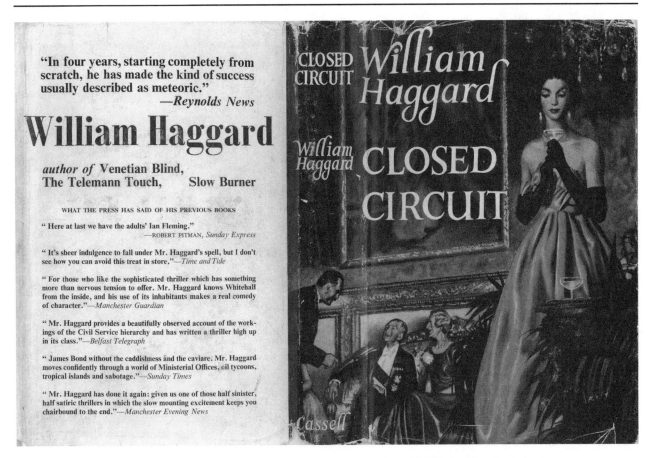

"In four years, starting completely from scratch, he has made the kind of success usually described as meteoric."
—*Reynolds News*

William Haggard

author of Venetian Blind,
The Telemann Touch,   Slow Burner

WHAT THE PRESS HAS SAID OF HIS PREVIOUS BOOKS

" Here at last we have the adults' Ian Fleming."
—ROBERT PITMAN, *Sunday Express*

" It's sheer indulgence to fall under Mr. Haggard's spell, but I don't see how you can avoid this treat in store."—*Time and Tide*

" For those who like the sophisticated thriller which has something more than nervous tension to offer. Mr. Haggard knows Whitehall from the inside, and his use of its inhabitants makes a real comedy of character."—*Manchester Guardian*

" Mr. Haggard provides a beautifully observed account of the workings of the Civil Service hierarchy and has written a thriller high up in its class."—*Belfast Telegraph*

" James Bond without the caddishness and the caviare. Mr. Haggard moves confidently through a world of Ministerial Offices, oil tycoons, tropical islands and sabotage."—*Sunday Times*

" Mr. Haggard has done it again: given us one of those half sinister, half satiric thrillers in which the slow mounting excitement keeps you chairbound to the end."—*Manchester Evening News*

CLOSED CIRCUIT William Haggard

William Haggard

CLOSED CIRCUIT

Cassell

Dust jacket for Haggard's 1960 novel, which takes his protagonist, Colonel Charles Russell, to South America, where Haggard served as a British government official in 1946 (Special Collections, Thomas Cooper Library, University of South Carolina)

proper British circles, making them inside accomplices. Against these ruthless campaigners, the old-fashioned banker Walter Hillyard (as well as his relatively principled way of life) is a doomed opponent and minor obstacle. Hillyard turns for comfort to his wife, Cynthia, and attempts to renew their marriage. Yet, the redemption of this long-neglected relationship in a finely drawn subplot intensifies Hillyard's movement toward destruction. Here, Haggard may well approach the "Jamesian complexity" that critic Julian Symons finds occasionally in the motivations of Haggard's characters. The later books seldom offer romantic love, replacing it more often with friendship or with simple passion—understood to be uncomplicated sexual appetite or "honest venery," as Haggard puts it in *The Money Men* (1981). Hillyard, however, does not meet Haggard's usual standards for consistency of characterization. *The Arena* concludes with such a swift decline in Hillyard from strength and decisiveness to despair that the book approaches melodrama. In later works Haggard is less inclined to

make strong, gifted characters sacrificial victims—even of themselves.

In his novels of the 1960s Haggard explores the tensions of the Cold War and the terrors of nuclear weapons. *The Unquiet Sleep* (1962) and *The High Wire* (1963) deal with themes of particular import to Haggard: the problem of balance in the modern world, where all must find their equilibrium among dangerous complexities. Failure in a Haggard novel brings death to the less capable; failure to recognize and foil the truly unbalanced threatens civilization itself. The balance Haggard maintains in Russell between political conservatism and moral pluralism is one of the many ways in which Haggard portrays difficult complexities in preference to simpler alternatives. In his novels Haggard clearly prefers individual merit over correctness in party, creed, or national origin. At the height of the Cold War, when *The Antagonists* (1964), *The Hard Sell* (1965), *The Powder Barrel* (1965), and *The Power House* (1966) maintained the steady confrontation of issues and backgrounds and of both Commu-

"William Haggard's name," says *Punch*, "is already made as a thriller writer with more to commend him than suspense making". The *New Statesman* has described him as "not so flash as Fleming, not so sad as Chandler, not as improbable as either, not too neat, not too nasty". His last book *The Arena*, was, said the *New Statesman*, "witty, intelligent, unflamboyant, poised with splendid balance between the 'novel of affairs' and the sophisticated thriller". These are indeed the qualities which have set Haggard in a special niche among this country's top thriller writers, qualities amply demonstrated in *The Unquiet Sleep*.

Dust jacket for Haggard's 1962 novel, about Cold War nuclear tensions (Special Collections, Thomas Cooper Library, University of South Carolina)

nism and Western values, Haggard was unafraid to admire a Communist enemy or criticize a sitting prime minister. *The Power House* so clearly indicts shortcomings that Haggard saw in Harold Wilson, prime minister at the time, that his publishers required extensive last-minute revisions.

Another Haggard favorite—*A Cool Day for Killing* (1968)—features the sophisticated Sheila Raden, one of a family of English adventurers who became sultans of the mythical kingdom of Shahbaddin. As the main character, Raden preserves her family's fortune, their honor, and the life of her lover after her father is assassinated. She executes a plan by which she blows up an insurer's vault, steals her family jewels (in danger of falling into the hands of her father's killers), and then hides them in plain view, a classic "purloined letter" plot device. Raden's plans require icy calm and a willingness to accept extreme personal danger. Russell's interest lies in preventing Shahbaddin from falling to the Chinese. With little help from Russell, Raden accomplishes both her goals and his. The admirable Mary Maguffy, Russell's operative, arrives

at the end of her protection detail to find a dead Chinese hit man and several files of interest to the security executive: "She gave the room a final searching stare. It wasn't a distinguished room but something distinguished had just occurred there. The wings of a simple justice had beaten powerfully in this little room, more than strongly enough to achieve what no Justice could have. She suppressed the moral judgment since she'd been taught to eschew it on duty." The language of this passage, like that of many throughout Haggard's writing, has a solemn, almost biblical, tone.

The son of a minister, Haggard undoubtedly absorbed the cadences of Scripture and prayer book. His code of values, however, as reflected in his plots and themes, is not based on a rigid set of religious views. Characters refer to God in passing (Russell prays briefly and desperately in *The Bitter Harvest*, 1971, as he takes the single shot that may save a man's life or lose it) but do so obliquely. In *The Doubtful Disciple* (1969), a Haggard character speaks directly to the nature and identity of God: "[He] hadn't expected his

God would be a fool. He'd be a senior administrator. . . . He wouldn't hold it against a colleague that he'd simply done his duty." Furthermore, Haggard takes careful note of other religions. The religion of Sheila Raden is that of a devout Muslim but not the "fiercely protestant Islam of the barren desert lands which had given it birth." In *Visa to Limbo* (1978) the pragmatic Haggard attends to the consequences of religion rather than to mysticism: a hedonistic sheik asks one of his ministers, Rifai, to "Consider how history might have changed if Christendom had been rather more sensible on the basically simple subject of sex and Islam less absurdly fanatical on the matter of taking a glass of wine." Religion complicates politics and fails to console individuals.

In *The Bitter Harvest* (published in the United States as *Too Many Enemies*, 1972), Russell exerts himself to preserve the life and reputation of a member of Parliament who was once married to one of Russell's former lovers, Miriam Meyer. His efforts are pale compared to those of Miriam herself, a woman who receives Russell's highest tribute: "I would hate to have you for an enemy." The blind loyalty of the Arab villain is not entirely dismissed by Russell: "The organization Georges Bresse had worked for was weak and divided, rather a poor joke," but "It would not remain a joke forever. . . . States would decay and . . . thrones might fall," and where earlier agents had failed, those who followed might succeed.

Russell appreciates the need for fastidiousness when discussing justice, even to the point of clarifying the motives of his enemies: "if your homes had been wretched, the land ill cared for, what answer was that to the men who had lost them, what answer that another race had watered your desert and made it bloom?" Life in India opened Haggard's mind to the dual perspectives of a person who has been immersed in two cultures and learned to see with other eyes.

In *The Old Masters* (1973; published in the United States as *The Notch on the Knife*), Russell not only is a witness to history; in his role as an "Old Master" of security he is also an agent of dramatic and sweeping changes in the balance of powers among nations. Authorized to act with broad authority and with absolute secrecy against enemies of his government, Russell fearlessly walks the tightropes of power that such influence demands. He commands events with panache, facilitated by a strong will and tightly controlled emotions. The ability of key characters to sway outcomes by speech as much as by action—suspense based upon style—is a Haggard hallmark.

Haggard's Paul Martiny novels, while not much of a departure from his other fiction in structure or technique, serve as a respite from the unrelentingly

Dust jacket for Haggard's 1968 novel, in which Colonel Russell helps a beautiful sultana preserve her family fortune (Special Collections, Thomas Cooper Library, University of South Carolina)

high moral tone of most of his other spy novels. Whereas Russell, Smith, and Mortimer are sworn to codes of highest conduct (if Smith's occasional marijuana smoking is disallowed), Martiny is amoral and bloodlessly violent against a power structure that he loathes. Martiny is an accountant who follows his secret bliss—generalized revenge against privilege—through the dangerous underworld of money laundering for criminal clients. In *The Kinsmen* (1974) he is drawn out of his need for secrecy by the claims of a distant cousin. What follows is an unlikely tale peopled by unlikable individuals whose only attraction is their improbable cleverness. Yet, its plot hurtles headlong through action that drives toward a suspenseful finish.

Russell's age, his core values about performance, and his innate lack of fear produce frequent self-examinations and testing of his abilities. On vacation in Greece as *The Scorpion's Tail* (1975) begins, he decides to swim to

Dust jacket for Haggard's 1969 novel, in which a biological weapon is developed that infects victims based on their race (Special Collections, Thomas Cooper Library, University of South Carolina)

a distant island and to undertake an unnecessarily dangerous ascent to the top of a cliff. Before he leaves the hilltop, Russell comes upon a clearing that he instinctively feels is sacred. He immediately identifies the resident spirit as feminine, "the goddess." His intuition is confirmed, he believes, by the fact that he encounters a scorpion at extremely close quarters that should have struck him instantly. The scorpion tolerates his presence, Russell senses, because of his proper conduct in the clearing. This Minoan moment reappears as an element of plot, recalling a force that outsiders do not sense or respect. In this atmosphere of watchful presences, Haggard achieves a new type of layering. This sense of power remains a novelty, however, for he returns in subsequent volumes to the direct and straightforward narrative style that relies little on mythic detail.

Yesterday's Enemy (1976) exploits old fears of nuclear terrorism as Russell foils a professional terror-

ist who has obtained plutonium. A stock phrase in diplomacy, "yesterday's enemies" denotes the speed with which alliances shift when new threats create common causes. Russell oversees a new alliance between the West and Russia against terrorist claims that Germany has nuclear capability and the will to use it.

In his midcareer novel *The Poison People* (1978), Haggard returns to India for his plot, creating a revenge story out of the Indian drug trade that poisons people from all strata of that country. Russell's wish to help his friend Fenwick, a member of Parliament, find and punish those responsible for the drug-related death of his son involves Russell in a chain of corruption reaching from England to a shadowy Indian drug overlord called "the Presence." Russell is professionally offended that diplomatic drug runners mock the guest-host relationship when they use their various immunities to set up pipelines for drugs. Haggard chooses an Indian from each level of the drug ladder to indicate a wider corruption; for example, Manerj, whose runner is Sen in England, is enslaved to another master called only the Man. All answer to "the Presence." The book is an indictment of fear and need on such a massive, hopeless scale that it seems eternal and unchangeable. Because Haggard's picture of India lacks even a shred of travel-poster appeal, *Poison People* has struck some reviewers as anti-India, but Haggard corrects this impression by briefly noting, "Charles Russell had seen service in India but had escaped the two traps which that country baited. One was the trap of contempt, the other of love." Indeed, Haggard himself has personally escaped this trap: understanding what has made India what it is, sympathizing, and yet maintaining an objective distance.

An early scene in *A Visa to Limbo* depicts a hedonistic sheik who dispatches an unfortunate boy, his catamite, describing him as "ugly as any woman alive." This opener must have seemed shocking to Haggard's readers, who might also have been taken aback that the disciplined Russell leaves England precipitously to join Lynne Hammer, recently the mistress of an oil sheik from Alidra (Libya), with plans to stay "indefinitely." Yet, Haggard writes of realities and truths he has seen abroad. Haggard's portrayal of Arab-Israeli tensions in *A Visa to Limbo* have become more timely over the years, so that the internecine conflicts, aborted coups, and constant plots against each other and outsiders seem taken from daily news reports. Haggard populates this terrain with sharply drawn characters, such as "The Admiral," a retired Israeli hawk who cannot or will not realize that he no longer wields legitimate power. Rifai, a Palestinian

Dust jacket for Haggard's 1973 novel, in which Colonel Russell has become one of the "old masters" of British intelligence
(Special Collections, Thomas Cooper Library, University of South Carolina)

who appears at the beginning of the novel as a colleague of the Admiral, disappears and resurfaces as a minister to the sheik who plots to ruin a Jewish oil company. It is realpolitik at its most self-interested. A thoughtful young heir to the aging sheik understands the limitations of his legacy within such formulations: "Some day we'll have to move closer to Israel. In watertight compartments, hating each other." Russell reflects, "It was a recipe for stifling stalemate, a passport to yesterday, visa to limbo." Here and elsewhere, Haggard uses generic or anonymous titles for characters who represent great evil: "the Admiral," "the Sheik," "the Presence." Mysterious sources of power carry an amplified sense of danger and omniscience. The unnamed character may be challenged and sometimes blunted but seldom defeated.

Haggard maintains his interest in Middle Eastern affairs with his next novel, *The Median Line* (1979). Russell says that "Arab opinion," the fiercely illogical force of Islamic conservatism among Middle Eastern nations, is as suspect and futile "as a Resolution in the United Nations." Both Arab men (especially the desert Berbers, whom Haggard calls "nature's light infantry") and women show high courage, however, in their protection of the affairs of the small country he describes. Starting with an elegant dinner in Belgravia, the book quickly devolves toward the "shootybangs," as reviewer Tim Heald, writing in the 28 January 1989 edition of *The Times* (London), called Haggard's more-active spy thrillers. During an after-dinner trip home in the president's bulletproof car, Russell saves him when an assassin showers them with gunfire and grenades. The president tells Russell, "I'll remember this forever," adding to the growing list of great men beholden to Russell. Honor requires a scrupulous quid pro quo in Russell's world—despite pleas that he is retired, he never ignores a call for help. *The Median Line* becomes a story of strong women, however, after the death of the president. His widow, Gael, the daughter of a legendary freedom fighter, takes immediate steps to enlist Russell in a plan to prevent her country from

Dust jacket for Haggard's 1976 novel, which pits Russell
against a professional terrorist with the capacity to make
nuclear threats (Special Collections, Thomas Cooper
Library, University of South Carolina)

and nations. His years of service also qualify him to speak with sharpness about the failings of governments, his own not excluded.

In *The Money Men* Haggard returns to banking for plot material, as Russell helps a woman friend use complicated international banking laws to save her small nest egg. Now forced into retirement, Russell exposes the sophisticated ways by which the famous citizens of England avoid monetary restrictions. Even the prime minister hides his funds in bearer bonds, a fact that Russell and Smith must handle in secret as Russell's replacement targets him for surveillance and dishonor. Without preaching about patriotism, Haggard makes a subtle point about honor. When Russell asks Smith why he is endangering his career to protect him, Smith replies, "I am your man." Against the setting of a corrupt Whitehall, the words have the sound of a true liegeman to a knightly mentor.

In *The Mischief Makers* (1982) Haggard makes particularly good use of a political hot spot, this time close to home. The racial tensions in London that form the backdrop of the book existed throughout the United Kingdom. In the 1970s large numbers of unemployed or underemployed immigrants from Africa and the Indian subcontinent fueled urban unrest and suffered injuries from street fighting. "The Market," a crowded area of shops and small stalls, serves the immigrant population in *The Mischief Makers* as both social center and a place for trading not-quite-legal goods. The scene is similar to Notting Hill, at that time an area of London where riots among racial minorities had broken out shortly before the novel was written. Herein, Haggard departs from his usual pattern of presenting Russell as the lead operative. Instead, Smith must confront the tangle of plots that will lead to anarchy if he is unsuccessful. Beginning with the determination of a sheik to avenge the rape of his favorite daughter by a British lout, the novel uses the cooperation of a hate-filled Anglo-Irishman to begin a racial upheaval that the sheik hopes will destroy the nation. In one of Russell's brief appearances in the book, he expresses a sympathetic understanding of the Anglo-Irishman's frustrations—he, too, came from a crumbling Anglo-Irish dynasty. "There but for the grace of God," confesses Russell, "go I."

Smith is a character through whom Haggard makes his best defense against accusations of racism, as Haggard's cutting remarks about cultural weaknesses have sometimes been called. Smith resents patronage because of his ethnicity and treasures his treatment by his former boss because he was yelled at, criticized, and praised exactly as were all other staffers. For Haggard, liberal ideas about making special allowances because of color are far more racist than

falling into the hands of its enemies. She is assisted by an extremely capable woman who, as Russell's bodyguard, is as athletic and fearless as any man Russell has known. Rounding out the roster of amazing women is Concerta, the mistress of one of the internal strongmen of the country. Concerta makes her living as a butcher, a fact that seasoned Haggard readers would find significant.

Russell frequently notes that golf and fishing are his only aims in retirement, but he seldom enjoys them. In *The Median Line* golf defines impending old age for him and for the president: "Both were once powerful strikers but lack of length made golf a different game." Russell's age is helpful to Haggard in several ways: it lends credibility to the political analysis—Russell has seen decades of political intrigues—and justifies his often jaundiced views of individuals, races,

expecting people of other races to meet successfully the high standards of equals. Russell and Smith equally understand the value of stereotyping to their work and exploit it: Russell often sends Smith in to accomplish a task that would strike other participants as inappropriate to a black man's role, but Smith knows how to use his race as an effective tool in the arsenal of the agency.

Following closely upon the success of *The Mischief Makers* were *The Heirloom* (1983), *The Meritocrats* (1985), and *The Martello Tower* (1986). Nearing the end of his career, Haggard maintained a competent level of craftsmanship, though Russell had become too familiar to create new interest. Indeed, in the later work, Russell's voice becomes indistinguishable from the words and thoughts of some other characters. H. R. F. Keating finds Haggard's worldview and tone of voice entering the minds and phrasing of almost all of his characters.

Comparing Haggard, then eighty-two years old, with several of his less worthy contemporaries, reviewer Chris Petit, writing in the 27 May 1989 *Times* (London), found *The Expatriates* (1989) to be "a perfectly adequate synopsis and structural analysis" of Greek-Turkish problems on a Mediterranean island, its detailed information on Near East politics "imparted concisely," with "none of the usual showing off." Petit further noted that Haggard "also shows evidence of real craft and proper composition" here, in "an extremely professional, unobtrusive piece of story-telling."

The judgments of this valedictory assessment (Haggard wrote only one more novel) were apt. Throughout his prolific career, William Haggard celebrated in his characters and plots the redeeming value of personal competence within flawed systems. Refined tastes and sensitive manners might strike the occasional reader as the essence of Russell, but they were not. Nor were they the essence of Haggard's craft. Ease of manner in both the writer and his character are the products of sustained attention. This preference for performance over belief is the ultimate key to Russell's values, the touchstone that lies deep beneath manners and style. His competence, discipline, and self-respect enable personal integrity to exist within systems that are too old, too complicated, and too compromised to promise hope. Russell does not even blink at the corruption of superiors; he has lived past such revelations to become his own focus of control. He places his standards of competence above the opinions of others and beyond the possibility of devaluation by their failures.

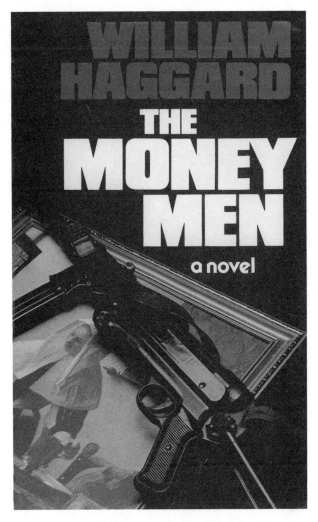

Dust jacket for Haggard's 1981 novel, in which Russell assists his former protégé, Willy Smith, in dealing with international financial scandals involving the British prime minister (Special Collections, Thomas Cooper Library, University of South Carolina)

References:

Julian Symons, *Mortal Consequences: A History, from the Detective Story to the Crime Novel* (New York: Harper & Row, 1972);

Robin Winks, "The Sordid Truths: Five Cases," in *Detective Fiction: A Collection of Critical Essays,* edited by Winks (Woodstock, Vt.: Countryman Press, 1988).

Papers:

William Haggard's papers are held at the Special Collections of the Thomas Cooper Library at the University of South Carolina in Columbia.

Adam Hall
(Trevor Dudley-Smith)
(17 February 1920 – 21 July 1995)

Gina Macdonald
Nicholls State University

and

Andrew Macdonald
Loyola University, New Orleans

BOOKS: *Animal Life Stories,* as Elleston Trevor, 3 volumes (London: Swan, 1943–1945)–comprises *Rippleswim the Otter, Scamper-Foot Pine Marten,* and *Shadow the Fox;*

Into the Happy Glade, as Dudley-Smith (London: Swan, 1943);

Over the Wall, as Dudley-Smith (London: Swan, 1943);

By a Silver Stream, as Dudley-Smith (London: Swan, 1944);

Double Who Double Crossed, as Dudley-Smith (London: Swan, 1944);

Elleston Trevor Miscellany (London: Swan, 1944);

Deep Wood, as Trevor, illustrated by David Williams (London: Swan, 1945); illustrated by Stephen J. Voorhies (New York: Longmans, Green, 1947);

Wumpus, as Trevor, illustrated by John McCail (London: Swan, 1945);

Heather Hill, as Trevor, illustrated by Williams (London: Swan, 1946); illustrated by Voorhies (New York: Longmans, Green, 1948);

The Immortal Error, as Trevor (London: Swan, 1946);

More about Wumpus, as Trevor, illustrated by McCail (London: Swan, 1947);

Badger's Beech, as Trevor, illustrated by Leslie Atkinson (London: Falcon Press, 1948; Nashville: Aurora, 1970);

Escape to Fear, as Dudley-Smith (London: Swan, 1948);

The Island of the Pines, as Trevor, illustrated by Williams (London: Swan, 1948);

Now Try the Morgue, as Dudley-Smith (London: Swan, 1948);

The Secret Travellers, as Trevor, illustrated by Williams (London: Swan, 1948);

Adam Hall (photograph © Elleston Trevor; from the dust jacket for the U.S. edition of Quiller Salamander, *1994)*

Where's Wumpus? as Trevor, illustrated by McCail (London: Swan, 1948);

The Wizard of the Wood, as Trevor, illustrated by Atkinson (London: Falcon Press, 1948);

Ants' Castle, as Trevor, illustrated by Williams (London: Falcon Press, 1949);

Badger's Moon, as Trevor, illustrated by Atkinson (London: Falcon Press, 1949; Nashville: Charterhouse, 1978);

A Spy at Monk's Court, as Trevor Burgess (London: Hutchinson, 1949);

Challenge of the Firebrand, as Trevor (London: Jenkins, 1950);

Chorus of Echoes, as Trevor (London & New York: Boardman, 1950);

Mole's Castle, as Trevor, illustrated by Atkinson (London: Falcon Press, 1950; Nashville: Charterhouse, 1978);

The Mystery of the Missing Book, as Burgess (London: Hutchinson, 1950);

Sweethallow Valley, as Trevor, illustrated by Atkinson (London: Falcon Press, 1950; Nashville: Charterhouse, 1978);

Dead on Course, as Mansell Black (London: Hodder & Stoughton, 1951);

Image in the Dust, as Warwick Scott (London: Davies, 1951); republished as *Cockpit* (New York: Lion, 1953);

Knight Sinister, as Simon Rattray (London & New York: Boardman, 1951); as Adam Hall (New York: Pyramid, 1971);

Redfern's Miracle, as Trevor (London & New York: Boardman, 1951);

Secret Arena, as Trevor (London: Jenkins, 1951);

Sinister Cargo, as Black (London: Hodder & Stoughton, 1951);

Tiger Street, as Trevor (London & New York: Boardman, 1951; New York: Lion, 1954);

A Blaze of Roses, as Trevor (London: Heinemann, 1952; New York: Harper, 1952); republished as *The Fire-Raiser* (London: New English Library, 1970);

The Domesday Story, as Scott (London: Davies, 1952); republished as *Doomsday* (New York: Lion, 1953);

Queen in Danger, as Rattray (London & New York: Boardman, 1952); as Hall (New York: Pyramid, 1971);

Bishop in Check, as Rattray (London & New York: Boardman, 1953; New York: Mill, 1961);

The Passion and the Pity, as Trevor (London: Heinemann, 1953);

The Racing Wraith, as Burgess (London: Hutchinson, 1953);

Shadow of Evil, as Black (London: Hodder & Stoughton, 1953);

Dead Silence, as Rattray (London & New York: Boardman, 1954); republished as *Pawn in Jeopardy,* as Hall (New York: Pyramid, 1971);

Naked Canvas, as Scott (London: Davies, 1954; New York: Popular Library, 1955);

Steps in the Dark, as Black (London: Hodder & Stoughton, 1954);

The Big Pick-Up, as Trevor (London: Heinemann, 1955); republished as *The Big Pick-Up: A Novel of Dunkirk* (New York: Macmillan, 1955);

Dead Circuit, as Rattray (London & New York: Boardman, 1955); republished as *Rook's Gambit,* as Hall (New York: Pyramid, 1972);

Forbidden Kingdom, as Trevor (London: Lutterworth, 1955);

Squadron Airborne, as Trevor (London: Heinemann, 1955; New York: Macmillan, 1956);

Gale Force, as Trevor (London: Heinemann, 1956; New York: Macmillan, 1957);

The Killing Ground, as Trevor (London: Heinemann, 1956; New York: Macmillan, 1957);

Dead Sequence, as Rattray (London & New York: Boardman, 1957);

Heatwave, as Caesar Smith (London: Wingate, 1957); republished as *Heat Wave* (New York: Ballantine, 1958);

The Pillars of Midnight, as Trevor (London: Heinemann, 1957; New York: Morrow, 1958);

Badger's Wood, as Trevor, illustrated by Atkinson (London: Heinemann, 1958; New York: Criterion, 1959);

Dream of Death, as Trevor (London: Brown, Watson, 1958);

The Crystal City, as Trevor, illustrated by Williams (London: Swan, 1959);

Green Glade, as Trevor, illustrated by Williams (London: Swan, 1959);

Silhouette, as Trevor (London: Swan, 1959);

The V.I.P., as Trevor (London: Heinemann, 1959; New York: Morrow, 1960);

The Billboard Madonna, as Trevor (London: Heinemann, 1960; New York: Morrow, 1961);

The Mind of Max Duvine, as Trevor (London: Swan, 1960);

The Burning Shore, as Trevor (London: Heinemann, 1961); republished as *The Pasang Run* (New York: Harper, 1962);

Squirrel's Island, as Trevor, illustrated by Williams (London: Swan, 1963);

The Volcanoes of San Domingo (London: Collins, 1963; New York: Simon & Schuster, 1964);

The Flight of the Phoenix, as Trevor (London: Heinemann, 1964; New York: Harper & Row, 1964);

The Berlin Memorandum (London: Collins, 1965); republished as *The Quiller Memorandum* (New York: Simon & Schuster, 1965);

The Second Chance, as Trevor (London: World, 1965);

Weave a Rope of Sand, as Trevor (London: World, 1965);

The 9th Directive (London: Heinemann, 1966; New York: Simon & Schuster, 1967);

The Shoot, as Trevor (London: Heinemann, 1966; Garden City, N.Y.: Doubleday, 1966);

A Blaze of Arms, as Roger Fitzalan (London: Davies, 1967);

The Freebooters, as Trevor (London: Heinemann / Garden City, N.Y.: Doubleday, 1967);

A Place for the Wicked, as Trevor (London: Heinemann, 1968; Garden City, N.Y.: Doubleday, 1968);

The Striker Portfolio (London: Heinemann, 1969; New York: Simon & Schuster, 1969);

Bury Him among Kings, as Trevor (London: Heinemann, 1970; Garden City, N.Y.: Doubleday, 1970);

The Warsaw Document (London: Heinemann, 1971; Garden City, N.Y.: Doubleday, 1971);

Expressway, as Howard North (London: Collins, 1973; New York: Simon & Schuster, 1973);

The Tango Briefing (London: Collins, 1973; Garden City, N.Y.: Doubleday, 1973);

The Mandarin Cypher (London: Collins, 1975; Garden City, N.Y.: Doubleday, 1975);

The Paragon, as Trevor (London: New English Library, 1975); republished as *Night Stop* (Garden City, N.Y.: Doubleday, 1975);

The Kobra Manifesto (London: Collins, 1976; Garden City, N.Y.: Doubleday, 1976);

Blue Jay Summer, as Trevor (London: New English Library, 1977; New York: Dell, 1977);

Seven Witnesses, as Trevor (London: Remplery, 1977);

The Theta Syndrome, as Trevor (London: New English Library, 1977; Garden City, N.Y.: Doubleday, 1977);

The Sinkiang Executive (London: Collins, 1978; Garden City, N.Y.: Doubleday, 1978);

The Scorpion Signal (London: Collins, 1979; Garden City, N.Y.: Doubleday, 1980);

The Sibling (New York: Playboy Press, 1979); as Trevor (London: New English Library, 1980);

The Damocles Sword, as Trevor (London: Collins, 1981; New York: Playboy Press, 1982);

The Pekin Target (London: Collins, 1981); republished as *The Peking Target* (New York: Playboy Press, 1982);

The Penthouse, as Trevor (London: Collins, 1983; New York: New American Library, 1983);

Deathwatch, as Trevor (New York: Beaufort, 1984; London: W. H. Allen, 1985);

Northlight (London: W. H. Allen, 1985; New York: Berkley, 1985); republished as *Quiller* (New York: Jove, 1985);

Siren Song, as Lesley Stone (London: W. H. Allen, 1985);

Riviera Story, as Stone (London: W. H. Allen, 1987);

Quiller's Run (London: W. H. Allen, 1988; New York: Jove, 1988);

Quiller KGB (London: W. H. Allen, 1989; New York: Charter, 1989);

Quiller Barracuda (New York: Morrow, 1990; London: W. H. Allen, 1991);

Quiller Bamboo (New York: Morrow, 1991; London: Headline, 1992);

Quiller Solitaire (New York: Morrow, 1992; London: Headline, 1992);

Quiller Meridian (New York: Morrow, 1993; London: Headline, 1993);

Quiller Salamander (New York: Otto Penzler, 1994; London: Headline, 1994);

Quiller Balalaika (London: Headline, 1996).

PLAY PRODUCTIONS: *The Search,* Bromley, U.K., 1953;

The Last of the Daylight, Bromley, U.K. 1959;

Murder by All Means, Madrid, 1960;

A Pinch of Purple, Bradford, U.K., 1971;

Just Before Dawn, London, 1972;

A Touch of Purple, London, 1972.

SELECTED PERIODICAL PUBLICATIONS– UNCOLLECTED: "Last Rites," *Espionage Magazine,* 2 (April 1986);

"Why Spy?" *Espionage Magazine* (September 1987).

Adam Hall wrote more than a hundred books for adults and children–some science fiction, fantasies, and horror tales but mostly war, mystery, and spy novels. He also published under the pseudonyms Elleston Trevor, Mansell Black, Trevor Burgess, Roger Fitzalan, Simon Rattray, Warwick Scott, Caesar Smith, Howard North, and Lesley Stone, as well as his real name, Trevor Dudley-Smith. His five-novel Hugo Bishop mystery series, published in England under the name Rattray in the 1950s, is striking for its psychological studies of deviant behavior. Hall's eighteen-novel Quiller espionage series, however, begun in the 1960s and continued throughout his lifetime, made his fame. These novels feature the psychology and exploits of a British secret agent, the Quiller of some of the titles in the series. In *The 9th Directive* (1966) one of Quiller's agency supervisors aptly describes him as "obstinate, undisciplined, illogical, and dangerously prone to obsessive vanities and wildcat tactics, very difficult to handle in the field and an embarrassment in London," whenever he chooses to report there in person.

Adam Hall was born Trevor Dudley-Smith on 17 February 1920 in Bromley, Kent, England, the son of Walter and Florence Elleston Smith. Remembering their constant strife during his childhood, Hall described his parents as devoted to him but not to each other. He was sent away to school at age eight, first attending Yardley Court Preparatory School in Tonbridge, Kent, from 1928 to 1932 and then Sevenoaks Public School, in Sevenoaks, Kent, from 1932 to 1938. His experiences led to a deep-seated loathing for the British public schools, an attitude that shows up in his books as characters recall knuckle-cracking blows and other school abuses that haunt their adult lives. Beaten at school, Hall sought a safe place to hide away and write. He later told his son that the swish of the cane left a mark on his soul. Looking back on those years, Hall said that if his fictional Quiller had experienced similar abuse in the public schools, his neuroses and antisocial instincts would be understandable. As a consequence of these experiences, Hall dropped out of school, never even considered university, and for the next two years worked as an apprentice race-car driver, an experience that provided insights into the psychological attractions of speed and danger and the physiological responses to both. He started writing at age nineteen and by twenty-one was producing two short children's novels a month.

In 1940 Hall joined the Royal Air Force hoping to fly Spitfires, but an eye problem (light sensitivity) thwarted that goal. Instead, he served as a flight engineer for Spitfires throughout World War II. Thus, the discussions in his fiction of planes, flight, pilots, and flight mechanics are informed and technical. He filled the hours off duty writing and published his first adult novels, *Over the Wall* (1943) and *Double Who Double Crossed* (1944), under his real name. He also turned out several quality children's books as well, including *Rippleswim the Otter* (1943), *Scamper-Foot Pine Marten* (1944), and *Shadow the Fox* (1945). Hall joked that, despite the wartime paper shortage, his publisher, Gerald George Swan, had plenty of paper in his warehouse and could therefore take a chance on new writers. Although Swan paid poorly, Hall had a genuine liking for him and remained loyal to him years later, still publishing a few titles with Swan despite the interest of major publishers in his works.

During the war Hall met his future wife, Jonquil Burgess. Both were bombed on a bus on London Bridge in 1943. Hall landed on top of her and, when she proved disoriented and in shock, carried her to safety at the first-aid station, where they were struck by another blast. Three weeks later they had their first dinner date. A former beauty queen who worked for Royal Air Force Intelligence, Jonquil was posted to Croydon, a key target of German bombing raids, and meeting became difficult. Hall has described the camaraderie of the wartime years and the quiet, shared anger that brought people together in the midst of terrifying circumstances.

Dust jacket for Hall's 1966 novel in which his series character, British secret agent Quiller, attempts to rescue a kidnapped member of the British royal family in Bangkok (Richland County Public Library)

In the meantime, Hall was still turning out books. For his third adult novel, *The Immortal Error* (1946), a fantasy tale of the survivor of an accident who wakes up with the wrong soul in his body, Hall adopted the pen name under which he became famous, a combination of his mother's maiden name and his own first name, Elleston Trevor. He went on to become a career writer, producing at least a book a year for the rest of his life. With time, he eventually adopted Elleston Trevor as his legal name. His early books were mainly war stories about important arenas of Allied action.

Jonquil became an editor with Swan and braved a blizzard to fly in from the Channel Islands for a publisher's dinner and a date with Hall. In 1947 the couple married while Hall was on a forty-eight-hour leave and promised to meet on London Bridge on the first day of peace. At that time, however, Hall was on a mopping-up assignment in Germany, and their rendezvous had to be postponed. He left the military only with demobilization after the war. Asked if he had ever worked as a spy, he chose silence rather than a denial, which has led some to believe that his final assignments in Germany involved more than simple soldiering.

Reunited after the war, the Halls had one son, Jean-Pierre Trevor. Hall was proud of his son and determined to provide him with a loving family, in contrast to his own. They built model airplanes and studied the martial arts together, and they remained close throughout Hall's lifetime. During the 1950s the family lived in Roedean, near Brighton, where father and son flew kites and raced miniature cars. Hall read avidly on a wide variety of topics ranging from Zen philosophy, motivational psychology, and performance under stress to physiology, brain research, and quantum mechanics. He passed on to his son his belief in widespread reading and meditation as keys to knowledge. Later in life, Jean-Pierre served as his father's literary manager.

In 1951 Hall began his Hugo Bishop mystery series under the name Rattray. (All but one of the American editions were published in the early 1970s under the name Hall.) The first novel in the series, *Knight Sinister* (1951), introduces Bishop, an amateur detective and a fashion plate with a love of the intellectual challenges of chess and a penchant for intrigue, danger, and fast women. He enjoys women, nightlife, and the study of human behavior in extremes. His intelligent assistant, the plump, middle-aged Miss Vera Gorringe, finds seemingly unsolvable mysteries for him, which he explores to their solution. A friendly local policeman and old school friend, Detective Inspector Frisnay of New Scotland Yard, confides information in hopes of having insights shared.

The books in the Bishop series share a tongue-in-cheek narrative voice and commentaries on the relationship between chess and life, leading some reviewers to describe the novels as elaborate chess games, with predetermined opening moves, a variety of gambits, pawns and rooks sacrificed, and checkmates. Hall was an avid chess player, and the series titles include the name of the chess piece that most closely approximates a key character. Bishop plays chess throughout the novels, referring to people involved in the case as a white knight, a dead pawn, and so on.

Knight Sinister explores the London theater world as Bishop seeks a missing actor who seems to be blackmailing his lover, the wife of a famous London theater director. Bishop reassures his client that his motives are purely personal: he finds the human animal and the effects of stress fascinating and the knowledge gleaned from his investigative experiences sufficient recompense for his exertions. One character says of Bishop, "I've never met anyone quite so magnificently callous," as she concludes that he is the murderer behind the scenes and is such a consummate actor that he is wasted off-stage; he uses her fanciful speculation to provide him with insights into the personalities involved in his investigation. The director's production of *Othello* proves brilliant in its understanding of baseless jealousy, for, as his diary and dying statement reveal, the psychology of William Shakespeare's play parallels his own response to the imagined love triangle of his marriage. *Queen in Danger* (1952) also features a homicidal husband, whose wife, the "queen" of the title, needs Bishop's protection despite her wealth and lavish lifestyle.

Bishop in Check (1953) begins with an apparent car accident that ends in death. Bishop, who witnesses the event on a lonely Surrey road and sees a sultry beauty confirm the victim as dead and drive away, investigates Brazilian-born Melody Carr, the enticing member of an exclusive private gambling club, the Beggar's Roost, where all the key players meet. The coroner's inquest raises questions that leave Bishop dissatisfied; a dead moth proves a clue to murder; and Bishop's study of Melody leads to the discovery of a second murder. Bishop toys with two women and discovers three would-be murderers, each working independently and with quite different motives—revenge, jealousy, and possessiveness—any one of whom could have caused the initial car wreck and resulting death.

In *Dead Silence* (1954), republished in the United States as *Pawn in Jeopardy* (1971), a Professor Scobie, just returned from an Antarctic expedition and scheduled to dine with Bishop, is flung to his death from a speeding train. A second member of the expedition dies from a poisonous snakebite. Threats, disappearances, and deaths that seem like accidents or suicides suggest a shared underlying cause, a secret and valuable discovery guarded by the dead men and their threatened fellow expedition members. A final suicide resolves all issues.

In *Dead Circuit* (1955), republished in the United States as *Rook's Gambit* (1972), the sudden, puzzling deaths of a murderer in England and three political prisoners in Spain (all supposedly from heart failure shortly before their executions) arouse Bishop's curiosity. A trip to Madrid allows for the introduction of exotic regional details (such as Andalusian dancers) and gives Bishop a clue: the presence of a German physicist at the death scenes. When a local girl who has been dating the German's foster son is shot dead and a military man shares the sinister secret of the German's scientific experiments, Bishop finds himself expendable, dependent for survival on an ambitious newspaperwoman seeking a scoop.

Disenchanted with English socialism and with what they saw as the breakdown of the work ethic and of other traditional values in his country, Hall set out with his family for warmer territory, choosing life in Spain for a while before moving to a place they consid-

Dust jacket for Hall's 1969 novel, which pits Quiller against East German nationalists seeking to reunify Germany outside NATO (Richland County Public Library)

ered more civilized, France. They settled in a village near Cannes and resided there from 1958 to 1972. Hall normally wrote about places he had not visited, so when he tried to set a new Quiller novel in the south of France, he got only a third of the way through before realizing that he knew the territory too well to write effectively about it in the Quiller style.

Hall found life too interesting to seek escape and concluded that if he were trying to escape something "deep in the subconscious," perhaps "some imprisoning memory of infancy," "Why not take others along with me?" His novels reflect his personal interest in games, puzzles, travel, astronomy, flight, the psychology of humans pushed to extremes, and the techniques of Eastern wisdom for controlling body and mind.

Hall had not planned to initiate a new series, but while writing the book that became the first Quiller novel, he saw reviews of John le Carré's *The Spy Who Came in from the Cold* (1963) and understood that le Carré was making a breakthrough in the spy novel, producing something far more serious than Ian Fleming's James Bond series. Hall started thinking about the broader possibilities of the genre and of Quiller in particular. He purposely put off reading le Carré's novel

until he finished his own so that he would have his own formula and plan of attack. Hall published the first Quiller novel, *The Berlin Memorandum,* in 1965, choosing his hero's name to honor the English author Sir Arthur Thomas Quiller-Couch. Mystery writer John Dickson Carr called it one of the best spy novels he had ever read. Republished in the United States as *The Quiller Memorandum* (1965), the title by which it is now most commonly known, the novel captures postmodern angst in Quiller's narrative voice. In this passage he speaks for his fellow agents:

> We are alone. We are committed to the tenets of individual combat and there is no help for him who fails. Save a life and we save a man who will later watch us through the cross-hairs and squeeze the trigger if he gets the orders or the chance. It's no go.
> The car burned and the man screamed and I sat watching.
> We are not gentlemen.

The concluding pages return to the final phrase: "the work had been quicker than expected. I had not taken a gun with me, nor any weapon at all; but we are not gentlemen, and we have our little ways. He had held out for close on twenty minutes and then broken, asking for mercy. Then he had told me everything." Quiller has played this Nazi war criminal psychologically, knowing the inevitability of his suicide.

The Quiller Memorandum sets the pattern of multiple betrayals and plots, with Quiller thrust into the midst of the action and not telling the reader all he knows. A door slams; a motor turns over; a plane lifts off; a gunshot rings out; and the novel is over. Readers are left to reconsider the action and piece together exactly what happened and when Quiller knew what he ultimately acts on. In *The New York Times Book Review* (22 January 1967) Anthony Boucher praised the novel as "a grand exercise in ambivalence and intricacy, tense and suspenseful at every moment." *The Quiller Memorandum* won the 1965 Mystery Writers of America Edgar Allan Poe Award and the Grand Prix Littérature Policière.

Quiller (a code name; his real name remains unknown) learned his craft infiltrating Nazi concentration camps and setting up escapes. Rumored to have been a doctor who was denied his license and who served a prison term, he is anonymous, with no dependents and with next of kin unknown. He exists only to perform and survive missions narrowly defined for his particular expertise. A "shadow executive" with a different cover name for every mission, he works for a secret organization with extraordinary powers, the nameless "Bureau" (irreverently dubbed the Sacred Bull by Quiller), which answers only to the English prime minister. Called "the quintessential corporate operator" by Otto Penzler, Quiller is a superagent, a sharpshooter, a practitioner of Zen mind control, a martial-arts expert, a jet pilot, and a self-described nihilist. A skilled linguist, versatile in a several languages, he sometimes repeats brief conversations in German, French, and other languages. Although critics often compare Quiller to Bond, Hall has said Quiller would consider Bond "a clown," a show figure, not the real thing.

In *The Quiller Memorandum,* as Quiller watches a musical production touted as representative of the new liberal Germany, he learns of the assassination of a fellow agent and the sighting of a Nazi officer, some of whose war crimes against starving, helpless Jews he witnessed personally. After the war Quiller testified in war-crime inquiries, but now prosecution witnesses are being found shot dead and facially mutilated in reprisal for their testimony. The neo-Nazis are on the rise in Berlin, and Quiller must face the nightmare of another German threat to world peace. His guide through Nazi conspiracies is a young woman obsessed with Adolf Hitler from childhood, when she witnessed the burning of his body. Today she pledges her life to his bones, on worshipful display for a modern Nazi elite bent on creating chaos and confusion, with plans to release a bacteriological

plague in Russia and detonate a nuclear device near the Mediterranean as first steps in a move to retake Europe and the Western world. Quiller must walk a tightrope of alliances and use all of his knowledge of psychological probing with drugs in order to thwart the Nazi need for vital information that only he possesses.

Through the novel Hall exorcizes his own postwar memories of Auschwitz and the horrors perpetrated by Nazis against the Jews. He writes to a generation for whom these memories have grown dim or never existed, so he re-creates them with passionate force: the white lamp shade, gloves, and book covers made of human skin; the mattresses filled with human hair; and the "scientific" experiments that depended on barbaric cruelties. Quiller saw these horrors firsthand because his agency activities took him to the concentration camps, where, for every two thousand Jews executed, he rescued seven or eight whose knowledge and skills made them valuable enough for Allied nations to take chances to save them.

Hall's 1966 novel *The 9th Directive,* set in Bangkok and the surrounding area, begins with a directive for Quiller to outwit a would-be assassin by predicting possible plans to kill a visiting member of the British royal family. As soon as he spots a known assassin in place and clearly preparing for action, his control directs him to shoot the man seconds before he pulls the trigger, one of the rare instances in which Quiller uses a gun. When the dead man proves a decoy, however, the action changes to Quiller's discovery and rescue of a kidnapped member of the royal family. The Bureau's decision to provide operatives only with knowledge limited to the scope of their narrow assignment prevented Quiller from seeing the broader picture of kidnapping rather than murder. The Red Chinese are behind the assassination ruse to cover their real plan: to obtain the release of a Chinese spy who stole key laser-weapon schematics and has a photographic memory. Quiller must somehow prevent the Chinese from getting the laser secrets and get the kidnapped royalty back safely.

In *The Striker Portfolio* (1969) Quiller is in Germany again, this time to investigate fighter planes that have crashed despite extreme precautions to protect them. While others concentrate on possible technological failure, Quiller seeks human causes and quickly finds them in the Zeller, an East German organization aimed at a reunified Germany outside of NATO and American control. This organization has in place a reeducation center to prepare future leaders, and it draws on old alliances and family ties to make key West Germans pliant. A German airbase psychiatrist who helps pilots deal with trauma is vital to assuring the crashes that are intended to embarrass Americans into pulling out of German bases. *The Striker Portfolio* is not as credible as other novels in the Quiller series, but it includes hair-raising car-chase scenes, a walk through a minefield separating East and West, torture through dehydration in an East German insane asylum, and a not-so-benign German clock maker.

In *The Warsaw Document* (1971) Hall pits Quiller against the Soviets, who have fabricated evidence of Western support of Polish dissidents in order to justify an invasion of Warsaw. The Russians are blackmailing the troubled son of an important politician and plan to use him as the scapegoat in a scheme set to coincide with an important multinational East-West conference. With Quiller in place in Warsaw, the Russians rely on their blackmail victim and a longtime British defector (reminiscent of Kim Philby) to set Quiller up for a fall. Quiller, however, whose sympathies for the amateur Polish rebels he encounters make him take risks counter to his training, concentrates on his assignment to protect the blackmailed youth (despite his betrayals). Against seemingly impossible odds he does so, at one point driving wildly through ice and snow and sliding into a frozen river, later inching up the walls of a narrow broom closet to hide from pursuers, killing a martial-arts expert with a difficult move he had learned shortly before taking on the mission, and finally conning the British defector who had conned so many. Quiller stops Soviet tanks in their tracks by destroying the blackmail evidence and disappearing from the country at a time when he seemed completely under Russian control. A director with Heinemann, the firm that published *The Warsaw Document,* congratulated Hall on the convincingly detailed background that he assumed to have been the result of weeks of research on location, only to learn that Hall had never been to Warsaw and had simply depended on a good guidebook, a street map, and his imagination.

The Halls had stayed in the United States for three months while Hall supervised the building of the airplane used in the filming of the 1966 movie adaptation of his novel *The Flight of the Phoenix* (1964) in Yuma, Arizona. They had fallen in love with the openness of Americans, the friendliness of Southwesterners in particular, and the warmth of the sun, so by the winter of 1972 they were ready to move to Phoenix, where Hall and his wife remained for the rest of their lives. They built a white, stucco, Spanish-style house in a rural area near Fountain Hills, a Phoenix suburb. Jonquil became Trevor's informal business manager and worked on a doctorate in English at Arizona State University.

In *The Tango Briefing* (1973) Quiller is on a mission his own people think could be his last. He must parachute from a glider into the Sahara Desert and race Arab agents to the site of a crashed plane carrying British-

Dust jacket for the U.S. edition of Hall's 1973 espionage thriller, in which Quiller parachutes into the Sahara Desert to find a crashed British airplane (Richland County Public Library)

manufactured nerve gas. He must then use a tactical nuclear device to detonate the deadly cargo. After viewing secret flight photos over Algeria, Quiller moves swiftly to Tunis, where the opposition (two separate groups) is already active, wiping out a fellow operative, shooting at Quiller, and hitting him with a car bomb before his mission even begins. He must deal with the agoraphobia that the empty desert brings on, the heat and cold, the sand and wind, an attack by buzzards, blood loss, and blackouts. With the mission incomplete the first time and a female agent in need of assistance, he must parachute in again, deal with the opposition, the buzzards, and a building sandstorm, and somehow survive the blast he sets off.

The Quiller novels that followed *The Tango Briefing* reflect Hall's progress in the field of martial arts and his increased knowledge of the specialized terminology of the field. His early descriptions of the martial arts were faked, drawing on his study of yoga and his read-

*Dust jacket for the U.S. edition of Hall's 1976 novel, in which
Quiller travels to the Amazon to rescue the kidnapped
daughter of the U.S. secretary of defense
(Richland County Public Library)*

ing, but mainly, he admitted, simply inventing a form of martial arts supposedly secret to the Bureau's training center. Later, he brought greater knowledge to his descriptions, as is seen in *The Mandarin Cypher* (1975). The novel opens with an agent's suicide. Countering the ignorance that causes nonfield operatives to dismiss suicides with such easy clichés as "He simply didn't have what it takes," Quiller imagines the torture, trauma, and mind games such an agent would have endured before finally breaking. Quiller's restless desire to get quickly back into action prompts him to volunteer for a minor assignment that actually jump-starts a more serious task. A British agent whose beautiful but grasping wife pushes him into selling secrets to the Chinese is being held on an oil rig that is actually a cover for a state-of-the-art missile site located near Hong Kong. Quiller, whose picture has circulated among the opposition, is attacked repeatedly and must call on his quick wits, fast reflexes, and martial-arts skills in order

to overcome several assailants. Swimming from a submarine to the oil rig at night, he surfaces in a minefield but turns the mines to his advantage in order to extract the traitor from Chinese control. The BBC television miniseries *Quiller* aired the same year the novel was published and ran for thirteen episodes, which followed the action of *The Tango Briefing*.

The Kobra Manifesto (1976) begins with a racetrack crash in Monaco, followed by a fast police escort and a London intelligence flap that hurtles Quiller from the French Riviera to the Amazon jungle. At the end of the novel he rescues the kidnapped daughter of the American secretary of defense and blows up the Kobra cell of multinational terrorists and the Boeing airliner they have hijacked. In between, Hall provides more background on other agents than in previous novels, explaining, for example, that unlike Quiller, who is a penetration agent, Heppinstall prefers "a difficult objective with a complicated access" requiring positive and negative feedback, while Vickers opts for a palace garden party, white gloves, and a carnation to catch a KGB mole. Quiller has chosen a dangerous occupation, but he is not alone in his competence and courage.

In 1973, thirty years after Hall had promised his newlywed wife that he would meet her on London Bridge when peace was declared, he kept his promise in a romantic way. He took her on a mystery trip to Lake Havasu City, where the London Bridge of their proposed meeting had been rebuilt in Arizona two years earlier.

In 1978 Hall began his study of Shotokan karate and quickly progressed in skills toward a black belt. With this study his descriptions of Quiller's martial arts became more informed and began to move from the simply physical to include a spiritual element. One day this year, Hall was standing alone in the Arizona desert savoring the songs of desert birds when a military jet flew overhead, low and fast, creating a loud sound wave. This experience was the inspiration for *The Sinkiang Executive* (1978). The commanding officer of Luke Air Force Base in Glendale lent Hall two pilots to brief him on such flying, so he would know enough to put Quiller in a plane.

In *The Sinkiang Executive* Quiller has offended government sensibilities by executing an opposition agent he recognizes as the killer of a woman he cared for. In retribution he is offered resignation or the acceptance of a seemingly impossible mission: to learn to fly a Soviet Finback (a MiG-28D) without ever actually flying one; to cross the Soviet border on his first real flight, under radar; and to avoid detection until he can take aerial photographs of three key Russian bases. The plan is then for Quiller to crash the plane, pass the pictures to a courier, and somehow make his way out of the country. The laconic, highly technical military briefing session on how to cross Soviet airspace, contrasting with the passionate description of the actual event in progress, is a tour de force. Throughout the entire mission, Quiller expects betrayal by his own side. Instead of sticking to the plan, he avoids ground-to-air missiles as long as possible, ejects moments before a missile blasts his plane to pieces, gives the courier photographs showing that the bases are decoys, escapes detection despite Soviet advanced knowledge, and uncovers a triple agent and the secrets he has acquired from three nations. Quiller uses his fake identity as a Russian pilot and his knowledge of Russian-Chinese border conflicts to bluff base officials and steal a MiG.

The writing style in *The Sinkiang Executive* is like that of Ernest Hemingway: terse and understated; communicating essentials in hard, driving prose; explaining little; and leaving the reader to intuit situation, character, relationships, and the moral of the story. In a stream-of-consciousness narrative, syntactical parallelism hurtles the action forward with amazing rapidity:

At three hundred and fifty I blew the canopy off and triggered the seat and felt the cartridge fire and thought *Christ we're hit* and then the windblast sent me whirling in the sky and in the middle of a visual sequence I saw the Finback and the long thin missile closing on it in the final seconds before the detonation boomed and the shock wave kicked me away and fragments came fluting through the smoke of the sunburst that had been the aircraft, picking at my body and whining past and picking again until I felt the jerk of the harness as the main chute deployed, a sense of life after death and the reek of chemicals, a glimpse of a torn panel turning like a falling leaf, a numbness creeping and then cold, intense cold, embalming the consciousness.

The technological devices important in a James Bond novel receive short shrift in *The Sinkiang Executive*. Rather, the human machine takes precedence, trained and honed to perform efficiently and effectively, yet betrayed by circumstances and by panic:

I became aware of my position here in the air and my relationship with the data streaming into the senses: the undulating hills and the idea of green grass and the summertimes of youth, kite-flying under the drifting cumulus; the sound of the engines that were driving me tumultuously across the planet's surface toward the point of extinction; the feel of the pressure suit and the back of the seat connecting me to the mundane world of engineering while the psyche began its last long scream of terror inside the organism.

In *The New Republic* Robin W. Winks called *The Sinkiang Executive* "stunningly well done, tense, elliptical, without a misplaced word."

In *The Scorpion Signal* (1979) Quiller is rushed to Moscow after only two weeks of recovery time from a previous traumatic mission, and his nerves are even rawer because a friend and fellow agent is thought to be in Lubianka Prison giving up a Leningrad cell it took eleven years to put in place. When Quiller himself is taken prisoner and tortured in Lubianka, he learns that his fellow agent escaped and, physically debilitated by hideous torture, is now on a personal vendetta against the Kremlin. Quiller, who also manages to escape, thinks that his friend may be responsible for his having been taken prisoner, and now he must stop a bomb from killing Leonid Brezhnev and the rogue agent from being recaptured and revealing everything. The interest in the novel lies in questions of loyalty and revenge, the Bureau's readiness to sacrifice the individual for the group, and the point at which a respected field agent becomes too great a liability.

Hall dedicated *The Pekin Target* (1981; republished in the United States as *The Peking Target*, 1982) to his *sensei* (master), Shojiro Koyama, a sixth-dan black belt in Shotokan karate. Hall said Koyama made a major difference in his life, and so he showcased in the novel the extrasensory powers he believed high-level martial-arts training and meditation could produce. By this time, Hall and his son had earned their third-kyu brown belts and together were teaching white-belt karate, involving what Hall called "the limitless capabilities of the bare hands, fine-tuned for work at close quarters in deadly silence," the tools Quiller exploits in the novels. Hall found karate more than just physical training, however, and spoke of learning to transcend physical limits so that, although in his early sixties at this time, he did things that were impossible for him at age sixteen.

In *The Pekin Target* agents of the KGB have kidnapped the beloved son of a Chinese warlord, the head of a tong, and they are blackmailing the warlord into committing acts of sabotage against the West, particularly the United States, in order to disrupt Sino-American relations. Quiller, posing as a Scots guard, is standing beside the British secretary of state when the coffin on which the secretary places a wreath blows up. The Chinese bomber is later found ritually killed and decapitated for targeting the wrong Westerner: his assignment was to kill the American secretary of state. Once Quiller discovers who the target is and who seems responsible, he parachutes in near the warlord's fortress and, though captured, connects with the blackmailed Chinese leader, Kuo-feng, a specialist in mind-projection meditation and martial arts so attuned to the power

*Dust jacket for the U.S. edition of Hall's 1978 novel, in which
Quiller steals and crashes a Russian spy plane
(Richland County Public Library)*

of *ki* (spirit or energy) that the air around him becomes a telekinetic weapon. Together, they use the Eastern arts of mind control to con the Russians into allowing Quiller to communicate in code with his base, supposedly in the exact words dictated to him. In fact, by means of clever interpretation across three languages, they actually direct the rescue of the kidnapped son. Quiller escapes in a Russian airplane, flies into the take-off path of a hijacked airliner carrying the youth, and leaps from the wrecked plane to rescue the boy and kill his captors, thereby freeing the warlord to wreak terrible vengeance on the KGB plotters.

When a Soviet naval officer sinks an American submarine monitoring Russian naval activity at Murmansk at the beginning of *Quiller* (1985; originally published as *Northlight*), the question is whether the American ship was in international or Soviet waters. As the CIA, KGB, and the Bureau work to affix blame, an important Soviet-American summit hangs in the balance, and Quiller must find out what really happened and who is to blame in order to save the summit meet-

ing and preserve peace. A Bureau mole long in place suddenly runs with a tape of the encounter, and Quiller must bring him (and the tape) in from the cold. The Bureau has promised the KGB their mole, but, shot dead by trigger-happy soldiers, he has lost his value. Quiller's new task is to get out of Russia the Soviet officer who caused all the trouble. Their secret flight out turns into a massacre and, downed in a small rubber dinghy with the shot-up Soviet naval officer, an idealist who acted out of a sense of patriotism but was made a scapegoat by his own side, Quiller discovers a sense of brotherhood in shared adversity and a mutual sense of betrayal as they wait to hear if their maritime rescuers are Soviet or Norwegian.

Jonquil, Hall's wife, died from a brain tumor in 1986. Hall and his son battled to save her with healers from Mexico and Hawaii and with rare herbs from Tokyo, but it was too late. Grief-stricken, Hall turned to a young family friend, Chaille Anne Groom, who helped him cope with his loss. A year later, with his son's approval, Hall married Chaille, a painter and a trainer of Arabian horses, and they settled down on an Arabian-horse ranch in Arizona.

In *Quiller's Run* (1988) Quiller, angry at having been treated as expendable in his last assignment, has quit the Bureau and is freelancing in Southeast Asia, tracking down his nemesis, an international arms dealer named Mariko Shoda. Shoda is a seductive but deadly Cambodian beauty, a man-hating mercenary with a stiletto. The action cuts frenetically from scene to scene, from Singapore to Phnom Penh and finally to the jungles of Cambodia. The tension is high, the action taut, and the ending surprising.

With *Quiller KGB* (1989) Hall responded to the changes being wrought in the Soviet Union by perestroika. Quiller must cooperate with a KGB operative to prevent Kremlin hard-liners from assassinating Mikhail Gorbachev in East Berlin and thereby ending his reformist policies. Losing Bureau and KGB tails, Quiller makes himself a target in the hope of nabbing his would-be killers. After several near-death experiences, one with a sniper, he targets the location and single-handedly saves Gorbachev.

In *Quiller Barracuda* (1990), set mostly in Miami but also in Nassau and along the Miami coast, Trilateral Commission–like conspirators try to subvert the American presidential election through subliminal persuasion while a Miami mafioso and his clan engage in drug running and mayhem. Hall describes horrific encounters with sharks, scenes clearly informed by research and conveyed with chilling immediacy—a naked woman swimming with the school of thresher sharks that killed her father; a setup for Quiller's own face-off with the deadly predators. Hall's Miami, while appropriately steamy and decadent, has few distinctive features, and several key characters, notably a nationally broadcast television news commentator visiting the city and a Miami undercover detective of Caribbean descent, seem more like devices to support a plot overburdened with characters and themes rather than genuine South Florida types. These diverse plot elements remain diffuse background material, never credibly integrated into the coherent story line that is a Hall trademark. Despite constant references to Toufexis, the feared Mafia chief, for example, he never appears as a character. Hall found that the openness of American culture made it hard to keep to the cunning and cover-up essential to a British spy story.

In *Quiller Bamboo* (1991), when the Chinese ambassador to England defects to the West, only to be assassinated, and another key leader in a free China movement dies in Calcutta, Quiller must help a noted Chinese astrophysicist and dissident, a refugee from the massacre at Tiananmen Square, Beijing, escape a trap in Hong Kong, where the Chinese have in place a plan to recapture, brainwash, and showcase him. Since this scientist may hold the key to a more democratic China, he gets his way when he insists that Quiller use his resourcefulness and survival skills to get him to Tibet.

Quiller Solitaire (1992) returns Quiller to Germany, now reunified, to investigate the apparent assassination of a British cultural attaché in Berlin and then the killing of another agent assigned to the case. Almost thirty years after the series began, Hall still has Quiller praise the psychological power of instinct:

> I don't like the nerves pulling tight when there's no reason, but I never ignore them. There are vibrations in human affairs that have nothing to do with speech or contact; they are there because the primitive brain stem still protects us in a world of technological sophistication, analyzing the environment, interpreting data that the senses have picked up even without our knowing, and on that level we don't understand the signals; we just feel uneasy, on edge.

The title of the novel would be appropriate for any of the books in the series, for Quiller is indeed on his own throughout the series. Here, however, his mission itself is code-named Solitaire and, although he half falls in love with the attaché's wife and must struggle against his own bureaucracy to gain freedom to derail the plot he uncovers, only he can save the day. The culprits prove to be members of the Red Army Faction working as "Nemesis" in a plot to blow up the White House with a hijacked Pan Am airliner loaded with explosives. Dieter Klaus, the head terrorist, is well drawn as a ruthless former East German secret-police officer gone independent, and the plot eerily foreshadows the 2001

Dust jacket for Hall's 1994 novel, in which Quiller goes to Cambodia and is drawn into a power struggle within the Khmer Rouge (Richland County Public Library)

attacks on the World Trade Center and the Pentagon, with fanatical Islamic suicide pilots, bitter hatred of the West, and the desire for maximum publicity.

In *Quiller Meridian* (1993) a blown rendezvous and a dead British agent in Bucharest bring Quiller to Moscow to meet a Russian agent aboard a Trans-Siberian Railroad express train in order to salvage an operation on which the survival of the free world depends. The Russian, however, is shot, and Quiller, detained for murder, escapes to Novosibirsk, Siberia, where the train has derailed and three Russian generals (part of a group meeting secretly on the train) are missing. The Red Chinese, disgruntled factions of the Russian army, and the die-hard communist underground organization Podpolia, which opposes perestroika, have joined forces with a former KGB agent who specializes in bombs. Quiller, caught between opposing factions, must battle the clock amid the physical restraints of the train setting to thwart conspiracy, prevent a coup, and save a girl.

After six weeks of inactivity, Quiller accepts a rogue control for a mission kept secret from the Bureau head himself in *Quiller Salamander* (1994). He flies once again to a politically volatile Cambodia, where the Khmer Rouge remain a force to be reckoned with. With Pol Pot in poor health, his would-be successor plans a missile attack on Phnom Penh to seize power, and Quiller, working alone as usual and with an inflexible deadline, must deal with the frustration created by his unreliable, inexperienced field director, who has his own parallel mission. A young Eurasian photojournalist on a personal vendetta against the Khmer Rouge proves Quiller's only ally. Nonetheless, he shows himself equal to the task, prevents disaster, and saves countless Cambodian lives.

The last Quiller novel is the nineteenth in the series, the posthumously published *Quiller Balalaika* (1996). Quiller returns to Russia, where the chief of signals asks him to take a suicide mission. He is to infiltrate the Russian mafia and locate a British national, a criminal genius who heads a powerful, lawless faction that could undermine Western efforts to shore up the declining Russian economy. Hall captures the viciousness and deadly powers of the Russian mafia, as judges, policemen, and ministers of state yield to their ruthless assault or die. Quiller must find his way through a deadly labyrinth and destroy the Minotaur that threatens both Russia and the West. Hall's son takes the last line of the novel–"And left a faint note floating on the air"–as his father's final message about his life and contributions.

Hall's reading in the last years of his life was in metaphysics, and he envisioned a more compassionate Quiller with the minor characters more well rounded. He completed *Quiller Balalaika* only three days before he died of stomach cancer on 21 July 1995 in Cave Creek, Arizona. Since Hall's son saw some semblance of his father in Quiller and actually called his father Quiller in describing his death, psychological parallels between the fictional character and the real author must have existed to some degree. Jean-Pierre Trevor buried his father's ashes in an Indian casket on a mountain in northern Arizona.

Adam Hall might have followed a pattern in both his Bishop and Quiller series, but he was never predictable. His novels are wide-ranging in setting, characters, and action. Intellectual, physical, and emotional challenges test the wit, endurance, and psychological soundness of his protagonists. Hall's works have been translated into nineteen languages and are highly popular in Russia. *Life* magazine has called Quiller "the most successful literary double agent in the business." Hall claimed that he wrote merely for entertainment, but ultimately he admitted that his appeal was, in fact, emotional: an appeal to a wish to understand inner drives, motivations, and neuroses and to discover personal truths through Quiller. Hall spent a lifetime spinning tales of the human psyche's resilience in the face of danger. He predicted that there would always be a place for the spy novel because "man is a warring animal" in need of information about the challenges that test his troubled soul.

Interviews:

Georgi Tolstiakov, "The Man Who Was Quiller," *Armchair Detective* (Winter 1996): 80–84;

Dan Hagen, "Profile: Adam Hall," *Espionage Magazine* (September 1987).

References:

John Ball, "Editor's Note: Concerning Two Authors," in *A Coffin for Dimitrios,* by Eric Ambler (New York: Knopf, 1977);

R. Jeff Banks and Harvey D. Dawson, "The Quiller Report," *Mystery Fancier,* 4 (January–February 1980): 8–11.

Papers:

Adam Hall's pre-1980 manuscripts are in the Mugar Memorial Library at Boston University. His post-1980 materials are at Arizona State University.

Reginald Hill
(3 April 1936 –)

James Hurt
University of Illinois at Urbana-Champaign

BOOKS: *A Clubbable Woman* (London: Collins, 1970; Woodstock, Vt.: Countryman, 1984);

Fell of Dark (London: Collins, 1971; New York: New American Library, 1986);

An Advancement of Learning (London: Collins, 1971; Woodstock, Vt.: Countryman, 1985);

The Castle of the Demon, as Patrick Ruell (London: Long, 1971; New York: Hawthorn Books, 1973);

A Fairly Dangerous Thing (London: Collins, 1972; Woodstock, Vt.: Countryman, 1983);

Red Christmas, as Ruell (London: Long, 1972; New York: Hawthorn Books, 1973);

Ruling Passion (London: Collins, 1973; New York: Harper & Row, 1977);

Heart Clock, as Dick Morland (London: Faber & Faber, 1973); republished as *Matlock's System,* as Hill (Sutton: Severn House, 1997);

A Very Good Hater: A Tale of Revenge (London: Collins, 1974; Woodstock, Vt.: Countryman, 1982);

Death Takes the Low Road, as Ruell (London: Hutchinson, 1974; New York: Mysterious Press, 1987);

Albion! Albion! as Morland (London: Faber & Faber, 1974); republished as *Singleton's Law,* as Hill (Sutton: Severn House, 1997);

An April Shroud (London: Collins, 1975; Woodstock, Vt.: Countryman, 1986);

Urn Burial, as Ruell (London: Hutchinson, 1975; Woodstock, Vt.: Countryman, 1987); republished as *Beyond the Bone,* as Hill (Sutton & New York: Severn House, 2000);

Another Death in Venice (London: Collins, 1976; Woodstock, Vt.: Countryman, 1987);

A Pinch of Snuff (London: Collins, 1978; New York: Harper & Row, 1978);

Captain Fantom: Being an Account of Sundry Adventures of Carlo Fantom, Soldier of Misfortune, Hard Man and Ravisher, as Charles Underhill (London: Hutchinson, 1978; New York: St. Martin's Press, 1980);

Pascoe's Ghost (London: Collins, 1979; New York: New American Library, 1989);

Reginald Hill (from the dust jacket for the U.S. edition of Singing the Sadness, *1999)*

The Forging of Fantom, as Underhill (London: Hutchinson, 1979);

The Spy's Wife (London: Collins, 1980; New York: Pantheon, 1980);

A Killing Kindness (London: Collins, 1980; New York: Pantheon, 1981);

Who Guards a Prince? (London: Collins, 1982); republished as *Who Guards the Prince?* (New York: Pantheon, 1982); republished as *Guardians of the Prince* (London: Fontana, 1983);

Traitor's Blood (London: Collins, 1983; Woodstock, Vt.: Countryman, 1986);

Deadheads (London: Collins, 1983; New York: Macmillan, 1984);

Exit Lines (London: Collins, 1984; New York: Macmillan, 1985);

No Man's Land (London: Collins, 1985; New York: St. Martin's Press, 1985);

The Long Kill, as Ruell (London: Methuen, 1986; Woodstock, Vt.: Countryman, 1988);

Child's Play (London: Collins, 1987; New York: Macmillan, 1987);

The Collaborators (London: Collins, 1987; Woodstock, Vt.: Countryman, 1989);

There Are No Ghosts in the Soviet Union: A Novella and Five Short Stories (London: Collins, 1987; Woodstock, Vt.: Countryman, 1988);

Death of a Dormouse, as Ruell (London: Methuen, 1987; New York: Mysterious Press, 1987);

Underworld (London: Collins, 1988; New York: Scribners, 1988);

Dream of Darkness, as Ruell (London: Methuen, 1989; Woodstock, Vt.: Countryman, 1991); republished, as Hill (London: HarperCollins, 1997);

One Small Step (London: Collins, 1990; New York: Delacorte, 1990);

Bones and Silence (London: Collins, 1990; New York: Delacorte, 1990);

The Only Game, as Ruell (London: HarperCollins, 1991; Woodstock, Vt.: Countryman, 1993);

Recalled to Life (London: HarperCollins, 1991; New York: Delacorte, 1992);

Blood Sympathy (London: HarperCollins, 1993; New York: St. Martin's Press, 1994);

Asking for the Moon (London: HarperCollins, 1994; New York: Countryman, 1996);

Pictures of Perfection (London: HarperCollins, 1994; New York: Delacorte, 1994);

Born Guilty (London: HarperCollins, 1995; New York: St. Martin's Press, 1995);

The Wood Beyond (London: HarperCollins, 1996; New York: Delacorte, 1996);

Killing the Lawyers (London: HarperCollins, 1997; New York: St. Martin's Press, 1997);

On Beulah Height (London: HarperCollins, 1998; New York: Delacorte, 1998);

Singing the Sadness (London: HarperCollins, 1999; New York: Thomas Dunne/St. Martin's Minotaur, 1999);

The Turning of the Tide, as Ruell (Sutton: Severn House, 1999);

Arms and the Women: An Elliad (London: HarperCollins, 2000; New York: Delacorte, 1999);

Dialogues of the Dead, or, Paronomania!: A Word Game for Two Players (London: HarperCollins, 2002; New York: Delacorte, 2002);

Death's Jest-Book (London: HarperCollins, 2002).

PRODUCED SCRIPTS: *An Affair of Honour,* television, 1972;

Ordinary Levels, radio, 1982.

OTHER: "The Educator: The Case of the Screaming Spires," in *Murder Ink: The Mystery Reader's Companion,* edited by Dilys Winn (New York: Workman, 1977);

"Sherlock Holmes: The Hamlet of Crime Fiction," in *Crime Writers: Reflections on Crime Fiction,* edited by H. R. F. Keating (London: BBC Publications, 1978);

"A Pre-History: Crime Fiction before the 19th Century," in *Whodunit?: A Guide to Crime, Suspense, and Spy Fiction,* edited by Keating (London: Windward, 1982; New York: Van Nostrand Reinhold, 1982);

"Proxime Accessit," in *New Crimes 2,* edited by Maxim Jakubowski (London: Constable Robinson, 1988);

"A Shameful Eating," in *A Suit of Diamonds,* edited by Robert Barnard (London: Collins, 1990);

"The Running of the Deer," in *Christmas Stalkings,* edited by Charlette McLeod (London: HarperCollins, 1992);

"Strangers on a Bus," in *Midwinter Mysteries 2,* edited by Hilary Hale (New York: Little, Brown, 1992);

"Market Forces," in *Northern Blood,* edited by Martin Edwards (London: Didsbury Press, 1992);

"Where the Snow Lay Dinted," in *Northern Blood 2,* edited by Edwards (London: Flambard Press, 1995);

"The Italian Sherlock Holmes," in *Holmes for the Holidays,* edited by Martin Harry Greenberg (New York: Berkley, 1996);

"Dalziel's Ghost," in *Detective Duos,* edited by Marcia Muller and Bill Pronzini (New York: Oxford, 1997);

"On the Psychiatrist's Couch," in *Perfectly Criminal 2: Whydunit?* edited by Keating (Sutton: Severn House, 1997);

"The Thaw," in *Northern Blood 3,* edited by Edwards (Birkenhead: Countyvise, 1998);

"The Cancellation," in *Cutting Edge,* edited by Janet Hutchings (London: Carroll & Graf, 1999);

"The Perfect Murder Club," in *Crime after Crime,* edited by Joan Hess (London: St. Martin's Press, 1999);

"True Thomas," in *Master's Choice 2,* edited by Lawrence Block (New York: Berkley, 2000).

SELECTED PERIODICAL PUBLICATIONS—
UNCOLLECTED: "A Little Talent, Lots of Practice,"
      Writer (November 1985);
"Serial Rites," *Writer* (December 1988).

Since 1970, Reginald Hill has written about fifty
books. Even though the Dalziel-Pascoe novels make
up less than half of Hill's work, he is nonetheless best
known for this series, nineteen novels so far about the
crude but canny Detective Superintendent Andy
Dalziel and his college-educated, sophisticated protégé, Peter Pascoe, members of the Mid-Yorkshire
Criminal Investigation Division (CID). Hill has also
written a dozen nonseries books and four books in a
second series (the Joe Sixsmith books) under his own
name, seven thrillers under the name Patrick Ruell,
three suspense novels as Dick Morland, and a pair of
fantasy novels as Charles Underhill.

In his detective novels Hill is a classicist, adher-
ing strictly to the structure of an initiating crime, a
period of investigation and a series of carefully spaced
clues, and a climactic revelation of the identity of the
criminal. His novels are often referred to as "police
procedurals," since they are written from the point of
view of the police. The term is inadequate, as Hill has
commented:

> Tell a British cop that my books are Police Procedur-
> als and his or her response is likely to be I wish!
> They are certainly "crime novels," and when I look
> at the great writers whose names appear on the
> genre's roll of honor, I am happy and flattered to fig-
> ure somewhere among them. I try to live up to the
> genre's great traditions of offering a complex puzzle
> honestly solved. At the same time, my work is fiction
> and it is contemporary fiction. The function of genres
> in the arts ought to be a shorthand indication of a
> broad unity of subject, style or approach among cer-
> tain practitioners. Only in prose fiction, and much
> less so I believe in America than in Britain, has it
> come to imply a value judgement, but usually, I am
> glad to say, by those whose judgement I admire.

Hill's work shakes loose the constrictions of the
crime-fiction genre and has claim to be considered
simply as contemporary British fiction for many reasons, among them his distinctive comic sense and his
keen observation of contemporary British life.

Hill likes to tell an anecdote about his hometown of Hartlepool, in far northeastern England. Its
main claim to fame, he says, is that "its inhabitants
are alleged to have put a shipwrecked monkey on trial
during the Napoleonic wars and when it answered all
their questions in what they presumed was French,
they hanged it as a spy." Hill alludes, without explanation, to "the Hartlepool monkey" in several of his

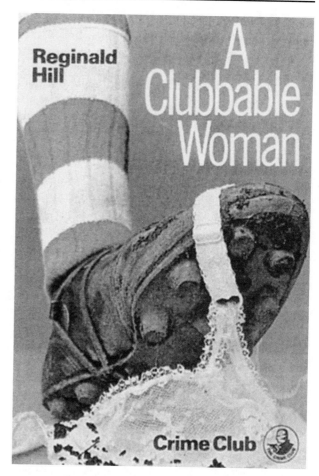

*Dust jacket for Hill's first novel (1970), which introduces
Yorkshire police inspectors Andy Dalziel and Peter
Pascoe (from John Cooper and B. A. Pike,
Detective Fiction: The Collector's
Guide, second edition, 1994)*

novels, and it serves as a convenient shorthand for
several of the sources of his comedy: the unexpected
entanglement of "crime" and social attitudes, English
provinciality and xenophobia, and the results of crime
investigation carried out with rigid preconceptions.

Another comment by Hill encapsulates another
side of his work, his continuing critique of British
society. When critics suggested that his novel *Pictures
of Perfection* (1994) was not a crime novel, Hill
responded, "I don't agree. You could say that in a
sense it is about the greatest crime of the century—the
destruction of community spirit and a whole way of
life in England during the past fifteen years." Hill's
England is the England of the 1970s and since, the
England of political and economic retrenchment, of
the rise of the welfare state and its fall at the hands of
the Tory government, of the growing pains of a newly
multicultural society, and other slings and arrows of
the period. Despite the seeming nostalgia of his

remark about *Pictures of Perfection,* Hill does not idealize the traditional "English way of life." His view of English society, both old and new, is for the most part a view from the bottom, or near the bottom, the view from the Mid-Yorkshire CID and, in the Joe Sixsmith series, from the position of a black lathe operator turned private investigator from Luton. The old England, for all its social injustices, did have some degree of "community spirit"; the challenge to the new England is to regain that sense of social cohesiveness as traditional boundaries of class, gender, and ethnicity are dissolved. So prominent is the strain of social criticism in Hill's crime fiction that his novels might be regarded not only as "contemporary fiction" but also as contemporary comedies of manners.

Reginald Charles Hill was born on 3 April 1936 in Hartlepool, in County Durham, in the northeast of England. When he was three years old, his parents, Reginald and Isabel (née Dickinson) Hill, moved west to what was then County Cumberland (now renamed Cumbria), seat of William Wordsworth's Lake District. He attended the grammar school in Carlisle, Cumberland, and then did two years of compulsory military service, from 1955 to 1957, in the British army. The army financed his university education at St. Catherine's College, Oxford, where he earned a B.A. (honors) in English in 1960. In the same year he married Patricia Ruell and accepted a job teaching high-school English in Essex. After five years of high-school teaching he became a lecturer at the Doncaster College of Education in Yorkshire. Here he began his writing career with *A Clubbable Woman,* published in 1970. In 1981, eleven years and nineteen novels later, he felt secure enough to resign his teaching job and since then has been a full-time writer, living in the small town of Ravenglass, Cumbria.

A Clubbable Woman is an impressive debut novel, not only in its polished mastery of novelistic technique but also in its anticipation of Hill's later work. Set in a small Yorkshire town, it deals with the clubbing murder of Mary Connon while she sat alone in her sitting room with her husband asleep upstairs. The novel introduces the characters of Dalziel and Pascoe (as Hill has written, "Andrew Dalziel, pronounced Dee-ell, and Peter Pascoe, pronounced Pascoe"), superintendent and detective-sergeant, respectively, of the Yorkshire CID. They are described for the first time in *A Clubbable Woman:*

> Superintendent Andrew Dalziel was a big man. When he took his jacket off and dropped it over the back of a chair it was like a Bedouin pitching camp. He had a big head, greying now; big eyes, short-sighted, but losing nothing of their penetrating force

behind a pair of solid-framed spectacles; and he blew his big nose into a khaki handkerchief a foot-and-a-half square. He had been a vicious lock forward in his time, which had been a time before speed and dexterity were placed higher in the list of a pack's qualities than sheer indestructibility. The same order of priorities had brought him to his present office.

> He was a man not difficult to mock. But it was dangerous sport. Perhaps therefore all the more tempting to a Detective-Sergeant who was twenty years younger, had a degree in social sciences and read works of criminology.

Dalziel and Pascoe change considerably over the years, but the basic dynamics of their relationship remain roughly the same, reminiscent of the many odd couples of fiction, from Don Quixote and Sancho Panza to Sherlock Holmes and Doctor Watson. On the most general level the earthy Dalziel and the cerebral Pascoe suggest flesh and spirit, body and mind. Less abstractly (and far more usefully), Dalziel and Pascoe embody several provocative historical contrasts. For one thing, they represent two approaches to criminal investigation: an old-fashioned, personal, intuitive approach (Dalziel) versus a modern, systematic, "scientific" approach (Pascoe). Dalziel has come up through the ranks, while Pascoe has a social-science degree. Dalziel is an insider in the society he polices—a native Yorkshireman—while Pascoe is an outsider, transferred to Yorkshire from the South Midlands CID. Dalziel is in his mid forties when the series begins, Pascoe in his mid twenties. This generational contrast is perhaps the most important to the thread of social commentary that runs through the Dalziel-Pascoe books. Dalziel speaks for an older England of traditional, settled values (though he often views them with a working-class skepticism); Pascoe for a contemporary England in flux, with blurred class boundaries, diminished imperial claims, economic woes, and rapid social change. Dalziel is the product of the England of the 1940s. Pascoe is a child of the 1960s, with all the changes that decade wrought in British life, including the rise of a distinctive youth culture, the women's movement, racial conflict, a diminished role in world affairs, and a corresponding concern with the local and even the regional within the home island.

An even earlier chapter in the Dalziel-Pascoe saga is supplied in the 1994 short story "The Last National Service Man," published in *Asking for the Moon* (1994). Pascoe, newly arrived in Mid Yorkshire, meets Dalziel for the first time, and the two of them are immediately kidnapped by a psychopath named Trotter who wants vengeance on Dalziel for repeatedly sending him back to the army when he went

Dust jacket for Hill's 1973 novel in which Pascoe investigates the murders of a group of his university classmates
(from Cooper and Pike, Detective Fiction: The Collector's Guide, *second edition, 1994)*

AWOL and thus making him "the last National Service man" through punitive extensions of his term of service. Locked together in a room in an isolated farmhouse, Pascoe learns that Dalziel is not the rustic ignoramus he has taken him for, while Dalziel learns that Pascoe, beneath his soft, college-boy manner, has a tough streak and can give as good as he gets. (Another short story—"One Small Step," also collected in *Asking for the Moon*—projects Dalziel and Pascoe into the year 2010 and has them investigating the first murder on the moon.)

This mystery-of-manners element that runs throughout the Dalziel-Pascoe novels is anticipated in *A Clubbable Woman,* along with the establishment of the central characters. The novel is set on the edge of a government-subsidized postwar council estate along a street called Boundary Drive. The Connons live on one side of the street, in a comfortable 1930s house

that used to mark the boundary of the town. Across the street, though, lie the cheaply built houses of the council estate, Woodfield Estate, which is itself isolated from the countryside by even newer construction. Connon is on the lower boundary of the middle class—he is assistant personnel manager of a small factory—and he has been able to buy his house only because the proximity of council estate has depressed prices. The Connons' neighbors, across the street in Woodfield Estate, are the Fernies. Dave Fernie is a worker in the factory where Connon is assistant personnel manager, and both the Connons and the Fernies are uneasy about their relative social status.

In a sense, *A Clubbable Woman* not only is set in Woodfield Estate but also is about Woodfield Estate and the social uneasiness of 1970s postimperial Britain. As Dalziel and Pascoe discover, the solution to Mary Connon's murder lies in the social environment of the estate and its surroundings, in the endemic ills of urban crowding: voyeurism, exhibitionism, jealousy, and social climbing. The theme is further complicated and enriched by another social unit basic to the novel, a rugby club, an all-male enclave to which Connon, Dalziel, and several of the other characters belong and which provides the context of the punning title of the novel. The juxtaposition of male club and largely female housing estate adds the dimension of gender politics to the pervasive though unobtrusive social satire of the novel.

The eighteen books that followed *A Clubbable Woman* during the decade of the 1970s, while Hill was still teaching at the Doncaster College of Education, developed the materials introduced in his first novel, while also exploring other modes. A Dalziel-Pascoe novel appeared every few years, with as many as four nonseries novels published between them. The other Dalziel-Pascoe novels of the 1970s include *An Advancement of Learning* (1971), *Ruling Passion* (1973), *An April Shroud* (1975), and *A Pinch of Snuff* (1978). The team also appear in the 1979 short-story collection *Pascoe's Ghost*. *An Advancement of Learning* is Hill's "campus novel," set at Holm Coultram College, formerly an all-girl seminary and recently converted to a state-subsidized coeducational teacher's college. Holm Coultram is not even a "Redbrick" institution but more a "poured-concrete" one, and higher education is not high on its list of priorities, especially in the midst of the student revolutions of the 1970s. After a few days of observing student apathy, faculty pomposity, and administrative incompetence, Dalziel remarks: "You know, I'm sick of this place and most of the people in it. I don't understand it, that's my trouble. My generation, most of 'em, worked bloody hard, and accepted deprivation, and fought a bloody war, and put our trust in politicians, so our kids could have the right to come to places like this. And after a few days here, I wonder if it was bloody well worth it."

To Dalziel's criticism, Pascoe can only rather lamely reply, "These places don't just train people, you know. They help them to grow up in the right kind of mental environment." *Ruling Passion, An April Shroud,* and *A Pinch of Snuff* continue the pattern of confronting Dalziel and Pascoe with situations charged with the possibility of both crime and contemporary social conflict: the worlds of London post-university yuppies, decayed aristocrats trying to recoup their fortunes through a nostalgic "theme" restaurant, and London "snuff-film" pornographers.

An Advancement of Learning also introduces Ellie Soper to the Dalziel-Pascoe saga. A college sweetheart of Pascoe's, she teaches at Holm Coultram College. They resume their romance and marry, and over the next few novels, they deal with the adjustments necessary for newlyweds, separate, get back together, and eventually have a child, Rosie. The Ellie-Pascoe dynamic is as important to the novels as the Dalziel-Pascoe dynamic. Pascoe has shocked Ellie and all their university friends by suddenly renouncing academic life and joining the police force. His reasons are unclear even to himself. When he finds himself among academics in *An Advancement of Learning,* he reflects, "He might have ended up like them if . . . if what? If there hadn't been something in him which made it necessary to be a policeman." The "something," as the series continues, seems to be a need to confront the real world rather than the abstract version of it found in school. A child of the 1960s, Ellie retains a negative view of the police, despite being married to a policeman. An ardent feminist and political activist, she regards Dalziel as sexist and reactionary, while at the same time nursing a secret affection for him. Positioned thus, between the cynical Dalziel on one side and the idealistic Ellie on the other, Pascoe becomes more and more the central, mediating figure in the series.

During his first decade as a writer Hill published not only the first five Dalziel-Pascoe novels but also twelve other novels: four thrillers under his own name (*Fell of Dark,* 1971; *A Fairly Dangerous Thing,* 1972; *A Very Good Hater: A Tale of Revenge,* 1974; and *Another Death in Venice,* 1976); four horror novels as Patrick Ruell (*The Castle of the Demon,* 1971; *Red Christmas,* 1972; *Death Takes the Low Road,* 1974; and *Urn Burial,* 1975); two thrillers as Dick Morland (*Heart Clock,* 1973, and *Albion! Albion!,* 1974); and two fantasy novels as Charles Underhill (*Captain Fantom: Being an Account of Sundry Adventures of Carlo Fantom, Soldier of Misfortune, Hard Man and Ravisher,* 1978, and *The Forging of Fantom,* 1979). In addition, he published a collection of short stories, dealing in part with Pascoe and Dalziel: *Pascoe's Ghost.* The most complex and interesting of these novels are the four published under his own name, and they give the impression of a young writer exploring various strings of his bow and suggest the question of what direction Hill's career might have taken if the Dalziel-Pascoe novels had not become such a popular success. In *Fell of Dark,* for example, he experiments with a first-person narrative, placing the focus not on the hunters but on the hunted, a young man named Harry Bentink who, on a walking trip through the Lake District, finds himself suspected of the rape and murder of two girls. *A Fairly Dangerous Thing,* though in third person, similarly deals with an ordinary man who finds himself caught up in someone else's crime, though the tone here is not sinister but farcical; a timid antiquarian finds himself in a criminal gang raiding an historical Great House in the midst of a videotaped orgy.

Hill's novels of the 1980s include five more Dalziel-Pascoe novels (*A Killing Kindness,* 1980; *Deadheads,* 1983; *Exit Lines,* 1984; *Child's Play,* 1987; and *Underworld,* 1988); five more thrillers published under his own name (*The Spy's Wife,* 1980; *Who Guards a Prince?,* 1982; *Traitor's Blood,* 1983; *No Man's Land,* 1985; and *The Collaborators,* 1987); three more novels as Patrick Ruell (*The Long Kill,* 1986; *Death of a Dormouse,* 1987; and *Dream of Darkness,* 1989); and a second collection of short stories that includes a novella (*There Are No Ghosts in the Soviet Union,* 1987). The second pentad of Dalziel-Pascoe novels shows a gradual but marked mellowing and enrichment of tone. Both Pascoe and Dalziel are more fully fleshed out, and while their dynamic remains the same, the contrast of head and heart is more complex and ambiguous than in the first novels. Comedy begins to shade into humor, as Pascoe reveals contradictions in his emphasis on rationality and Dalziel shows sides of his personality that belie his bluff manner. These qualities are most evident in *Underworld,* a novel set in the coal mines of Yorkshire in the aftermath of the national miners' strike. The title refers not only to the dark world of the mines but also to the buried passions of the characters in this tale of a missing child, an old man whose apparent suicide throws suspicion on him, and his son who returns to Yorkshire to clear his father's name. Like *Child's Play, Underworld* was recognized by the British Crime Writers Association by being short-listed for its Golden Dagger Award. (In 1990 he won the award for *Bones and Silence,* as well as a Cartier Diamond Dagger award for lifetime achievement.) Hill's nonseries novels, too, showed a steady progress toward complexity of characterization and skill in plotting, especially *Death of a Dormouse,* in which a man's death triggers his wife's exploration both of her husband's secret life and of herself.

The most notable event since 1990 in Hill's work has been the introduction of a new series, the Joe Sixsmith books. First introduced in a short story called "Bring Back the Cat!" in *There Are No Ghosts in the Soviet Union,* Sixsmith is a middle-aged, black lathe operator who has lost his job and has stumbled into private detection almost by accident, by happening to be present when bad things happen. A bachelor, he lives with his cat, Whitey, and loves singing and full English breakfasts. Hill denies ever having been to Luton, a medium-sized city a few miles northwest of London, but it is as inspired a choice of a setting as Yorkshire was for the Dalziel-Pascoe novels, offering as it does a view of contemporary British society from the margins. Luton's "mean streets" are equally far

Dust jacket for the U.S. edition of Hill's 1999 novel, the fourth to feature the character Joe Sixsmith, a lathe operator turned private eye (Richland County Public Library)

from the cosmopolitan glamour of London and the pastoral fields of English rural fantasy. Unemployment is rampant; the dole check is the high point of the month; and the town is plagued by all the social ills of modern Britain: drug addiction, homelessness, street crime, and racism. In *Born Guilty* (1995) Joe muses about the changes in Luton since he grew up there: "before the sand got in the social machine and civilization started grinding to a halt . . . Create a society which didn't offer help to the helpless or hope to the hopeless, and where did you expect them to go?" Through all the privations of Luton life, though, Joe's good sense and sense of social justice hold out a hope that community can be rebuilt, as a passage from the third Sixsmith novel, *Killing the Lawyers* (1997), indicates: "Even through his anger, Joe felt the familiar pang of affection and pride. This was his town. And he was going to leave it better than he found it."

Despite the grimness of their settings and subjects, though, the Joe Sixsmith novels are consistently comic in tone, with a light touch reminiscent of the early Dalziel-Pascoe novels. The move to an urban setting is perhaps Hill's response to the changing demography of British life, in which the residual class consciousness of the housing estate is less urgent an issue than teenage homelessness. The Sixsmith series complements the Dalziel-Pascoe books in other ways as well. As the Dalziel-Pascoe books became longer, darker, and more substantial, the Sixsmith novels fill their earlier place as lighter, more-comic entertainments.

The first Sixsmith novel, *Blood Sympathy,* appeared in 1993; that novel and its two immediate successors, *Born Guilty* and *Killing the Lawyers,* explore the world of Luton. *Singing the Sadness* (1999) sends Joe farther afield, to Wales, to sing with his choir in a singing competition. The title comes from a conversation Joe has with a gay schoolteacher:

> As a people we know a deal about sadness in all its many and sometimes horrifying forms. All kinds of ways to deal with such knowledge. Drink your way out of it, if that's your fancy. Try to spend your way out of it, if you have the money. Politicize your way out of it, maybe, if you have the vote. We realized a long time ago there's no real way out of it, so we sing it. I don't mean sing our way out of it, more sing our way into it so we can make something different of it. Singing the sadness, that's what most of our music is about.

The speech could serve as an epigraph to all the Sixsmith novels, which stress joking as well as singing as a defense against the sadness of life.

Despite the artistic success of the Sixsmith novels, Hill's supreme achievement thus far is probably the Dalziel-Pascoe novels published since 1990, which include *Bones and Silence, Recalled to Life* (1991), *Pictures of Perfection, The Wood Beyond* (1996), *On Beulah Height* (1998), *Arms and the Women: An Elliad* (1999), and *Dialogues of the Dead, or, Paronomania!: A Word Game for Two Players* (2002). The shift in what might be categorized as the later Dalziel-Pascoe novels does not correspond precisely to the turn of the decade; *Underworld* anticipates the shift and might reasonably be included in the group. The most superficial marker of the later Dalziel-Pascoe novels is a fairly dramatic increase in their length. The early novels in the series run to about 100,000 words; the Dalziel-Pascoe novels of the 1990s run about half again as long. This greater capaciousness changes the nature of the novels: the earlier novels typically provided an evening's quick read; the later ones unfold more slowly, and though they main-

tain the classic detective-story structure, the interest shifts somewhat away from the puzzle to the development of character and situation.

Along with this greater weight, the later Dalziel-Pascoe novels have become steadily more self-consciously literary and even self-referential, so that they can be read not only as ingenious variations on the detective-story structure but also in the context of the tradition of English literature as a whole. Hill has always been a rather bookish writer; even the early *An Advancement of Learning* has a title, a general epigraph, and chapter epigraphs from Sir Francis Bacon's *The Advancement of Learning* (1605), and the subtitle of *Child's Play* tells readers that it is "A Tragi-Comedy in Three Acts of Violence, with a Prologue and an Epilogue." Perhaps the most dazzling bit of literary homage in Hill's early work, though, is the short story "Exit Line" (collected in *Pascoe's Ghost*), which begins with a close (and hilarious) pastiche of Samuel Beckett's *Molloy* (1951): a character in a bare room is watched over by mysterious keepers and forced to write his life story over and over. Then, three-quarters of the way through the story, the perspective abruptly changes; the reader is forced to reevaluate what has gone before; and the seemingly fantastic, existential Beckettian allegory turns out to be a perfectly credible realistic situation.

These "conversations" with the traditions of English fiction become more integral and important in Hill's Dalziel-Pascoe novels of the 1990s. *Bones and Silence* draws its title from an epigraph from Virginia Woolf's *The Waves* (1931), and the plot is interwoven with the York Cycle of mystery plays, which is being produced in the course of the novel (with Dalziel in the role of God). The title of *Recalled to Life* is a phrase from Charles Dickens's *A Tale of Two Cities* (1859), which provides the chapter epigraphs. *Pictures of Perfection* is Hill's Jane Austen novel; the title, the epigraph, and the chapter headings are all taken from her letters. The title of *The Wood Beyond* alludes to William Morris's *The Wood Beyond the World* (1894), while the epigraphs are from Andrew Marvell's "The Nymph Complaining for the Death of Her Faun" (first published in 1681). The songs of Gustav Mahler's *Kindertotenlieder* (1904) are an important intertext in *On Beulah Height. Arms and the Women,* Hill's "Elliad," centered on Ellie Pascoe, is perhaps the most bookish of Hill's novels, with a title that plays on the first line of Virgil's *Aeneid,* epigraphs from Sir Thomas Browne's *Hydriotaphia: Urn Burial* (1658), Petronius's *Satyricon,* and Stevie Smith's "Girls!" (1942), and interspersed chapters from Ellie's feminist rewriting of Homer's *Odyssey.* The title of *Dialogues of the Dead* alludes not only to the dialogues within the novel but also to *Dia-*

logues of the Dead (1721), by the minor eighteenth-century English poet Matthew Prior.

The proliferation of literary allusions in Hill's late novels might be regarded as mere decoration, and indeed in the early novels they usually do not amount to much more than that. The Bacon allusions in *An Advancement of Learning* are of interest mainly for their amusingly anachronistic parallels to the current academic scene. In the later novels, though, they often take on structural significance, creating implied intertexts as alternatives to the contemporary actions of the novels. In *Pictures of Perfection* and *The Wood Beyond,* two novels that offer alternative versions of the English pastoral myth, the Austen allusions and the ones from Marvell offer versions of the myth against which the rural scenes of the contemporary action are compared. In *Recalled to Life* the evocation of *A Tale of Two Cities* suggests a parallel between Dickens's Doctor Manette and Hill's Cissy Kohler, both released after long terms in prison and, more generally, between the justice of pre-Revolutionary France and that of the England of the 1963 Profumo scandal. Hill's evocations of the portrayals of England of past literature are seldom at the expense of the present; more often they find in the idealizations of the past the same flaws as in the England of the present.

Also during the 1990s, the readership of the Dalziel-Pascoe novels was greatly extended by the adaptation of the series for British Broadcasting Corporation television. The television series extended over five seasons, from 1996 to 2000, and starred Warren Clarke as Dalziel and Colin Buchanan as Pascoe. Of the nineteen episodes, the first thirteen were based on the novels (though adapted by other writers), and the last six were original scripts using Hill's characters and written by a variety of other writers, including David Ashton, Michael Chaplin, Michael Jenner, Steve Attridge, Malcolm Bradbury, and Matthew Hall. The series was enormously popular and was later shown in the United States on the Public Broadcasting System series *Mystery!*. Hill has expressed "lukewarm opinions (at best)" about the series: "they have used good actors, good directors, and good scriptwriters, and they've made some very good shows," but "TV is too self-absorbed to enter into an equal partnership" with viewers. Hill's (and most Hill fans') chief reservation about the television series is the characterization of Dalziel, younger, thinner, and more polite than in the original. "I love Warren Clarke (who plays Dalziel) as an actor," Hill has said, "but his is not the face I see as I write my books."

Walter Mosley, Hill's distinguished American contemporary (whose character Easy Rawlins is an American cousin to Hill's Joe Sixsmith), has observed that of all fictional genres, crime fiction offers the most comprehensive view of society, since crime knows no social boundaries. Few contemporaries have taken more advantage of this fact than Reginald Hill, whose body of work offers not only suspenseful plots, compelling characters, and vigorous language but also a view of contemporary England that is searching and critical but warm and humane, even in the midst of mayhem and murder.

Michael Innes
(J. I. M. Stewart)
(30 September 1906 – 12 November 1994)

Charles L. P. Silet
Iowa State University

BOOKS: *Death at the President's Lodging* (London: Gollancz, 1936); republished as *Seven Suspects* (New York: Dodd, Mead, 1937);

Hamlet, Revenge! (London: Gollancz, 1937; New York: Dodd, Mead, 1937);

Lament for a Maker (London: Gollancz, 1938; New York: Dodd, Mead, 1938);

Stop Press (London: Gollancz, 1939); republished as *The Spider Strikes* (New York: Dodd, Mead, 1939);

The Secret Vanguard (London: Gollancz, 1940; New York: Dodd, Mead, 1941);

There Came Both Mist and Snow (London: Gollancz, 1940); republished as *A Comedy of Terrors* (New York: Dodd, Mead, 1940);

Appleby on Ararat (London: Gollancz, 1941; New York: Dodd, Mead, 1941);

The Daffodil Affair (London: Gollancz, 1942; New York: Dodd, Mead, 1942);

The Weight of Evidence: A Detective Story (New York: Dodd, Mead, 1943; London: Gollancz, 1943; New York: Dodd, Mead, 1944);

Educating the Emotions (Adelaide: Hunkin, Ellis & King, 1944);

Appleby's End (London: Gollancz, 1945; New York: Dodd, Mead, 1945);

From London Far (London: Gollancz, 1946); republished as *The Unsuspected Chasm* (New York: Dodd, Mead, 1946);

What Happened at Hazelwood (London: Gollancz, 1946); republished as *What Happened at Hazelwood?* (New York: Dodd, Mead, 1946);

A Night of Errors (New York: Dodd, Mead, 1947; London: Gollancz, 1948);

The Journeying Boy (London: Gollancz, 1949); republished as *The Case of the Journeying Boy* (New York: Dodd, Mead, 1949);

Character and Motive in Shakespeare, as Stewart (London & New York: Longmans, Green, 1949);

Michael Innes (from the dust jacket for the U.S. edition of Appleby and the Ospreys, *1987)*

Three Tales of Hamlet, by Innes and Rayner Heppenstall (London: Gollancz, 1950);

Operation Pax (London: Gollancz, 1951); republished as *The Paper Thunderbolt* (New York: Dodd, Mead, 1951);

A Private View (London: Gollancz, 1952); republished as *One-Man Show* (New York: Dodd, Mead, 1952);

Christmas at Candleshoe (London: Gollancz, 1953; New York: Dodd, Mead, 1953);

Appleby Talking: Twenty-Three Detective Stories (London: Gollancz, 1954); republished as *Dead Man's Shoes* (New York: Dodd, Mead, 1954);

Mark Lambert's Supper, as Stewart (London: Gollancz, 1954; New York: Norton, 1954);

The Man from the Sea (London: Gollancz, 1955; New York: Dodd, Mead, 1955);

The Guardians, as Stewart (London: Gollancz, 1955; New York: Norton, 1957);

Appleby Talks Again: Eighteen Detective Stories (London: Gollancz, 1956; New York: Dodd, Mead, 1957);

Old Hall, New Hall (London: Gollancz, 1956); republished as *A Question of Queens* (New York: Dodd, Mead, 1956);

Appleby Plays Chicken (London: Gollancz, 1956); republished as *Death on a Quiet Day* (New York: Dodd, Mead, 1957);

A Use of Riches, as Stewart (London: Gollancz, 1957; New York: Norton, 1957);

James Joyce, Writers and Their Work Series, no. 91 (London: Longmans, Green, 1957);

The Long Farewell (London: Gollancz, 1958; New York: Dodd, Mead, 1958);

Hare Sitting Up (London: Gollancz, 1959; New York: Dodd, Mead, 1959);

The Man Who Wrote Detective Stories: And Other Stories, as Stewart (London: Gollancz, 1959; New York: Norton, 1959);

The New Sonia Wayward (London: Gollancz, 1960); republished as *The Case of Sonia Wayward* (New York: Dodd, Mead, 1960);

Silence Observed (London: Gollancz, 1961; New York: Dodd, Mead, 1961);

The Man Who Won the Pools, as Stewart (London: Gollancz, 1961; New York: Norton, 1961);

A Connoisseur's Case (London: Gollancz, 1962); republished as *The Crabtree Affair* (New York: Dodd, Mead, 1962);

The Last Tresilians, as Stewart (London: Gollancz, 1963; New York: Norton, 1963);

Thomas Love Peacock, as Stewart, Writers and Their Work Series, no. 156 (London: Longmans, 1963);

Eight Modern Writers, as Stewart, Oxford History of English Literature, volume 12 (Oxford: Clarendon Press, 1963);

Money from Holme (London: Gollancz, 1964; New York: Dodd, Mead, 1965);

An Acre of Grass, as Stewart (London: Gollancz, 1965; New York: Norton, 1966);

The Bloody Wood (London: Gollancz, 1966; New York: Dodd, Mead, 1966);

A Change of Heir (London: Gollancz, 1966; New York: Dodd, Mead, 1966);

The Aylwins, as Stewart (London: Gollancz, 1966; New York: Norton, 1967);

Rudyard Kipling (London: Gollancz, 1966; New York: Dodd, Mead, 1966);

Vanderlyn's Kingdom, as Stewart (London: Gollancz, 1967; New York: Norton, 1968);

Appleby at Allington (London: Gollancz, 1968); republished as *Death by Water* (New York: Dodd, Mead, 1968);

Joseph Conrad (London: Longmans, 1968; New York: Dodd, Mead, 1968);

A Family Affair (London: Gollancz, 1969); republished as *Picture of Guilt* (New York: Dodd, Mead, 1969);

Cucumber Sandwiches, and Other Stories, as Stewart (London: Gollancz, 1969; New York: Norton, 1969);

Death at the Chase (London: Gollancz, 1970; New York: Dodd, Mead, 1970);

An Awkward Lie (London: Gollancz, 1971; New York: Dodd, Mead, 1971);

Avery's Mission, as Stewart (London: Gollancz, 1971; New York: Norton, 1971);

Thomas Hardy: A Critical Biography, as Stewart (London: Longman, 1971; New York: Dodd, Mead, 1971);

Shakespeare's Lofty Scene, as Stewart (London: Oxford University Press, 1971);

A Palace of Art, as Stewart (London: Gollancz, 1972; New York: Norton, 1972);

The Open House (London: Gollancz, 1972; New York: Dodd, Mead, 1972);

Mungo's Dream, as Stewart (New York: Norton, 1973; London: Gollancz, 1973);

Appleby's Answer (London: Gollancz, 1973; New York: Dodd, Mead, 1973);

Appleby's Other Story (London: Gollancz, 1974; New York: Dodd, Mead, 1974);

The Gaudy, as Stewart (London: Gollancz, 1974; New York: Norton, 1975);

The Mysterious Commission (London: Gollancz, 1974; New York: Dodd, Mead, 1975);

The Appleby File: Detective Stories (London: Gollancz, 1975; New York: Dodd, Mead, 1976);

Young Pattullo, as Stewart (London: Gollancz, 1975; New York: Norton, 1976);

A Memorial Service, as Stewart (London: Gollancz, 1976; New York: Norton, 1976);

The Gay Phoenix (London: Gollancz, 1976; New York: Dodd, Mead, 1977);

The Madonna of the Astrolabe, as Stewart (London: Gollancz, 1977; New York: Norton, 1977);

Honeybath's Haven (London: Gollancz, 1977; New York: Dodd, Mead, 1978);

Full Term, as Stewart (London: Gollancz, 1978; New York: Norton, 1979);

The Ampersand Papers (London: Gollancz, 1978; New York: Dodd, Mead, 1979);

Our England Is a Garden and Other Stories, as Stewart (London: Gollancz, 1979);

Andrew and Tobias, as Stewart (London: Gollancz, 1980; New York: Norton, 1980);

Going It Alone (London: Gollancz, 1980; New York: Dodd, Mead, 1980);

Lord Mullion's Secret (London: Gollancz, 1981; New York: Dodd, Mead, 1981);

The Bridge at Arta and Other Stories, as Stewart (London: Gollancz, 1981; New York: Norton, 1982);

Sheiks and Adders (London: Gollancz, 1982; New York: Dodd, Mead, 1982);

A Villa in France, as Stewart (London: Gollancz, 1982; New York: Norton, 1983);

Appleby and Honeybath (London: Gollancz, 1983; New York: Dodd, Mead, 1983);

My Aunt Christina, and Other Stories, as Stewart (London: Gollancz, 1983; New York: Norton, 1983);

Carson's Conspiracy (London: Gollancz, 1984; New York: Dodd, Mead, 1984);

An Open Prison, as Stewart (London: Gollancz, 1984; New York: Norton, 1984);

The Naylors, as Stewart (London: Gollancz, 1985; New York: Norton, 1985);

Appleby and the Ospreys (London: Gollancz, 1986; New York: Dodd, Mead, 1987);

Parlour 4 and Other Stories, as Stewart (London: Gollancz, 1986; New York: Norton, 1986);

Myself and Michael Innes, as Stewart (London: Gollancz, 1987; New York: Norton, 1987).

Editions and Collections: *Appleby Intervenes: Three Tales from Scotland Yard* (New York: Dodd, Mead, 1965);

The Michael Innes Omnibus (Harmondsworth, U.K.: Penguin, 1983);

The Second Michael Innes Omnibus (Harmondsworth, U.K.: Penguin, 1983).

OTHER: Michel de Montaigne, *Montaigne's Essays: John Florio's Translation,* edited by Stewart (London: Nonesuch, 1931; New York: Random House/Modern Library, 1931);

"Strange Intelligence," in *Imaginary Conversations: Eight Radio Scripts,* edited, with an introduction, by Rayner Heppenstall (London: Secker & Warburg, 1948);

Rudyard Kipling, *Kim,* introduction by Innes (London: Macmillan/St. Martin's Library, 1961; New York: Dodd, Mead/Great Illustrated Classics, 1962);

Wilkie Collins, *The Moonstone,* edited by Innes, as Stewart (Harmondsworth, U.K.: Penguin, 1966);

John B. Priestly, *Thomas Love Peacock,* introduction by Innes, as Stewart (Harmondsworth, U.K.: Penguin, 1966);

William M. Thackeray, *Vanity Fair,* edited, with an introduction, by Innes, as Stewart (Harmondsworth, U.K.: Penguin, 1968);

Thomas Hardy, *Stories and Poems,* Everyman's Library, no. 708, introduction by Innes, as Stewart (London: Dent, 1970);

William M. Thackeray, *The History of Pendennis,* introduction by Innes, as Stewart (Harmondsworth, U.K.: Penguin/English Library, 1971).

PRODUCED SCRIPTS: "Strange Intelligence," radio, *Third Programme,* BBC, 30 June 1947;

"The Hawk and the Handsaw," radio, *Third Programme,* BBC, 21 November 1948;

"The Mysterious Affair at Elsinore," radio, *Third Programme,* BBC, 26 June 1949.

SELECTED PERIODICAL PUBLICATIONS–UNCOLLECTED: "Death as a Game," *Esquire,* 63 (January 1965): 55–56;

"An Edinburgh Boyhood," *Holiday,* 30 (August 1965): 60–71.

The name Michael Innes is synonymous with the witty, academic crime novel beloved in the British tradition of mystery fiction. His Inspector Appleby series, which was published over half a century, set a standard for decades and earned for its author a singular place in the annals of the genre. Starting out at the tail end of the "Golden Age" of crime writing in the 1930s, Innes, the pen name of J. I. M. Stewart, crafted among the best of the old-style, densely plotted detective stories. Throughout the years of his career his mysteries continued the British countertradition to the American hard-boiled crime story. Although perhaps less well known in the United States, the crime novels of Michael Innes remain enjoyable and instructive. Critical reviews have included such descriptive terms as "mischievous," "donnish," "fantastical," "bookish," "mannered," "whimsical," "extravagant," "operatic," "idiosyncratic," and "very very English."

Michael Innes was born John Innes Mackintosh Stewart in Edinburgh, Scotland, on 30 September 1906. His father, John Stewart, was a lawyer, and his mother, Elizabeth Jane (née Clark) was from Nairn, Scotland. John Innes Stewart grew up in the genteel environment of Edinburgh's Georgian New Town and attended the New Town's Edinburgh Academy, where he spent, by his own recollection, eleven years subject to the philological pedagogy and spartan routine of the grim school, interrupted only by "disagreeably muddy games." The austerity of the academy was leavened by

Innes, circa 1912, with his mother, Elizabeth Jane Stewart
(*from* Myself and Michael Innes, *1987*)

his occasional visits to the Scottish National Gallery, where he was first exposed to the wonders of painting: "Italian light on Scottish walls," as Stewart later described the experience in *Holiday* (August 1965) in "An Edinburgh Boyhood." He nearly decided to read for a degree in art history, and the later creation of the portrait-painting detective, Charles Honeybath, attests to his love for art.

In 1925 Stewart received a scholarship to Oriel College, Oxford, and received a first in English language and literature in 1928. Oxford in the 1920s was still a highly conservative institution run on the most "antique conventions," he later recalled, but Stewart's undergraduate years proved a rich source of fictional material for both his mysteries and for the "Oxford Quintet" that he wrote under his own name. After leaving the university, he spent a year in Europe, some of the time studying psychoanalysis in Vienna (references to psychoanalysis often appear in his fiction). Returning to England, Stewart received his earliest academic publication when the Nonesuch Press hired him to edit John Florio's translation of Michel de Montaigne. That job helped to secure his initial academic position as a

postgraduate fellow at his old Oxford college, Oriel. Stewart's first full-time academic post, however, came when he was appointed a lecturer in English at the provincial University of Leeds.

Stewart's experience at Leeds is important for two reasons: he met and married his wife, Margaret Hardwick, a medical student, during this period, and the five years he spent there provided him with a setting for several of his "Redbrick" mysteries, most notably *The Weight of Evidence: A Detective Story* (1943) and *Old Hall, New Hall* (1956; published in the United States as *A Question of Queens*). In 1936 he accepted a post as the jury professor of English at the University of Adelaide in South Australia. On the long sea voyage to Australia, Stewart created the character of John Appleby. During the six-week trip Stewart completed the first of the novels, *Death at the President's Lodging* (1936; published in the United States as *Seven Suspects,* 1937), that made him famous as a writer of crime fiction. During the next ten years Stewart, writing under the pseudonym of Michael Innes, a play on his two middle names, wrote twelve of the Appleby books, but only two of them, *Lament for a Maker* (1938) and *What Happened at Hazelwood* (1946), had much to do with Australia. The rest were solidly British in setting.

After the war Stewart and his family (he eventually had five children, three sons and two daughters) returned to the British Isles when he accepted a position at the Queen's University, Belfast, Northern Ireland, where he spent two years. Although he continued to write his Appleby novels, Stewart also published an academic work under his own name, *Character and Motive in Shakespeare* (1949). The publication of his first scholarly book along with a contract to write the final volume for the Oxford History of English Literature secured him an appointment in 1949 as a student of Christ Church, Oxford, which he held until his retirement as professor emeritus in 1973. In 1969 he also became a reader of English literature at Oxford.

At the time of his appointment to Christ Church, Stewart began to write more or less conventional fiction as J. I. M. Stewart, and for the rest of his career he alternated these novels and stories with his crime fiction. In addition, he turned out a steady stream of academic monographs on such writers as James Joyce, Thomas Love Peacock, Rudyard Kipling, Joseph Conrad, and Thomas Hardy, as well as scholarly editions, introductions, essays, and book reviews. For a few months, from October 1949 to February 1950, he contributed a column called "Radio Notes" to the *New Statesman and Nation*. Stewart also wrote some radio plays for the British Broadcasting Corporation (BBC) in the late 1940s, two of which were published in *Three Tales of Hamlet* (1950), written with Rayner Heppenstall.

In one of the sections of *Myself and Michael Innes* (1987), in which he discusses the origins of his crime fiction, Stewart notes that during the period of mystery writing known as the Golden Age, the period when he began his career in the field, the reader was challenged to read detective fiction with some concentration, through a "vigilant attention" to minutiae not unlike that of a scholar in more exacting spheres of criticism. This quality may be one of the reasons why so much crime fiction has historically been written by academics, at least in the British tradition. Although initially he planned a less rigorous method for his mysteries, when he actually got down to writing them, he discovered that he needed to "buckle down" and construct a narrative both complex and intricate. Even though throughout his career as Michael Innes, Stewart regarded his mysteries as recreational reading, he nevertheless devised his fiction with attention to detail, careful plotting, and a literary style worthy of his other calling as a scholar.

The Inspector Appleby stories are often most aptly described as donnish. From the first in the series, *Death at the President's Lodging,* to the last, *Appleby and the Ospreys* (1986), Innes maintained a consistently high level

of crime writing: a grand style, even perhaps a touch academic, with careful, intricate plotting (Innes retained elements of the puzzle mystery throughout the run), and copious literary references (in keeping with the donnish tradition), aesthetic asides, and a goodly dash of wit and humor. This winning combination kept readers coming back for more through the years. Although the critics often quibbled over various details of the novels, they, too, in general applauded his efforts.

As critic George L. Scheper points out in the only book-length study of Innes, *Michael Innes* (1986), the Inspector Appleby mysteries came along at a particularly auspicious time in the history of the genre, just as the period of the Golden Age was coming to a close. Dorothy Sayers and others had re-wed the crime story to the novel of manners, rescuing the crime story from the well-worn ruts of the "puzzle mystery" and the "novel of sensation." In the process these novels reintroduced a comic mode that diverged from the other tradition emerging during that time, the hard-boiled school of fiction, which, along with the police procedural and the thriller, portrayed a world of disorder, realistically delineated, that was both threatening and ironic. Scheper goes on to note that the novels of Sayers and Innes differ fundamentally from the ethos of the hard-boiled school in that their more comic vision presents a world ordered, innocent, and happy, only temporarily threatened by the forces of evil and malevolence, which would be put right by the investigations of the detective.

The tradition of the comedy of manners relies on social satire, which exposes the ridiculousness, hypocrisy, and vanity of human behavior. It is a tradition, Scheper notes, that evolved not from Edgar Allan Poe, Eugène François Vidocq, Daniel Defoe, and Newgate Callendar but rather from the fiction of Wilkie Collins, Henry Fielding, and Charles Dickens, "the great masters of the comedy of manners." Scheper also points out that although Innes took his novels in several genre directions, including the thriller, he generally worked within this tradition of British crime fiction. The Appleby books explore with variations the conventional mystery types—the locked-room and country-house mysteries, and those set in other isolated locales such as an island or the confines of a university campus—to great effect. Innes did so, however, with his own brand of fantasy, of a society remembered, and of literary form.

Innes wrote sparingly about his own craft, but in "Death as a Game," which he wrote for *Esquire* in 1964, he acknowledged that his books were less topical and more understated than was typical of the genre. He described them as more of the "Missing Masterpiece order: very British, very restrained." He also might have added that they were funny. Since the stories were

Innes with his wife, Margaret Stewart (from Myself
and Michael Innes, *1987)*

meant to be entertaining, Innes limited the reader's scope and worked to eschew specific social or political concerns. In spite of his denial, however, Innes's mysteries, as does all crime fiction if only indirectly, ultimately do touch on a wide variety of pressing cultural issues, including power relations, social classes, racial and gender questions, as well as general notions of crime and punishment.

In the same essay Innes also denied that the mystery was the place to examine complex motivations or expose psychological truths. Nor was it the place to explore new values or to promote the reevaluation of old ones. He felt that the mystery was the form par excellence for promoting an intellectual exercise to be enjoyed as a process in and for itself—which may explain why readers are often mystified by his endings that seem unnecessarily abrupt and fanciful, by literary non sequiturs and illogical plot elements, and by the oddball characters who crop up at strange moments in his stories. Wordplay, literary and cultural allusions, satirical portraits of his characters, and the pleasures of a plot well or bizarrely turned were more to the keeping of his stated intention of writing mere entertainments.

Innes has left an interesting clue to the background from which he derived his crime novels. In the chapter titled "Excursions on the Detective Story" from *Myself and Michael Innes,* he pauses in his narrative to explain the more traditional literary origins of some of his mystery fiction. He discusses Sir Arthur Conan Doyle's use of clues in the Sherlock Holmes stories, clues that when explained impress readers with the detective's powers of observation and inference. However, Innes remarks, there is no contest between the reader and Holmes. For clues to be fair to the reader they must fall within the common knowledge, "things so generally known to be true that evidence need not be led to validate them." The writer, relying on social tact, then endeavors to estimate the extent of the readers' knowledge. Innes turns to Agatha Christie with somewhat the same argument and finally to Sayers, who maintained that the essential rules for writing detective fiction were laid down in Aristotle's *Poetics* and further refined by Ronald Knox, for whom Greek drama provided the model. Next, Innes explores the literary precedents of mystery fiction from Henry Fielding to William Godwin to Collins and from Anthony Trol-

lope, Conrad, and Dickens to Lord Peter Wimsey. Since Innes had previously mentioned William Shakespeare, Robert Louis Stevenson, and George Gissing in formulating his detective novels, it becomes apparent that although he may have claimed to have written only for entertainment when producing his mystery fiction, in fact much more actually went into its production than he had previously admitted.

Myself and Michael Innes was written at the end of his life after he had stopped writing fiction of any kind, and it must therefore take precedence in any evaluation of his crime fiction. "Excursions on the Detective Story" and other references in his reminiscence show that Innes not only thought carefully about how to construct his own mystery stories and was well versed in the history of the genre but that he also drew heavily on the traditions of the literary British novel as well when writing his crime novels. Anyone who has carefully read the Appleby books will not be overly sur-

prised by Innes's remarks, but having him set them down in black and white adds a measure of confirmation. Clearly, from his own remarks, his background supplied the breadth of learning and depth of insight that characterizes his fiction and elevates it beyond the run-of-the-mill crime story.

In the course of his career as a writer of crime fiction Innes wrote several different kinds of books: three dozen of the Inspector Appleby series, for which he is best remembered, four other "series" novels featuring the art historian Charles Honeybath, including one book featuring both detectives, *Appleby and Honeybath* (1983), and his thrillers, some ten in number, including *The Secret Vanguard* (1940) and *The Journeying Boy* (1949). In addition, he published two compilation volumes of his novels, several collections of short stories, and a collaborative book that included his "Hamlet" plays for the BBC. In a career that spanned fifty years he wrote fifty volumes of crime fiction plus his conventional novels and his academic work. Leaving aside his professional academic work, Stewart is now best remembered for his Michael Innes Appleby stories.

Because Innes wrote so many of the Appleby novels, it is somewhat difficult to review them wholesale. Scheper divides Innes's novels by category: the first Appleby mysteries, *Death at the President's Lodging, Hamlet, Revenge!* (1937), and *Lament for a Maker;* the thrillers, including flight-and-pursuit stories, thriller-fantasies, and impersonation tales, which include some novels in which Appleby does not appear, such as *The Man from the Sea* (1955); the novels that involve academic settings such as Oxford or the Redbrick universities, private scholars, and public schools, including *Operation Pax* (1951), *Mark Lambert's Supper* (1954), and *A Family Affair* (1969); and the satirical novels set around salons, particularly the Honeybath books such as *The Mysterious Commission* (1974), *Honeybath's Haven* (1977), and *Lord Mullion's Secret* (1981). One could also, of course, categorize the same books by subgenres of mystery fiction: the academic novel, the closed- or locked-room tale, and the country-house murder, for example. No matter how they are arranged, though, these stories all feature the same erudition and wit.

In his initial three novels Innes established the tone that he maintained throughout his career as a mystery author. Much as does Sherlock Holmes in *A Study in Scarlet* (1888), Appleby is introduced as a fully developed character in *Death at the President's Lodging*. The novel is set in a fictional Oxford/Cambridge college, revolves around intellectual rivalries, is peopled by the usual academic types that Innes returned to time and again, and makes use of a traditional crime subgenre, the locked-room mystery, complete in the original pub-

Dust jacket for the U.S. edition of Innes's 1986 novel, the last to feature his most popular character,
Inspector Appleby (Richland County Public Library)

lication with a map. In the third novel in the series, *Lament for a Maker,* Innes moves from the more elite Oxbridge setting to a Redbrick one and again reprises a cast of academics, this time exiled to a provincial university. The university-college locale became one of the staples of Innes's crime fiction, and, indeed, he is credited for establishing the conventions of this resilient mystery subgenre.

John Appleby is an erudite policeman with a donnish turn of mind who is fond of literary allusions and is as comfortable in a senior common room as is Colin Dexter's later creation, Inspector Morse. Initially, at least, he solves his crimes through the application of logic and careful reasoning much as would an academic in solving a scholarly problem. In the first of the series, *Death at the President's Lodging,* the solution to the conventional puzzle mystery comes to him through a literary/philosophical clue, and the second, *Hamlet, Revenge!,* relies on an analysis of Shakespeare's play along with other Elizabethan texts. Appleby's academic bent also accounts for the many novels set in university locales,

both at Oxford and at Redbrick institutions, in not only the first Appleby mystery but also such later books in the series as *The Weight of Evidence, Old Hall, New Hall,* and *Appleby Plays Chicken* (1956).

Appleby first appears as a young policeman but later rises to become Commissioner of the Metropolitan Police. And as Appleby develops as a character, Innes gives his policeman more latitude and permits him to develop his sense of intuition. His more unconventional side is reflected in his marriage to the sculptor Judith Raven, who comes from a eccentric literary family. She first appears in *Appleby's End* (1945), and their marriage provides Appleby with an introduction to the country life, which features in many of the later novels—the Palladian thrillers—such as *Appleby at Allington* (1968), *The Open House* (1972), and *Appleby's Other Story* (1974).

Innes did not restrict Appleby to investigating only within the groves of academe and frequently created more exotic or fanciful settings and plots. In *Appleby on Ararat* (1941), he is among the characters shipwrecked on a seemingly deserted island in the

South Pacific when the ocean liner on which they were traveling is torpedoed. Appleby interacts with a bizarre cast of characters, including some foreign spies. In spite of Innes's disavowal that he avoided social issues in his crime fiction, the novel touches on issues of race (one of the characters is a black African), gender (there are contrasting female types), the social prejudices engendered by British empire, the current world war, and psychology. As with all of the Appleby novels, literary references dot the narrative as the detective refers to everyone from D. H. Lawrence to Kipling with the additional references to Johann Rudolf Wyss's *Swiss Family Robinson* (1812–1813), Defoe's *Robinson Crusoe* (1719), and the stories of Robert Louis Stevenson. Innes uses his usual inimical prose style, part academic formal and part British Golden Age modern. He continued this format until his last Appleby book, *Appleby and the Ospreys,* set in the same country house, Clusters, that was featured in *Hamlet, Revenge!,* bringing the series full circle at the end of his writing career.

After Stewart's retirement from academic life he moved to a modest home at Fawler Copse, outside Wantage, Oxfordshire. His wife died in 1979. Stewart died on 12 November 1994 after some years of declining health. He was survived by three sons and two daughters.

In an interview quoted by Scheper, Stewart summed up his legacy by remarking that he conceded that the fictional works of Michael Innes would probably outlast those of J. I. M. Stewart. "Innes," he said, "is rather better at what *he* does than Stewart is at what *he* does." This assessment is probably fair. Michael Innes, primarily through his Inspector Appleby novels, has earned a considerable reputation in the history of crime fiction as a writer who not only, along with Agatha Christie, maintained the traditions of the Golden Age period long after it had lost ground to the competing American hard-boiled tradition but also developed the genre in distinctive ways in his own right. Innes contributed a solid body of work that has shaped the traditions of the mystery. He established the outlines of academic crime fiction, which still flourishes. He introduced elements of the absurd into the genre, an approach that has been much imitated. He combined wit with learning that bridged the years of the mystery from the 1930s to the present. Moreover, he did it all in a high literary style that was both erudite and accessible.

References:

Jane S. Bakeman, "Advice Unheeded: Shakespeare in Some Modern Detective Novels," *Armchair Detective,* 14 (Spring 1981): 134–139;

David L. Jacobs, "Photo Detection: The Image as Evidence," *Clues,* 1 (Fall/Winter 1980): 18–32;

Agate Nesaule Krouse and Margot Peters, "Murder in Academe," *Southwest Review,* 62 (Autumn 1977): 372–373;

John D. Neville, "Michael Innes," *Clues,* 5 (Fall/Winter 1984): 119–130;

LeRoy Panek, "The Novels of Michael Innes," *Armchair Detective,* 16 (Spring 1983): 116–130;

George L. Scheper, *Michael Innes* (New York: Ungar, 1986).

P. D. James
(3 August 1920 –   )

Andrew F. Macdonald
Loyola University, New Orleans

See also the James entry in *DLB 87: British Mystery and Thriller Writers Since 1940, First Series.*

BOOKS: *Cover Her Face* (London: Faber & Faber, 1962; New York: Scribners, 1966);

A Mind to Murder (London: Faber & Faber, 1963; New York: Scribners, 1967);

Unnatural Causes (London: Faber & Faber, 1967; New York: Scribners, 1967);

The Maul and the Pear Tree: The Ratcliffe Highway Murders, 1811, by James and T. A. Critchley (London: Constable, 1971; New York: Mysterious Press, 1986);

Shroud for a Nightingale (London: Faber & Faber, 1971; New York: Scribners, 1971);

An Unsuitable Job for a Woman (London: Faber & Faber, 1972; New York: Scribners, 1973);

The Black Tower (London: Faber & Faber, 1975; New York: Scribners, 1975);

Death of an Expert Witness (London: Faber & Faber, 1977; New York: Scribners, 1977);

Sparky and Family, illustrated by Cora E. M. Paterson (Ilfracombe: Stockwell, 1978);

Innocent Blood (London: Faber & Faber, 1980; New York: Scribners, 1980);

The Skull beneath the Skin (London: Faber & Faber, 1982; New York: Scribners, 1982);

A Taste for Death (London: Faber & Faber, 1986; New York: Knopf, 1986);

Devices and Desires (London: Faber & Faber, 1989; New York: Knopf, 1990);

What's So Special about Books? or, How to Answer the Child Who Says That Dickens Would Have Written for Video if He'd Had the Chance, W. H. Smith Contemporary Papers, no. 3 (London: W. H. Smith, 1990);

The Children of Men (London: Faber & Faber, 1992; New York: Knopf, 1993);

Original Sin (London: Faber & Faber, 1994; New York: Knopf, 1995);

A Certain Justice (London: Faber & Faber, 1997; New York: Knopf, 1997);

P. D. James (courtesy of the author)

Murder and Mystery: The Craft of the Detective Story, Adam Helms Lecture, no. 4 (Stockholm: Wahlström & Widstrand, 1997);

Time to Be in Earnest: A Fragment of Autobiography (London: Faber & Faber, 1999; New York: Knopf, 2000);

Death in Holy Orders (London: Faber & Faber, 2001; New York: Knopf, 2001).

Collections: *Crime Times Three: Three Complete Novels Featuring Adam Dalgliesh of Scotland Yard* (New York: Scribners, 1979)–comprises *Cover Her Face, A Mind to Murder,* and *Shroud for a Nightingale;*

Murder in Triplicate: Three Complete Novels by the Queen of Crime (New York: Scribners, 1980)–comprises *Unnatural Causes, An Unsuitable Job for a Woman,* and *The Black Tower;*

P. D. James Omnibus (London: Faber & Faber, 1982)–comprises *Unnatural Causes, Shroud for a Nightingale,* and *An Unsuitable Job for a Woman;*

Trilogy of Death: Three Complete Novels (New York: Scribners, 1984)–comprises *Death of an Expert Witness, Innocent Blood,* and *The Skull beneath the Skin;*

The Omnibus P. D. James (London: Faber & Faber, 1990)–comprises *An Unsuitable Job for a Woman, Death of an Expert Witness,* and *Innocent Blood;*

Trilogy of Death (London: Penguin, 1992)–comprises *An Unsuitable Job for a Woman, Innocent Blood,* and *The Skull beneath the Skin;*

A Second Dalgliesh Trilogy (London: Penguin, 1993)–comprises *A Mind to Murder, A Taste for Death,* and *Devices and Desires;*

The Omnibus P. D. James (London: Faber & Faber, 1998)–comprises *A Taste for Death, Devices and Desires,* and *Original Sin.*

PLAY PRODUCTION: *A Private Treason,* London, Palace Theatre, 12 March 1985.

OTHER: "Moment of Power," in *Ellery Queen's Murder Menu,* edited by Ellery Queen (New York: World, 1969), pp. 167–184;

"The Victim," in *Winter's Crimes 5,* edited by Virginia Whitaker (London: Macmillan, 1973);

"A Very Desirable Residence," in *Winter's Crimes 8,* edited by Hilary Watson (London: Macmillan, 1976), pp. 154–167;

"A Fictional Prognosis," in *Murder Ink: The Mystery Reader's Companion,* edited by Dilys Winn (New York: Workman, 1977), pp. 339–342;

"Ought Adam to Marry Cordelia?" in *Murder Ink,* edited by Dilys Winn (New York: Workman, 1977), pp. 68–69;

"Great-Aunt Allie's Flypapers," in *Verdict of Thirteen,* edited by Julian Symons (New York: Harper & Row, 1978), pp. 1–24;

"Dorothy L. Sayers: From Puzzle to Novel," in *Crime Writers: Reflections on Crime Fiction,* edited by H. R. F. Keating (London: BBC, 1978), pp. 64–75;

James Brabazon, *Dorothy L. Sayers,* foreword by James (New York: Scribners, 1981);

"A Series of Scenes," in *Whodunit?: A Guide to Crime, Suspense and Spy Fiction,* edited by Keating (London: Windward, 1982), pp. 85–86;

"The Girl Who Loved Graveyards," in *Winter's Crimes 15,* edited by George Hardinge (London: Macmillan, 1983), pp. 51–65;

"Address Given at the Centenary Luncheon at the Park Lane Hotel, Piccadilly on 24th November, 1990," in *Encounters with Lord Peter,* edited by Christopher Dean (Hurstpierpoint: Dorothy L. Sayers Society, 1991);

Wilkie Collins, *The Moonstone,* introduction by James (London: Folio Society, 1992);

"The Man Who Was Eighty," in *The Man Who . . . ,* edited by Keating (New York: Macmillan, 1992);

800 Years of Women's Letters, foreword by James, edited by Olga Kenyon (Boston: Faber & Faber, 1993);

"Is There Arsenic Still for Tea?" in *Anglian Blood,* edited by Robert Church and Martin Edwards (Norwich: Rampant Horse, 1995);

"The Mistletoe Murder," in *A Classic Christmas Crime,* edited by Tim Heald (London: Pavilion, 1995);

"The Odour of Anglicanism," in *Our Childhood's Pattern: Memories of Growing Up Christian,* edited by Monica Furlong (London: Mowbray, 1995);

Stuart Kind, *The Sceptical Witness: Concerning the Scientific Investigation of Crime against a Human Background,* foreword by James (Harrogate, U.K.: Forensic Science Society, 1999);

Sightlines, edited by James and Harriet Harvey Wood (London: Vintage, 2001).

SELECTED PERIODICAL PUBLICATIONS–
UNCOLLECTED: "Writing a Mystery," *Writer,* 83 (April 1970): 11–14;

"Mysteries within Mysteries," *Writer,* 89 (October 1976): 20–22.

P. D. James is the inheritor of some of the most distinguished literary mantles in popular fiction, those previously worn by detective-story writers who achieved near perfection in their craft. James's works hearken back to Agatha Christie's ingenious plotting, evocative settings, and quirky series detective Hercule Poirot, sometimes faintly echoing her predecessor's models but updating them and making them uniquely her own. A James plot, like Christie's best, is a well-oiled machine, efficient and balanced in a style many modern detective-fiction writers hardly aspire to attain. Her settings, like Christie's, reflect an impressive variety of interests, often esoteric and sometimes obscure. Like her predecessor, she speaks for a certain social class and way of life, one quintessentially English, without excluding readers who are different from the persona suggested by the narrative voice, as her success in the United States attests. By James's time, however, the detective genre had matured into a

James with her husband, Conner White, and daughter Jane at Chigwell Row, Essex, circa 1944
(*from the U.S. edition of* Time to Be in Earnest: A Fragment of Autobiography, *2000*)

vehicle that could take many directions, playing against the stock protagonists of Christie's time to suggest both the diversity of realism and the rich well-roundedness of serious fiction.

Phyllis Dorothy James was born on 3 August 1920, in Oxford, England, the daughter of Inland Revenue officer Sidney Victor and Dorothy May Amelia Hone James. Her mother suffered from recurrent bouts of depression and had to be hospitalized on a regular basis. The family moved to Cambridge, where James attended Cambridge High School for Girls. She left school at age sixteen to work in a tax office and then became an assistant stage manager at the Festival Theatre in Cambridge. (This stage experience led to her own play, *A Private Treason*, staged in 1985 in London's West End.) When World War II began, she worked for the Red Cross as a nurse and then for the Ministry of Food.

On 8 August 1941 James married Ernest Conner Bantry White, a physician with the Royal Army Medical Corps. The couple had two daughters—Clare, born in 1942, and Jane, born in 1944. White returned from his wartime service suffering from post-traumatic stress syndrome and was diagnosed as a schizophrenic, a circumstance that forced James to work full-time to support her family as her husband went in and out of hospitals. She says of the experience, "No one who has never had to live with a partner who is mentally ill can possibly understand" and further explains that the couple lived in "separate hells," with each intensifying the other. Needing to support her family after the war, she worked for the North West Regional Hospital Board in London, where she served as the principal administrative assistant from 1949 to 1968.

During this period of her life James began to write seriously, two hours every morning before work. In an interview with David Lehman and Tony Clifton of *Newsweek,* James says that she realized that if she did not make the effort to write that first book, time would slip by, and eventually it would be too late: "I would be saying to my grandchildren, 'Of course I really wanted to be a novelist.'" In an interview with Connie Lauerman of the *Chicago Tribune,* James observed that working full-time provided her with a wide variety of experiences impossible to encounter by simply staying at home—so many experiences that she considers the struggles of those working years as vital to her success as a writer. She learned about the inner workings of hospitals, nursing homes, psychiatric clinics, and forensic laboratories, as well as the harrowing effects of corrosive poisoning and other such specialized medical knowledge. James's first novel, *Cover Her Face* (1962), took her three years to write but was accepted by the first publisher to whom she sent it; the story built on her hospital experiences. James was in her early forties when it was published. The title comes from John Webster's tragedy *The Duchess of Malfi* (1623).

Cover Her Face sets up James's first series detective, Adam Dalgliesh, as highly competent, intelligent, sensitive, and superior to his fellows. By the time of *A Mind to Murder* (1963) the poet-detective is less certain and somewhat defensive, almost as if James were refusing to grant him an easy, successful career arc as a series detective. Dalgliesh's poetry, however, is going well in *A Mind to Murder,* and he comes to the crime scene from a publishing party.

James's husband died in 1964, and in 1968, having qualified on an open examination, she moved into a civil-service position that provided invaluable experience relevant to her crime stories. She became the principal administrative assistant in the police department under the Department of Home Affairs in London. The year before taking this position, she had published her third novel, *Unnatural Causes* (1967), in which Dalgliesh's aunt, Jane Dalgliesh, first appears. She provides the one stable family member in the chief inspector's life. (His romantic relations are in continual disarray.) Never married, she inherited family furniture that Dalgliesh remembers from his youth, as he recalls when he visits her for rest and recuperation. Like him she is tall, lean, and ascetic, a lover of serious music and good books. Jane is a serious amateur ornithologist who occasionally contributes to scholarly publications in the field, and aunt and nephew enjoy tramping the coastal areas in pursuit of her hobby and his mental well-being.

While still employed in the police office, James cowrote, along with T. A. Critchley, a nonfiction work titled *The Maul and the Pear Tree: The Ratcliffe Highway Murders, 1811* (1971). This true-life detective story presents an investigation of the brutal murders that occurred at the London Docks, near Wapping Old Stairs, a rough neighborhood where pirates were once hanged at low tide. The victims were two shopkeepers, their baby, a shop boy, and, twelve days later, a pub owner, his wife, and a servant. James and Critchley capture the Regency law enforcement system grappling with a major murder investigation and use modern knowledge of forensics and criminal detection to question the credibility of the original evidence and the validity of the official verdict. The authors conclude that it "seems unlikely that we shall ever know the full truth" but speculate about complications never considered in the original investigation.

That same year James published *Shroud for a Nightingale* (1971). In the introduction to *Crime Times Three: Three Complete Novels Featuring Adam Dalgliesh of Scotland Yard* (1979) James says that by the period when *Shroud for a Nightingale* was written, she and Dalgliesh were "well established in the ambiguous and complicated partnership which exists between a writer and a continuing creation." The mystery centers on the death of student nurses and teaching nuns in a nursing school and illustrates that even women who are innocent of murder may, through egotism, manipulative behavior, and ambition, set off events that lead to the murder of others—sometimes, in fact, to their own. *Shroud for a Nightingale* received a Silver Dagger Award from the Mystery Writers' Association and an Edgar Award from the Mystery Writers of America.

James remained in her administrative-assistant position until 1972, when she transferred to the criminal police department. That same year she published *An Unsuitable Job for a Woman,* introducing the series detective Cordelia Gray. While there had been many fictional female detectives before her, Cordelia is surely the first of her youth and inexperience to operate in such gritty, sometimes hard-boiled circumstances. (Ida in Graham Greene's 1938 novel *Brighton Rock* is an unremarked precursor.) With Cordelia, James takes her most-daring chances in creating a series detective. As has been observed by critics, the novels in which Cordelia appears combine the bildungsroman, or coming-of-age, genre with the detective story, almost necessarily since Cordelia is so young and has received an otherworldly academic education at a convent school. Less often remarked is how Cordelia fails in *An Unsuitable Job for a Woman* by becoming obsessed with the victim, Mark Callender, to the point of wearing his clothes, living in the shack where he died, and appropriating as her talisman the leather strap with which he was hanged. Although she "solves the murder" by enabling rough justice when Mark's mother uses Cordelia's gun to achieve vengeance, Cordelia's behavior seems entirely intuitive and reac-

Dust jacket for James's 1963 novel, the second to feature police inspector and poet Adam Dalgliesh
(from John Cooper and B. A. Pike, Detective Fiction: The Collector's Guide, *1988)*

tive, a repudiation of the calculated rationality of Dalgliesh. Cordelia as a character seems more a wish fulfillment than a serious attempt to lay out a plan for a successful female detective. She is fiercely loyal and empathetic to the weak, but these humane virtues serve her poorly in *An Unsuitable Job for a Woman.* If James found herself frustrated with Dalgliesh's increasing sourness and lack of empathy, then creating a young, empathetic female character might have seemed a welcome counter. As she said in a 1985 interview, "There's a great body of unused talent for detection" among women, and while the upper ranks of the world's police are predominantly male, "some women would certainly excel there." In spite of Cordelia's failures, she remains a wonderful character, especially in *An Unsuitable Job for a Woman,* which earned a Scroll Award from the Mystery Writers of America.

James's next novel, *The Black Tower* (1975), earned her a second Silver Dagger Award from the Mystery Writers' Association. As the novel opens, Dalgliesh has been misdiagnosed as suffering from a fatal disease.

When he learns the truth he takes a brief holiday to sort through his conflicts about his profession as well as his love life. His drive to succeed has diminished by this point in his career, and his mellow, somewhat nostalgic musings contrast sharply with the two alpha males in the novel, Wilfred Anstey and Julius Court. The former is the charismatic leader of a cult-like organization that operates a home for incurables, a place supposedly inspired by a miraculous cure at Lourdes in France. Wilfred, like many such characters in James's books, is basically fraudulent, arrogantly self-convinced, and competent. Julius is another one-note personality, a modern humor character driven by a will to act out his power over others. Dalgliesh, even when he pays a courtesy call to the local police, is restrained to the point of tentativeness; he is reluctant to play the role of take-charge detective when he has no formal assignment to the case, and he silently deplores the pressure from his host to be a tame poet-in-residence, performing for his less-than-appetizing meal. James is clearly fascinated by these forces pulling in opposite directions, on

Dust jacket for James's third novel (1967), in which Dalgliesh's Aunt Jane helps him solve a mystery (from Cooper and Pike, Detective Fiction: The Collector's Guide, *second edition, 1994)*

the one hand toward submersion in a professional role, on the other toward independence from social groups, whether they be the police or a religious-medical cult. Dalgliesh asserts an independent identity set apart from those suggested by the groups in which he moves, and this freedom from stereotypical roles provides him with a continuing interest as a main character and gives him staying power over a long series of books.

The mystery in *Death of an Expert Witness* (1977) involves the death of the chief scientific officer at an isolated forensics laboratory. The novel employs some of the elements of the conventional village mystery—the secret, unacknowledged sin that triggers a murder, the corruption beneath a benign, bucolic exterior, and the complexities of true social relations underlying overt social roles—but the characters are higher up in the social scale. Once the unlikely premise of a nationally famous forensics laboratory set among rural villages is accepted by the reader, the interplay of competitive jealousies among the highly competent staff allows James

to show how intelligent and successful people, specialists in difficult, esoteric disciplines, handle the disappointments, frustrations, and opportunities that work in any corporate structure inevitably brings. Their isolation on the gloomy, closed landscape of the fens of East Anglia (an area known to James from her childhood) draws attention to their plight in a way that a London setting would not allow.

In 1979 the success of her literary efforts led James to devote herself to writing full-time, although she continued to serve in positions relevant to her interests in crime and punishment. In her next novel, *Innocent Blood* (1980), a young woman, Philippa Palfrey, who was adopted as a child into a privileged family, fantasizes about her possibly scandalous origins, such as being the daughter of a parlor maid and an aristocrat, but the truth is far less benign. Opening doors to the past, in her case, means danger, betrayal, and long-buried horror. Daniel Aaron, the Jewish detective in the novel who is losing his heritage but is still not embraced by the police force, illustrates the problem of inclusiveness, an issue with which English culture continues to struggle.

In *The Skull beneath the Skin* (1982) Cordelia Gray has been hired to protect Clarissa Lisle, a beautiful but fading actress whose life is being threatened in a series of poison-pen letters. Clarissa is a memorably drawn figure, an archetypal actress in her love of dramatic gestures and personal emotional drama, yet also a particularized and sadly human character as well. For all her emotional wisdom on the stage, she is unable to care for others or relate to them in any way that does not pay large benefits to herself, as her arbitrary treatment of her psychologically fragile stepson shows. Her encounters with Cordelia show the great range in the repertoire of James's female characters, with Clarissa an almost eighteenth- or nineteenth-century type of the powerful actress, unabashedly using her femininity to manipulate others to get what she wants; and, in contrast, the polite, restrained, modern Cordelia. The sea between Courcy, the island setting of the novel, and the mainland to which characters and police regularly return is emblematic of the special status of the small, temporary island community, its separation and distance from normal human rules and behavior. When the characters cross the strait on the ferry, they are undergoing a literal sea change to a place where the bonds of mother and son, husband and wife, and friendship can be broken with comparative ease. (The island is the site of an earlier ghastly torture killing of a German war prisoner at the hands of his fellows; such isolated settings in coastal areas tend to suspend civilized restraints in James.)

In *The Skull beneath the Skin* Cordelia lives in style in an upscale Victorian setting, far removed from the shack of *An Unsuitable Job for a Woman,* but her fellow inhabitants of the faux "castle" on Courcy outmaneuver her again and again. As in *An Unsuitable Job for a Woman,* the villain almost kills her in a terrifying, claustrophobic drowning attempt. Although she has been hired to protect Clarissa from harm, Cordelia fails miserably and is more a pawn of circumstances than an assertive private detective. She is somewhat intimidated by the formidable group that surrounds Clarissa and shows her youth and inexperience in her inability to force the willful theatrical folk to change their behavior to accommodate her mission of protection. As in *An Unsuitable Job for a Woman,* Cordelia ultimately figures out the murder, but the conclusion remains unsatisfactory, the goal of justice unfulfilled.

In her introduction to *The Skull beneath the Skin* in *Trilogy of Death: Three Complete Novels* (1984) James suggests that Cordelia's youthful freshness renewed the writer's energy for finding new ways to deal with the clichés of the mystery genre. As she told Olga Kenyon, it is "easier to have a woman as a chief character [since] with a woman detective you are free." Cordelia encounters a variety of eccentric characters, from her flawed mentor, Bernie Pryde, to the creepy Ambrose Gorringe, a tax fraud obsessed with Victorian memorabilia of death. With all she meets, Cordelia is honest, brave, tough, intelligent, open, and sweet. If, in the complex relationship between author and series character, Dalgliesh is a simulacrum of James as a professional administrator reluctantly sorting out recalcitrant subordinates, then Cordelia is a representation of a more personal, domestic side, an idealized portrait of how the author might have liked to have been as a young woman. Cordelia's mistakes come from inexperience, never from failures of character.

The deaths of Paul Berowne, an important political figure, and a lowly tramp in an Anglican church form the mystery in *A Taste for Death* (1986). Whether the two deaths were a murder-suicide or a double murder by an outsider is debated well into the novel, with Berowne's mental state being of crucial importance to understanding the crime: if he were not depressed or suicidal, he and the tramp must have been killed by a third party. (Forensic evidence shows the tramp could not have killed Berowne.) Any discussion of motive presupposes a definition of human nature, of how the investigators believe human beings behave, their range of possible behavior. Dalgliesh's role as lead investigator becomes particularly important, since the crime in question is the first case for a new squad investigating politically sensitive cases, which he heads. His two subordinates are complete opposites. Chief Inspector John

Dust jacket for James's 1971 novel, in which Dalgliesh solves a series of murders at a nursing school (from Cooper and Pike, Detective Fiction: The Collector's Guide, *second edition, 1994)*

Massingham, with whom Dalgliesh worked in *Death of an Expert Witness,* is the son of a peer, educated at his father's renowned public school, the scion of a venerable family for whom public service is the appropriate career choice. While such young men would once have joined the army to protect the empire abroad, Massingham serves justice in London, an ambitious policeman who, like Dalgliesh, can never be one of the gang because of his background and education. Inspector Kate Miskin is excluded because of her gender. Abandoned by her father and raised in miserable public housing by her impoverished mother, Kate is a completely self-made woman, an up-through-the-ranks officer who understands how policing can mean keeping rough order among the poor and disenfranchised. Despite their diverse backgrounds and professional misgivings, the team works smoothly and competently thanks to Dalgliesh's discipline and refusal to countenance self-seeking. (Massingham is jealous of Kate's rapid rise and ascribes it to gender preference.)

A Taste for Death provides several descriptions of Dalgliesh's investigative methods. Apart from running down every lead, no matter how tedious and apparently pointless, he has disciplined himself and his team to observe closely and to resist quick inferences: "There's no difficulty in recognizing the obvious. One should be slower to believe it." In the Berowne case, for example, Dalgliesh makes himself take his time:

> Before he concentrated on the actual scene of the crime, Dalgliesh always liked to make a cursory survey of the surroundings to orientate himself and, as it were, to set the scene of murder. That exercise had its practical value, but he recognized that, in some obscure way, it fulfilled a psychological need. Just so in boyhood he would explore a country church by first walking slowly round it before, with a frisson of awe and excitement, pushing open the door and beginning his planned progress of discovery to the central mystery. And now, in these few remaining minutes, before the photographer, the fingerprinting officers, the forensic biologists arrived at the scene, he had the place almost to himself. Moving into the passage, he wondered whether this quiet air tinctured with the scent of incense, candles and the more solidly Anglican smell of musty prayer books, metal polish and flowers had held for Berowne also the promise of discovery, of a scene already set, a task inevitable and inescapable.

In *Devices and Desires* (1989) Dalgliesh visits an isolated stretch of the Norfolk coast to settle the effects of his aunt Jane (introduced in *Unnatural Causes*) at the same time that a serial killer known as The Whistler is murdering women in the area. A ruined Benedictine abbey shares the coast with the "great, grey bulk" of Larksoken Nuclear Power Station. Dalgliesh muses to another character about the presence of the station, which seems to be establishing its right to dominate this natural space. Its lasting power, however, is double-edged, its nuclear waste permanent, but its massive concrete structure just another potential ruin against the action of the sea, which has devoured not just World War II fortifications but also whole chunks of headland. James's well-ordered prose forces the reader's eye to linger over severed or brutalized body parts. Miles Lessingham, a power-station employee who has just discovered the latest victim of The Whistler, nervously recounts what it was like: "More shocking than terrible. Looking back, my emotions were complicated, a mixture of horror, disbelief and, well, shame. I felt like a voyeur. The dead, after all, are at such a disadvantage. She looked grotesque, a little ridiculous. . . . Horrible, of course, but silly at the same time. I had an almost irresistible impulse to giggle." The odd marriage of reserved prose and graphically vivid bloody detail serves James well, inoculating against the charge of sen-

sationalism and capturing the melancholy consequences of murder as few detective fiction writers have ever managed to do.

James's next novel was a futuristic dystopia, *The Children of Men* (1992). Set in 2021, the setting is no brave new world but a time when the human species, suddenly sterile, faces total annihilation. Despair reigns, democracy yields to the easy security of paternalistic tyranny, and strange cults spring up, engaging in flagellation, human sacrifice, and assisted suicides. The novel becomes a paean to a lost world and lost possibilities—that is, the loss of James's world and of English culture—as the bones of plague victims pile high and the aged are drugged and placed aboard barges, which are then sunk at sea. Then a child is born—a miraculous birth. Despite James's assertion that she belongs to no political party, her conservatism is clear in this science-fiction tale with its biblical imagery and names and Christian symbols. The novel makes a political and religious statement of hope amid the ruins of a grasping modern society. It ends with a baptism in tears, a cross made in human blood on the forehead of the newborn boy, and the pronouncement "So it begins again."

After *The Children of Men* James returned to her forte, the crime novel. In *Original Sin* (1994) Dalgliesh and Miskin investigate multiple deaths at a publishing house, Peverell Press, with offices in the ironically named Innocent House. *A Certain Justice* (1997) is a classical locked-room mystery. Brilliant, ambitious Inner Temple criminal trial lawyer Venetia Aldridge successfully defends a smoothly presentable, cold-eyed young sociopath, appropriately named Ashe (the product of foster homes and institutions), who has been accused of murdering his slatternly aunt. Aldridge is convinced of his guilt, but, by calling into question the testimony of an eyewitness, wins his release. Ashe, who understands Aldridge's competitiveness and culpability, invades her home and wins the heart of her troubled eighteen-year-old daughter, Octavia. The daughter, who loathes her mother for neglecting her, naively believes that acquittal means innocence. In a short time, partly in defiance of her mother, Octavia announces her plans to marry Ashe.

After confrontations with Ashe; with her married lover, who is ending their relationship; with a colleague whose jury tampering she has uncovered; and with some fellow barristers at Pawlet Court who are determined to keep her from becoming head lawyer, Aldridge turns up stabbed to death in chambers. The door is locked from the inside. Commander Dalgliesh is called in, assisted by Inspector Miskin and her new partner, Piers Tarrant. This detective team probes Aldridge's personal history and recent actions, finding several suspects and motives. (Even the cleaning lady disliked Aldridge for her failures in a case dear to her.) When a second murder follows and Ashe and Octavia disappear, the complicated threads of a case involving thwarted ambition, childhood neglect, obsession, and revenge pull together to reveal an intricately woven pattern with death at its center. As always, James brings to life the intricate social relationships of people acting within an intimate and volatile workplace–in this case, the closed world of a legal community with its rivalries, alliances, compromises, slights, and unspoken hatreds.

In 1999 James published an abbreviated autobiography of sorts, an account of her seventy-eighth year, *Time to Be in Earnest: A Fragment of an Autobiography*. Although critics found it too public a work for an autobiography, with private matters kept private, it reflects the author's solid traditional values and stoical endurance of adversity and her belief in personal responsibility and character building in schools. She observes,

> We were taught as much by example as precept, to respect our minds and to use them to examine the evidence before rushing in with our opinions, to distinguish between fact and theory, to see history through the eyes of the poor and vanquished, not merely those of the powerful and the conquerors, not to believe that something is true simply because it would be pleasant or convenient if it were, and, when exposed to propaganda, to ask ourselves, "In whose interest is it that I should believe this?"

James speaks out for decorum, courtesy, dignity, and generosity and attacks modern "political correctness" as "pernicious linguistic fascism." She criticizes modern feminists for fashionably presenting themselves as victims when they, like those of her generation, could seize opportunities if they wished.

In *Death in Holy Orders* (2001) Dalgliesh investigates the deaths of three people associated with a training school for the priesthood. St. Anselm's is a High Anglican theological college located on an eroding cliff above the windswept East Anglian coast. This setting allows James to voice again the personal pleasure she takes in the pounding of the North Sea and isolated shores. It also allows her to articulate the religious debate between the traditional and the modern, with the latter calling for the church to adapt itself to twenty-first-century needs in order to survive and the former clinging to the mystery of the faith, ceremony, hymns, liturgy, and the the old-fashioned virtues of Anglicanism. Dalgliesh, the son of a pastor, remembers with nostalgia the innocent summers he spent at St. Anselm's as a teenager. When a rich and powerful industrialist asks him to investigate the questionable circumstances of the death of his son, Dalgliesh agrees. The son, Ronald Treeves, a young ordinand at the

James in New York City in 1980, on the occasion of the U.S. publication of her novel Innocent Blood *(photograph by Susan Gray; from the U.S. edition of* Time to Be in Earnest: A Fragment of Autobiography, *2000)*

remote and privileged college, was found suffocated in a sandbank. His death is reported as accidental, but an anonymous note points to murder. When a retired nurse with a bad heart is also found suffocated, perhaps to silence her about an event from twelve years earlier, and then evangelical Archdeacon Crampton, who championed ecclesiastical modernity and advocated closing the college, has his head bashed in–in a locked room–Dalgliesh brings in his full murder team and begins the inevitable investigative process of exposing the secrets of the college and its inhabitants. As *A Certain Justice* focused on a law office, so *Death in Holy Orders* explores the closed world of an ecclesiastical community, continuing James's study of how such a closed environment shapes motive and behavior.

James's priests and acolytes are fallible beings. An elderly priest accused of sexual molestation is indeed a homosexual but is innocent of the charge of molestation. Others, however, are not so innocent, as arrogance and repressed passions hide situations such as incest, secret marriage, and illegitimacy. A valuable

2

reported, that the whole house was waiting. Gregory hadn't shown himself. He had, at

Dalgliesh's request, handed over his passport after the last interrogation and there was no

fear that he would abscond. But flight had never been an option. It was no part of

Gregory's plan to be hauled back ignominiously from some ~~seedy~~ *inhospitable* foreign refuge.

It was a cold day and he smelled in the London air for the first time the metallic

tang of winter. A biting but fitful wind scoured the City and by the time he reached the

A12 it was blowing in strong, more sustained blasts. The traffic was unusually light

except for the trucks on their way to the east coast ports, and he drove smoothly. *and felt, his*

hands lightly on the wheel, his eyes fixed ahead. What had he but two guys hairs [...]

His thoughts moved from the arrest to the trial and he found himself rehearsing

the case for the defence. The DNA could not be challenged; Gregory had worn Ronald

Treeves's cloak. But the defence counsel would probably claim that Gregory ~~had~~

~~complained of feeling cold~~ *perhaps complaining of feeling cold.* when giving that last Greek lesson to Treeves, and had

borrowed it. Nothing was less likely, but would a jury believe that? Gregory had a

strong motive, but so had others including ~~his son~~ *Raphael*. The twig found on the floor of

Raphael's sitting room could have blown in unseen when he left his set to go to Peter

Buckhurst; *His prosecution would probably be wise not to make too* The telephone call to Mrs Crampton, put through from the box in the

College, was dangerous to the defence but it could have been made by five other people,

and possibly by ~~Henry Bloxham~~ *Raphael.* ~~if he had run at speed from the College to the church.~~

And then there was a case to be made against Miss Betterton. She had motive and

opportunity, but had she the strength to wield that heavy candlestick? No one now would

know; Agatha Betterton was dead. *Gregory had [...] her been accused [...] of the murder of murdering Margaret Monroe [...] neither can [...] the official evidence ever to justify his arrest*

Page from the revised typescript for James's 2001 novel, Death in Holy Orders
(Collection of P. D. James)

altar triptych and a missing cloak figure in a murder equation beleaguered by red herrings. Dalgliesh, realizing he has been "a detached observer of life" for too long and in danger of stifling any personal "quickening of the spirit," makes tentative moves toward a personal love relationship, promising a resolution of his long-standing love conflicts.

James has been repeatedly recognized for her contributions to the crime-fiction genre ever since winning first prize in the Crime Writers' Association's 1967 short-story contest for "Moment of Power." In 1987 she received the Diamond Dagger from the association for outstanding lifetime contributions to crime writing. James's honorary degrees include doctorates from the University of Buckingham (1992) and the University of London (1993). She was awarded the Order of the British Empire (OBE) in 1983 and in 1991 was created a life peer of the United Kingdom with the title Baroness James of Holland Park. In 1992 she was made a Commander of the British Empire. James is a fellow of the Royal Society of Literature, the Royal Society of Arts, and the Institute of Hospital Administration. She is a member of the Detection Club and the Society of Authors, for which she served as chair from 1985 to 1987.

If P. D. James has been misunderstood at times and appropriated by groups she would not wish to spend any time with, it is perhaps because, like her greatest creation, Dalgliesh, her fiction is complex, multifaceted, and quite human beneath a cool, orderly narrative voice. In a world in which popular fiction is often seen as promoting a single, simple thesis or advancing a particular view of the world, James, in the words of Bernard Benstock, "creates a vast and intricate cross section of English life . . . and probes the hidden corners" of the various characters who inhabit it. This depiction of England must be all the more manifold given the enormous changes wrought after World War II, as a homogenous, class-ridden, and stable society became increasingly fragmented and fluid. James depicts some responses to this change, beginning in the 1960s and 1970s, and although she can be caustic about the excesses of those periods of radical chic and ideological purity, she is in fact quite evenhanded about revealing upper-class arrogance and remains open to the claims of the dispossessed and alienated.

Detective fiction has always occupied an odd niche in popular writing, set apart from "serious" fiction, but, because of its forays into questions of social justice and social class, the moral struggle between forces of good and evil, justice and retribution, social manners, and secrets the general public barely dreams of, and its anatomizing of human motive, the genre is frequently beloved of "serious" readers. Such readers may have interests in social policy questions, particularly the practical ones in criminal justice, or they may simply be curious about the many ways in which human nature manifests itself. Such readers show the current inadequacy of the definition Dorothy L. Sayers gave of the detective genre, the literature of "escape" as opposed to the literature of "expression." Readers of James may well be escaping, in the sense that all reading takes one away from action, but they are certainly also experiencing the full range of expression. P. D. James is not alone in having raised crime fiction to literary levels at the end of the twentieth century, but she certainly deserves much of the credit.

Interviews:

Barbara Bannon, "PW Interviews: P. D. James," *Publishers Weekly,* 209 (5 January 1976): 8–9;

Jane S. Bakerman, "From the Time I Could Read, I Always Wanted to Be a Writer," *Armchair Detective,* 10 (January 1977): 55–57, 92;

Patricia Craig, "An Interview with P. D. James," *TLS: The Times Literary Supplement,* 5 June 1981, p. 4079;

Dale Salwak, "An Interview with P. D. James," *Clues,* 6 (Spring–Summer 1985): 31–50;

Rosemary Herbert, "A Mind to Write," *Armchair Detective,* 19 (1986): 340–348;

"Detective Stories Affirm the Sanctity of Life," *U.S. News & World Report,* 101 (24 November 1986): 78;

M. Stassio, "No Gore Please–They're British: An Interview with P. D. James," *New York Times Book Review,* 9 October 1988, pp. 1, 18–20;

Lynn Barber, "The Cautious Heart of P. D. James," *Vanity Fair,* 56 (March 1993): 80–94;

Herbert, "P. D. James," in her *The Fatal Art of Entertainment: Interviews with Mystery Writers* (New York: G. K. Hall, 1994), pp. 55–83;

Shusha Guppy, "P. D. James: The Art of Fiction CXLI," *Paris Review,* 135 (Summer 1995): 52–75.

References:

Jane S. Bakerman, "Cordelia Gray: Apprentice and Archetype," *Clues,* 5 (Spring–Summer 1984): 101–114;

Sue Ellen Campbell, "The Detective Heroine and the Death of Her Hero: Dorothy Sayers to P. D. James," *Modern Fiction Studies,* 29 (Autumn 1983): 497–510;

M. Cannon, "Mistress of Malice Domestic," *New York Times Book Review,* 27 April 1980, p. 50;

S. L. Clark, "*Gaudy Night's* Legacy: P. D. James's *An Unsuitable Job for a Woman,*" *Sayers Review,* 4 (1980): 1–11;

Kathryn Flett, "Murder, She Writes," *Harper's Bazaar,* 122 (September 1989): 94;

Richard B. Gidez, *P. D. James* (Boston: Twayne, 1986);

Donald Goddard, "The Unmysterious P. D. James," *New York Times Book Review,* 27 April 1980, p. 28;

Bruce Harkness, "P. D. James," in *Essays in Detective Fiction,* edited by Benstock (London: Macmillan, 1983), pp. 119–141;

Carolyn G. Heilbrun, "The Detective Novel of Manners," in her *Hamlet's Mother and Other Women* (New York: Columbia University Press, 1990), pp. 231–243;

Erlene Hubly, "Adam Dalgliesh: Byronic Hero," *Clues,* 3 (Fall–Winter 1982): 40–46;

Hubly, "The Formula Challenged: The Novels of P. D. James," *Modern Fiction Studies,* 29 (Autumn 1983): 511–521;

Joyce Carol Oates, "Inside the Locked Room," *New York Review of Books,* 45 (5 February 1998): 19–21;

Dennis Porter, "Detection and Ethics: The Case of P. D. James," in *The Sleuth and the Scholar: Evolution of Current Trends in Detective Fiction,* edited by Barbara A. Rader and Howard G. Zetler (Westport, Conn.: Greenwood Press, 1988), pp. 11–18;

Norma Siebenheller, *P. D. James* (New York: Ungar, 1981);

Christine Wick Sizemore, "The City as Mosaic: P. D. James," in her *A Female Vision of the City: London in the Novels of Five British Women* (Knoxville: University of Tennessee Press, 1989), pp. 152–187;

Julian Symons, "The Queen of Crime," *New York Times Magazine,* 5 October 1986, pp. 48–50, 54, 58, 60, 70;

Patricia A. Ward, "Moral Ambiguities and the Crime Novels of P. D. James," *Christian Century,* 101 (16 May 1984): 519–522;

Robin W. Winks, "P. D. James: Murder and Dying," *New Republic* (31 July 1976): 31–32.

Alistair MacLean

(28 April 1922 – 2 February 1987)

Chris Willis

BOOKS: *H.M.S. Ulysses* (London: Collins, 1955; Garden City, N.Y.: Doubleday, 1956);

The Guns of Navarone (London: Collins, 1957; Garden City, N.Y.: Doubleday, 1957);

South by Java Head (London: Collins, 1958; Garden City, N.Y.: Doubleday, 1958);

The Last Frontier (London: Collins, 1959); republished as *The Secret Ways* (Garden City, N.Y.: Doubleday, 1959);

Night without End (London: Collins, 1960; Garden City, N.Y.: Doubleday, 1960);

Fear Is the Key (London: Collins, 1961; Garden City, N.Y.: Doubleday, 1961);

The Dark Crusader, as Ian Stuart (London: Collins, 1961); republished as *The Black Shrike* (New York: Scribners, 1961);

All About Lawrence of Arabia (London: W. H. Allen, 1962); republished as *Lawrence of Arabia* (New York: Random House, 1962);

The Satan Bug, as Stuart (London: Collins, 1962; New York: Scribners, 1962);

The Golden Rendezvous (London: Collins, 1962; Garden City, N.Y.: Doubleday, 1962);

Ice Station Zebra (London: Collins, 1963; Garden City, N.Y.: Doubleday, 1963);

When Eight Bells Toll (London: Collins, 1966; Garden City, N.Y.: Doubleday, 1966);

Where Eagles Dare (London: Collins, 1967; Garden City, N.Y.: Doubleday, 1967);

Force 10 from Navarone (London: Collins, 1968; Garden City, N.Y.: Doubleday, 1968);

Puppet on a Chain (London: Collins, 1969; Garden City, N.Y.: Doubleday, 1969);

Caravan to Vaccarès (London: Collins, 1970; Garden City, N.Y.: Doubleday, 1970);

Bear Island (London: Collins, 1971; Garden City, N.Y.: Doubleday, 1971);

Captain Cook (London: Collins, 1972; Garden City, N.Y.: Doubleday, 1972);

The Way to Dusty Death (London: Collins, 1973; Garden City, N.Y.: Doubleday, 1973);

Alistair MacLean (photograph by Godfrey Argent; from the dust jacket for the U.S. edition of River of Death, *1981)*

Breakheart Pass (London: Collins, 1974; Garden City, N.Y.: Doubleday, 1974);

Circus (London: Collins, 1975; Garden City, N.Y.: Doubleday, 1975);

The Golden Gate (London: Collins, 1976; Garden City, N.Y.: Doubleday, 1976);

Goodbye California (London: Collins, 1977; Garden City, N.Y.: Doubleday, 1978);

Seawitch (London: Collins, 1977; Garden City, N.Y.: Doubleday, 1977);

Athabasca (London: Collins, 1980; Garden City, N.Y.: Doubleday, 1980);

River of Death (London: Collins, 1981; Garden City, N.Y.: Doubleday, 1982);

Partisans (London: Collins, 1982; Garden City, N.Y.: Doubleday, 1983);

Floodgate (London: Collins, 1983; Garden City, N.Y.: Doubleday, 1984);

San Andreas (London: Collins, 1984; Garden City, N.Y.: Doubleday, 1985);

The Lonely Sea: Collected Short Stories (Glasgow: Collins, 1985; Garden City, N.Y.: Doubleday, 1986);

Santorini (London: Collins, 1986; Garden City, N.Y.: Doubleday, 1987).

Collections: *Five Great War Stories* (London: Collins, 1978)—comprises *H.M.S. Ulysses, The Guns of Navarone, South by Java Head, Where Eagles Dare,* and *Force 10 from Navarone;*

Four Great Adventure Stories, introduction by Carl Foreman (London: Collins, 1981)—comprises *When Eight Bells Toll, The Golden Gate, Caravan to Vaccarès,* and *Circus.*

PRODUCED SCRIPTS: *Where Eagles Dare,* motion picture, M-G-M, 1968;

Puppet on a Chain, by MacLean, Don Sharp, and Paul Wheeler, motion picture, Scotia-Barber, 1971;

When Eight Bells Toll, motion picture, Rank, 1971;

Breakheart Pass, motion picture, United Artists, 1975.

OTHER: *Alistair MacLean Introduces Scotland,* by MacLean and others, edited by Alastair M. Dunnett (London: Deutsch, 1972; New York: McGraw-Hill, 1972);

John Denis, *The Hostage Tower,* based on a story outline by MacLean (London: Fontana, 1980);

Denis, *Air Force One Is Down,* based on a story outline by MacLean (London: Fontana, 1981);

Alastair MacNeill, *Alistair MacLean's Death Train,* based on a story outline by MacLean (London: Collins, 1989);

MacNeill, *Alistair MacLean's Night Watch,* based on a story outline by MacLean (London: Collins, 1989);

MacNeill, *Alistair MacLean's Red Alert,* based on a story outline by MacLean (London: Collins, 1990; South Yarmouth, Mass.: Curley, 1992);

"The Cruise of the Golden Girl" (1954), in *Alistair MacLean: A Life,* by Jack Webster (London: Chapmans, 1991), pp. 305–317;

MacNeill, *Alistair MacLean's Time of the Assassins,* based on a story outline by MacLean (London: HarperCollins, 1991);

MacNeill, *Alistair MacLean's Dead Halt,* based on a story outline by MacLean (London: HarperCollins, 1992);

Simon Gandolfi, *Alistair MacLean's Golden Girl,* based on a screenplay by MacLean (London: Chapmans, 1992);

MacNeill, *Alistair MacLean's Code Breaker,* based on a story outline by MacLean (London: HarperCollins, 1993);

MacNeill, *Alistair MacLean's Rendezvous,* based on a short story by MacLean (London: HarperCollins, 1995).

SELECTED PERIODICAL PUBLICATION–UNCOLLECTED: "Rewards and Responsibilities of Success," *Glasgow Herald,* 19 June 1982.

Despite being one of the world's best-selling writers, Alistair MacLean was consistently modest about the literary merits of his twenty-eight novels of action and adventure. He always insisted that he was a storyteller rather than a novelist, and he felt great regret that he had never written what he regarded as a "good" book. MacLean was, however, proud of his ability to create fast-moving, exciting action-adventure stories. In a 1971 interview he told Barry Norman, "Basically I'm a person who tells stories. . . . the basic secret is speed—keep the action moving so fast that the reader never has time to stop and think. . . . That's why there is never any sex in my books; it holds up the action." MacLean added that he disapproved of "permissiveness and pornography. It's a matter of satisfaction to me that I can produce bestsellers without resorting to these things." He disdained what he referred to as the "sex, sadism and snobbery" of the Ian Fleming school of writing.

Alistair Stuart MacLean was born on 28 April 1922 in Glasgow, Scotland. His mother, Mary Lamont MacLean, a deeply religious woman, was also a prize-winning singer. His father, also named Alistair MacLean, was a Church of Scotland minister. A writer himself, the Reverend MacLean published books of Christian meditations, most notably *High Country* (1928) and *Hebridean Altars: The Spirit of an Island Race* (1937), which was republished in 1999. Young Alistair was the couple's third child. He had two older brothers, Lachlan and Ian. A younger brother, Gilleasbuig (known as Gillespie), was born in 1926. Soon after Alistair's birth, the family moved to the country district of Daviot, six miles south of Inverness.

The MacLeans were Gaelic speakers. At his father's insistence, Alistair did not learn English until he

Stars of the 1961 motion-picture adaptation of MacLean's 1957 novel The Guns of Navarone:
Irene Papas, James Darren, Anthony Quayle, David Niven, Gregory Peck, Anthony Quinn,
Stanley Baker, and Gia Scala (Everett Collection)

was seven and spoke only Gaelic at home until the age of fifteen. He was educated at the local primary school in Daviot. In his 1991 biography of the novelist, Jack Webster records that the MacLean brothers wore kilts to school and went barefoot all summer and that Alistair's first teacher, Barbara Mackintosh, recalled Alistair as "a quiet little boy who gave me no trouble."

In 1936, when Alistair was fourteen, his father died. By this time both his older brothers had left home, Lachlan to study medicine and Ian to serve in the merchant marine. Mary MacLean moved back to Glasgow in spring 1937 with Alistair and Gillespie. Alistair obtained a bursary to Hillhead High School in Glasgow. When he was sixteen, his oldest brother, Lachlan, died of stomach cancer a few weeks before turning twenty-one. Alistair was deeply distressed by Lachlan's death, which left a lasting impression. As a successful novelist many years later, he became heavily involved with cancer charities.

MacLean left school in the summer of 1939, just before the start of World War II. He had had good exam results in English, history, Latin, mathematics, and science, and his teachers had hoped he would go on to further education. As he had to support his wid-

owed mother, however, he decided to take a job in the offices of F. C. Strick, a shipping firm that ran services between Glasgow and the Persian Gulf.

In 1941 MacLean joined the Royal Navy, enlisting as a volunteer rather than waiting to be conscripted. His war experiences were to provide valuable material for his fiction. After initial training he became a leading torpedo operator on HMS *Royalist,* an escort ship for convoys taking supplies to Russia. These Arctic convoys were notoriously dangerous. Naval vessels joined the supply ships north of Scotland and escorted them through hostile Arctic waters to Murmansk, braving German submarines, destroyers, and airplanes. The crews also faced fearful cold, which could cause frostbite within minutes. MacLean fictionalized his experiences vividly in his first novel, *H.M.S. Ulysses* (1955).

After this stint with the convoys, the *Royalist* served in the Mediterranean and the Aegean. In September 1944 the ship took part in the bombardment of shore targets on Nazi-occupied Greek islands. MacLean used this experience as source material for his second novel, *The Guns of Navarone* (1957), and its sequel, *Force 10 from Navarone* (1968). In 1945 the *Royalist* was sent to the Far East, playing an important part in the liberation of Singapore. This theater of war provided the background for MacLean's third novel, *South by Java Head* (1958).

MacLean told his shipmates that he regretted not having continued his education and that he hoped to resume his studies after the war. On 26 March 1946 he was officially released from the navy and went back into civilian life with the intention of taking a degree. In the autumn of 1946 he began to study English literature at Glasgow University, supporting himself by working in a post office and sweeping streets. Narrowly missing a first because of a hand injury shortly before his final exams, MacLean gained a good second-class honors degree and graduated with an M.A. in 1950. (Under the Scottish educational system a four-year course results in an M.A. or M.S.)

During the summer vacation of 1949 MacLean worked as a hospital porter at the King George V Sanatorium at Godalming in Surrey, where he met his future wife, Gisela Heinrichsen. She was a German from Schleswig-Holstein who had come to Britain to learn English, despite the widespread hostility to Germans in postwar England. She soon moved to Glasgow to work in Mearnskirk Hospital, while MacLean trained as a teacher at Jordanhill College, also in Glasgow. Disregarding opposition from some members of MacLean's family, they married on 2 July 1953, at St. Columba's Church in Glasgow. Gisela might have provided the inspiration for at least one of MacLean's later heroines. In *San Andreas* (1984), Margaret Morrison is a half-German nurse working on a World War II hospital ship. Another sympathetic German female character is Helene Fleming in *Night without End* (1960).

By the time of his marriage MacLean had a secure job as a teacher at Gallowflat Secondary School in Rutherglen, south of Glasgow. He taught English, history, and geography at the boys-only school. His pupils recall him as a good teacher, although MacLean later said that he did not enjoy the work. In his 1971 interview with Norman he said that he became a teacher because "It seemed the logical thing to do if you had an honours degree in English. . . . I had no sense of vocation. . . . I didn't enjoy teaching." Meanwhile, MacLean had begun writing in his spare time. His efforts were rewarded early in 1954, when his short story "The Cruise of the Golden Girl" was published in *Blackwood's Magazine*. The story was a slightly fictionalized account of a disastrous sailing trip that he had taken with three friends. Written in plain, clear prose, the story combines excitement and humor, foreshadowing the technique MacLean was to use in his best novels.

MacLean's career soon took a dramatic turn for the better. In March 1954 he won first prize in a short-story competition organized by *The Glasgow Herald*. His story, "The Dileas," was the dramatic tale of a sea res-

cue off the West Highland coast, with a tear-jerking and highly improbable conclusion. The prize of £100 made a substantial difference to the income of a teacher taking home a salary of about £24 per month. More important, it led to MacLean's being sought out by a publisher eager to publish more of his work. Ian Chapman, who worked for the Glasgow publishing firm Collins, noticed his wife crying over MacLean's story in *The Glasgow Herald*. Intrigued, he read "The Dileas" himself and decided to seek out the author. Chapman met MacLean several times during the spring and summer of 1954 and urged him to write a novel. Although initially reluctant, MacLean began to write *H.M.S. Ulysses* in September 1954, shortly after the birth of his first son, Lachlan. A mere ten weeks later he presented Chapman with the finished manuscript. Chapman's initial reaction was that "he's written so fast it can't possibly be any good." He changed his mind as soon as he read it, becoming MacLean's publisher and lifelong friend.

Collins gave MacLean an advance of £1,000, and *H.M.S. Ulysses* was published in September 1955. By spring 1956 it had sold a quarter of a million copies. Motion-picture rights were sold for £30,000 (though the movie was never made); an American edition was published in 1956; and serial rights were sold to the popular British magazine *Picture Post* for £5,000. *H.M.S. Ulysses* became one of the best-selling British novels of the twentieth century.

A largely autobiographical account of MacLean's time in Arctic convoys, *H.M.S. Ulysses* remained MacLean's favorite book. Tautly written, it recounts four days in the working life of a destroyer escorting an Arctic convoy. In one moving (if melodramatic) sequence, the ship's captain has to order a torpedo operator to fire on another British ship—an oil tanker that is ablaze and must be sunk before the fire reveals the convoy's position to the enemy. The crew of the *Ulysses* is aware that all the men on board the tanker will be killed if this order is carried out. MacLean adds a dramatic twist worthy of Thomas Hardy: the operator, a minor character who fires the fatal torpedo, is the son of the tanker's captain, and he knows that he is killing his own father. Perhaps this episode reflects one of MacLean's own fears during his time as a torpedo man. His brother Ian was a merchant seaman and could well have been sailing on any of the vessels that MacLean's ship escorted. In the dedication to the novel MacLean thanks Ian (by now a master mariner) for helping him with maritime technical details.

MacLean intended *H.M.S. Ulysses* to be an expression of his admiration for the men who had served in the Royal Navy. But according to later press coverage—notably, MacLean's obituary in the *Times* (London)—the Admiralty was not pleased with MacLean's gritty, unsentimental description of the horrors of the Arctic convoys and his depiction of the senior officers on shore as completely out of touch with the harsh realities faced by the men risking their lives on board the ships. In the opening chapter a naval officer says at a disciplinary hearing that, in the convoys, "you're keyed up to snapping point, sometimes for seventeen days on end, when you have constant daily reminders of what may happen to you in the shape of broken, sinking ships and broken, drowning bodies." Accusing the Admiralty of knowing nothing about life on the convoys, the officer then asks,

Do you know what it's like when the wind, twenty degrees below zero, comes screaming off the Polar and Greenland ice-caps and slices through the thickest clothing like a scalpel? When there's five hundred tons of ice on the deck, where five minutes' direct exposure means frostbite, where the bows crash down into a trough and the spray hits you as solid ice, where even a torch battery dies out in the intense cold? . . . And do you know what it's like to go for days on end without sleep, for weeks with only two or three hours out of the twenty-four . . . every nerve in your body and cell in your brain stretched taut to breaking point, pushing you over the screaming edge of madness?

This passage, one of MacLean's most vivid and evocative, continues for several pages. He contrasts the speaker's highly emotional state with the callous and phlegmatic attitude shown by his deskbound superiors. The Admiralty representative's response to the officer is merely to comment, "You are quite obviously overwrought."

Thriller writer Hammond Innes described *H.M.S. Ulysses* as "the Navy's war with the lid right off—blood, toil, tears and sweat—all the horror of war and none of the boredom." As Angus Shaw in the *Glasgow Evening News* commented, it was "not for the squeamish." Shaw had served on the Arctic convoys himself and praised the grim realism of MacLean's novel, as did *Picture Post* reviewer Godfrey Winn, another Arctic-convoy veteran. The reviewer for *The Birmingham Post* was even more lavish in his praise, calling *H.M.S. Ulysses* "the grandest novel of the sea ever written." But not all the reviews were favorable. The Scottish *Daily Record* condemned the book as "drivelling melodrama," comparing it to "a horror comic strip" and complaining that it insulted the Royal Navy. In an article for *The Glasgow Herald* twenty-seven years later, MacLean wrote, "I had paid the Royal Navy the greatest compliment of which I could conceive: this dolt thought it was an act of denigration. This was the first so-called literary review I read: it was also the last."

Dust jacket for the U.S. edition of MacLean's 1963 novel, in which an American nuclear submarine carries a British agent to the Arctic (Richland County Public Library)

Encouraged by the phenomenal success of *H.M.S. Ulysses,* MacLean began a second novel, *The Guns of Navarone.* In 1971 he told Norman that he

wrote it with more method than inspiration. . . . First I drew up a list of the characters, then I drew a diagram of the plot. There were a number of squares to represent the chapters and in the squares were circles to show where the characters came in—and red crosses to show where they died . . . [there were] too many crosses in the middle and not enough at the end, so I rearranged it until there were crosses all the way through . . . I've never written a book that way since.

Ever cautious, MacLean kept his job as a schoolteacher, being uncertain as to whether the success of his first book was just a flash in the pan. He need not have worried: *The Guns of Navarone* was a resounding success.

Published in 1957, *The Guns of Navarone* was another World War II story, inspired by the six months MacLean had spent in the Aegean Sea while serving on the *Royalist*. Based partly on the wartime exploits of the Special Boat Service, the novel concerns a small group of Allied servicemen sent on a mission to sabotage German heavy artillery on a Nazi-occupied Greek island. The group includes two world-class mountaineers, who take the landing party up a supposedly unclimbable cliff on the island. MacLean himself was not a mountaineer, but he had researched the subject well, and this part of the narrative is vivid and convincing. *The Guns of Navarone* is probably the most male-dominated of MacLean's novels. Every character is male, and women are mentioned only three times: one character mentions that he has a daughter; another has witnessed the death of his grandmother; and the wife and children of another are reported to have been killed. None of these women are named, and it transpires that one of them never actually existed. Such an all-male cast was convincing in *H.M.S. Ulysses,* reflecting the reality of naval life during World War II, but it is less convincing in a novel set on a Greek island and with many civilian characters. MacLean, however, never seems entirely at ease when writing about women, and all his books are similarly male-dominated.

In 1961 *The Guns of Navarone* was made into a highly successful movie starring Gregory Peck, David Niven, and Anthony Quinn. It won the 1962 Oscar for special effects and was nominated for several other Academy Awards. MacLean had wisely distanced himself from the making of the movie, in which some events and characters from the novel were changed, introducing female characters and a love interest. Later, however, he requested a copy of the script, marking the start of a fascination with screenwriting and the mechanics of motion-picture production, which he put to good use in a later novel, *Bear Island* (1971), as well as in his own screenplays.

Although war was his subject matter, MacLean was at pains to emphasize that he held strong antiwar views. In an article for the Companion Book Club, quoted in Webster's biography of MacLean, he wrote, "On the positive side, I wanted to write a war story–with the accent on the story. Only a fool would pretend that there is anything noble or splendid about modern warfare, but there is no denying that it provides a great abundance of material for a writer, provided no attempt is made to glorify it or exploit its worst aspects."

Despite MacLean's protests, *The Guns of Navarone* does indeed glorify the larger-than-life heroes who destroy the Nazi guns. He makes no attempt, however, to glorify war itself. His antiwar sentiments also became evident at the premiere of the movie version of one of his later war books, *Where Eagles Dare* (1967). Chapman, who sat beside MacLean at the premiere, recalled

the author wryly commenting, "This is terrible! I didn't kill as many Germans as this. I was writing an anti-war film." MacLean's scruples did not prevent him from pocketing the profits from his works, but, as his career progressed, he wrote less and less about war, concentrating on crime thrillers instead.

The Guns of Navarone was as successful as its predecessor, prompting MacLean to give up teaching and become a full-time writer. To escape England's punitive tax system, he and Gisela moved to Switzerland with three-year-old Lachlan before the publication of his third novel, *South by Java Head,* in 1958. Unlike MacLean's first two books, this exciting wartime adventure is not concerned solely with military protagonists. It recounts the adventures of a mixed group of civilians and military personnel fleeing from the 1942 Japanese invasion of Singapore. Like all MacLean's books, *South by Java Head* is male-dominated but less so than his previous works. Two major characters are female, and the group includes a child. The mixed race of the heroine is unusual for British fiction of the 1950s, and at the end of the book it is made clear that she will marry the hero. Marriage was the standard fate for any MacLean heroine lucky enough to survive two hundred pages of murder, mayhem, and hair's-breadth escapes. The book has a strong (if understated) antiracist message. In one telling passage, the heroine tells the hero that many white people in Singapore snubbed her because of her dark skin. *South by Java Head* cannot be described as an antiracist book, however, as MacLean's deeply unsympathetic portrayal of the Japanese military commander reflects many of the commonly held anti-Japanese prejudices of the time. The well-publicized suffering of British soldiers in Japanese prisoner-of-war camps meant that English readers had little sympathy for the Japanese. MacLean's stereotyping is fairly typical of the portrayal of the Japanese military in British fiction for many years after World War II.

Collins disliked *South by Java Head* and sent Chapman to Switzerland to tell MacLean that they would reject the book unless he made substantial changes. But Chapman arrived to find a telegram reporting that the movie rights to *South by Java Head* had just been sold for a substantial sum, prompting Collins to accept the manuscript unchanged.

From this time onward MacLean usually wrote a novel per year. Generally speaking, the critics disliked his work, but the public loved it, and his books sold by the million. Written at the height of the Cold War, MacLean's next novel, *The Last Frontier* (1959), is an espionage thriller in which a British agent sent on a mission behind the Iron Curtain becomes increasingly disillusioned with Cold War politics. Unlike most of MacLean's work, this novel carries a strong moral

Clint Eastwood, Richard Burton, and Mary Ure in the 1968 motion-picture adaptation of MacLean's novel
Where Eagles Dare *(1967), in which a group of elite soldiers attempts to rescue a captured American
general from a German mountain stronghold during World War II (Everett Collection)*

message. One of the main characters, a concentration-camp survivor, makes an impassioned plea for humanity and tolerance between nations and for understanding between East and West:

> The desperate, most urgent need this world knows or will ever know is the need for an effort without parallel in history to get to know ourselves and the other people of this world even as we know ourselves. . . . we must always remember that a nation is made of millions of little human beings just like we are, and to talk about national sin and guilt and wickedness is to be wilfully blind. . . . The intolerance of ignorance, not *wanting* to know–that is the last real frontier left on earth.

The same character voices MacLean's own antiwar views and expresses fears about nuclear weapons, condemning military scientists as "those luckless, brilliant creatures who have long since traded in their birthright of independence, buried their consciences, and sold out to the governments of the world–so that they can strive harder and still harder until they have in their hands the ultimate weapon of destruction." After *The Last Frontier* MacLean decided that thrillers were no place for overt moralizing. Summarizing his career

in *The Glasgow Herald* in 1982, he commented, "I should have listened to Sam Goldwyn's dictum that messages are for Western Union."

Night without End (1960) is a story of survival. An airplane crash leaves a mixed group of passengers stranded in the Arctic with no hope of rescue. With the aid of members of a scientific expedition, they must make a grueling journey in subzero temperatures to reach safety. The hero soon discovers that the airplane was sabotaged and that two of the group must be murderers, but he has no way of telling who they are. Like the later *Ice Station Zebra* (1963), also set in the Arctic, *Night without End* features one of MacLean's innovative variations on the Agatha Christie formula of placing a small group of suspects in a closed environment. The murderers, of course, turn out to be the least likely suspects. Despite the grim setting, the novel includes some humorous observations on the class system. One of the least sympathetic characters is Phyllis Dansby-Gregg, a rich society beauty who, even in such extreme circumstances, refuses to lower her standards so far as to call her maid by her first name instead of her surname. That Phyllis's character develops and changes convincingly over the course of the novel is a measure of MacLean's skill.

Beginning in the 1960s, MacLean's novels featured an increasing number of American characters and settings—perhaps in a bid to maintain and increase his phenomenal sales in the United States. *Fear Is the Key* (1961) is a gripping revenge thriller set on an oil rig in the Gulf of Mexico. It opens with an airplane crash (as in *Night without End*) and the kidnapping of an oil heiress. As in *Night without End,* the main character's wife and child are killed before the action begins. The denouement takes place on a submarine—a setting that MacLean used again in *Ice Station Zebra.* Exciting and violent, *Fear Is the Key* ends with the hero meditating on the hollowness of revenge. Having avenged the deaths of his family, he reflects that "It was all over and done with and empty now, and it all meant nothing."

With *Night without End* and *Fear Is the Key* MacLean began using first-person rather than third-person narrative. As he told Chapman, "The old alleged technique that carried me so miraculously through *Ulysses* to *The Last Frontier* has had its day. . . . What I'm trying to do is develop a technique of completely impersonal story-telling in the first person." MacLean's laconic, first-person narrative style owed something to the writing of Raymond Chandler, whose works he greatly admired. Following MacLean's success, later thriller writers such as Dick Francis and Desmond Bagley developed similar styles. Collins, however, expressed dissatisfaction with MacLean's new work. Annoyed by this criticism, MacLean announced his intention to write under another name in order to prove that his writing ability, not just his name, sold books. To Chapman's intense annoyance, MacLean took the pseudonym Ian Stuart, the name of Chapman's son. MacLean published two crime/espionage novels under this name, one in 1961 and one in 1962. *The Dark Crusader* features a tough, male secret agent and his beautiful female sidekick investigating the disappearance of British weapons scientists on a Polynesian island. *The Satan Bug* concerns the disappearance of a lethal toxin from a laboratory that is loosely based on the notorious British government laboratories at Porton Down. Neither is among MacLean's best work, and without the MacLean name, sales were poor. They were later republished under his own name and sold well.

In 1961 the MacLeans adopted a baby, Michael. Like Gisela, he was German. She had assumed that she could not have another child, but shortly after adopting Michael, she became pregnant. In October 1963 she gave birth to another son, named Alistair Stuart after his father.

After his unpropitious attempt at publishing pseudonymously, MacLean returned to writing under his own name. For his next two novels he returned to one of his favorite subjects, the sea. *The Golden Rendez-* *vous* (1962) is a tale of crime on the high seas and was adapted as a motion picture starring Richard Harris in 1977. A beautiful heiress provides the love interest, and the denouement involves a stolen atomic missile. Despite MacLean's skill at maritime writing, *The Golden Rendezvous* is not one of his best books, and the action is at times formulaic and unconvincing. His next book, however, is one of his best. *Ice Station Zebra* is set on a United States Navy nuclear submarine that takes the protagonist, a British government investigator, to the Arctic to investigate the mysterious disappearance of members of a scientific expedition. As always, MacLean researched meticulously. The book gives a detailed and convincing picture of life aboard a submarine. In one particularly terrifying chapter, an engine-room fire leaves the broken-down submarine trapped under the polar icecap, with the crew facing almost certain death from suffocation as their air slowly runs out. Again written in the first person, the book combines excitement, humor, and suspense, ending with a surprise denouement worthy of Christie at her best.

Even *The Times Literary Supplement* (*TLS*), which usually denigrated MacLean's work, praised *Ice Station Zebra,* although the reviewer, Stephen Kroll, commented that the hero "sounds at times too much like an American private detective." For many of MacLean's readers, however, this characteristic is one of the attractions of the novel. The hero's wry asides enliven the book and add humor to what would otherwise be a grim tale of privation and mass murder. John Sutherland sees the book as acknowledging the decline of British military power, commenting that "There is a certain geopolitical realism in *Ice Station Zebra*'s tacit acknowledgement that it is the superpower America which now has the ships that matter. But there is also a nostalgia for past power in the evident intellectual superiority of the sophisticated Briton over this technologically advanced, well-meaning but essentially naive ally."

MacLean was becoming increasingly disillusioned with writing for a living. In 1963 he shocked his publishers by announcing his intention to give up writing and set up as a hotelier. Delivering the manuscript of *Ice Station Zebra* to Collins, he told Chapman, "That's the last book you are getting out of me. . . . I've never enjoyed writing and was only doing it to make money." MacLean returned to England, moved to Cornwall, and bought the famous Jamaica Inn (the setting of Daphne du Maurier's best-selling 1936 novel of the same name), intending to run it himself. He also bought two other hotels, Bank House near Worcester and the Bean Bridge in Somerset. He later explained that he had become "disillusioned with writing. . . . At the time it seemed empty and meaningless. I thought that owning property would be a more worthwhile occupation."

Dust jacket for the U.S. edition of MacLean's 1974 novel, about a train that becomes snowbound in the Nevada mountains in 1873 (Richland County Public Library)

Friends recalled his tremendous enthusiasm for his new project. After an afternoon selling trinkets in Jamaica Inn's souvenir shop, MacLean gleefully told a friend, "I've been more in contact with real life in the last hour than during nine years of writing novels."

Unfortunately, the hotel project proved a disaster. MacLean was not a good businessman, and he lost money hand over fist. Meanwhile, he found that "writing had become attractive again," and he felt the urge to write another book for Chapman, "just to show him what he'd been missing all those years." In 1966 MacLean moved back to Switzerland and began writing again. The result was *When Eight Bells Toll* (1966), which was adapted as a movie starring Robert Morley and Anthony Hopkins in 1971. MacLean set the novel in one of his favorite areas–the islands off the West Coast of Scotland. As a young man he had sailed those waters for pleasure, and many of the locations are instantly recognizable to anyone familiar with the area. The plot concerns hijacked ships, and much of the action takes place at sea. *When Eight Bells Toll* features a typical MacLean hero, a laconic British secret agent who is able to handle beatings, near drowning, sleep deprivation, and large amounts of whiskey without any visible effect. Like many of MacLean's protagonists, he is a

cynical, world-weary widower who falls in love with the heroine after initially suspecting her of being in league with the villain.

Before *When Eight Bells Toll* was published, American motion-picture producer Elliot Kastner approached MacLean and asked him to write an original screenplay for a World War II adventure movie. MacLean was reluctant at first but allowed himself to be persuaded. The result was the successful *Where Eagles Dare,* published as a novel in 1967 and released as a movie the following year. The title, which was suggested by Kastner, is taken from William Shakespeare's *King Richard III:* "the world is grown so bad / That wrens make prey where eagles dare not perch" (act 1, scene 3). The action takes place in a German castle called Schloss Adler–Eagles' Castle. The story involves an elite group of soldiers who parachute behind enemy lines to rescue a captured United States Army general. One of the paratroopers is a woman, as is a British secret agent who helps them. This use of female characters probably reflects the demands of the movie producers rather than MacLean's own inclinations, as he was always more comfortable writing about male characters. Both the book and movie versions of *Where Eagles Dare* feature a complex plot involving many double crosses by double and triple agents with multiple identities. In *Simon Rose's Classic Film Guide* (1995) Rose observes, "You have to put your brain on hold to watch this, so many are its implausibilities."

Kastner later recalled that MacLean sometimes seemed guilt-ridden about the large amounts of money he was now making, even though he declared that he wrote purely to make money. Chapman made a similar observation in 1971, telling Norman that "Alistair started writing to make money. . . . But now he's made it, he has a conscience about it. It seems to him sinful that he should earn such vast amounts for doing something that comes so easily to him." By now MacLean was one of the world's richest and best-selling authors and was running into trouble with the British tax authorities. He decided to retain control of his own copyrights rather than handling them through a corporation, but this demonstration of principles cost him large sums in income tax.

A visit to Amsterdam gave MacLean the idea for *Puppet on a Chain* (1969), a thriller about drug smuggling. Passing a warehouse near the docks, he saw a puppet hanging by the neck from a chain. In the novel the puppet becomes a dead body. The title is also a reference to Sandy Shaw's song "Puppet on a String," which won the 1967 Eurovision Song Contest, but MacLean's story is infinitely darker than Shaw's jaunty love lyric. A reviewer in *The New York Times* described the book as "filled to bursting with murder and mayhem, grit and gore." The hero's sidekicks are two beautiful female Interpol agents, but their part in the action is largely passive. They are there to provide a love interest and to be rescued (or not) by the hero, who always patronizingly refers to them as "the girls." At the end of the book he proposes marriage to one of them and tells her that if she agrees to marry him she must retire from her job, even though she is only in her twenties.

Puppet on a Chain features many striking images, some of which verge on the surreal. The hero and heroine break into a warehouse and find a room full of near-life-size puppets, which appear to be watching them. One character meets a grisly end while taking part in a murderously choreographed folk dance. Another is first maddened and then killed by the sound of a room full of simultaneously chiming clocks, which are amplified to earsplitting volume through his headphones—a scene that might have been inspired by Dorothy L. Sayers's *The Nine Tailors* (1934), in which a man is killed by the noise in a belfry while the bells are ringing. MacLean wrote all these scenes with a view to how they would look in a movie. He wrote the screenplay for the adaptation and was furious when some scenes were rewritten by a more experienced screenwriter employed by the production company. MacLean complained that the movie was a "rubbishy travesty of what I wrote" and disassociated himself from the project.

MacLean had little faith in his own writing abilities at this time. Webster quotes him as saying, "If I went on writing the same stuff, I'd be guying myself. As it is, I can hardly keep a straight face sometimes when I'm putting the words down." MacLean's next novel, *Caravan to Vaccarès* (1970), was badly received. A tale of crime and espionage during a Gypsy festival in Provence, it lacked the verve and wit of his earlier work. *Sunday Express* reviewer Graham Lord described it as "the worst-written, feeblest and most boring novel I have read by an established author this year." Such judgments did not affect sales, however: *Caravan to Vaccarès* was as successful as any of MacLean's earlier best-sellers.

In 1970 MacLean and his family moved to the Villa Murat, near the Swiss village of Celigny, fourteen miles from Geneva. They hoped that the villa would become their permanent home. It was an apt residence for a writer who had expressed worries about the nuclear threat so convincingly in *The Last Frontier*. MacLean joked that the thickness of the walls of the sixty-year-old house made it "the only atom-bomb-proof residence on the shores of Lake Geneva." His neighbors included Richard Burton, who had starred in the motion-picture version of *Where Eagles Dare*. The two men had met on the movie set, where there had been considerable friction between them. MacLean never felt entirely at ease among his rich neighbors, telling Norman in 1971 that "I don't belong in this class. It's ridiculous."

MacLean returned to form with *Bear Island,* published in 1971. Dealing with the misadventures of a motion-picture crew on location in the Arctic, the novel satirizes the movie industry. Shortly before it was published, MacLean told Norman that he had become disillusioned with the motion-picture business because it contained "So many entrepreneurs and promoters and uncreative people. . . . I couldn't get along with them." The book features another Chandler-like first-person narrative, in which the hero makes wry jokes about the follies of the movie industry. MacLean assured Norman that the characters were not based on anyone he knew: "The characters come out of my head. I'll never use people I know because you can't betray friendship that way."

MacLean's experience of moviemaking and his wartime experience of the Arctic combined to make *Bear Island* one of his best and most convincing thrillers. The novel also reflects another aspect of his life. He had been battling a drinking problem for a long time, and one of the most sympathetic characters is the alcoholic Lonnie Gilbert, a production manager who has taken to drink after losing his wife and children in a road accident (a common MacLean plot device for establishing the world-weariness of male characters). Lonnie, however, is a somewhat sanitized and charming alcoholic. He does not vomit, pick fights, or become abusive when drunk; he merely becomes more cynical than usual. Alcoholics in MacLean's fiction are usually sympathetic characters, unlike drug addicts, who are almost invariably portrayed as morally or physically repulsive.

By 1971 MacLean's books had sold twenty-three million copies, earning him millions of pounds. He was one of the world's highest-paid novelists. That year he told Norman, "There's Simenon, there's Agatha Christie and there's me." But he had considerable family worries. His marriage to Gisela was running into problems, and their son Lachlan was seriously ill. MacLean had initially feared that the illness might be leukemia; however, it was eventually diagnosed as a blood disorder that was not fatal but required several operations. MacLean was deeply distressed by his son's illness and often said that he would willingly give away all his money in exchange for a cure.

Around this time MacLean agreed to write a thirty-five-thousand-word pamphlet for a cancer charity, with the proceeds to go to cancer research. The subject was one on which he felt strongly. His elder brother Lachlan had died of cancer. More recently, his close friend, journalist Robert Pitman, had died slowly and painfully from the same cause. MacLean, afraid that he would be accused of writing the pamphlet for publicity or money, told Norman that he was "doing it because, in Britain alone, fifteen thousand people died unnecessarily of cancer last year." "A Layman Looks at Cancer" was never published. Cancer specialists who saw the manuscript objected to some of MacLean's conclusions and to his statement that euthanasia could be justified, "when people are grey and just vegetables."

MacLean made another venture into nonfiction in 1972. *Captain Cook* is a readable and well-researched biography, skillfully written in plain, straightforward language. In the preface he insists that the book is not meant to be a definitive biography of Cook: "A true biography is a fully-rounded portrait, but there are colours missing from my palette. I do not know enough about the man." MacLean set high standards for himself as a biographer. As a former history teacher he understood the value of historical accuracy and disliked some biographers' habit of speculating wildly about their subjects' lives rather than relying on fact. As he observes in the preface, "Extrapolation and uninspired guesses are no substitute for historical accuracy."

In 1972 MacLean divorced Gisela and married Marcelle Georgeus, a French movie executive and former actress. The wedding took place in a London registry office on 13 October 1972. The marriage was

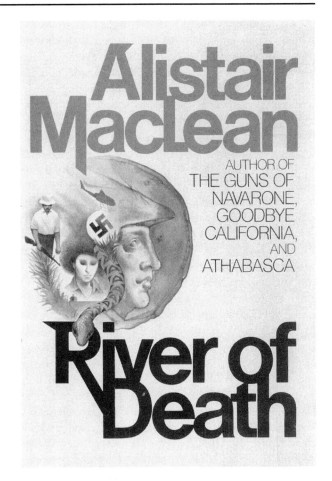

Dust jacket for the U.S. edition of MacLean's 1981 novel, about a search for Nazi gold in the Amazon jungle (Richland County Public Library)

not a happy one, and the couple separated in 1976. Soon after the marriage, MacLean began to research *The Way to Dusty Death* (1973). The title is taken from Shakespeare's *Macbeth:* "And all our yesterdays have lighted fools / The way to dusty death" (act 5, scene 5). The novel is a gripping (if implausible) tale of race fixing, sabotage, and drug smuggling among Grand Prix drivers. The hero is a British world-champion race-car driver who pretends to be an alcoholic in order to trap a gang of criminals. At first, the reader is given the impression that he is in fact an alcoholic, albeit an exceptionally clever and charming one. Inevitably, the reader feels some sympathy for the driver's friends and colleagues, who are unable to cope with his behavior. Some of them try to help, while others virtually disown him. In an early chapter MacLean reveals that the hero is in fact virtually a teetotaler and that the alcoholism is an act. At this stage the reader's sympathies switch to the hero, and the concerned friends are seen as hypocritical or misguided. In *The Way to Dusty Death* MacLean returned to writing in the third person, allowing for episodes that take place when the hero is absent, such as scenes in which other characters discuss his supposed alcoholism. The drawback, however, was the loss of the first-person narrative that had made many of his previous novels effective. MacLean's writing style in *The Way to Dusty Death* is noticeably less polished than in his previous novels written in the first person.

MacLean's friend the race-car driver Jackie Stewart gave him inside information about life on the Grand Prix circuit and might have been the model for the hero. The villain, Nicola Tracchia, was named after another of MacLean's friends, a Swiss hotelier. Planning to collaborate on a motion-picture version of *The Way to Dusty Death,* Stewart and MacLean toured Europe's Grand Prix racetracks and filmed part of the Monaco Grand Prix, but in the end their plans came to nothing, and the movie was not made.

Kastner gave MacLean the idea for his next novel, *Breakheart Pass* (1974), an historical adventure set in Nevada in 1873. Written in the third person, it features the typical MacLean action hero, transplanted to the Wild West. The story, which takes place on a snowbound train and involves smuggling and murder, is reminiscent of Christie's *Murder on the Orient Express* (1934), but the violence and cynicism in MacLean's novel are far removed from Christie's cozy, middle-class world. In 1975 *Breakheart Pass* was successfully adapted as a motion picture starring Charles Bronson.

By the time of the publication of *Breakheart Pass,* MacLean was losing his struggle with alcoholism. Kastner felt that MacLean's heavy drinking accounted for the declining quality of his later books. Webster suggests a different cause, suggesting that the falling-off dated back to "when he transposed his habits and began to think of film scripts first." As Chapman pointed out, MacLean was now "writing with the screen in mind and neglecting to build up the atmosphere and description a book requires." Screenwriter David Osborn, who worked with MacLean in the late 1960s, told Webster that MacLean's "early work showed a great sense of adventure, but he suffered a long downward slide. He was a lovable oddball with all the hallmarks of a real British eccentric." The tight plotting and stylish humor of MacLean's mid-1960s thrillers, such as *Ice Station Zebra* and *When Eight Bells Toll,* had given way to the melodramatic implausibilities of *Where Eagles Dare* and *Force 10 from Navarone,* both of which had begun life as movie scripts. Significantly, his only real return to form came in *Bear Island,* which satirizes the motion-picture industry and features movie tycoons as its villains. Whatever the cause, there is no denying that by the mid 1970s MacLean's books were steadily getting worse. Plots became more and more implausible, and the dialogue was often stilted or melodramatic.

Circus (1975) was a tale of espionage, with a circus performer as the protagonist, giving MacLean scope to describe some unlikely physical and mental acrobatics. Bruno Wildermann is a high-wire walker and trapeze artist who performs blindfolded. He has a photographic memory and is an expert in karate and judo as well as a skilled magician. This unlikely combination of skills leads to his being recruited by the CIA. MacLean strained readers' credulity even further with *The Golden Gate* (1976). An Arab oil sheikh is traveling with the president of the United States when armed criminals hijack the presidential motorcade and hold it for ransom on the Golden Gate Bridge. The book is written in the third person, and MacLean's usual dry wit is absent from the narrative, apart from one memorable passage. In front of television cameras, the president loses his temper and tells the criminal mastermind exactly what he thinks of him. His sentiments are eloquent and admirable, but his bad language costs him the next election.

By this time MacLean's second marriage was beginning to break up. He and Marcelle moved restlessly between Europe and the United States, with homes in Switzerland, California, and the south of France. Marcelle wanted to make a permanent home of California, but MacLean did not share her enthusiasm for the United States. After their separation in June 1976, he moved back to Europe. He wryly titled his next book *Goodbye California* (1977). The novel deals with a terrorist threat to cause an earthquake along the San Andreas Fault. MacLean was evidently latching on to the 1970s trend for disaster movies and novels, but he soon returned to writing straightforward thrillers. *Seawitch* (1977) is set on an oil rig and has similarities with the earlier and much better *Fear Is the Key.* MacLean's writing was becoming formulaic and repetitive, but his books continued to sell well.

Soon after MacLean's return to Europe, movie producer Peter Snell approached him with the suggestion of writing a television series. Typically self-deprecating, MacLean told Snell, "I don't know anything about television. I don't even watch it." But not long afterward, he sent Snell an eighty-seven-page novella titled "Air Force One Is Down," which he felt could be adapted for television. The story involved the hijacking of the American president's private jet and revealed some similarities with *The Golden Gate.* The novella was extended by screenwriter Burt Nodella, and the two authors agreed to collaborate on a set of outlines for television. Nodella visited MacLean in the south of France, where the work went well, but Nodella was worried about MacLean's drinking and insecurity. In his diary he noted that MacLean told him, "I write rubbish. . . . I want to write a really good book," and that he seemed obsessed with his failed first marriage. Around this time, MacLean attempted a reconciliation with Gisela. She did not want to remarry him, but the couple remained friends, and their sons divided their time between both parents.

The planned television series did not materialize. MacLean retained the rights to his outlines, but he decided not to rewrite them as novels. He employed another writer, John Denis, to novelize two outlines as *The Hostage Tower* (1980) and *Air Force One Is Down* (1981). MacLean made no pretense of having written the books, but it was easy to gain a wrong impression from the covers. His fans complained, and MacLean decided that no more novels were to be adapted from these outlines during his lifetime. With an income now reaching about £800,000 per year, he valued his reputation more than the extra money these novelizations would have brought him. Determined to make good use of his money, he became one of the founding members of the World Wildlife Fund. Through this venture he met Sir Peter Scott, founder and owner of the Slimbridge Wildfowl Sanctuary, on the Severn River between Gloucester and Bristol. MacLean hoped to write a biography of Scott's father, Antarctic explorer Robert Falcon Scott. Scott promised him unrestricted access to the family archives, but MacLean never completed the project.

In 1978 MacLean and his secretary, Sabrina Carver, visited Yugoslavia to research a wartime adventure novel. MacLean was impressed with Dubrovnik and bought a flat there. He became involved in local life and contributed large sums to Yugoslav charities. He spent eight months of each year in Dubrovnik until his death in 1987. During the other four months MacLean spent time with Gisela and his sons and enjoyed trips to India, Peru, and Brazil, conducting research for future novels. Carver was initially concerned by his failure to take notes on these trips, but when he began writing, she was amazed at his powers of memory.

MacLean's next novel, *Athabasca* (1980), is about an attempt by saboteurs to destroy an Alaskan oil pipeline. He had researched the novel meticulously–perhaps too meticulously. The result is so bogged down with technical detail as to be almost unreadable in parts. *River of Death* (1981) concerns a search for stolen Nazi gold in modern South America. MacLean included moving descriptions of the plight of the Amazonian Indians, threatened by Western greed and deforestation. *Partisans* (1982), the result of MacLean's research in Yugoslavia, is a tale of World War II espionage. Like *The Guns of Navarone,* it features a group of agents on a special mission, and like *Where Eagles Dare,* it involves double agents and false identity.

Floodgate (1983) is set in the Netherlands and features a dramatic opening, in which a gang of terrorists floods Schiphol Airport in Amsterdam. MacLean was again following the fashion for disaster novels, but the book also displays a strong detective element. It reintroduces one of the minor characters from *Puppet on a Chain,*

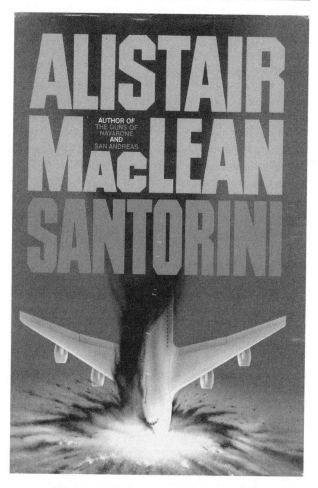

Dust jacket for the U.S. edition of MacLean's last published novel (1986), in which a British naval officer must locate a nuclear bomb-laden airplane that has crashed into the ocean and come to rest on an underwater volcano (Richland County Public Library)

Colonel van de Graaf, the Amsterdam chief of police. The protagonist, Peter van Effen, is a senior police detective who goes undercover to infiltrate a terrorist group. *Floodgate* also features two typical MacLean heroines, van Effen's sister Julie and his colleague Anne Meijer. Young and beautiful, they are kidnapped by the terrorists. Despite the fact that Meijer is supposedly a top-grade undercover agent, the women make no attempt to escape but wait passively to be rescued by van Effen.

In 1983 Glasgow University awarded MacLean an honorary doctorate. Some academics and literary figures felt that his writing did not qualify him for this degree, but the university overruled their objections. Reporting on the ceremony, *The Scotsman* of 16 June 1983 noted that MacLean's novels had been translated into seventeen languages and that at least sixteen of his books had sold more than one million copies. Ever modest, MacLean was convinced that he did not deserve the honor, and he made it clear that he did not want to be known as "Dr. MacLean." He told *The Glasgow Herald,* "I saw no reason why I should have been chosen. I could not believe it." In a letter accepting the degree, MacLean joked that in the Royal Navy, "even a ranker can be awarded a Good Conduct Medal for 21 years of undiscovered crime." The university's response was that the degree was not a mere reward for "good conduct" but was offered in recognition of "a formidable talent to amuse, in the best sense of that term."

MacLean returned to familiar territory in 1984 with *San Andreas,* another novel about the Arctic convoys in World War II. The *San Andreas* is a hospital ship with saboteurs on board and German U-boats in hot pursuit. Gripping and fast-paced though the book is, it lacks the realism of *H.M.S. Ulysses,* and the main characters are thinly drawn and unconvincing compared to those in MacLean's earlier work. *San Andreas* was followed by an anthology of MacLean's short stories, *The Lonely Sea: Collected Short Stories* (1985). The collection included an interesting postscript, an article in which MacLean discussed his career. Originally written for *The Glasgow Herald* in 1982, the article opens with his tribute to that newspaper for launching his career twenty-seven years earlier. "During those twenty-seven years," he continues, "I have written twenty-seven books, fourteen screenplays and numerous magazine and newspaper articles. It has been, and remains, a fair enough way of earning a living."

On 16 May 1985 MacLean's estranged second wife, Marcelle, died of cancer at age fifty. Although they had been on bad terms for many years, MacLean paid for her funeral. By this time his own health was failing. His eyesight was deteriorating, he was diabetic, and he regularly forgot to take his insulin. His family was concerned about him, but, as he lived alone, there was little they could do.

MacLean's last novel, *Santorini* (1986), is set in the Aegean Sea. In one of MacLean's most extravagant plots, a plane carrying nuclear bombs crashes into the sea, coming to rest above a quiescent volcano that is on a tectonic fault. The hero must prevent what another character describes as "the combined and simultaneous effects of a massive thermo-nuclear detonation, a volcanic eruption and an earthquake." The protagonist is a naval officer, and much of the action takes place on board a NATO frigate, giving MacLean scope to display his knowledge of seafaring.

In January 1987 MacLean suffered a series of strokes and collapsed while on a visit to Munich. Although he was immediately rushed to a hospital, nothing could be done to save him. He died on 2 February 1987 and was buried near Gisela's home in Celigny.

MacLean left four book outlines that were completed after his death. *Alistair MacLean's Death Train* (1989), *Alistair MacLean's Night Watch* (1989), *Alistair MacLean's Red Alert* (1990), and *Alistair MacLean's Time of the Assassins* (1991) were based on the plots he had created for Snell's proposed television series in the 1970s. MacLean's obituary in *The Scotsman* described him as "the most successful Scottish novelist since the Second World War" and summed up his achievement: "he wrote books to make air journeys tolerable and to take people out of themselves for a few hours. He did it very well . . . he gave countless hours of pleasure to millions of people. There are worse epitaphs."

Interview:

Barry Norman, "The Best-selling Sceptic," *Observer* (London), 5 September 1971, color supplement.

Biography:

Jack Webster, *Alistair MacLean: A Life* (London: Chapmans, 1991).

Reference:

John Sutherland, "Alistair MacLean and James Clavell," in his *Bestsellers: Popular Fiction of the 1970s* (London & Boston: Routledge & Kegan Paul, 1981), pp. 96–107.

James McClure

(9 October 1939 –)

Andrew F. Macdonald
Loyola University, New Orleans

and

Gina Macdonald
Nicholls State University

BOOKS: *The Steam Pig* (London: Gollancz, 1971; New York: Harper & Row, 1972);

The Caterpillar Cop (London: Gollancz, 1972; New York: Harper & Row, 1973);

Four and Twenty Virgins (London: Gollancz, 1973);

The Gooseberry Fool (London: Gollancz, 1974; New York: Harper & Row, 1974);

Snake (London: Gollancz, 1975; New York: Harper & Row, 1976);

Killers (London: Fontana, 1976);

Rogue Eagle (London: Macmillan, 1976; New York: Harper & Row, 1976);

The Sunday Hangman (London: Macmillan, 1977; New York: Harper & Row, 1977);

The Blood of an Englishman (London: Macmillan, 1980; New York: Harper & Row, 1980);

Spike Island: Portrait of a Police Division (London: Macmillan, 1980; New York: Pantheon, 1980);

The Artful Egg (London: Macmillan, 1984; New York: Pantheon, 1985);

Cop World: Policing the Streets of San Diego (London: Macmillan, 1984); republished as *Cop World: Inside an American Police Force* (New York: Pantheon, 1984);

Imago: A Modern Comedy of Manners (New York: Penzler, 1988);

The Song Dog (London: Faber & Faber, 1991; New York: Mysterious Press, 1991).

OTHER: "Scandal at Sandkop," in *Winter's Crimes 7,* edited by George Hardinge (London: Macmillan, 1975);

"Book One: To Be Continued" and "Corella of the 87th," in *Murder Ink: The Mystery Reader's Companion,* edited by Dilys Winn (New York: Workman, 1977).

James McClure (photograph by George Resetzer; from the dust jacket for the U.S. edition of The Song Dog, *1991)*

British colonialism in Africa provided a rich field for detective fiction on the African scene, an inevitable result of the collisions of different races and cultures that raised questions of crime, punishment, justice, and injustice as filtered through dramatically different perceptions. With books such as *Murder on Safari* (1938), Elspeth Huxley provides early versions of colonial and native interaction, while Stuart Jackman and Brian Cleeve explore the nasty side of colonialism and apartheid in spy novels characterized by violence and brutality and dreadful scenes of the dehumanization of African natives. Employing an ancient Egyptian setting, Lynda Robinson makes her detective the ancient lord chief investigator for Pharaoh Tutankhamen, and P. C. Doherty makes his the chief judge in Thebes. Elizabeth Peters places her Victorian archaeological detective team in Egypt, and Michael Pearce follows the investigations of the British head of Cairo's criminal-investigation department. Karin McQuillan traces the adventures of an American safari guide, while Lawrence Sanders's amateur detective Peter Tangent troubleshoots for an American oil company in Africa. Against the artificiality of such mysteries trading on an exotic and fashionable locale, some of the plots of which could, in fact, have been set anywhere, the detective stories of James McClure provide a sociological, political, and humanistic examination of the injustices of apartheid. McClure's fiction could not be set anywhere but South Africa in the days of formal racial segregation. His plot premises arise out of the particular conundrums that racial separation created, and his biracial investigative team must tread a wary path through the minefields of a country in which four mutually antagonistic cultures—Afrikaner, Bantu, English, and mixed race—attempt to coexist while speaking to each other in at least three languages. Although witty and often humorous, McClure's mysteries plainly exhibit the degradation of people based on color, a recurring theme tightly integrated into his plots and settings.

Like Arthur Upfield, H. R. F. Keating, and Tony Hillerman, McClure employs the detective genre to contrast a colonialist culture with the native culture it dominates: a Western, individual-based technological society with a non-Western, nontechnological tribal- and community-centered society. McClure's depiction of the confrontation between a modern, European culture with an ancient tribal one is unique in its even-handedness, a quality few of his predecessors have been able to achieve; colonial perspectives dominate in most of the European writers who wrote about Africa. McClure, a native South African, manages to give each side its due while never shrinking from dramatizing the brutality and absurdity of the racial system. In doing so, he raises questions about identity, ethnicity, government-imposed segregation and isolation, linguistic hegemony, and marginalization.

McClure's police procedurals mainly play off British against Afrikaner and Afrikaner against Zulu/Bantu, although East Indians and other "colored" people move in and out of the plot. The books communicate details of daily life that make readers feel they really know the amazing mix of people, the land against which they struggle, and the cultures that mold them all too well. McClure teams Afrikaner Tromp Kramer with Zulu Mickey Zondi, a detective duo whose discovery of commonalities and growing respect for each other's intelligence, amid a culture whose deep-seated racial and ethnic biases condemn such friendship, challenge the premises of apartheid. Through character, incident, and situation, McClure captures the inhumanity of systems that reject one segment of their population as inferior and apply the "one drop of blood" rule of racial categorization with insidious intent and dehumanizing effect. Critics have compared McClure's crime fiction in sociological and humanistic importance to the works of Alan Paton, Nadine Gordimer, and André Brink. Unlike those authors, however, McClure finds shared humor a contrast to human absurdity; amid his bleakest, most horrific scenes he always infuses some comedic lightness to counter the darkness. In that way his writing is closer to the native African oral tradition of humor amid hardship. His works, although written in English and exploiting the European police-procedural genre, blend colonial heritage and South African joie de vivre. They remain optimistic, infused with the glorious landscape and the bright yellow sunlight of the continent, even as they describe appalling crimes. McClure's works brought a freshness and newness to a sometimes tired genre and paved the way for the wealth of cross-cultural detective novels that followed in the 1980s and 1990s. They reflect the deep-seated humanism of their creator.

Born James Howe McClure in Johannesburg, South Africa, on 9 October 1939 to British parents, army officer James Howe McClure and Isabella Cochrane McClure, from an early age he learned to look back to an England he had never lived in as "home," to identify birds from there, and to see English values as his own. At the same time, he has childhood memories of listening with pleasure and shared amusement to Zulu men digging ditches and singing comic and ironic descriptions of the whites who walked along the pavement next to them. McClure attended school in Pietermaritzburg, Natal: Scottsville School from 1947 to 1951, Cowan House from 1952 to 1954, and Maritzburg College from 1955 to 1958. Upon graduation he worked as a commercial photographer until he obtained a position in 1959 as a teacher of English and art at a boys' preparatory school in Pietermaritzburg, where he worked until 1963. On 6 January 1962 he married Lorellee Ellis. They have two sons and one daughter: James Howe, Alistair Francis, and Kirsten Anne. McClure next worked as a reporter, first for *The Natal Witness* from 1963 to 1964, then for *The Natal Mercury* from 1964 to 1965, and finally for *The Daily News*

(Natal) in 1965. His job as a crime reporter and his acquaintance with local police gave him access to the Pietermaritzburg townships that he would not have had otherwise. There he learned that a South African police officer could get away with a great deal that would never be permitted elsewhere, but he also came to understand that the apartheid laws and the pass laws were evil and not the police, who, by and large, acted to protect the interests and properties of black complainants against black criminals.

McClure reports that by 1965 he had simply seen too much and could not determine how to continue living in South Africa without seeming to condone acts and attitudes of apartheid that repulsed him. He loved the beauty of the country and the excitement of his work, but as a crime reporter he had a much broader experience with a cross-section of people than did most citizens, and what he saw and experienced became more and more unbearable. Consequently, McClure and his family moved to Edinburgh, Scotland, the five of them living in a two-room flat until he could reestablish himself in this familiar, yet new, country. He became a subeditor for the *Daily Mail,* working there from 1965 to 1966, and then moved to Oxford, where he worked as subeditor of the *Oxford Mail* for three years and then as deputy editor for the Oxford Times Group from 1969 to 1974. When he first moved to England, McClure voted for Labour Party candidates but was put off by the failure of the party to do anything about suffering working-class citizens; instead, he felt they were simply riding their hobbyhorses into Parliament. He told interviewer Sarah Nuttall in 1994 that he did not become a conservative, but he did become cynical about British politics.

While in Oxford, McClure turned to crime fiction as a means of channeling the anger he had experienced in South Africa. He had been searching for the right medium, and reading the books of black American author Chester Himes (one of his personal favorites) made him realize the potential of the crime-fiction genre, particularly its broad scope. Police detectives have access to every level of society and can cross social, racial, and economic barriers otherwise closed to most South Africans. Thus, McClure deliberately set out to make real his experiences and understandings in a manner that would reach a wide audience and give him scope to explore what was hidden. He asserts that his books are each "about something that is uniquely South African," often something that generates anger in the black population. Yet, at the same time, he sees himself as basically an entertainer, hoping to win a good laugh and to keep readers interested so that he can "punch home" what he wants to get across.

Dust jacket for the U.S. edition of McClure's first novel (1971), which introduces his series characters: South African police detectives Tromp Kramer and Mickey Zondi (Richland County Public Library)

When McClure wrote *The Steam Pig* (1971), he toyed with the opening sentence for some time and then just began typing, not thinking about plot or order but just letting his ideas flow. He typed for two weeks right through to the end, put the typescript in the mail to the publishers, and ended up receiving the Crime Writers' Association's Gold Dagger Award as a result. This writing pattern has varied, however, according to the situation. McClure recalls one instance later in his career when he went through more than sixty rewrites of the same page until he got it the way he wanted it.

The Steam Pig introduced McClure's two key series detectives. Through the growing respect and affection that his Afrikaner detective develops for his Bantu partner, McClure demonstrates the racial split that he personally witnessed time after time on the reporter's beat in South Africa, a pattern that both horrified and offered hope of change. South African policeman Tromp Kramer, a tall, blonde, broad-shouldered Afrikaner, the son of a farmer from a dorp (village) in the Orange Free State, is brutal, heavy-handed, and crude, and yet somehow likable. Kramer secretly shares the opinion of the Kalahari bushmen that shelter and clothing are less important than food, believing that "a man's duty was to invest his labors in his belly so to labor again." His response to the city of Durban tells readers much about him:

> Durban had never appealed to Kramer. She was not his kind of city. He liked his women to be big and strong and primitive, yes; but also dignified and clean. Durban was a whore.
>
> A cheap whore, who sprawled lush, legs agape at the harbor mouth, beside the warm Indian ocean, which was not a sea but a favor that she sold.

Kramer is drawn from the prejudices and attitudes of policemen McClure encountered as a journalist. Kramer's Bantu assistant, Mickey Zondi, who is fluent in three languages and has the ability of total recall common to those raised in an oral tradition, knows when to shuffle and play the subservient native fool faced with a white "boss" and when to share with Kramer his complex understanding of motives and acts. Kramer is a bachelor, whose deepening relationship with the Widow Fourie and her children is occasionally offset by sexual attractions elsewhere. Zondi, in contrast, is a happily married man, proud of his wife, Miriam, and concerned for the future of his intelligent, curious children. He regularly skimps to bring them a map, an atlas, or a reference book that they can study together.

Zondi and Kramer share a curiosity and an urge to discover patterns and relationships in the world around them, qualities that make them good detectives. Both are tough-minded in their approach to criminals, in one case tacitly letting a would-be murderer electrocute himself when he lifts his weapon to shoot them. Zondi is clever and competent, but on occasion he forgets the lessons of his rural youth, such as the need to travel with two hardwood sticks, one for fending off blows and one for striking. His lack of these sticks on a cross-country trek makes fellow Bantus suspect that he is a government spy. Kramer, for all his inspiration and insights into the criminal mind, at times misunderstands English phrasing, once mistaking "sabbatical" for "Sabbath." McClure typically refers to the detective's method with a touch of cynicism: "Kramer made a number of astute deductions based on obscure references—perception being relative, too."

Though the "neutrality" of the police genre constituted much of its initial appeal for McClure, from the beginning of his series he has brought to life through character and action the bitterness, the hatreds, and the moral consequences of apartheid. *The Steam Pig* is a powerful expression of the distortions created by racist

government policies. Kramer and Zondi have developed elaborate public facades to avoid demonstrating politically inappropriate sympathy between white and black, though in private Zondi is clearly a professional and his partner's equal. Zondi comes at crime from a different perspective, understands the responses of the native communities, and can intimidate natives in ways that Kramer never can. The normal give-and-take of friends and colleagues on a case together would be interpreted as "cheekiness" on Zondi's part and abnormality on Kramer's part. Thus, when Zondi is caught recumbent in Kramer's office, Kramer must explain, "My boy's sick," and when Zondi is badly injured, Kramer must stifle his desire to rush to his aid. He knows enough about his fellow Afrikaners to disguise his concern behind racist comments about inherent laziness or mental denseness and the need to patch Zondi up in order to get him back in the field. When Zondi recounts events, he does it the Zulu way, beginning at the beginning, explaining eating patterns and other irrelevant details, giving no additional weight to particulars until he arrives at the chronological moment at which their significance becomes apparent. This oral storytelling pattern provides Kramer with an opportunity to feign impatience, though beneath his rough exterior he is clearly proud of Zondi's powers of observation and courage. Anyone who has experienced a truly cross-cultural friendship will recognize the dynamics that bond this pair, the sense of difference that intrigues but sometimes frustrates, the need to justify to conventional observers just what is appealing about someone so different. In the 1994 interview with Nuttall, McClure talked about the realities that inspired his creation of this pair. He said he never saw blacks sitting in the fronts of cars except in the police force, where "blacks and whites were very much closer," having bonded to such a degree that because a lot of Afrikaners took a pride in speaking Zulu, "it was almost effeminate not to, it was sissy not to be able to speak Zulu. Puts a funny twist on it, doesn't it?"

Everything is distorted, shaded, or touched by race, and all of Kramer's cases throughout the Kramer-Zondi series from the first are either race driven or racially tinged. One Afrikaner colonel tells Kramer, "I never allow a wog to touch my delphiniums," and another, in a later novel, asks Kramer, "How many coons do you know that have ever even dreamed of so much money coming their way?" Kramer replies with irony, "Oh, I think they all dream." In *The Steam Pig,* upon an emergency trip to the hospital, the fair-skinned father of a white family is reclassified as black because of something that shows up in his blood tests, and the family members, who have led privileged lives, are plunged into the nightmare of their new identity, one where college and professions are no longer options, and they live in fear with no hopes for the future. A reviewer of *The Steam Pig* in *TLS: The Times Literary Supplement* asserted, "Any white fool in South Africa could enjoy it [this novel] and see nothing subversive in it at all," a criticism McClure takes with a grain of salt since "books just find their level." If readers miss the implicit ironies, it just means that the books are "reasonably truthful." A Swedish reviewer called the novel "a searing indictment of apartheid."

The Caterpillar Cop (1972) begins with an amusing seduction scene involving a tennis star and a groupie, one that turns grim when the couple find they are sharing the bushes with a castrated corpse, a youth ritually mutilated with a sickle. A search for a Land Rover that Kramer spotted leaving the area leads to blood on a jacket sleeve and a knowledgeable ecologist who applies his understanding of nature to assist with the case and prove premeditation. Further investigation reveals that the boy was a member of a South African detective club and, like members of the Hitler Youth, took admonitions to be on guard against violations of the apartheid rules seriously, spying on his neighbors to expose liberals and harassing black workers by checking their passbooks and their rooms at night. The case eventually turns on a difference in meaning between Afrikaans and English. When events come to a head, Kramer saves Zondi's life by killing an ax-wielding, maniacal witch doctor but arranges the scene to look as if a fellow Bantu had somehow speared the villain. In that way, as a white man, Kramer appears to be uninvolved in black violence.

In 1973 McClure tried another creative direction with the novel *Four and Twenty Virgins,* set in England. The story postulates a secret vigilante group of conservatives with visions of reforming English politics, returning England to the English by clamping down on immigration, and setting the country back on a right-wing course. An unplanned execution, however, produces such violent infighting that the plan is short-lived. *Four and Twenty Virgins* simply does not have the driving force and humanistic power of the novels in the Kramer-Zondi series, and McClure, realizing that fact, returned to the series.

The Gooseberry Fool (1974) opens with the graphically described brutal murder of a seemingly upright churchgoer and teetotaler. As Zondi tracks a suspect, the novel meticulously describes the human cost of "black spot" evictions, in which whole black villages are ripped up, their citizens transported to seemingly uninhabitable new tent towns in "homelands," a euphemism for land without water, food, or humanizing amenities. Whereas before they had a hard land "that gave nothing for nothing," "a good place for puff adders and lizards," now they have bedrock on which nothing grows. A mob of angry adults

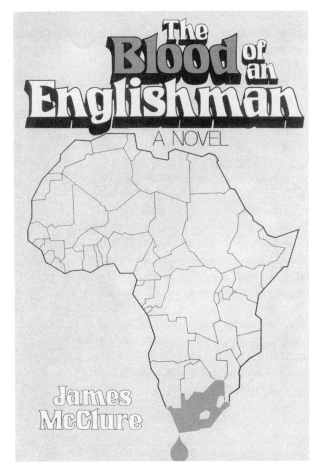

Dust jacket for the U.S. edition of McClure's 1980 Kramer and Zondi novel (Richland County Public Library)

evicted from their homes by the white security forces riots in the streets, chasing Zondi with murderous intent because he has let the children into the food stores, forgetting that in their hunger they will eat all and leave nothing for future meals. When Zondi is hospitalized after this mob scene, Kramer must keep his fears for his friend's recovery hidden if he is to function effectively as a superior officer. Eventually, Kramer learns that the murdered man was a government spy ferreting out liberals among his Catholic congregation. In *The Gooseberry Fool,* as in the rest of the series, McClure shows insight into cultural distinctions that, though seemingly minor, represent a world of difference in perceptual understanding. Zondi, seeking confirmation of the time period when a criminal passed through a village, realizes that the villager he interviews "had lived all her life without knowing that time was divisible, like a bowl of porridge between her children, into a number of small and exact parts," and that he must therefore seek other means to measure time.

In 1974, on his first trip back to South Africa in ten years, McClure found that he had put out of his mind the degree of social restrictions and thus failed to obtain a permit to visit a friend in Sobantu, a slip that could have caused much trouble for his friend. At this time the success of his detective series enabled McClure to work full-time as a writer, and his visit to South Africa renewed the sense of outrage that fuels his books.

McClure's *Snake* (1975) features two crimes, one white, one black. A Trekkersburg nightclub performer with a reputation for teasing suitors about their manhood is found strangled, supposedly by her pet python. When an autopsy on the snake reveals a broken back, however, it is clear that the creature was a murder weapon, not a killer. The second investigation concerns a series of robbery-murders, but the extortionist protection racket that seems to motivate them proves a false trail. When Kramer finally tracks down the real killer, his life depends on Zondi's wit and shooting expertise. Kramer's relationship with the Widow Fourie is at first somewhat rocky in this story because of a psychiatrist who blames her son's surly behavior on an Oedipal complex, but when Kramer buys the widow a house large enough for the boy to have his own room and teaches him to use a rifle, complexes go out the window, and Kramer finds himself more tightly bound to the widow's family than ever before. Heartbreaking tales of apartheid are as inseparable a part of the background of *Snake* as they are of McClure's other series novels. A Bantu teacher and class, for example, are turned away from a nearly empty museum theater because of the fine print that designates it "Whites Only." A black-white criminal partnership thrives because investigators are blind to the possibility of a cross-racial alliance, a racially forbidden mother-son relationship.

McClure once again departed from his detective series pattern to write *Rogue Eagle* (1976), a tale of espionage, terrorism, and political obsession that received the Silver Dagger Award from the Crime Writers' Association. The spy team of this novel is an unlikely pair. Nancy Kitson is a stunningly beautiful socialite who covers her low-level CIA assignments with the patter of a wide-eyed innocent, while Finbar Buchanan, a Scots secret agent formerly stationed in Saigon, plays a deadly game against Boer terrorists while posing as a carefree photojournalist doing human-interest stories in remote villages. The setting is Lesotho, the home of the Basotho people, a racially and culturally "liberal" island in the western center of South Africa, but some of the participants are from nearby Rhodesia, and the terrorist plot begins there. The villains are members of the Broederbond (Brotherhood), a real and powerful secret Afrikaner society that often operated as a shadow government for South Africa. In 1944, Jan Smuts, then the South African prime minister, had banned this white racist brotherhood as a "dangerous," "fascist" organization. (McClure provides a history of the Boers, their historical reasons for hating the British, and their pro-

Nazi sympathies and attitudes.) The novel begins with the initiation of one of the villains into the group by plunging a dagger into a form draped with a black shroud embroidered with the word "Treason." For Americans, the images are reminiscent of Ku Klux Klan rallies and lynchings. In fact, hatred of blacks lies at the heart of the Broederbond and their terrorist plot to assassinate the prime minister of Lesotho and to blame the wholesale butchery of tribesmen on extremist black groups.

The success of these novels provided McClure with more freedom of choice about his journalism than ever before. In 1976 he became the managing editor of Sabena Gakulu, a publishing business that he runs out of his home, and he has continued in this position ever since.

The Sunday Hangman (1977) marks a return to the Kramer-Zondi series. An amateur who seems to have insider knowledge of the art of hanging as practiced in South Africa is killing off victims as if he were an official executioner. The novel begins with the point of view of a black victim, a longtime offender who thinks he has had a blackout but recognizes the signs of an official execution and then shifts to the point of view of the police, who initially believe they are investigating a suicide. Once they have evidence that the hangings are murders, not suicides or accidents, they seem to have a limited number of suspects since South Africa bans distribution of any information concerning the techniques of state executions (techniques based on the British method of hanging). Since the murdered victims are people whose criminal acts were not punished by the courts, the detectives can narrow their search even more. Kramer is bothered by what he sees as the softness and laxity of Durban, and Zondi recognizes the glossiness of skin that indicates good food consumed regularly in quantity and attitudes unusual and "inappropriate" in native servants. Zondi is suffering from a bullet wound that has been slow to heal, but this does not keep him from active investigation. He is entrusted with information about a stolen child that no one else could pry out of the locals. McClure's novels cover a range of South African topics, but his descriptions of racial relationships and the language and restraints of apartheid, which made (and still make) them so shocking for outside readers, made them seem realistic to South Africans. Surprisingly, *The Sunday Hangman* is the only one of McClure's novels to be banned in South Africa, and even then it was not banned because of its controversial depiction of black-white relationships but instead because government censors found the detailed description of prisons and official hangings too realistic and accurate.

In both *The Sunday Hangman* and the novel that followed it, *The Blood of an Englishman* (1980), a pathologist and his assistant (recurring series figures) who are Holocaust deniers have plans to find identifying components that will enable them to distinguish the red blood of a

black man from that of a white man, a difference they assume must exist, and the discovery of which they further assume will be of great scientific value. In the latter novel Zondi asks Kramer, "When will you learn that a black child is only seven years old when he stops wondering at the ways of white persons?"

In *The Blood of an Englishman* separate investigations of two violent murders dovetail, both tied to blackmail, fake war stories, and English-Afrikaner wartime enmities. Kramer must deal privately with a wartime murder his own father committed (with justification), and Zondi must play dead in order to catch a crafty killer. The novel captures the complexities of human behavior and of justice, as well as the redeeming power of man's ability to laugh at his own absurdity.

The same year that *The Blood of an Englishman* was published, McClure also published a documentary-style study of a real-life police department in Liverpool, England, titled *Spike Island: Portrait of a Police Division* (1980). In a review of this book crime novelist P. D. James argues that McClure "shows us the truth of a policeman's job through the eyes of the men and women who actually do it, and in their own words," in "1,417 blighted acres of tough, humorous, rambunctious lawlessness in the heart of Liverpool." Yet, argue both James and McClure, the job has "more to do with human inadequacy, frailty and failure than with positive evil" and requires "dedication and compassion, cunning and guile as much as courage and physical strength." Most of all it requires "a measure of detachment since, without this saving armor, one suspects that a policeman in an inner-city area might break his heart." James writes that McClure makes readers experience "the challenge, the humor, boredom, dangers and fascination" of being a policeman. In doing so he makes his book more than just a sociological report. James calls it "a book about ourselves, about the society we have created, and about the precariousness of the bridges we have so painfully erected over the chasm of poverty and crime."

McClure followed his close examination of the Liverpool police force with a similar study, *Cop World: Policing the Streets of San Diego* (1984). He was particularly impressed with the progressive nature of the police department in the California city. His cinematic style in the book consists of quick takes of street policing and terse chapters that create the suspense one expects in a police-procedural mystery, an approach that has led critics to compare his writing in *Cop World* to that of Joseph Wambaugh. Throughout his writing career McClure has never sought to produce grim sociological tracts, though his details have often been grim and realistic. Instead, he strives for a complex mixture of cultures, tones, and psychologies. Thus, his police nonfiction is as much a mix of good humor and realism as are his South African mysteries.

Dust jacket for the U.S. edition of McClure's 1991 novel, a flashback to the 1962 murder case that brought Kramer and Zondi together as partners (Richland County Public Library)

In the mysteries, McClure tempers the dark side of apartheid with the daily give-and-take of likable human beings. Kramer's earthy Afrikaner humor matches that of Zondi, and Zondi's understated Zulu humor humanizes him and his people in a way that lectures about oppressed humanity never could. In *The Sunday Hangman* he falls down and feigns injury in order to induce some children to feel comfortable enough to talk to him, and then he flirts outrageously with a large woman laundering clothes in a river, exchanging bawdy comments in order to win the confidence of the group of washerwomen. To a fellow Zulu's conversational gambit that a mutual acquaintance spoke of him with great respect, Zondi replies in a tongue-in-cheek, self-effacing manner—"I do not remember that he owed me money"—and the two share a hearty laugh. When terrified to board a helicopter for his first ride and taunted by Kramer—"afraid to fly . . . ? You, a bloody Zulu warrior, the bravest of the brave, scaring everyone shitless in your monkey skins and snazzy leopard trimmings, hey?"—Zondi replies with aplomb: "The

Lieutenant has placed his finger *right* on the problem, boss! As he can see, I am simply not dressed for the occasion."

Despite such comedy and even slapstick humor throughout his detective series, McClure is at his most humorous in *The Artful Egg* (1984). Published between his two nonfiction works, the novel mines the riches of African and European humor. The ingenuousness of rural people with urban jobs is touching and funny, as when a gardener asserts, "I am a Presbyterian, which protects me from ignorant superstition." *The Artful Egg* is more playful than any of McClure's other novels. In his 1994 interview with Nuttall, McClure said that he never believed in the books by Gordimer and J. M. Coetzee because they preached to the converted, and in this novel he takes on such writers. He is particularly put off by Gordimer's lack of a sense of humor. Hence, the death of a famous author noted for her social realism and for her brave stance against apartheid (her books capture the day-to-day realities of Bantu life) provides McClure with an opportunity to investigate the hypocrisy of her stance. Kramer discovers that the author's preference for sleeping comfortably on a bed was what generated an empathetic response when she toured native areas. In *The Artful Egg* McClure suggests that a writer who misses the humor that helps the natives survive their deplorable conditions and even more deplorable treatment has missed the human heart of her subjects.

In proof of this proposition, McClure sets grim facts against playful interracial encounters. Kramer takes joy in pulling over a rich Englishman in a pale-green safari suit for using the change of a red light to green as an excuse not to pay a poor newspaper seller whose paper he has taken. McClure sets a less competent racially mixed team in competition with McClure and Zondi. The Bantu detective of this team has persuaded his white partner that he cannot drive safely and then brags to his fellow Bantus about his "pink" chauffeur. Through the same team McClure also parallels Bantu and Afrikaner cruelty, with one native detective enjoying an interrogation carried out after dark "well away from squeamish people" in a lively, uninhibited way and then planning on dropping a powerful aphrodisiac into his arrogant white partner's drink in order to discredit him. Zondi takes advantage of whites' inability to distinguish between natives in order to misdirect this other team and bring down the wrath of the superintendent on them. McClure has fun with Zondi's ability to imitate the verbal style of the most rural and bigoted Afrikaner police officers. At the same time, Zondi has his first encounters with white liberals, who see him as a fellow human being.

Between the two final novels in the Kramer-Zondi series McClure turned to lighter fare, publishing *Imago: A Modern Comedy of Manners* (1988). Set in England, it is a funny, poignant story of a man in his forties falling in love with a teenager, understanding the absurdity of the relationship but unable to stop himself.

The Song Dog (1991) is a prequel to the Kramer-Zondi series. Set in 1962, the novel presents the murder case that brought Lieutenant Tromp Kramer and Sergeant Mickey Zondi together and introduced them to Widow Fourie and Miriam. McClure worked on *The Song Dog* for thirteen months in the evenings, after his regular workday. His goal was to minimize and compress his vision into a tightly focused unit that would make the unfamiliar familiar to his readers and make them recognize basic human realities. Such tightness is the signature of a McClure novel. Plot, character, and setting come tumbling at the reader nonstop, with no wasted words and little explanatory apparatus, a real achievement given the wealth of background material necessary for a setting alien to most readers of English. In *The Song Dog* Kramer has gone to a backwater town in Zululand to investigate an unusual pair of deaths caused by the dynamiting of an isolated home. The victims are a respected police officer and the licentious young wife of a noted local hunter. Kramer is initially uncertain whether the husband was the intended target or the perpetrator (acting out of jealousy), nor whether the policeman came to the house in the course of his duties or to carry on a clandestine affair. The local police and medical staff seem incompetent and out of their league, unsure of how to protect the scene of the crime from contamination and how to conduct an investigative autopsy that will hold up in court. In the process of his investigation Kramer observes an odd Zulu who always seems to be in the background, with matchsticks in his earlobes, an inside-out coat, and eyes and manner too sharp not to be suspect. The man Kramer suspects of criminal involvement is, of course, Zondi, on the scene to carry out an investigation of his own. He is tracking down a native killer from the area, his own cousin. Zondi later tells Kramer (after saving his life), "I would prefer to kill Mslope myself. . . . There would be some dignity in such a death, which would greatly benefit the spirits of our ancestors." The dynamics between the disgruntled and wary Kramer and the clever, intelligent Zondi suggest the commonalities of competence and intuitive understanding of the criminal mind that make them such a formidable team. At the same time, the image of cane cutters—always in the background, "blacker than black, hooded by their sacks, long knives motionless, watching him drive by, just the whites of their eyes showing"—suggests how much Kramer needs a partner such as Zondi, who can bridge the gap between the worlds of whites and blacks and draw on native resources forever closed to Kramer. Zondi consults a local witch in the traditional manner, crawling into her secret abode in a scene that captures the power of tribal religion and oracle-like pronouncements; he thereby gains information vital to the case and to finding his cousin's hiding spot.

McClure says that in *The Song Dog* he intentionally made Kramer more "uncouth," "much more Afrikaner and hard-line in some ways" than he is in the other novels because he is not supposed to have been in Natal long enough to have been changed by the experience. At one point Kramer says, "The only thing that's fair about me is the color of my hair," adding, "People should remember that." From the beginning of the novel he suspects the husband because of his too-perfect British good looks and superior manner. Kramer calls the South Africans of British descent "a race apart" and becomes angry at the names he knows they call Afrikaners. Ultimately, the murderer turns out to be someone quite different from Kramer's despised suspect, and, again, Zondi must come to Kramer's rescue. McClure calls *The Song Dog* the alpha and omega of the series because it explains how the team began and is the final book in the series. The novel ends with the Song Dog witch's cryptic predictions of a future that readers of the earlier books in the series might recognize.

McClure was in the right place at the right time to produce a detective series that will endure, both for historical and modern reasons. Character and plot arise out of the milieu. McClure's books are unthinkable in any other locale, even though overt discussion of apartheid as a theme is avoided. His works are possibly the best examples of multiethnic, multicultural detective novels in English. They are primers on purely South African psychological states, emotional responses, and even crimes involving black Africans, Afrikaners, the English, and "colored" or mixed-race peoples. The choice of an Afrikaner-Zulu police-detective team is inspired; it is the only credible way for McClure to move characters out of their racially prescribed neighborhoods to cross between the four state-designated racial categories. Thus, readers meet Asian shopkeepers, Indian postal officers, Zulu farmhands, Afrikaner farmers, coloreds passing for white, intensely committed English reformers, and English-hating Boers. In 1996 McClure reported that he hears distinctive voices and cadences as he re-creates in his mind the speech patterns of specific character types. Ultimately, character drives plot as McClure explores the complicated relationships and mix of feelings that make the twists of plot inevitable.

Although he was raised in a British commonwealth and lives and works in England, McClure's detective fiction shares far more with the American hard-boiled genre than with cozy English mysteries. His South African mysteries and spy stories provide a harsh look at either the literal frontier or the urban areas where frontier values still prevail. His milieu is the opposite of the civilized settings of Golden Age mysteries; rather, he is interested in those areas of society where structures break down and where law and humanity clash. Like Dashiell Hammett, Himes, and Raymond Chandler, McClure sees the supposed orderly and domesticated face of modern life as a veneer covering violence and disarray, where the role of the police is to protect the interests of the rich and powerful without losing all claim to decency, honor, and self-respect. The world is a nasty place, and it is delusive to be sentimental about it, but the detective can earn his pay, do some small measure of good, and have a laugh at the end of the day.

James McClure's influence in the United States has been important, with his models of ethnic detectives providing the matrices of character and plot that American writers have followed up on to create the multicultural detective. Himes excepted, most writers focused on the white, Anglo-Saxon majority until the 1960s and 1970s, which ushered in phalanxes of ethnic detectives—Native American, African American, Asian, and Jewish—a rainbow coalition of crime busters who paved the way for female, gay, and other diverse detectives who more accurately reflect the North American melting pot. McClure, whose books sold well in the United States, did not cause this phenomenon, but it might have developed differently without his model of a black-and-white team, apparently unequal but in practice mutually respectful and similarly capable. What cannot be denied is McClure's educational influence on American understandings of apartheid and the chilling parallels to the equally real, if not institutionalized, racial segregation in the United States. Many white Americans learned to recognize their own racial shortcomings in the harsher but uncannily similar situations McClure captured in his novels. He achieved true international status, not simply interpreting Africa to outsiders but also showing readers around the world the face of their own humanity, or lack of it. A member of the Detection Club, the Crime Writers' Association, and Mystery Writers of America, McClure resides and works in Headington, Oxford, England.

Interview:

Sarah Nuttall, interview with McClure, *Southern African Review of Books,* 30 (March–April 1994).

Reference:

Edward Tomarken, "James McClure's Mickey Zondi: The Partner of Apartheid," in *The Post-Colonial Detective,* edited by Ed Christian (New York: Palgrave, 2000).

James Melville
(Roy Peter Martin)
(5 January 1931 –)

Ellen Kocher Plaisance
Dillard University

BOOKS: *Japanese Cooking,* by Melville, as Peter Martin, and Joan Martin (Indianapolis: Bobbs-Merrill, 1970);

The Wages of Zen (London: Secker & Warburg, 1979);

The Chrysanthemum Chain (London: Secker & Warburg, 1980; New York: St. Martin's Press, 1982);

A Sort of Samurai (London: Secker & Warburg, 1981; New York: St. Martin's Press, 1982);

The Ninth Netsuke (London: Secker & Warburg, 1982; New York: St. Martin's Press, 1982);

Sayonara, Sweet Amaryllis (London: Secker & Warburg, 1983; New York: St. Martin's Press, 1984);

Death of a Daimyo (London: Secker & Warburg, 1984; New York: St. Martin's Press, 1985);

The Death Ceremony (New York: St. Martin's Press, 1985);

Go Gently, Gaijin (New York: St. Martin's Press, 1986);

The Imperial Way (London: Deutsch, 1986; New York: Fawcett, 1988);

Kimono for a Corpse (London: Secker & Warburg, 1987);

The Reluctant Ronin (New York: Scribners, 1988);

A Haiku for Hanae (New York: Scribners, 1989);

A Tarnished Phoenix (London: Barrie & Jenkins, 1990);

Miss Seeton, by Appointment, as Hampton Charles (New York: Berkley, 1990);

Advantage, Miss Seeton, as Charles (New York: Berkley, 1990;

Miss Seeton at the Helm, as Charles (New York: Berkley, 1990);

The Bogus Buddha (London: Headline, 1990; New York: Scribners, 1991);

The Body Wore Brocade (New York: Scribners, 1992);

Diplomatic Baggage (London: Severn House, 1995);

The Reluctant Spy (London: Severn House, 1995);

The Chrysanthemum Throne: A History of the Emperors of Japan, as Martin (Honolulu: University of Hawaii, Latitude 20, 1997).

James Melville (photograph by Carole Rawcliffe; from the dust jacket for The Body Wore Brocade, *1992)*

OTHER: "Santa-San Solves It," in *Crime at Christmas,* edited by Jack Adrian (London: Equation, 1988);

"Otani Has a Haircut," in *New Crimes 2,* edited by Maxim Jakubowski (London: Robinson, 1990);

"Gambling on Ganymede," in *Midwinter Mysteries 2,* edited by Hilary Hale (London: Little, Brown, 1992);

"Programmed for Murder," in *First Culprit,* edited by Liza Cody and Michael Z. Lewin (London: Chatto & Windus, 1992);

"Night Flight," in *Third Culprit,* edited by Cody, Lewin, and Peter Lovesey (London: Chatto & Windus, 1994);

"Dodgy, Very," in *Anglian Blood,* edited by Robert Church and Martin Edwards (Norwich, U.K.: Rampant Horse Limited, 1996).

SELECTED PERIODICAL PUBLICATIONS–UNCOLLECTED: "Living with Series Characters," *Writer,* 104 (August 1991): 12;
"Shakespeare in Japan," *TLS: The Times Literary Supplement,* 6 September 1991, p. 13.

James Melville, like James McClure, Arthur Upfield, and H. R. F. Keating, paved the way for the modern ethnic mystery. Appealing to readers' curiosity about foreign lands and foreign cultures, his cross-cultural detective stories capture Japanese, Americans, and British in situations that call attention to their different values and their different ways of perceiving the world around them. Melville teaches readers about Japanese culture and provides insights into a community-centered culture that distrusts the "eccentric," individualistic Western culture. He dramatizes the dynamics of Japanese social and business relationships and, while telling interesting stories that turn on the traditional questions of motive and evidence, opens doors into a world quite different from the reader's. While his settings are indeed exotic, they are not meant to be simply background; instead, they provide the basis for a study of manners. Thus, Melville brings to detection a new function: using questions of crime and justice as ways to explore cultural values and differences.

Melville was born Roy Peter Martin on 5 January 1931 in London, England. His parents were Walter Martin, a postal worker, and Annie Mable (née Cook) Martin, a dressmaker. He attended Highbury Grammar School from 1942 to 1948 and Birkbeck College, University of London, in 1948 and 1949, majoring in philosophy and political philosophy. While at Birkbeck he began his political career as a local government officer in the London County Council. From 1950 to 1951 he served with the Royal Air Force Education Branch as a sergeant instructor. He married Marjorie Peacock in 1951, the same year that he resumed his studies at the University of London, while teaching in a local school to pay his way and again serving as a local government officer in the London County Council. He received a B.A. with honors in philosophy in 1953, quit teaching in 1954 in order to study full-time, and graduated with an M.A. in political philosophy in 1956. He next became a publicity officer for the Royal Festival Hall in London from 1956 to 1960, with time out to study in West Germany at the University of Tübingen in 1958–1959. In 1960 he divorced Marjorie Peacock and married Joan Drumwright, with whom he later had two sons, James and Adam. That same year he made an important career move, working in cultural diplomacy and educational development for the British Council. His work took him from London to Indonesia, Hungary, and Japan.

During his first post in Japan from 1963 to 1970, he served as director of the British Cultural Institute in Kyoto. There he completely fell in love with Japan and with the Japanese, as he stated in a 1987 interview with *Contemporary Authors:* "I was waking up in the morning and thinking I ought to pinch myself, wondering if I was really being paid to live in such a fascinating place." In 1970, after his years in Kyoto, he wrote his first book, *Japanese Cooking,* with his second wife, Joan Martin. Also in 1970 he became a Member of the Order of the British Empire (MBE). After working in Budapest as a cultural attaché at the British Embassy from 1972 to 1973, he was sent back to London. There he divorced Joan Martin in 1977 and married singer-actress Catherine Sydee in 1978.

During the 1970s he spent some years writing essays and articles and then, while in London in the middle of the decade, he wrote his first two novels, *The Wages of Zen* (1979) and *The Chrysanthemum Chain* (1980). Having been a fan and an avid reader of classic British mystery writers such as Sir Arthur Conan Doyle and of such American crime writers as Dashiell Hammett and Raymond Chandler and hearing of an interesting murder case while in his position in Kyoto, he realized that he might be able to write a mystery that exploited his interest in the Far East and that would teach his readers about a culture he personally found fascinating. These books, the first in the popular Inspector Otani mystery series, were designed to entertain readers while exposing them to conflicts between East and West, against the backdrop of everything Melville loves about Japan.

Moreover, what Melville loves most is characters and their philosophical pondering. The series includes a set of repeating characters: Inspector Otani; his side-kicks, Jiro Kimura and Hachiro "Ninja" Noguchi; Otani's wife, Hanae; and a collection of recurring policemen and criminals, Japanese and foreign. *The Wages of Zen* was published in the summer of 1979, just when Martin was due to return to Japan as a cultural counselor with the British embassy in Tokyo. He served in this position from 1979 to 1983. As a senior member of the embassy, he and his superiors thought that he should use a pen name so as not to offend any Japanese officials. He chose his new name by combining the names of his two sons, Adam Melville and James Peter. He published four more of his Inspector Otani mysteries during his second stay in Japan: *The Chrysanthemum Chain, A Sort of Samurai* (1981), *The Ninth Netsuke* (1982), and *Sayonara, Sweet Amaryllis* (1983).

After his return to London, Melville became a professional writer. He continued to visit Japan during

Dust jacket for Melville's first novel (1979), which introduces Kyoto police inspector Tetsuo Otani (from John Cooper and B. A. Pike, Detective Fiction: The Collector's Guide, *second edition, 1994)*

the 1980s while writing prolifically, publishing eight more Otani mysteries between 1984 and 1992, including *Death of a Daimyo* (1984), *The Death Ceremony* (1985), and *Go Gently, Gaijin* (1986). His first historical novel, *The Imperial Way* (1986) was published next, followed by three more Otani mysteries, *Kimono for a Corpse* (1987), *The Reluctant Ronin* (1988), and *A Haiku for Hanae* (1989). In 1990 Melville published not only *The Bogus Buddha* in the Otani series and the historical novel *A Tarnished Phoenix* but also three novels in the series of Miss Seeton mysteries created by Heron Carvic—*Miss Seeton, by Appointment; Advantage, Miss Seeton;* and *Miss Seeton at the Helm*—under the pseudonym Hampton Charles. His last Otani mystery, *The Body Wore Brocade* (1992), was followed in 1995 by two new mysteries featuring hero Ben Lazenby of the British Foreign Service, *Diplomatic Baggage* and *The Reluctant Spy*. In 1997 he published a history, *The Chrysanthemum Throne: A History of*

the Emperors of Japan, under his real name. Melville lives in Herefordshire, England. He is a member of the British Academy of Film and Television Arts, the Mystery Writers of America, the Crime Writers Association, the Detection Club, and Travellers' Club.

Melville's most popular novels are his Inspector Otani series, thirteen novels written between 1979 and 1992, which are notable for their portrayal of Japan and what it means to live in the crossroads of several cultures. The settings, themes, and characters reflect Melville's entire life studies and experiences—his knowledge of politics and philosophy, his experiences traveling abroad in the diplomatic corps, and his delight in the history, beauty, idiosyncrasies, and struggles of the Japanese people. Superintendent Tetsuo Otani deals with murders within the context of Hoygo Prefecture and more specifically the city of Kobe, the most international city in Japan. Melville depicts Japan at its most beautiful and traditional, describing cherry blossoms, tea ceremonies, and temples, while he includes plenty of the modern, from fashion shows to love motels. Melville writes of a variety of characters who have experienced life as he has, characters who must deal with the dichotomies of life: history and the present, truth and lies, the outside world and the inside view, foreigners and countrymen. Melville's understanding of culture is reflected in his characters, who use traditional ways to maintain their relationships with each other and to preserve the order of society while ultimately uncovering the murderer.

To a certain extent, all of the central characters in the series are some facet of Melville himself. As the work of a student of philosophy and political philosophy, his writing is distinguished by his ability to think and see each character fully, to be each character while he writes it, while in his life in the diplomatic corps he was exposed to all kinds of foreign nationals and became an expert on many aspects of the Japanese. Otani is the character the reader inevitably associates with most, however, and Melville follows his activities and his musings. Like Melville when he began to write the series, Otani is middle-aged, middle-class, and knowledgeable about the world of politics and proper decorum. He is also conservative, mild mannered, and caring. Married to Hanae, he is proud of her beauty and the conventionality of their marriage—she is a housewife who takes cooking classes and washes his back. Yet, he is also proud of his unconventional way of treating her as a confidante and adviser to his cases. He also shares a close relationship with his son-in-law, Akira Shimizu, who is married to his daughter, Akiko. During the 1960s Akiko and Akira were student protesters and Otani arrested Akira several times, but Otani now trusts his advice implicitly. His father, Professor Otani of Osaka Imperial University, always disapproved of his son joining the American postwar police force, because the old man had been a victim of the "thought police" of the war days. Though many Japanese distrust and dislike the police because of similar memories, Otani does become a member of the Rotary Club, and, being sponsored by a Rotarian of position, a baron, as tradition requires, he earns respect for his profession. Otani always has a sense of history and of his place in the hierarchy of Japanese modern society whenever he looks at the portraits of his predecessors—from the nineteenth-century Maiji Period to those of imperial Japan and postwar Japan. Mostly it is Otani's place to support the status quo of the culture. As a traditional Japanese, he lives in history and in the modern world and must make both work.

Maintaining the social level of each relationship and the respect it is due is also a part of Otani's police world, as he struggles with governors, diplomats, other precincts, the odd foreigners, and the gangster lords of the Yakuza. Melville deeply understands the difficulty of maintaining balance within Japanese culture, which means understanding that each stratum is a culture of its own with its own rules. Otani is uncomfortable with those who break the rules of society but breaks a few himself by considering his associates, detectives Ninja Noguchi and Jiro Kimura, to be friends as well as subordinates. His affection for them is strong despite the fact that they live outside of society, Noguchi among the marginalized Japanese of Korean descent and Kimura among foreigners. Their unconventional social placement makes them, as Otani puts it, "very useful." Otani also breaks with convention to disassociate himself from Detective Sakamoto, a by-the-book man of the old school, inheritor of the thought-police tactics.

Ultimately, Otani is an everyman, imperfect, trying to do right and follow the rules of his culture, realizing that he cannot always choose the middle ground. He must deal with unsavory people, even with gaijin (foreigners), for whom "he has no taste"; he must be un-Japanese and go beyond convention yet know that he will not always get his culprit despite the sacrifices that he makes. Although the mysteries are resolved in each book, because of Japanese conventions people are often willing to confess a crime they did not commit, or they commit suicide to protect another. Therefore justice is served in a way, but only Otani and those close to him—and the reader—get to share in the inside secret of the true plots and criminals, while the rest of Japan gets the official outside view. For Westerners, sometimes Japanese justice as so described is no justice, and yet order and harmony are restored and the community is satisfied. As a policeman Otani must strive to preserve the social order through his wit and personal relation-

ships. He must use his feelings yet control them in order to get his man. Readers feel what he feels toward the other characters and appreciate his divergent feelings about the gaijin who unsettle society.

Influenced by his training as a philosopher, Melville presents two philosophies, the ancient and the modern, at crossroads, by including several fascinating Japanese women characters in the novels. Hanae represents Japanese tradition, though she breaks tradition often. The home is her domain, and being a wife and grandmother is her essence. Yet, she manages to get kidnapped; travels to England, where she handles being a foreigner much better than does her husband; and even discovers a body while at a fashion show. On the other hand, Junko Migishima, a detective in Otani's squad, marries a fellow detective through *omiai*—an arranged marriage—but does not give up her career to stay home. Otani admires Junko's professionalism and accepts her as being within the norm for modern Japanese women. Hanae and Junko are representative of Japan in the process of change. Melville makes quite clear that culture is always being influenced by outside forces and ideas from beyond one's sphere or country, that culture is always evolving.

Otani's two principal subordinates, Kimura and Ninja Noguchi, both live on the margins of Japanese culture. Kimura, a fortyish bachelor born in Chicago, is comfortable among gaijin, a social ability Otani cannot fathom. Yet, for all of his ease with women and the world in general, he cannot settle down. Both Otanis have soft spots for him, though they are often scandalized by his sexual relationships with foreign women and his unorthodox methods of following a case. He often flaunts convention in speaking to Otani, while Otani refers to him with the affectionate "Kimura-kun."

Melville used one of his own relatives as a basis for the untidy, likable Noguchi, who is a puzzling hero. He blends into the Japanese "underbelly" of "Koreans"—Japanese of Korean descent—who are still completely unaccepted in Japan. Noguchi can appear unnoticed on a scene, hence his nickname "Ninja," a reference to the black-clad warlords' spies of former days. When Otani needs to contact a Yakuza leader, Noguchi disappears into this foreign world to make the contact. Noguchi is mysterious and beyond the understanding of Otani or the reader and follows no socially "acceptable" Japanese standards. He barely speaks to Otani, dresses deplorably by Japanese standards, and has had a common-law Korean wife and son by her, unthinkable acts of social rebellion in a country where even third- and fourth-generation Koreans remain "foreigners" and are denied citizenship. Yet, Otani and all detectives respect him and even view him with awe. Living in a culture that is not the acceptable one has a price; in *Sayonara,*

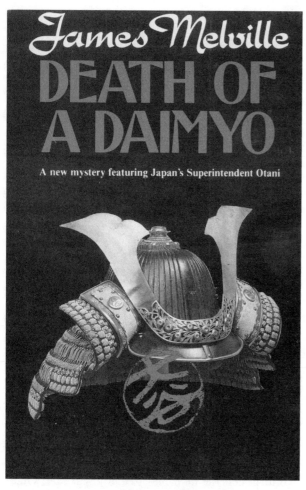

Dust jacket for the U.S. edition of Melville's 1984 mystery, in which Otani and his wife solve a murder in London (Richland County Public Library)

Sweet Amaryllis, Noguchi encounters his own son involved in a drug-smuggling ring and must have him arrested. Beyond these few details of his life, Otani and the reader know no more but remain outsiders looking into a way of life forever incomprehensible and foreign. Through the character of Noguchi, Melville philosophizes that no matter the experience, language ability, or knowledge about the country one lives in, much will still remain hidden and unknowable.

Melville's experiences in living abroad have also influenced the wide array of gaijin characters that appear in the novels. From the most important British diplomats to eccentric Brits who will never fit in Japan, from Americans studying Zen to sadistic former Nazis, Melville shows the variety of the types that those who travel may meet abroad. This number includes plenty of homosexuals, escaping derision or simply discomfort at home. The majority of his Westerners are in Japan living privileged lives that they could not live at home.

Some are misfits who can hide their idiosyncrasies while living in Japan, but they cannot hide from the foreign community. Melville juicily describes them for the readers' enjoyment.

Other foreigners are respected types within their country, diplomats, such as Melville, on their way up the ladder. They are all types that Melville would have met through the diplomatic corps and that he satirizes to greater and lesser degrees in the series. Some choose not to be engulfed by Japan but spend most of their time within their own foreign community until they go on to mix into another foreign community in another country. Others are exchange students, such as Rosie, the Suzukis' babysitter in London, featured in *Death of a Daimyo* and *The Death Ceremony,* who visits the Otanis and flaunts the conventions of Japanese culture: she wears nothing but jeans and T-shirts, comes home at all hours of the night, and lectures them on the value of brown rice. She does speak some Japanese but is the foreigner who never even notices that she is breaking every rule, and she provides comic scenes as well as more-serious dilemmas for the Otanis.

Also prominent in the series are those businessmen or models who are there to take from Japan, to make money, perhaps legally and perhaps not. This wide variety of foreigners in Kobe makes the Superintendent Otani series an examination of conflicting cultures, one that does not always show the West at its best. Otani and his detectives must learn to understand these aliens, "read their faces" as Otani puts it, in order to uncover hidden plots and solve murders. The reader witnesses the struggles to comprehend and remain polite on all sides.

The first novel in the series, *The Wages of Zen,* introduces the main series characters, who are called in to solve the murder of a foreigner studying Buddhism at a Zen temple. What appears to be corruption from without—a variety of eccentric foreigners, some of them lesbians—turns into the discovery of corruption from within the most sacred traditions of the temple. In *The Chrysanthemum Chain* Otani uncovers true corruption caused by foreigners when a prominent English teacher is murdered. While observing the traditional funeral and inquiring within the ranks of Yakuza gangsters, Otani discovers just how many Japanese of importance are within the chain involved in blackmail. Suicide turns out to be the solution to even modern problems of honor. *The Chrysanthemum Chain* also features a young British diplomat, Andrew Walker, perhaps a self-portrait of the young Melville. He is seeking his position within the expatriate British community and the diplomatic corps and is also dazzled by Japan. He must decide how far to delve into Japan and a relationship with a beautiful but dangerous young woman. The reader identifies with the young Brit's discovery of Japan through exciting character development, plot twists, and beautiful descriptions.

A Sort of Samurai features an earthquake, the death of a former Nazi, a mysterious woman interesting to Kimura, and a Bunraku (traditional puppet theater) performer. Otani uncovers a man of noble intentions, a modern "samurai" knight who fights for honor and the defense of a lady. In *The Ninth Netsuke* Otani and Hanae discover a statuette, a netsuke, hidden in a "love hotel," a Japanese hotel used for sexual trysts. The plot involves the loss of national treasure during World War II and the connections between important Japanese, Philippine love slaves, and their descendants. *Sayonara, Sweet Amaryllis* is also full of gaijin who are "ruining" Japan. The poisoning of a woman at a madrigal rehearsal leads to Kimura's uncomfortable relationships with a bubbly, middle-aged British woman, a character of great panache, and with a beautiful young woman, while it also involves Noguchi's discovery of his son's involvement in the underworld of the Yakuza.

Death of a Daimyo is an exciting turning point in the series, as the Otanis become the foreigners when they visit England. During their visit to St. Cuthbert's College in Cambridge, a famous Japanese tycoon is found murdered. His death could be connected to some Yakuza deaths in Japan, so Otani telephones Kimura to investigate in Japan. While in England, Hanae frets over her daughter's family's Western lifestyle and their babysitter, Rosie. She also meets Japanese expatriates and an academic who speaks Japanese. Each of these delightful characters makes readers see England through Japanese eyes, as a puzzling, exotic locale. In Japan, young Detective Migishima encounters unsavory underworld characters when she dresses as a Yakuza madam to fool a yacht full of gangsters. In *The Death Ceremony* Rosie comes from England to stay with the Otanis and disturbs their life. When a tea ceremony master is killed and an Irish tea student is suspected, the Irishman turns out to be Rosie's boyfriend. Otani wonders if the Irish Republican Army might have infiltrated his home and been responsible. Jealousy and revenge turn out to be the true cause of the murder, proving the gaijin are not always responsible for waves of rebellion in traditional Japan. Sometimes tradition produces murder.

Go Gently, Gaijin reveals the presence of the Israeli-Arab conflict in Japan. Someone from the Takarahaza All-Girl Opera may be involved in murder, but so might Kimura's new American girlfriend and Hanae's sister's international club. Otani's investigation uncovers characters experiencing old conflicts and tragic love. In *Kimono for a Corpse* the Japanese fascination with fashion and appearances turns deadly. Otani and his detectives have been investigating reports of blackmail and threats at the international fashion show when Hanae discovers a body decked out in a beautiful kimono. Otani must look beyond the facades to see what ugliness lies beneath the world of haute couture.

In *The Reluctant Ronin* a Dutch woman on a sponsored business exchange is found dead with a picture of the Otani family in her purse. Gangsters are suspected. Hanae thinks she saw her son-in-law kiss this woman before he suddenly disappeared. A *ronin* is a samurai on the run, a man who has lost his master and is an outsider in society. Because of the possible family involvement, Otani does not confide much to his detective friends and must therefore rely on the underworld and the spirit world to solve the case. Turning to the spirit world for information and sometimes justice is traditional in both China and Japan. The Akira Kurosawa motion picture *Rashomon* (1950), for example, based on the 1915 novella by Ryūnsuke Akutagawa, includes a ghost that testifies in a court hearing.

Greed lies behind the murder in *A Haiku for Hanae*. Otani investigates the twenty-year-old murder of an American missionary killed in front of a Shinto shrine. No one can explain how or why the man has been murdered, but an ancient Japanese fable provides clues, as does the world of the beyond. In *The Bogus Buddha* an international summer school on Japanese culture is receiving death threats, and an important archaeologist is murdered. Not coincidentally, a well-known gangster who has just been released from prison disappears about the same time. Since Hanae's sister is teaching at the school, the Otanis are personally involved when the students meet gangsters and are introduced to a cultural view they had not intended to learn about.

In *The Body Wore Brocade,* the last of the series to date, marital discontent flares up between Hanae and Otani, who is now getting on in years. Otani is hit by a sniper's bullet and is in the hospital pondering his life. The only witness to the shooting was the nephew of a wealthy software developer who is also a Nō theater performer. The software developer is found dead in full costume just after the nephew's attempted suicide. As usual, the new and the old Japan meet, and a pensive Otani ponders his past as well as his future.

Each book in the Superintendent Otani series is entertaining on its own, but reading them in order is even more interesting, for there is a constant moving forward and unfolding of the characters. This fact focuses the reader on what the books are really about: personal relationships and cross-cultural experiences. Otani must pay dues within the social structure of Japanese culture and Japanese relationships. Because modern Japan still exists within its feudal history, Otani must negotiate this maze of hierarchy (politicians, Yakuza, and subordinates alike) in order to solve a case

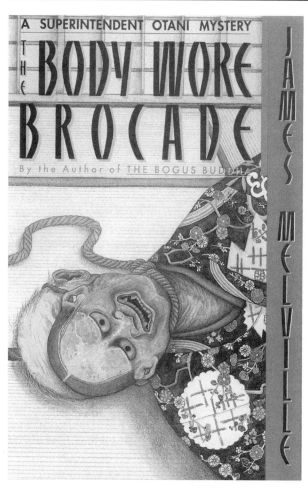

Dust jacket for Melville's novel in which Otani tracks a sniper who wounded him (Richland County Public Library)

and keep every individual secure within his position. Through Otani's visits to different social strata, the reader sees the many cultures within Japan. In the encounters he has with foreigners, Koreans from within Japan or Westerners from without, Otani must use Kimura and Noguchi to help him untangle, understand, and know. Therefore, his relationship with his subordinates are most important to his success. The three characters care about each other most of all and undertake interestingly Japanese solutions to keeping their relationships comfortable and stable. Otani values those who are bridges to other cultures and worlds, as does Melville, whose entire series encompasses the philosophical and political dilemmas of an ever changing global world. Only an author with Melville's background could have presented the moral and cultural dilemmas of the Japanese people in such an entertaining, interesting way.

In general, the Otani books are light and pleasurable to read, full of humor, Japanese coinages of English phrases, pompous officials, and domestic concerns. Even readers who are not interested in Japan can enjoy the series's look at human character, for James Melville's uppermost goal is to entertain readers. The earlier books in the series are the best, with some of the later books slightly weaker. The Otani novels have been translated into Japanese and have a following in Japan, as well. When his Japanese acquaintances discovered that Melville was the same Peter Martin working at the British Embassy, they were quite pleased that he had honored them with the attention. According to Melville in the *Contemporary Authors* interview, "Japanese are perhaps unique in feeling rather flattered when a foreigner writes books about them." He has also been interviewed in Japan, and according to Melville, "people regard me as something of a freak, because so far as I know, I'm the only British crime writer, at least, who's writing murder mysteries set in Japan and involving Japanese people in the most important roles." This setting and Melville's understanding of the Japanese and of the way culture affects crime and justice make Melville's detective novels a valuable contribution to cross-cultural understanding.

Interview:

"Melville, James," *Armchair Detective,* 16 (1983): 340–347.

Patricia Moyes

(19 January 1923 – 2 August 2000)

Cynthia A. Bily
Adrian College

BOOKS: *Dead Men Don't Ski* (London: Collins, 1959; New York: Rinehart, 1960);

The Sunken Sailor (London: Collins, 1961); republished as *Down Among the Dead Men* (New York: Holt, Rinehart & Winston, 1961);

Death on the Agenda (London: Collins, 1962; New York: Holt, Rinehart & Winston, 1962);

Murder à la Mode (London: Collins, 1963; New York: Holt, Rinehart & Winston, 1963);

Falling Star (London: Collins, 1964; New York: Holt, Rinehart & Winston, 1964);

Johnny under Ground (London: Collins, 1965; New York: Holt, Rinehart & Winston, 1966);

Murder Fantastical (London: Collins, 1967; New York: Holt, Rinehart & Winston, 1967);

Death and the Dutch Uncle (London: Collins, 1968; New York: Holt, Rinehart & Winston, 1968);

Helter-Skelter (New York: Holt, Rinehart & Winston, 1968; London: Macdonald, 1969);

Who Saw Her Die? (London: Collins, 1970); republished as *Many Deadly Returns* (New York: Holt, Rinehart & Winston, 1970);

Season of Snows and Sins (London: Collins, 1971; New York: Holt, Rinehart & Winston, 1971);

The Curious Affair of the Third Dog (London: Collins, 1973; New York: Holt, Rinehart & Winston, 1973);

After All, They're Only Cats (New York: Curtis, 1973);

Black Widower (London: Collins, 1975; New York: Holt, Rinehart & Winston, 1975);

To Kill a Coconut (London: Collins, 1977); republished as *The Coconut Killings* (New York: Holt, Rinehart & Winston, 1977);

How to Talk to Your Cat (London: Barker, 1978; New York: Holt, Rinehart & Winston, 1978);

Who Is Simon Warwick? (London: Collins, 1978; New York: Holt, Rinehart & Winston, 1979);

Angel Death (London: Collins, 1980; New York: Holt, Rinehart & Winston, 1981);

A Six-Letter Word for Death (London: Collins, 1983; New York: Holt, Rinehart & Winston, 1983);

Patricia Moyes (photograph © 1989 by Jim Haszard; from the dust jacket for Black Girl, White Girl, *1989)*

Night Ferry to Death (London: Collins, 1985; New York: Holt, Rinehart & Winston, 1985);

Black Girl, White Girl (New York: Holt, 1989; London: Collins, 1990);

Twice in a Blue Moon (London: Collins, 1993; New York: Holt, 1993);

Who Killed Father Christmas? and Other Unseasonable Demises (Norfolk, Va.: Crippen & Landru, 1996).

Edition: *Murder by 3's,* introduction by Anthony Boucher (New York: Holt, 1965)—comprises *Dead Men Don't Ski, Down Among the Dead Men,* and *Falling Star.*

PLAY PRODUCTION: *Time Remembered,* translated by Moyes from Jean Anouilh's *Léocadia,* London, Lyric Hammersmith, 2 December 1954; New York, Morosco Theatre, 12 November 1957.

PRODUCED SCRIPT: *School for Scoundrels,* motion picture, by Moyes, Peter Ustinov, and Hal E. Chester, Continental Pictures, 1960.

OTHER: Jean Anouilh, *Time Remembered: A Romantic Comedy,* translated by Moyes (London: Methuen, 1955; New York: S. French, 1959).

SELECTED PERIODICAL PUBLICATIONS–
UNCOLLECTED: "Writing a Mystery," *Writer,* 83 (April 1970): 11–14;
"Mysteries within Mysteries," *Writer,* 89 (October 1976): 20–22.

Although her work falls into the broad category sometimes called the "British detective story" or the "British police procedural," and although her detective is undeniably British (in fact, a high-ranking inspector with Scotland Yard), Patricia Moyes's nineteen mystery novels have always been more popular in the United States than in Great Britain. Even into the 1970s and 1980s, when conventional wisdom held that readers had lost interest in formal detective stories, Moyes continued to sell well. As Anthony Boucher noted in his introduction to the omnibus volume *Murder by 3's* (1965), there are still readers ready to be taken "back in happy nostalgia to the prime vintage years of Ngaio Marsh and Margery Allingham in the 1930s."

Moyes's novels arise from a worldview that is ordered–some have said "cosy." Her plots have distinct beginnings, middles, and endings; authority figures are generally to be trusted; people commit murder because of greed or revenge or other basic human instincts. Clues are sprinkled throughout the text, so that the denouement makes sense and feels right. While each book involves at least one murder, the violence happens offstage; there are no scenes of torture or brutality, although many of the criminals are ruthless and evil. In a 15 October 1989 review for *The New York Times,* Jack Sullivan commented admiringly that Moyes "somehow manages to make drug dealing seem more like bad manners than bad morals." Readers follow the adventures of Henry and Emmy Tibbett because they are interested in a good puzzle: For thirty years many reviewers and most of her book jackets quoted an early review by Vivian Mort in the *Chicago Tribune Magazine of Books,* referring to her as the writer who put "the 'who' back in who-dunit."

Perhaps the most cogent description of Moyes's work is in her own voice. As she says in *Twentieth-Century Crime and Mystery Writers* (1991), "My preference is for mystery stories that are well-plotted (and never cheat the reader), that are ingenious, and amusing rather than vicious, and that are placed in a setting which the author clearly knows well, and peopled with characters who are more than dummies to be pushed around by the exigencies of the plot." True to her own standards, Moyes has been consistently praised for her plots, her settings, and her rounded characters.

Patricia Moyes was born Patricia Pakenham-Walsh on 19 January 1923 in Dublin, Ireland. To her family and friends she was known all her life as "Penny." Her parents were Marion (née Boyd) and Ernst Pakenham-Walsh, part of a large and influential Anglo-Irish family. Her father was a member of the Indian Civil Service, eventually becoming a high court judge in Madras. Pakenham-Walsh was educated from 1934 to 1939 at Overstone School, an academy for girls, in Northamptonshire, England. She was an excellent student and showed a talent for writing early on. In fact, at the age of eight she had already chosen her career and made herself the editor and sole writer of a family newspaper.

Her formal education ended in 1939, when World War II began. Although she was too young to serve, she lied about her age in order to join the Women's Auxiliary Air Force (WAAF). In the early days of shortwave-length radar, she worked from 1939 to 1945 as a radar controller and flight officer (the same positions her fictional Emmy Blandish Tibbett held). Still interested in writing, she also wrote amusing sketches for entertainment in the barracks.

In 1945 the WAAF released her to become a technical adviser to Peter Ustinov, who was producing a motion picture, *School for Secrets* (1946), about the uses of radar. Pakenham-Walsh was selected for the job because she knew about radar and had some writing experience. She learned a great deal about the movie industry, working on everything from scriptwriting to managing small production details. She later used this inside knowledge to create the background for her mystery novel about the movie business, *Falling Star* (1964). She became Ustinov's personal assistant, a job she held until 1953.

The following year she joined *Vogue* magazine in London as an assistant editor and stayed there until 1958. Among her duties she wrote a regular column called "Shophound." Her experiences in the fashion industry formed the backdrop for another mystery novel, *Murder à la Mode* (1963). During her years at *Vogue* she was married to photographer John Moyes, acquiring the surname she used as an author. They married in 1951 and divorced in 1959. During these years she also began taking on full-length writing projects. Fluent, like Henry Tibbett, in various European languages, she translated Jean Anouilh's French 1940 play *Léocadia* as *Time Remembered* (1955); it was produced in London in 1954 and on Broadway in 1957

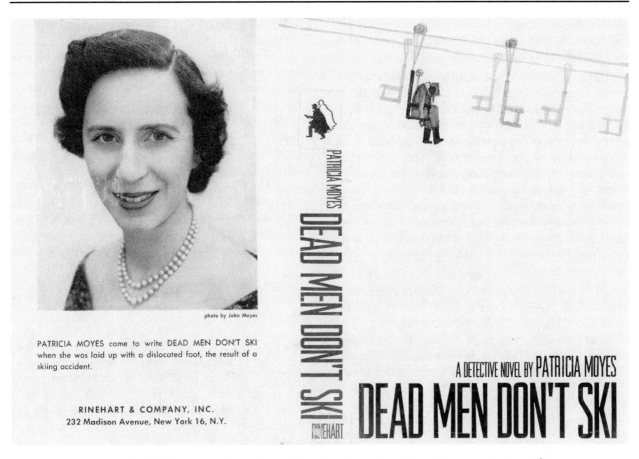

PATRICIA MOYES came to write DEAD MEN DON'T SKI
when she was laid up with a dislocated foot, the result of a
skiing accident.

RINEHART & COMPANY, INC.
232 Madison Avenue, New York 16, N.Y.

photo by John Moyes

*Dust jacket for the U.S. edition of Moyes's first novel (1959), which introduces Scotland Yard Inspector Henry Tibbett
and his wife, Emmy (Bruccoli Clark Layman Archives)*

with Helen Hayes and Richard Burton in the lead roles. The play gave her enough money to quit her job and move to Switzerland. She was there, recovering from a skiing accident, when she decided to try her hand at writing a mystery novel. The result was *Dead Men Don't Ski* (1959), set at a ski resort in the Dolomites and introducing Chief Inspector Henry Tibbett of the C.I.D. and his wife, Emmy.

With the first Henry Tibbett novel, Moyes firmly establishes "facts" of Henry's and Emmy's biography and demonstrates the methods by which Henry solves all his crimes. Henry is forty-eight years old in *Dead Men Don't Ski* and described from the first as "a small man, sandy-haired and with pale eyebrows and lashes which emphasizes his general air of timidity." To put it another way, "Henry Tibbett was not a man who looked like a great detective," a point that Moyes repeats in every novel. This quality of being nondescript serves Henry well, for he is never recognized as a policeman until he reveals his identity, and he is able to gain the confidence of people who are hiding informa-

tion. In *Dead Men Don't Ski* he and Emmy have been sent by Scotland Yard to a remote ski lodge in northern Italy, in the guise of normal vacationers. By the time the murder has been committed and Henry's true position is revealed, he has already won the confidence of several of the suspects.

Henry is paired *in Dead Men Don't Ski* with an Italian police official, Capitano Alfredo Spezzi. Typically, Henry is drawn into the investigation of a murder on foreign soil; in this case he speaks better English than Spezzi and so is pressed into interrogating the British suspects. The two men work together to solve the mystery of a murdered man found on a ski lift, and they become good friends, but their methods are dramatically different. Spezzi is a methodical man who puts together elaborate and precise timetables of the actions of everyone involved in the murder. Henry, on the other hand, is a man of instinct, who relies on an intuitive quality he refers to as his "nose." When he tells his wife, "You know, Emmy, my nose tells me we're approaching this case from the wrong end altogether," she knows that he will soon have the solution. Moyes highlights Henry's "nose" by pairing him with a man who does not trust it.

In this first novel the murder is solved through a series of insightful interrogations and through moments of quiet contemplation. Most of the "action" takes place in the hotel bar, or in coffee shops in town, or in the office where the police conduct their interrogations, but there are also thrilling scenes of skiing action. There are no fistfights or disguises; Henry never even raises his voice, although he sees clearly that he is being lied to repeatedly. He does not discover a secret document or missing treasure. Instead, he ponders the evidence and, in his hotel room away from the others, he realizes what must have happened.

By his side as he ponders and realizes is Henry's wife, Emmy. Emmy is forty years old and a bit plump, and she and Henry appear to have been married for some time. They are comfortable together and know each other well. They both smoke, like the same drinks, and enjoy each other's company. Boucher observed that Moyes herself had been married only a short while when *Murder by 3's,* which includes *Dead Men Don't Ski,* was published, and he commented, "How she understands so intimately and truly the problems (and the special happinesses) of two people who are nudging fifty after decades of marriage is simply one of those minor miracles that born writers can rear back and pass." Emmy knows what Henry is thinking, what his facial expressions mean, what it means when he refers to his "nose" or rubs the back of his neck. She is ready at all times to assist him in whatever way she can, from sitting in on interrogations and taking notes in shorthand (and then staying up all night to type up the reports) to running into town to ask questions of the shopkeepers. Henry is noticeably appreciative of her contributions.

Emmy is not just subservient to Henry, however; she has talents of her own, which she willingly uses to help Henry with his work. When the couple arrive at the Bella Vista Hotel, Henry has never skied before, but Emmy has tried it twice. In a few days the athletic Henry is still in the beginners' course, while Emmy has been promoted to the third class. Between them, they are able to observe both the experienced and the novice skiers in their party. Henry relies on her brains, as well. When he thinks he has the answer to the mystery, he carefully relates every detail to Emmy. While he speaks, she listens "intently, occasionally putting a question, but never a comment." When he is finished, however, he asks, "Now, tell me what you think of it all." The twenty-first-century reader may cringe occasionally, as when Henry asks another man to "Look

after the old lady," but for the most part Emmy is a bright, probing, and equal partner.

Dead Men Don't Ski introduces other elements that later become plot staples: the secondary characters who reappear in later volumes (Spezzi and his love interest and chief suspect, Gerda); the young woman of a wealthy family who is about to enter an unsuitable marriage (Trudi Knipfer); the smuggling of drugs as motive for murder; and Henry's fluency in Italian, German, and other European languages.

The success of *Dead Men Don't Ski* did not immediately turn Moyes into a novelist. For her next project she collaborated with Ustinov and Hal E. Chester on the movie script for *School for Scoundrels* (1960). The witty satire stars Ian Carmichael as a weak man who tries to hang on to the girl of his dreams by learning the skills of "gamesmanship" and "one-upmanship" at the school. The movie was a success, but the script was Moyes's last.

Her next novel was *The Sunken Sailor* (1961; published in the United States as *Down Among the Dead Men*). In this novel Moyes draws on her love of sailing instead of skiing, as Henry investigates the death of an experienced yachtsman. Just as Henry (and so the readers) learned the rudiments of skiing in *Dead Men Don't Ski,* this case gives Henry and Emmy their first experiences at sailing, and the novel is full of technical description, terminology (the old-timers say "sailing" or "boating," but never "yachting"), and action. For the first time (but not the last) Emmy is kidnapped and narrowly escapes death but comes away with an important clue.

On 13 October 1962 Moyes married James Haszard, who worked as a lawyer and an interpreter at the International Court of Justice in the Hague. They met when he answered an ad she had placed looking for crew for her boat. With him she settled down into something resembling a normal domestic life, and wrote books—mostly Henry Tibbett mysteries—for the rest of her life. She and her husband were excellent skiers and sailors, and Moyes continued to use technical knowledge of both these sports in her mysteries. The couple also shared an appreciation for fine food and wine and for cats. They lived in Switzerland and then in a restored eighteenth-century house on the Rhine River, perhaps resembling the house that plays such an important role in *Death and the Dutch Uncle* (1968).

Death on the Agenda (1962), published the year of her marriage to Haszard, is set in Geneva, Switzerland, where she and her husband were living and where Henry Tibbett participates in an International Narcotics Conference. Just before a meeting, one of the officials is murdered in a locked room, and the only possible suspect is Henry himself. The plot involves interpreters whose work resembles that of James Haszard, and again Moyes creates a strong sense of place and time by carefully presenting precise details of the layout of Geneva and the workings of the Palais des Nations. Like all of her plots, this one could only take place in the setting she creates for it, and the motive for the murder arises logically from that setting.

Geneva presents more challenges for Henry and Emmy than simple murderers and international drug organizations. In *Death on the Agenda* their marriage is threatened. First, Henry is attracted to the beautiful Mary Benson, an Australian who works at the Palais des Nations as a verbatim transcriber, assigned to Henry's conference. Giddy as a teenager, Henry lies to Emmy and takes Benson on a secret picnic on the beach, where they kiss passionately. Hurt and angry, Emmy goes to dinner with the wealthy and handsome Paul Hampton. By contrast, Henry's old friend Spezzi of the Italian police has come to the conference with his wife, Gerda, with whom he fell in love in *Dead Men Don't Ski,* and their marriage still bears the glow of newness. Of course, Henry and Emmy find their way back to each other in the end, with their tempters safely out of the way. As it turns out, Hampton is the head of the drug-selling organization; he is killed while resisting arrest. Benson is the murderer, and she kills herself rather than face death at the hands of the organization. Henry realizes Emmy's importance to him: "If it was true that their relationship would henceforth be different, it was true in the best possible sense. Their interdependence had never been more clearly demonstrated, and it had been spiced with the possibility, which would now always be with them, that each was capable of finding adventure elsewhere."

Henry is also confronted with the realization that crimes and criminals are more rich and complicated than he had considered. Even his own motives are unclear to him when he tells Benson that he knows she is the murderer and gives her the opportunity to choose her own death. Although he has been an inspector for many years, "Henry knew that his life could never be quite the same again. Old, unquestioned values had been turned upside down. The black and white view of morality which he had accepted as his middle-class heritage had gone forever." Perhaps Moyes's greatest strength as a writer is her ability to create rounded characters whose emotions and motives are complex enough to seem real.

For *Murder à la Mode* Moyes drew on her years with British *Vogue,* setting the murder in the offices of *Style,* a London fashion magazine. Readers are treated to a beginner's course in the workings of the fashion industry, with intricate explanations of the toile, the cotton copy of a designer original sold to manufacturers, and the financial decisions designers must make. The

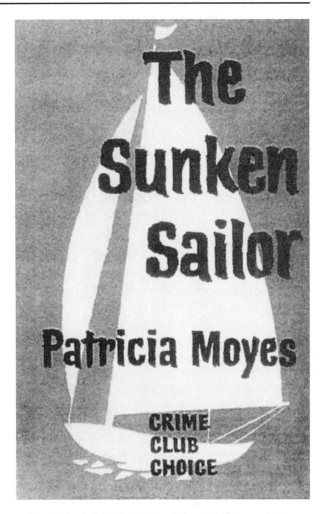

Dust jacket for Moyes's 1961 novel, in which Tibbett and Emmy solve the case of a murdered yachtsman (from John Cooper and B. A. Pike, Detective Fiction: The Collector's Guide, second edition, 1994)

characters in Moyes's fashion world are eccentric and proud of it, and critics have often pointed to this novel as one of Moyes's and the genre's best.

Compared with Moyes's earlier works, *Murder à la Mode* is remarkable for the amount of sexual material; by modern standards, however, it can only be considered quaint. Emmy's niece, Veronica Spence, appears in the novel as a fashion model. She is a grown woman, living on her own in London, and she has apparently been known to travel overnight with Donald McKay. This travel, and the unspoken worry that the two might have had sexual relations, is a great concern to the entire family. (To everyone's relief, Veronica and Donald decide to marry at the end of the book.) There is also a scandal involving the murder victim, an unmarried woman. Some believe that she might have been pregnant when she died, and this possibility is so shocking that even the police are timid about mentioning it

Dust jacket for Moyes's 1964 novel, the fifth Inspector Tibbett mystery, involving murder on a motion-picture set
(from Cooper and Pike, Detective Fiction: The Collector's Guide, 1988)

among themselves. Typically, though, there are no actual sex scenes in the book.

Murder à la Mode offers the first of many gay characters in the Henry Tibbett series. Nicholas Knight, a dress designer, is easily identified by his calm objectivity when surrounded by a roomful of nearly naked models (a room that drives Henry to distraction), and by his "strange, almost skipping step" and his "high-pitched voice." The magazine publisher, Henry learns, has a long-standing rule against hiring homosexuals "however brilliant they may be. This is not a question of morals. It's simply that there are few enough men on the creative side of the magazine, and each one must contribute one hundred percent masculinity, as a balancing factor against the predominantly female element." Although there is some stereotyping in Knight's description, Moyes and her "good" characters seem to accept easily his homosexuality. Throughout the novels

there are several gay men but no overt condemnation or advocacy by the characters or through the workings of the author. Knight is at first a suspect in the murder, but he turns out to be more foolish than evil, and this pattern follows many of the gay characters in the series.

This novel also offers the best view yet of Henry's and Emmy's home life. For the first time Henry is assigned a case while he is at home, at work. Henry and Emmy live, it is revealed, in an unfashionable section of Chelsea on the ground floor of a shabby Victorian house converted to apartments. The Tibbetts have bad taste in furnishings, and they know it. Henry sometimes wishes he could provide better for Emmy, but their home is a happy one, even though throughout the series their house is referred to as "ugly."

Moyes's life again provided the setting for her next novel, *Falling Star,* in which the murder is committed on a movie set. The title is a pun: the star of the movie dies by falling down a flight of steps and under a train. With this book Moyes experiments with point of view. Instead of the third-person narrator she has used before, *Falling Star* is told by Anthony "Pudge" Croombe-Peters, the producer of Northburn Films. Pudge fills his pages with technical information, warning that "readers of this book are going to have to learn quite a bit about film-making before they are through." Henry, whose body of knowledge is becoming as expansive as his author's, also must learn to understand the process before he can solve the mystery.

The moral ambiguity that Henry encountered in *Death on the Agenda* echoes at the end of *Falling Star*. In a dramatic scene high above the ground on a catwalk, Pudge and Henry try to stop Sam, the murderer, from killing Sonia, the victim's widow. As Pudge pulls Sonia to safety, he reports, "at first I was not aware of the sound of another scuffle going on further down the gallery, in the black darkness beyond the arc lamp. The first I knew was a shattering, wrenching sound, and then a terrible dull thud." Sam has fallen to his death. When it is all over Pudge asks, "'Henry, up there on the gallery what actually happened?' Henry looked at me sadly. 'He jumped, of course,' he said. 'As soon as he saw me he realized . . . ' There was a pause. . . ." Henry does not explain the scuffling sounds—nor does Moyes—and the idea of Henry taking justice into his own hands is never raised again.

Emmy is in the spotlight in the sixth novel, *Johnny under Ground* (1965). Like Moyes herself, Emmy served as a section officer in the WAAF during World War II. A reunion with her Royal Air Force (RAF) comrades sets the stage for a murder, and this time Emmy is the chief suspect. In this novel Emmy feels restless. Henry and Emmy have never been able to have children, and Emmy's volunteer work is not sufficiently fulfilling. The reunion dredges up memories of her first true love, Beau Guest, a married flying hero who apparently committed suicide in 1943 just after a meeting with Emmy.

Emmy's innocence is a key element in all that happens. Because she was so innocent when she was young, she was easily fooled by the murder of Guest, disguised as suicide. Her innocence as an adult makes her an obvious target for those who try to pin the next murder on her and leads to her being kidnapped and almost killed. Finally, her innocence prevents her from seeing basic qualities in people she considers friends. Arthur Price, an RAF comrade of whom she has always been especially fond, is homosexual, but she has never known it. As they are discussing the murders, she suddenly notices "his neat, plump hands and feet, his gestures, his tendency to fuss—'a bit of an old woman,' they had called him in the Mess. 'Why didn't I see it then?' Emmy wondered. 'I suppose I was too innocent.'"

Dust jacket for the U.S. edition of Moyes's 1973 novel, an Inspector Tibbett mystery set in the milieu of London greyhound racing (Richland County Public Library)

In the end Henry convinces Sammy, the murderer, not to kill Emmy, but Sammy turns his gun on himself. Again Henry reflects on the essential ambiguity of humans and their actions: "For a moment Henry looked down at Sammy—a pathetic, gay, amoral, criminal, kind, cruel, funny human being. A gallant pilot. A cheat. A murderer. An ordinary man."

In *Murder Fantastical* (1967) Moyes introduces some of her most endearing characters, the eccentric but kind Manciple family. As the Manciples debate fine points of linguistics and regional accents, Henry demonstrates that he is nearly as quick-witted as they are. He has always enjoyed crossword puzzles and spends an entire train ride working on one in *Dead Men Don't Ski*. Edwin Manciple, who routinely completes *The Sunday Times* crossword in a matter of minutes, respects Henry's ability to solve the clues. Moreover, Henry is well read, gaining the trust of one suspect by comparing the philosophies of Xenophanes and Karl Marx.

The novel touches briefly on another thematic thread that runs through several novels: the struggles faced by newly independent Third World nations. Several former colonies of the British Empire declared their independence during the 1960s, and through the Henry Tibbett novels Moyes illustrates the nobility of the native peoples and the pressures that threaten to corrupt their new political power. The brilliant and eccentric missionary Edwin Manciple, former bishop of Bugolaland, sums up the feelings of many former colonists who have returned home: "Horrible country. . . . I miss it very much. Charming people. Appalling climate. Independent now, and very good luck to them."

The theme of postcolonial politics is central to *Death and the Dutch Uncle,* which concerns a border dispute between two newly independent African nations, Mambesi and Galunga. The action takes place in the Netherlands, at the International Court of Justice at the Hague, where Moyes's husband was working. The details of canals, canal boats, and windmills provide a rich setting. Again Moyes provides an insider's look at the work of the interpreters and the legal staff, as she explores the complicated question of the obligation a newly independent nation has to honor treaties formed earlier by the colonial government.

Henry, who has been promoted to superintendent of New Scotland Yard, speaks French and Dutch in solving this case, as easily as he spoke German and Italian in *Dead Men Don't Ski.* Emmy does not speak Dutch, so Henry has to interpret for her. Yet Emmy's role has become increasingly stronger over the years, and the marriage is sound. Henry and Emmy still live in an "ugly" house with unfashionable furniture and unimpressive wine, but when Henry notices the beautiful Madeleine la Rue he also notices, with satisfaction, that he prefers Emmy. Emmy is content to be the assistant and follows Henry's spoken and unspoken orders, but she is quick-witted enough to leave a message on a hair ribbon, and this time when she is kidnapped and about to be killed it is because she has bravely stayed behind to protect a little girl. Henry saves her just in time, but not before he receives the first in a series of shots clean through the shoulder that barely slow him down.

Moyes continued to create a mystery every year or two for several years. In 1968 she published her only novel for young adults, *Helter-Skelter.* Her next Henry Tibbett novel, *Who Saw Her Die?* (1970; published in the United States as *Many Deadly Returns*) won the Edgar Allan Poe Special Award from the Mystery Writers of America. It features another of Moyes's elderly eccentrics, this time an old woman celebrating her birthday. In *Season of Snows and Sins* (1971), set in the small scenic village of Montarraz, Switzerland, Henry has been pro-

moted again, to detective chief superintendent. On a skiing vacation he finds himself solving in a murder case that involves drugs, adultery, and child prostitution.

For her eleventh Henry Tibbett mystery, *The Curious Affair of the Third Dog* (1973), Moyes entered a world that was completely new to her: the world of dog racing. A chance meeting with a man involved in the sport inspired her to the research she needed to flesh out the novel. *The Curious Affair of the Third Dog* is full of vivid details of place, technical descriptions, and a cast of characters that readers have met in earlier books, including Veronica Spence's parents (the passage of time is marked by a conversation about Veronica and Donald's new baby); Major George Weatherby, a two-bit crook; and Sergeant Derek Reynolds, Henry's right-hand man at Scotland Yard. This time it is Henry who is kidnapped; he escapes with only one shot, which passes cleanly through his shoulder.

Moyes had been a cat fancier all her adult life, and in 1973 she published a humorous memoir centered on her pets, *After All, They're Only Cats.* This book was followed in 1978 by *How to Talk to Your Cat,* an entertaining and informative guide to understanding vocal and nonvocal cat communication. With *How to Talk to Your Cat* Moyes reached a large audience completely unaware of her mystery books.

In the early 1970s James Haszard was transferred to Washington, D.C., to work with the International Monetary Fund. He and Moyes moved to Georgetown (taking along their boat and their cats), and Moyes subsequently set much of *Black Widower* (1975) there. *Black Widower* is another title with a pun in it: the central character, Sir Edward Ironmonger, is black, and his wife is murdered. Ironmonger is the ambassador to the United States from the newly independent Caribbean nation of Tampica, a beautiful, unspoiled island in the fictional British Seaward Islands (patterned after the British Virgin Islands, where Moyes and Haszard vacationed frequently and eventually lived year-round). As in *Death and the Dutch Uncle,* the plot revolves around a treaty signed before independence and the conflicts between those who can profit personally from honoring it versus the national interest in abandoning it.

In *Black Widower* Moyes confronts the issues of race and gender. As she has done previously with homosexual characters, she stakes out a position by the casualness with which she presents her black characters, refusing to notice anything unusual in bright and competent Tampicans. Several white characters in *Black Widower* mean well but cannot help thinking themselves superior to the black Tampicans. Many of the white tourists at the most expensive resort on Tampica are casually racist and see no reason to couch their feelings in polite words. In all cases the racist characters are on the side of the criminals; Moyes does not create racists and homophobes who are in all other respects decent people. Emmy's role here is to subvert female stereotypes. In order to conceal the reason they are staying on in Tampica–to investigate murder and corruption–Henry and Emmy allow the others to think that Henry has been bullied into staying by the "little woman" who could not resist a free vacation. Between themselves the two are amused at being able to fool people so easily by playing to convention.

When Haszard retired, he and Moyes settled in Virgin Gorda, one of the islands in the British Virgin Islands. Henry Tibbett returns to the Caribbean for *To Kill a Coconut* (1977; published in the United States as *The Coconut Killings*), *Angel Death* (1980), and *Black Girl, White Girl* (1989), as the fragile new democracy of Tampica struggles to build an honest tourism industry without attracting a drug trade and the accompanying corruption. This concern was a strong one for Moyes, who treasured her new island home. In the introduction to *Angel Death* she writes, "The plot may seem outrageous, and yet it is not beyond the bounds of possibility. Fortunately, the authorities are alert and vigilant, and I am convinced that in no territory would things reach the point described here without official intervention. Those of us who love the islands and their people pray that this will always be so."

Angel Death gives Emmy her biggest role, when Henry is given PCP ("angel dust") without his knowledge and undergoes a dramatic personality change. He turns against Emmy, telling her "I don't give a damn what you do," resigns from Scotland Yard, and embarks on a wild sailing tour with drug dealers. Emmy, holding onto her belief that the real Henry, her husband of twenty years, is still reachable, discovers the murderers, breaks into an office, operates a radio (drawing on her WAAF experience), and rescues Henry in the middle of a hurricane. When one of the suspects calls Emmy "quaint" and asks her "are you Victorian enough to stay at home, Emmy, or do you have a job like so many women these days?" Emmy replies, "I don't think I'm particularly Victorian . . . but I don't have a job. . . . I look after my husband." (When Emmy is kidnapped in *Black Girl, White Girl* she does not need to be rescued; she tricks her captors and gets away. Henry is relieved: "He had, as usual, underestimated her. How had she done it?")

In *Who Is Simon Warwick?* (1978) Moyes offers one of the few entirely sympathetic transsexual characters in mainstream fiction. The story hinges on a missing heir; the long-lost Simon Warwick does not come forward because he has undergone medical treatments and become Sally Warwick. Sally and her husband ultimately decide to give up the inheritance rather than face

Dust jacket for Moyes's 1989 novel, one of four Inspector Tibbett mysteries set in the fictional Caribbean island nation of Tampica (Richland County Public Library)

condemnation from the family. Another character, Denton Westbury, is a homosexual interior decorator, the true illegitimate son of the dead millionaire, Lord Charlton, who never knew he had a son. Westbury is also kept hidden, because it is taken for granted that his father would not have accepted him ("Can you imagine Mr. Alexander turning control of Warwick Industries over to a homosexual interior decorator? Don't be silly.").

In *A Six-Letter Word for Death* (1983) Moyes brings back the Manciple family to help Henry solve a crossword puzzle that provides clues to a murder. The story takes place on the Isle of Wight, and Moyes dedicates the book to the isle where she spent two years in the RAF. As Henry works toward the solution, he encounters a missing heir, a young woman who is engaged to an unsuitable man, a suspect who is "as queer as a three-dollar bill" but who helps reveal the murderer, and the Guess Who club, an organization of mystery writers. Moyes herself made frequent appearances at mystery writers' conventions toward the end of her career, often accompanied by her friend and fellow mystery writer Sarah Caudwell.

Night Ferry to Death (1985) concerns diamond smuggling on the ferry between England and the Netherlands, giving Moyes one last chance to revisit Amsterdam. Although Henry and Emmy do not appear to have aged since *Dead Men Don't Ski,* Ineke, a little girl in *Death and the Dutch Uncle,* is now eighteen years old and taking advice from Emmy about how to rendezvous with a young man her parents do not approve of. *Twice in a Blue Moon* (1993), the last of Moyes's novels, allows the author to indulge in one more of her personal interests, fine food and wine, as the story revolves around a gourmet restaurant.

James Haszard died in 1994, shortly after the publication of *Twice in a Blue Moon.* In 1996 Moyes published *Who Killed Father Christmas? and Other Unseasonable Demises,* a complete collection of her short mystery stories. Although reviewers noted sadly that Henry and Emmy Tibbett did not appear in the collection, the volume was highly and universally praised. At the end of her life Patricia Moyes devoted most of her energy to the cats she had always loved. Although she was ill in her last years, she was active in a campaign to neuter and innoculate the large population of feral cats that lived on the British Virgin Islands. She died at her home on Virgin Gorda on 2 August 2000.

Through nineteen mystery novels and dozens of short stories, Moyes created solid plots and likable characters, placed them in interesting settings, and allowed them to demonstrate intuition and mental agility rather than physical strength. She will be remembered as one of a small group of writers who extended the Golden Age of the detective novel into the second half of the twentieth century.

Interviews:

Ellery Queen's Mystery Magazine (June 1982): 92–93;

Ellery Queen's Mystery Magazine (July 1982): 105–107.

Reference:

Anthony Boucher, Introduction to *Murder by 3's,* by Patricia Moyes (New York: Holt, 1965).

Anne Perry
(28 October 1938 –   )

Marilyn Rye
Fairleigh Dickinson University

BOOKS: *The Cater Street Hangman* (New York: St. Martin's Press, 1979; London: Hale, 1979);

Callander Square (New York: St. Martin's Press, 1980; London: Hale, 1980);

Paragon Walk (New York: St. Martin's Press, 1981; London: HarperCollins, 2000);

Resurrection Row (New York: St. Martin's Press, 1981; London: HarperCollins, 2001);

Rutland Place (New York: St. Martin's Press, 1983; London: HarperCollins, 2001);

Bluegate Fields (New York: St. Martin's Press, 1984; London: Souvenir, 1992);

Death in the Devil's Acre (New York: St. Martin's Press, 1985; London: Souvenir, 1991);

Riders, Ready: A Story of BMX, with Advice from the Experts (Houston: Tadpole, 1985);

Cardington Crescent (New York: St. Martin's Press, 1987; London: Souvenir, 1990);

Silence in Hanover Close (New York: St. Martin's Press, 1988; London: Souvenir, 1989);

Bethlehem Road (New York: St. Martin's Press, 1990; London: Souvenir, 1991);

The Face of a Stranger (New York: Fawcett Columbine, 1990; London: Headline, 1993);

A Dangerous Mourning (New York: Fawcett Columbine, 1991; London: Headline, 1994);

Highgate Rise (New York: Fawcett Columbine, 1991; London: Souvenir, 1992);

Belgrave Square (New York: Fawcett Columbine, 1992; London: Souvenir, 1993);

Defend and Betray (New York: Fawcett Columbine, 1992; London: Headline, 1994);

Farrier's Lane (New York: Fawcett Columbine, 1993; London: Collins Crime, 1994);

A Sudden, Fearful Death (New York: Fawcett Columbine, 1993; London: Headline, 1993);

The Hyde Park Headsman (New York: Fawcett Columbine, 1994; London: HarperCollins, 1996);

The Sins of the Wolf (New York: Fawcett Columbine, 1994; London: Headline, 1994);

Anne Perry (photograph by Robert Clark; from the dust jacket for The Whitechapel Conspiracy, *2001)*

Traitor's Gate (New York: Fawcett Columbine, 1995; London: HarperCollins, 1996);

Cain His Brother (New York: Fawcett Columbine, 1995; London: Headline, 1995);

Pentecost Alley (New York: Fawcett Columbine, 1996; London: HarperCollins, 1997);

Weighed in the Balance (New York: Fawcett Columbine, 1996; London: Headline, 1996);

Ashworth Hall (New York: Fawcett Columbine, 1997; London: HarperCollins, 1999);

God's Part (London: Avon, 1997);

The Silent Cry (New York: Fawcett Columbine, 1997; London: Headline, 1997);

Whited Sepulchres (London: Headline, 1997); republished as *A Breach of Promise* (New York: Fawcett Columbine, 1998);

Brunswick Gardens (New York: Fawcett Columbine, 1998; London: Collins Crime, 1999);

The Twisted Root (New York: Fawcett Columbine, 1999; London: Headline, 1999);

Bedford Square (New York: Ballantine, 1999; London: Headline, 1999);

Tathea (London: Headline, 1999; Salt Lake City: Shadow Mountain, 2001);

Half Moon Street (New York: Ballantine, 2000; London: Headline, 2000);

The One Thing More (London: Headline, 2000);

Slaves of Obsession (New York: Ballantine, 2000); republished as *Slaves and Obsession* (London: Headline, 2000);

The Whitechapel Conspiracy (New York: Ballantine, 2001; London: Headline, 2001);

Funeral in Blue (New York: Ballantine, 2001; London: Headline, 2002);

A Dish Taken Cold (New York: Carroll & Graf, 2001);

Come Armageddon (London: Headline, 2001);

Southampton Row (New York: Ballantine, 2002; London: Headline, 2002);

Death of a Stranger (New York: Ballantine, 2002);

Seven Dials (New York: Ballantine, 2003).

OTHER: "Hostage to Fortune," in *The New Adventures of Sherlock Holmes,* edited by Martin H. Greenberg and Carol-Lynn Rössel Waugh (New York: Carroll & Graf, 1987);

"Digby's First Case," in *Women of Mystery,* edited by Cynthia Manson (New York: Carroll & Graf, 1992);

"Dorothy L. Sayers on Dante," in *Dorothy L. Sayers: The Centenary Celebration,* edited by Alzina Stone Gale (New York: Walker, 1993), pp. 109–121;

"The Blackmailer," in *Murder for Love,* edited by Otto Penzler (New York: Delacorte, 1996);

"The Watch Night Bell," in *Holmes for the Holidays,* edited by Greenberg, Waugh, and Jon L. Lellenberg (New York: Berkley, 1996), pp. 1–17;

"The Escape," in *The Year's 25 Finest Mystery and Crime Stories* (New York: Carroll & Graf, 1996);

"The Christmas Gift," in *More Holmes for the Holidays,* edited by Greenberg, Waugh, and Lellenberg (New York: Berkley, 1997);

"Daisy & the Archaeologist," in *Canine Crimes,* edited by Jeffrey Marks (New York: Jove, 1997);

"Uncle Charlie's Letters," in *Crime through Time,* edited by Miriam Grace Monfredo and Sharon New-

man (New York: Berkley Prime Crime, 1997), pp. 273–288;

"The Case of the Santo Nino," in *Crime through Time II,* edited by Miriam G. Monfredo and Newman (New York: Berkley, 1998), pp. 84–99;

"Daisy and the Silver Quaich," in *Midnight Louie's Pet Detectives,* edited by Carole Nelson Douglas (New York: Forge, 1998);

"Madam President," in *First Lady Murders,* edited by Nancy Pickard (New York: Pocket Books, 1999);

"Heroes," in *Murder and Obsession: A Century of British Mystery & Suspense,* edited by Penzler (New York: Delacorte, 1999);

"The Reverend Collin's Visit," in *Unholy Orders: Mystery Stories with a Religious Twist,* edited by Serita Stevens (Philadelphia: Intrigue Press, 2000);

"Daisy and the Christmas Goose," in *Malice Domestic 10,* edited by Nevada Barr (Dresdon, Tenn.: Avon, 2001), pp. 168–192;

Chapter 10 of *Naked Came the Phoenix: A Serial Novel,* edited by Marcia Talley (New York: St. Martin's Minotaur, 2001), pp. 169–184.

SELECTED PERIODICAL PUBLICATIONS– UNCOLLECTED: "The Profiteer," *Mary Higgins Clark Mystery Magazine,* 1 (1996);

"A Matter of Blackmail," *Mary Higgins Clark Mystery Magazine,* 3 (Summer–Fall 1997);

"An Affair of Inconvenience," *Mary Higgins Clark Mystery Magazine,* 5 (Fall 1998);

"A Letter from the Highlands," *Meridian* (June 2000 –) <http://www.meridianmagazine.com/anneperry/ index.html>.

Anne Perry specializes in historical mysteries set in England in the Victorian period. She explores the dramatic contrasts in Victorian society between its oppositions of rich and poor, public and private, and respectability and disgrace. Her choice of period provides an ideal setting to explore the contrast between illusion and reality at the heart of the mystery story. In her two series Perry features investigative teams composed of a professional male and an amateur female detective who pursue solutions to crimes in different but complementary ways. Her first mystery novel, *The Cater Street Hangman* (1979), begins the series of twenty-two novels featuring the husband-and-wife team of Inspector Thomas and Charlotte Pitt. *The Face of a Stranger,* published in 1990, initiates the Inspector Monk and Hester Latterly series, which includes eleven additional titles. In both series the upper-class status of the women and the professional contacts of their working-class husbands connect the detectives to all levels of their societies. Both series examine the development and construction of identity in a society divided along rigid class lines.

Perry's works are notable for introducing a range of independent and unconventional women characters and plots that highlight controversial social issues, especially in regard to the positions of women and the poor in nineteenth-century British society. Extensive historical research underlies the detailed descriptions of Victorian life to portray the niceties of upper-class etiquette, the grim poverty of the workhouses, the endless domestic routines of servants, and the confining roles of upper- and middle-class women. Perry's novels briefly introduce historical figures and touch on historical events such as the Crimean War, the American Civil War, and the Revolutions of 1848. As Perry noted when interviewed by Diana Cooper-Clark in 1983, "My novels focus on the political power struggle." Perry's plots highlight the need for political reform, and while her characters challenge many social norms, they seek to improve, not overturn, basic social structures. Female characters develop a protofeminist awareness of the injustices faced by women; yet, as Victorians they share many of the values of their society. Their desires for the same legal and political rights held by men does not preclude their fulfilling to some degree traditional roles as companions, lovers, and wives. Perry's villains often kill to maintain their outward appearances of respectability, social status, or political power. Yet, Perry frequently creates sympathy for these murderers, a high proportion of whom are women, as well as for their victims. No sympathy exists, however, for characters that put political or abstract ideas ahead of the life or welfare of any individual or for those who corrupt justice. Accusations of murder against several major series characters create empathy for those caught in a justice system that equates power with innocence and crime with lower social status. Many of Perry's novels present suspenseful trial scenes that end in unexpected reversals of this equation. Her complex plots are designed to reveal the secrets of many characters' lives, not just the murderer's act. As she told Cooper-Clark, she designs each plot by "constructing a mystery and then peeling it off bit by bit."

Although Perry's novels focus more on upper-class characters, critics have compared her work to Charles Dickens's in its demonstration of the hidden connections between the various classes and the London neighborhoods they inhabit. Critical response to Perry's mysteries has been positive and her reputation among mystery fans has grown steadily, if slowly. Her audience has been primarily American, with many of her novels published first, or only, in the United States; since 1998 her work has received much more attention in Britain, however, and her audience there has

Dust jacket for the 1990 novel in which Perry introduced detective William Monk (Bruccoli Clark Layman Archives)

increased substantially. Perry fans are loyal and were uninfluenced in their opinions by disclosures in 1994 of Perry's own conviction for a crime when she was an adolescent in New Zealand.

Anne Perry, née Juliet Marion Hulme, was born in Blackheath, London, on 28 October 1938. Her mother, H. Marion Reavley Hulme, was a teacher; her father, Walter Hulme, a scientist, became rector of Christchurch University College when his family moved to New Zealand because of Perry's respiratory health problems. Perry's early education was private; later she attended a private high school. As Sarah Lyall's and Geraldine O'Brien's 1994 articles in *The New York Times* document, Perry's early years were masked by a false identity. In 1994, after the release of *Heavenly Creatures,* a movie about a well-known murder case in New Zealand, Perry was identified as Juliet Hulme. Perry and her friend, Pauline Parker, had murdered Parker's mother. At the time Perry was on medication later found to impair judgment. After her release from prison at age eighteen, Perry had a range of jobs. Although she always wanted to write, she was an airline hostess from 1962 to 1964, an assistant buyer from 1964 to 1966, and a nanny and property underwriter in California from 1967 to 1972. Since 1972 she has been a full-time writer. When in California she became a member of the Church of Latter Day Saints (Mormon) and is an active church member. Perry lives in Portmahomack, Scotland, with a dog and four cats. Her short story "Heroes," set during World War I, won the Mystery Writers of America award for best short story in 2000. Her fantasy novel *Tathea* (1999) won the Association of Mormon Letters Award for excellence in LDS (Latter-day Saints) letters in 2001. Perry usually publishes one novel in both the Pitt and Monk series every year. She has also written two novels about the French Revolution.

When Perry turned from historical fiction to write her first mystery novel, she did not envision the ensuing series. Many of the key characters and themes in the series appear in *The Cater Street Hangman,* however, although in seminal form. In 1881 Inspector Thomas Pitt, the educated son of an estate caretaker, arrives in Cater Street to investigate the murders of several young women, including the maid of the Ellison family, and, later, their eldest daughter, Sarah. His perfect diction identifies him as a gentleman, while his appearance negates that conclusion, making it hard for many people to define his exact niche in the social hierarchy. He insists that he be treated as a middle-class professional, showing that he aspires to a higher social class.

Pitt falls in love with Charlotte Ellison, an unconventional and outspoken young woman whose character is loosely modeled on Jane Eyre, and whose outward rebellion is limited to reading newspapers surreptitiously, conversing with a tactless honesty, and refusing a "suitable" marriage. Her mother, Caroline, sees the need "to school Charlotte in the art of dissembling, masking her feelings." Charlotte's frankness, which challenged Victorian gender conventions about women, was a social liability, since Charlotte's "feelings were far too violent to be becoming in a lady." Pitt's presence allows Charlotte access to the broader knowledge of the world that her social status denies her. He expands her horizons by telling her about the real poverty and crime in London and challenging her class prejudices. Knowing she may be living with a potential murderer, Charlotte questions how much people can see of the individual behind the social mask. While Pitt proceeds in his investigation, Charlotte does not help solve this crime, although she does gather some useful information. This novel suggests that Charlotte's potential to grow as a person and as an investigator are intertwined. Since during this novel Charlotte's sister,

Emily, becomes engaged to Lord Ashworth, this investigation paves the way for Pitt to learn how tactfully to pursue cases among the upper classes, knowledge that helps him advance his career throughout the series.

The motivation for crime in *The Cater Street Hangman,* as in many novels in the first half of the series, suggests the Victorians' exaggerated desire for respectability hid a multitude of sins. Additionally, since women's social status required accepting social conventions, Charlotte's outspoken nature and instant moral indignation suggest her life will not resemble the useless, confining, and emotionally repressed lives of other Victorian women of her class. She is the moral lightning rod of the series. In her review of *Pentecost Alley* (1996) for *The New York Times* (7 April 1996), Marilyn Stasio wrote that it is Perry's "fine bladed outrage that draws blood in this series," and in her 16 March 1997 review of *Ashworth Hall* (1997), she suggested that the "subtle play on sex roles, a constant in this rewarding series, may well be the secret of its profound appeal." These elements appear in *The Cater Street Hangman* and continue throughout the series. The targets of outrage change, though, as political themes come to predominate in the later novels of the series. Perry also continues to name novels after specific London neighborhoods.

After her marriage to Pitt, Charlotte and her family become increasingly engaged in his investigations, not always with his knowledge or approval. Marrying beneath her socially gives Charlotte the freedom of an unconventional marriage while she retains some of her upper-class privileges through family connections. As Myles L. Clowers observed in 1995, Charlotte and her sister Emily's main tool of investigation is the social call, used to gather information informally in contrast to Pitt's more official procedures. For example, in *Callander Square* (1980), when the bodies of two infants are unearthed, Emily calls on acquaintances in the titular neighborhood and arranges for Charlotte, presented as Miss Ellison, to work assisting General Balantyne, a resident, with his memoirs. Charlotte gathers and shares information with Pitt about the residents' secret sexual liaisons and less respectable private lives. The novel examines the precarious nature of women's lives: working women such as maids, governesses, and secretaries have little protection against licentious employers, while wives fear loss of social status if their husbands' indiscretions are exposed. Although Pitt puts the pieces of the puzzle together, Charlotte plays an active role in this investigation, which serves as her apprenticeship and gives her the chance to develop her skills of observation and information gathering.

The rape and murder of a respectable young woman in another upper-class neighborhood occurs in *Paragon Walk* (1981), which examines Victorian attitudes toward rape and again reveals the secret liaisons and desires hidden behind masks of social respectability. The neighbors reiterate that respectable women are not raped and therefore believe the victim must have had a moral flaw. This novel introduces a major series character, Lady Vespasia Cummings-Gould, Emily's great-aunt by marriage, who lives in the neighborhood. At nearly eighty years old, the wealthy and elegant Lady Vespasia, daughter of a duke, inspires fear and terror in some people and inspiration and admiration in others, especially Charlotte. Her acidic comments introduce elements of a comedy of manners into the series. Lady Vespasia's social and political connections become increasingly important as the series develops, especially since she is active in the cause of reform. This case also marks Charlotte's continuing development as a detective, since she now finds herself able to adopt social roles with increasing ease and skill.

The next novel, *Resurrection Row* (1981), begins Perry's more serious exploration of the poverty of the working classes and the need for social reform. Pitt pursues an investigation to discover why recently buried citizens are being disinterred. These bizarre events have a hidden connection to the efforts of Lady Vespasia and her friend, Somerset Carlisle, M.P., in their current campaign to influence parliamentary legislation to improve working conditions for children. For the first time Perry's mystery makes an explicit connection between the political power and wealth of the aristocracy and the exploitation of the poor. The original and bizarre plot twist at the end demonstrates Perry's comedic skills and her interest in viewing moral decisions in more nuanced terms, as Pitt weighs his need to punish one murderer against the lives of a million working-class children.

In her first four novels Perry examines the illicit love affairs of the upper classes; in the next five she explores the secret sexual perversions of Victorian society. In *Rutland Place* (1983) Charlotte's mother acknowledges Charlotte's accomplishments as a detective when she requests help in finding a lost locket with a picture that could compromise her reputation. While investigating the theft and its connection to murder in the neighborhood, Charlotte solves many neighborhood mysteries, such as the story behind the death of Ottilie Carrington. In reality, Ottilie has run off to have a successful career in London music halls, but her respectable family has told its neighbors that she has died. Pitt is not pleased when Charlotte returns home one evening singing risqué songs and slightly drunk on champagne. As Charlotte untangles the emotional relationships that explain Pitt's identification of the murderer, she exposes the brother-sister incest in the

Dust jacket for the 1992 novel in which Perry's Inspector Thomas Pitt has his first confrontation with the powerful secret organization known as the Inner Circle (Richland County Public Library)

Lagarde household and the sexual abuse suffered by Eloise Lagarde at the hands of her brother.

Bluegate Fields (1984) centers around the murder and homosexual abuse of a young aristocrat by his uncle. His body turns up in a sewer in poverty-stricken Bluegate Fields. It is impossible to identify where his body was thrown into the sewer, for the system "is a labyrinth . . . that stretched out under the whole of London." Thus, it represents the hidden and criminal connections among all elements of the city. Pitt's career is jeopardized as his superiors pressure him to construct a case against an innocent tutor instead of exposing ugly secrets. Pitt does not want Charlotte pursuing the case, although she does identify the murderer in the end. In response, she learns to lie by omission, marking her growing assertiveness as a woman and detective. Pitt

The critics applaud
Anne Perry and her William Monk novels

A SUDDEN, FEARFUL DEATH

"Absorbing...Anne Perry continues her
excellent renderings of Victorian manners and mayhem."
—*Chicago Sun-Times*

"Perry's narrative is as stately and elegant as a royal barge on the
Thames...with a final courtroom confrontation that's a humdinger."
—*The Washington Post Book World*

DEFEND AND BETRAY

"Engaging and sharply observed...
The climactic trial, and its ugly disclosures, are well wrought."
—Frederick Busch
The New York Times Book Review

"A richly textured and timeless novel of suspense.
Her Victorian England pulsates with life and is peopled with
wonderfully memorable characters."
—Faye Kellerman

THE FACE OF A STRANGER

"First-rate."
—*The New York Times Book Review*

"Richly textured with the sights and sounds
of London and its countryside...Solidly absorbing."
—*Kirkus Reviews*

ISBN 0-449-90638-8

ANNE PERRY

AUTHOR OF
THE HYDE
PARK HEADSMAN

THE SINS
OF THE
WOLF

*Dust jacket for Perry's 1994 novel, in which Monk must clear the name of his crime-solving partner,
nurse Hester Latterly, when she is accused of murdering one of her patients
(Richland County Public Library)*

notes this striking change in her character: "Her ability to deceive was entirely new, and he was not used to it."

Death in the Devil's Acre (1985) explores the same connections between classes after respectable men are found murdered in an area where institutionalized prostitution supports the local economy. Thus, this novel again attacks the hypocrisy of Victorian values that result in a double moral standard for men and women and economic exploitation of poor women by upper-class men. Even though they seem respectable, all the murdered men have some hidden economic tie to the exploitation of poor women for whom prostitution is the best economic option. Furthermore, the work critiques the Victorian ideal of the upper-class woman as an aesthetic object, beautiful but useless, because it suggests the smothering boredom of women deprived of any real achievements. Charlotte, returning to Callander Place and inadvertently rekindling General Balantyne's affection toward her, learns that upper-class women such as his daughter seek excitement by selling their services as prostitutes.

Charlotte's involvement in this case tests Pitt's tolerance for her detective work. His approval evapo-

rates when she crosses the geographical boundary separating a respectable London neighborhood from the slums in Bluegate Fields, thus entering a dangerous world outside the sphere of respectable women. After Charlotte attempts to wrest a gun away from the general's daughter in a brothel during the closing scene of the novel, he redraws the lines of his authority and forcefully tells her, "you damn well do as you're told." Charlotte's testing of limits and confrontation with physical danger underlines her expanding authority as a detective figure, however.

One of the most important titles in the series is *Cardington Crescent* (1987) when Emily, now Lady Ashworth, seems certain to be arrested for the murder of her husband, George, during their visit to his cousins' house. Aunt Vespasia, also present, supports Charlotte in her efforts to clear Emily. Investigation of the murder reveals that the family patriarch both belittled his artistic son and forced his daughter-in-law into a sexual liaison. With so much at stake, Charlotte is fiercely combative in her efforts to keep the patriarch from pinning the crime on Emily to spare his own family's reputation. Pitt understands and supports Charlotte's detective work, which furthers his own investigation. Her access to the family's private quarters results in her identification of the murderer and her revelation of the incest motivating him to act.

In *Silence in Hanover Close* (1988) Pitt investigates an unsolved murder that occurred several years earlier. He and Charlotte discover that false evidence was planted during an accidental murder of a government official to conceal his secret life as a cross-dressing homosexual. In this novel, detecting is clearly described as acting, when Charlotte and Emily assume fictive personalities during their investigation. Emily, who is hired as a lady's maid, learns to view the aristocracy from a new perspective, while Charlotte plays the role of a visitor from the country. Pitt's superiors hope this sensitive case will damage his career, but he survives their machinations.

The series takes a more serious turn as Perry continues to link individual crimes with the theme of the need for social reforms. Women's suffrage takes the foreground in several novels that address in more depth the struggle to gain legal rights for women. Since Charlotte has enjoyed more freedom than many women of her day, she becomes more aware of the extent of other women's powerlessness before the law.

In *Bethlehem Road* (1990) Charlotte learns of men's right to control their wives' religious beliefs, lock them away in homes or mental institutions, or divorce them while keeping their children and possessions. In this novel, which begins with Charlotte at a meeting to support women's franchise, Perry draws her most critical picture of the treatment of women in Victorian society. Yet, as Cathy Leaker and Julie Anne Taddeo point out, Perry's indignation on behalf of women is tempered by ambivalence, as reflected in her negative characterization of a feminist character. Later, in *Brunswick Gardens* (1998) Perry again presents a negative portrait of a "new" woman. In *Bethlehem Road* Charlotte takes an independent role in the investigation, but her independence is slightly undermined when she pays insufficient attention to danger and barely escapes being killed. Although she is shaken after being attacked, she reacts like a more modern detective figure and attacks in return, causing the killer to plunge into the Thames River.

Highgate Rise (1991) returns to the theme of the exploitation of the poor by the rich when a strong woman reformer is killed to protect the reputation of her grandfather, a bishop who knew that the family money came from slum housing in the poorest section of London. After Clemency Shaw gives away her inheritance, she becomes the victim of an arsonist who kills to preserve the bishop's untarnished memory. *Farrier's Lane* (1993), one of the darker novels in the series, explores in some depth Victorian anti-Semitism when

Pitt reexamines the case of a young Jewish actor hanged earlier for the murder and crucifixion of his sister's Christian lover.

By this point in his career Pitt's success as an investigator and his tact in dealing with the aristocracy ensures that all politically sensitive cases will be assigned to him. The novels place a new emphasis on the growth of his career and reputation. Despite his success, the delicate nature of his investigations places his career, and later, his family in danger. In *Belgrave Square* (1992) Pitt first learns of a nefarious and powerful political organization called the Inner Circle. Although it appears to its new members as a beneficial organization, it uses its members' allegiance to control governmental and economic affairs. Positing its existence leads Perry to create Byzantine plots on occasion; in this novel, a blackmailer is murdered to conceal that a leader of the Inner Circle murdered his wife many years earlier when she threatened to reveal his homosexual love affair. This novel marks a pivotal point in the development of the moral consciousness of characters in the series, who make conscious choices not to abandon their principles to obtain power. Emily's new husband makes his first attempt at Parliament but fails because he will not join the Inner Circle. Pitt is offered a promotion to superintendent but turns it down because he wants to remain involved in actual investigations.

In *The Hyde Park Headsman* (1994) Charlotte again plays an active role. Her discovery that one of the victims has physically abused his wife helps Pitt solve the case, as does her ability to save Pitt, newly promoted to superintendent, from being blindsided by a charming murderess. Just as importantly, Emily's husband, Jack Radley, gets elected to Parliament, which broadens the scope and range of action of the series. For example, in *Ashworth Hall* Jack and Emily host a select group of preeminent Irish and English politicians as they attempt to arrive at a solution for Irish home rule, a situation that generates the murder plot.

The members of the Inner Circle challenge Pitt again in *Traitor's Gate* (1995). The complex plot of this novel centers on British choices regarding the colonization and economic development of Africa and raises the issue of where one's ultimate loyalties should lie. Sir Michael Desmond, the son of Pitt's childhood protector, Sir Arthur Desmond, asks Pitt to investigate treason in the Colonial Office. Desmond has proof of German access to British intelligence on Africa, a situation that recalls Sherlock Holmes's challenge in Arthur Conan Doyle's "The Adventure of the Naval Treaty" (1893). Desmond also asks Pitt to investigate his father's alleged suicide. He believes Sir Arthur was murdered because he betrayed the Inner Circle by openly criticizing its attempts to control British foreign

Dust jacket for Perry's 1996 novel, in which Monk and Latterly investigate the murder of a German prince in England (Richland County Public Library)

policy in Africa and exploit the continent for its own gain. Pitt's investigation is a direct challenge to the circle's power, which is built on the blind loyalty of its members. It puts him at great personal risk but does not deter him. His investigations allow him and Charlotte to circulate in aristocratic society and meet interesting characters with African connections. Pitt proves that the secretary of state for colonial affairs murdered his wife, considering her a traitor when she no longer supported his political views. The killing of Desmond's murderer by Pitt's superior in the police department demonstrates the power of the organization to corrupt justice and hide the group from public scrutiny, a power that threatens Pitt's own safety. In this novel Pitt and Charlotte demonstrate their growing mastery of political intrigue and consider the ways they have changed during the course of their relationship. When Pitt returns to Sir Arthur's memorial service and is identified by local gentry as "the caretaker's son," his reply insists on recognition of his professional achievements and new identity. He answers coldly that he is "Superintendent Pitt of Bow Street." Charlotte remembers her innocence about the world when she met Pitt, particularly her tendency to see the world in black and white before she gained "an understanding of the shades of gray that only experience could teach."

Perry has referred to the greatest crime spree of Victorian England, the bloody murders of Jack the Ripper, in several of her novels. In *The Whitechapel Conspiracy* (2001), which demonstrates Perry's ability to sustain intricate plots, she offers her own imaginative explanation of these horrific deaths. The novel opens as Pitt inadvertently thwarts the Inner Circle by arresting one of its members for murder. In retaliation, the circle effects the reassignment of Pitt to the Secret Branch. He goes undercover in Spitalfields in London's East End to investigate a revolutionary plot. The Inner Circle plans to incite the revolution, bring down the monarchy, and then replace it with a republic under its control. Plots and counterplots complicate the action as Pitt, Aunt Vespasia, and her former lover, an Italian revolutionary, defuse the situation with a brilliant plan that foils the leader of the Inner Circle. In a plot reversal reminiscent of Edgar Allan Poe's "The Purloined Letter" (1845), the novel reveals the moral bankruptcy of the English governing classes.

This novel again shows the interconnections among all levels of English society when historical characters such as the duke of Windsor and Randolph Churchill make cameo appearances; and Pitt's assignment necessitates detailed descriptions of Jewish immigrant life and the living conditions of the working poor. The novel once more reveals significant corruption within the police force. Pitt's knowledge of it forces him to make difficult moral choices that shape him into a more complex character. For the first time he must step outside of the boundaries of the law to fight injustice and safeguard the state. When he discovers a second murder framed as a suicide, he destroys evidence calculated to incite a working-class uprising. Although Pitt's investigation isolates him, the number of characters involved in collaborative detection reaches a new high. In addition to Charlotte and Lady Vespasia, Pitt's maid and his Bow Street assistant participate in unraveling the conspiracies. Their loyalty and his moral decisions contrast sharply with the values of those they investigate.

In *Southampton Row* (2002), members of the Inner Circle continue to seek revenge against Pitt, again forcing his reassignment to the Special Branch and causing his family's retreat to Dartmoor. The machinations of Charles Voisey, the leader of the Inner Circle, to win a seat in Parliament in the pending elections seem much less threatening than the circle's earlier plot; nonetheless, the head of the Special Branch believes Voisey, a respected judge, will achieve enough power to thoroughly corrupt the court system. Although Voisey uses blackmail and a smear campaign to win the election and to destroy Pitt's reputation, Pitt becomes increasingly competent in dealing with Machiavellian plots, learning to use political power to prevent harm to him or his family. Since Charlotte is in the country with the children, she plays no detective role in this novel. The dynamics of detection established throughout the series suffers from her absence.

The collaborative detective work of Pitt and Charlotte, their high regard for each other, and their compassion for others create a partnership that helps each of them escape boundaries of class and gender. While Pitt sometimes worries that Charlotte misses the luxuries and status she enjoyed before marriage, she is more than willing to trade them for the adventures of detecting. Eventually, Pitt's successful career helps him provide Charlotte with more material advantages as well. Charlotte seeks reforms for women, but she does not express the outrage of some women characters presented as embittered feminists in the series. The feminist view of the series places ideology second to human relationships. Perry's feminism is, however, strongly present in her restructuring of detective-fiction conventions. Thomas Pitt is intelligent and psychologically

astute, but he is not a superhero like some earlier detectives. Charlotte is not a sidekick but a true partner, just as necessary as her husband in solving the crimes. Furthermore, throughout the series the novels include many other characters involved in detection that contribute to the success of the investigations. Perry's novels, then, support Margaret Kinsman's observation that feminist authors deemphasize the importance of the central detective character and attach more importance to the results of collaborative efforts.

In 1990, just as Perry's Pitt series began to explore in more depth some of the injustices in later Victorian society, Perry began publishing a second series set in the earlier Victorian period. This series, darker in tone, is much more critical of the restrictions and abuses of the society in which it is set. Perry again uses a male-female detective team, but the characters, Inspector William Monk and a nurse, Hester Latterly, are fiercer individualists, highly volatile, and more traumatized by their past experiences. Personal antagonism and romantic tension characterize their early relationship, and only slowly do they develop an understanding and appreciation of each other apart from professional respect. Hester, from a genteel background, left home to nurse in the Crimean War. Her experiences in the Crimea change her values and make her critical of British society when she returns home. Inspired by her work with Florence Nightingale, Hester would like to use Nightingale's ideas to reform medical practices at home. The medical establishment's refusal to change is symptomatic of the larger society's inability to view itself with critical and impartial eyes. Hester, another outspoken heroine, is quick to anger when she finds her work and ideas constantly dismissed because of her gender.

Whereas Hester is a more intellectual and independent version of Charlotte, Monk is a more polished, more insecure version of Pitt. Monk, like Pitt, is intelligent and successful, and he possesses a beautiful voice, but he has a more arrogant and colder personality. As the series opens, Monk suffers from amnesia and is hospitalized as the result of a serious accident. He has no memory of his life before the accident, and he is always trying to find out what kind of man he has been. As the series progresses, Monk is able to fill in more gaps about his identity. Eventually he learns that he was born in a fishing village in Northumberland. After Monk came to London, a prominent businessman became his mentor and taught him to speak, dress, and act like a gentleman. The sartorial elegance that distinguishes Monk's appearance apparently consumed most of his policeman's salary before his accident. The imprisonment of Monk's mentor spurred Monk to join the police to become an agent of justice. Joan Warchol Rossi's description of him

Eoin McCarthy as Inspector Pitt and Keeley Hawes as Pitt's wife, Charlotte, in the 1998 Arts & Entertainment Network adaptation of Perry's first novel, The Cater Street Hangman *(Everett Collection)*

Perry's second series continues to examine the schizophrenic nature of Victorian society and the way respectable appearances hide the deepest social and familial sins. Investigations reveal that since characters lead double lives, they are in fact strangers to those around them. The title of the first novel in the series, *The Face of a Stranger,* demands a double interpretation. The stranger is both the unidentified murderer and Monk, who seeks to learn what kind of man he was before his accident. Monk's dual investigations to identify these two strangers run parallel. For a while he has good reason to believe that he may be the murderer. The victim, a swindler, has presented a false face to society for a long time, as well as to his mother and other women who have loved him. This novel introduces several of the major characters and themes of the series, including the hypocrisy of the upper classes, Monk's search for his identity, Hester's passion for medical reforms, and her need for independence.

When Monk first wakes up after a serious accident, his past identity has been erased so completely that he does not even know his name. After returning to police work, he learns that he is vain, methodical, solitary, brilliant, ambitious, and unkind. Many of his subordinates fear his sharp tongue, and his immediate superior, Runcorn, fears his ambition. Monk is assigned to investigate the death of Major Jocelyn Grey, an aristocrat, because he is considered the best detective and also has the manners and appearance to least offend the aristocracy. Yet, if he fails or antagonizes Grey's aristocratic family, many on the force will take pleasure in his downfall. When Monk meets Hester, who is visiting her friend Lady Callandra Daviot, Jocelyn's aunt, he immediately antagonizes her by saying he hates clever women. She retorts, "I love clever men. . . . It seems we are both to be disappointed." The dialogue between them is antagonistic and witty, but eventually Monk confides in Hester and depends on her help to solve the mystery. Simultaneous feelings of antagonism and deep trust underlie their early ambivalent relationship. Hester's comments deflate many pompous male characters, including Monk, at times and provoke discussions about the gender stereotypes in Victorian society and women's lack of legal rights. Lady Callandra, who shares Hester's point of view, is a loyal friend to Hester and Monk throughout the series.

In the second novel, *A Dangerous Mourning* (1991), the unfolding events again reveal social hypocrisy and the use of power to corrupt justice. The novel describes the human damage caused by the arrogance of patriarchal and aristocratic power, and the plot carefully draws parallels among doctors who practice medicine blindly, fathers who use their power to control their daughter's lives, and generals who send troops to be

in *Great Women Mystery Writers: Classic to Contemporary* (1994) illuminates his essential nature: Monk "is equally capable of cruelty and suffering, . . . a Byronic hero in a Gothic novel world filled with the terrors of uncertainty and obscurity." Early in the series Monk loses his position on the police force and becomes an agent of inquiry; Hester is dismissed as a hospital administrator and takes on private cases. As in Mary Roberts Rinehart's work, a nurse and a detective make a good investigative team. Hester is often able to provide Monk with information to solve his cases since she has access to his clients' private lives, and she solves many of the mysteries. Since both characters live financially precarious lives, the settings of the novels frequently reflect lives on the mean streets of London as well as the lives of those who lead a comfortable upper-class existence. As a result of their experiences and the precarious nature of their existence, both characters view their society through the lens of outsiders.

slaughtered. When Hester acts on her own in defiance of a doctor's orders and successfully alleviates the pain of a patient, she is fired for disobedience and knowing more than the doctor.

Monk's second assignment again catches him in the double bind of reconciling the pursuit of justice with preserving the reputation of a powerful aristocratic family, since Monk's superiors expect him to exonerate the family and find the murderer among the servant class. Instead, Monk and Hester uncover the Moidore family's shameful secrets, including Sir Basil Moidore's moral, if not legal, crimes against his daughters, committed to maintain the family's power and reputation. He has betrayed one daughter by sending her fortuneless husband to certain death in one of England's military disasters and married his other daughter to a wealthy but licentious and abusive man. After Sir Basil's widowed daughter learned of his greed and betrayal, she committed suicide, and the family disguised this dishonorable act as murder, covering up one more scandal. When Monk refuses to compromise his principles by arresting an innocent servant, he is fired from the police force. Since Monk's investigation suffers from his impaired memory and Hester's nursing position in the home gives her a more accurate view of family relationships and the ability to understand the significance of a crucial detail, she plays the more active role in arriving at the truth after Monk eliminates other possible solutions. This novel introduces the accomplished barrister Oliver Rathbone, who works with Hester and Monk on many future cases, but his romantic interest in Hester infuses tension into his relationship with Monk.

The next novel, *Defend and Betray* (1992), once again underscores the powerlessness of women in Victorian society, laying out its consequences in an even darker and more shocking fashion than before. The novel centers around the trial of Alexandra Carlyon, who admits from its opening that she has murdered her husband, the respected military man General Carlyon. Rathbone tries to develop a defense but gets no help from his client, who has no apparent motive and will not explain her actions. Eventually, however, Hester deduces that the general was sodomizing his son and that murder was Alexandra's only option to defend her child. Now if she defends her action, she will betray her son's shame. Alexandra's helplessness reflects the appalling situation of Victorian women, who had no legal rights over their children and could not challenge their husband's total authority. The novel paints a negative picture of a masculine culture that devalues women and makes men uncomfortable in their presence. Monk's investigation keeps going over the same ground without producing any insight, especially since

it is interrupted by his need to retrace three of his earlier cases to find a woman he once loved. He is bitterly disappointed in his discoveries and himself, because he must confront his attraction to feminine women who lack the courage of Hester and Alexandra. Perry's ability to slowly build suspense and create a dramatic reversal at the conclusion of the trial turns the indictment of Alexandra into an indictment of her culture and society.

Perry's continually developing tableaux of Victorian society connects the fact of women's powerlessness in the domestic setting with the denial of professional opportunities in the public world. For instance, Sir Basil has complete power over his daughters because they are economically dependent on him. Perry reexamines the theme of women's lack of career opportunities and its effects on their lives in *A Sudden, Fearful Death* (1993) and in a later novel, *Whited Sepulchres* (1997; published in the United States as *A Breach of Promise*, 1998). In *A Sudden, Fearful Death* a Crimean nurse and acquaintance of Hester, Prudence Barrymore, is murdered in the hospital where Hester has worked. Nurse Barrymore's passion for medicine and the quality of her work for Dr. Stanhope mistakenly lead her to believe he will help her enter medical school, even though women are never admitted. He kills her when she demands his help in return for her silence about the abortions he has performed for rich women. Prudence's letters to her sister reflect her passion for medicine, but the prosecution interprets them as a passion for Stanhope since woman's passion for knowledge is beyond the prosecution's comprehension. Hester understands that false assumptions about women's nature have confused the issue, and Monk finds the means to incriminate Stanhope. Also, Monk begins to understand that his own similar misconceptions about women have made him undervalue Hester's strength, courage, and dedication to her ideals.

The Sins of the Wolf (1994) is a key novel in the series because it places its characters in extremely dangerous situations that test the true nature of their relationships. When Hester travels to Scotland on a private nursing assignment, the family of her patient frames her for the woman's murder. Monk does some of his best investigative work to unravel the duplicitous layers of the wealthy and respected Farraline family's history, revealing the corruption at its core. Set in a different country, the novel restates in new terms the familiar theme of hypocrisy behind respectable appearances. In her discussion of Dorothy L. Sayers's translation of Dante's *Inferno,* Perry identifies the wolf as representative of the deepest sins, sins of the intellect, "malice and fraud, the perversion of that which should have been good, the betrayals." The Farralines' wealth stems not

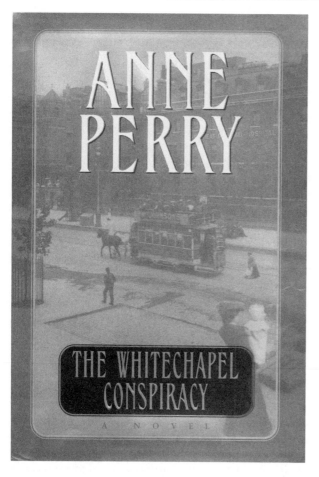

Dust jacket for Perry's 2001 Pitt mystery, in which the inspector investigates an anti-monarchist Inner Circle plot with links to the Jack the Ripper murders (Richland County Public Library)

from their legitimate business but from a highly successful counterfeiting operation, and counterfeiting is the thematic symbol of the perversion of truth and the falsity of all appearances. Hester's guilt is counterfeit; the unconsummated marriage of Mary and Hamish Farraline is a counterfeit relationship, and the acknowledged paternity of the children is another fiction as well. Furthermore, Alistair, the eldest son, who holds a high position in the Scottish justice system, takes bribes and condones the counterfeiting operation. In contrast to the fraud of these relationships, Hester, Monk, the Rathbones, and Callandra Daviot have relationships of true value. When Hester and Monk believe they are going to die, they reveal their intense attraction to each other in a scene that marks a turning point in their relationship, although afterward they are not ready to abandon their need for independence. Setting the novel in Scotland allows Perry to describe the countryside where she now lives and also provides variety in her continuing use of a cast of established characters.

Perry's descriptions of the familiar setting of London in *Cain His Brother* (1995) invest that novel with a mood reminiscent of Dickens's work. Like Dickens, Perry demonstrates the hidden connections among the social classes of London. The unreconciled dualities of Victorian society are symbolized by the opposite natures of the twin brothers raised by Lord Ravensbrook. One, Angus Stonehold, is a respectable businessman; the other brother, Caleb, is a vicious man and part of the criminal underworld of Limehouse and the marshes farther downriver. Since Hester, Lady Callandra, and her friend Dr. Kristian Beck are aiding typhus victims in Limehouse, Hester is able to gather information for Monk to help him locate Angus for his distraught wife, Genevieve, who believes Caleb has killed him. In reality Caleb is not a twin but one of Angus's dual personalities, the representation of repressed insanity caused by the abuse inflicted by Ravensbrook during his childhood. Angus's dual personality represents the human damage caused by the social and geographical divisions of London into rich and poor, respectable and criminal, ill and healthy, as well as the two-faced nature of Lord Ravensbrook. This novel also provides Monk with more insight about his past harshness in the pursuit of justice and his mistaken judgment in valuing conventional femininity and charm over Hester's qualities of independence, honesty, and courage. Monk's realization that he can rely on Hester and admit his weakness and foolishness to her, as well as his increasingly accurate judgment about women, strengthens their relationship.

Perry's early interest in writing historical fiction with foreign settings predominates in shaping the plots of several novels in the Monk series, the first of which, *Weighed in the Balance* (1996), addresses events influenced by Prussia's impending unification of German states. Her novel *Slaves of Obsession* (2000) follows Hester and Monk to the United States in pursuit of stolen armaments in a case in which Hester again nurses wounded and dying soldiers on American battlefields. In *Funeral in Blue* (2001) Monk travels to Vienna to explore his client's role in the Revolution of 1848 and hears heroic tales about idealistic revolutionaries.

The inspiration for *Weighed in the Balance* may have come from the Sherlock Holmes story "A Scandal in Bohemia" (1891), since its central interest is the love story of a minor (and exiled) German prince from Felzburg who has been murdered in England. Monk travels to Venice and Felzburg and an English country estate during an investigation to clear the name of Rathbone's client, Countess Zora Rostova. Although the action is set primarily in England, the story centers on the romantic marriage of Prince Frederick and Princess Gisela and the political intrigue surrounding it. Unlike previous novels, this one offers little commentary on English society, except for the suggestion that all royalty is open to scrutiny. As before, the joint talents of Monk, Hester, and Rathbone turn an apparently hopeless trial case into an explosive indictment of a murderer, again demonstrating Perry's skill in building suspense and creating courtroom drama. Thematically, the novel depicts the developing romance between Hester and Monk, which contrasts sharply with the actual relationship between Frederick and Gisela. Hester rewrites the royal legend with the observation that they were not great lovers but two people using each other to fulfill their needs. Her definition of love, a relationship between individuals true to themselves and thus capable of loving others, foreshadows the course of Hester and Monk's developing relationship and supports the thematic insistence in the series on the necessity of women's pursuit of self-fulfillment.

As the series progresses, the novels question the nature of the relationship between a constructed social identity and an individual's personal sense of identity built upon experience and ability. They show the disorientating consequences of losing a social identity or the damaging results of subsuming a personality into a socially constructed role. In addition to Monk's quest for knowledge about his own past, which appears in many novels, plot structures entailing exploration of characters' past lives raise this issue as a major theme in *The Silent Cry* (1997), *Whited Sepulchres, The Twisted Root* (1999), and *Funeral in Blue.*

The Silent Cry, like *Bluegate Fields* in the Pitt series, begins with the murders of respected men who had hidden connections to the sexual pleasures for sale in the London slums. Two respectable citizens, one dead and one barely alive, are found savagely beaten in the slums of St. Giles. Hester nurses the survivor, Rhys Duff, who cannot explain why he and his dead father went to those slums or who attacked them there. He is incapable of speech, having been traumatized into silence. When Rhys is charged with murder, Monk investigates and learns that Rhys's father, doctor, and schoolmaster routinely went to the slums and raped prostitutes for pleasure. They rape Rhys because they do not recognize him, identifying him only as a young male and possible victim. His rape, as well as his loss of familial and social status, associates him with the area prostitutes, whom the men regard as a class of human beings, anonymous and interchangeable, that they can treat as objects. The son's silence and the stripping of the protection of his social status identifies him with the prostitutes, victims who cannot speak against their exploiters and reveal them as dishonorable men.

An interesting twist on the theme of identity shapes the plot and unexpected revelations at the end

of *Whited Sepulchres.* This novel, like the earlier *A Sudden, Fearful Death,* suggests gender roles are social constructions that impose distorted and constricting identities on individual women. As in *Defend and Betray* and *Weighed in the Balance, Whited Sepulchres* centers on Rathbone's defense of a client who provides no information or explanation of his behavior. Killian Melville, a brilliant young architect, is sued in a breach-of-promise case because he refuses to wed his patron's daughter. An autopsy performed on him after his death at the end of the trial reveals that Killian was a woman cross-dressing as a man in order to practice her profession. The unyielding prejudice of the Victorians against women who try to enter the "male" sphere outside the home assigns the remarkable designs left by Killian a lesser value: she is a woman who will never be used. The descriptions in the novel of the hysteria of the marriage market coupled with Killian's desperate strategy to pursue a career concretely convey the Victorian assumption that women have no career alternatives to marriage, which confers upon them the status and identity of their husbands. Although Mrs. Lambert kills Killian to halt Monk's investigation before he discovers damaging information that would ruin her daughter's chances of marriage and her own reputation, Monk and Hester uncover her lower-class origins and the murders that fed her ambition. As a result of this investigation, Monk's character becomes more empathetic, which enables him to admire Hester's concern for her patients. Spurred by his new appreciation, he proposes marriage and Hester accepts, giving a definitive shape to the romance that propels the series forward. In contrast to their society's conventional ideas of marriage, the description of their relationship suggests marital happiness depends upon valuing each partner's autonomy.

The opening pages of *The Twisted Root* bring to mind the opening of the Sherlock Holmes story "The Adventure of the Noble Bachelor" (1892), since in each case young women vanish in the middle of celebrations marking their highly desirable marriages. In the Conan Doyle story the bride leaves after seeing the husband she had believed dead; in the Perry novel the fiancée flees after recognizing her fiancé's uncle as the man who raped and impregnated her when she was twelve. The title *The Twisted Root* refers to the complicated relationships in the background of Lucius Sturbridge, which, if revealed, would disinherit Lucius, strip him of his legitimacy, and radically alter his identity. The detective work in the novel again underscores the collaborative nature of Monk and Hester's investigations. Monk quickly succeeds in finding the missing fiancée, while Hester, through her connections as a nurse, finally per-

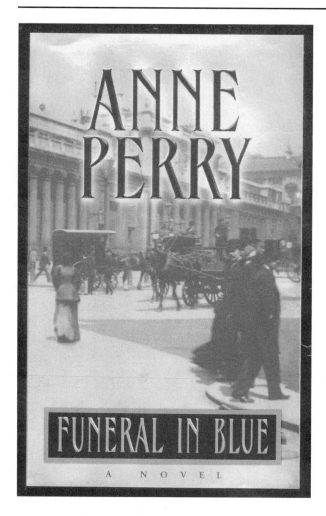

Dust jacket for Perry's 2001 William Monk mystery, in which the detective travels to Vienna to solve a murder mystery involving the German Revolution of 1848 (Richland County Public Library)

suades her to explain her behavior and clear an innocent woman from a false charge of murder. In addition to the usual theme of murder to preserve wealth and reputation, the novel examines the nature of parent-child bonds and the complicated relationships of duty, sacrifice, and love. Monk's mentoring relationship with a young detective and Hester's new cause of providing medicine to elderly soldiers also suggest the importance of accepting moral obligations.

This novel also describes Monk and Hester's period of adjustment as a newly married couple. Monk is enough of a Victorian to insist that Hester cannot earn a salary, so her nursing is limited to volunteer work and visits to elderly soldiers, but he still values her detective work. Although she is married, Hester remains independent, willing to take risks for a good cause, and persistent in her fight to train nurses as professionals.

In *Funeral in Blue* the murder investigation centers on Hester's small circle of friends at the hospital where she has worked occasionally during the six years after her return from Crimea. It reprises themes from earlier novels: the difficulty of truly knowing other people who keep so much of themselves hidden behind their everyday faces; the continuing hold of the past upon the present; the emptiness of women's lives when they have little to occupy their time, the issue of women's property rights, and the need to distinguish love from dependency or selfishness. Familiar settings include the hospital and the courthouse, but Monk's investigation also takes him to London's gambling houses and the coffeehouses of Vienna in his quest to uncover the passions and history that may make sense of murder.

When two women, the wife of Hester's colleague Dr. Beck and an artist's model, are found dead in a London artist's studio, Hester, Monk, and Lady Callandra investigate to clear Beck of murder charges. The title of the novel refers to a portrait of his wife, Elissa, called *Funeral in Blue,* which Monk believes captures the essence of her identity as a passionate revolutionary in Vienna in 1848. The stories Monk hears about the Becks' revolutionary past broaden the historical scope of the novel and draw a pointed contrast between Elissa's past life, full of purpose and activity, and her stifling life in London as a middle-class woman with no interesting occupation. She becomes addicted to gambling, as does Hester's sister-in-law, and the stories of the two women show the destructive consequences of the Victorian ideology that defined women only as "angels of the house," expected to confine their activities to the domestic sphere.

Hester's decision during this investigation to broaden the scope of her detective work extends another challenge to the Victorian conception of a woman's place. After Monk leaves for Vienna, Hester pursues the investigation in the streets of London, placing herself in danger to gather information as Monk would have done had he been present. Her successful results show her acting with increased agency despite the fears she experiences. Another significant development is Monk's changed relationship with his former superior, Runcorn, opening up the possibility that Monk may work more closely with the police in future investigations. In the end Runcorn, Monk, and Hester confront the real murderer together.

Monk's investigations continue to show the importance of the past in defining an individual's identity and also how that identity must be continually reconceived. Perry's use of a Romantic definition of identity as organic, fluid, and stemming from the individual underlies the critical view presented in her novels of the Victorian definition of identity as socially constructed and class-based. Monk's discovery of new information alters the legendary image of Elissa and presents Beck with the need to reconstruct his sense of himself. Monk's changed relationship with his former enemy, Runcorn, is possible only when Monk understands his past history and can use it to reshape others' perceptions of him to understand the man he has become. The belief that an individual's identity is fluid, shaped but not fixed by the past, results in characters whose response to change and ability to grow continue to interest readers.

Anne Perry's works succeed in blending conventions of mystery, romance, and historical fiction in novels that create detailed portraits of Victorian life. Her Pitt series charts a map of London neighborhoods as each novel adds to her increasingly complex portrait of the city at a particular moment in history. Her Monk series investigates in more depth a range of social and political issues that shaped England into a modern society. Like Perry, who considers her writing a temporary escape into a different time period, readers can experience temporarily the sensibility and mores of an earlier time while recognizing in its outlines similar issues and problems in the modern world. Perry's accomplishment as a detective writer is to reconceive detective work as a highly moral endeavor. The Victorian setting of her novels makes the moral tone of her characters' belief in their causes sound idealistic, but not anachronistic, as such discussions would be in contemporary works. Furthermore, Perry's use of detective couples extends the possibilities of earlier models. Men and women collaborate as equals, and their different approaches allow them to build on each other's discoveries. The necessity of two detectives working together gives each a more human face and less heroic stature, as does their need for additional assistance from friends and colleagues.

Interviews:

Diana Cooper-Clark, "Interview with Anne Perry," in her *Designs of Darkness: Interviews with Detective Novelists* (Bowling Green, Ohio: Bowling Green State University Popular Press, 1983), pp. 205–223;

Dean James, "Anne Perry," *Mystery Scene,* 42, no. 14 (1994): 71–72;

Elisabeth Sherwin, "Perry's Peaceful Writing Life No Longer a Mystery," *Davis Virtual Market* (13 April 1997) <http://virtual-markets.net/~gizmo/1997/perry.html>;

"A Conversation with Anne Perry," in Perry's *Brunswick Gardens* (New York: Fawcett Columbine, 1998);

Linda Richards, "The Mysteries of Anne Perry." *january magazine* (November 1998) <http://www.januarymagazine.com/profiles/perry.html>.

References:

Myles L. Clowers, "She Snoops to Conquer: The Historical Detective Novels of Anne Perry," *Clues: A Journal of Detection,* 16, no. 1 (1995): 25–34;

Margaret Kinsman, "Band of Sisters," in *The Art of Detective Fiction,* edited by Warren Chernaik, Martin Swales, and Robert Vilain (New York: St. Martin's Press, 2000), pp. 153–169;

Cathy Leaker and Julie Anne Taddeo, "Defend and Preserve: Imminent Nostalgia in the Victorian Mysteries of Anne Perry," *Clues: A Journal of Detection,* 17, no. 1 (1996): 77–106;

Sarah Lyall, "Mystery Writer's Hidden Mystery," *New York Times,* 17 August 1994, p. C9+;

Geraldine O'Brien, "From New Zealand, Heavenly Murderous Creatures," *New York Times,* 13 November 1994, section 2, p. 15+.

Ellis Peters
(Edith Pargeter)
(28 September 1913 – 14 October 1995)

Gina Macdonald
Nicholls State University

with

Michele Theriot
Nicholls State University

BOOKS: *Hortensius, Friend of Nero,* as Edith Pargeter (London: Lovat Dickson, 1936; New York: Greystone, 1937);

Iron-Bound, as Pargeter (London: Lovat Dickson, 1936);

Day Star, as Peter Benedict (London: Lovat Dickson, 1937);

Murder in the Dispensary, as Jolyon Carr (London: Jenkins, 1938);

Freedom for Two, as Carr (London: Jenkins, 1939);

The City Lies Four-Square (London: Heinemann, 1939; New York: Reynal & Hitchcock, 1939);

Death Comes by Post, as Carr (London: Jenkins, 1940);

Masters of the Parachute Mail, as Carr (London: Jenkins, 1940);

The Victim Needs a Nurse, as John Redfern (London: Jarrolds, 1940);

Ordinary People, as Pargeter (London: Heinemann, 1941); republished as *People of My Own* (New York: Reynal & Hitchcock, 1942);

She Goes to War, as Pargeter (London: Heinemann, 1942; West Seneca, N.Y.: Ulverscroft, 1993);

The Eighth Champion of Christendom: Lame Crusade, as Pargeter (London: Heinemann, 1945);

Reluctant Odyssey: Being the Second Volume of the Eighth Champion of Christendom (London: Heinemann, 1946);

Warfare Accomplished: Being the Third Volume of the Eighth Champion of Christendom (London: Heinemann, 1947);

The Fair Young Phoenix, as Pargeter (London: Heinemann, 1948);

By Firelight, as Pargeter (London: Heinemann, 1948); republished as *By This Strange Fire* (New York: Reynal & Hitchcock, 1948);

Edith Pargeter (from the dust jacket for the U.S. edition of Brother Cadfael's Penance, *1994)*

The Coast of Bohemia (London: Heinemann, 1950);

Fallen into the Pit, as Pargeter (London: Heinemann, 1951; New York: Mysterious Press, 1994);

Lost Children, as Pargeter (London: Heinemann, 1951);

Holiday with Violence, as Pargeter (London: Heinemann, 1952; West Seneca, N.Y.: Ulverscroft, 1994);

This Rough Magic, as Pargeter (London: Heinemann, 1953);

Most Loving Mere Folly, as Pargeter (London: Heinemann, 1953);

The Soldier at the Door, as Pargeter (London: Heinemann, 1954);

A Means of Grace, as Pargeter (London: Heinemann, 1956);

The Assize of the Dying, as Pargeter (London: Heinemann, 1958; Garden City, N.Y.: Doubleday, 1958);

Death Mask (London: Collins, 1959; Garden City, N.Y.: Doubleday, 1960);

The Will and the Deed (London: Collins, 1960); republished as *Where There's a Will* (Garden City, N.Y.: Doubleday, 1960);

The Heaven Tree (London: Heinemann, 1960; Garden City, N.Y.: Doubleday, 1960);

Death and the Joyful Woman (London: Collins, 1961; Garden City, N.Y.: Doubleday, 1962);

Funeral of Figaro (London: Collins, 1962; New York: Morrow, 1964);

The Green Branch (London: Heinemann, 1962);

The Scarlet Seed (London: Heinemann, 1963);

Flight of a Witch (London: Collins, 1964; New York: Mysterious Press, 1991);

A Nice Derangement of Epitaphs (London: Collins, 1965); republished as *Who Lies Here?* (New York: Morrow, 1965);

The Lily Hand and Other Stories (London: Heinemann, 1965);

The Piper on the Mountain (London: Collins, 1966; New York: Morrow, 1966);

Black Is the Colour of My True-Love's Heart (London: Collins, 1967; New York: Morrow, 1967);

The Grass-Widow's Tale (London: Collins, 1968; New York: Morrow, 1968);

The House of Green Turf (London: Collins, 1969; New York: Morrow, 1969);

Mourning Raga (London: Macmillan, 1969; New York: Morrow, 1970);

The Knocker on Death's Door (London: Macmillan, 1970; New York: Morrow, 1971);

Death to the Landlords! (London: Macmillan, 1972; New York: Morrow, 1972);

A Bloody Field by Shrewsbury (London: Macmillan, 1972; New York: Viking, 1973);

City of Gold and Shadows (London: Macmillan, 1973; New York: Morrow, 1974);

The Horn of Roland (London: Macmillan, 1974; New York: Morrow, 1974);

Sunrise in the West: The Brothers of Gwynedd I (London: Macmillan, 1974);

The Dragon at Noonday: The Brothers of Gwynedd II (London: Macmillan, 1975);

The Hounds of Sunset: The Brothers of Gwynedd III (London: Macmillan, 1976);

Never Pick Up Hitch-Hikers! (London: Macmillan, 1976; New York: Morrow, 1976);

Afterglow and Nightfall: The Brothers of Gwynedd IV (London: Macmillan, 1977);

A Morbid Taste for Bones: A Mediaeval Whodunnit (London: Macmillan, 1977; New York: Morrow, 1978);

Rainbow's End (London: Macmillan, 1978; New York: Morrow, 1979);

One Corpse Too Many: A Mediaeval Whodunit (London: Macmillan, 1979; New York: Morrow, 1980);

The Marriage of Meggotta (London: Macmillan, 1979; New York: Viking, 1979);

Monk's-Hood: The Third Chronicle of Brother Cadfael (London: Macmillan, 1980; New York: Morrow, 1981);

Saint Peter's Fair: The Fourth Chronicle of Brother Cadfael (London: Macmillan, 1981; New York: Morrow, 1981);

The Leper of Saint Giles: The Fifth Chronicle of Brother Cadfael (London: Macmillan, 1981; New York: Morrow, 1982);

The Virgin in the Ice: The Sixth Chronicle of Brother Cadfael (London: Macmillan, 1982; New York: Morrow, 1983);

The Sanctuary Sparrow: The Seventh Chronicle of Brother Cadfael (London: Macmillan, 1983; New York: Morrow, 1983);

The Devil's Novice: The Eighth Chronicle of Brother Cadfael (London: Macmillan, 1983; New York: Morrow, 1984);

Dead Man's Ransom: The Ninth Chronicle of Brother Cadfael (London: Macmillan, 1984; New York: Morrow, 1984);

The Pilgrim of Hate: The Tenth Chronicle of Brother Cadfael (London: Macmillan, 1984; New York: Morrow, 1985);

An Excellent Mystery: The Eleventh Chronicle of Brother Cadfael (London: Macmillan, 1985; New York: Morrow, 1986);

The Raven in the Foregate: The Twelfth Chronicle of Brother Cadfael (London: Macmillan, 1986; New York: Morrow, 1986);

The Rose Rent: The Thirteenth Chronicle of Brother Cadfael (London: Macmillan, 1986; New York: Morrow, 1986);

The Hermit of Eyton Forest (London: Headline, 1987; New York: Mysterious Press, 1988);

The Confession of Brother Haluin (London: Headline, 1988; New York: Mysterious Press, 1989);

A Rare Benedictine: The Advent of Brother Cadfael (London: Headline, 1988; New York: Mysterious Press, 1989);

The Heretic's Apprentice: The Sixteenth Chronicle of Brother Cadfael (London: Headline, 1989; New York: Mysterious Press, 1990);

The Potter's Field (London: Headline, 1989; New York: Mysterious Press, 1990);

Smart Moves (London: Headline, 1990; New York: Mysterious Press, 1994);

The Summer of the Danes (London: Headline, 1991; New York: Mysterious Press, 1991);

Shropshire: A Memoir of the English Countryside, text by Peters, photographs by Roy Morgan (Stroud, U.K.: Alan Sutton, 1992; New York: Mysterious Press, 1993);

The Holy Thief: The Nineteenth Chronicle of Brother Cadfael (London: Headline, 1992; New York: Mysterious Press, 1993);

Strongholds and Sanctuaries: The Borderland of England and Wales, text by Peters, photographs by Morgan (Stroud, U.K.: Alan Sutton, 1993);

Brother Cadfael's Penance: The Twentieth Chronicle of Brother Cadfael (London: Headline, 1994; New York: Mysterious Press, 1994).

Editions and Collections: *A Rare Benedictine: The Advent of Brother Cadfael,* introduction by Peters (New York: Mysterious Press, 1988);

The Brothers of Gwynedd Quartet (London: Headline, 1990)—comprises *Sunrise in the West, The Dragon at Noonday, The Hounds of Sunset,* and *Afterglow and Nightfall;*

The Benediction of Brother Cadfael, introduction by Peters (New York: Mysterious Press, 1992)—includes *A Morbid Taste for Bones* and *One Corpse Too Many;*

The Heaven Tree Trilogy (New York: Mysterious Press, 1993; London: Warner, 1994)—comprises *The Heaven Tree, The Green Branch,* and *The Scarlet Seed.*

PRODUCED SCRIPT: *The Heaven Tree,* radio, 1975.

TRANSLATIONS (as Pargeter): Jan Neruda, *Tales of the Little Quarter* (London: Heinemann, 1957; Westport, Conn.: Greenwood, 1976);

František Koik, *The Sorrowful and Heroic Life of John Amos Comenius* (Prague: State Educational Publishing House, 1958);

A Handful of Linden Leaves: An Anthology of Czech Poetry, edited by Jaroslav Jas (Prague: Artia, 1958);

Joseph Toman, *Don Juan* (New York: Knopf, 1958);

Mojmir Otruba, Zdenek Pesat, and others, eds., *The Linden Tree: An Anthology of Czech and Slovak Literature, 1890–1960,* translated by Pargeter and others (Prague: Artia, 1962);

Bôzena Nêmcová, *Granny: Scenes from Country Life* (Prague: Artia, 1962; Westport, Conn.: Greenwood Press, 1976);

Josef Bor, *The Terezin Requiem* (New York: Knopf, 1963);

Alois Jirásek, *Legends of Old Bohemia* (London: Hamlyn, 1963);

Karel Hynek Macha, *May* (Prague: Artia, 1965);

Vladislav Vanura, *The End of the Old Times* (Prague: Artia, 1965);

Bohumil Hrabal, *A Close Watch on the Trains* (London: Cape, 1968); republished as *Closely Watched Trains* (Evanston, Ill.: Northwestern University Press, 1995);

Josefa Slanska, *Report on My Husband,* introduction by Pargeter (London: Hutchinson, 1969);

Ivan Klíma, *A Ship Named Hope: Two Novels* (London: Gollancz, 1970);

Jaroslav Seifert, *Mozart in Prague* (Prague: Artia, 1970).

Like more-recent writers, such as Anne Perry, Elizabeth Peters, and Peter Lovesey, who have followed her lead, Ellis Peters has made the historical mystery novel her own special domain; but unlike these three, with their nineteenth-century settings, she chose a much more distant historical setting, the Middle Ages, particularly the twelfth and thirteenth centuries. Although the first of her two detective series was contemporary, featuring Detective-Sergeant George Felse, his wife, and their son, after thirteen novels of domestic crime, Peters was ready for a more challenging series, one that allowed her to use her scholarship, the familiar locale of her region, and her training and interest in history. The result was innovative, intriguing historical crime stories set in twelfth-century Shrewsbury, their amateur detective a monk, Brother Cadfael. Begun in 1977, this popular series, which includes twenty novels—several of them filmed for the BBC *Mystery Theater* series and starring Derek Jacobi—educates readers about medieval life, its hierarchies and structures, its daily concerns and hardships, its conflicts and intrigues, its joys and fears. Peters is a prolific, versatile, accomplished writer, with a passion for bringing the past to life in meaningful ways that touch on modern lives and with a strong sense of the flowing, almost musical, prose of the period of which she writes.

Peters asserts in *The Writer* that she has never been attracted to the "pure puzzle, with a cast of characters kept deliberately two-dimensional and all equally expendable at the end." Instead, she is interested in the "paradoxical puzzle, the impossible struggle to create a cast of genuine, rounded, knowable characters caught in conditions of stress," and then "to let the readers know everything about them, feel with them, like or dislike them, and still to try to preserve to the end the secret of which of these is a murderer." Consequently, she believes a good detective novel should be a good novel, multidimensional with serious themes involving politics, religions, family, and society; a study of human development and change; a portrait of the individual within a community; and a treatment of universal concerns such as love and death. Peters's mysteries guarantee accurate, concrete historical details, a strong, upright, intuitive detective, convincing character studies, believable teenagers, a cunningly contrived mystery linked to the psychology of the characters and the distinctive setting of the story, a knowledge of easily acquired herbs and poisons, an experienced understanding of the harsh realities of war, and authenticity of place.

Ellis Peters was born Edith Mary Pargeter on 28 September 1913 to Edmund Valentine and Edith Hordley Pargeter in Horsehay, near Shrewsbury in Shropshire. Her works reflect her ties to this land, with Shropshire and the Marches of Wales, especially Shrewsbury, central to her work. For more than a thousand years this border territory has been a focal point for Welsh-English tensions. Peters claims her Welsh grandmother created in her an affinity for Wales and its squabbling factions and for the accommodations locals made in order to survive conflicts with the wealthier, better-armed English. *A Bloody Field by Shrewsbury* (1972), set near early-fifteenth-century Shrewsbury, captures a significant moment in this conflict: Harry "Hotspur" Percy's rebellion against Henry Bolingbroke, who had seized the English throne and had begun the line that produced the first Queen Elizabeth. *The Brothers of Gwynedd* series and the Brother Cadfael mysteries depend on Peters's intimate knowledge of this region and her vivid descriptions of the wild terrain and the rural beauty.

The nom de plume Ellis Peters, used solely for her mysteries, has provided her with anonymity and a masculine cover, a practice common for women writers of her generation; and, in fact, Pargeter has also written under the pseudonyms Peter Benedict, Jolyon Carr, and John Redfern. She attended Dawley Church of England Elementary School, then the Coalbrookdale High School for Girls, where, at age twelve, she began her first novel, having been encouraged by teachers impressed by her writing. Rudyard Kipling and Thomas Mallory were among her favorite authors. Instead of an Oxford Higher School Certificate and first-class honors in English leading to further academic pursuits, at age twenty she began to work as a pharmacist's assistant, dispensing medications to customers in a shop in Dawley, a seven-year experience (from 1933 to 1940) that taught her much about pharmaceuticals and herbs and that prepared her to make Brother Cadfael and his apprentices authorities on the healing arts, especially herbal medicine as practiced in medieval times. Thus, when she names poisons or elaborates on the effects of a particular leaf or flower, she knows of which she speaks. During this period, Peters published *Hortensius, Friend of Nero* (1936), her first historical novel, and "The Face of Wax," her first short

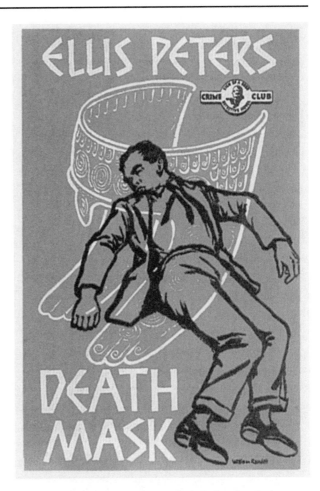

Dust jacket for Pargeter's 1959 novel, the first that she wrote under her best-known pseudonym (from John Cooper and B. A. Pike, Detective Fiction: The Collector's Guide, *1988)*

story (published in *Good Housekeeping*). When World War II broke out, Peters entered the Women's Royal Naval Service and was promoted to the rank of petty officer. King George VI awarded her the Medal of the British Empire in 1944 for outstanding service in communications. She left the military in 1945, but her military service had provided new areas of interest and expertise with which to develop military images of the past. Her military position had allowed her to continue to write and publish romances and contemporary novels throughout the 1940s, including four World War II novels. One of these, *She Goes to War* (1942), tells Peters's own story through the eyes of her impulsive protagonist, Catherine Saxon, who travels to Devonport to join the Women's Royal Navy Service; young Saxon's decision is sudden, her reasons ill-defined, and the consequences unforeseen. Peters turned the events of the war around her into prose; the trilogy comprising *The Eighth Champion of Christendom* (1945), *Reluctant Odyssey* (1946), and *Warfare Accomplished* (1947), for example, depicts the maturation

*Dust jacket for the U.S. edition of Peters's 1976 novel in which
a young hitchhiker gets entangled with a gang of bank robbers
(Richland County Public Library)*

successful movie. These activities led to an award she treasured most highly because of her fellow feeling for the people of Czechoslovakia–the Czechoslovak Society for International Relations Gold Medal and Ribbon, awarded during the Prague Spring of 1968. She also had received and continued to receive other awards. For instance, in 1961 the International Institute of Arts and Letters made her a fellow in recognition of her scholarly contributions in history and translation, and the same year she received the Edgar Allan Poe Award from the Mystery Writers of America for her fourth mystery novel, *Death and the Joyful Woman* (1961). She had published her first mystery novel, *Fallen into the Pit,* in 1951 and her second, *Death Mask,* in 1959. The first she wrote under her own name, but for the second she created the pseudonym by which she is best known to mystery fans: "Ellis" (her Welsh grandmother's maiden name and her brother's name) and "Peters" (a variation of Petra, a Czech friend's daughter's name). In this way she hoped readers could distinguish her mystery creations from her other writing. From 1960 to 1979 Peters wrote a play, short stories, historical novels, five nonseries mysteries, and twelve more Felse mysteries, and from 1977 to 1995 twenty Brother Cadfael mysteries, confirming the aptness of her description of herself as "essentially a story-teller." During this productive period Ellis demonstrated that she had learned to combine her love for puzzles and intrigue with her love of history.

Fallen into the Pit introduces Detective Sergeant George Felse of the Comerford, Midshire, Criminal Investigation Division (CID), whose thirteen-year-old son, Dominic, has stumbled over a corpse. Dominic had been taught logic and self-defense by a former soldier, now mentor, who warned that fighting is a life-and-death matter that proves nothing, settles nothing, and solves nothing. Now, Dominic must put his lessons into practice in order to solve the murder and tackle a villainous evildoer. Music, adolescence, and family all play integral roles in the Felse novels from the start. The novels demonstrate how an active, loving family can nurture a youth and smooth the path of maturation, in contrast to the strained and terrifying experiences of children in less protective environments. Peters's pattern in this series is to show young people who are a touching mixture of innocence and knowledge finding their way through nightmare experiences to adult understanding. Her outlook is ultimately optimistic, with a focus on human potential taking precedence over evil and mayhem.

of a hero who moves from the peace of village life to the horrors of war and the nightmare experiences of Jewish refugees. *A Means of Grace* (1956), in turn, grows out of the aftermath of the war, with its heroine, a teenage German refugee, returning to a changed and divided nation and finding her friends suffering under the restraints of Communism.

Czechoslovakian attachés whom she befriended during her wartime service with the Royal Navy taught Peters the Czech language. After the war, guilt and anger over the Western nations' betrayal of Czechoslovakia at Munich led her to study the Czech language in greater depth on her own and to translate Czechoslovakian literary works to help educate English speakers about the plight of Czechoslovakia and the suffering of the Czech and Slovak peoples. She began with Jan Neruda's *Tales of the Little Quarter* (1957) and continued with, among others, works by Jaroslav Seifert, Josef Bor, and Bohumil Hrabal, whose *Ostre sledované vlaky* (which Pargeter translated as *A Close Watch on the Trains,* 1968) was made into a

In the second Felse novel, *Death Mask,* Dominic is again caught up in mystery in which a young boy has witnessed his guardian's death in a questionable accident and then has been whisked away by his estranged mother, only to find that danger threatens. In *Death and the Joyful Woman* a resilient sixteen-year-old Dominic falls in love with an heiress, who becomes his father's chief suspect in the murder of a beer baron, a complication that strains the father-son relationship but that turns out well in the end as the father steps in and concludes the investigation. Music lessons bring Dominic into the case initially, and the lessons provide the cover for a trap for the real murderer. Peters captures the turmoil of an adolescent on the verge of adulthood and a concerned father's difficulties dealing with his son's troubled maturation. These early efforts at detective fiction follow traditional patterns of clues and misdirection, with more of a focus on plot and less on characterization than Peters's later, more complex mysteries. The fact that the Felse series has been reprinted in the 1990s, however, suggests that Peters's take on family relationships and adolescent perspectives continues to ring true.

As the series progresses, Dominic and Felse's wife, Bunty, play amateur detective more and more in their own right, but the involvement of the whole family in the mysteries, though in varying degrees, makes the series an interesting study in family dynamics. In *Flight of a Witch* (1964) Dominic's English teacher asks Felse, now an inspector, to find a young woman mysteriously gone, missing on a Welsh hillside reputed to be the abode of witches, a woman Felse connects with a burglary and murder. Through the English teacher's reactions to the conservatism and superstition of the Welsh community in which he teaches, Peters sheds light on cultural differences. Both *Flight of a Witch* and *A Nice Derangement of Epitaphs* (1965; published in the United States as *Who Lies Here?*) tackle parent-child tensions and questions of identity and belonging in families with an adopted child or one born late in a marriage. In *A Nice Derangement of Epitaphs* eighteen-year-old Dominic, vacationing with his parents in Cornwall, provides vital clues to a mystery involving two skeletons in a two-hundred-year-old tomb and becomes involved in the plight of a fifteen-year-old Cornish lad whose world is turned upside down.

In *The Piper on the Mountain* (1966) Dominic, who has been studying at Oxford, travels with friends to Czechoslovakia, where he is much attracted to a vacationing Theodosia Barber, nicknamed Tossa, who hopes to solve the unexplained death of her stepfather in the Low Tatras in Slovakia and instead gets caught up in espionage and political intrigue. Tossa and Dominic become romantically involved; he brings her home to meet his family, and they are inseparable in later books. As its title suggests, in *Black Is the Colour of My True-Love's Heart* (1967) love affairs and betrayals are at the heart of a mystery when Dominic and Tossa attend a weekend course in folk music at a Welsh college, and the college warden and the star of the seminar both suspiciously disappear. Dominic (now twenty) goes it alone without his family in *Mourning Raga* (1969) and *Death to the Landlords!*

(1972). In *Mourning Raga* he and Tossa escort a young girl home to New Delhi only to discover that her father has been missing for more than a year; the novel provides Peters an excuse to explore an exotic setting and its inhabitants and to comment on the commonalities that unite, despite cultural differences. Again, music plays a significant role, with the whistled notes of an Indian raga a musical clue. Upon graduating, Dominic works for a swami's mission, and in *Death to the Landlords!* he investigates terrorist attacks on wealthy landowners. This novel captures the complexities of an impoverished multicultural nation, with major religious, political, racial and economic differences. Despite the attractions of India, Peters is clearly ambivalent about the nation as a whole.

Bunty Felse, in turn, is the primary detective in *The Grass-Widow's Tale* (1968), called one of Peters's best by critic Dell Shannon. Bunty was a concert contralto before her marriage, and in this novel, with husband and son away on her forty-first birthday, she rethinks the life she gave up for marriage. Depressed and feeling her years, she goes to a local pub to cheer herself up and ends up leaving with an unhappy young man, in the trunk of whose car lies a girl's body. The novel serves as a means for Peters to reaffirm Bunty's place as a beloved member of her family circle, but first she and the young man must escape from murderous professional criminals who hold them captive. George Felse takes Bunty on vacation to Austria in *The House of Green Turf* (1969), where they meet a famous opera singer who firmly believes a dead man threatens her life, and this time George investigates.

Back in England, on the Welsh border, Felse must deal with gothic trappings, superstitions, and the death of a photographer in *The Knocker on Death's Door* (1970), the disappearance of a well-known archaeologist in *City of Gold and Shadows* (1973), and the death of the "squire" in another Welsh border village in *Rainbow's End* (1978). Now a superintendent, Felse finds his solution in old manuscripts and a ruined abbey.

Peters's eight mysteries from this time without the Felse family, published under the pseudonyms Jolyon Carr and John Redfern, differ greatly from her series mysteries. Despite their concern with the music world that Peters loves, *The Will and the Deed* (1960; published in the United States as *Where There's a Will*) and *The Horn of Roland* (1974) are weakly plotted, and their characters are only sketchily developed. More successful works in this set are *Funeral of Figaro* (1962), in which a baritone is murdered during a performance of Wolfgang Amadeus Mozart's *Le nozze di Figaro* (The Marriage of Figaro, 1786) and *Never Pick Up Hitch-Hikers!* (1976), with its humorous portrait of domineering parents. In the latter, included in Garland Press's "Fifty Classics of Crime Fiction 1950–1975" series, a likable young Willie Banks, leaving home, accepts a ride with a stranger and ends up amid bank

*Dust jacket for the U.S. edition of Peters's 1984 novel,
the tenth chronicle of Brother Cadfael, the author's
most popular creation (Richland
County Public Library)*

thieves planning a criminal caper involving £250,000 in stolen money. Luckily, a clever young lady rescues him from great unpleasantness, only to get caught up with him in campy drama.

In 1977, with the publication of *A Morbid Taste for Bones: A Mediaeval Whodunnit* some twenty-five years since her first detective novel, Peters discovered the perfect fit for her varied interests, values, and inclinations—a forum for history, war, romance, religion, and mystery, all amid familiar landscapes, and for the exploration of universal concerns and esoteric medieval lore. Her crusader-turned-monk detective Brother Cadfael, her most memorable character, shares features with her earlier interest in soldiers readjusting to peacetime, dealing wisely with civilian worries, and mentoring troubled youths despite a generation gap (Cadfael recalls all too vividly his own mischievous behavior as a youth). Peters continues to explore father-son relationships, family dynamics, and the maturation process, as well as cultural distinctions,

but in this series she mainly distinguishes between the Welsh and the English. Brother Cadfael, like George Felse, calmly evaluates the crime scene and studies the suspects for physical signs and "tells" of their hidden natures; yet, he is also a man of action, hardened by years of wartime service and wise in the ways of warriors and politicians. Peters created Brother Cadfael after researching the early history of the Benedictine abbey in Shrewsbury. She made him a fifty-seven-year-old Welshman from Gwennet, who was a crusader and a seaman before becoming a convert and a cloistered monk serving at Shrewsbury Abbey. Brother Cadfael battles superstition in the community, hypocrisy and religious intolerance within the Church, and ambition, greed, and cruel indifference in the aristocracy while fostering concern for the poor, the downtrodden, the young, the weak, and the ill (for example, lepers who once were brave crusaders). As in the Felse series, the villains in the Brother Cadfael series are despoilers of youth, those who prey on, threaten, or injure the young, the inexperienced, and the defenseless.

In the Brother Cadfael series the complexity of medieval society within its hierarchical structures, the violence of the age, the contrast between static and thrusting change, the limits of village life and the exotic possibilities and dangers of travel, and the clash between classes and regions all make for an interesting combination of the predictable and the unpredictable. Noted Chicago Catholic author Andrew M. Greeley, in *Armchair Detective* (Summer 1985), observes that Peters so effectively reconstructs the religion, history, social structure, culture, politics, and lifestyle of twelfth-century England in her Cadfael series that she makes readers feel as if they know personally the monks, townsfolk, squires, and nobility as they know their "friends and neighbors." He adds that Peters makes readers feel "the common humanity which links us to these inhabitants' world, so very different from our own." Peters captures the sense that modern man can contemplate the Marches with the same pleasure that a medieval human would have contemplated them, and that, despite the distance of time, place, and humanity, remain in essence much the same. Her crusader-turned-monk, like her soldiers-turned-teachers, brings to the contemplative life the harsh experiences of war, the widened perspective of the world traveler, and the humility of the man who has been debased by experience and survived.

In keeping with their medieval setting, Peters builds her Cadfael stories around the medieval chronicle and the frame tale. In fact, most of her Brother Cadfael novels have the subtitle "The Chronicles of Brother Cadfael" to call attention to the time progression as season follows season, bitter civil war continues, and claimants to the English throne (rival cousins King Stephen and Empress Maud) battle each other across the land. Civil war rends the social fabric and gives rise to injustices and crimes perpetrated against the ordinary citizenry. Eileen Tyler, writing in *Critical Survey of Mystery and Detective Fiction* (1988), calls Peters "a social novelist" and her mysteries "a set of concentric circles" with the detective at the center, by which she means that murder enables her to dramatize human interactions, explore social, familiar, and personal relationships, and place the individual and his or her actions in a social context. In a 1991 *Publishers Weekly* interview with Rosemary Herbert, Peters put it this way: "Many perfectly good historical novels somehow set their characters at a terrible distance from us, as though they're not the same species." Instead, she writes to bridge the ages and recognizes that doing so successfully means striking "a balance between modern, colloquial speech and the archaic."

A Morbid Taste for Bones introduces Brother Cadfael's background, personality, and nature, all of which Peters explores in greater detail and drama from mystery to mystery. Drawing on the true story of moving the bones of Welsh St. Winifred from Holywell, Wales, to the Abbey of Saint Peter and Saint Paul, Shrewsbury, Peters makes Welsh-born Cadfael the English monks' guide and interpreter of language and culture. In particular Cadfael must deal with the greedy, arrogant Prior Robert, who hopes to bribe the Welsh community into giving up its beloved saint to Shrewsbury for safekeeping. The murder of a local clan leader takes place almost a hundred pages into the story, and while investigating it and defending a wrongly accused English youth in love with a Welsh lass, Cadfael must also deal with Church politics (in the form of an overly ambitious and fanatical monk) and with the political situation (by coming up with a sensible plan for moving the saint's bones without giving offense). At the same time, he nurtures the maturation and spiritual growth of a young novice monk, an assistant whom Cadfael helps choose love and a normal life over a celibate vocation to which the assistant has no calling. Folklore and superstition play their part, as does excessive devotion and ambitious scheming.

One Corpse Too Many (1979), based on the siege of Shrewsbury in August 1138, depicts the ruthlessness of civil war as King Stephen seizes the castle and hangs defenders from the ramparts. An extra body among the executed puts Cadfael in pursuit of a criminal who had hidden behind political upheaval. Hugh Beringar, the clever and upright undersheriff to Sheriff Gilbert Prestcote, assists Cadfael and learns from his seasoned experience. The team must deal with the distinctions and points of intersection between secular and canonical law, and as the two grow to trust and respect each other their cooperation and interaction becomes a significant part of the series. Loyalty and love effectively counter murder, violence, and chaos.

Derek Jacobi as Brother Cadfael in the BBC television series based on Peters's medieval mysteries (Everett Collection)

Winner of the Silver Dagger Award from the British Mystery Writer's Association, *Monk's-Hood* (1980), set in December 1138, begins with Brother Cadfael's herbal remedies being used to murder Gervase Bonel, whose widow, Richildis, was once Cadfael's fiancée. Cadfael's large, flourishing garden, with its herbs for both seasoning food and healing sicknesses and injuries, is important throughout the series, but most especially in this novel, where the suspect died after being served a dinner seasoned and prepared at the monastery and laced with Cadfael's own special monkshood (wolfsbane) liniment. Three suspects have motives: the victim's quarrelsome stepson, Edwin; a brooding youth, Bonel, forced into serfdom; and a Welshman, a disgruntled bastard. Cadfael's encounter with Richildis (whom he has not seen in forty-two years) makes him reexamine his calling briefly. Deputy Sheriff Hugh helps Cadfael uncover the true murderer and prove the accused innocent. Cadfael calls Bonel "a child of his time and place." Solving this crime is most important to Cadfael, for, as in William Shakespeare's history plays, his garden serves as a metaphor for Cadfael's function in the community as healer and nurturer, controlling and channeling the dangerous to make it serve benign social ends.

Saint Peter's Fair (1981) makes Shrewsbury's annual merchant's fair in 1139 a crime center and the backdrop for various intrigues. Economic recovery from a debilitating siege has heightened tensions between town and abbey, and the death of a well-respected merchant threatens to lead to open conflict. A down-to-earth and humane Cadfael metes out justice to those guilty of deadly sins, but most particularly greed, envy, and hatred.

In *The Leper of Saint Giles* (1981) a leper, newly come to the lazarhouse (leprosarium) of Saint Giles, proves to be Lazarus, a former crusader who was a hero to Cadfael and who is mysteriously connected to a rich young woman being forced into an unwanted marriage by her ambitious and indifferent uncle. When a squire she loves faces accusations of theft and the murder of the man she was to wed, she rightly seeks Cadfael's help and receives it. With characteristic unrelenting curiosity and the desire to aid those in need, Cadfael links leper and youth and makes a leap of the imagination.

Praised by both Edward D. Hoch and Greeley, *The Virgin in the Ice* (1982) reveals a kinship between a mysterious forester, Olivier de Bretagne, and Brother Cadfael. A winter landscape and thick, dark forest create a bleak and threatening atmosphere, one intensified by a woman's body frozen in a pond, two children and the nun who escort them mysteriously missing, and a fellow monk severely beaten and suffering amnesia. Olivier surreptitiously helps Cadfael and Hugh rescue the kidnapped children. The selflessness of Cadfael, Hugh, and Olivier counter the brutal lawlessness of civil war.

The Sanctuary Sparrow (1983) takes place a month after Easter in 1140, when a poor traveling performer, a jongleur, accused of theft and murder, flees a lynch mob and claims sanctuary at the Abbey of Saint Peter and Saint Paul. Cadfael believes his tale, examines the evidence and, with Hugh Beringar's help, proves his innocence, despite the suspicions his poverty arouses.

In *The Devil's Novice* (1983), set in September 1140, both the abbot and Brother Cadfael distrust the motives of fathers who dedicate their young children as oblates to the order. They doubt that the newest member of the abbey has a genuine religious calling, though he is overly anxious to expedite the taking of his vows. Cadfael sorts through clues to link a murder to the new novice. In his role of gardener he must not only nurture the plants he wants to grow, but he must also weed out those that threaten his garden. In this case he also nurtures a youth, Brother Meriet, who has been unjustly banished to the monastery for a crime he did not commit, and the true culprit must be weeded out.

In *Dead Man's Ransom* (1984) a wounded Sheriff Prestcote, taken prisoner by the Welsh in the battle of Lincoln (February 1141), is murdered before a prisoner exchange, and Hugh, who succeeds Prestcote as sheriff,

seeks Cadfael's help locating the culprit. At the same time, Cadfael helps star-crossed young lovers.

Events in *The Pilgrim of Hate* (1984) begin to unfold at the end of May of 1141. Although there has been three years of civil war between King Stephen and Empress Maud, the abbey still attracts a large crowd for the celebration of the Feast of Saint Winifred. Of the many pilgrims to the feast, Brother Cadfael finds two seemingly close companions disconcerting: Ciaran, who has vowed to walk from one end of England to the other barefoot, and Matthew, who dogs Ciaran's every step. News of the murder of a knight in distant Winchester reinforces Cadfael's suspicions that something is amiss, something bound up in the Machiavellian politics of the day.

In *An Excellent Mystery* (1985), a surprisingly tender love story, two refugees from the recently destroyed abbey at Winchester arrive together at Shrewsbury in August 1141: one a mute, the other a former crusader severely wounded in the battle for Jerusalem and dying a lingering death. Cadfael's close observation of detail and his knowledge of the ways of soldiers makes him wary of these two, especially when he learns that a young woman missing from a convent she was supposed to enter is thought to be dead.

The Raven in the Foregate (1986) personifies religious fanaticism in the shape of Father Ailnoth, a political appointee to vicar of the parish of Holy Cross. This harsh, intolerant man lacks Christian compassion, treats children with cruelty, delivers fire-and-brimstone tirades from the pulpit, and in every way proves himself the reverse of what a good parish priest should be. During Christmas 1141 he arrives and is drowned in the millpond. To find his murderer, Cadfael, urged on by Hugh, sets a trap, tests identities, and examines motives.

As the title *The Rose Rent* (1986) suggests, the murder relates to an unusual rental arrangement: wealthy young widow Judith Perle rents her house from the abbey for the annual price of a single white rose cut from a bush in her yard. In spring 1142, however, when Brother Eluric goes to collect the rose rent, he meets death instead. The rose bush and its owner are both gone, and Brother Cadfael's search for a killer who would profit from ending the rent agreement with the abbey leads to another death. Judith's suitors initially seem the most likely suspects, yet the best clue comes in a different form: a pair of shoes seemingly for someone with two left feet.

In keeping with her interest in history, in *The Hermit of Eyton Forest* (1987) Peters focuses on the ill effects of ravaging civil war on a local family in the fall of 1142, when Empress Maud was under siege at Oxford. The family is that of Richard Ludel, fatally wounded in the battle of Lincoln. His death leaves his ten-year-old son, also named Richard, heir to the family manor at Eaton. Richard's grandmother approaches the new resident of the hermitage near her land for advice about her conflict with the abbey for her grandson's custody. When the resident is found dead in the forest, locals believe his errand boy to be the best suspect, because of rumors that he is a runaway villein fleeing a ruthless master. In fact, the identity of the killer is fairly clear from the start, for Peters is more interested in the history of the period than in any classic murder formula.

A Shrewsbury monk's personal internal turmoil becomes the focus of *The Confession of Brother Haluin* (1988). In this mystery Brother Haluin, who had nearly died in the snows of the winter of 1142, feels compelled to confess that, as a youth, he was tangentially involved in the death of the young woman he had loved and impregnated. His confession marks just one step in his quest for personal peace, for he promises as penance for past wrongs to visit the woman's mother, beg forgiveness, and pay his respects at the grave site. After Haluin recovers from his injuries, he and Cadfael set out on this journey, only to find that their pilgrimage to make up for past wrongs leads to new complications—a new murder and the need for careful investigation.

A Rare Benedictine: The Advent of Brother Cadfael (1988), a collection of three short mysteries about Cadfael's earlier life, marks a departure for Peters in style. "A Light on the Road to Woodstock" is historically vital to readers of Cadfael mysteries, for it explains how and why he decided to devote his life to the monastic brotherhood even as he pursued his avocation as an amateur detective. In "The Price of Light" Hamo FitzHamon of Lydyate presents the abbey with a pair of high-quality candlesticks in order to assure his soul a place in heaven, but FitzHamon is deceiving God and the Church, for the candlesticks are not really his, and soon Brother Cadfael must discover what wrongs lie behind FitzHamon's pious facade. In "Eye Witness" Cadfael traps a thief who has taken the rents collected by the abbey steward and has thrown the steward himself into the river.

In *The Heretic's Apprentice* (1989) two visitors to the Abbey of Saint Peter and Saint Paul in June 1143 raise broad questions of Church reform. The rich and rigidly doctrinaire Augustinian Canon Gerbert of Canterbury fears the negative impact of heresy. Loyal young Elave, who has brought home for burial the body of his master, William of Lythwood, after a seven-year pilgrimage together, finds his master and himself accused of heresy and himself of murder. While the bishop deals with the heresy charges, Cadfael and Hugh deal with the murder charge. Realizing that William's daughter's finely carved wooden box, which Elave brought back for her dowry, may have been filled with valuables worth a

Dust jacket for the U.S. edition of the final novel in Peters's series about the crime-solving Benedictine monk (Richland County Public Library)

murder, they search first for a robber. Peters uses the heresy charges to explore theological controversies that led to the Protestant Reformation, and her allusions to such significant religious reformers as Peter Abelard and Martin Luther inform readers of the sweep of abuses that demanded change.

Nominated for the Agatha Award in 1991 as best "domestic" mystery novel, *The Potter's Field* (1989), the seventeenth Brother Cadfael chronicle, depicts dreadful crimes and twisted motives, yet optimism, truth, and, justice prevail. In October 1143 plowing for planting exposes the shallow grave of a woman. Brother Cadfael's close observation of the natural world makes him also a close observer of human behavior. Experience has taught him to trust an intuition born of hardship and danger; yet, his solutions to crime draw on logical and careful thought. Ultimately, his decisions about how to act on his knowledge are based on his religious understanding of the need for compassion and a personal sym-

Pargeter in 1991 (photograph by Ed Christian; from
Clues, *14 [Fall/Winter 1993])*

pathy with the underdog. As an amateur detective who is also a man of God, he is less concerned with how a crime was committed than with why, the complex human motivations that lie behind surface appearances. Thus, Cadfael deals with overweening ambition and a lust for power, religious intolerance and hypocrisy, secret passions, and the overwrought responses of adolescents for whom the adult world is a mystery, a promise, and a threat. A key to the dead woman's identity and killer may be a ring. Among those characters caught up in the investigation are an abbey brother, supposedly abandoned by his wife; a young novice with the responsibility of tending his dying mother; a peddler and his traveling companion; and a young woman fearful of her future.

In *The Summer of the Danes* (1991) Cadfael and Brother Mark travel into Wales as guests of the Welsh chief Owain Gwenedd in the summer of 1144. Their assignment is to strengthen the power of the English Church over the Welsh Church. Gwenedd has exiled his treacherous brother, Cadwaladr, in an attempt to prevent civil war, but the suspicious death of Cadwaladr's emissary while under Owain's protection provides Cadwaladr an excuse to bring an invading Danish force from

Dublin. The meeting of English and Welsh provides Peters an excuse once again to discuss differences between the two peoples and their respective Church doctrines and structures. Peters takes time for parent-child relationships, as usual: a Welsh clergyman and his rebellious daughter.

The Holy Thief (1992), the nineteenth chronicle of Brother Cadfael, provides Cadfael an interesting puzzle: a stolen reliquary and then a murder, coupled with the inordinately zealous activities of a novice and a bondwoman to rescue the relics of Saint Winifred from spring floodwaters. Cadfael has extra motivation to uncover the guilty in order to keep a secret of his own.

Brother Cadfael's Penance (1994), the final series chronicle, repeats Peters's recurring concerns, including the anguish and destruction wrought by war, its toll on communities, families, and individuals, complex father-son relationships (those of Cadfael and his son, Olivier de Bretagne, and Robert of Gloucester and his son), and the struggle for justice. The double plot of the novel probes the two father-son relationships. Robert of Gloucester, as brother to and primary supporter of the Empress Maud, is most significant to the action. At the end of 1145, England is once again ravaged by war, the aristocracy uncaring that their political ambitions are destroying homes and citizens and disrupting farming and commerce. When Cadfael learns that Olivier has been captured and is being held without ransom, he publicly declares his kinship with Olivier by petitioning the abbot for time off from his duties to find and free his son. The discovery that Robert of Gloucester's rebellious and pigheaded son has Olivier brings Olivier's brother-in-law, Yves Hugonin, to aid Cadfael in the rescue. In the meantime the clever and conniving Empress Maud schemes to revenge a murdered knight, regardless of the consequences.

Of her fictive hero, Brother Cadfael, Peters told Herbert that while she had retained throughout the series his compassion and his feeling for young people, she focused less and less on his faith: "It's rather casual, you know. He believes; he's a monk. He's living the monastic life, and he means it, but he's not dwelling on it. Since then, he's had a few more things to say about how deeply he feels about his religion." She went on to reflect, "He's really made me think about what I believe. I say that I created him, but he's been busy ever since creating–or recreating–me. To try to get into his mind and make him real I have to think the way he would–as a real believer. I think he's confirmed me in beliefs I already rather likely held."

The last years of her life marked a period of reverence being paid, as when in 1994, in a ceremony before the House of Lords, the Crime Writer's Association and Cartier awarded Peters the Diamond Dagger for lifetime achievement and Queen Elizabeth II honored her with the Order of the British Empire. That same year fellow author Margaret Lewis published her biography, *Edith Pargeter/Ellis Peters,* part of the Seren Border Lines Series. In April 1995 Peters was guest of honor at Malice Domestic VII, an annual mystery conference, and in June she received the first Grand Master Award at Historicon I, a conference for historical mystery lovers. When Peters died in her home in Shropshire on 14 October 1995, she left behind a remarkable canon that speaks to her versatility, intellect, knowledge, and understanding of human frailty and strength.

In all of the books in the series young men stand falsely accused of crimes they did not commit and young women have their virtue threatened by powerful men in authority and are often kidnapped or forced into loveless engagements and need rescuing. Thwarted young love as a central theme is one reason many critics have compared the Cadfael novels to the works of another historical mystery writer, Mary Stewart. As Tyler notes, the literary tradition Peters follows is that of social comedy, in which young lovers are blocked by unsympathetic adults, but these often ambitious and greedy blocking figures are eventually outwitted and overcome, and young love wins out; the social order is restored, and its continuance is confirmed by a final wedding.

Unlike most other of her fellow authors in the mystery genre, Ellis Peters has won critical acclaim and has been widely written about in scholarly circles. In addition, this popularity has extended far beyond the scholarly and the critical. Thus, one can find references in Fodor's guide to Great Britain to Cadfael's Shrewsbury; an Ellis Peters Appreciation Society with a newsletter; a website called *Brother Cadfael's World;* and a full-length scholarly work, Robin Whiteman's *The Cadfael Companion: The World of Brother Cadfael* (1991; revised, 1995), which explains the world of Cadfael with appendices of plants and herbs mentioned in the chronicles and a glossary of places and terms. The details of place, the idea of historical continuity and of enduring communities in which historical tensions are repeated again and again at family, city, and national levels, the commentary on war and how it changes people and communities, the universal struggle between good and evil worked out in daily struggles and in shades of gray make Peters's series familiar and inviting despite the time span that separates her characters from modern readers. This quality is both her strength and her weakness: she interprets the past in ways modern readers can relate to, but in doing so she changes the past in greater and lesser degrees to fit the needs, ideas, obsessions, and spirit of the present. By setting her studies of crimes amid past ages and long-past civilizations, Peters gains a distance on her subject and, while entertaining readers with challenging puzzles and intriguing ratiocination, brings to life a world that is both vitally different from the modern world and yet, in significant ways, no better and no worse. Thus, despite her inherent optimism, Peters does not view history as a progression toward a better society but instead as evidence that as a species humanity has learned little from the past and repeats its patterns.

Interview:

Rosemary Herbert, "Ellis Peters: the Novelist cum Historian," *Publishers Weekly,* 238 (9 August 1991): 40–41.

References:

Mary K. Boyd, "Brother Cadfael: Renaissance Man of the Twelfth Century," *Clues: A Journal of Detection,* 9 (Spring/Summer 1988): 39–48;

Andrew M. Greeley, "Ellis Peters: Another Umberto Eco?" *Armchair Detective,* 18 (Summer 1985): 238–246;

Edward D. Hoch, "The Priestly Sleuths," in *Synod of Sleuths: Essays on Judeo-Christian Detective Fiction,* edited by Jon L. Breen and Martin H. Greenberg (Metuchen, N.J.: Scarecrow Press, 1990), pp. 1–7;

Anne K. Kaler, ed., *Cordially Yours, Brother Cadfael* (Bowling Green, Ohio: Bowling Green State University Popular Press, 1998);

Robert S. Paul, Introduction to *Whatever Happened to Sherlock Holmes: Detective Fiction, Popular Theology, and Society* (Carbondale: Southern Illinois University Press, 1991), pp. 1–27;

Barbara G. Peters, "Collecting Edith Pargeter/Ellis Peters," *Firsts,* 5:11 (November 1995): 32–41;

Fred E. H. Schroeder, "Landscapes of Fear in English Mysteries," *Clues: A Journal of Detection,* 2 (Fall/Winter 1990): 65–84;

William David Spencer, *Mysterium and Mystery: The Clerical Crime Novel* (Ann Arbor, Mich.: UMI Research Press, 1989);

Robin Whiteman, *The Cadfael Companion: The World of Brother Cadfael,* introduction by Peters (London: Macdonald, 1991; revised and updated edition, London: Little, Brown, 1995; New York: Mysterious Press, 1995).

Raymond W. Postgate

(6 November 1896 – 29 March 1971)

William Reynolds
Hope College

BOOKS: *The International during the War* (London: Herald, 1918);

Doubts Concerning a League of Nations (London: Herald, 1919);

The Bolshevik Theory (London: Richards, 1920; New York: Dodd, Mead, 1920);

The Workers' International (London: Swarthmore / New York: Harcourt, Brace & Howe, 1920);

The New Russia, by Postgate and T. A. Jackson (Madras: Arka, 1922);

Out of the Past: Some Revolutionary Sketches (London: Labour Publishing, 1922; Boston: Houghton Mifflin, 1923); republished as *Revolutionary Biographies* (Madras: Arka, 1922);

Chartism and the "Trades Union" (London: Labour Research Department, 1922);

The Builders' History (London: National Federation of Building Trade Operatives, 1923; New York: Garland, 1984);

Murder, Piracy and Treason: A Selection of Notable English Trials (London: Cape, 1925; Boston: Houghton Mifflin, 1925);

A Short History of the British Workers (London: Plebs League, 1926);

A Workers' History of the Great Strike: Written, from Material Supplied by Plebs Correspondents in All Parts of the Country, by Postgate, Ellen Wilkinson, and J. F. Horrabin (London: Plebs League, 1927);

That Devil Wilkes (New York: Vanguard, 1929; London: Constable, 1930; revised edition, London: Dobson, 1956);

Robert Emmet (London: Secker, 1931); republished as *Dear Robert Emmet* (New York: Vanguard, 1932);

No Epitaph (London: Hamilton, 1932); republished as *Felix and Anne* (New York: Vanguard, 1933);

Karl Marx (London: Hamilton, 1933);

How to Make a Revolution (London: Hogarth Press, 1934; New York: Vanguard, 1934);

What to Do with the B.B.C. (London: Hogarth Press, 1935);

Raymond W. Postgate (from J. R. Postgate and Mary Postgate,
A Stomach for Dissent: The Life of
Raymond Postgate, *1994)*

A Pocket History of the British Workers to 1919 (London: Fact, 1937);

Those Foreigners: The English People's Opinions on Foreign Affairs as Reflected in Their Newspapers since Waterloo, by Postgate and Aylmer Vallance (London: Harrap, 1937); republished as *England Goes to Press: The English People's Opinions on Foreign Affairs as*

Reflected in Their Newspapers since Waterloo (Indianapolis: Bobbs-Merrill, 1937);

The Common People, 1746–1938, by Postgate and G. D. H. Cole (London: Methuen, 1938); republished as *The British Common People, 1746–1938* (New York: Knopf, 1939); revised and enlarged as *The Common People, 1746–1946* (London: Methuen, 1946); revised edition republished as *The British People, 1746–1946* (New York: Knopf, 1947);

Verdict of Twelve (London: Collins, 1940; New York: Doubleday, Doran, 1940);

Let's Talk It Over: An Argument about Socialism for the Unconverted (London: Fabian Society, 1942);

A Pocket History of the British Working Class (Tillicoultry, Scotland: NCLC Publishing Society, 1942; second edition, 1947; third edition, 1964);

Somebody at the Door (London: Joseph, 1943; New York: Knopf, 1943);

The Life of George Lansbury (London & New York: Longmans, Green, 1951);

The Plain Man's Guide to Wine (London: Joseph, 1951; New York: Eriksson-Taplinger, 1960; revised and enlarged edition, London: Joseph, 1965; revised again, edited by John Arlott, London: Joseph, 1970; New York: Eriksson, 1976);

The Ledger Is Kept (London: Joseph, 1953);

An Alphabet of Choosing and Serving Wine (London: Jenkins, 1955);

Story of a Year: 1848 (London: Cape, 1955; New York: Oxford University Press, 1956);

Every Man Is God (London: Joseph, 1959; New York: Simon & Schuster, 1960);

The Home Wine Cellar (London: Jenkins, 1960);

Story of a Year: 1798 (London: Longmans, 1969; New York: Harcourt, Brace & World, 1969);

Portuguese Wine (London: Dent, 1969).

OTHER: *Revolution from 1789 to 1906, Documents Selected and Edited with Notes and Introductions by R. W. Postgate* (London: Richards, 1920; Boston: Houghton Mifflin, 1921);

Karl Marx, *The Civil War in France Preceded by Two Manifestos of the General Council of the International on the Franco-Prussian War,* historical introduction by Postgate (London: Labour Publishing, 1921), pp. 1–5;

Pervigilium Veneris: The Eve of Venus, edited and translated by Postgate (London: Richards, 1924; Boston: Houghton Mifflin, 1924);

"Papers of the First International Communication about the George Howell Collection preserved at the Bishopsgate Library, London," in *Marx-Engels-Archiv. Band I: Marx: Werke bis September 1844* (Frankfurt am Main: Marx-Engels-Archiv Verlagsgesellschaft MBH, 1926), pp. 442–447;

The Conversations of Dr. Johnson Extracted from the "Life" by James Boswell, edited by Postgate (London: Knopf, 1930; New York: Vanguard, 1930);

"Radio, Press and Publishing," in *Twelve Studies in Soviet Russia,* edited by Margaret I. Cole (London: Gollancz, 1933), pp. 227–247;

Detective Stories of Today, edited by Postgate (London: Faber & Faber, 1940);

Moray MacLaren, *"By Me . . .": A Report upon the Apparent Discovery of Some Working Notes by William Shakespeare in a Sixteenth-Century Book,* edited by Postgate (London: Redington, 1949);

H. G. Wells, *The Outline of History, Being a Plain History of Life and Mankind,* revised by Postgate, 2 volumes (Garden City, N.Y.: Garden City Books, 1949; London: Cassell, 1951); revised again by Postgate (London: Cassell, 1961; Garden City, N.Y.: Garden City Books, 1961); revised again by Postgate and G. P. Wells (Garden City, N.Y.: Doubleday, 1971; London: Cassell, 1972);

The Good Food Guide, edited by Postgate (London: Cassell, 1951–1968);

Edward Ott, *From Barrel to Bottle: Notes on the Home Bottling of Wine,* foreword by Postgate (London: Dobson, 1953), pp. 9–15;

Sidonie Gabrielle Colette, *Mitsou; or, The Education of Young Women,* translated by Postgate, volume 10 of *Works of Colette* (London: Secker & Warburg, 1957); republished in *"Mitsou" and "Music-Hall Side Lights"* (New York: Farrar, Straus & Cudahy, 1958);

Paul Reboux, *Food for the Rich,* edited and translated by Margaret Costa, wine revisions by Postgate (London: Blond, 1958; New York: Barnes, 1960), pp. 6–15;

R. S. Magowan, *Oxford and Cambridge: A Book of Photographs,* introduction by Postgate (London: Spring Books, 1961), pp. 7–8;

H. G. Wells, *A Short History of the World,* revised by Postgate and G. P. Wells (London: Collins, 1965);

The Good Food Guide to London, edited by Postgate (London: Consumers' Association and Hodder Paperbacks, 1968);

The Agamemnon of Aeschylus, edited and translated by Postgate (Cambridge: Rampant Lions, 1969).

SELECTED PERIODICAL PUBLICATIONS–UNCOLLECTED: "Who Won Waterloo?" *Nation,* 41 (24 September 1927): 802–803;

"Iron Tonic for Labour," *New Statesman and Nation,* 6 (7 October 1933): 410–411;

"How to Make a Revolution," *American Mercury*, 32 (May 1934): 12–20;

"Critique of Communist Tactics," *American Mercury*, 32 (July 1934): 281–289;

"Echoes of a Revolt," *New Republic*, 83 (22 May 1935): 44–45;

"Revolution in Sparta," *New Republic*, 83 (31 July 1935): 329–332;

"What Chance for Revolutions?" *New Republic*, 103 (22 July 1940): 111–114;

"Problem of International Language," *Political Quarterly*, 14 (January 1943): 46–59;

"Britain's Political Scene," *New Republic*, 113 (22 October 1945): 520–521;

"Wines from the Commonwealth," *New Statesman*, 50 (12 November 1955): 622;

"Gallipoli: The End of a World," *Nation*, 183 (29 September 1956): 270–271;

"How to Invest in Wine," *Spectator*, 199 (22 November 1957): 691;

"Travel in Germany," *Holiday*, 36 (October 1964): 131–138;

"Which Wine?" *New Statesman*, 68 (20 November 1964): 784–786.

The multitalented Raymond W. Postgate achieved distinction as classical scholar, economist, social historian, food and wine connoisseur, and journalist while, almost as a sideline, drawing upon his expertise in these areas to secure a limited yet clearly defined and probably lasting place among the detective-fiction novelists of his generation. Postgate was not a uniformly successful literary artist. Except for *Verdict of Twelve* (1940), his plots are not exceptional; and, even in his best novels, only a few of the main characters are fully alive. What distinguishes Postgate is his ability to give life to his characters' social and historical milieu and a talent for showing readers the effects these external factors have on human action.

The eldest son of renowned Latin scholar Professor John Percival Postgate and his wife, Edith (née Allen) Postgate, Raymond William Postgate at first seemed destined for an academic career, winning a scholarship to St. John's College, Oxford, in 1915. While at Oxford he became a Marxian Socialist and in 1916 was jailed for refusing conscription. He was disinherited by his conservative father in 1918 when he married Daisy Lansbury, the daughter of George Lansbury, who led the Labour Party from 1931 to 1935. The Postgates eventually had two sons, John Raymond, born in 1922, and Richard Oliver, born in 1925.

After the war Postgate tried to support himself and his family by socialist journalism—serving as a sub-editor of the *Daily Herald* from 1919 to 1923, assistant editor of *Lansbury's Labour Weekly* from 1925 to 1927, editor of *Fact* from 1937 to 1939, and editor of the *Tribune* in 1940–1941–and through more-conventional positions as an internal editor for the fourteenth edition of the *Encyclopaedia Britannica* (1927–1928) and European representative for Alfred A. Knopf from 1930 to 1949. In addition, from 1942 to 1950 Postgate held a position as civil servant in the Board of Trade.

Postgate began writing books with the dual purposes of furthering socialism and augmenting the meager income his devotion to the cause brought him. His early works deal primarily with Labour Party theory and history; three stand out as atypical: *Pervigilium Veneris: The Eve of Venus* (1924), an edition/translation of an anonymous late-classical poem; *Murder, Piracy and Treason* (1925), an account of what Postgate called "notable English trials," which foreshadows his later interest in detective fiction; and *No Epitaph* (1932; published in the United States as *Felix and Anne*, 1933), his first novel.

Postgate uses *No Epitaph* to argue for the view that the popular press is more concerned with advertising revenue and circulation figures than with truth. By combining the knowledge of characterization he had accumulated in writing two full-length biographies and a book of biographical sketches with his firsthand knowledge of journalism and socialism, Postgate succeeded in making Felix Queagh (a young socialist journalist), his wife, Anne, and his editor, Sheringham, recognizable at least as types a contemporary reader would not have been surprised to encounter in Fleet Street or at a Labour Party meeting.

The plot is simple. After slowly working himself into a secure position at the *Daily Tribune*, Felix makes love with Sheringham's wife. Once Sheringham finds out what Felix has done, he makes it impossible for Felix to stay on. Though Felix achieves some success with his *Life of Briand*, his career soon begins a downward spiral, culminating in his death in a traffic accident. Postgate includes enough action to retain his readers' interest in characters so controlled by their environments that it is difficult to identify with them. The course of events, particularly after Felix's personality begins to disintegrate, is easy to predict, however; and at key moments readers are denied access to the characters' inner selves or presented set-piece speeches in place of human communication. Further, *No Epitaph* has typical first-novel problems with structure and proportion. To downgrade Sheringham, Postgate elaborately demonstrates that his success is largely because of the work of brilliant subordinates, but the theme disappears entirely halfway through the novel. The most insightful section of the whole novel–an overly long but compelling account of a labor dispute in a midland

Postgate in 1937, during his tenure as editor of the journal Fact *(from Postgate and Postgate,* A Stomach for Dissent, *1994)*

town–has almost nothing to do with anything else in the novel.

The next eight years were Postgate's most productive as a social critic and historian; he did not turn again to fiction until 1940, editing an anthology of detective stories and publishing his first detective novel, *Verdict of Twelve.* It is impossible to say how much freedom Postgate had in deciding which stories and which authors to include in *Detective Stories of Today* (1940), but all twenty stories have something, if only entertainment value, to recommend them. Moreover, the anthology furnishes a good cross section of British detective fiction at the end of the Golden Age and provides easy access to worthwhile stories not anthologized elsewhere.

By 1940 many writers of detective fiction had attempted realistic characterization in their novels, though none had anticipated Postgate's stress on the controlling power of social forces, so some of the popularity of *Verdict of Twelve* is surely because of the novelty of Postgate's approach. In brief, Postgate narrates the events leading up to Rosalie van Beer's trial for murdering her nephew Philip, the principal prosecution and defense arguments presented during the trial itself, and Rosalie's first-person account of what actually took place. Equally essential to the book are its prefatory account of how and why Rosalie became a murderer and character studies of the twelve jurors, which reveal that each person's verdict is determined not so much by questions of truth or justice as by such factors as reli-

gious fanaticism, class prejudice, and the dynamics of the discussion carried on in the jury room. Novelty within the genre aside, *Verdict of Twelve* deserves the praise it has been accorded: though flat, its characters are vivid; its social history compelling; and its plot a masterpiece of elegant simplicity that distracts readers from asking the key question before Postgate unleashes it on the last page.

More surprising, much of the success of the novel derives from the demands of the genre itself. While *No Epitaph* was so open-ended that Postgate at times seemed uncertain about what to emphasize and even about what should happen next, no such problems are evident in *Verdict of Twelve.* The murder-trial format provides an organizational framework as well as a standard by which to eliminate extraneous material. While the portraits Postgate gives of Rosalie and the four or five jurors from whom the others take their lead are less comprehensive than those of Felix and Anne, readers' attention is so concentrated on whether Rosalie is the murderer and on whether the others will vote to convict or to acquit that they neither notice nor care much that they are shown nothing of any other aspect of the characters' personalities.

Postgate's second detective novel, *Somebody at the Door* (1943), is a less successful variation on the basic pattern of *Verdict of Twelve,* with the trial format replaced by the more familiar formula of murder, investigation, and solution. In *Somebody at the Door*

Postgate and his wife, Daisy, in the mid 1960s (from Postgate and Postgate, A Stomach for Dissent, *1994)*

Inspector Holly (who is briefly introduced in *Verdict of Twelve*) must find the murderer of Henry James Grayling, who dies at home in suburban Croxburn following a train journey from London. As in *Verdict of Twelve,* Postgate adopts the linked biography format, this time atomizing Grayling, his wife, and several of the people who shared the railroad carriage with Grayling on his last journey.

All the characters have life stories worth recounting, but Postgate becomes so absorbed in small-scale excellence that he loses track of the larger picture. The reader encounters a series of brilliant scenes but waits in vain for more than a few of them to be connected, all the while laboring through a detective plot with a solution that, if not obvious from the beginning, is clear chapters before Holly so much as begins to be aware of it.

After World War II, Postgate began a new stage in his career, one that extended to the end of his life. Even as a young man Postgate had made himself a connoisseur of both food and wine; during the rationing days of 1949 he began organizing a Good Food Club

with himself as president and compiling an amateur guide in which volunteers would report on British hotels and restaurants to try to pressure owners into improving standards. The first *Good Food Guide,* edited by Postgate, appeared in 1951; he continued to supervise new yearly editions until late 1968, when poor health forced him to retire.

Moving with the times, Postgate set his last detective novel, *The Ledger Is Kept* (1953), in a British atomic-research station at Chellerton and chose as the murder weapon radioactive sodium phosphate secretly placed in the victim's food over a period of time. Postgate limits the number of suspects so drastically that readers must again wonder why Inspector Holly takes so long to work things out, and a major subplot involving the betrayal of atomic secrets to the Russians reveals the existence of an agent whose actions have no connection with the murder and whose motives are so poorly defined that they can be revealed only in a lecture Holly delivers after the spy's arrest.

Despite these problems, *The Ledger Is Kept* is a better novel than *Somebody at the Door* and, except for a less original plot, arguably superior to *Verdict of Twelve*. Concentrating on the life of the victim, Henry Proctor, Postgate enables the reader to understand and sympathize with a man who dies before the reader can meet him. Postgate effectively captures the conflict the young Proctor experiences between the demands of the Southampton Gospel Fellowship, the puritanical Christian sect in which he was raised, and the liberating academic and social atmosphere of an Oxford depopulated by World War I. Postgate uses some of the later sections of the book as places to lecture on his own political and social ideas. But the parts of the novel that detail the control Proctor's repressed and repressive sister, Dorothy, exerts over her brother further deepen the reader's sympathy for Henry and make understandable his affair with Doreen Thompson, a teenage housemaid so callow that she bases her view of reality on the cinema, even going so far as to rename herself Lana Larmoor (the surname being derived from those of Dorothy Lamour and Hedy Lamarr).

Postgate is equally convincing in his portraits of Dorothy Proctor as a woman so convinced of her own rectitude that she is prepared to murder Henry for violating the dictates of her conscience and of Doreen Thompson as one who has loved to the best of her ability and who has been shattered by Proctor's death. Particularly moving is the account Postgate, ever the social historian, gives of Doreen's encounter with the bureaucracy of the welfare state when she visits a labor exchange to seek a new job. The improbably fast-moving subplot that details the evolving love of Proctor's assistant, Ronald Aldridge, for Proctor's secretary, Olive Myers, is surprisingly tender and sincere–the sort of story Postgate could probably have made the centerpiece of another novel and a typical example of his constant tendency to force his fiction to carry too many burdens.

Postgate similarly overextends himself in his final novel, *Every Man Is God* (1959). The book simultaneously tries to serve as a modern counterpart for the Orestes-Agamemnon myth; a social history of, among other things, the pre-1914 British army, the introduction of electricity into the residences of the wealthy, and the decline of the country house during World War I; an interpretation of the changes that the British upper classes–and to a large extent Britain itself–underwent between 1880 and the 1930s; a multigenerational family saga; and a statement of Postgate's own philosophy of life.

The parallel to the ancient myth is rather mechanical, but sections of *Every Man Is God* rank among the best in Postgate's fiction. The social history is, as ever, fascinating, and integrated with the rest of the novel. Postgate's account of the role women played in World War I raises Iris Alderton to the level of Iphigenia, whose innocent death she reenacts, while details about the electrification of country houses are central to the variation of Clytemnestra's murder of Agamemnon that Clarissa Alderton employs to dispatch her husband, Arthur. Nowhere does Postgate depict characters more thoroughly or more sympathetically than Arthur and Clarissa's son, Oswald, and Patrick Calcraft, who in the course of the novel develops from a caricature of the military doctor into a human being capable of loving and of being loved. Moreover, though both Oswald and Patrick are portrayed as products of their environments, their triumphs and their defeats are so clearly their own that readers simply cannot view them as anything but free.

As sales of his *Good Food Guide* grew, Postgate became a celebrity, appearing on radio and television programs to discuss the fine points of gastronomy and publishing many articles and several books on food, wine, and travel. On a more modest scale, Postgate also continued his career as a social historian with *Story of a Year: 1848* (1955) and *Story of a Year: 1798* (1969)

before bringing himself full circle in his final book, also published in 1969, an edition and translation of the *Agamemnon* of Aeschylus. He died on 29 March 1971, at the age of seventy-four.

Postgate moved from an early fascination with Karl Marx, whose dictum "It is not the consciousness of men that determines their existence, but on the contrary their social existence determines their consciousness" serves as an introduction to *Verdict of Twelve,* to a vision of an Aeschylean universe where circumstances force people into crimes, crimes inevitably answered by punishments that often as not destroy the innocent along with the guilty. His novels often provide a vision other than what Postgate intended, however. The personae of *No Epitaph* are puppets, but in *Verdict of Twelve* the characters are autonomous enough that it is impossible for readers not to judge that Rosalie van Beer has chosen, and chosen not just unlawfully but immorally, to take her nephew's life. *The Ledger Is Kept* and *Every Man Is God* not only espouse a more muted brand of determinism but also provide characters whose strengths and weaknesses so clearly mirror the reader's that the focus becomes not so much what has caused characters to behave as they have as what effect these actions will have on the characters.

Raymond W. Postgate is not a great novelist, but an achievement such as his deserves to be noticed. As a writer of detective fiction he merits particular recognition for his efforts to provide new, convincing, and psychologically reasonable answers to a question that the genre often ignores and just as often answers with one cliché or another: "What reason could the murderer have had for acting that way?"

Reference:

J. R. Postgate and Mary Postgate, *A Stomach for Dissent: The Life of Raymond Postgate* (Staffordshire: Keele University Press, 1994).

Papers:

A collection of Raymond W. Postgate's papers is held at the International Institute of Social History in Amsterdam, the Netherlands.

Anthony Price

(16 August 1928 –   )

Gina Macdonald
Nicholls State University

BOOKS: *The Labyrinth Makers* (London: Gollancz, 1970; Garden City, N.Y.: Doubleday, 1971);

The Alamut Ambush (London: Gollancz, 1971; Garden City, N.Y.: Doubleday, 1972);

Colonel Butler's Wolf (London: Gollancz, 1972; Garden City, N.Y.: Doubleday, 1973);

October Men (London: Gollancz, 1973; Garden City, N.Y.: Doubleday, 1974);

Other Paths to Glory (London: Gollancz, 1974; Garden City, N.Y.: Doubleday, 1975);

Our Man in Camelot (London: Gollancz, 1975; Garden City, N.Y.: Doubleday, 1976);

War Game (London: Gollancz, 1976; Garden City, N.Y.: Doubleday, 1977);

The '44 Vintage (London: Gollancz, 1978; Garden City, N.Y.: Doubleday, 1978);

Tomorrow's Ghost (London: Gollancz, 1979; Garden City, N.Y.: Doubleday, 1979);

The Hour of the Donkey (London: Gollancz, 1980);

Soldier No More (London: Gollancz, 1981; Garden City, N.Y.: Doubleday, 1982);

The Old Vengeful (London: Gollancz, 1982; Garden City, N.Y.: Doubleday, 1983);

Gunner Kelly (London: Gollancz, 1983; Garden City, N.Y.: Doubleday, 1984);

Sion Crossing (London: Gollancz, 1985; New York: Mysterious Press, 1985);

Here Be Monsters (London: Gollancz, 1985; New York: Mysterious Press, 1985);

For the Good of the State (London: Gollancz, 1986; New York: Mysterious Press, 1987);

A New Kind of War (London: Gollancz, 1987; New York: Mysterious Press, 1988);

A Prospect of Vengeance (London: Gollancz, 1988; New York: Armchair Detective Library, 1990);

The Memory Trap (London: Gollancz, 1989; New York: Armchair Detective Library, 1991);

The Eyes of the Fleet: A History of Frigate Warfare, 1793–1815 (London: Hutchinson, 1990; New York: Norton, 1996).

Anthony Price (from the dust jacket for The Hour of the Donkey, *1980)*

Although often compared to the works of such illustrious writers of British spy fiction as John Buchan, Eric Ambler, John le Carré, and Len Deighton, the espionage novels of Anthony Price add an unexpected twist. They are firmly based on historical precedent, and the leading intelligence operatives from both England and Russia are trained historians and archaeologists who see past patterns at work in modern conflicts. The British spies are old-school fellows from Oxford or Cambridge; from personal experience with eccentric and intellectually challenging professors, they recognize the difference between allegiance to liberal or leftist ideas and betrayal of country. They also understand, however, that the British universities are recruiting grounds for Russian spies and that the Russians might well have inserted moles to replace students from foreign nations (such as Rhodesia, New Zealand, Canada, or Australia) with few or no surviving relatives. The British themselves recruit among the top students whose intellect, curiosity, and physical prowess may suit them for national service. H. R. F. Keating places Price in "the third generation among the modern" spy writers, one who has gone past the simplicity and straightforward action of Ian Fleming and the double- and triple-crosses of le Carré to even more-intricate puzzles whose solutions depend on an understanding of obscure literary works and minor historical events. Cushing Strout aptly calls Price "the modern master of blending military history with fictional mystery" and associates him with Buchan's vision of "patriotic gentlemen and women," while Peter Lewis calls Price "the author who has most consistently and most successfully introduced historical dimension into his novels," inspiring a new generation of writers such as Julian Rathbone, Ken Follett, and Robert Littel.

Price's readers delight as much in the flow of quotations from unexpected voices and the historical and archaeological details as in the twists, turns, and crosses of plot. Price's main characters find erudite explanations of intellectual puzzles, only to see the information turned on its head or reconfigured. Thus, self-congratulation turns to bitter panic when a new piece of information forces reconsideration of the evidence and its significance. Unlike historical novels set in the past with a medieval monk or an historical figure such as Jane Austen as the detective, or the pattern illustrated by Josephine Tey's *Daughter of Time* (1951), in which a bedridden modern detective investigates an historical conundrum or mystery by piecing together clues from the literary and historical record, Price creates the allure of history without the historical setting. In his novels the past is the clue to the present, and those who fail to learn the lessons of history are doomed to repeat the past. The Russians feared a German invasion in the fourteenth century, and that fear had not changed much by 1940. Price is interested in questions of loyalty, a natural concern in a system known for its sellouts to the Soviet Union. He explains that his goal is to explore what William Faulkner called "truths of the heart," the wellsprings of comradeship, love, and personal loyalties to people, places, and ideas, those qualities of heart and mind that have endured through the ages. There is a refreshing idealism in Price's works, an old-fashioned sense that there is a good side and a bad side and that one must never confuse the two. American and English critics speaking of Price's canon employ such phrases as "unsentimental," "convoluted," "unique," "deft," "polished," and "immensely enjoyable," "a blend of the spy novel and the classic whodunit" with "post-Philby" "moral riddles," "as engrossing as a chess game."

Anthony Price was born on 16 August 1928 in Hertfordshire, the son of Walter Longsdon Price, an engineer, and Kathleen Lawrence Price, an artist. As a youth Price attended King's School, Canterbury. He went straight from school into the Royal Army, enlisting in 1947, in time for brief postwar service during the detentions and interrogations on the Continent. He attained the rank of captain and demobilized in 1949. His military service ended, Price returned to school, attending Merton College, Oxford, where he was an exhibitioner (recipient of a study grant); he received a B.A. with honors in history in 1952. Upon graduating, Price worked as a journalist for the Westminster Press, beginning in 1952 and continuing until 1988. He began his lifetime journalism career as a reviewer of historical books and married Ann Stone, a registered nurse, on 20 June 1953. They have three children: James, Simon, and Katherine. Eventually, Price became the crime reviewer for the *Oxford Mail*, a position that prepared him intellectually for his avocation as a spy-mystery writer and taught him about the intricacies of the craft. With time he advanced in his career to become deputy editor of the *Oxford Times*.

In 1970 Price published his first novel, *The Labyrinth Makers*, which won the Silver Dagger Award from the Crime Writers' Association in 1971. His aim was to combine elements of the spy thriller with those of the detective mystery and to create a set of characters who would recur throughout an ongoing series, with all of the books to follow linked to one key Machiavellian character, David Audley. The wide-ranging historical interests of this character permitted Price to include in future novels whatever private research or hobby he was engaged in at the time. The unifying concept was that spymaster Audley would link all of Price's novels, either as the central investigative officer or as an intelligence presence behind the scenes, taking on tasks no one else will touch. Audley has studied history and regularly produces historical tomes. He poses as a university professor or an obsessed historian gathering materials for a book about the past while engaging in espionage activities that are concerned with the present. In most cases, an artifact from the past or even clues suggestive of surviving artifacts play significant roles.

An insatiably curious maverick, Audley, says his associate Colonel Jack Butler, was "born into the wrong age," seeing himself "as a prince-bishop from his beloved Middle Ages, mediating between God and

Dust jacket for Price's 1972 novel, inspired by the case of the British traitor Kim Philby (from Armchair Detective, *19 [Fall 1986])*

man, and meddling happily in the affairs of both to their discomfort"—without regard to "good order," "discipline," or "common sense." At times, however, Audley comes to an easy conclusion based on his knowledge of the past, only to realize that, like some historical figure, he has been misdirected and has missed the true historical parallel, the parallel that forces him to reconsider his interpretation of present characters and events. Various characters describe Audley as hard as nails, "a mailed fist in a velvet glove." His forte is constructing houses of cards from miniscule evidence, brainstorming to find the pattern and significance behind the tiniest of indicators. At times he thinks of himself as a puppet master or as the spoiler who breaks the pattern into which he has fallen in order to foil or at least disturb the opposition. Audley has an apt quotation from the works of Rudyard Kipling for every situation and understands other cultures in terms of their historical or literary patterns (for instance, the Russian love of the cryptic nature of *Hamlet,* with its "dark vein of self-destruction").

Price decided that the narrative voice could shift from volume to volume but that, whatever the point of view, Audley and a running cast of characters were to provide continuity and a solid background or history to lend a depth of characterization and complexity difficult to achieve in any one volume. The result is what Keating calls "the life-history of a spy-catcher," "a dyed-in-the-wool intelligence man." That portrait takes the form of multiple perspectives, conflicting points of views and interpretations, with the seeming reality of events and actions shifting in kaleidoscopic fashion depending on the shifts in time and personalities.

The Labyrinth Makers begins in Berlin and the final days of the Third Reich, when many national loyalties succumbed to the personal need to survive or the desire to ease the future with the spoils of war. Royal Air Force Flight Lieutenant John Steerforth planned to ease his future by stealing Trojan treasure from Berlin, but, with success in his grasp, he and his airplane crashed in unknown waters. Soviet interest in a World War II Dakota (DC-3) transport recently discovered at the bottom of a drained Lincolnshire lake, combined with evidence that something valuable was smuggled out of Berlin, leads Audley, a ministry advisor, to investigate. What he finds is a lost, supposedly Trojan, treasure (the Schliemann Collection, stolen Nazi treasure) and the love of his life, the gutsy Faith Steerforth, the daughter of the dead pilot-thief. He also finds himself caught up in a battle of wits with a Russian figure who threads his way throughout the series, causing mayhem and diplomatic consternation: archaeologist and KGB agent Professor Nikolai Andreivich Panin. Price equates him with J. R. R. Tolkien's Dark Lord, a "very ordinary little man, totally without any aura of power or menace," a "sheep-face" with a bent nose and deeply lined cheeks, and a disconcerting neutrality of manner that hides a sharp intellect, a predilection for puzzles, and a strong personal commitment to undermining the West in every way feasible. Panin has an operation of his own in play against extreme military elements in his own system and sends Audley on a wild-goose chase as a diversion to disguise his own activities and to discredit rogue military officers who might have been involved in a 1937 plot against Joseph Stalin.

No one believes there is a real treasure, nor do they think that Audley can find it. Both sides, however, underestimate his cleverness with puzzles, his understanding of human psychology, and his ability to operate under time restraints. Thus, when he successfully completes his assignment and figures out how the West is being manipulated for Panin's ends and what to do about it, officials on both sides of the Iron Curtain are taken aback. As *The Labyrinth Makers* progresses, personal concerns begin to take precedent over Audley's assignment, even though understanding the pilot's daughter is clearly a way of understanding her long-dead father. The couple find themselves pursued, hide in an early-sixteenth-century priest's cell in the Audley family home while murderous thugs search diligently for them, and fall in love amid danger. Price writes convincing love stories and makes budding romance a quiet feature of each of his novels.

The Labyrinth Makers establishes the patterns that Price continued to use to good effect in the novels that followed. His heroes and heroines, as he himself points out, are "not secret agents so much as secret policemen (and women)," and his themes are "the virtues of a free man in a free country"–"loyalty, duty, honor and patriotism." He looks with a forgiving eye on human limitations, demonstrating that Faith is not really the arrogant snob her manner suggests but a saddened woman who has lost her father twice, in effect, and whose nearsightedness without her glasses makes her look at people literally without seeing them clearly. Likewise, Price reports that an elderly woman was not trying to be offensive: "hers was simply the narrowed viewpoint of the elderly, the self-comforting assumption that her feelings would be shared by all sensible people." He also believes, however, that people should learn from experience. Thus, his characters often have sudden flashes of insight that make them reevaluate past interpretations of deeds and events, as when Faith suddenly realizes that her father's gift to her of a beautiful, expensive book on Troy and Heinrich Schliemann's treasures was not the carefully chosen present of a loving father but a book left over from his investigation of riches he planned to steal.

Another characteristic that The Labyrinth Makers establishes as central to Price's concerns is quite English in nature. He emphasizes his characters' ties to the land, and his descriptions of place make clear that his appreciation for it is akin to that of the pursued hunter hero of Geoffrey Household's classic Rogue Male (1939). Price has his key characters observe the contours of the land with a soldier's eye, looking for the high ground and the defensive position, the vulnerable open spaces, and the comforting hiding spots. On the Downs, Audley sees "down below him the neat patchwork of fields, the squat churches and neat houses with smoking chimneys," a scene that he calls "the rich, fat, peaceful land of England" in contrast to the "more ancient and hostile" ambience of the Downs: "The downlands could be creepy on a hot still day. And in the evenings there always seemed to be things moving outside the circle of a man's vision." As an historian Audley walks the fields of battle, notes the slight shifts of terrain that are matters of life and death with the enemy close at hand, and

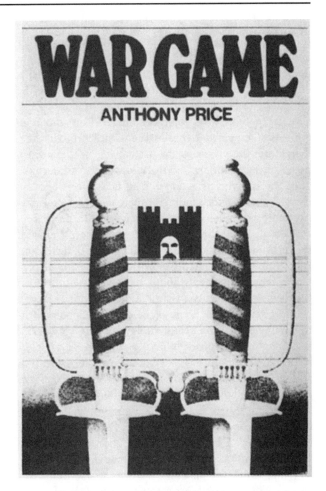

Dust jacket for Price's 1976 novel, in which re-creations of English Civil War battles become the setting for Cold War conflicts between England and the Soviet Union (from Armchair Detective, 19 [Fall 1986])

speculates as to the character of the men who would set up camp in one location over another.

In The Labyrinth Makers Price introduced relationships and characters who appear in later volumes, particularly "think tank" personnel, such as director Sir Frederick and agents Hugh Roskill and Jack Butler. Sketched in superficially here, they grow in importance over the course of the series. By presenting them from different perspectives and showing them through admiring or censorious eyes, Price provides a depth of characterization and complexity normally missing in such a series. Where other writers simply repeat their featured characters' basic qualities, Price probes deeply to show them in different roles depending on shifting situations and combinations of personalities.

The Alamut Ambush (1971) demonstrates another characteristic of Price's series. Instead of proceeding chronologically, the action leaps forward and back, from Audley's and his cohorts' memories of their personal experiences in World War II, their parents' and professors' memories of World War I, and their studies about Roman England and Hadrian's war to a student demonstration inspired by modern Russia. Fragments of the past make intuitive sense of fragments of the present as Price argues that human nature in all its facets—war, politics, love, comradeship, idealism, and cynicism—has remained basically the same through time. Therefore, the classicist, the archaeologist, the anthropologist, the historian, and the literary scholar all make good spies, spymasters, and intelligence officers because they have an understanding of the complexity, simplicity, and predictability of human behavior. In *The Alamut Ambush* the main threat comes from northern Persia, a region Audley considers the original home of terrorism. Although set in a small English town, the novel provides interesting details about the entire Middle East (Audley's pet specialty), Islam, and Arab versus Aryan cultural heritages. A bomb planted in the car of a British intelligence officer sends Audley, along with Roskill, searching for the cause. What they discover is a highly respected institution, funded to promote education among middle-class Arabs from a variety of nations, being manipulated by terrorists who find its respectability a useful cover for their activities. Egyptians and Israelis secretly join forces to thwart the schemes of the master terrorist Hassan and his cohorts. Ultimately, young Roskill must shed his blood in defense of homeland and family friends as the terrorist attack occurs too close to home and he comes to understand the risk and guilt that compelled the original bombing murder.

A British look at the radicalization of universities in the 1970s, inspired by the real-life betrayals of Oxford graduate Kim Philby, *Colonel Butler's Wolf* (1972) moves from the comfortable reading rooms of Oxford to the desolate moors and Hadrian's Wall. The Russians are active at Oxford, promoting student protest and misguiding British youths. Audley must expose a Russian wolf, a sleeper who is laying the groundwork for future trouble. With squadron leader Roskill out of the picture owing to injuries, Butler is nearly burned to death when he breaks into the school records of a dead youth, a KGB sleeper. He does not realize at the time that the records provide a clue to the identity of another sleeper, alive and active. The way Butler pulls himself together to make his escape is typical of the way Price integrates past and present: "He had always prided himself on his calm self-discipline, the Roman virtue of the British infantryman. Others might be cleverer, quicker to charge—and quicker to fly. But he had conditioned himself over the years to do within himself what the redcoats had so often done in tight corners: to form square unhurriedly and without panic." Promoted from major to colonel, Butler finds that Audley has set him

up to replace his namesake, also a Colonel Butler, an authority on Roman siege warfare and Byzantine mechanical weapons, who had been invited to help with the excavations at the Cumbria University study center near Hadrian's Wall.

The redheaded Butler, a soldier's soldier, with his prizefighter's face, his devotion to his three precocious daughters, and his distrust of women thanks to an unfaithful wife, makes an interesting contrast to the scholarly Audley. Butler is blunt where Audley is indirect, disturbed by deception where Audley takes pride in his inventiveness. Amid the showy and competitive conversation of Oxonians, with their obscure quotations and arcane lore, Butler understands one image that applies to the situation: Grendel is loose at the university; the stronghold Heorot is threatened; and a Beowulf is needed to stop the monster. With a Polish American at his side and a young woman descended from the tough-minded medieval founders of Cumbria, Butler takes a stand at Hadrian's Wall as college youths, like Picts assaulting the Romans, charge up the hill in angry protest of a missile range, having been manipulated into a situation that could cover an assassination or strengthen the position of the Russian sleeper, intent on conquest. The Beowulf of the day, supposedly a Rhodesian, brings down the Russian sniper but is himself exposed as one of three sleepers, a murderous villain, contemptuous of the English, their traditions, and their spirit. Price makes his final warning through Audley, who tells Butler, "You and I—we're on our Wall when it's weak. Weak on the Wall, and weak behind it. . . . Some of our people don't believe there are any savages out there." The Russians are the savages trying to tear down hundreds of years of British tradition and civilization. Butler, proud of his nickname, "The Thin Red Line," stands firm in defense of bright young people, full of enthusiasm for good causes, their sense of right manipulated by the enemy within.

In 1972 Price became editor of the *Oxford Times* and an employee of the Oxford Times Group, positions that overlapped with his employment with Westminster Press. He continued to write his espionage series while working full-time as a journalist. His stories grew out of the headlines and out of his personal historical studies.

The title of *October Men* (1973) comes from the notion of late-middle-aged men desperately seeking ways to atone for their youth, secure wealth for their families, or reap long-delayed revenge. The main October man of the story is an aging courier in Russia, who used German and Russian rumors of North Sea oil to play on the greed of a wealthy entrepreneur in order to win a commitment that his wife and child would be gotten out of East Germany and financially cared for thereafter. As irrefutable evidence of the value of his information, the courier arranged his own death. It turns out that his information fit the facts, making the entrepreneur's fortune and now setting a pair of vengeful October men to find a nonexistent Russian traitor.

Price frequently alludes to or builds his story around events in France during World War II, drawing on his personal knowledge of the time and the region. Thus, he speaks authoritatively of weapons, ammunition, tactics, insignias, the makeup of particular regiments, and the place of a minor skirmish in the broader picture. He calls the British and German soldiers killed in the Battle of the Somme "the cream" of their nations, the former "irreplaceable as men," the latter, "irreplaceable as soldiers." *Other Paths to Glory* (1974), which many call his best effort, received the Golden Dagger Award from the Crime Writers' Association in 1975 and the Swedish Academy of Crime Fiction Award for best foreign crime book in translation in 1979. The historical focus of the novel is World War I, particularly the Battle of the Somme, the details of which could directly affect a summit meeting in the 1970s. The title comes from John Masefield's "The Old Front Line" (1917), about the wartime paths to glory being "deep under the corn" and the war "a romance in memory." The book introduces ambitious young military historian Paul Mitchell. Two strangers approach and throw him into a weir, and he barely escapes with his life.

A suicide note causes the police to mistrust Mitchell's story of attempted murder until Audley shows up with the information that Mitchell's professor, another World War II expert just back from the battlefields of France, has been murdered. The police write Mitchell up as missing and, assuming the identity of one Captain Lefevre, he draws on his knowledge of the battles, personalities, regiments, and particular topography to help prevent a bombing in the present. Mitchell's knowledge of the network of underground caverns that still lie cut into the chalky hillsides is the secret a network of terrorists plans to use to their advantage. Ultimately, Mitchell proves his mettle and thwarts an assassination. Despite his scholarly desire to rush out and write articles based on his discoveries, he is tempted by the possibility of a new career working alongside Audley.

Our Man in Camelot (1975), a study in KGB misdirection, intertwines a modern tale of a United States Air Force plane missing on a flight from its British base with Arthurian legend. The only sign of something amiss is the pilot's sudden enthusiasm for books on Arthurian England and his search for a reference to Mount Badon in the Nizhni Novgorod manuscript of the Venerable Bede (held by Panin). The perspective in the novel is that of Mosby Singleton Shelby, an

Dust jacket for Price's 1978 novel, tracing his series character David Audley's origins as an intelligence agent during World War II (from Armchair Detective, *19 [Fall 1986])*

American dentist turned CIA agent who must work with his British counterparts to solve the mystery. Accompanied by his assigned partner and pretend wife, Shirley, on his mission to England, Shelby observes the Audley family relaxing on the beach and assists them when their sabotaged car fails to function. Audley, in the midst of a book on the twelfth-century earl of Pembroke, is drawn into Shelby's interest in the sixth-century Mount Badon, the site of Arthur's most important battle victory. The CIA knows the Russians sabotaged the airplane and, exploring all the available manuscripts referring to Badon, tempts Audley with artifacts and aerial photographs into finding the elusive, legendary Mount Badon; in this way the agency hopes to draw out the KGB. In a quiet English churchyard Shelby kills two British agents, thinking they are KGB operatives, and then finds that the British are far ahead in the espionage game and that American-Brit-

Dust jacket for Price's novel in which an ill-matched pair of British soldiers are caught up in the fall of France and the evacuation of the British army from Dunkirk in 1940 (Collection of Anthony Price)

ish relations are the real target as Panin schemes to put the two allies at odds.

War Game (1976) sets a modern conflict between the Soviets and the British in the midst of a modern re-creation of English Civil War battles. The historical Cavaliers and Roundheads are played by their modern political equivalents.

The '44 Vintage (1978) is a prequel to the books in the Audley series. It looks to the characters' pasts, with German-speaking Corporal Butler, age nineteen, suffering from athlete's foot in the wet fields of World War II and taken from the Lancashire Rifles to join a secret unit called the Chandos Force, after a fourteenth-century English soldier and cutthroat marauder of the French countryside, Sir John Chandos. Young Audley is conscripted for special duty for a similar reason, his French language skills. When the two meet, they dis-cover in different ways that all is not what it seems. But-

ler, after clearly demonstrating his honesty and patriotism, kills his first enemy in a life-or-death knife fight, and the enemy turns out to be a British officer. The Chandos Force is in fact a group of rogue soldiers who are taking advantage of their special status to reach a French chateau and extract a fortune hidden there from the Germans. As the Germans pull out and the Chandos Force advances, Butler and Audley, who were misdirected into the midst of the retreating German forces and are thought dead, race to reach the hiding place first, having learned from a local French doctor the truth of what is hidden there: a pestilence that could destroy them all. The pleasure from the story is multi-ple: an interesting historical study of a multinational war winding down, an exciting war story with a sur-prising twist, a bildungsroman, and a psychological study of Audley and Butler as youths. Regular readers of Price's novels can see in the two young men the raw, unformed characters that, with time and experience, become the two Cold Warriors of Price's other novels.

Price was much taken by the ideas and values expressed in Faulkner's 1949 Nobel Prize acceptance speech and quotes lines from it in *Tomorrow's Ghost* (1979) to sum up the nature of two of the central char-acters, Butler and Frances Fitzgibbons, citing "the old verities and truths of the heart, the old universal truths . . . love and honor and pity and pride and com-passion and sacrifice." These values are the essence of this sad and poignant tale, and it is the message Price wishes to convey throughout his series about the men and women who daily put their lives on the line as secret agents, their heroism unknown and unsung except in private circles. Coming straight from an aborted assignment where she had to look quite differ-ent from her usual professional self, Fitzgibbons, through whose eyes readers see the action, must move directly into a university setting, assume the role of a scholar specializing in Tolkien and fairy tales, and at the same time run the security controls to protect a visiting minister from Ulster. Required to remove a bomb from the men's cloakroom, she performs her terrifying duty with quiet heroism, at the same time sharing with read-ers her irritation with Mitchell, a heroic figure in other Price novels, but from her view "insufferably pomp-ous," "a cold fish" with an "irritating habit of trying to reduce every situation to some obscure military analogy."

An army widow and former typist recruited by Colonel Butler, Fitzgibbons has a natural aptitude for espionage and an uncanny knack for judging others, both of which make her invaluable as an investigator. In *Tomorrow's Ghost,* however, she receives a nightmare assignment—to investigate her mentor, Butler, and to put to rest, one way or another, the rumors that still link him to the unsolved murder of his wife. To lay to rest "tomorrow's ghosts" and free Butler from the cloud over his career, she uses all of the resources at her command, interviewing the police inspector in charge of the murder investigation nine years earlier, going to great lengths in order to interview Butler's children, and finally ferreting out his secret and honorable alibi. In doing so, she sees to the heart of this earnest man and falls in love with him. Thanks to Israeli assistance, she also discovers that she has been manipulated by agents in the British ranks who fear that Butler's promotion was Audley's way of paving the way for his own higher appointment.

Set in postwar France, *Soldier No More* (1981) is tied to the Algerian and Suez crises; involves Russians, Israelis, and the English; and is told from the interesting perspective of a traitor, a double agent who cannot make up his mind about which side deserves his loyalty. David Roche has been assigned to recruit Audley by both his masters, British and Communist. He has been working for the opposition ever since a woman he loved supposedly died, and now he is looking for the right way to insinuate himself into Audley's crowd in order to approach him. He has met with Audley's teachers and studied Kipling, but he is unprepared for the power of the intellect with which he must deal. While readers follow Roche's self-justifications and his careful manipulation of others to create the proper image for each side, Audley is already working for British intelligence, and they are playing with Roche to glean information vital to their cause. When Algerians, who have misread the intelligence signals, attack, Roche redeems himself somewhat by defending Audley's friends, but after debriefing, he can soldier no more.

The Old Vengeful (1982) typifies Price's interest in history for its own sake. This interest is not limited to one historical event, problem, or region but plays off a series of time periods, in this case the recurring name of a naval vessel that figured significantly in several historical settings and wars and has direct application to Russian-British relations in the 1970s. Almost the entire book is a case of misdirection, with Audley sending his people out on missions he hopes will keep the Russians from knowing that he is onto their plot. Mitchell is assigned to insinuate himself into the good graces of Elizabeth Loftus, the plain but intelligent daughter of a retired naval commander, whose book on the ships named *Old Vengeful* throughout English naval history somehow ties in with the name of an ongoing Russian operation, Project Vengeful. When Audley sets Mitchell to recruit Elizabeth for government work, he takes the opportunity to recruit her as his wife (her interest in Mitchell has been clear from the start).

In *Gunner Kelly* (1983), when Colonel Butler's nineteen-year-old daughter, Jane, confesses to involving her godfather, Audley, in a school friend's murder plans, Butler takes her seriously, and the quiet hamlet of Dunstisbury Royal becomes a fortress, with villagers on patrol, traps laid, and an unknown terrorist or terrorists expected. The town hero, General Maxwell, has recently died in a car bombing, and his servant and fellow soldier, Gunner Kelly, thinks that he was the intended target. The Irish Republican Army (IRA) is suspected, but KGB operatives are the real perpetrators, seeking one Aloysius Kelly, an Irish traitor and a KGB teacher who trained spies and then defected. When Kelly's brother, Gunner, died from a bomb, Aloysius assumed his name and hid out with Maxwell. Now he has played the villagers' love of the general to buy himself time to escape KGB executioners. Aloysius almost escapes, but villagers turn on him when he needlessly kills one of their own. Through Audley, Price attacks the Irish as lacking a sense of historical perspective and, instead of laughing at the follies of their ancestors, obsessing over them to the point of re-creating their tragedies in boring and senseless repetition.

In *Sion Crossing* (1985) a trap set for Audley instead closes on Olivier St. John Latimer, who is in competition with Audley for the deputy directorship of the intelligence service. Latimer is an overweight, out-of-shape British intelligence officer with no real field experience and certainly none involving physical exertion and danger. According to a CIA contact, American senator Thomas Cookridge, the chairman of the New Atlantic Defense Committee, needs a Civil War expert, and Latimer, anxious for American allies in his quest for promotion, steps in to gain an advantage on his competition. This action takes him to a former cotton plantation at Smithville, near Atlanta, Georgia, where he finds himself hot, unintelligible, and out of his depth. Price has great fun as Latimer dredges up pieces of half-remembered American history and tries to seem knowledgeable.

Latimer becomes caught up in a serious Civil War reenactment that turns deadly. He proves his mettle by rescuing from churning waters a seriously injured professional hitman who has protected him and by holding off an attack by Russians dressed as Confederate soldiers. Back in England, Mitchell has been trying to make sense of Latimer's actions. He, Audley, and Butler connect events to a secret Soviet finishing school for Communist sleepers being sent to Western nations. They call in a timely British rescue team led by Wing Commander Roskill. Though Price has his history right, his southerners are rather odd, but then most of them turn out to be Russians. Latimer is horrified by the heat and humidity, has no reference points for

3

I [cap as text for roman numeral

"Mad," murmured Captain Willis at the Adjutant's departing back. "Quite mad."

Everyone at the breakfast table pretended to take no notice, except Captain Henry Bastable, who disliked Captain Willis almost as much as he did Hitler.

"Quite mad." Now that the Adjutant was out of earshot Willis spoke louder. "Probably certifiably mad, too."

One day, when the war had been won and the washing *hung* on the Siegfried Line, and the Prince Regent's Own South Downs Fusiliers returned to its proper and more agreeable amateur status, there was going to be a new breakfast rule at the annual Territorial Army camp, Basable vowed silently to himself: to the existing <u>Officers will not talk shop</u>, it would add <u>and at breakfast</u> <u>officers will not talk at all.</u>

"Mad as a bloody hatter," said Willis, more loudly still.

It was wrong to hope that Willis would be the first P.R.O. battle casualty of the Second World War. And anyway, Willis would probably bear a charmed life, he was that sort of person. So that new rule would be needed to shut him up. But in the meanwhile, the best Bastable could do was to glower at him over his crumpled copy of <u>The Times</u>, and grunt disapprovingly in the hope that Major Tetley-Robinson would notice, and take the appropriate action.

"Drill!" exclaimed Willis, in a voice no one could pretend to fail to hear.

"Eh?" Major Tetley-Robinson looked up for a moment from the piece of bread which he had been examining, but then looked down again at it. "You

25

Corrected typescript pages for the opening of The Hour of the Donkey
(Collection of Anthony Price)

4

know, we'll never get decent toast from this stuff, the composition's all wrong. We'll have to find a way of baking our own."

"I said 'drill'," said Willis clearly. "'Drill'."

"Eh?" Major Tetley-Robinson looked up again, but this time at Lieutenant Davidson. "No more of this damn Froggie stuff, Dickie - I won't have it! It's all crust and air, and you can't make toast out of crust and air." He switched the look to Willis at last. "Talking shop, Wimpy? Or did I mishear you, eh?"

Bastable was disappointed to observe that Tetley-Robinson was trying to let Willis off. Normally the Major could be relied on to savage Willis at every opportunity, his dislike of the man dating from the discovery that Willis's fluent French stemmed from the possession of a French grandmother, and from Alsace moreover, which was dangerously close to the German frontier. 'Fellow doesn't look like an Alsatian - more like a cross between a greyhound and a rat,' the Major had observed <u>sotto voce</u> on receiving this intelligence. 'Probably runs like a greyhound too.'

But now the prospect of action appeared to have mellowed this enmity, for the Major was regarding Wimpy with an expression bordering on tolerance.

Willis returned the look obstinately. "No. I said 'drill'. My company - "

"I heard." The Major lifted his chin and looked down his nose at Willis. "Shop - and you know the rule." He leaned back in his chair and half-turned towards the mess waiter without taking his eyes off Willis. "Higgins - fetch Captain Bastable's steel helmet."

Willis licked his lips. "My company - "

"Not until you're wearing your steel helmet, <u>if</u> you please, Wimpy," snapped the Major. "Then you can talk as much as you like, if you can find anyone to listen to you... " He pointed down the table. "Pass me the marmalade, will you, <u>Bar</u>stable?"

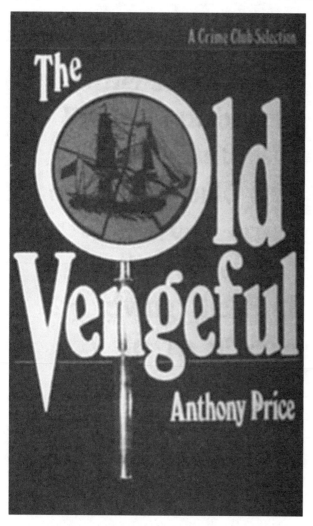

Dust jacket for Price's 1982 novel, in which the history of various British warships named The Old Vengeful *figures in a Russian spy plot (from* Armchair Detective, *19 [Fall 1986])*

understanding American black-white conflicts and interaction, misunderstands Southern diction, and is out of his element in almost every way.

In *Here Be Monsters* (1985) Loftus is the central investigating official, with her talents and her self-control tested in several ways. Latimer is once more gunning for Audley, this time by proving that men Audley vetted in 1958 were actually traitors connected to the KGB sleeper operation. The plot begins with the murder of a would-be suicide at a World War II battle site on the French coast where he had once plucked a downed flyer from rough seas. The circumstances force an investigation that Audley cannot resist joining. He and Loftus interview key figures from the past and even travel to France in search of evidence. There, the now-retired Captain Peter Richardson helps them evade CIA watchers and almost elude their

French counterparts. Ultimately, their strongest suspect makes them realize that Panin has once again deliberately set agents at odds as a distraction while he gets his own agent out of England and eliminates a British agent that has troubled him. Loftus sees in Audley a modern Sir Francis Walsingham, a clever Renaissance schemer and master spy, and speculates that Mitchell, whose marriage proposal she rejected and whose love she continues to reject, could, with time, become another Audley. Yet, she fails to see in herself what her superiors recognize, her toughness, strength, and determination amid adversity, as well as her too great pleasure in pushing others to the edge. To awaken Loftus to her own monster within, they plan to send her back into the fray against an adversary who will make her question her basic nature. On a personal note, Price comments on American McCarthyism, believing that indeed America was beset by Communist tools in the 1950s but that Senator Joseph R. McCarthy, in his self-righteous fury against them, became a monster more dangerous than those he pursued. Price suggests that every government agent must guard against the loss of humanity and the unwillingness to forgive weakness in others or to acknowledge that one's best theories and judgments may be wrong.

For the Good of the State (1986) captures the interagency jealousies that set British against British as top intelligence officer Henry Jaggard, jealous of Audley's successes, places him in the midst of a Russian confrontation that both Panin and Jaggard hope will result in Audley's expulsion from the service. Jaggard's self-justification is "Quis custodiet ipsos custodes?" (Who will mind the minders?). His willingness, however, to have a sharpshooter take potshots at Audley at his family home and to leave Audley exposed to Russian violence at a medieval site suggests that Jaggard is the minder who needs minding. He also miscalculates when he chooses the Polish-English Sir Thomas Arkenshaw as Audley's minder (in the sense of armed protector) for several reasons. Arkenshaw has a ready sympathy for Audley because of their shared enthusiasm for medieval fortifications; Audley had a youthful love affair with Arkenshaw's flamboyant and passionate mother; and Audley understands and appreciates Polish history, heritage, and doomed courage. Arkenshaw is an interesting study in clashing cultural behavior, his British reserve coupled with a Polish instinct to charge when danger threatens, his academic enthusiasm for medieval castles coupled with his highly competent knowledge of weapons and of all the skills necessary to protect those he guards from unexpected attack. The mystery elements come from Audley and Arkenshaw's deduction that a declared accident is murder and that they are being set up to excuse a Russian assassination as an act of self-defense and to take the fall for a bungled operation. The conclusion is all about payback, with Arkenshaw's decision to change over to the Department of Intelligence Research and Development not only confirming the value of that department but also thwarting Jaggard.

A New Kind of War (1987) is a flashback to Audley's youth and the beginnings of the research-and-development think tank. Set in Germany immediately after World War II, as the title suggests, it marks the change from hot war to Cold War, from the clarity of a visible enemy to the enemy in the ranks, as the European nations prepare for a secret war of spies, sleepers, and the other intelligence apparatus by which nations prepare themselves against any future attack. The novel begins with Audley's troops surprising a Captain Fred Armstrong Fattorini of the Royal Engineers, who is hiding with a Greek captain in Canadian battle dress on a hilltop near Delphi. The opening is from Fattorini's point of view, and no one knows whom to trust until the Greek mentions the eve of Scobiemas, a reference only someone with strong English ties would know about. It turns out that the Greek has been testing Fattorini for a possible intelligence position. Fattorini is soon transferred into Audley's corps, a special unit with a focus on recruitment and vetting, acquiring trained German university and scientific personnel with valuable skills (a "braindrain" operation), and ferreting out sleepers being put in the British and American ranks by Russians (and possibly Germans) to pave the way for future potential confrontations. Audley is young, cocky, and seemingly all too verbal for a position involving secrets, but there is method in his constant yammering. As he pretends to be researching German tank development, he puts his life on the line for more-important causes, and his troops are loyal. The British are keeping secrets from the Americans, who want to be in on all mop-up activities. The Russians already have Communist sympathizers in place, and everyone is trying to keep important German scientists from going over to another side since wartime allies may prove peacetime enemies. A seemingly "mad" British officer provides effective cover by demanding aerial photographs, supposedly to find the location of a battle, "Herrmannscholact," where the German "barbarians" under Arminius (or Herrmann) ambushed and slaughtered three Roman legions under Varius in A.D. 9. These operations enable Audley and Fattorini to engage in odd, "cooperative" maneuvers to keep the Americans out of the intelligence loop and deal with traitors in their midst who are assisting the Russians in acquiring or eliminating German brainpower. Price, through Audley, draws on his own end-of-war experiences, discusses a favorite book (Robert Graves's 1934 novel *I, Claudius*) and contrasts the

Dust jacket for Price's 1983 novel, in which the Soviet KGB becomes involved in political violence in Ireland (from Armchair Detective, 19 [Fall 1986])

fall of the Nazi regime with the fall of Rome. Through his characters, Price takes positions on the war that are meant to teach modern readers about the realities of World War II that time is erasing. The result is an effective genre mix that helps readers to see with new understanding a segment of the war rarely treated (the inglorious shut-down operations) and that argues Price's message throughout his canon: the present grows out of the past and produces the future, and one cannot fully understand today or tomorrow without knowing yesterday.

A Prospect of Vengeance (1988) and *The Memory Trap* (1989) were the last two novels in the Audley series. In 1988, for reasons of health, Price retired from journalism. These books look to the changes taking place in the Cold War world of espionage and to the more modern focus on terrorism as the next major threat to the free world.

In 1990 Price published an historical study on a topic that had clearly intrigued him for many years, *The Eyes of the Fleet: A History of Frigate Warfare, 1793–1815,* preparatory materials for which he had used to good effect in *The Old Vengeful.* At age sixty-two, he took what he called "an annually renewable holiday," a sabbatical from writing, saying, "no use being a bit richer but a lot more dead with so many fine things still to be seen and so many good wines still to be tasted." Besides, as a Cold War writer, he felt that his war and the enemy of his generation were past and that "no other villains seemed to measure up." He has not published since. Price remains a member of the Guild of British Newspaper Editors, the Crime Writers' Association of England, and the Detection Club. He and his family live in Horton-cum-Studley, Oxford, England.

Newgate Callendar, mystery critic for *The New York Times Book Review,* describes Price as "a unique contributor to a genre in which British authors have always excelled," juggling convoluted intrigues and making sense of them so that the structural, historical, literary, and personal dimensions merge into a challenging whole. Price's goal is a combination of entertainment and instruction. He teaches enduring values and the necessity of people in a democracy to struggle against forces that would undermine their values, government, and way of life. Price assumes that his readers are, like some of his characters, "innocent" about the world of politics: "Always trying to transpose their safe, cozy world with that other, very different one, brave

old Uncle Joe [Stalin], puffing his pipe; cuddly Mr. Krushchev, dandling his grandchildren on his knees; mild, worried-looking Mr. Kosygin, playing the dove to Brezhnev's hawk," the nightmare reality ready to dissolve such fantasies in the morning sun. Price's most significant contribution to the mystery and espionage genres is his creation of spymaster-historian Audley, whose fascination with archaeology and historical conundrums makes him quite good at his job of puzzling out the intricacies of modern espionage. No single volume captures Audley's essence, but he lurks in the background or moves into the foreground of every book in the series. Price traces Audley from a young soldier at the end of World War II, through his early assignments; his romance with his wife, Faith; his recruiting, testing, and training of colleagues; his battles of wits with his Russian opposite number, Panin; his promotions up the rank; his enthusiasms for different historical puzzles; his failures; his successes; and his purposeful refusal to engage in power-grabbing strategies. The result is a multivolume life history of a modern humanist and scholar, who, like the Renaissance masterminds behind the reign of Elizabeth I of England, guards the realm with the mastery of Walsingham and the ruthlessness of the Machiavellian Sir William Cecil. Together the Audley novels provide insights into how an historian develops evidence, examining different personalities in different periods and from different political positions to extrapolate a realistic portrait of an historical figure.

Ruth Rendell
(Barbara Vine)
(17 February 1930 –)

Patricia A. Gabilondo
Nicholls State University

See also the Rendell entry in *DLB 87: British Mystery and Thriller Writers Since 1940, First Series.*

BOOKS: *From Doon with Death* (London: Long, 1964; Garden City, N.Y.: Doubleday, 1965);

To Fear a Painted Devil (London: Long, 1965; Garden City, N.Y.: Doubleday, 1965);

Vanity Dies Hard (London: Long, 1966); republished as *In Sickness and in Health* (Garden City, N.Y.: Doubleday, 1966);

A New Lease of Death (London: Long, 1967; Garden City, N.Y.: Doubleday, 1967); republished as *Sins of the Fathers* (New York: Ballantine, 1970);

Wolf to the Slaughter (London: Long, 1967; Garden City, N.Y.: Doubleday, 1968);

The Secret House of Death (London: Long, 1968; Garden City, N.Y.: Doubleday, 1969);

The Best Man to Die (London: Long, 1969; Garden City, N.Y.: Doubleday, 1970);

A Guilty Thing Surprised (London: Hutchinson, 1970; Garden City, N.Y.: Doubleday, 1970);

No More Dying Then (London: Hutchinson, 1971; Garden City, N.Y.: Doubleday, 1972);

One Across, Two Down (London: Hutchinson, 1971; Garden City, N.Y.: Doubleday, 1971);

Murder Being Once Done (London: Hutchinson, 1972; Garden City, N.Y.: Doubleday, 1972);

Some Lie and Some Die (London: Hutchinson, 1973; Garden City, N.Y.: Doubleday, 1973);

The Face of Trespass (London: Hutchinson, 1974; Garden City, N.Y.: Doubleday, 1974);

Shake Hands Forever (London: Hutchinson, 1975; Garden City, N.Y.: Doubleday, 1975);

A Demon in My View (London: Hutchinson, 1976; Garden City, N.Y.: Doubleday, 1977);

The Fallen Curtain, and Other Stories (London: Hutchinson, 1976); republished as *The Fallen Curtain: Eleven Short Stories by an Edgar-Award Winning Writer* (Garden City, N.Y.: Doubleday, 1976);

Ruth Rendell (photograph © by Jerry Bauer; from the dust jacket for the U.S. edition of Adam and Eve and Pinch Me, *2001)*

A Judgment in Stone (London: Hutchinson, 1977; Garden City, N.Y.: Doubleday, 1978);

A Sleeping Life (London: Hutchinson, 1978; Garden City, N.Y.: Doubleday, 1978);

Make Death Love Me (London: Hutchinson, 1979; Garden City, N.Y.: Doubleday, 1979);

Means of Evil (London: Hutchinson, 1979; Garden City, N.Y.: Doubleday, 1980);

Three Cases for Chief Inspector Wexford (Helsinki: Eurographica, 1979);

The Lake of Darkness (London: Hutchinson, 1980; Garden City, N.Y.: Doubleday, 1980);

Put on by Cunning (London: Hutchinson, 1981); republished as *Death Notes* (New York: Pantheon, 1981);

The Fever Tree and Other Stories (London: Hutchinson, 1982; New York: Pantheon, 1982);

Master of the Moor (London: Hutchinson, 1982; New York: Pantheon, 1982);

Matters of Suspense (Helsinki: Eurographica, 1983);

The Speaker of Mandarin (London: Hutchinson, 1983; New York: Pantheon, 1983);

The Killing Doll (London: Hutchinson, 1984; New York: Pantheon, 1984);

The Tree of Hands (London: Hutchinson, 1984; New York: Pantheon, 1984);

An Unkindness of Ravens (London: Hutchinson, 1985; New York: Pantheon, 1985);

The New Girl Friend and Other Stories of Suspense (London: Hutchinson, 1985; New York: Pantheon, 1986);

A Dark-Adapted Eye, as Barbara Vine (London: Viking, 1986; New York: Bantam, 1986);

Live Flesh (London: Hutchinson, 1986; New York: Pantheon, 1986);

Collected Short Stories (London: Hutchinson, 1987; New York: Pantheon, 1988);

A Fatal Inversion, as Vine (Harmondsworth, U.K.: Viking, 1987; New York: Bantam, 1987);

Heartstones (London: Hutchinson, 1987; New York: Harper & Row, 1987);

Talking to Strange Men (London: Hutchinson, 1987; New York: Pantheon, 1987);

The House of Stairs, as Vine (London: Viking, 1988; New York: Harmony, 1989);

The Veiled One (London: Hutchinson, 1988; New York: Pantheon, 1988);

The Bridesmaid (London: Hutchinson, 1989; New York: Mysterious Press, 1989);

Undermining the Central Line, by Rendell and Colin Ward (London: Chatto & Windus, 1989);

Ruth Rendell's Suffolk, photographs by Peter Bowden (London: Muller, 1989);

Gallowglass, as Vine (London: Viking, 1990; New York: Harmony, 1990);

Going Wrong (London: Hutchinson, 1990; New York: Mysterious Press, 1990);

The Strawberry Tree, published with *Flesh and Grass,* by Helen Simpson (London: Pandora, 1990);

The Copper Peacock, and Other Stories (London: Hutchinson, 1991; New York: Mysterious Press, 1991);

King Solomon's Carpet, as Vine (London: Viking, 1991; New York: Harmony, 1991);

Kissing the Gunner's Daughter (London: Hutchinson, 1992; New York: Mysterious Press, 1992);

Asta's Book, as Vine (London: Viking, 1993); republished as *Anna's Book* (New York: Harmony, 1993);

The Crocodile Bird (London: Hutchinson, 1993; New York: Crown, 1993);

No Night Is Too Long, as Vine (London: Viking, 1994; New York: Harmony, 1994);

Simisola (London: Hutchinson, 1994; New York, Crown, 1995);

Blood Lines: Long and Short Stories (London: Hutchinson, 1995; New York: Crown, 1996);

The Brimstone Wedding, as Vine (London: Viking, 1995; New York: Harmony, 1995);

In the Time of His Prosperity, as Vine (London: Penguin, 1995);

Ginger and the Kingsmarkham Chalk Circle (London: Phoenix, 1996);

The Keys to the Street (London: Hutchinson, 1996; New York: Crown, 1996);

Road Rage (London: Hutchinson, 1997; New York: Crown, 1997);

The Chimney Sweeper's Boy, as Vine (London: Viking; 1998; New York: Harmony, 1998);

A Sight for Sore Eyes (London: Hutchinson, 1998; New York: Crown, 1999);

Thornapple (London: Travelman, 1998);

Harm Done (London: Hutchinson, 1999; New York: Crown, 1999);

Grasshopper (London: Viking, 2000; New York: Harmony, 2000);

Piranha to Scurfy and Other Stories (London: Hutchinson, 2000; New York: Crown, 2001);

Adam and Eve and Pinch Me (London: Hutchinson, 2001; New York: Crown, 2001);

Babes in the Wood (New York: Crown, 2002);

The Blood Doctor, as Vine (New York: Shaye Areheart, 2002).

OTHER: *A Warning to the Curious: The Ghost Stories of M. R. James,* edited by Rendell (London: Hutchinson, 1987; Boston: Godine, 1989);

Anthony Trollope, *Barchester Towers,* introduction by Rendell (London: Folio Society, 1989);

Wilkie Collins, *The Woman in White,* introduction by Rendell (London: Folio Society, 1989);

Trollope, *Dr. Thorne,* introduction and notes by Rendell (London & New York: Penguin, 1991);

The Reason Why: An Anthology of the Murderous Mind, edited, with an introduction, by Rendell (London: Cape, 1995; New York: Crown, 1996).

SELECTED PERIODICAL PUBLICATION–
UNCOLLECTED: "A Voyage among Misty Isles," *New York Times Magazine,* 16 May 1993, pp. 28–34.

In the world of mystery and detective fiction, Ruth Rendell is considered by most critics as one of the leading, if not the leading, practitioners of the genre. Often hailed as the "Queen of Crime" or "the First Lady of Mystery," she has also been called the "new Agatha Christie," a label that, given the vast difference in her work from Christie's, annoys Rendell. In an interview in *Maclean's* (6 November 1989) with Diane Turbide, Rendell complained, "It's all so much rubbish, these tags. My books are nothing at all like Agatha Christie's, and the Queen of Crime–I mean, really." Despite any inaccuracy or the extravagant flash of such tags, they promiscuously flourish because of Rendell's unparalleled publishing success and eminence in the field of mystery and detective fiction. For more than thirty-five years this prolific writer, with more than forty-five novels and seven short-story collections to her credit, has enthralled readers and critics alike with her ability to make out of what might, in a less skillful writer's hands, fall into the formulaic, something always suspenseful and viscerally compelling. More than sixteen million of her novels (published in twenty-five languages) have been sold worldwide, several of which have been adapted as motion pictures, including eight television series in the United Kingdom.

Her work has received not only the recognition of substantial international sales but also the praise of fellow writers and reviewers. P. D. James, although on the other side of the political bench, has stated of her good friend that, when it comes to mystery fiction, "No one has explored with greater sensitivity and compassion those dark recesses of the human psyche. She is one of the remarkable novelists of her generation" (quoted in *People,* 18 December 1995). Val McDermid, who has called her "an anatomist of the human psyche," declared in *Crime and Mystery Fiction Journal,* "No-one can equal her range or her accomplishment; no-one has earned more respect from her fellow practitioners." Like so many other reviewers, Francis Wyndham of *TLS: The Times Literary Supplement* (1994), praising her "highly developed faculty for social observation" and her "masterly grasp of plot construction," has written that "Ruth Rendell's remarkable talent has been able to accommodate the rigid rules of the reassuring mystery story (where a superficial logic conceals a basic fantasy) as well as the wider range of the disturbing psychological thriller (where an appearance of nightmare overlays a scrupulous realism)."

Ruth Barbara Grasemann was born on 17 February 1930 in South Woodford, London, to an English

Dust jacket for Rendell's 1967 novel in which her series detective, Inspector Wexford, investigates the disappearance of an eccentric artist's socialite sister (from John Cooper and B. A. Pike, Detective Fiction: The Collector's Guide, second edition, 1994)

father, Arthur Grasemann, and a Swedish mother, Ebba Elise Kruse Grasemann, both schoolteachers with great interest in literature and the arts. Despite her parents' nurturing of their only daughter's artistic gifts, Ruth led a lonely childhood, made more lonely by the unhappiness of her parents' marriage. The strife in her home and her resultant need to escape, however, spurred the young Rendell to re-create in her imagination the unhappiness around her into fictive accounts that allowed her to distance herself from the pain and to lay the foundation for her later creative technique. When she was seven her family moved to Loughton in Essex, where she lived until she graduated high school.

Instead of following her parents into teaching, Grasemann decided to forgo the expected university route to try her hand instead at journalism. Writing for the *Chigwell Times,* she eventually became its chief editorial writer and later worked as reporter and subeditor for the West Essex newspapers the *Express* and the *Independent*. She never felt comfortable or adept at writing journalism, however, for, as she has indicated in interviews, she is a natural storyteller and always felt limited by the facts, having to suppress a desire "to rearrange the endings." In an unpublished interview with Rendell, B. J. Rahn reports that she "enraged the owners of a house by stating it was haunted," and allegedly she wrote an article about a guest speaker's speech at a tennis-club dinner without having attended the dinner, only to find that the speaker had expired before he could finish the speech. Grasemann is said to have resigned honorably after the snafu. During her stint as journalist, she met her husband, Don Rendell, a political reporter, and, after marrying in 1950, she quit journalism in 1953 to raise her son, Simon.

During this time Rendell embarked upon a program of intensive reading and of learning French and classical Greek. She also experimented with writing various forms of fiction, from the short story to the comedy of manners to the historical novel, with no intention of publishing, writing them simply for her own pleasure. After several years of writing, she began to submit her short stories to magazines with no success. She finally submitted a comedic novel to a publisher, and, although this manuscript was not accepted, it did attract the publisher's interest enough for Rendell to be invited to submit another novel. The novel subsequently submitted was a psychological study that, although well received, had to be revised for acceptance into a detective novel—and so her best-known character, Chief Inspector Reginald Wexford, was at first merely part of an apparatus that Rendell had to impose upon her novel for quite practical reasons. The result was her first published novel, *From Doon with Death* (1964). That Rendell was, in a sense, obliged to create Wexford for other than aesthetic reasons explains why the characterization of the inspector in the first three Wexford novels is not quite solid.

Almost immediately after the publication of her first Wexford novel, Rendell began a second line of fiction that has resulted in the publication of twenty novels—psychological suspense novels that explore the psychology of crime, especially murder, outside the world of the detective. Ten years after the publication of *From Doon with Death,* after several prestigious awards and the favorable attention of important reviewers, Rendell's work quickly achieved international fame, so much so that, in 1983, Rendell and her husband were able to purchase a fifteenth-century cottage in Polstead, Suffolk, where Rendell writes much of her work, an area that is the subject of *Ruth Rendell's Suffolk* (1989). Always interested in extending the boundaries of her own work, Rendell was not content to pursue the same

directions in her art and in 1986 began publishing lengthier and more-complicated psychological thrillers under the pseudonym Barbara Vine (Barbara being her middle name, Vine, her grandmother's name). Multi-generational in scope and far more experimental than her other novels, the Vine novels sealed Rendell's reputation as an accomplished writer of fiction. Her novels have been awarded several Edgar Allan Poe Awards from the Mystery Writers of America, Silver Dagger and Gold Dagger Awards from the Crime Writers Association in England, have been short-listed for the prestigious Whitbread Prize, and have been awarded the Arts Council National Book Award and the *Sunday Times* Award for literary excellence. A fellow of the Royal Society of Literature, Rendell has been honored with several doctorates from British and American universities and in 1996 was made Commander of the Most Excellent Order of the British Empire. In 1997 she joined the House of Lords as a working peer under Tony Blair's administration. Although the title of "Queen of Mystery" may make her flinch, Rendell is content as the baroness of Babergh (Babergh is a Suffolk district) both to lead and to support activism in causes ranging from environmentalism, adult literacy, children's rights, and, most recently, in the campaign against female circumcision.

Rendell, often compared to Patricia Highsmith, has been praised for her ability to expose the menace that shadows the sunlit world of ordinary lives. In Rendell's work, the roots of psychopathology are found within the psyche of Everyman: the potential for, and consequently, the actuality of, murderous violence, mindless cruelty, and self-destructive obsession. In Rendell's world "we are capable of anything," as a character puts it in *The Bridesmaid* (1989). Although Rendell never shies away from gritty portraits of the underclass, she reminds readers that what appears as the polite and smooth fabric of middle-class society is actually knotted with the potential explosion of violence because of the frustrations of desire, or, more frighteningly, to the unexpected slipup, the chance occurrence, the trivial event that serves as the catalyst for unforeseen chaos. Intensely interested in the psychological, Rendell always puts more emphasis on character than plotting, her interest in the internal lives of her characters. "The old-fashioned detective story, which is so much a matter of clues and puzzles," according to Rendell in a 1996 interview in the *Irish Times,* "is certainly on the way out, if not already gone. Crime novels now are much more novels of character, and novels which look at the world we live in."

Rendell established her reputation on the Wexford novels, a series that developed from her love of what she described to Susan L. Clark as "the old-fashioned format—not terribly Golden Age but a format that includes a wonderful and interesting detective." She "wanted a middle-aged, ordinary detective, rather literary," and Reginald Wexford certainly meets the criteria. A lover of poetry with a penchant for the apt literary quotation, Wexford exhibits none of the cynicism, eccentricity, or misanthropy of so many other literary detectives. Married happily to his devoted Dora, Wexford, the father of two grown daughters, lives a centered and middle-class life in the fictional town of Kingsmarkham in Sussex.

Kingsmarkham serves as a constant reminder of the pastoral dream of rural England, a dream fully realized in so many places of classic English mystery, but Rendell places such pastoral reference within the context of the sprawling suburbanization and the encroachment of urban culture on the rhythms of country life. Unlike Miss Marple's St. Mary Mead, Kingsmarkham is a microcosm of contemporary sociological dynamics, allowing Rendell to paint a full portrait of what she has described to Susan Rowland as the "social stratification in rural England." Rendell, fascinated both by nature and by architecture, by botanical details and the way that architecture embodies both human desire and wretchedness—whether the stark, barren bungalows of the working class or the country homes of the affluent— pays great attention to locale. Her meticulous description of setting serves to create atmosphere and, more important, to communicate the intimate relation between the physical and the psychological, especially in terms of the way that landscapes, whether urban or rural, take on the imprints of sociological change and personal conflict. Thus, for example, in *Kissing the Gunner's Daughter* (1992), aristocrat Davina Flory's restoration of the ancient copses once part of Cheriton Forest that extended into her estate lies incomplete, interrupted by a household mass murder that ends all her attempts to keep both the history of her family and the future of her granddaughter under the control of aristocratic ideology.

Influenced in her portrayal of Wexford by Hilary Waugh's Fred Fellows, Rendell described Wexford to Clark as "quite witty . . . a big solid type, very cool and calm," a man who, though unattractive according to conventional standards, attracts both women and men alike because of his "lively intelligence and zest for life," as he is characterized in *A Sleeping Life* (1978). What is unusual, however, about the often fatherly Wexford is the high degree of empathy with which he treats his fellow human beings, whether in the interrogation room or in the street. This openness makes him strongly attractive to women, and many times the faithful Wexford has had to dodge the amorous interests of attractive women in the series, most dangerously in *Shake*

MVRDER BEING ONCE DONE
RVTH RENDELL

A Crime Club Selection

Dust jacket for the U.S. edition of Rendell's 1972 novel, in which Wexford, recovering from a heart attack, investigates a murder involving a London religious cult (Richland County Public Library)

Hands Forever (1975), when the manipulative Nancy Lake comes close to turning Wexford's life upside down. Strongly philosophical, Wexford is a level-headed idealist with a sometimes curmudgeonly contempt for the inanities of modernity. Through Wexford's often ironic eye, Rendell paints a remarkably specific portrait of the changes that have occurred in English life—the encroachment of suburban sprawl, the banal homogenization of consumer culture, the dispossessed youth, the problems with unemployment, and the growing complexities of civil bureaucracies. Able to see both sides of any issue, as well as to grasp the essential poignancy of the human condition, Wexford finds himself often at odds with his official role, for his reliance on intuition and the imagination usually runs counter to the official line, offering a rich resource of dramatic tension.

Wexford, like Colin Dexter's Morse and Joyce Porter's Dover, has his sidekick, the archly conservative, stiffly principled, and emotionally repressed Inspector Michael Burden, who serves as a foil in many ways. Burden, unlike the intuitive and open-minded Wexford, is a creature of convention and procedure, whose narrow views on gender, race, and class, as well as his rigid morality, conflict with Wexford's willingness to ponder other points of view, however radical or disconcerting, in his attempt to understand the complexities of contemporary life. Belying his conservative views, Burden is a snappy dresser, priding himself on never looking the policeman, while Wexford, willing to recognize the messiness of modern life, lumbers through his life looking the epitome of the low-paid civil servant in his rumpled suits and beloved stained raincoat. Burden follows the practical line, Wexford the unusual; yet, typical of detective duos, they represent dialectical sides of the human personality and of methods of investigation. In the Wexford novels the detective tradition allows for a constant tension between the importance of solution and thus restoration of order and the sense that once murder has occurred, nothing can ever be truly restored to what it was before. Burden's efficiency and smarts represent that essential emphasis on solution, yet Wexford's intuitive and philosophical methods are rooted in his knowledge that solving the murder, although important in the process of justice, never solves what is wrong at the heart of things. The murderer may be caught, but the consequences of his or her crime leave a sad wreckage of human life that always has unforeseen and long-term consequences.

While Burden, in true police procedural fashion, seeks to find his man or woman, Wexford begins by understanding the conditions that made the crime possible. Like his creator, Wexford always works from ultimate causes, not simply reconstructing the crime but reconstructing and understanding the psychic forces and conflicts in the people involved so as to understand *why* much more than *how*. Understanding the former leads Wexford to a sad, often prison-like, network of dysfunctional relationships, usually familial, always rooted in the conflict between socio-economic restrictions and the definitions that limit and therefore frustrate desire. Crime, in most classic examples of the detective genre, arises out of aberrancy, that which is antithetical to the social order, which must be wiped out to reaffirm the ultimate reasonableness of the world within which we live. In Rendell's world, however, crimes such as murder seem to be the almost logical by-products of human relationships because of the oppressive and victimizing dynamics of social structures—the dynamics of the contemporary nuclear family, of gen-

der and racial definitions and strictures, and, perhaps most important, of socio-economic class conflict that do not control or efface aberrancy but effect it because they suppress and impede fundamental desires.

While Rendell's later Wexford novels are more politically direct in their presentation of social problems, the early ones tend to deal more with the conflict between social restraint and forbidden desire. In Rendell's first novels she experiments with what became her trademark use of parallel plots and the intersection of perspectives to deepen her exploration of the psychological underpinnings of crime. In *From Doon with Death* Rendell subverts assumptions about social identity and gender in a mystery that explores the tragic discrepancies between public personas and private realities through the device of literary and photographic texts. The unlikely murder victim, Margaret Parsons, a dowdy, ordinary housewife, seems to have lived a nondescript life of drudgery, with her dull husband in her equally dull house, except for the sudden violence of her death, which has all the marks of a crime of passion. The only testimony to any possibility of passion lies in a series of romantic novels and collections of poetry inscribed by the mysterious Doon to Minna and an old faded photograph of Margaret and her schoolmates. Searching for old lovers in a past that seems remarkably empty of passionate relationships, Wexford must walk through the upper-class, polished homes of two of Margaret's former schoolmates, more beautiful, more glamorous, more successfully married than she, yet eminently more unhappy. Only when Wexford is able to see beyond the surface of convention and to ignore the red herring of adulterous relationships can he recognize the possibility that Doon might be a woman. After that leap of logic, literary identity and literary inscriptions reveal their long-held private meanings, and the photograph, with its long-frozen gestures, communicates to Wexford the murderer's years of lonely desire. The murderer's confession is given to Wexford because "he is the only one who understands."

If *From Doon with Death* deals with the then-taboo subject of lesbianism, Rendell's second Wexford novel—*A New Lease of Death* (1967; republished as *Sins of the Fathers,* 1970)—explores the ancient assumption that the sins of the father are visited upon the children, here not only through environmental influence but, more troublingly, through genetic taint. A concerned father of a young man determined to marry the daughter of a convicted and executed murderer, the eminently respectable and usually liberal-minded Reverend Henry Archery arrives in Kingsmarkham to trace the forgotten path of the murderer, hoping to find that the wrong man had been convicted and thus to be assured of the suitability of his potential daughter-in-law. Parallel plots concerning parentage, both legitimate and illegitimate, of two young girls—one the daughter of the accused murderer, the other the witness to the murder—expose the complexity of environmental influences as well as afford Rendell the opportunity for brutally accurate portraits of the misery that childhood trauma can inflict upon the adult. It is in this novel that we can detect Rendell's gift of describing rooms and houses so as to convey both socio-economic class and psychological portrait. The worn-out lives of alcoholic mother and drug-addicted daughter are mirrored in the mise-en-scène of broken and dirty crockery sticky with congealing egg yolks, the smell of unwashed and greasy bedsheets, the spoiled milk and ashtrays filled with cigarette butts, all presented through the middle-class perspective of Burden, who cannot fathom why people "choose" to live this way.

This intersection of perspectives is more successfully developed in *Wolf to the Slaughter* (1967), a Wexford novel that, surprisingly enough, seems to present little of Wexford's point of view, as Rendell experiments with multiplying perspectives and plotlines to create a much more complex novel than her previous two. A cryptic initial prologue, in which a nameless man and woman stagger away in obvious fright and confusion from a dark tenement, sets up the donnée whose truth we cannot understand until the very end of the novel. Although a murder seems to have occurred, there is no body, yet much blood has been spilled in a room anonymously rented from charwoman Ruby Branch for a few hours of undisturbed sex on the night when socialite Ann Margolis, the promiscuous, jet-setting sister of the eccentric and famous avant-garde London artist, Rupert Margolis, has gone missing. In Rendell's hands, what could conventionally serve as devices for a neat and tidy solution—a blood-stained carpet; a lighter inscribed to an "Ann" found in the possession of Branch's boyfriend, petty criminal Monkey Matthews; and an anonymous note naming killer and victim—serve only to confuse and complicate, leading the police in multiple directions that give Rendell the opportunity to explore the power relations of men and women from different social classes. In the working-class life of Ruby Branch, small-time criminal Monkey Matthews has exploited Ruby's neediness, living as a parasite off her wages and playing on her fear and ignorance, while in the cocoon-like security afforded by wealth and celebrity, Rupert Margolis exhibits a pathological dependency on his sister, without whom he is absolutely helpless. Two potential suspects supply the middle-class perspective—Cawthorne, the auto mogul, and his wife represent the vulgar flash

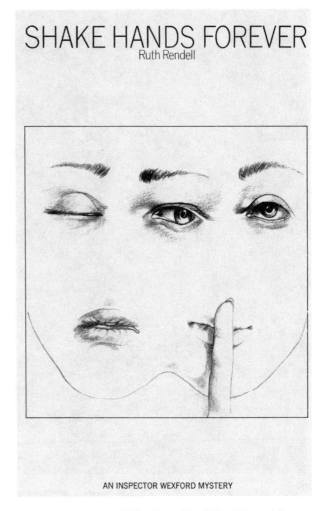

Dust jacket for the U.S. edition of Rendell's 1975 novel, in which Wexford tries to prove that a seemingly innocent man murdered his wife (Richland County Public Library)

of the newly rich, the sterility of their marriage providing fodder for adultery, while Kirkpatrick, another adulterous businessman, this time the proverbial traveling salesman, and his increasingly shrill wife live in a suburban hell of repressed anger and sexual frustration.

These conflicted relationships provide a frame for the irrational sexual obsession that Detective Drayton suffers throughout the novel. Drayton—a recognizable character type that Rendell utilizes in several later psychological thrillers—takes much of the focus of the novel as he battles an overpowering sexual obsession with Linda Grover, the intellectually empty and physically delicate daughter of a grubby shopkeeper. Emotionally repressed and ruthlessly narcissistic, Drayton has little control in the presence of Linda, despite the fact that her shop-girl manners and the vulgarity and slumminess of her world repulse him; this mixture of vulgarity and beauty attracts him, however—she is as "something

Dust jacket for the U.S. edition of Rendell's 1978 novel, in which Wexford investigates the murder of a lonely woman who had an alternate identity as a popular male novelist (Richland County Public Library)

beautiful in an ugly setting," and nausea and desire are as inseparable as the "bluish transparency" of her Madonna-like skin is from the cobwebbed, dirty glass-paneled, pornography-ridden shop within which she lives and works. Drayton's repulsion and attraction border on the masochistic and lead inevitably to professional ruin. Drayton's confusion of love with sexual need, his sadomasochistic conflation of love with power, parallels the confusion of the women who have fallen prey to the sexual charisma of Ray Ansty, the apparent murderer who can become aroused only after a bit of bloodletting, an unfortunate requirement for his partners.

When Wexford finally solves the murder—or, more accurately, when Wexford proves that a murder has occurred through the discovery of a body and the resultant sorting of identities and roles—he discovers, as in *From Doon with Death,* the ease with which appearance

can deceive. Even more striking is that the complexity of plot in the novel serves not so much to enhance the puzzle-solving skills of the detectives as it does to demonstrate the primacy of chance and coincidence: without any police investigation all would have been revealed in a matter of days—Anne Margolis would have returned from her vacation and Ray Ansty's body would have been discovered in the back of Grover's car. Indeed, Wexford's solving of the mystery turns on a matter of luck.

In *A Guilty Thing Surprised* (1970), Rendell continues to examine conflicts with desire and taboo, this time bringing in Wexford's own struggles with the discrepancy between erotic desire and the vicissitudes of age. The central plot concerns a brother and a sister, who, after an early unhappy childhood spent in much discord, meet many years later as strangers and fall in love. Learning of their true relation, they each marry other people, attempting thereby to live separate lives but falling back together and covering their affair by a public animosity that, although a charade, is obviously rooted in long-repressed sibling rivalry. Discovery, inevitably, leads to murder, one that reveals other secret relationships, most notably between a much older, wealthy man and a Lolita-like German au pair, whose own flirtation with Wexford only serves to remind him of his helplessness before his growing old— "the only tragedy of life, the pain beside which every other pain dwindled into insignificance." Age does not lessen desire but only makes it, in the eyes of the world, seem grotesque. It is Wexford's gift to be able to relate his own conflicts, however different in degree or kind, to those that he investigates, as when readers are told that "for the first time in his career he understood what impelled those men he questioned and brought to court, the men who forgot for a while chivalry and social taboo and sexual restraint, the rapists, the violaters." Here the solution, as in *From Doon with Death,* comes through the literary word, specifically through Wexford's reading of a biography of William Wordsworth, in which a reference to Lord Byron—one who also loved a sister too well—opens the doors of perception, again, into what lies beneath the surface of convention.

Throughout the series Rendell develops the lives of Wexford and Burden, their experiences often mirroring or serving as counterpoints to the central murder plot. In *Murder Being Once Done* (1972) Rendell is most skillful in weaving parallel plots out of Wexford's private conflicts and those of the murder plot. Wexford, recovering from a heart attack, is forced by doctor's orders, as well as by the tyranny of familial concern, to convalesce in the modern home, uncomfortably centrally heated, of his nephew in Chelsea under the too watchful eye of his wife and niece who, in their anxiety over him, seem determined to strip him of any shred of independence. Wexford's deterioration in health has led to a painful but necessary regime of physical reformation, yet reformation of the body—the taking of dry toast and carrot juice—does not here lead to spiritual reformation but to a profound sense of helplessness and, more painfully, of irrelevance.

In keeping with its theme of reformation, more specifically, of utopia, the novel is set in Chelsea, the site where Sir Thomas More's home once stood, and Wexford has More's *Utopia* (1516) on his mind throughout the work—although he cannot help but see an annoying similarity between the expression on the Chelsea More statue and the face of the infamous murderer Dr. Crocker. That Wexford imagines the features of a murderer upon the features of a saintly would-be reformer reminds readers of all the reasons utopias are never possible, and Rendell sensitively uses geography in this regard, juxtaposing the security and beauty of upscale Chelsea with the fictional London neighborhood of Kenbourne Vale where the crime takes place, where "miles of moldering terraces" hold "two classes of people: *Threepenny Opera* crooks and the undeserving poor." Kenbourne Vale also holds the body of a murdered young woman, a former member of a religious cult, the Children of Revelation, led by a sadist who, in the name of redemption, enslaves his followers, mostly women, into a psychological and physical dependence that necessitates their complete withdrawal from the world, a counterpoint to Wexford's semi-imprisonment as convalescent.

Although Rendell gives a brilliant study of cult psychology, her emphasis is broader, specifically as to how the natural desire to protect and to nurture can transform so easily into the need to control and to direct, and in so doing to kill, intentionally or not, that which threatens that control. Parental love, or a grotesque perversion of it, and the devastating fear of loss of that role drive most of the characters in the novel—from the murder victim, who seeks the return of the child she has just given away, to the newly adoptive father who attempts suicide upon loss of his daughter to the murderer who kills for a few thousand pounds to keep his child near him. The Children of Revelation stands as the obscene parody of parental love, the women kept as eternally passive children, unable to survive without the direction, however abusive, of their leader.

Wexford himself, like the murder victim alien in a strange land, must stumble about in London and desperately try to regain his self-respect. To do so he secretly investigates the crime, eventually joining forces with the official investigation of his nephew; yet, he suf-

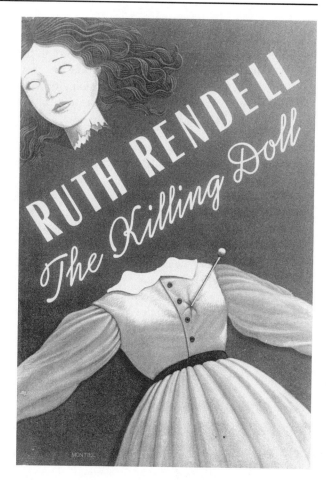

Dust jacket for the U.S. edition of Rendell's 1984 novel in which a schizophrenic woman believes that her brother has dangerous magical powers (Richland County Public Library)

fers several humiliating defeats because of embarrassing miscalculations that brand him as the country bumpkin to the more polished and cynical London officers. Ultimately, because of Wexford's stubbornness and persistence, and his ability to accept his mistakes as just that and not as signs of diminished capacity, the crime is solved, restoring his self-confidence and showing him that working without sleep, drinking a few scotches, and tramping about Kenbourne Vale at all hours of the day and night will not indeed kill him.

An important part of the suspense of many of the Wexford novels lies in Rendell's use of the deadline—in *Murder Being Once Done* Wexford must solve the case before his train leaves for Kirkingham, and in *Shake Hands Forever* he must prove that Robert Hathall has murdered his wife before Hathall leaves the country for a new job in Brazil. In this novel, as in others, Rendell puts emphasis not only on Wexford's dogged persistence but also in his intuition. Wexford, absolutely convinced that Hathall has killed his wife, has nothing to base his certainty on except for an intuition that borders on the psychic. Because he has no evidence—indeed, every fact seems to point to the banal normalcy of Hathall—Wexford's obsessive investigation of his man leads to charges of harassment and his being taken off the case; yet, Wexford, as in the beginning of *Murder Being Once Done,* slips easily enough into the role of private detective, taking it upon himself to have Hathall shadowed in London and to follow his intuitions, even when he miscalculates, running into dead end after dead end. As the murderer is finally caught because of his inability to "shake hands forever" with his lover-accomplice, Wexford in a subplot is faced with the option of following through with a guilt-ridden but thrilling passion for Nancy Lake, who is persistent in her attempts at seduction. Wexford is able to refuse, finally, her offer; following "his own standards and what is right for him," he acts as "a man of sense," accepting that although "the whole of his recent life" has "seemed to him a long series of failures, of cowardice and caution," he has yet "been bent towards doing what he believed to be right and just." Here Rendell uses Wexford's own private concerns as counterpoint to the choices of the criminal to show not only the difference between good and evil but also the ease with which one can slip from one to the other.

In *A Sleeping Life* and *An Unkindness of Ravens* (1985) Rendell continues to complicate and therefore to deepen her thematic concerns through parallel plots between Wexford's and Burden's personal lives, but her interest in the conflict between desire and social constraint becomes more and more enlivened by her increasing concern with social and political commentary. These two novels squarely focus on feminist concerns.

In *A Sleeping Life* the central murder plot involves gender-identity conflicts, while the personal subplot concerns Wexford's elder daughter Sylvia's newly found feminist awareness, an awareness that results in her leaving her husband and moving in with her parents, two sons in tow. The resultant conflict between Wexford, who struggles to understand Sylvia's deep unhappiness, and Sylvia, who is overwhelmed with anger and frustration at her husband's and father's inability to understand her needs, has sparked the charge that Rendell is antifeminist, because it is quite clear that Wexford finds Sylvia's radical feminism abhorrent and irrational. Wexford, despite his sensitivity to women's issues, still believes that being an attractive woman "had certain advantages," and he is unable to ignore that Sylvia's radical politics seem a luxury that she can easily afford given the middle-class advantages provided by family. Wexford's ability to solve the central crime of the novel derives from his sensitivity to the often subtle lines of oppression of women, however,

despite Sylvia's charge (and some critics') of chauvinism.

Rhoda Comfrey, an unattractive, unmarried, and middle-aged woman—three adjectives that brand her as useless in a sexist society—is found murdered on a lonely path. Nothing about Comfrey, other than the location of her senile father in the Kingsmarkham nursing home and a boozing aunt in town, can be found. A Londoner with a false address, she seems to have no immediate past and no locatable present, only a few acquaintances, one of whom is the successful and handsome historical novelist Grenville West. Comfrey's remote past spells a story of loneliness, poverty, and neglect, her physical unattractiveness reason enough for her family to reject her. Rendell uses Wexford's love of words to lead him to the solution of Comfrey's hidden life when Sylvia, in a shouting match with her father, declares that a woman would have to be an eonist to reach true equality with a man. When he goes to his reference books he reads of the long and curious history of eonism—men or women posing as the other sex—and he understands the tragedy of Comfrey, who, because of her lack of beauty and charm, "had none of a woman's advantages over a man," but "by posing—or passing—as a man had everything to gain." Comfrey, as Grenville West, is able to exhibit a confidence that she was not allowed as a woman and to enjoy great professional success. Comfrey's real identity was discovered by one who dedicated all her love and trust in West, who kills her not so much because of betrayal but because of fear of the inevitable loss of a reality by which she has lived. Wexford's sympathy with both murderer and murder victim arises from his growing understanding of what people are driven to do by this need to protect the reality by which they live. The lines from Francis Beaumont and John Fletcher's *The Maides Tragedy* (1619) appropriately supply the title—"Those have most power to hurt us, that we love; We lay our sleeping lives within their arms."

After the publication of *An Unkindness of Ravens, Ms.* magazine declared Rendell "the biggest anti-feminist there is." More intelligent, although no less critical, readings have come from critics such as Sally R. Munt, who concedes that *An Unkindness of Ravens* is Rendell's most "feminist text"—because it is "focused intently on women and sexual violence, covering assault, rape, incest, bigamy and pedophilia"—but who then critiques it as being not only "part of that decade's hostility towards the feminist activism of the 1970s" but also "a reaction against radical and lesbian feminism specifically, which was expressing itself in the form of cultural feminism in the early 1980s." Organized feminism does indeed receive at Rendell's hands an almost over-the-top critique as the object of Wexford and Burden's investigations: a militant feminist society ARRIA (Action for the Radical Reform of Intersexual Attitudes), its logo a woman-faced raven, its mission, to "defy men by intellectual and also by physical means." Members are to carry weapons, are never to marry, some even demanding that a true initiation should require the murder of a man. Munt argues that "by identifying the Women's Liberation movement with five hundred fervent adolescent schoolgirls, led by their lesbian games mistress and her man-hating fanatical love, Edwina Klein, Rendell implies feminism is merely an immature stage which hysterical minors may undergo."

Most galling to the feminist critic, however, is that Rendell creates a plot that for the most part seems the perfect vehicle for a feminist manifesto, yet that, at the last moment, in a characteristic turning of the screw, subverts this expectation. A bigamist, who for many years has managed to keep two wives and two households ignorant of each other, is found murdered. Upon their discovery of the two wives, Wexford and Burden also discover that each household includes two teenage daughters, one (possibly both) the victim of their father's incestuous attacks. That each is a member of ARRIA and that two men in Kingsmarkham have narrowly escaped being knifed to death by an unknown young woman lead the detectives and the readers to believe that the murderer has been motivated by revenge, self-defense, and, given the sexual violation, an understandable hatred against men. At the end of the novel, however, instead of fulfilling expectations and satisfying what some might consider proper ideological focus, Rendell reveals that the father was no pedophile, that there was no incest, no sexual violence. Sarah Williams, the elder teenage daughter, has killed to protect her chances of receiving a grant for medical school. The opportunity for murder has also provided her and her half sister, Veronica, a moment to express "all kinds of murder" in a rather theatrical tableaux—a revenge killing straight out of classical myth. Motives attributed to exploitation by the father, to the patriarch, are mere adolescent fantasy; the real motives are gain and the satisfaction of psychopathic curiosity.

Although politically liberal, Rendell will never sacrifice in her fiction either the complexity of human motive or the formal demands of her plotting to a political agenda; thus, in *Kissing the Gunner's Daughter,* improvising off the country-house theme of so much British literature, she subverts the liberal assumption that Britain's class system no longer had the stranglehold that it used to have. In a 1999 interview with Rowland, Rendell explained that she "wanted to show otherwise," that, at the time she wrote the novel, "Britain was trying to pretend that the social class system was no longer

Dust jacket for the U.S. edition of Rendell's 1985 novel, in which a radical feminist group seems to have a role in a series of violent assaults and a murder (Richland County Public Library)

as rigid as earlier times." In *Kissing the Gunner's Daughter* Rendell again builds strata of plots—concerning a bank robbery, AIDS, and a mass murder at the magnificent Tancred House, not to mention Wexford's problems with his daughter Sheila's new lover, an elitist, post-postmodern novelist—plots that expose the reality and consequences of class division.

Although Rendell refused in her interview with Rowland to label *Kissing the Gunner's Daughter* a "political novel," she has called her next Wexford novel, *Simisola* (1994), the first of the "political Wexfords." *Simisola* confronts racism in rural England, particularly within the context of the exploitation of immigrant workers, of modern-day slavery, and of the unconscious—and therefore possibly more dangerous—forms of racism. Dr. Akande's family is part of a handful of black people who live in Kingsmarkham, and when Akande's daughter Melanie disappears after visiting the unemployment office, Wexford finds himself treating the Akandes with a degree of personal attention and solicitousness that he would not have normally paid to a white family in a similar situation because of his guilt over how, as he argues with Burden, "We're all racist. We were conditioned that way and it's in us still, it's ineradicable." Despite his intellectual understanding, Wexford, nevertheless, is utterly floored and horrified at himself and his fellow officers when they mistakenly assume that the body of a badly beaten black young woman is that of Melanie Akande, even though it should have been quite obvious that the dead woman was years younger than Melanie. They could not see beyond the blackness of her skin, and the outraged, anguished cries of Melanie's parents as they view the battered body of a strange woman whom they had been led to believe was their daughter batter Wexford in a novel that links racism not only to the unspoken cruelties but also to sexual and economic exploitation.

In *Simisola,* according to Guy Walters of the *London Times* (1994), "Wexford's Kingsmarkham patch is a subtly different place. The town has a more recessionary feel; the unemployed and the halt are more in evidence, and it has lost its comfortable atmosphere of sated bourgeois life. Wexford himself is a gloomier figure; irritated by his family, and emotionally drained by the nature of his work." Such irritation and gloom, however, is unexpectedly mitigated by the personal crisis of *Road Rage* (1997). The title *Road Rage* refers not to the explosive violence of the modern commuter but to the anger and subsequent violence of a proposed bypass that, although designed to promote efficiency, will cut through and thus devastate a bucolic landscape, not to mention compromise local businesses as well as views purchased at great cost by wealthy landowners. This road rage brings together an unlikely assortment of citizens—those upright of the middle-class, many of whom have never been politically involved, and long-active environmentalists, some of whom constitute a radical and eccentric subculture, politically seasoned by regular and often violent skirmishes with public authority. Rendell, although herself a dedicated environmentalist, presents environmental issues within the context of social stratification that inevitably must expose conflicting economic interests. Such disparate and yet related interests serve to complicate the plot when a radical ecoterrorist group, Sacred Globe, kidnaps five people, one of whom happens to be Wexford's wife, Dora. The terrorists' ingenious and cruel techniques of hostage-taking, of manipulating those hostages, and of making their demands upon the government form a chillingly accurate portrait of the dynamics of terrorism. When Dora is surprisingly released, she, for the first time in the Wexford series, crosses into Wexford's professional world, serving as the only witness and thus playing a key role in the

investigation. Wexford, not only disturbed about having to subject his wife to seemingly endless interrogation, is also unsettled because of his own sympathies with the ecoterrorists' goals. Despite his revulsion at their techniques, Wexford is aware that "this wasn't the first case of an investigating officer being entirely in agreement with the aims of hostage-takers while hating the way they tried to secure their ransom."

Ultimately, the source of conspiracy, kidnapping, and murder has been neither the politically disenfranchised nor the idealist, as assumed by Wexford's fellow officers, but the wealthy owners of a country house whose view from their beveled windows would be "devastated . . . laid waste" by the "incessant roar of the bypass users" and their property values grievously threatened. Similar to Sarah Williams's theatrical turn in the killing of her father, Rendell has her criminals, a seemingly dull and upright middle-aged couple, put on a convincing performance as terrified hostages while all along directing the entire conspiracy as one would an elaborate costume drama.

In *Harm Done* (1999) Rendell continues to address social problems but goes further than in *Road Rage* to explore their psychological sources. The title of the novel plays off the common phrase "no harm done," here in the context of knocking the wife about, reflecting the apathy of society toward a crime most often not treated as a crime and most often hidden by the victim, who takes the guilt and shame upon herself. Rendell probes both the overt and insidious effects of domestic abuse through a disturbing portrait of a wealthy couple, the Devenishs, who live in a large and opulent house kept perfectly, perhaps too perfectly, by the terrified Fay Devenish. Edward Devenish is the model honorable family man to the world, but to his wife he is a batterer, who not only has beat her for years but who also, as is usual for the batterer, kept her in a state of mind-numbing fear and bovine passivity. Fearing her three-year-old daughter will suffer the same abuse as she grows older, Fay arranges the girl's kidnapping to save her from the damage that her two older sons have already incurred. The kidnapping occurs immediately after the mysterious disappearance of two young women—one a mentally impaired girl from a working-class neighborhood, the other an intelligent university student from a middle-class household. Both girls surface, each giving a clearly fabricated story of her abduction. Although no harm seems to have been done, Wexford, characteristically, cannot leave things alone, and his investigations are complicated by the news that a convicted pedophile, upon finishing his sentence, has moved into a public-assisted housing complex right before the abduction of the three-year-old girl. Hysteria hits the complex; the press adds fuel to the fire; and mob mentality rules, culminating in riots, one of which leads to the throwing of a kerosene bomb and the death of one of Wexford's officers.

Wexford's focus is sharply divided by the mystery of the two girls' disappearance, the kidnapping of the three-year-old, the role, if any, of the pedophile, the source of the kerosene bomb, and eventually, the murder of Edward Devenish. Whether they are all connected or whether coincidence makes for false connections adds to the suspense of this novel, and the solution to the disappearance of the two young girls provides one of Rendell's most bizarre yet entertaining subplots.

The Wexford series has allowed Rendell the opportunity to explore her interest in psychology and in social commentary through the tradition of detective fiction, but the rigid requirements of the mystery formula have restricted how far she has been able to take her investigations into the psychopathological. In the detective story, no matter how disturbing things have been, logic and common sense must triumph over irrationality, and, although Rendell's Wexford novels are unusual because they do not leave readers with a tidy sense of things, readers can, nevertheless, no matter how dark the world has been shown to be, always hang on to the sanity, goodwill, and humanity of Wexford. Further, because the popularity of this series is to a certain extent based on the ongoing development of Wexford's character, Rendell must always give attention to Wexford, as well as to his family and fellow officers. Rendell's psychological suspense novels, however, have allowed her to erase that generic frame of order and to erase as well the restricted point of view of Wexford. The detective apparatus having been removed, Rendell is free to explore the psychology of both victimizers and victims, the arm of the law only a distant complication, in plots that share the same intricacy as the Wexford series.

The characters of Rendell's suspense novels are driven and tortured by obsession, paranoia, anxiety, and guilt. One important purpose of her plumbing of these psychopathologies, according to Rendell, "is to present a person who is odious, has obvious emotional imbalance, but yet is pitiable." Not "want[ing] to portray characters who are wholly hateful," Rendell, through her sensitive characterization, is able to force readers to feel an empathy that inevitably makes them aware of the fluid border between sanity and insanity, between the merely disordered and the deeply depraved. For example, *A Demon in My View* (1976) depicts the emotionally and socially alienated Arthur Johnson, who, on the surface, leads the life of a quiet, unassuming bachelor. In reality, however, he struggles daily to control psychotic explosions of violence, some

Dust jacket for the U.S. edition of Rendell's 1986 novel, the first she published under the pseudonym that combines her middle name and her grandmother's surname (Richland County Public Library)

of which have resulted in the strangulation of women, by elaborate obsessive-compulsive rituals involving housekeeping and organization and by exacting his murderous rages on a dressmaker's dummy kept in the basement.

In *A Judgment in Stone* (1977), Eunice Parchman, a simple housekeeper, has never been able to read and, because of that, has lived a life of isolation, shame, and both emotional and intellectual regression. "A stone age woman petrified into stone," she has had to live on the edge of community, her nickname, appropriately enough, "Miss Frankenstein," and her alienation has been further aggravated by her position as servant to employers whose patronizing attempts to help her are interpreted as part of the mockery from which she has struggled to protect herself. The extent of her petrifaction is clear from her inability to feel any remorse for murdering her employers: "No pity stirred her, and no regret. She did not think of love, joy, peace, rest, hope, life, dust, ashes, waste, want, ruin, madness, and death, that she had murdered love and blighted life, ruined hope, wasted intellectual potential, ended joy, for she hardly knew what these things were. . . . She thought it a pity about that good carpet getting in such a mess, and she was glad none of the blood had splashed onto her." In *The Killing Doll* (1984) the schizophrenic Dolly Yearman, tormented by delusions, leads a life of fear and alienation that culminates in murder, while *Live Flesh* (1986) is told from the viewpoint of Victor Jenner, a convicted rapist and murderer, who, upon release from prison, enters into a strange, symbiotic relationship with the police officer that he shot and paralyzed. Rendell has stated that with Jenner she "was consciously trying to push understanding as far as possible, to create someone who is as far as can be from our sympathy but who can yet command it."

Several of Rendell's psychological suspense novels focus on ordinary protagonists who, under the pressures of the extraordinary, confront their own potential for irrationality and violence. One such character, Philip Wardman of *The Bridesmaid,* a novel about sexual obsession, leads a dull but happily ordered life with his widowed mother and two sisters and his position with an interior-design firm in London until his life intersects with that of Senta, a beautiful yet psychotic woman who bears an uncanny resemblance to Philip's mother's garden statue of Flora, the Roman pagan goddess, a statue who, to Philip, represents an ideal feminine beauty, the only woman he feels he could truly love. Before Philip meets Senta, he feels forced, in a move full of Oedipal significance, to "kidnap" the statue from the garden of his mother's former lover and to hide the statue in his closet, where it stands as a symbol of all of his deeply held desires. In this twist on the Pygmalion story Senta seems to be the statue come to life, and, just as the statue's beautiful face is marred by a green stain and chip, so is Senta's mind damaged by narcissism and paranoid schizophrenia.

Rendell probes both the psychology of sexual obsession and of self-deception with Philip, who gradually becomes implicated in Senta's bizarre demand that they prove their love by committing murder, forever sealing the bond between them through the spilling of blood. Senta, as expected, fulfills her side of the contract, murder not new to her as illustrated by Philip's horrifying discovery of the putrefying body of Senta's former rival grotesquely sitting in one of the upper recesses of the ramshackle, labyrinthine house in which she lives. The creepiness of the central Senta plot certainly pulls the narrative into the Gothic, but Rendell carefully balances the mythic and irrational power of the Gothic with the ordinariness of a subplot concerning Philip's mother and her failed romance with Gerard

Arnham, a man whose wealth and taste sadly contrast with the lower-middle-class Wardman household.

Going Wrong (1990) is another of Rendell's novels that presents a vivid portrait of physical and social London landscapes, landscapes that represent deadly class differences. She also returns to the viewpoint of the criminal, although protagonist Guy Curran is as much victim as victimizer. Curran, like so many of Rendell's characters, is consumed by a sexual obsession, one that has blighted his young life with delusional expectations that have prevented him from any meaningful emotional relationship. The object of his obsession is Leonora Chisholm, a young woman with whom he had a fleeting adolescent romance years before they entered different social worlds. A child of the streets, Guy quickly amassed great wealth through drug dealing, moving by his early twenties into the slightly more respectable business of kitschy art reproductions. In his attempt to win Leonora, Guy becomes a connoisseur of the best that money can buy—his attraction to material luxury the legacy of early, intense experience with poverty. His money and attentions, however, cannot buy acceptance into Leonora's higher-class world, her preference for the intellectually shabby-chic lifestyle an affront to Guy's Gatsby-like equation of luxury with class. Because Leonora does not have the strength to cut things off, her weakness probably aggravated by her fear of Guy's underworld connections, she limits their relationship to lunch on Saturdays, while Guy continues to believe that nothing has changed, even as Leonora makes plans to marry someone else. Unable to recognize her fear of him, Guy gradually falls into paranoid projections as he convinces himself that Leonora is being held back from him by her family, who look at him as nothing but a thug, and by her less attractive roommates, who are jealous of their love. His rage at their rejection, fueled by his need to wipe out any impediment to the fulfillment of his obsession, leads to a hysterical rampage of pursuit and a murder for hire gone terribly wrong.

The plotting of Rendell's psychological thrillers always involves, as in the Wexford novels, two or more parallel stories that link a common theme or concern. With no detective and police investigation to provide the unifying focus, such parallel plots serve in the suspense novels to allow the reader the pleasure of anticipating how Rendell will bring these disparate plots together, plots that usually involve characters from radically different levels of society living radically different lives, whose paths will inevitably cross in rather dramatic ways. Her technique has been described as Dickensian not only because of her interest in portraying characters from a variety of social classes and contexts, but also because of her emphasis on the interconnectedness of human lives. Because such a strategy inevitably involves the intersection of multiple points of view, it also encourages readers to defer judgment as they move through a variety of identifications, leading into a deeper awareness of the complexity and essential mystery of the human psyche. In the Wexford series this intersection more than likely serves to expose how criminality is not something outside the civilized order but the product of civil order itself. In the suspense novels, however, it exposes the varieties of private hells, the dark, twisted fantasies that lie behind the faces of what seem to be quite ordinary people. According to the 1989 *Maclean's* interview with Turbide, Rendell has observed that she need not go far to find the material for her disturbing psychological portraits: "It's only necessary to stand beside somebody in a bus queue, or sit in a pub listening to other people's conversations."

The dramatic potential for random "intersections" is, of course, most present in the city where the movement of crowds makes proximity unavoidable and intersection likely. For this reason, *The Keys to the Street* (1996), set in the Regent's Park area of London with its design of concentric circles connected by paths and roads, is Rendell's most successful attempt to integrate setting with her theme of the interconnectedness of human lives. In the circles and on the paths of Regent's Park, the novel follows the lives of several persons, lives that seem at first to have no possible connection. Each person holds a drama within, certainly not apparent one to another, as they cross each other's paths. One of these is Roman, in the recent past a successful publisher, a happily married father who suddenly lost his entire family in an auto accident. Committing a type of suicide, he kills off one life and takes up another as a "dosser," taking to the streets as a kind of penance for having survived. Despite his camaraderie with other homeless and his raw experience of the streets, he is always conscious of being fraudulent because he is able to draw money from his bank account when absolutely necessary, and, unlike the mentally shattered around him, he can always return to the affluent life that he once knew. Mary, a shy, placid young woman, house-sits in the chic neighborhood of Park Village West, having fled so as to discover a new way of defining herself outside of her former boyfriend's denigration. She agrees to donate her bone marrow to a dying young man as a way of asserting her fledgling independence and as a way of meaning something to someone. When she meets the young man whom she has saved, she feels, as do Senta and Philip in *The Bridesmaid,* that she has met her twin, her other half. They fall in love, but Mary's former boyfriend, Alistair, once he realizes he is losing her, turns violent, stalking her through the park.

Dust jacket for the U.S. edition of Rendell's 1997 novel, in which Wexford's wife is taken hostage by a gang of ecological terrorists (Richland County Public Library)

Each character lives in a different world, yet, as their paths cross in the park, their lives intersect. Although these intersections are sometimes random and inconsequential except for the irony produced by the characters' being unaware of each other's dramas, they lead, at other times, to unforeseen dramatic consequences even when governed by chance. For example, one poignant crossing occurs when Mary, quickly walking through the park, terrified that Alistair is in pursuit, sees Roman. When their eyes meet for just a second, Mary does the unusual. She politely nods, a nod inconsequential to her but which Roman takes as an unexpected recognition of his humanity. At this point, Roman makes himself her protector, and, for most of the novel, unknown to Mary, he guards her, again a father to now an unsuspecting daughter. Eventually, Roman and Mary's lives do meaningfully connect, each able to give the other something that has been missing from life, but, in this novel, most intersections, although they do reveal unexpected connections in the characters' lives, also represent the essential separateness of human beings.

Regent's Park, with its expansive areas, accessible to anyone during the day, offers a democratic leveling that allows for the interaction of people from all classes; yet, its misaligned, concentric circles symbolize the distinction and division of lives. It is, however, the massive iron gates with their magisterial spikes that surround the park, gates locked at night to keep out both criminals and the homeless, that remind readers of the importance of boundaries in this novel and the tenuousness of the democratic dream in a frenetic city where so many green places are gated against the unsavory or the unsuitable. When homeless men are found stabbed and then impaled on these great iron spikes, the brutality of the city is grotesquely and profoundly exposed—the image of the homeless man, the disposable man, impaled upon that which forms the boundary between the grit and grime of city street and the pastoral green within. Rendell, however, chooses not to emphasize the serial murder plot but instead to foreground the private dramas of individual persons. Walking through the park, none of the characters is what he or she seems, the identity and drama locked behind the facade imposed by social definitions of class and gender.

The Keys to the Street may be Rendell's most compassionate and most complex treatment of the human condition; yet, it has not been well received, most reviewers disappointed in her failure to bring all the strands together. The effectiveness of the structure, however, lies in this intentional failure to make everything connect. In Rendell's psychological thrillers, those avenues of emotional connection, like the misaligned arcs of Regent's Park, often do not meet, frustrating the hopes and dreams of her characters' lives.

In *A Sight for Sore Eyes* (1998) and *Adam and Eve and Pinch Me* (2001), Rendell returns to a more streamlined structure of parallel plots, with fewer characters and narrative strands than in *The Keys to the Street,* although her meticulous drawing of contemporary life in Britain's capital through the juxtaposition of different classes is certainly in full evidence. *A Sight for Sore Eyes,* like many of Rendell's novels a study in sexual obsession, is also a novel in which the latent interest that runs throughout many of her novels is made explicit—on the one hand, the potentiality of the aesthetic object to provide sustenance to the human soul; on the other, its capacity to mystify and thus to deceive by providing an alternate dimension ungrounded by reality. Teddy Brex grows up in a ramshackle, working-class neighborhood where he suffers a peculiar abuse. His physical needs are met, but, unwanted and unloved, he is totally ignored and must scratch out his existence in a chaotic

household where Pyrex dishes filled with cigarette butts sit next to the piles of dirty and loud knitting with which his mother is obsessed. Teddy has an artistic sensibility and an exaggerated capacity to appreciate and to make beautiful things. He meets Francine, a sheltered young public-school girl from a much more prosperous and gracious world, the only person whom he has ever seen who embodies the beauty, grace, and perfection that art holds.

Francine's mother was killed by a drug addict who happened to go to the wrong address. Since then, for many years her entire life has been lived under the irrational certainty held by her father and her psychotic stepmother that Francine, the only witness to her mother's murder, is still in imminent danger, not to mention the equal certainty that she must be mentally "damaged." The result has been a kind of imprisonment, from which Teddy is determined to rescue her. A murder allows him to appropriate the gentrified London cottage full of beautiful things for Francine, but Teddy is incapable of making love to her, for she is not a woman to him but a doll that he dresses in velvet and silk and photographs before a mirror. Teddy, only able to buy time by murder, piles up the bodies in the proverbial cellar, using his cabinet-making skills to seal them in a plaster tomb, only to find, later, through an ironic series of mishaps, himself trapped in the tomb of his own making.

In *Adam and Eve and Pinch Me* Rendell puts her familiarity with Westminster's fear of scandal and with the dogged pursuit by the British press of any whiff of sexual impropriety to good use in a novel that manages to blend the titillation of the political scandal with the suspense of a ghost story. She once again brings disparate social classes together, this time through the nefarious but good-humored Jerry Leach (a.k.a. Jock Lewis, a.k.a. Jeff Leigh), whose confidence game involves the solicitation, through temporary marital engagements, of lonely women's affections and monies. His machinations draw together the lives of three very different women—the beautiful but down-on-her-luck Zillah Leach, his abandoned working-class wife, struggling to support herself and her two children; Fiona Harrington, a hardworking and successful professional single woman; and Minty Knox, upon whom the plot focuses, an obsessive-compulsive, psychotic laundry worker. When Jerry (or Jock) fakes his own death by allowing everyone to believe that he has been killed in a train wreck, Zillah and Minty are left with fast-moving consequences that approach the bizarre and sometimes the grotesquely humorous.

Rendell's emphasis falls on a carefully plotted contrast between the flashy saga of Zillah's tenuous rise into high society as the chic wife of a Tory member of

Parliament and the grisly tale of Minty's slow fall into deeper psychoses. Zillah, still married to Jerry, agrees to marry "Jims" Melcombe-Smith, one of Rendell's typically narcissistic males, so that she might provide a cover for his gay lifestyle. Zillah finds herself caught in a web of scandal as her connection to her murdered first husband and the public disclosure of her husband's homosexuality throw her into the limelight of celebrity, of which she has always dreamed but now finds much more uncomfortable than the dumpy life from which Jims rescued her.

Despite the concern and care of her neighbors, Minty lives an isolated life in a lonely, dark house where what she believes to be the ghosts of Jock and her mother torment her. Her isolation and her psychoses are made worse by an obsessive-compulsive neurotic obsession with hygiene, and Rendell's portrait of what it is like to look at everything around oneself, from the clothes on one's body to the food on one's plate, as colonized by filth and germs is both textbook-accurate and moving in its sensitivity. She learns to keep the ghosts at bay with the strong plunge of a large knife, a strategy that works for a while until Minty, because of Rendell's wicked use of coincidence, begins to confuse real people for ghosts. Murder, as expected, connects the women's lives and throws the plotting into a dizzying spin of ironic and grotesquely humorous twists.

While working on her first Barbara Vine novel, Rendell told *Contemporary Authors,* "I understood that what I was going to do would be an semi-historical novel with a great deal of research in that period, and that my readers would find this quite strange. They might find it acceptable, but I thought they would want to know what was going on. So I chose a pseudonym, but at the same time deciding not to keep my own identity a secret." As complex as the plotting of Rendell's other novels are, the Barbara Vine novels are even more so, as their length, which typically runs hundreds of pages longer than her other novels, testifies. Although the Barbara Vine novels have been often described by reviewers as darker than her others, Rendell herself, in the 1989 interview with Clark, described them as "gentler," not "as terrifying" as the non-Wexford novels. They are more psychologically subtle and much more uncertain in their lack of closure and in their greater emphasis on the indecipherability of human behavior. Although the hold of the past upon the present—especially the influence of childhood trauma and neglect—informs all of Rendell's novels, in the Vine novels the relationship of past to present is much more complicated because of much more experimental structures, such as the sophisticated uses of point of view. This experimentation with narrative

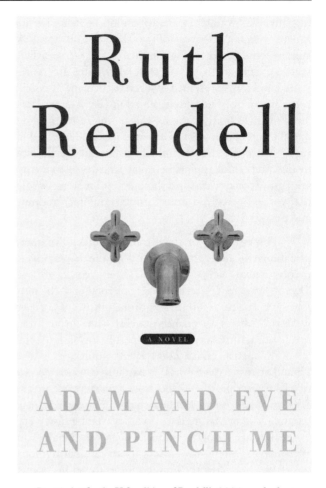

Dust jacket for the U.S. edition of Rendell's 2001 novel, about
three women who all marry the same confidence man
(Richland County Public Library)

voice, especially the multiplying of first-person perspectives, complicates and thus deepens Rendell's pervasive concern with the remote past, with the time of consciousness and the related processes of memory, and the struggle to interpret the past with any degree of certainty.

Many of the novels are structured around the protagonist's explorations and reinterpretations of events buried in the remote past, usually involving undiscovered crime. In several of the Vine novels, such as *A Dark-Adapted Eye* (1986) and *A Fatal Inversion* (1987), the past, reinterpreted differently by a group of intimates, holds much more sway over their present lives, lives caught in the unconscious playing out of consequences of concealed or forgotten trespasses. The narrative of *A Dark-Adapted Eye* is poised between the execution of a woman for murdering her young niece and the attempts by her other niece thirty-five years later to reconstruct the story of that murder from eyewitness accounts and from the faded photographs and yellowing letters left waiting for interpretation. *A Fatal Inversion* moves from the discovery of two skeletons on a Suffolk country estate to an idyllic summer eleven years earlier, whose events, in the recollective aftermath, are represented and misrepresented by each participant. Rendell, referring to the Vine novels, stated in *Contemporary Popular Writers* (1997) that she has been "interested in guilt and the fictional process of moving back and forward in time." Murder, incest, infanticide, mysteries of paternity or maternity, kidnapping, betrayal, suicide—all make up the jigsaw pieces that form the puzzle of a larger whole that can be perceived only through multiple accounts and perspectives.

This emphasis on the provisional quality of interpretation explains why so many of the Vine novels involve texts and writing. The premise of *A Dark-Adapted Eye* concerns the reconstruction of the past for a journalistic account. The protagonist of *The House of Stairs* (1988) is a romance novelist who, through the process of writing an account of past betrayal, finds the truth of a past. *Asta's Book* (1993; published in the United States as *Anna's Book*) is partially constructed out of trial transcripts of excerpts from a diary, while in *The Chimney Sweeper's Boy* (1998), a character's research for a biography of her father leads to a devastating discovery involving her father's unfinished novel. Finally, in *Grasshopper* (2000), the letters from an anonymous writer will not allow the protagonist to forget his crime. In *Mystery and Suspense Writers: The Literature of Crime, Detection, and Espionage* (1998) B. J. Rahn traces Rendell's conscious debt in the Vine novels to Henry James: "Rendell uses various rhetorical devices to lead the reader along the path the narrator takes into the dark heart of the mystery and out again into the light of knowledge, from intriguing remarks about mistaken assumptions in the past ('I believed then') to remorse about not recognizing the significance of the moment ('Had I but known') to ominous hints of impending disaster ('The diaries lay waiting') to full insight in the present ('I realize now') to regret at not being able to see into the future ('I wish I knew')." Rendell has been accused of duplicating in the Vine canon many of the same themes of her psychological thrillers; however, she has countered such criticism, if it is criticism, by conceding that if "the Rendells are starting to resemble the Vines . . . it was bound to happen. There is, after all, one of me."

Ruth Rendell has produced a body of work that has extended the boundaries of the detective and mystery genre, thus redefining possibilities and strategies for future writers, as well as making more permeable that quickly disappearing boundary between "popular" and "serious" fiction. She began her career with the detective novel, and, although she has admitted to having long lost interest in the Wexford series, she seems reconciled to continuing the series because of to its enormous popularity, assuring concerned fans that Wexford will be killed off only in a posthumously published novel. In 1989 Rendell, admitting in the Clark interview that writing the Wexford series had become more of a duty than a pleasure, explained, "It is not interesting to me; I write the other books for my pleasure; I write the Wexfords and Burdens because they are popular—People ask for them." Whether Rendell, in her stretching of the boundaries of whatever genre to which she turns her attention, will find the need to reinvent herself remains to be seen, although, for the time being, she seems content to continue in her pattern of alternating Vine and Rendell novels every year. Rendell's greatest contribution, in addition to her gifts as a storyteller, has been to track the social and the psychological circulation of that vast system—political, familial, cultural, and genetic—in which people are forced to play out their lives, through a body of work that takes readers not into the cozy drawing rooms of traditional English mystery but into the lives and psyches of men and women in a vividly contemporary Britain.

Interviews:

Susan L. Clark, "A Fearful Symmetry," *Armchair Detective,* 22 (1989): 228–235;

Diane Turbide, "Murderous Secrets," *Maclean's,* 102 (6 November 1989): 94.

References:

Sally R. Munt, *Murder by the Book? Feminism and the Crime Novel* (London: Routledge, 1994);

Susan Rowland, *From Agatha Christie to Ruth Rendell: British Women Writers in Detective and Crime Fiction* (London: Palgrave, 2001);

Julian Symons, *Bloody Murder: From the Detective Story to the Crime Novel* (London: Viking, 1985), pp. 177–180.

Colin Watson

(1 February 1920 – 17 January 1983)

Daryl Y. Holmes
Nicholls State University

BOOKS: *Coffin Scarcely Used* (London: Eyre & Spottiswoode, 1958; New York: Penguin, 1967);

Bump in the Night (London: Eyre & Spottiswoode, 1960; New York: Walker, 1962);

Hopjoy Was Here (London: Eyre & Spottiswoode, 1962; New York: Walker, 1963);

The Puritan (London: Eyre & Spottiswoode, 1966);

Lonelyheart 4122 (London: Eyre & Spottiswoode, 1967; New York: Putnam, 1967);

Charity Ends at Home (London: Eyre & Spottiswoode, 1968; New York: Putnam, 1968);

The Flaxborough Crab (London: Eyre & Spottiswoode, 1969); republished as *Just What the Doctor Ordered* (New York: Putnam, 1969);

Snobbery with Violence: Crime Stories and Their Audience (London: Eyre & Spottiswoode, 1971; New York: St. Martin's Press, 1972); revised edition (London: Eyre Methuen, 1979);

Broomsticks over Flaxborough (London: Eyre Methuen, 1972); republished as *Kissing Covens* (New York: Putnam, 1972);

The Naked Nuns (London: Eyre Methuen, 1975); republished as *Six Nuns and a Shotgun* (New York: Putnam, 1975);

One Man's Meat (London: Eyre Methuen, 1977); republished as *It Shouldn't Happen to a Dog* (New York: Putnam, 1977);

Blue Murder (London: Eyre Methuen, 1979);

Plaster Sinners (London: Eyre Methuen, 1980; Garden City, N.Y.: Doubleday, 1981);

"Whatever's Been Going on at Mumblesby?" (London: Methuen, 1982; Garden City, N.Y.: Doubleday, 1983).

Edition: *Lonelyheart 4122,* foreword by Peter Lovesey (Bath, U.K.: Chivers, 1993).

OTHER: "Interview with a Character," in *Murder Ink: The Mystery Reader's Companion,* edited by Dilys Winn (New York: Workman, 1977), pp. 79–80;

"Mayhem Parva and Wicked Belgravia," in *Crime Writers: Reflections on Crime Fiction,* edited by H. R. F. Keating (London: BBC Publications, 1978).

Praised by critic Ian Ousby as one of the most energetic and entertaining comic writers, Colin Watson might be deemed the master of the "anti-cozy" for his Inspector Purbright series. In deliberate contrast to what Watson called the "Mayhem Parva" school of writers like Agatha Christie, in his novels he delights in painting out the unromantic aspect of country life in the town of Flaxborough, where, according to H. R. F. Keating, "corruption was endemically rife, sexuality more or less unbridled and modest Inspector Purbright trie[s] valiantly to cope."

Colin Watson was born on 1 February 1920 in Croydon, Surrey. He attended Whitgift School in Croydon from 1930 to 1936, "one of the smaller public schools," he recalled in "Interview with a Character," "and that nearly always has the effect of putting one up against authority." In 1936 Watson began working in advertising in London. After two years he switched to journalism, working in London and the surrounding provinces from 1938 to 1940. Watson then worked for an engineering firm that kept him busy in London and its surrounding provinces from 1940 to 1945. He reentered the newspaper field, this time working as a leader-writer for Thomson Newspapers from 1952 to 1960. From 1957 to 1960 he also worked for the BBC in Newcastle-upon-Tyne. Watson's first novel, *Coffin Scarcely Used,* was published in 1958, and after 1960 he devoted himself full-time to mystery writing. Watson married twice, first to Peggy Swift and second to Anne Watson, and had three children, Michelle, Jennifer, and Jeremy.

The first novel in the Flaxborough series, *Coffin Scarcely Used,* introduces the Flaxborough police force as it comes up against murder, an event so unlikely that the chief constable of the town, Harcourt Chubb, knows of only one other within his memory, and that by a man of the "old school" who, in Chubb's mind, played by the rules, turning himself in and rendering police investigation virtually unnecessary. In this instance, however, and in spite of Chubb's best efforts to see Marcus Gwill's death as nothing but a suicide, the murderer is of the new school. Inspector Walter Purbright, by pointing out that he has never "encountered a suicide who has been in the mood for confectionary at the last moment," forces Chubb to involve himself and his men in the hunt for a killer. Chubb is "a slow thinker and late eater . . . , silver-haired, composed and misleadingly aesthetic-looking." His voice is "thin, cultured . . . , dried up with calming important citizens and lecturing Flaxborough Historical Association on Bronze Age burial." So unsuitable is Chubb to his career that Purbright suspects that "Chubb had donned the uniform of head of the Borough police force in a moment of municipal confusion when someone had overlooked the fact that he was really a candidate for the curatorship of the Fish Street Museum." Although his infinitely preferred activities are gardening and the breeding of Yorkshire terriers, Chubb is unusually active in this novel: he speaks with the town's senile coroner and so keeps an inquest from derailing. This first novel includes the one instance of the chief constable sitting down at work in the presence of his men; throughout the rest of the series he stands, and his motivations for doing so are explained.

Inspector Purbright is "a large, but unassuming-looking man in neutral-shaded clothes" with "a bland, pleasant face beneath springy, corn-coloured hair that not even relentless cropping could bring to conformity." Although happily married, his wife is never named, never seen, and rarely mentioned. Purbright appears only in his work environment, which includes the Fen Street police station where his upper-story, shabby office is separated from the modernized downstairs offices by a rickety spiral staircase. More often out of his office than in it, his investigative manner is best summarized by a character who has been upset by it, undertaker Jonas "Nab" Bradlaw: "I know that man Purbright. He may not be brilliant but he perseveres. He makes himself a thorough nuisance and rubs it in by constantly apologizing. I had him to put up with this morning. I tell you he'll be on our back until kingdom come, with his 'I hate to trouble you' and 'Mightn't it be so' and 'Perhaps you'd care to tell me.'"

Purbright is most outstanding for his amiability, humility, tenacity, and sharply ironic wit. A sample of this wit comes when interviewing Bradlaw, whose television-informed ideas about policemen are apparent to Purbright: "'He's the one,' said Purbright to Love, jerking his thumb at Bradlaw. 'Got the bracelets, Sid? Bracelets,' he explained to the now peeved undertaker, 'are what we call handcuffs. Very slangy.'" Likewise, Pur-

bright's exchange with his right-hand man, Sergeant Sidney Love, at the scene where a body has been found indicates his typical response to lack of thought:

"Nothing round here, Sid?"
"What had you in mind, sir?"
Purbright looked at Love from under his brows. "Clues," he said.

If Love is not as mentally fleet as the detective inspector, he is clearly a far cry swifter than many of his fellow subordinates, such as police constable Pook, whose name, Purbright says in *Lonelyheart 4122* (1967), is "like a formula in physics expressive of the nearest thing to non-existence." Love's perennially youthful face is his most outstanding physical feature, one that Purbright sometimes finds irritating and always finds puzzling: "Purbright looked upon it thoughtfully; he could never quite decide whether that cleanly shining feature properly belonged to a cherub or an idiot." The final officer of note who appears regularly throughout the series is "florid, fat, catarrhal and kindly" Sergeant Malley (spelled without the *e* in some of the later novels). He is the officer for the senile coroner, Albert Amblesby, and a match for the bad-tempered, unsympathetic old man. Additional characters who reappear or are referenced in later works are Mrs. Popplewell, a Flaxborough justice of the peace, and Dr. Heineman, a pathologist at the General Hospital.

Plot-wise, Purbright and his men must sift through ghost and vampire sightings, advertisements for odd antiques, town history, a surgeon's office, and a bag of marshmallows for clues to the deaths of members of an intimate circle of friends. Purbright's fine deductive powers are evidenced in his application of what Chubb refers to as "a wealth of psychology" and his interpretation of evidence that Love has seen but not understood the significance of. Besides showcasing Purbright's techniques of detection and some of the more exciting, fast-paced elements of criminal investigations, Watson reveals the drudgery of police work and the depth of knowledge he gained of police investigations when working as a reporter in his depiction of the thoughts of detective constables Harper and Pook while they are canvassing for information: "It did not strike them as at all reasonable that a murder could have been committed so privately as to have escaped entirely the notice of upwards of sixty householders, most of them patently inquisitive insomniacs with a keen sense of the significance of every passing footstep and every distantly slammed door."

In the second mystery in the series, *Bump in the Night* (1960), public statues and a shop sign are bombed, an action that initially seems to be the work of one of the town's more illustrious troublemakers and its chief prankster, Stanley Porteous Biggadyke. When Biggadyke himself is blown up, Purbright is not convinced that his end, however fitting the townspeople of Chalmsbury might find it, was accidental. The first half of the novel describes the inhabitants and goings-on in Chalmsbury. Of particular note, besides Biggadyke are Barrington Hoole, an optometrist who, in *Lonelyheart 4122,* is cited as the author of a descriptive history of Flaxborough; Walter Grope, a movie-theater doorman with a knack for rhyming who later retires and moves to Flaxborough, where he plays a significant part in *The Flaxborough Crab* (1969; published in the United States as *Just What the Doctor Ordered*); and Leonard Leaper, a young man who turns up in a variety of professions throughout the course of the series.

In *Bump in the Night,* Leaper is a reporter, providing Watson opportunities not only to poke fun at small-town newspaper journalism, but also to offer a comical contrast to the methods and manners of professional detectives. With characteristic wit, Watson describes Leaper's reasoning after a second bomb goes off in Chalmsbury:

> His reasoning was conditioned by regular absorption of radiation from the *Daily Sun.*
>
> This vital journal, the joining of whose staff was Leaper's idea of ultimate beatitude, had taught him that any two consecutive events that displayed the slightest similarity were a series. So he knew that what had disturbed Chalmsbury was a succession of crimes that promised the indefinite recurrence in headlines of phrases like "strikes again." This was satisfactory for, like all true devotees of the *Daily Sun,* Leaper cherished continuity and liked life's amazements to conform to established definitions.

Thinking to catch the criminal in action and get a great story, Leaper carefully selects an outfit that will render him unobtrusive for his espionage. The first person he encounters notes, "I like your sleuthing set, Len." Not particularly subtle, neither is Leaper cautious, mature, or professional in his spying.

Only after the third bomb goes off and the police are no closer to solving the mystery than they were before does Purbright get called in. Purbright's sojourn out of town allows him to witness a sane and "decently conducted" inquest, a notable rarity for Purbright and for the series, and introduces a theme that is picked up in several later novels, particularly in *Broomsticks over Flaxborough* (1972; published in the United States as *Kissing Covens*)—advertising psychology. Doubtlessly drawing on his own experience in advertising, Watson captures the appeal of magazine story ideals for their readers. Purbright's landlady, Mrs. Crispin, uses what

Dust jacket for Colin Watson's first novel (1958), which introduces his series character, Inspector Walter Purbright of the town of Flaxborough (from John Cooper and B. A. Pike, Detective Fiction: The Collector's Guide, *1988)*

she has learned from magazine stories about "happily integrated husbands" rather than what her own experience might suggest as the basis for the decor in her gentlemen's sitting room.

Hopjoy Was Here (1962) builds on the elements of espionage introduced in *Bump in the Night* to create a spoof on Ian Fleming's James Bond series, popular at the time. Like Bond, Hopjoy, as his name suggests, takes joy in bed-hopping. Hopjoy's conquests are not fabulously beautiful or extremely intelligent women, however, and he does not suavely step away, unscathed. As often as not, jealous husbands and boyfriends do him bodily harm. Further, unlike the Bond series, it is not a question of the secret agent seeking to foil an enemy's plot for world destruction; *Hopjoy Was Here* revolves around the search for the secret agent. Set in Flaxborough, the novel adds depth to several characters already introduced. Sergeant Malley, for example, smokes a pipe "in which seemed to be smouldering a compound of old cinema carpet and tar," a fact that indicates his down-to-earth nature when contrasted with the description of a special agent's smoking equipment—a pouch made of "Andalusian doeskin (which honey curing makes the softest hide in the world)" and "pure Latakia" tobacco—and the lengthy, sensual description of his smoking.

Sergeant Love, his perennial youthfulness once again noted, reveals another side of himself, "editor Love," beginning what becomes a trademark and highlighting Love's Walter Mittyish imagination: "The sergeant, one of whose private dreams accommodated editor Love, waistcoated and dynamic, appraising a re-plated page one, set off again for Pawson's Lane with his mind embannered by SCARFACED PLAYBOY SOUGHT IN WARD TEN: MUST RENEW MIRACLE DRUG." Beyond the usual noting of Chief Constable Harcourt Chubb's desire not to be put to any trouble, readers are given an example of the way Chubb serves to stimulate Purbright's thinking: "Purbright carried Warlock's report to the Chief Constable not in confidence that Mr. Chubb possessed a superiority of intellect consonant with his rank but rather as a man with a problem will seek out some simple natural scene, the contemplation of which seems to set free part of his mind to delve more effectually towards a solution."

In the next novel in the Flaxborough series, *Lonelyheart 4122,* Watson introduces a character noted by critics as one of the most charming and entertaining in the series, genteel con artist Lucilla Edith Cavell Teatime. In her early fifties, trim, handsome, and of the belief that "self preservation" is "as much a public duty as a private pleasure," Miss Teatime has found herself getting a little too old to continue her operations in the faster-paced climate of London and has chosen Flaxborough as her next center for operations. As part of her preparation for adjustment to the new town, Teatime reads Barrington-Hoole's *Guide to Eastern England,* which describes the town as prosperous from its rich farmland, a navigable river, and food and plastics factories and offers an historical explanation of the eccentricities of the current inhabitants: "Flaxborough was a market town of some antiquity with a remarkable record of social and political intransigence. The Romans had lost a legion there; the Normans had written it off as an incorrigible and quite undesirable bandit stronghold; while the Vikings—welcomed as kindred spirits and encouraged to settle—had fathered a population whose sturdy bloodymindedness had survived every attempt for eight centuries to subordinate and absorb it."

The plot of *Lonelyheart 4122* intimately involves Teatime as the target of a scheme that has led to the disappearance of two of the town's women. A schemer herself, Teatime is adept at investigating this particular brand of crime; in fact, her uncovering of the perpetrators of the homicides comes only moments before Purbright's own. Watson seems to suggest in his juxtaposition of Teatime and Purbright's investigative efforts that Teatime is Purbright's equal in intelligence, tenacity, nerve, resource, and knowledge of human nature. Peter Lovesey, in his introduction to the 1993 Chivers edition of the novel, goes so far as to suggest that she is "Watson's answer to Miss Marple," though wittier and more entertaining. Purbright's appreciation for her talents is evidenced in future novels, in which he often relies on her insights, experience, and contacts to help with his investigations. For the reader, besides the pleasure of watching her work against those who would take advantage of her, including a delightful game of dominoes mentioned again in *"Whatever's Been Going on at Mumblesby?"* (1982), Teatime also gives readers the pleasure of watching her outwalk Sergeant Love and easily outwit Constable Pook.

Leaper reappears, this time as a preacher at a mission, though Purbright clearly remembers him as the "carrot-nosed reporter seven years before in Chalmsbury." When Leaper greets him with "Hello there, brother," Purbright also remembers when Leaper used to greet him with a "Hello, chief" and concludes that "obnoxious modes of address seemed endemic to his nature." Though never shown to be of any particular faith, Purbright, brought into the realm of God during his visits to the mission to talk with Leaper, does speculate about people's treatment of God: "It was the baleful keening of the mission's congregation (its apparently permanent session embraced the rarest intervals of silence) that droned through the thin walls to Purbright's ear as he entered Northgate from Farrier Street. Drawing nearer its source, he wondered why religion—the western kind, anyway—laid such stress upon giving God praise. Never sympathy."

Also reappearing is Detective Constable Harper, last seen canvassing a neighborhood in *Coffin Scarcely Used,* now responsible for fingerprinting the business office in Mrs. Staunch's Handclasp House and apparently much happier at this task: "The outing was clearly a treat for him. He loped around the little room like an exploring Gibbon and happily spooned great quantities of grey powder on all accessible surfaces, including several that took account of the possibility of the intruder's having been eight feet tall." Chief Constable Chubb can only stand a limited amount of Purbright's theorizing before he drifts off to leave Purbright happily to his own devices; Chubb has nine Yorkshire terriers, a number that horrifies Purbright and that even fellow breeders find borderline immoral. Sergeant Love, who has twice been bitten by some of Chubb's terriers, is noted to have grown up in the town of Flaxborough and to have returned to work there after brief stints in other police divisions. Finally, Watson returns to the idea of advertising, again through room decor. Two rooms for clients, one for men, the other for women, at Handclasp House are carefully designed to appeal through the senses to all the ideal, romanticized notions of domestic happiness touted by dating agencies and in "happy home" magazines. The room for male clients, for example, has scents of freshly baked bread, flowers, and clean laundry, while the room for female clients hints of pipe tobacco and has carefully placed "well worn leather slippers." The visitors, Purbright first and Teatime later, are, however, too analytical and content with their respective lives to be susceptible to the onslaught of emotional appeals.

Advertising and emotional appeals are central to *Charity Ends at Home* (1968) as well. Flaxborough supports forty-three known charities, thirty of which are devoted to animals, most of those to dogs. In considering just what charity means to the trapped and penned animals, orphans, and old people when throngs of people appear weekly to pet them, talk inanely to them, rumple their curls, and smile mercilessly, Purbright finds himself feeling as sorry for the recipients of charity as he did for God in *Lonelyheart 4122*. He finds charities quite useful, though, as a means for people to direct their hostilities against something other than their neighbors. Hostility does, however, become directed against citizens of Flaxborough, and in the case of Mrs. Palgrove, who is found drowned in her own well, the result is the criminal investigation around which the story is built. Hostility has its comical side, too, as Sergeant Malley exacts what he considers a little fitting revenge for Coroner Amblesby's cruelty to others. Malley's "private and carefully guarded opinion was that the coroner was 'a wicked old sod and a damned disgrace.'" His revenge includes making sudden stops, ostensibly to avoid hitting animals and children, that send the coroner sliding off the seat. Charities are also of interest to Lucy Teatime, who has founded one of her own to help the San Francisco ponies that work beneath the streets pulling the cable for the cable cars. Once again she helps Purbright, providing him not only insight into the workings of charities but also access to her wide range of friends and acquaintances.

In *The Flaxborough Crab* young and middle-aged women alike are attacked by erotically charged but physically inept older men, one of whom comes to be known as the "Flaxborough Crab." Also central to the story is the appeal to the elderly of certain drugs and herbal supplements. Juniform, for example, a drug manufactured by a company named Elixon, promises to inhibit the aging process and is, on patient demand,

Dust jacket for the third of Watson's Flaxborough novels, a spoof of Ian Fleming's James Bond stories (from Cooper and Pike, Detective Fiction: The Collector's Guide, *second edition, 1994)*

being prescribed by physician Dr. Meadow. Also in demand is "Samson's Salad," a product of Teatime's "Moldham Mere Laboratories" that purportedly harnesses "The Secret of the Amazing Virility of Boadicea's Warriors." Mr. Grope, former commissionaire of the Rialto theater in Chalmsbury and now retired and living in Flaxborough, is worrying his wife with his suddenly altered behavior, demanding his "conjuggling rights" and stealing women's underwear from clotheslines, behavior she thinks may have something to do with the "Samson's Salad" he has been taking. Alderman Steven Winge also suddenly begins to exhibit erotic impulses. When Winge ends up drowning and Meadow is murdered, Purbright must sort the truth from the hype and determine which product was responsible for the deaths of these two men.

The night watches for the Flaxborough Crab involve the introduction of Policewoman Sadie Bellweather and several new constables. Constable Fairclough "looked capable of giving a good account of himself in a chase, provided he did not actually have to get out of the car." Constable Brevitt seems more likely to chase a suspect, because he stands listening to Purbright's instructions "with one eye on the door as if it were a racetrack starting gate." Constable Braine (spelled with the *e* in later novels) is the opposite of what his name promises. The literal-minded Constable Burke strolls on past a scene of two women trying to drag a third into a fire because "the prevention of cremations was not in his brief." Suggested as well is one of the differences between the uniformed policemen and the plainclothes detectives: when all the officers are instructed to show up that night in dark clothes, "the men from the uniformed branch . . . had responded . . . by donning their best Sunday suits."

Watson followed *Snobbery with Violence: Crime Stories and Their Audience* (1971), a witty and enlightening study of nineteenth- and twentieth-century crime fiction, with the novel *Broomsticks over Flaxborough,* which reflects his research into witchcraft and his experience with advertising. The coven of witches, under the acceptable banner of the "Flaxborough, Chalmsbury and Brocklestone Folklore Society," consists of people whose ideas of the nature and purpose of witchcraft are so diverse as to cause discord among them. Some members of the coven simply want to celebrate nature while others enjoy the orgiastic aspects of their quarterly sabbaths. Some members cannot manage to get the appropriate words right, calling Pan "Pen," Belial "Billy Boy," and pentagrams "pentagons." Still, when reveler Edna Hillyard disappears one sabbath and, later, anti-witchcraft activist Bertram Persimmon winds up dead, the coven provides plenty of suspects for Purbright. The activities of the folklore society also provide Teatime with a new channel for her energies, the Edith Cavell Psychical Research Foundation. In fact, she helps the distraught Lucillite advertisers who have come to test-market their product in "Flickborough," offering to clear the filming area of the unusually high levels of paranormal activity through "TeleRadiation."

In a scene in which the Lucillite advertising executives provide a Freudian analysis of the washing detergent itself, taking on the identity and voice of the detergent and expounding on the symbolic meaning of washday (renewed virginity) for the "washwives" and "drudgegrudges" who will buy the product, Watson hilariously satirizes advertising jargon. He likewise contrasts the promises on a cookie package with the ingredients again to highlight the appeal of advertising to the imagination: Constable Pook bites into a Kreemi-Krunch Kookie, which promises to "release the real taste of the country in the first bite," allowing "his taste buds to be beguiled by the country-style combination of

dehydrated milk solids, soya rusk, sodium monostearate and saccharin."

The equally absurd and misleading aspects of print journalism do not escape Watson's barbs, either. The depiction of the press conference after Hillyard's disappearance and the subsequent newspaper story in which "Parbright" is misquoted and his statements taken out of context demonstrate journalistic sensationalism and irresponsibility. Watson seems to express contempt for the loss of ethical and intellectual integrity among journalists when he has Purbright note to Chubb that "newspapers are a branch of the entertainment industry, not a research foundation." Set against all the fraudulence, however, is Sid Love's honesty and careful, if plodding, work. Readers learn Love has been faithfully engaged to the same girl for fourteen years—the duration of their courtship, he theorizes, a function of their mutual passivity. More important, his attention to detail when listening to taped interviews of two different suspects answers the question of who actually murdered Persimmon.

Likewise, in *The Naked Nuns* (1975; published in the United States as *Six Nuns and a Shotgun*), an underling provides the necessary information for Purbright to solve a case involving a threat from an American mobster and the death of Arnold Hatch, owner of Flaxborough's Floradora Club. Chief Constable Chubb has experienced a mild stretch of his mental facilities as a result of his years working with Purbright. No longer absolutely convinced that crime is simply a product of his officers' imaginations or a characteristic of the working class, Chubb now occasionally fantasizes that the wealthy and nobly born have taken up crime as a "fashionable demonic hobby." Chubb is no better at understanding a case, however, allowing Purbright the opportunity to graciously (and with tongue in cheek) help Chubb save face: "'You will, of course, have raced ahead and deduced the conclusions that Captain West and I reached,' said Purbright, 'but I shall outline them nonetheless, if you don't object, sir.'"

Meanwhile, Lucy Teatime is now the director of Famtrees, a lineage-tracing agency, and once again advertising language is comically explored when a "medieval banquet" at the Floradora Club offers deep-frozen chicken sprayed with a stain as "capons," cheap Spanish wine with some raisins tossed in as "sack," an instant whipped-cream dessert as "possets and syllabubs," and "a species of electronic lute" that makes noises that sound alternately "like the snapping of two-inch steel cables in Alpine valleys," "a chimney stack falling through a corrugated roof," and "a prolonged railway accident."

In the next novel in the series, *One Man's Meat* (1977; published in the United States as *It Shouldn't Hap-*

pen to a Dog), Woof brand dog food, known as "the caviar of the canine world"; the Happy Endings Agency, with its goal "to ease the path of true divorce"; and a young man's fall to his death from a securely locked ride in the amusement park are the main threads of the convoluted murder plot. Solving the mystery takes the combined efforts of Inspector Purbright and Lucy Teatime. Intertwined with the main mystery are updates on recurring characters. First, Coroner Albert Amblesby has died, "choked, it was said, upon the honor of knighthood belatedly bestowed for the political skullduggery of his long-gone prime, as a dehydrated miser may choke upon a rich tidbit." Second, Leaper reappears, now age thirty-five, as the warden for Northern Nutritionals, makers of Woof. Since his stint as a minister in *Hopjoy Was Here,* he has also been a gas fitter and valet, among other jobs. His frequent career shifts are credited to his "having failed from his earliest years to develop any sense of relationship between ambition and capability." Third, Chubb continues to reveal his prejudices, assessing intelligence by district, and the defensive shield he uses against Purbright is described as "specially pliable" and capable of taking on "as seemed apposite at the moment, the shape of wisdom absolute, of a democratic willingness to learn, of the remembrance of an important engagement elsewhere, or even of a good-humored and altogether spurious stupidity."

After an adventure novel centering on journalist Clive Grail, *Blue Murder* (1979), Watson refocuses on the Flaxborough police in *Plaster Sinners* (1980). Love is "coshed" over the head as he admires the plaster model of a cottage, one of many worthless items in lot 34 at an antiques auction. To Purbright's surprise, the bidding for the lot begins at £4.00 and ends at a remarkable £370.00. Equally intriguing is the fact that the highest bidder for the lot, Mrs. Moldham-Clegg, faints as soon as she learns the police will be examining the items she has bought before she will be able to take them home. The developing case takes on even darker overtones for Purbright when an inept London criminal is tracked to Flaxborough, where he has disappeared. The disappearance of a London parolee brings Detective Inspector Eric Bradley to Flaxborough, introducing the most compatible detective with whom Purbright has ever worked.

Bradley has a superior officer similar to Chubb and shares Purbright's sense of humor, eye for the absurd, and ironic manner of expression. Yet, as an outsider and a city person, he can say to Chubb and of people in the community things that Purbright can only think. For example, he directly accuses Chubb of partiality based on social stature and notes Constable Brain's resemblance to a frog. Bradley is certainly a necessary antidote to Chubb in this work, because the case

Dust jacket for Watson's 1968 novel, in which the activities of Flaxborough's charitable organizations lead to murder (from Cooper and Pike, Detective Fiction: The Collector's Guide, *second edition, 1994)*

involves a member of the "quality" in Mrs. Moldham-Clegg, and "ancient and private loyalties . . . had been stirred" in Chubb's mind, putting him in a mood "which would prove obstructive, perhaps even dictatorial, in the face of novelty or radicalism." Indicative of his sentiments about the upper class, Chubb believes Mrs. Moldham-Clegg's fainting to have been "rather nice" because it indicates highly developed sensitivity. "Dogs were much the same: the better the pedigree, the greater the propensity to have fits." Sergeant Malley also plays a pivotal role in the story. His large circle of acquaintances makes him a veritable "Who's Who in Flaxborough and district," and a particularly fruitful resource when Purbright and Bradley's inquiries are stymied by the Moldhams.

Finally, several references to the passage of time occur in this work, something that does not seem to happen in the "Mayhem Parva" world. Teatime has branched out into the antiques field and is now proprietress of the House of Yesteryear. Sergeant Malley is deemed "promotion-proof," having served for twenty-three years without advancing. Purbright has given up smoking; his hair has gotten considerably grayer; and he has so recently acquired reading glasses that wearing them still makes him feel self-conscious. Among the items on Mrs. Chubb's shopping list is Chubb's All-Bran.

Casually mentioned in *Hopjoy Was Here,* Mumblesby becomes the site of murder in the last of Watson's novels, *"Whatever's Been Going on at Mumblesby?."* Purbright's initial reason for traveling to the hamlet is to represent Chubb at the funeral of Richard Daspard "Rich Dick" Loughbury, wealthy solicitor and highly respected member of the Flaxborough community. By virtue of sitting by the back door of the church, Purbright is called upon to rescue the widow of the deceased, who has been locked in a bathroom in her own home. While searching for a key to unlock the door, Purbright further discovers that a fire has been set to a pile of clothes and a bottle of gas placed on a chair near the pile. That nobody in the village takes any of this mischief seriously seems to Purbright more than what the widow, Zoe, thinks it is: simply another indication of the locals' general hostility toward her because they see her as a gold digger and an interloper. Purbright's attempts to dig beneath appearances soon lead him into a tangle of adultery, extortion, suicide, murder, and layers of deceit that requires the assistance of Love, Teatime, and Malley to untangle. Teatime is still proprietress of the House of Yesteryear in Flaxborough, though she has opened a subsidiary shop in Mumblesby called Gallery Ganby. Purbright calls on her in her shop in Flaxborough to make use of her expertise in antiques, an illuminating adventure that takes him amid "pine furniture that appeared to have been assembled by mad axemen and priced by mad accountants" and biscuit tins supposedly signed by Lawrence of Arabia. Chief Constable Chubb retains his presumption of innocence by social status. Despite his claim that he "should be the last . . . to discourage tenacious pursuit and prosecution of a criminal, whatever his social standing," in the next breath he blames the working-class victim of a high degree of "contributory negligence" and a short while later is relieved to learn that the criminal got away. The book ends, however, with an optimistic challenge to snobbery. When Zoe's mother tells her that the people in Mumblesby who go riding are not going to want Zoe along, Zoe replies, "They're going to have to get used to it, then, aren't they?"

During his lifetime Watson held memberships in the Detection Club, the Crime Writers' Association of England, the Society of Authors, and the Horncastle Allotment Holders Association. He also was the recipient of the prestigious Silver Dagger Award for his mysteries. Several of the Flaxborough mysteries became the basis for the BBC television series *The Flaxborough Chronicles.* Watson died on 17 January 1983, at the age of sixty-two.

Consistently sharp and funny, the entire Inspector Purbright series offers readers a host of delightfully eccentric characters, an unforgettable town, and original, well-developed plots. Colin Watson's mysteries serve as a corrective to what he saw as problematic in crime fiction, namely that the appeal of crime stories stems from their affirmation of readers' cherished prejudices. Relying on the role of humor as a provoker of thought, Watson employs the mystery genre to burrow beneath the surface of those prejudices and to expose their absurdity. His major strategy is reductio ad absurdum, a satire ploy that has won many readers' affection.

Checklist of Further Readings

Adey, R. C. S. *Locked Room Murders and Other Impossible Crimes: A Comprehensive Bibliography.* London: Ferret, 1979; revised edition, Minneapolis: Crossover, 1991.

Aisenberg, Nadya. *A Common Spring: Crime Novel and Classic.* Bowling Green, Ohio: Bowling Green State University Popular Press, 1979.

Albert, Walter. *Detective and Mystery Fiction: An International Bibliography of Secondary Sources.* Madison, Ind.: Brownstone, 1985.

Allen, Dick, and David Chacko, eds. *Detective Fiction: Crime and Compromise.* New York: Harcourt Brace Jovanovich, 1974.

Atkins, John. *The British Spy Novel: Studies in Treachery.* London: Calder, 1984.

Bakerman, Jane S., ed. *And Then There Were Nine: More Women of Mystery.* Bowling Green, Ohio: Bowling Green State University Popular Press, 1985.

Ball, John, ed. *The Mystery Story.* San Diego: University of California Press, 1976.

Bargainnier, Earl F. *Comic Crime.* Bowling Green, Ohio: Bowling Green State University Popular Press, 1987.

Bargainnier, ed. *Ten Women of Mystery.* Bowling Green, Ohio: Bowling Green State University Popular Press, 1981.

Bargainnier, ed. *Twelve Englishmen of Mystery.* Bowling Green, Ohio: Bowling Green State University Popular Press, 1984.

Bargainnier and George N. Dove, eds. *Cops and Constables: American and British Fictional Policemen.* Bowling Green, Ohio: Bowling Green State University Popular Press, 1986.

Barnes, Melvyn. *Best Detective Fiction: A Guide from Godwin to the Present.* London: Bingley/Hamden, Conn.: Linnet, 1975.

Barnes. *Murder in Print: A Guide to Two Centuries of Crime Fiction.* London: Barn Owl, 1986.

Barzun, Jacques, and Wendell Hertig Taylor. *A Catalogue of Crime: Reader's Guide to the Literature of Mystery, Detection, and Related Genres.* New York: Harper & Row, 1974; revised edition, New York: Harper & Row, 1989.

Benstock, Bernard, ed. *Essays on Detective Fiction.* London: Macmillan, 1983; republished as *The Art of Crime Writing: Essays on Detective Fiction.* New York: St. Martin's Press, 1985.

Benvenuti, Stefano, and Gianni Rizzoni. *The Whodunit: An Informal History of Detective Fiction,* translated by Anthony Eyre. New York: Macmillan, 1981.

Binyon, T. J. *Murder Will Out: The Detective in Fiction.* Oxford: Oxford University Press, 1989.

Bloom, Clive, ed. *Spy Thrillers: From Buchan to Le Carré*. New York: St. Martin's Press, 1990.

Borowitz, Albert. *Innocence and Arsenic: Studies in Crime and Literature*. New York: Harper & Row, 1977.

Bourgeau, Art. *The Mystery Lover's Companion*. New York: Crown, 1986.

Breen, Jon L. *Novel Verdicts: A Guide to Courtroom Fiction*. London: Scarecrow Press, 1984.

Breen. *What about Murder? A Guide to Books about Mystery and Detective Fiction*. London: Scarecrow Press, 1981.

Browne, Ray B. *Heroes and Humanities: Detective Fiction and Culture*. Bowling Green, Ohio: Bowling Green State University Popular Press, 1983.

Burns, Rex, and Mary R. Sullivan, eds. *Crime Classics: The Mystery Story from Poe to the Present*. New York: Viking Penguin, 1991.

Cadogan, Mary, and Patricia Craig. *The Lady Investigates: Women Detectives and Spies in Fiction*. Oxford: Oxford University Press, 1986.

Carr, John C. *The Craft of Crime: Conversations with Crime Writers*. Boston: Houghton Mifflin, 1983.

Cassiday, Bruce, ed. *Roots of Detection*. New York: Ungar, 1983.

Cawelti, John C. *Adventure, Mystery, and Romance: Formula Stories as Art and Popular Culture*. Chicago: University of Chicago Press, 1976.

Cawelti, and Bruce A. Rosenburg. *The Spy Story*. Chicago: University of Chicago Press, 1987.

Charney, Hannah. *The Detective Novel of Manners: Hedonism, Morality and the Life of Reason*. Rutherford, N.J.: Fairleigh Dickinson University Press, 1981.

Cox, J. Randolph. *Masters of Mystery and Detective Fiction*. London: Scarecrow Press, 1989.

Dale, Alzina Stone, and Barbara Sloan-Hendershott. *Mystery Reader's Walking Guide: London*. Lincolnwood, Ill.: NTC Contemporary, 1987; reprinted, 1994.

DeMarr, Mary Jean, ed. *In the Beginning: First Novels in Mystery Series*. Bowling Green, Ohio: Bowling Green State University Popular Press, 1995.

Denning, Michael. *Cover Stories: Narrative and Ideology in the British Spy Thriller*. Routledge, N.Y.: Routledge University Press, 1987.

Dilley, Kimberly J. *Busybodies, Meddlers and Snoops: The Female Hero in Contemporary Women's Mysteries*. Westport, Conn.: Greenwood Press, 1998.

Dove, George N. *The Police Procedural*. Bowling Green, Ohio: Bowling Green State University Popular Press, 1982.

Dove. *The Reader and the Detective Story*. Bowling Green, Ohio: Bowling Green State University Popular Press, 1997.

Dove. *Suspense in the Formula Story*. Bowling Green, Ohio: Bowling Green State University Popular Press, 1989.

East, Andy. *The Cold War File*. London: Scarecrow Press, 1983.

Freeling, Nicholas. *Criminal Convictions: Errant Essays on Perpetrators of Literary License*. London: Godine, 1994.

Gordon, Kelly R. *Mystery Fiction and Modern Life.* Jackson: University Press of Mississippi, 1998.

Gorman, Ed. *Speaking of Murder: Interviews with Masters of Mystery and Suspense.* New York: Berkley, 1998.

Gosselin, Adrienne Johnson, ed. *Multicultural Detective Fiction: Murder from the "Other" Side.* New York: Garland, 1998.

Green, Joseph, and Jim Finch. *Sleuths, Sidekicks and Stooges: An Annotated Bibliography of Detectives, Their Assistants and Their Rivals in Crime, Mystery and Adventure Fiction, 1795–1995.* London: Scolar, 1997.

Haining, Peter. *Mystery! An Illustrated History of Crime and Detective Fiction.* London: Souvenir, 1977.

Harding, Phil, ed. *The BFI Companion to Crime.* Berkeley: University of California Press, 1998.

Harper, Ralph. *The World of the Thriller.* Cleveland: Press of Case Western Reserve University, 1969.

Hauer, Margaret L. *Scene of the Crime: A Mystery Lover's Reference Guide.* Tijeras, N.Mex.: Blue Diamond, 1998.

Haycraft, Howard. *Murder for Pleasure: The Life and Times of the Detective Story.* New York: Carroll & Graf, 1984.

Heising, Willeta. *Detecting Men: A Reader's Guide and Checklist for Mystery Series Written by Men.* Dearborn, Mich.: Purple Moon, 1998.

Heising. *Detecting Women: A Reader's Guide and Checklist for Mystery Series Written by Women.* Dearborn, Mich.: Purple Moon, 1996.

Henderson, Lesley, ed. *Twentieth Century Crime and Mystery Writers.* London: St. James Press, 1991.

Herbert, Rosemary, ed. *The Fatal Art of Entertainment: Interviews with Mystery Writers.* New York: Macmillan, 1994.

Herbert, ed. *The Oxford Companion to Crime and Mystery Writing.* Oxford: Oxford University Press, 1999.

Herman, Linda, and Beth Steil. *Corpus Delecti of Mystery Fiction: A Guide to the Body of the Case.* London: Scarecrow Press, 1974.

Hilfer, Tony. *The Crime Novel: A Deviant Genre.* Austin: University of Texas Press, 1990.

Hubin, Allen J. *Crime Fiction II, A Comprehensive Bibliography, 1749–1990,* revised edition. London: Garland, 1984.

Irons, Glenwood, ed. *Feminism in Women's Detective Fiction.* Toronto: University of Toronto Press, 1995.

Jakubowski, Maxim, ed. *100 Great Detectives, or, The Detective Directory.* New York: Carroll & Graf, 1991.

Jarvis, Mary J. *A Reader's Guide to the Suspense Novel.* New York: G. K. Hall, 1997.

Johnson, Timothy W., and Julia Johnson, eds. *Crime Fiction Criticism: An Annotated Bibliograpy.* New York: Garland, 1981.

Keating, H. R. F. *The Bedside Companion to Crime.* London: O'Mara, 1989.

Keating. *Crime and Mystery: The 100 Best Books.* New York: Carroll & Graf, 1987.

Keating, ed. *Crime Writers: Reflections on Crime Fiction.* London: British Broadcasting Corporation, 1978.

Keating, ed. *Whodunit? A Guide to Crime, Suspense & Spy Fiction.* New York: Van Nostrand Reinhold, 1982.

King, Nina. *Crimes of the Scene: A Mystery Novel Guide for the International Traveler*. New York: St. Martin's Press, 1997.

Klein, Kathleen Gregory, ed. *Diversity and Detective Fiction: Race, Gender, Ethnicity*. Bowling Green, Ohio: Bowling Green State University Popular Press, 1999.

Klein, ed. *Great Women Mystery Writers: Classic to Contemporary*. Westport, Conn.: Greenwood Press, 1994.

Klein, ed. *The Woman Detective: Gender and Genre*. Urbana: University of Illinois Press, 1995.

Klein, ed. *Women Times Three: Writers, Detectives, Readers*. Bowling Green, Ohio: Bowling Green State University Popular Press, 1995.

La Cour, Tage, and Harold Morgensen. *The Murder Book: An Illustrated History of the Detective Story*, translated by Roy Duffell. London: Allen & Unwin, 1971.

Lambert, Gavin. *The Dangerous Edge*. London: Barrie & Jenkins, 1975.

Landrum, Larry N., Pat Browne, and Ray B. Browne, eds. *Dimensions of Detective Fiction*. Bowling Green, Ohio: Bowling Green State University Popular Press, 1976.

Mackler, Tasha. *Murder . . . by Category: A Subject Guide to Mystery Fiction*. London & Metuchen, N.J.: Scarecrow Press, 1991.

Magill, Frank N., ed. *Critical Survey of Mystery and Detective Fiction*. Pasadena, Cal.: Salem, 1988.

Mandel, Ernest. *Delightful Murder: A Social History of the Crime Story*. London: Pluto, 1984.

Mann, Jessica. *Deadlier than the Male: Why Are Respectable English Women so Good at Murder?* New York: Macmillan, 1981.

McCormick, Donald. *Who's Who in Spy Fiction*. London: Elm Tree, 1977.

Melling, John Kennedy. *Murder Done to Death: Parody and Pastiche in Detective Fiction*. London: Scarecrow Press, 1996.

Menendez, Albert J. *The Subject Is Murder: A Selective Subject Guide to Mystery Fiction*. 2 volumes. New York: Garland, 1986–1990.

Merry, Bruce. *Anatomy of the Spy Thriller*. Dublin: Gill & Macmillan, 1977.

Modern Fiction Studies, special "Detective & Suspense" issue, 29 (Autumn 1983).

Most, Glenn W., and William W. Stowe, eds. *The Poetics of Murder: Detective Fiction and Literary Theory*. New York: Harcourt Brace Jovanovich, 1983.

Mundell, E. H., Jr., and G. Jay Rausch. *The Detective Short Story: A Bibliography and Index*. Manhattan: Kansas State University Library, 1974.

Munt, Sally R. *Murder by the Book? Feminism and the Crime Novel*. London & New York: Routledge, 1994.

Niebuhr, Gary Warren. *A Reader's Guide to the Private Eye Novel*. New York: G. K. Hall, 1993.

Olderr, Steven. *Mystery Index: Subjects, Settings and Sleuths of 10,000 Titles*. Chicago: American Library Association, 1987.

Oleksiw, Susan. *A Reader's Guide to the Classic British Mystery*. New York: Mysterious Press, 1989.

Ousby, Ian. *The Crime and Mystery Book: A Reader's Companion*. London: Thames & Hudson, 1997.

Palmer, Jerry. *Thrillers: Genesis and Structure of a Popular Genre*. London: Arnold, 1978.

Panek, Leroy L. *An Introduction to the Detective Story*. Bowling Green, Ohio: Bowling Green State University Popular Press, 1987.

Panek. *The Special Branch: The British Spy Novel, 1890–1980*. Bowling Green, Ohio: Bowling Green State University Popular Press, 1981.

Pate, Janet. *The Book of Sleuths: From Sherlock Holmes to Kojak*. London: New English Library, 1977.

Pederson, Jay P., and Taryn Benbow-Pfalzgraf, eds. *St. James Guide to Crime and Mystery Writers*. London: St. James Press, 1996.

Porter, Dennis. *The Pursuit of Crime: Art and Ideology in Detective Fiction*. New Haven: Yale University Press, 1981.

Pronzini, Bill, and Marcia Muller, eds. *1001 Midnights: The Aficionado's Guide to Mystery and Detective Fiction*. New York: Arbor House, 1986.

Pyrhönen, Heta. *Murder from an Academic Angle: An Introduction to the Study of the Detective Narrative*. Columbia, S.C.: Camden House, 1994.

Rader, Barbara A., and Howard G. Zettler, eds. *The Sleuth and the Scholar: Origins, Evolution and Current Trends in Detective Fiction*. New York: Greenwood Press, 1988.

Reddy, Maureen T. *Sisters in Crime: Feminism and the Crime Novel*. New York: Continuum, 1988.

Reilly, John M., ed. *Twentieth-Century Crime and Mystery Writers*, revised and enlarged edition. New York: St. Martin's Press, 1985.

Sauerberg, Lars Ole. *Secret Agents in Fiction: Ian Fleming, John Le Carré, and Len Deighton*. New York: St. Martin's Press, 1984.

"Senior Sleuths," *Mystery Readers Journal*, 10, no. 3 (Fall 1994).

Skene Melvin, David, and Ann Skene Melvin. *Crime, Detective, Espionage, Mystery and Thriller Fiction and Film: A Comprehensive Bibliography of Critical Writing through 1979*. Westport, Conn.: Greenwood Press, 1980.

Slung, Michele B., ed. *Murder and Other Acts of Literature*. New York: St. Martin's Press, 1997.

Smith, Myron J., and Terry White. *Cloak and Dagger Fiction: An Annotated Guide to Spy Thrillers*. Westport, Conn.: Greenwood Press, 1995.

Spencer, William David. *Mysterium and Mystery: The Clerical Crime Novel*. Carbondale: Southern Illinois University Press, 1992.

Steinbrunner, Chris, Otto Penzler, and Marvin Lachman, eds. *Detectionary: A Biographical Dictionary of the Leading Characters in Detective and Mystery Fiction*, revised edition. Woodstock, N.Y: Overlook, 1977.

Steinbrunner and Penzler, eds. *Encyclopedia of Mystery and Detection*. New York: McGraw-Hill, 1976.

Stewart, R. F. . . . *And Always a Detective: Chapters on the History of Detective Fiction*. Newton Abbot, U.K.: David & Charles, 1980.

Swanson, Jean, and Dean James. *By a Woman's Hand: A Guide to Detective Fiction by Women.* New York: Berkley, 1994.

Symons, Julian. *Bloody Murder: From the Detective Story to the Crime Novel.* New York: Viking, 1984.

Thompson, Jon. *Fiction, Crime, and Empire: Clues to Modernity and Postmodernism.* Urbana: University of Illinois Press, 1993.

Walker, Ronald G., and June M. Frazer, eds. *The Cunning Craft: Original Essays on Detective Fiction and Contemporary Literary Theory.* Macomb: Western Illinois University, 1990.

Wark, Wesley K., ed. *Spy Fiction, Spy Films, and Real Intelligence.* London & Portland, Ore.: Cass, 1991.

Watson, Colin. *Snobbery with Violence: Crime Stories and Their Audience,* revised edition. London: Eyre Methuen, 1979.

Waugh, Hillary. *Hillary Waugh's Guide to Mysteries and Mystery Writing.* Cincinnati: Writer's Digest Books, 1991.

Winks, Robin W., ed. *Colloquium on Crime: Eleven Renowned Mystery Writers Discuss Their Work.* New York: Scribners, 1986.

Winks, ed. *Detective Fiction: A Collection of Critical Essays.* Englewood Cliffs, N.J.: Prentice-Hall, 1980.

Winks, ed. *Modus Operandi: An Excursion into Detective Fiction.* Boston: Godine, 1982.

Winks, and Maureen Corrigan, eds. *Mystery and Suspense Writers: The Literature of Crime, Detection, and Espionage.* New York: Scribners, 1998.

Winn, Dilys. *Murder Ink: The Mystery Reader's Companion,* revised edition. New York: Workman, 1984.

Woeller, Waltraud, and Bruce Cassiday. *The Literature of Crime and Detection: An Illustrated History from Antiquity to the Present,* translated by Ruth Michaelis-Jena and Willy Merson. New York: Ungar, 1988.

Contributors

Cynthia A. Bily . . . . *Adrian College*

J. Randolph Cox . . . . *St. Olaf College*

Mary Jean DeMarr . . . . *Indiana State University*

Patricia A. Gabilondo . . . . *Nicholls State University*

Daryl Y. Holmes . . . . *Nicholls State University*

James Hurt . . . . *University of Illinois at Urbana-Champaign*

Margaret Kinsman. . . . . *South Bank University*

Andrew F. Macdonald. . . . . *Loyola University, New Orleans*

Gina Macdonald . . . . *Nicholls State University*

Ellen Kocher Plaisance . . . . *Dillard University*

B. J. Rahn . . . . *Hunter College, City University of New York*

William Reynolds . . . .*Hope College*

Marilyn Rye . . . . *Fairleigh Dickinson University*

Marie D. Sheley. . . . .*Nicholls State University*

Charles L. P. Silet . . . . *Iowa State University*

Marcia J. Songer . . . . *East Tennessee State University*

Katherine Staples. . . . .*Austin Community College*

T. R. Steiner . . . . *University of California at Santa Barbara*

Nancy Ellen Talburt . . . . *University of Arkansas*

Michele Theriot. . . . .*Nicholls State University*

Michael J. Tolley . . . . *University of Adelaide*

Anita Tully . . . .

Chris Willis . . . .

Anna Wilson . . . .*Birmingham University*

L. R. Wright . . . . *East Tennessee State University*

Juana R. Young . . . . *University of Arkansas*

Cumulative Index

Dictionary of Literary Biography, Volumes 1-276
Dictionary of Literary Biography Yearbook, 1980-2001
Dictionary of Literary Biography Documentary Series, Volumes 1-19
Concise Dictionary of American Literary Biography, Volumes 1-7
Concise Dictionary of British Literary Biography, Volumes 1-8
Concise Dictionary of World Literary Biography, Volumes 1-4

Cumulative Index

DLB before number: *Dictionary of Literary Biography,* Volumes 1-276
Y before number: *Dictionary of Literary Biography Yearbook,* 1980-2001
DS before number: *Dictionary of Literary Biography Documentary Series,* Volumes 1-19
CDALB before number: *Concise Dictionary of American Literary Biography,* Volumes 1-7
CDBLB before number: *Concise Dictionary of British Literary Biography,* Volumes 1-8
CDWLB before number: *Concise Dictionary of World Literary Biography,* Volumes 1-4

Grey, Lady Jane 1537-1554 . . . . DLB-132

Grey Owl 1888-1938 . . . . DLB-92; DS-17

Grey, Zane 1872-1939 . . . . DLB-9, 212

Grey Walls Press DLB-112

Griboedov, Aleksandr Sergeevich
1795?-1829 . . . . DLB-205

Grier, Eldon 1917- DLB-88

Grieve, C. M. (see MacDiarmid, Hugh)

Griffin, Bartholomew flourished 1596 . . . . DLB-172

Griffin, Gerald 1803-1840 . . . . DLB-159

The Griffin Poetry Prize Y-00

Griffith, Elizabeth 1727?-1793 . . . . DLB-39, 89

Preface to The Delicate Distress (1769) DLB-39

Griffith, George 1857-1906 . . . . .DLB-178

Griffiths, Ralph [publishing house] DLB-154

Griffiths, Trevor 1935- DLB-13, 245

Griggs, S. C., and Company DLB-49

Griggs, Sutton Elbert 1872-1930 . . . . DLB-50

Grignon, Claude-Henri 1894-1976 . . . . DLB-68

Grigorovich, Dmitrii Vasil'evich
1822-1899 . . . . DLB-238

Grigson, Geoffrey 1905- DLB-27

Grillparzer, Franz
1791-1872 . . . . DLB-133; CDWLB-2

Grimald, Nicholas
circa 1519-circa 1562 . . . . DLB-136

Grimké, Angelina Weld 1880-1958 . . . DLB-50, 54

Grimké, Sarah Moore 1792-1873 . . . . DLB-239

Grimm, Hans 1875-1959 . . . . DLB-66

Grimm, Jacob 1785-1863 . . . . DLB-90

Grimm, Wilhelm
1786-1859 . . . . DLB-90; CDWLB-2

Grimmelshausen, Johann Jacob Christoffel von
1621 or 1622-1676 . . . . . DLB-168; CDWLB-2

Grimshaw, Beatrice Ethel 1871-1953 . . . . .DLB-174

Grin, Aleksandr Stepanovich
1880-1932 . . . . DLB-272

Grindal, Edmund 1519 or 1520-1583 . . . . DLB-132

Gripe, Maria (Kristina) 1923- DLB-257

Griswold, Rufus Wilmot
1815-1857 . . . . DLB-3, 59, 250

Grosart, Alexander Balloch 1827-1899 . . . DLB-184

Gross, Milt 1895-1953 . . . . DLB-11

Grosset and Dunlap DLB-49

Grossman, Allen 1932- DLB-193

Grossman Publishers DLB-46

Grossman, Vasilii Semenovich
1905-1964 . . . . DLB-272

Grosseteste, Robert circa 1160-1253 . . . . . DLB-115

Grosvenor, Gilbert H. 1875-1966 . . . . DLB-91

Groth, Klaus 1819-1899 . . . . DLB-129

Groulx, Lionel 1878-1967 . . . . DLB-68

Grove, Frederick Philip 1879-1949 . . . . . . DLB-92

Grove Press DLB-46

Grubb, Davis 1919-1980 . . . . DLB-6

Gruelle, Johnny 1880-1938 . . . . DLB-22

von Grumbach, Argula
1492-after 1563? DLB-179

Grymeston, Elizabeth
before 1563-before 1604 . . . . DLB-136

Gryphius, Andreas
1616-1664 . . . . DLB-164; CDWLB-2

Gryphius, Christian 1649-1706 . . . . DLB-168

Guare, John 1938- DLB-7, 249

Guerra, Tonino 1920- DLB-128

Guest, Barbara 1920- DLB-5, 193

Guèvremont, Germaine 1893-1968 . . . . . . DLB-68

Guglielminetti, Amalia 1881-1941 . . . . . . DLB-264

Guidacci, Margherita 1921-1992 . . . . DLB-128

Guide to the Archives of Publishers, Journals,
and Literary Agents in North American
Libraries Y-93

Guillén, Jorge 1893-1984 . . . . DLB-108

Guilloux, Louis 1899-1980 . . . . DLB-72

Guilpin, Everard
circa 1572-after 1608? DLB-136

Guiney, Louise Imogen 1861-1920 . . . . . . DLB-54

Guiterman, Arthur 1871-1943 . . . . DLB-11

Günderrode, Caroline von
1780-1806 . . . . DLB-90

Gundulić, Ivan
1589-1638 . . . . .DLB-147; CDWLB-4

Gunesekera, Romesh 1954- DLB-267

Gunn, Bill 1934-1989 . . . . DLB-38

Gunn, James E. 1923- DLB-8

Gunn, Neil M. 1891-1973 . . . . DLB-15

Gunn, Thom 1929- DLB-27; CDBLB-8

Gunnars, Kristjana 1948- DLB-60

Günther, Johann Christian
1695-1723 . . . . DLB-168

Gurik, Robert 1932- DLB-60

Gurney, A. R. 1930- DLB-266

Gustafson, Ralph 1909-1995 . . . . DLB-88

Gustafsson, Lars 1936- DLB-257

Gütersloh, Albert Paris 1887-1973 . . . . . . DLB-81

Guthrie, A. B., Jr. 1901-1991 . . . . DLB-6, 212

Guthrie, Ramon 1896-1973 . . . . DLB-4

The Guthrie Theater DLB-7

Guthrie, Thomas Anstey (see Anstey, FC)

Gutzkow, Karl 1811-1878 . . . . DLB-133

Guy, Ray 1939- DLB-60

Guy, Rosa 1925- DLB-33

Guyot, Arnold 1807-1884 . . . . .DS-13

Gwynne, Erskine 1898-1948 . . . . DLB-4

Gyles, John 1680-1755 . . . . DLB-99

Gyllensten, Lars 1921- DLB-257

Gysin, Brion 1916- DLB-16

H

H.D. (see Doolittle, Hilda)

Habermas, Jürgen 1929- DLB-242

Habington, William 1605-1654 . . . . DLB-126

Hacker, Marilyn 1942- DLB-120

Hackett, Albert (see Goodrich, Frances)

Hacks, Peter 1928- DLB-124

Hadas, Rachel 1948- DLB-120

Hadden, Briton 1898-1929 . . . . DLB-91

Hagedorn, Friedrich von 1708-1754 . . . . . DLB-168

Hagelstange, Rudolf 1912-1984 . . . . DLB-69

Haggard, H. Rider
1856-1925 . . . . DLB-70, 156, 174, 178

Haggard, William 1907-1993 . . . . . .DLB-276; Y-93

Hagy, Alyson 1960- DLB-244

Hahn-Hahn, Ida Gräfin von
1805-1880 . . . . DLB-133

Haig-Brown, Roderick 1908-1976 . . . . DLB-88

Haight, Gordon S. 1901-1985 . . . . DLB-103

Hailey, Arthur 1920- DLB-88; Y-82

Haines, John 1924- DLB-5, 212

Hake, Edward flourished 1566-1604 . . . . DLB-136

Hake, Thomas Gordon 1809-1895 . . . . . . DLB-32

Hakluyt, Richard 1552?-1616 . . . . DLB-136

Halas, František 1901-1949 . . . . DLB-215

Halbe, Max 1865-1944 . . . . DLB-118

Halberstam, David 1934- DLB-241

Haldane, J. B. S. 1892-1964 . . . . DLB-160

Haldeman, Joe 1943- DLB-8

Haldeman-Julius Company DLB-46

Haldone, Charlotte 1894-1969 . . . . DLB-191

Hale, E. J., and Son DLB-49

Hale, Edward Everett
1822-1909 . . . . .DLB-1, 42, 74, 235

Hale, Janet Campbell 1946- DLB-175

Hale, Kathleen 1898- DLB-160

Hale, Leo Thomas (see Ebon)

Hale, Lucretia Peabody 1820-1900 . . . . . . DLB-42

Hale, Nancy
1908-1988 . . . . DLB-86; DS-17; Y-80, Y-88

Hale, Sarah Josepha (Buell)
1788-1879 . . . . .DLB-1, 42, 73, 243

Hale, Susan 1833-1910 . . . . DLB-221

Hales, John 1584-1656 . . . . DLB-151

Halévy, Ludovic 1834-1908 . . . . DLB-192

Haley, Alex 1921-1992 . . . . DLB-38; CDALB-7

Haliburton, Thomas Chandler
1796-1865 . . . . DLB-11, 99

Hall, Adam 1920-1995 . . . . .DLB-276

Hall, Anna Maria 1800-1881 . . . . DLB-159

Hall, Donald 1928- DLB-5

Hall, Edward 1497-1547 . . . . DLB-132

Hall, Halsey 1898-1977 . . . . DLB-241

Hall, James 1793-1868 . . . . .DLB-73, 74

Hall, Joseph 1574-1656 . . . . DLB-121, 151

Hall, Radclyffe 1880-1943 . . . . DLB-191

Hall, Samuel [publishing house] DLB-49

Hall, Sarah Ewing 1761-1830 . . . . DLB-200

Hall, Stuart 1932- DLB-242

Hallam, Arthur Henry 1811-1833 . . . . DLB-32

I

L

S